TROLLOPE

For Mary —

VICTORIA GLENDINNING

TROLLOPE

Victoria Glendinning.

HUTCHINSON
LONDON

© Victoria Glendinning 1992

The right of Victoria Glendinning to be
identified as Author of this work has been asserted
by Victoria Glendinning in accordance with the
Copyright, Designs and Patents Act, 1988

This edition first published in 1992 by
Hutchinson

RANDOM CENTURY GROUP LTD
20 Vauxhall Bridge Road, London SW1V 2SA

RANDOM CENTURY AUSTRALIA (PTY) LTD
20 Alfred Street, Milsons Point, Sydney, NSW 2061, Australia

RANDOM CENTURY NEW ZEALAND LTD
18 Poland Road, Glenfield, Auckland, NEW ZEALAND

RANDOM CENTURY SOUTH AFRICA (PTY) LTD
PO Box 337, Bergvlei, 2012, South Africa

A CIP catalogue record for this book is
available from the British Library

ISBN 0 09 173896 2

Set in Baskerville by Deltatype Ltd,
Ellesmere Port, Cheshire
Printed and bound in Great Britain by
Butler and Tanner Ltd, Frome, Somerset

In discussing the character of a man, there is no course of error so fertile as the drawing of a hard and fast line. We are attracted by salient points and seeing them clearly we jump to conclusions, as though there were a lighthouse on every point by which the nature of the coast would certainly be shown to us. And so it will if we accept the light only for so much of the shore as it illumines. . . .

The man of letters is, in truth, ever writing his own biography. What there is in his mind, is being declared to the world at large by himself. And if he can so write that the world at large shall care to read what is written, no other memoir will perhaps be necessary.

Anthony Trollope, The Life of Cicero

The desire is common to all readers to know not only what a great writer has written, but also of what nature has been the man who produced such great work.

Anthony Trollope, Thackeray

CONTENTS

LIST OF ILLUSTRATIONS

PLATES

TEXT ILLUSTRATIONS

ACKNOWLEDGEMENTS

The author and publishers gratefully acknowledge the following sources of the illustrations: *Plates*: 1, Orley Farm School, Harrow; 2, *Country Life*; 3 and 44, National Portrait Gallery, London; 4, 35, 48–50, Hugh Trollope; 5 and 14, Mansell Collection; 6, Victoria and Albert Museum, London; 7, Guildhall Library, London; 10 and 36, N. John Hall; 11, *Charles Bianconi* by Mrs Morgan John O'Connell, Chapman and Hall, 1878; 12, 15, 17 and 25–7, Mary Evans Picture Library; 13, 29 and 42, Trustees of the Boston Public Library; 18, 19 and 45, The Post Office; 20 and 21, *Kate Field* by Lilian Whiting, Samson Low Marsten & Co, 1899; 22, 43 and 47, Morris L. Parrish Collection, Princeton University Library; 23, *Framley Parsonage* by Anthony Trollope, Smith, Elder, 1861; 24, Punch Publications; 28, Mrs Ayres; 30–33 and 46, Robert Cecil; 34, Bodleian Library; 37–9, Willoughby Norman; 40, Jarndyce Antiquarian Bookshop; 41, Robert Fairley. Plates 8, 9 and 16 are from the author's personal collection. *Text illustrations*: 1, Margaret Tilley; 2, University of Illinois Library; 3, Morris L. Parrish Collection, Princeton University Library; 4, Willoughby Norman.

The stag device which appears in the chapter headings is a detail from the Trollope family's coat of arms. Anthony had it engraved on his personal letter-paper.

ACKNOWLEDGEMENTS

MY first thanks must go to Richard Cohen, formerly of Hutchinson, who proposed this book to me and, after he left the firm, continued as my editor. I could not have managed without his support and his editorial rigour. My particular thanks too to Robyn Sisman of Hutchinson; to Judith B. Jones of A. A. Knopf; to Bruce Hunter, best and kindest of agents; to Gabrielle Allen, for inspired picture research; to Christine Shuttleworth, who compiled the index; and to Professor Roy Foster, who read my typescript and was generous with his special knowledge of Irish and English nineteenth-century political history, and with his time, and with the loan of books and additional material. (Any errors of fact are my own.)

I should particularly like to thank Tom Phillips RA for the intuitive sympathy of his portrait of Anthony Trollope in his younger days – when no portrait of him was ever painted.

Robert A. Cecil, Anthony Trollope's great-great-nephew, kindly allowed me to use his private collection of family letters, photographs and portraits. Equally generous was Hugh Trollope, Anthony's great-great-grandson, whom I visited in New South Wales and who lent me family papers and photographs in his possession. I am grateful too to Margaret Tilley, grand-daughter of Anthony's brother-in-law John Tilley, who allowed me to use letters and documents preserved in her family; to the Earl of Rosse, who gave me access to the archive at Birr Castle, Co. Offaly, Ireland; and to Carron Greig and his son Geordie, who admitted me to their remarkable collection of Trollopiana and allowed me to use some rare items.

I would like to thank the Dean of the Faculty of Princeton University for a Visiting Fellowship which made my stay at Princeton very pleasant, and the following libraries and institutions for permission to quote from materials in their possession and for the helpfulness of their staff: first and foremost Princeton

University Library and Alexander D. Wainwright (for the Morris L. Parrish Collection) and Mark Farrell (for the Robert Taylor Collection); Nancy Romero, Head of the Rare Book and Special Collections Library at the University of Illinois at Urbana-Champaign; the Boston Public Library; the Bodleian Library, Oxford; the London Library; the Forster Collection at the Victoria and Albert Museum; the National Art Library at the Victoria and Albert Museum; the Library of the Chartered Institute of Bankers; the Archives and Local Studies Section of the Brian O'Malley Central Library and Arts Centre, Rotherham; the Miss Lewis Pharmaceutical Gallery at the Hitchin Museum; the Ulster Museum, Belfast.

Many other people in Britain, Ireland, Canada, the USA and Australia have contributed to this book by giving or lending photographs, books and other materials, sharing knowledge, experience and insight, and providing information, references, ideas, contacts, practical help, advice or hospitality: Mrs Ayres, Nina Bawden, Daphne Bennett, Carmel Bird, David Black, Ursula Bowlby, Alan Brissenden, David Caird, Jenefer Coates, Andrew Crawshaw, Frank Dickinson, Geoffrey Dutton, Rob Fairley, Norman Feltes, Greg Gatenby, Leslie Glazer, Hugo Glendinning, Simon Glendinning, Yasmine and Dr Brendon Gooneratne, John Gross, Selina Hastings, Belinda Hollyer, Cheveley Johnston, Hermione Lee, John Letts, Caroline Lippincott, Judith Luna, Alison Lurie, Russell McDougall, Willoughby Norman, Hailz-Emily Osborne, Josephine Pullein-Thompson, Fiona Russell, Jim Sait, John Saumarez-Smith, Richard Seebohm, Richard Shone, David Singmaster, Deborah Singmaster, Fabienne Smith, Hilary Spurling, Claire Tomalin, Emma Trevelyan, Joanna Trollope, Julian Watson, John de Vere White, Michael Wood, Patricia Zeppel, Philip Ziegler.

Last but first always, my deep gratitude to Terence de Vere White, who over the past four years has had to live with Anthony Trollope as well as with me. Between the two of them I have been in good company.

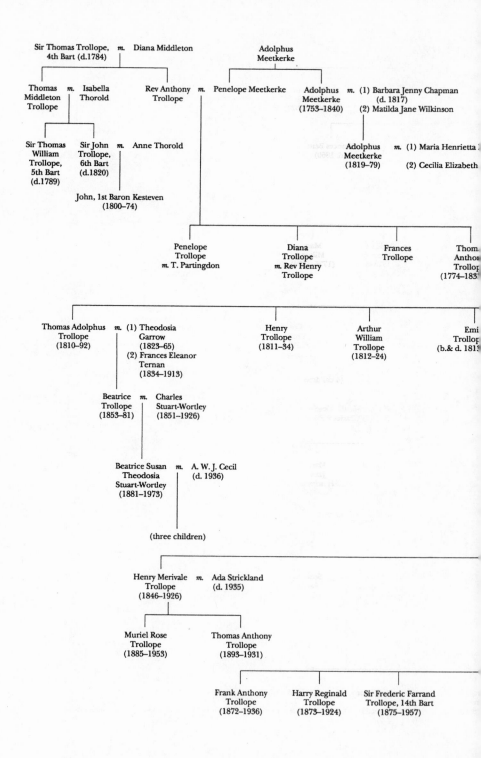

Sir Thomas Trollope, *m.* Diana Middleton
4th Bart (d.1784)

Adolphus
Meetkerke

Thomas *m.* Isabella   Rev Anthony *m.* Penelope Meetkerke   Adolphus *m.* (1) Barbara Jenny Chapman
Middleton   Thorold   Trollope   Meetkerke   (d. 1817)
Trollope   (1753–1840)   (2) Matilda Jane Wilkinson

Sir Thomas   Sir John *m.* Anne Thorold   Adolphus *m.* (1) Maria Henrietta
William   Trollope,   Meetkerke
Trollope,   6th Bart   (1819–79)   (2) Cecilia Elizabeth
5th Bart   (d.1820)
(d.1789)

John, 1st Baron Kesteven
(1800–74)

Penelope   Diana   Frances   Thom
Trollope   Trollope   Trollope   Antho
m. T. Partingdon   *m.* Rev Henry   Trollo
                     Trollope   (1774–183

Thomas Adolphus *m.* (1) Theodosia   Henry   Arthur   Emi
Trollope   Garrow   Trollope   William   Trollo
(1810–92)   (1823–65)   (1811–34)   Trollope   (b.& d. 181
                (2) Frances Eleanor   (1812–24)
                     Ternan
                     (1834–1913)

Beatrice *m.* Charles
Trollope   Stuart-Wortley
(1853–81)   (1851–1926)

Beatrice Susan *m.* A. W. J. Cecil
Theodosia   (d. 1936)
Stuart-Wortley
(1881–1973)

(three children)

Henry Merivale *m.* Ada Strickland
Trollope   (d. 1935)
(1846–1926)

Muriel Rose   Thomas Anthony
Trollope   Trollope
(1885–1953)   (1893–1931)

Frank Anthony   Harry Reginald   Sir Frederic Farrand
Trollope   Trollope   Trollope, 14th Bart
(1872–1936)   (1873–1924)   (1875–1957)

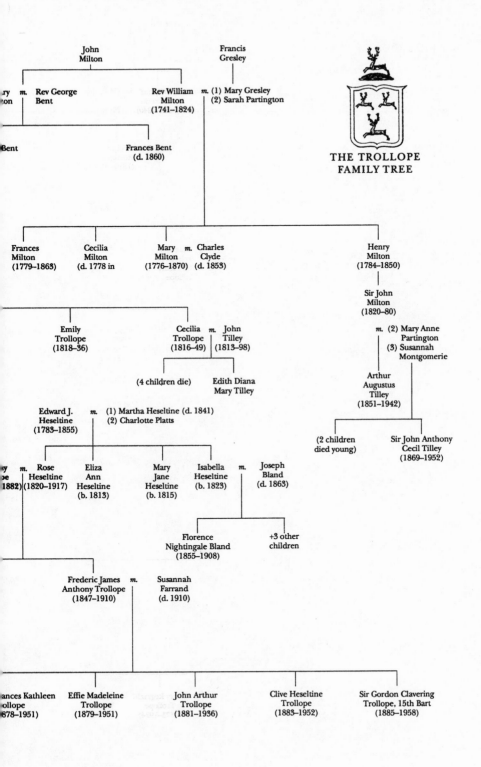

THE TROLLOPE
FAMILY TREE

John
Milton

Francis
Gresley

ᴬʳʸ   m.   Rev George
ᵗᵒⁿ   Bent

Rev William   m. (1) Mary Gresley
Milton   (2) Sarah Partington
(1741–1824)

Bent

Frances Bent
(d. 1860)

Frances   Cecilia   Mary   m.   Charles   Henry
Milton   Milton   Milton   Clyde   Milton
(1779–1863)   (d. 1778 in   (1776–1870)   (d. 1853)   (1784–1850)

Sir John
Milton
(1820–80)

Emily   Cecilia   m.   John   m. (2) Mary Anne
Trollope   Trollope   Tilley   Partington
(1818–36)   (1816–49)   (1813–98)   (3) Susannah
                                                                Montgomerie

                 (4 children die)   Edith Diana   Arthur
                                    Mary Tilley   Augustus
                                                          Tilley
                                                          (1851–1942)

Edward J.   m.   (1) Martha Heseltine (d. 1841)
Heseltine   (2) Charlotte Platts
(1783–1855)
                                                          (2 children   Sir John Anthony
                                                          died young)   Cecil Tilley
                                                                             (1869–1952)

ᵃʸ   m.   Rose   Eliza   Mary   Isabella   m.   Joseph
ᵖᵉ   Heseltine   Ann   Jane   Heseltine   Bland
1882)(1820–1917)   Heseltine   Heseltine   (b. 1823)   (d. 1863)
                      (b. 1813)   (b. 1815)

                                   Florence   +3 other
                                   Nightingale Bland   children
                                   (1855–1908)

          Frederic James   m.   Susannah
          Anthony Trollope   Farrand
          (1847–1910)   (d. 1910)

ᵃⁿᶜᵉˢ Kathleen   Effie Madeleine   John Arthur   Clive Heseltine   Sir Gordon Clavering
ᵒˡˡᵒᵖᵉ   Trollope   Trollope   Trollope   Trollope, 15th Bart
ᵇ78–1951)   (1879–1951)   (1881–1936)   (1883–1952)   (1885–1958)

INTRODUCTION

THE working title for this book was *Gypsy Lips*. It comes from the humorist J. B. Morton ('Beachcomber'):

Stampedes of wild elephants are becoming more common in Ahahaland, owing to the presence of film units up country, on the lower Zimbabwe. The film men have taught the elephants to stampede on the slightest provocation, as they needed such a scene for *Gipsy Lips*, the life story of Anthony Trollope.*

The joke lies in the disjunction between a tale of riproaring adventure and exotic sex, and the solid, unsensational Britishness of Anthony Trollope, as he is commonly perceived. What makes me laugh even more is that if a film were to be made of his life story, stampeding elephants might well be in order. On his second journey to Australia in 1874 he stopped off in Ceylon and rode out into the forest-covered mountains where wild elephants roamed. Anthony was no good with a gun but 'it had been my grand desire to see an elephant, – a real wild elephant, – and perhaps to shoot him.' The rest of the story is in this book. Suffice for now to reveal that 'we heard the rush of the brute close to us, within thirty yards I should say, crushing his way through the jungle. . . .'

When I began my research in early 1988 there had been no full-length biography of Anthony Trollope since James Pope Hennessy's (1971), and I believed that I was the only person to be embarking on such a project. Then I discovered that not one, not two, but three American academics – R. H. Super, Richard Mullen, and N. John Hall – were already engaged on full-scale scholarly biographies of Trollope, and had been for some years. Their books have all now been published. The net result is that an enormous amount of information about Trollope is now in the

* J. B. Morton, *The Misadventures of Dr Strabismus*, Sheed & Ward, 1949.

xvii

public domain. All three are authoritative 'chronicle' biographies, and each professor has his area of special expertise. Professor Super, already the author of a valuable monograph, *Trollope in the Post Office*, knows more than anyone about Trollope's Civil Service career. Dr Mullen brought a historian's objectivity and breadth of reference to his task. Professor N. John Hall, whose meticulous two-volume *Letters of Anthony Trollope* already consti-tuted a biography by other means, has a genius for the uncovering of fascinating minutiae, and is particularly good on Trollope's travel writing and on the publishing history. The new wave of biographical interest in Trollope coincided with the successful inauguration of the Trollope Society both in London and in New York and with the society's programme of publishing, between 1989 and the end of the century, in association with the Folio Society, a uniform edition of all the forty-seven novels plus five volumes of short stories. Added to this, in autumn 1991 the Dean of Westminster gave his consent for a memorial to Anthony Trollope to be placed in Poets' Corner in Westminster Abbey. This honour, and this enthusiasm for his books – unprecedented since his heyday – was long overdue.

It may well be imagined however that my confidence was shaken as news of the threefold wave of new Trollope biographies broke over me. But my book has turned out to be unlike the others. Sex, or at any rate gender, may account for the difference. Women critics have written about Trollope's work, but no woman had written his biography.*

Learning about Trollope the private man I soon found myself involved in family dynamics – particularly his relationships with his dominant mother, his hopeless father, his tubercular sisters, his two sons, his three nieces – and his eldest brother Tom, for whom I conceived a hostility which I have made every effort to temper with fairness.

Above all, I was curious about Anthony's wife Rose, about whom neither Anthony nor any of his friends and relations ever said much; his previous biographers, while in agreement that she was a good and loyal support to the great man, as indeed she was,

---

* Unless you count the collaboration of Lucy Poate Stebbins with her son Richard Poate Stebbins; they were joint authors of *The Trollopes: The Chronicle of a Writing Family* (1947).

have not found much to say about her either. Nathaniel Hawthorne's son Julian said of Trollope, surprisingly, that 'his wife was his books'; listening for her as I read them I have found this to be true. Her presence in my own book became stronger and stronger. The nature of marriage and the balance of power between the sexes, a central question in much of Trollope's fiction, is central to this book too. I have also been interested in his responses to the 'advanced', outspoken, independent American and English women he met in middle life, who attracted and frightened him and disturbed his notions of male supremacy. These women too he wrote into his novels.

The balancing of public and private, outer and inner, is a problem of all biography. It was a problem for Trollope in the management of his own life and one of his preoccupations as an author. In his fiction however and, as I hope, in this biography, the discourse is unitary whether the topic be personal politics and sexual morality or political institutions and public morality. I was never tempted, in my pursuit of the private man, to downplay his passionate interest in public life nor the face he presented to the world. That is the face that most people knew in his lifetime and still do know; for Anthony Trollope has to some extent been hijacked by those beguiled by a traditionally bluff, clubbish, roast-beef kind of masculinity. It is half the story. In the alternative universe of his fiction he could enact a subversive, a sceptic, a weeping man, a timid girl or a rebellious, tormented woman with equal wholeheartedness and precision.

Trollope is, in fact, inexhaustible. He is advocate both for the prosecution and for the defence of his characters and, as with the Bible or Shakespeare, the reader can extract from his work whatever reinforces his or her own social and political views. One must draw limits around the biography of even an inexhaustible man. I would have liked to write more about the sexual scandals of the 1840s and 50s which Anthony Trollope, leading a marginalised life in Ireland, picked up from his smarter acquaintances at second hand and which later contributed to his fiction: the case of Lady Lincoln, for example, who ran off to the Continent with Lord Walpole, hotly pursued by Lord Lincoln's best friend W. E. Gladstone, the future Prime Minister. Lord Lincoln, who had served in Peel's Cabinet, was as upright and sober as Plantagenet Palliser; his wife was as flighty as Lady

Glencora Palliser, Anthony's most bewitching and potent heroine. The Lincoln scandal would have had an added frisson for Anthony, living in Ireland, because the unfortunate Lord Lincoln was the minister in charge in Dublin during the Famine.

Some often-told stories were even older. In the 1840s a prominent London hostess was the fifth Countess of Jersey, notorious for the great escapade of her youth: heiress to the opulent banker Robert Child of Child's Bank at Temple Bar, she had escaped from her parents' house in Berkeley Square and eloped to make a secret marriage, as the poor little rich girl Marie Melmotte attempted to do in *The Way We Live Now*. One of lovely Lady Jersey's close friends was Lord Melbourne's sister Emily, who married the dull Lord Cowper at eighteen. The young, glamorous Lady Cowper was, with Lady Jersey, one of the society belles who controlled the membership of Almack's, an exclusive club for dancing and gambling which was founded to provide fun for the upper classes in the years just after the Battle of Waterloo. Lady Cowper met Lord Palmerston at Almack's in the days when they were both young and he was nicknamed 'Cupid'; he was unfaithful to her with her friend Lady Jersey and many others, but married her after Lord Cowper's death. As Lady Palmerston, she was an indefatigable party-giver with a finger in every political pie, and stories about her also contributed to Anthony's fantasy of Lady Glencora – as did stories about Lady Palmerston's wayward sister-in-law Lady Caroline Lamb, who waltzed at Almack's until forbidden to do so by her lover Lord Byron, 'mad, bad and dangerous to know'. More than one predatory Trollopian rake is Byronic, scar-faced where he was club-footed; and more than one stiff Trollopian husband forbids his wife to dance the waltz, which was considered shockingly lascivious.

Waltzing was introduced to Almack's by the young Russian Princess Lieven – a close friend of Lady Jersey and Lady Palmerston and someone who, with her dark exoticism, her thin flat figure, and her talent for discreet relationships with great men, bears a distinct resemblance to the fictional Madame Max Goesler. Thus this one tight social group provided Anthony's imagination with material for his fantasy to work on, and the examples cited here are but the tip of an iceberg.

Some of the other men and women who fuelled his novelist's imagination have their place in my narrative, but to illustrate all the ways in which his fiction echoed and was echoed by real-life people and their sexual or political imbroglios would result in a body of work equal in bulk to his fiction and without its artistry. He absorbed endless gossip about the generation before his own from talk in his clubs when he finally came back to live in England; only a knowledge of the Lady Lincoln story, for example, gives point to Anthony's remark (reported by his first biographer T. H. S. Escott with no explanation at all) that a well-known old Garrick Club anecdotist insisted how 'Lord Lincoln was quite the pleasantest of all Peel's followers'.

Reading Anthony Trollope, I have learned what and how he thought about flirting, democracy, picnics, age and ageing, digestion, Christmas, art and architecture, crinolines, hairstyles, dancing, wine, gardens, bad smells, illness and insanity, cigars, male friendships, spiritualism, swimming, women's teeth, and the way dinner should be served. A lot of this has found its way into the book, but I just could not find a place in the text to write about women's teeth.

I think Trollope looked after his own teeth; at least, he travelled with a toothbrush. No one can read his novels without noticing that he never describes a woman or a girl without describing her mouth and teeth – whether her lips are thick or thin, whether her teeth are large or small, how white they are, and whether she shows them when she smiles. He was not alone in this obsession. His mother in her travel books made the same kind of observations, attributing a sort of indecency to wide mouths and to teeth that were visible; and nearly all contemporary accounts of Queen Victoria's appearance remark that her upper lip left her teeth uncovered, but – it is always 'but' – her teeth were white and small.

What was all this about? I looked at some nineteenth-century books on dentistry. The most illuminating was *Opinions on the Causes and Effects of Diseases in the Teeth and Gums* by Charles Bew, an Irishman who was the Prince Regent's dentist and afterwards went on the Brighton stage. At the back of his book, which was published when Anthony Trollope was three, there are plates as exquisitely engraved and coloured as Redouté's roses or Audubon's birds – but they depict rotting stumps, putrefying molars, canines jutting at grotesque angles, and malformed jaws with just two or three decayed teeth attached.

Until the second half of the century, when vulcanised rubber and then porcelain gradually came into use, false teeth were made of gold, tin, ivory, wood, bone, or from real teeth taken from corpses. Sometimes the upper and lower sets were joined by a steel hinge, which sprang open or snapped shut at inconvenient moments. Sometimes the dentures were made in a single piece, with lines drawn down to simulate individual teeth. The teeth of Clara Van Siever in *The Last Chronicle of Barset* are described as being too perfect, 'like miniature walls of carved ivory'. That's no doubt exactly what they were, as Trollope's contemporary readers would have understood. 'She knew the fault of this perfection, and shewed her teeth as little as she could.'

Modest Victorian women, and not only those with bad or missing or false teeth, smiled with their mouths closed. Good teeth were rare enough to be startlingly sexy. To show healthy white teeth between full lips was provocative – a small nakedness. That was certainly how Anthony Trollope saw it. (Maybe *Gypsy Lips* was not such a ridiculous title after all.)

I have never been so happy researching and writing any book so much as this one. If twenty professors had declared themselves to be writing lives of Trollope I would not and could not have given mine up, once I had begun. If even part of my pleasure is conveyed to the reader, and if he or she is influenced thereby to read or re-read Trollope's work, I shall be well satisfied. Newcomers to Trollope often want to know which of his novels are the best. I would say, read them all; but if forced to pick out the 'great' ones, I would choose *The Small House at Allington, The Last Chronicle of Barset, Phineas Finn, He Knew He Was Right, The Eustace Diamonds, The Way We Live Now* and *The Prime Minister*. This is a personal matter, open to debate.

PART ONE

LEAPS IN THE DARK

CHAPTER ONE

WHEN Anthony Trollope visited South Africa in 1877, the Astronomer Royal at Capetown asked him if he was interested in the stars. 'In truth I do not care for the stars. I care, I think, only for men and women, and so I told him.'

In *The Belton Estate* he described how dull sermons, three times a day, Sunday after Sunday, exhorted the faithful to reject all the pleasures of this world in the hope of heaven to come. If that were right, 'then why has the world been made so pleasant? Why is the fruit of the earth so sweet; and the trees, why are they so green; and the mountains so full of glory? Why are women so lovely?'

That is Anthony Trollope. But then so is this: 'We are all of us responsible for our friends, fathers-in-law for their sons-in-law, brothers for their sisters, husbands for their wives, parents for their children, and children even for their parents. We cannot wipe off from us, as with a wet cloth, the stains left by the fault of those who are near to us. The ink-spot will cling' (*The Three Clerks*). For him the family drama was central. It would be some time before he discovered the world to be a pleasant place, and even then the ink-spot clung.

If Anthony were ever, as his eldest brother Tom claimed, their mother's favourite, her 'Benjamin', it was only for a short time in his babyhood. When he was born his mother already had three sons, the third one worryingly delicate, and she had lost a daughter who died soon after birth. This made the arrival fourteen months later of Anthony, on 24 April 1815, doubly precious.

The following year Mrs Frances Trollope gave birth to a daughter who lived, Cecilia; and less than two years after that, in February 1818, came Emily. Mrs Trollope was by then thirty-eight. She had six children living, and her family was complete.

Her two eldest boys, Thomas Adolphus (Tom) and Henry, born 1810 and 1811, made a pair. The third boy, Arthur, spent the latter part of his short life away from home. The two little girls at the end of the family made another pair, and were treated and educated differently. So Anthony had no natural ally within the family.

Mrs Trollope loved all her children. When in 1827 she went away to America in an attempt to save the family fortunes she took just the girls and Henry with her. Anthony did not see his mother at all between the ages of twelve and a half and sixteen, and he survived those years in circumstances which would depress and disturb the most robust adolescent. Frances Trollope can be seen as a feminist heroine, but she was not a comfortable mother for Anthony.

She was, for all her independence and initiative, a woman who needed a man's arm on which to lean. By the time her boys were young adults it was her eldest son Tom who was taking on the role of companion, confidant and husband-substitute – a role that he fondly sustained, with modifications, to the end of Mrs Trollope's long life.

Anthony was afraid, when he was young, that he would sink below the waves altogether. His adolescent fantasies were to be transformed into novels that brought him the security, the recognition and the friends that he craved, but he forgot none of the miseries of his youth. When he came to write his auto-biography, he emphasised his achievements by presenting a picture of appalling unhappiness and failure in childhood:

> My boyhood was, I think, as unhappy as that of a young gentleman could well be, my misfortunes arising from a mixture of poverty and gentle standing on the part of my father, and from an utter want on my own part of that juvenile manhood which enables some boys to hold up their heads even among the distresses which such a position is sure to produce.

'Keppel Street cannot be called fashionable, and Russell Square is not much affected by the nobility,' Anthony Trollope wrote in *Lady Anna*. Keppel Street in the Bloomsbury area of London was where he was born, but he can have had little memory of living there because the family moved out of London while he was still a baby. Bloomsbury was respectable but not smart, tenanted chiefly by clerks, lawyers and – in Russell Square – some judges, whose houses Mr Trollope would solemnly point out to his little boys. Keppel Street was convenient for the Inns of Court, and within reach of the countryside which began just beyond the New Road (now the Euston Road) at the top of Gray's Inn Lane.

Anthony's father was never a happy or an easy person. He married Frances Milton on his thirty-fifth birthday, 23 May 1809. She was twenty-nine – a mature bride. Trollope heroines who have reached that age are trawling for a husband with some desperation.

Thomas Anthony Trollope was a good match, on the face of it. He was educated at Winchester and at New College, Oxford, where he became a Fellow. A don's life might have suited his scholarly nervousness, but he became a barrister of the Middle Temple, with chambers in Lincoln's Inn in Chancery Lane.

He was living alone at 16 Keppel Street when Henry Milton, Frances's younger brother, found a job as a clerk at the War Office and moved into 27 Keppel Street. His sisters Frances and Mary came up from the country to keep house for him. The three Miltons got to know Mr Trollope as neighbours, and he found himself seriously interested in Frances, who was always known as Fanny.

She had pretty, widely spaced eyes and a pointed chin; a face that was at its best full on. In profile, both nose and chin were prominent. It is hard to tell whether Thomas Anthony Trollope was deeply in love with her. Years later, in 1869, Anthony received by post a bundle of his parents' letters dating from the time of their first meeting. There was no note with the letters to say who had sent them or where they had been found. They were probably left behind in one of the many lodgings and rented houses which Fanny Trollope occupied over the years.

Anthony, reading them, was impressed by how well his mother expressed herself, and by the natural poetic grace of her writing. He made no comment on those from his father. There is, in fact, something rigid and repressed about Thomas Anthony's letters to Fanny. In the 1890s Tom Trollope's second wife compiled a memoir of the mother-in-law she never knew; following what must have been the family line, she stressed that Thomas Anthony was not a cold man, but one who was afraid, or unable,

5

to show affection, and hated any kind of gush. The letters bear this out. 'I always feel afraid of raising doubts to the prejudice of my own sincerity,' he wrote to Fanny less than three weeks before their wedding, explaining why he did not write more lovingly.

Fanny was affectionate and spontaneous and made up the lack. She put her best efforts into being in love with him, and kept it up for about ten years, long after things began to go wrong. She called him her 'dearest, dearest Trollope'.

Where were the couple to live? Fanny thought that Mr Trollope's house was too big, and that her brother's was too small. Should they not buy something else? But Thomas Anthony wanted to hold on to the lease of 16 Keppel Street. He moved into his chambers so that Mr Melville the builder could do up the house. Since Fanny was at home preparing for the wedding, he had to concentrate on domestic details. 'I have given orders for the blinds, for the grates to be put in, and the pole to be made for curtains in the dining parlour.' The carpet had come. 'It is well we have some old tables and chairs that may suffice at present for a room or two.'

Sir John Trollope, he told her, wanted to know what to give them for a wedding present. He had suggested silver forks, and had been told 'how amply we were supplied in that respect'. But, added Thomas Anthony, '*being all alone by myself* I am perfectly at a loss what to think of'. He told Fanny about his dreadful headaches, which sometimes lasted for days.

He has the air of a man quick to find a grievance – not only about being left to deal with the dilatory Mr Melville and the fitting up of the house, but about Fanny's perhaps insufficient concern for Sir John Trollope's goodwill.

Sir John was important. He was the sixth baronet, of Casewick (pronounced Kezzick) near Stamford in Lincolnshire, and Thomas Anthony's first cousin. The Trollopes traced their line back to the 1300s, and had lived at Casewick since the sixteenth century. Several had been Lords Lieutenant of the county. Many had distinguished themselves – sometimes by falling out with their superiors – in the army and navy. There were bishops, archdeacons and vicars among the Trollopes, and most married the daughters of men of rank. Trollopes had large families. Trollope girls, latterly, had tended to marry clergymen.

Thomas Anthony called himself a Liberal, but the Lincolnshire Trollopes were, like so many country squires in Anthony's novels, Tories of the old school. A fifteen-year-old girl, a neighbour and an earl's daughter, visiting Casewick in the 1820s, found Sir John's daughters 'very Missy' and the evening 'very stupid'.* The Lincolnshire Trollopes were powerful landed gentry. Sir John's son, another John, became MP for the county and was created Baron Kesteven in 1868.

Outside Lincolnshire, the ridiculousness of the name had to be reckoned with. At school Anthony, defending himself against mockery, asserted that it was a corruption of 'Trois Loups', the nickname given to a Norman ancestor in tribute to his valour in overcoming three wolves. The legend was quoted, but questioned, by Anthony's cousin Archdeacon Edward Trollope, who preferred a topological explanation – Trolls-hope, meaning Elf-dale.

If one looks at Anthony Trollope's family and forbears there is no need to wonder how he came to write with such familiar ease about clergymen. Thomas Anthony's father was a clergyman. Fanny's father was a clergyman too, and like Thomas Anthony had been at Winchester and New College. The Miltons however did not belong to the same sphere of society as the Trollopes. Fanny was, like many of Anthony's most sympathetic fictional heroines, a 'lady' not by lineage but because she had been brought up as a lady. These heroines suffer by being considered unsuitable brides for the sons of the aristocracy.

Those who did not like Fanny Trollope called her vulgar. When the critic and essayist Frederic Harrison wrote† that 'good old Anthony had a coarse vein – it was in the family', it was Fanny Trollope he was thinking of. Fanny's mother – this was always mentioned with some emphasis – had been a Gresley. The Gresleys were a landed family in Staffordshire. Anthony gave his grandmother's name, Mary Gresley, to the eponymous heroine of one of his short stories; and a dull, rejected suitor in *Sir Harry Hotspur of Humblethwaite* is called Lord Alfred Gresley.

The real-life Mary Gresley, Fanny's mother, died young, and

* Revel Guest and Angela V. John, *Lady Charlotte: A Biography of the Nineteenth Century*, Weidenfeld & Nicolson, 1989. 'Stupid', here as in Anthony's novels, means boring.

† In *Early Victorian Literature* (1902).

Fanny's stepmother was a Miss Partington. Here at least she and Thomas Anthony found common genealogical ground; his sister Penelope had married a Partington. So far so good. But Fanny's father, the Rev. William Milton, vicar of Heckfield in Hampshire, was the son of a Bristol tradesman, variously described as a saddler and as a distiller – a combination which suggests resourcefulness.

The saddler's clever clerical son, Fanny's father, was a genial and eccentric man. He went in for schemes and inventions. His prototypes for traction engines and for carriages that would not overturn littered the vicarage lawn. He hated the scraping sound made by a knife on a china plate, and had a dinner service made with silver discs set in the middle of every plate, on which to cut the meat.

He was a loving father and grandfather, but he was still the son of a saddler. Frequently in his novels Anthony remarked that one could not make a silk purse out of a sow's ear. In *Is He Popenjoy?* the courtly Dean Lovelace's father had been a stable-keeper and tallow-chandler: 'The man looked like a gentleman, but still there was the smell of a stable.' The grand Germain ladies, whose brother Lord George married the Dean's daughter, accepted the Dean 'because holy orders are supposed to make a gentleman', but agreed that 'the Dean isn't quite. . . .' The Dean's aunt was simply vulgar. His daughter (who had been brought up as a lady) was accepted on terms of equality; 'but then there was a feeling among them that she ought to repay this great goodness by a certain degree of humility and submission.' She was neither humble nor submissive. It is possible that Anthony's mother had to put up with something like this at the hands of the Lincolnshire Trollopes, and she was not humble and submissive either.

Through his mother, Anthony had strong West Country connections. He knew Barsetshire from his earliest days. There were old family friends and relations around Bristol. His Milton grandparents had been living near there, in the village of Stapleton, when his mother was born. His mother's sister Mary made a late marriage to a naval commander, Charles Clyde, who lived at Ottery St Mary in Devon. A Gresley aunt of his mother's had married the rector of Crediton, also in Devon, and a daughter of that marriage, Fanny Bent, lived in Exeter, at 8 York Buildings.

Fanny Bent was a favourite with the Trollope children, and

West Country holidays were planned round visits to her. She was a strong-minded unmarried woman with reactionary political opinions, forcibly expressed, as Tom Trollope recalled, in a Devonshire accent. Her figure was 'as well known in Exeter as the cathedral towers', and she was very like Aunt Jemima Stanbury, who lived in the Close at Exeter, in Anthony's *He Knew He Was Right*. Staying with Fanny Bent was Anthony's first experience of the small, self-contained world of a cathedral town.

Intellectually, Anthony's parents were well enough matched. Fanny did not have her husband's classical education, but she was well read and a good linguist. It was she, an ardent reader of Dante, who composed a sonnet to her beloved in Italian. He confessed that he dared not risk trying to reply in kind.

Marriage relaxed Thomas Anthony, temporarily. Tom was born less than a year after the wedding, and around that time they were a close, loving couple. In Anthony's *Orley Farm*, the wife of the lawyer Mr Furnival, feeling neglected by her husband, recalled with nostalgia the struggles, and the love, of early married life: 'Ah me! I wonder if you ever think of the old days when we were so happy in Keppel Street?' In *Orley Farm* it was the husband's professional and social success that came between him and his wife. With the Trollopes, it was the husband's failure. But not yet. 'God bless you, my dearest Fanny, and our darling child,' Thomas Anthony wrote. 'Give him a kiss and tell him his papa sends it to him.' Fanny and the baby were staying at her father's house while her husband was away on circuit. Already he was looking round for a house out of London for his new family.

For like Fanny, Thomas Anthony had been brought up in the country. His mother died when he was only fourteen. His father, the Rev. Anthony Trollope, was for forty years the rector at Cottered, a pretty village in Hertfordshire. He died a couple of years before Thomas Anthony met Fanny, which may explain the ample supply of silver forks at 16 Keppel Street.

According to his memorial in Cottered church, the Rev. Anthony Trollope's 'Christian harmony and benevolence' gained him 'the Esteem of all good Men'. It also gained him a wife from a rich local family. For most of his incumbency he was also rector of St Mary's in the nearby village of Rushden, and he married

9

Penelope Meetkerke, daughter and sister of successive squires of Rushden. In childhood Thomas Anthony and his three sisters divided their time between Cottered rectory and Julians, the big house outside Rushden belonging to his mother's family.

Meetkerke is an unlikely name for an English country squire, but the family had been in Rushden since Adolphus Meetkerke, Flemish ambassador to Elizabeth I, had married a local heiress and acquired Julians. The third Adolphus Meetkerke, Thomas Anthony Trollope's uncle, was married but childless. It was officially understood that Thomas Anthony was to be his heir.

This comfortable prospect coloured all Thomas Anthony's thinking about the future. He would not only inherit Julians, the house, its contents and its land, but the rents from the farmers and cottagers of Rushden and its satellite hamlet Cumberlow Green. He would be an independent country gentleman. If his career at the Chancery Bar was not very successful, which so far it was not, it hardly mattered. Thomas Anthony and Fanny had great expectations.

Thomas Anthony always argued with his Uncle Adolphus when he was at Julians, which was not politic, especially as Thomas Anthony could not argue pleasantly. Fanny, staying at Julians when she was expecting Tom, wrote to her husband: 'This place is most beautiful. . . . I am sorry to tell you that your uncle is far from well.' Uncle Adolphus's health was naturally a matter of interest. Tom was christened Thomas Adolphus after this significant relative; as the eldest son, he was in line to inherit Julians in his turn, some time in the distant future.

The sweetness of early married life did not last. It is from Tom's memoirs that we know the daily routine at 16 Keppel Street. They kept up appearances, but money was short. The Trollopes had a manservant in the family livery, even though their evenings were lit by just two tallow candles – cheaper, and smellier, than wax. Mr Trollope started his boys on an old-fashioned text-book, the *Eton Latin Grammar*, by the age of six. In the early mornings, before breakfast, Tom and later the others would be learning their day's lesson, to be tested by their father. He did not hit them when they made mistakes, but he pulled their hair. Anthony's earliest memory – long before he was six – was of inclining his head towards his father 'so that in the event of guilty fault, he might be able to pull my hair without stopping his razor or dropping his shaving-brush'. Mr Trollope had the best of intentions, and he instilled much that was useful; he insisted, for example, on precision and economy both in speaking and in writing. He was a stickler for obedience and honesty; and family life did nothing for his bilious headaches and his moodiness.

The fun in the house came through their mother. She taught the children to read, and time spent with her was pleasure. Mrs Trollope was gregarious and hospitable, and the friends who came to Keppel Street were mostly hers. She had a penchant for romantic foreigners and political exiles such as the Italian revolutionary General Guglielmo Pepe, who brought the children mandarin oranges and figs. (Anthony did not like figs.)

By the time Anthony was born his father's plans to move out of London were already well advanced. They were to put a tenant in 16 Keppel Street and move to Harrow-on-the-Hill, sixteen miles out in the county of Middlesex. This was not a random choice. The boys were all destined for Winchester, their father's old school, but the great public schools then took boys from a very young age; most importantly, a number of sons of residents in Harrow parish could attend the famous school free, by the terms of the foundation. Harrow would serve as a preparatory school for Winchester, at no cost to the Trollopes.

Mr Trollope's plan was encouraged by a fellow barrister, John Herman Merivale, who lived near the Trollopes in Bloomsbury. Merivale's wife Louisa was the daughter of the Rev. Joseph Drury, a former headmaster of Harrow. Two of the Merivale boys, Herman and Charles – friends of the Trollope children, though a little older – were both starting at Harrow. John Merivale, a younger brother, who would follow suit, became Anthony's lifelong friend.

Harrow was a village, its steep street dominated by the school buildings, the masters' houses and the church, surrounded by farmland and belts of woodland. The local landlord was Lord Northwick, who was a governor of the school. He owned the big house, Harrow Park, but lived mostly in Worcestershire, leaving the management of his Harrow property to Quilton, his bailiff.

Mr Trollope leased at a high rent 157 acres around Illots Farm, down the hill south of the village, from the Northwick estate. 'That farm', wrote Anthony in his autobiography, 'was the grave

11

of all my father's hopes, ambition, and prosperity, the cause of my mother's sufferings, and of those of her children, and perhaps the director of her destiny and of ours.'

Mr Trollope intended to keep up his Bar practice, travelling into London in the gig, and to work the farm. He had absolutely no experience of farming, and agriculture was in any case suffering from the economic recession which followed the end of the war with France. Corn prices had crashed. (Anthony was born a couple of months after the Battle of Waterloo.)

What is more, instead of improving Illots farmhouse, Mr Trollope proceeded to build a large new house, with gardens, further up the hill on his holding. To build an ambitious and expensive house on land that would never be his own seems an unbelievably silly decision for anyone to take, let alone a lawyer. It can only be explained by Mr Trollope's confidence in the inheritance that was to come to him on the death of his Uncle Adolphus. An added advantage was that Lord Northwick reduced the rent, since the new house would, in the end, revert to the estate. The Trollopes called the new house Julians – by coincidence, one of the fields on his rented Harrow land had always been called Julians. The new house would be a foretaste of the Julians he would inherit.

Then something quite unforeseen happened. Uncle Adolphus's wife died. Uncle Adolphus was sixty; within a year, in 1818, around the time the Trollopes moved into their brand-new house, he married again. His new wife, Matilda Wilkinson, was a young woman, and the following year she produced a son, another Adolphus. She had four more children, all of whom died in childhood or young adulthood, but Adolphus, the natural heir, survived. The Trollopes no longer had any expectations at all.

This massive disappointment became part of the family legend, and an explanation, even an excuse, for the disasters that came after. The idea of obsessional grievance as an occupation for life was to pervade Anthony's novels. 'There is nothing perhaps so generally consoling to a man as a well-established grievance; a feeling of having been injured, on which his mind can brood from hour to hour, allowing him to plead his own cause in his own court, within his own heart, – and always to plead it successfully,' he wrote in *Orley Farm*, and went on to express the same idea, either in his editorial voice or through someone else, in at least

12

eight other novels over the next two decades. 'Next to a sum of money down, a grievance is the best thing you can have,' said Mr Curlydown the Post Office clerk in *John Caldigate*, a late novel. Anthony Trollope's plots hinge obsessively on problematic wills and inheritances. There are four characters called Adolphus in his opus, and they are all either cads or morons.

At the very end of his life he wrote *Mr Scarborough's Family*, about the malice of a testator. The subplot was set in the Rushden area of Hertfordshire, and included a meet of the Puckeridge Hunt at Cumberlow Green, which was on the Meetkerke property. This part of the story concerned Mr Peter Prosper, the elderly owner of a large house that he had willed to his nephew. Mr Prosper caused dismay when he courted a grotesque local spinster whose name, like Uncle Adolphus's real-life bride, was Matilda. Mr Prosper's nephew, who offended his uncle by showing 'his own intellectual superiority', gloomily foresaw 'half-a-dozen little Prospers occupying half-a-dozen little cradles'. But this Matilda was so vulgar and greedy that Mr Prosper changed his mind about marrying her, and the nephew came into his inheritance.

It was characteristic of Anthony to make amends and heal old sores in his fiction. In that parallel world, as in daydreams, he could invent alternative histories.

After he lost the hope of Julians, Mr Trollope's gloom and bad temper deepened. Every day he drove down to London in the gig, to what Anthony called his 'dingy, almost suicidal chambers' in Lincoln's Inn. (One of his pupils actually did commit suicide there.) Anthony was told later that his father had been a good and conscientious lawyer, but that his impatience and bad temper drove away the attorneys on whom he depended for briefs.

Tom, in his memoirs, confirmed that their father was 'not a popular or a well-beloved man'. What was worse, 'he was not popular in his own home'. The children avoided their father and preferred their mother, and their father knew it. He had more of them to support now. Cecilia was born in October 1816, soon after the move to Harrow, displacing Anthony as the 'Benjamin', and Emily in the year that Uncle Adolphus remarried.

By the time Emily was two, Mr Trollope was losing so much money on the farm he thought of moving back to Keppel Street.

Instead, he took the family – and Nurse Farmer, and George the manservant, and Neptune the Newfoundland dog (whom Anthony brought back to troublesome life sixty years later in *Dr Wortle's School*) – back to Illots farmhouse. It was an economy move, but he was unable to resist improving and enlarging the farmhouse, making it 'commodious, irregular, picturesque and straggling', as Anthony wrote. (He described it in detail as Orley Farm, the house which his fictional Lady Mason preserved for her son by forging a will.)

It was, when he had finished, a graceful Georgian country house in a good garden, very much a 'gentleman's residence', set well back down a wooded lane from the steep road into Harrow. They renamed the farmhouse Julian Hill.* Mr Trollope rented out the white elephant he had built, his Julians; they never lived there again.

Around the time of Emily's birth, Tom and Henry – who were given a good deal of freedom when their father was not around – contracted typhus from playing near a foul drain. The Harrow apothecary treated the little boys with calomel, which made them much worse. Only the intervention of a Dr Butt, introduced by a concerned friend of Mrs Trollope's, saved Tom's life. Calomel was what Mr Trollope himself habitually took, in large quantities, in an attempt to relieve his chronic headaches and stomach troubles. Tom, writing at the better-informed end of the nineteenth century, felt sure that it was calomel that shattered his father's nervous system.

Calomel is mercurous chloride, and mercury is toxic. Large doses lead to anaemia and damage the immune system, causing allergies and weakened resistance to physical or emotional stress. It was widely taken as a supposed cure for all manner of illnesses and conditions, from babies' teething troubles to intestinal worms and heart disease. It was the standard treatment for syphilis. Its most general family use was as a purgative, and it was the drug of choice in the Trollope household, as in many others.

Mr Trollope's excessive dependence on calomel exacerbated, if it did not cause, his neurotic irritability and poor health. Too much calomel in childhood may also have been a contributing

---

* Julian Hill still stands, and has been restored by owners with the Trollope connection in mind.

cause of the breathing problems, or 'asthma', from which Anthony suffered in later life.

Harrow was dominated by the great public school, which meant that Harrow was dominated by the Drury clan. Seldom can one family – all of them in holy orders – have had such a grip on any institution for so long.

The Merivale boys' grandfather, the Rev. Joseph Drury, who became headmaster back in 1785, had gone by the time Anthony started at the school. But Joseph's eldest son, the Rev. Henry Drury, known as Old Harry, was an assistant master for forty-one years, and one of Old Harry's sons, the Rev. Benjamin Drury, later taught there too. Old Harry was fourth master, and took the Lower School. He was Anthony's tutor. Tom Trollope remembered him as 'a coarse man, coarse in manner and coarse in feeling', though a good scholar; he was the most influential and energetic man around the place.

The Rev. Mark Drury, younger brother of the ex-headmaster, was second master; and Mark's son, the Rev. William Drury, was fifth master when Anthony first went there. Mark Drury had been a candidate for the headmastership in 1805, when his brother retired. Lord Byron, then a senior boy of seventeen, had campaigned passionately for Mark Drury, but the job went to an outsider, the Rev. George Butler. Mark Drury stayed on – he was Tom Trollope's tutor – and grew grossly fat, becoming virtually a prisoner in his chair. The Drurys had a genetic glandular disorder which made them all overweight.

Byron remained a legend in the school. He was, when the Trollope boys were there, Harrow's most glamorous and notorious old boy, because of his poetry – in which Anthony immersed himself as a boy – and his way of life. Much of Old Harry Drury's kudos came from the fact that Byron had been in his house, and had once sat up all night with him discussing the immortality of the soul.

The Drury clan even penetrated the Trollopes' West Country world. Their family house was near Dawlish, on the coast south of Exeter. One of Old Harry's sons, another Henry and a near contemporary of Anthony's, held various livings in Wiltshire before ending up in Salisbury as Archdeacon in the 1860s, 'full of anecdotes and badinage'.

These concatenations of clergymen, not only in Anthony's family but in his boyhood world, make even more superfluous any speculation about how he knew so much about clerical manners, clerical politics, and the whole 'black influx', as he called it in *Is He Popenjoy?*

Anthony was just eight when in the summer of 1823 he was plunged into Harrow School. Tom and Henry had already moved on to Winchester according to plan, so it was with Arthur that Anthony trudged up the hill to Harry Drury's house.

There were never more than seventeen day boys when Anthony was there, and sometimes as few as ten. Some of them the sons of local tradesmen and all of them 'charity boys', they were given a hard time by the fee-paying boarders, sons of peers and gentlemen. Anthony was the son of a gentleman too, but no one would have guessed it. Tom and Henry came in for their fair share of 'brutal bullying', but Anthony, in his autobiography, doubted whether they ever had to go through what he did. 'I was never spared; and was not even allowed to run to and fro between our house and the school without a daily purgatory.'

If he did not mention Arthur, it was because Arthur was soon too sickly to go to school. He went to stay with his Milton grandfather at Heckfield. In July 1824 the grandfather died. Arthur, aged twelve, died just ten weeks later. These losses had to be borne by little Anthony, already confused and demoralised by the bullying at school.

'No doubt my appearance was against me.' Anthony never, in all his life, learned to wear his clothes well. Anything he put on looked rumpled and too tight. In any case, the Trollope children were not turned out like little gentlemen. There was no money for good clothes. Mrs Trollope was sublimely uninterested in what she herself wore. Children's clothes were commonly made at home, but they were not often like the trousers and jackets put together by Mrs Trollope and Nurse Farmer.

Anthony recalled being stopped by the headmaster, Dr Butler, who pretended not to recognise him and asked in a roaring voice 'whether it was possible that Harrow School was disgraced by so disreputably dirty a little boy as I'. The mature Anthony thought that this was unnecessarily cruel. Dr Butler must have known who he was, 'for he was in the habit of flogging me constantly'.

Anthony, telling this story, could not resist the old joke: 'Perhaps he did not recognise me by my face.'

As at other public schools there was no teaching at all at Harrow, in the modern sense. It was simply a matter of reciting, translating, and learning by heart passages from Latin and Greek authors, and composing a few lines of Latin verse each day on a given theme. There were no other subjects on the curriculum.

To enable the boys to make any headway at all the masters acted as private tutors, by personal arrangement with parents, who paid them; Mr Trollope paid nothing to Old Harry for Anthony, a charity boy. New buildings had been added to the sixteenth-century Old Schools just before Anthony started there: the Speech Room, form rooms, the library. But pupil numbers were falling, and were to fall still lower, partly because of the economic recession and partly because morale was low, discipline non-existent apart from ritual beatings, and 'vice' rampant – though vice meant drinking, idleness, vandalising the village shops and going with the local girls every bit as much as it meant homosexuality.

The boys did exercise their sexuality on one another, energetic-ally; but it was seen, in the public schools, as just a regrettable overflow of sensual energy. The classification of homosexuals as a category was only made in the latter half of the century. For most of Anthony's lifetime, a 'pervert' was Anglican orthodoxy's word for a convert to the Church of Rome.

Mrs Trollope's way of dealing with troubles – bereavements, her husband's mental and physical ill-health, chronic money problems – was to plunge into vivacious activity. She was sociable; she liked young people and they liked her. In the boys' school holidays she entertained freely, organising picnics and amateur theatricals at Julian Hill, sending out her spontaneous notes of invitation on pieces of scrap paper. Before they were writers, the Trollopes all wrote. Among the family papers are full-length plays by Mrs Trollope and riddles, verses, acrostics and sketches by the family.

The younger generation of the Drury tribe were frequent visitors, while the nearest property to Julian Hill belonged to a family called Grant, who were the Trollopes' closest allies. Colonel James Grant and his wife Penelope had a son, Owen, and three daughters, Anna, Mary and Kate, who played with the Trollope children in and out of their adjoining gardens. After Anthony's death Tom had a letter of condolence from Mary Grant, then Mrs Christie, and replied to her: 'I have never forgotten and never can forget the days when – as you say, – Trollopes and Grants seemed to be one large family. They were happy days; and that intimacy made for me the happiest part of them. . . . How is Anna? How is Kate? . . . And you are a grandmother!! Heaven and Earth! Will you come out and swing under the old elm tree? Or will you let me wheel you down the hill in a barrow?' He was in love with Kate, Tom wrote, 'in those old boy and girl days, something more than half a century ago! Not that she ever knew it, dear innocent hearted child that she was!'

Five years younger than Tom, Anthony was a scruffy little boy, waiting for his turn on the swing, longing to wheel one of the Grant girls in the barrow, joining in the games as best he could. As a man in his sixties, after watching children playing in a park, he wrote: 'Oh, – how long ago it was since I played kiss-in-the-ring, and how nice I used to think it!' (*South Africa*).

When Anthony was only seven, before he started at school, Mrs Trollope caused a pleasurable social stir in Harrow by something she wrote. The vicar of Harrow for fifty years from 1811 was John William Cunningham, a prominent evangelical from that branch called the Clapham Sect. To the Trollopes and the Drurys, his kind of low-church evangelicalism was laughably bad form. Evangelicalism, an integral part of the Church of England, was a movement that grew from the bottom up, socially speaking; by the mid-century it had reached the upper classes, and was the source of the radical zeal and high seriousness that reformed not only social legislation but social attitudes. In the early 1820s, evangelicalism was still mainly urban, working-class and, to conventionally well-bred people, dreary when not dangerously subversive.

Mr Cunningham was much loved by the poor people in the parish. He was also, to all intents and purposes, chaplain of Harrow School, of which he was a governor. The boys attended the flint-built parish church beside the school at the top of the hill; there was as yet no school chapel. Cunningham had a wider fame, as the author of a successful book called *The Velvet Cushion*, which went into ten editions in the first two years after it was published in 1814.*

When in 1822 four-year-old Allegra, Byron's illegitimate daughter by Claire Clairmont, died in Italy, Byron gave instructions that her body was to be brought back to England and buried at Harrow, where he had been happy. But the vicar, Mr Cunningham, vetoed the placing of any tablet or inscription on her grave, on the grounds that such an indelicate and regrettable situation must not seem to be condoned. Harry Drury conducted Allegra's pathetic funeral, and there was no memorial stone.†

It was a complex moral delicacy, as well as evangelical puritanism, that determined Cunningham's behaviour. He was a friend of Byron's estranged wife, who sometimes visited him at Harrow. The Drurys and the Trollopes thought Cunningham had behaved badly – and found it hugely amusing when Cunningham tried to mend his hand, and keep in with Harrow's famous ex-pupil, by asking Harry Drury to convey to Lord Byron how much he admired his poem *Cain* (published the previous year, and regarded as scandalous by orthodox believers).

This drama surrounding Allegra's burial gave the small Harrow circle something to gossip about, and Mrs Trollope excelled herself by writing out the episode in verse, in the style and metre of Byron's *Don Juan*, in the course of which she satirically characterised everyone involved. Her poem was circulated and caused much amusement. Harry Drury was so delighted that he gave her the manuscript of a poem by Byron inscribed to himself.

When Anthony was in his early twenties he annotated his own copy of his mother's 'Lines Written on the Burial of the Daughter of a Celebrated Author'. It is the first known writing in his hand to have survived. He was quite critical of his mother's view of affairs, especially of her Byron-worship and her Conservatism. What mother and son shared was contempt for 'cant' – a favourite contemporary hate-word signifying, in this context, hypocrisy and the affected use of inflated religious phraseology which Cunningham went in for. 'Old Harry [Drury] had as little cant as

---

* *The Velvet Cushion* is an account, from the evangelical standpoint, of all the vagaries of the Church of England since the Reformation, as recounted by a pulpit cushion.

† An inscribed stone in memory of Allegra was erected beside the church porch by the Byron Society in 1980.

any man I knew,' wrote Anthony against the relevant stanzas. As for the headmaster, Dr Butler, Anthony noted that he had 'unbounded, interested reverence for all in power', was very severe with the small boys and unable to keep the big ones in order – 'rather feared them, than was feared by them'.

The public image was rather different. The Rev. Thomas Dibdin, an eccentric bibliophile and a close friend of Harry Drury's, described the scene at Harrow's speech day on 4 June 1822. The rows of prettily dressed ladies on the benches, he said, looked like 'beds of tulips'. 'Dr Butler is clothed in his academic robes, as indeed are all the masters. . . . Every parent's eye is fixed on his beloved child, who is to figure in this Marathon scene of classical competition. Hope, joy, delight, confidence, alternately possess and mark their countenances. . . . If hospitality, and a generous, Englishman-like feeling prevails anywhere, it prevails at HARROW.'*

This, for us, is deeply ironic. Mrs Trollope, a badly dressed woman, would not be greatly enhancing the 'beds of tulips'. Mr Trollope never went anywhere near the school. The Trollope boys did not distinguish themselves either in sport or academically. After nearly three years at Harrow, Anthony was still 'last boy', getting nowhere in his Latin and Greek, and very unhappy.

He thought, later, that Harry Drury must have suggested to his father that he ought to be taken away. At the time, his parents were more worried about their second son, Henry, who was doing conspicuously badly at Winchester.

Mr Trollope wrote long, nagging, niggling letters to Henry – 'just to read them seems to arouse a kind of irritable antagonism,' wrote Tom's wife many years later, before destroying them. Mrs Trollope wrote more encouragingly, sometimes in French or Latin. The little girls' education was proceeding at home, on progressive lines; Cecilia was studying algebra with a family friend, and Emily learning fractions with her father.

In early 1825, around the time Anthony turned ten, he was removed from Harrow and sent as a boarder to a private school at Sunbury, a village on the Thames south-west of London. The Sunbury school was run by the Rev. Arthur Drury, one of fat

* The Rev. Thomas Frognall Dibdin, 'A Day at Harrow', published in *The Museum* and quoted in his *Reminiscences of a Literary Life* (1836).

Mark Drury's fat sons, who had a bad stutter. During the two years Anthony was there, 'though I never had any pocket-money, and seldom had much in the way of clothes, I lived more nearly on terms of equality with other boys than at any other period during my very prolonged schooldays.'

This relative contentment was ruined by a school scandal. Four boys were accused of 'some nameless horror' – probably sexual experimentation. 'I was one of the four, innocent as a babe, but adjudged to be guiltiest of the guilty,' partly because he had come from a public school. The four were punished in every possible way for a whole term. Anthony hated the other three boys for not telling Mr Drury that he was not involved. He felt an added humiliation in the knowledge that they, the 'curled darlings of the school', would never have deigned to include him in their secret wickedness, whatever it was.

On the first day of the following term Mr Drury whispered to Anthony that perhaps a mistake had been made. 'With all a stupid boy's slowness, I said nothing.' Telling this story in his autobiography, he wrote: 'All that was fifty years ago, and it burns me now as though it were yesterday.'

When Anthony had been at Sunbury a year, the Trollopes took Henry away from Winchester. Mr Trollope wanted his three sons to go on to New College, Oxford, as he had done. 'But that suffering man was never destined to have an ambition gratified. We all lost the prize which he struggled with infinite labour to put within our reach' (*Autobiography*). Henry was the first disappointment. He was idle, and he was difficult. What interested him was natural science; he was a keen amateur geologist. The Winchester curriculum was of no help there.

The parents took Henry to Paris, and left him to board with a Swiss Protestant clergyman and to work translating letters in a counting-house, with a view to perfecting his French and acquiring some business experience.

Mr and Mrs Trollope had been in France, without the children, the previous two summers, staying with Mrs Garnett, a widowed friend of Mrs Trollope from her West Country world.* There the

---

* John Garnett (1750–1820) was a Bristol merchant who emigrated to America. After his death his widow and two of his daughters settled in Paris.

Trollopes got to know a woman called Frances Wright – another Fanny. Fifteen years younger than Mrs Trollope, she was to have an enormous influence on the Trollopes' family history.

Fanny Wright was Byronic and boyish, in so far as someone with a full figure can be boyish. She cut her hair short, and wore a knee-length tunic over Turkish trousers. In her early twenties she had taken ship to the United States, and on her return published an enthusiastic book about American society. Her book brought her the friendship of General Lafayette, hero of the French Revolution, who had fought with Washington in the American War of Independence. She visited him in France for extended periods, and they were delighted with one another. He became her romantic father-figure; Fanny Wright wanted him to adopt her as a daughter, but instead they sustained an intense *amitié amoureuse* which enraged the ageing general's family.

Mrs Trollope was dazzled by Fanny Wright, and by General Lafayette, to whom the Trollopes were introduced. Mrs Trollope was thought to have become a reactionary, after liberal beginnings; but it was only the romance and charm of foreign radicals and exiles that attracted her. She was clever, vital and responsive, but unanalytical. She was never a revolutionary. She adored Lafayette, and ignored his political philosophy.

With Fanny Wright, the Trollopes went to stay at La Grange, Lafayette's château near Rosay, twenty-five miles from Paris. He maintained a large household like a personal court, and there were dances, excursions, great dinners, and talk such as never came their way in Harrow. On the last night of their 1824 holiday, Fanny Wright gave a farewell dinner for them in Paris to which Lafayette came. This was a great compliment. With the Garnetts, they also met Mary Clarke, a sociable, unconventional young Englishwoman, a great friend of the elderly *salonnière* Madame Récamier, and someone who was later to be useful to Mrs Trollope.

The Continental connection enlarged the Trollopes' lives, but leaving Henry in Paris with the Swiss clergyman proved a failure. At fifteen, he was too young to benefit from being on his own in a foreign city, and within a few months he was home again. What to do with Henry became one of the Trollope parents' many worries.

The expected vacancy for Anthony at Winchester – as a scholar, living in College, not boarding in a master's house – came up in spring 1827, just before his twelfth birthday. The dread of yet another new school was mitigated by the fact that Tom was still there, and a praefect, so he could hope for some protection.

Winchester was, according to one historian, 'at its *worst*, the most sinister of all the [public] schools'.* Life in College was ruled absolutely by the 'praefect of hall', and under him by the praefects, each of whom was in charge of a chamber. Chambers, where boys slept, studied and played, were the basic social unit. There was no escape from ritual cruelties and inflexible rules and customs, and no privacy. Smaller boys and those who did not become praefects were 'inferiors' and, unless they were petted and popular, slaves.

Mrs Trollope wrote to Tom reminding him how much Anthony would depend on him:

I dare say you will often find him idle and plaguing enough. But remember, dear Tom, that, in a family like ours, *everything* gained by one is felt personally and individually by all. He is a good-hearted fellow, and clings so to the idea of being Tom's pupil and sleeping in Tom's chamber, that I think you will find advice and remonstrance better taken by him than by poor Henry. Greatly comforted I am to know that Tony has a praefect brother. I well remember what I used to suffer at the idea of what my 'little Tom' was enduring.

Tom described in his memoirs how every 'inferior' at Winchester was allocated a praefect as his tutor, to hear his Latin and Greek, supervise him generally and protect him from bullying. His account confirms the almost total authority that the praefects had in the life of the school. No one ever dreamed of appealing to a master in cases of injustice.

Anthony was Tom's pupil. In his autobiography, after stressing that in later life he and Tom were 'fast friends', Anthony wrote that at Winchester Tom was 'of all my foes, the worst'. Their mother had written about brotherly advice and remonstrance. Tom went further: 'as a part of a daily exercise, he thrashed me with a big stick. That such thrashings should have been possible at a school as a continual part of one's daily life, seems to me to argue a very ill condition of school discipline.'

* John Chandos, *Boys Together: English Public Schools 1800–1864*, Hutchinson, 1984.

Nor does it say very much for Tom, established in the family hierarchy as the 'good' brother. It is not clear whether these thrashings were a private practice, or in the course of the 'public tundings', carried out after dinner in hall 'with a tough, pliant ground-ash stick'. In any case, wrote Tom as an old man, 'my own impression is that the practice was eminently calculated to foster among us a high tone of moral and gentlemanlike feeling.' He wrote nothing about his persecution of his younger brother.

There were also casual and frequent 'scourgings' by the masters, with switches of applewood twigs sent specially from Herefordshire in bundles. Scourgings did not really hurt, said Tom. He himself was never subjected to a public tunding, but as a small boy was scourged as many as five times a day, for trivial offences such as lateness. Anthony claimed the same, in addition to fraternal and other thrashings. There was a story told at Winchester in the late 1820s that if you heard screams, they would be those of young Anthony Trollope being beaten by his brother, and if you heard particularly loud screams, they would be those of both the Trollopes being beaten by Bob Lowe.*

In the summer following Anthony's first term at Winchester all the family was at home – Mr and Mrs Trollope, Tom, Henry, Anthony, and the two girls Cecilia and Emily. There was someone else too – Mother's great new friend, Auguste Hervieu. He was a young Frenchman, an artist, whose father, it was said, had been a colonel in Napoleon's army and died in the retreat from Moscow. Auguste Hervieu had been involved in underground activities against Louis XIII, and feared arrest in France. No one in the family quite knew how he became Mrs Trollope's *protégé* – they were too young at the time to take an interest in such details – but she probably met him with Lafayette and Fanny Wright.

He was in London, penniless, when Mrs Trollope invited him to Harrow to teach the girls drawing. She wrote to Mary Russell Mitford† about him: 'I wish you knew this young man, and you

* Robert Lowe, First Viscount Sherbrooke, 1811–92: an albino with defective eyesight and a sarcastic tongue; Chancellor of the Exchequer 1868, Home Secretary 1873. A violent reactionary.

† Mary Russell Mitford, 1787–1855: poet, playwright and author, best known for *Our Village* (1832), and an indefatigable letter-writer. Mrs Trollope had met her in Hampshire before her marriage, when Miss Mitford had found her 'a very lively, pleasant young woman'.

would then feel as we do. . . . Imagine a being full of lofty
aspirations, conscious of high powers, yet dragged to earth by the
pitiful necessity of earning his daily morcel.' While working on a
painting which had then been 'badly hung by the academicians',
he had 'more than once gone without his dinner, that he might
buy colours – he hoped this picture would get him known'.

Nothing would ever get Hervieu known. He remained and
remains obscure. Before long, he was a member of the Trollope
household, and remained so for over a decade, sometimes
appearing to be Mrs Trollope's chief solace and support and
sometimes a demanding hanger-on.

After the holidays Tom and Anthony returned to Winchester
and Fanny Wright came to stay at Julian Hill. She and Mrs
Trollope had much to discuss. Three years before, she had
attached herself to the Lafayette entourage when he went on a
semi-royal tour of America; while there, she had seen chained
blacks up for sale in Savannah, and the cooperative community
New Harmony, founded by the British socialist Robert Owen.
These experiences determined her to free Southern slaves and
train them for their freedom in an experimental utopian community.

Fanny Wright had a personal fortune from her Scotch linen-
merchant father. She bought 2,000 acres at nine cents an acre in
virgin woodland on the Wolf River in Tennessee, and called her
holding Nashoba. Then she bought slaves in Nashville and settled
them at Nashoba along with some Quakers, to fell trees, build
cabins, and establish the multi-racial commune. Free love and the
abolition of marriage and religion were also part of her plan. But
she herself became ill – Nashoba was a malarial swamp – and had
to return to Europe.

Now Fanny Wright, with her sister Camilla, was going back to
Nashoba. There had been some question of one of Mrs Garnett's
daughters going too. Fanny had also tried to persuade Mary
Shelley, the widow of the poet, to join her mission. Both these
young women declined.

Incredibly, Mrs Trollope, aged forty-seven, a married woman
with five children, decided to go with her. She would take Henry
and the girls and Hervieu. Fascinated by Fanny Wright, she
ignored the enthusiastic talk of free love and racial equality, in
neither of which she believed. She was taking a leap in the dark.

CHAPTER TWO

TOM and his second wife, the principal family historians, both wrote that it was Mr Trollope's idea that Mrs Trollope should go to America. They may have been fudging the real issues here, just as they fudged the long association of Mrs Trollope with Auguste Hervieu. Anthony, as an adult, brooded and speculated about his parents' marriage. His novels pick away at marriages where the wife is better equipped for the business of life than the husband, and ambiguous triads consisting of husband, wife, and wife's male friend, in which the wife is technically innocent but self-willed and, in the eyes of the world, culpable. Nor has anyone written about obsessional jealousy with more understanding than Anthony Trollope.

Mrs Trollope was certainly not broken-hearted at the thought of leaving Mr Trollope for an extended period. As Tom wrote, 'I do not think it would be an exaggeration to say that for many years no person came into my father's presence who did not forthwith desire to escape from it.' Tom always took his mother's part. Anthony saw both sides of every question. In his autobiography, betraying no one, he characteristically stressed the money angle. His mother's chief aim, he wrote, was to find work in America for Henry, and to settle him there; 'and perhaps joined with that was the additional object of breaking up her English home without pleading broken fortunes to the world.' For something had to be done.

Mr Trollope's income from the Bar was almost non-existent. The farm was plunging them deeper into debt. The children believed that it was their father who decided to sink his remaining capital (which was probably the capital of Mrs Trollope's marriage settlement, which he should not have touched) in a commercial enterprise in America. His idea was to start a 'bazaar', to supply the raw American West with small, useful household items – such as pin-cushions, pocket-knives and pepper-boxes, or so Anthony rather vaguely thought. Mrs Trollope was to find a suitable site and Mr Trollope was to send money and follow her out later. Neither of the Trollope parents intended to emigrate, but they hoped Henry would stay on and make a career running the bazaar.

Mrs Trollope, with Henry, Cecilia, Emily, Auguste Hervieu, a manservant and her maid Mrs Cox, set sail for the United States on 4 November 1827, reaching the mouth of the Mississippi on Christmas Day. Mrs Trollope's disenchantment with Fanny Wright began on the voyage, and one look at the badly organised, primitive, disease-ridden rural slum near Memphis that was Nashoba finished her off. She, Hervieu and her troupe moved on to Cincinnati.

Soon after his wife's departure Mr Trollope abandoned his law practice, and abandoned Julian Hill as well. He did not give up Julian Hill and the farm altogether, being bound by the terms of the lease. He let the house and rented an additional farm at Harrow Weald, a hamlet three miles north, and tried to work both holdings, compounding his difficulties.

Tom came home after his final term at Winchester to the Harrow Weald farm. This may have been the summer that Anthony spent all by himself in his father's chambers in Lincoln's Inn. 'There was often a difficulty in the holidays, – as to what should be done with me.' He remembered passing the time by wandering around the deserted buildings – the law too was in summer recess – 'and in reading Shakespeare out of a bi-columned edition which is still among my books. It was not that I had chosen Shakespeare, but that there was nothing else to read' (*Autobiography*).

Shakespeare infiltrated his imagination,* along with the concerns of his father's moribund Chancery practice: disputed wills, mismanaged trusts, guardianships, bigamy, illegitimacy.

---

* For example, Louis Trevelyan in *He Knew He Was Right* is Trollope's Othello; Mrs Proudie is a spawn of Lady Macbeth, as is Lady Glencora, who in *The Prime Minister* is described as feeling in regard to her husband 'somewhat as Lady Macbeth did towards her lord'. Mr Scarborough in *Mr Scarborough's Family* is a perverse King Lear, and there are many little Lears in Trollope, worrying how to bequeath their lands and possessions, and making wrong choices.

Nothing was wasted, in the end. But to Anthony, Lincoln's Inn always spelt doom. When he was in his fifties he wrote a story, 'The Spotted Dog', in which the narrator walked with a drunken, degraded gentleman scholar, who afterwards cut his own throat, through the Old Square of Lincoln's Inn, 'than which we know of no place in London more conducive to suicide'; and on through New Square, 'which has a gloom of its own, not so potent, and savouring only of madness'.

How did the child that he was, dumped there, find his food, and who got his clothes washed? Was there some wretched caretaking clerk, as much a prisoner as Anthony himself? Was it really a whole summer holidays, or just a few dreadful days burned into a thirteen-year-old's memory?

No letters reached Mrs Trollope in America for six months. She and her little group were desperate for money. She wrote to Tom, from whom she did not hide her marital difficulties: 'Is your father ill? Is he dead? Have his affairs fallen into such confusion that he has not been able to procure the money necessary to send us a remittance?' It was Hervieu, she told Tom, who was paying for everything, including their food; he was making a little money by teaching drawing and selling the odd picture. She herself had decided to write a book about her American adventures, to be illustrated by Hervieu.

When she had been away a year, in autumn 1828, Mr Trollope sailed to join her. He travelled steerage, to save money, in gross discomfort, and was ill for the whole voyage.* He took Tom with him. Of the whole family, only Anthony was left in England and, as he wrote in his autobiography, 'another and different horror fell to my fate'.

Mr Trollope had gone off without paying Anthony's school bills. (The boys were supplied with a daily allowance of bread, butter and milk from the college buttery; other food had to be paid for.) The shopkeepers who supplied the Winchester boys were instructed by the school to extend Anthony no credit. His shilling-a-week pocket money, issued to all the boys and added to the school bill, was stopped. He had no money to give the

* The Atlantic crossing, under sail, took over a month. The first steamship crossing was not until 1838.

statutory tips to college servants, which filled him with shame and embarrassment. 'My schoolfellows of course knew that it was so, and I became a Pariah.' He had, he said in his autobiography, no close friend in whom to confide.

He was not a puny adolescent. All the Trollope boys were heavily built and quite tall (Anthony grew to five feet ten inches), and had loud voices. 'I was big, and awkward, and ugly, and, I have no doubt, skulked about in a most unattractive way. But ah! how well I remember all the agonies of my young heart; how I considered whether I should always be alone; whether I could not find my way up to the top of that college tower, and from thence put an end to everything?'

Both as a dirty little boy at Harrow and as a hulking, skulking, bigger boy at Winchester, Anthony saw himself as a Caliban figure, and blamed his appearance (as well as his poverty) for his unpopularity. In *Can You Forgive Her?* he wrote about the way he observed one man dominating another in social life, concluding that it was 'the outward look of the man' that did the trick. 'Among boys at school the same thing is even more conspicuous, because boys have less of conscience than men, are more addicted to tyranny. . . .'

Those who domineer are not stronger, or braver, or cleverer. 'Here again I think the outward gait of the boy goes far towards obtaining for him the submission of his fellows.' Anthony as a youth looked with incredulous envy at those he called 'curled darlings'.* Good-looking, privileged, confident, easy-mannered, sexually attractive young men – born into the purple, or at least into inherited acres – stalk and laze and flirt their way through his novels. Sometimes he took his revenge by making them venal, shallow and treacherous. Sometimes, entering into their triumphs and indiscretions, he enacted them, becoming in fantasy, in the parallel world of his books, a curled darling himself.

The bazaar project was going ahead in Cincinnati. The site for the building was bought for $1,635 in Mr Trollope's name. He was to

---

* The phrase is from *Othello*, where Brabantio, Desdemona's father, is aghast that his daughter can forsake 'the curled darlings of our nation' for 'the sooty bosom' of the Moor. Trollope quoted the passage in *The Prime Minister*, apropos of Mr Wharton's loathing of his daughter's passion for Ferdinand Lopez, a Portuguese Jew, and the phrase is used repeatedly in other novels.

go home and despatch the stock; Mrs Trollope and the others stayed on.

If nothing has survived about what was said and thought at home about Mrs Trollope's relationship with young Hervieu, America was not so discreet. When she was back in England and the American edition of her *Domestic Manners of the Americans* came out in 1832, causing a scandal and touching every raw nerve in the young Republic's self-esteem, what Cincinnati thought of her during her sojourn there came out too. One local paper criticised her for travelling with a younger man apparently devoted to her and on whom she was dependent for money. Mr Trollope was pitied as a deceived husband. Another Cincinnati paper denounced her liaison with the 'big whiskered Frenchman' (thus providing the only description of Hervieu that we have). She had complained in her book that there were no dinner parties given in Cincinnati; Cincinnati riposted that she had never been admitted into polite society in the city.

The caricaturists underlined the message. In one ingenious drawing, a family group, Mr Trollope was shown wearing a hat out of which appear to sprout cuckold's horns – in fact, antlers belonging to a stag in a half-hidden picture on the wall. Mrs Trollope was described in an article as 'short, thick and vulgar-looking . . . in a green calash* and a long plaid cloak dragging at her heels'. In the caricature she was depicted as long-chinned, knobby-nosed, toothless, thin-lipped and squint-eyed.

Hervieu's portrait of her – done to publicise them both in the year that *Domestic Manners of the Americans* came out, and hung in the Royal Academy exhibition at Somerset House – was very different, as was his sketch of her in her book *Vienna and the Austrians* a few years later. His Mrs Trollope had a girlish, appealing, heart-shaped face, with wide-spaced eyes, just like her daughter Cecilia. No doubt Hervieu flattered her outrageously. Anthony's wife Rose, who first met Mrs Trollope more than a decade later, insisted that Hervieu's portrait was a good likeness. Whatever the truth of the matter Mrs Trollope in middle age, as seen by the Americans, was no figure of romance, no matter what

* A calash was a particularly large and ugly bonnet, stiffened by hoops. It could be pulled forward or pushed back like the hood of a cab or a pram. An example – green, like Mrs Trollope's – is on display in the Victoria & Albert Museum.

they assumed about her relationship with the bewhiskered young Frenchman.

Did jealous suspicion, as well as calomel, poison Mr Trollope? There is no way of knowing whether these American articles and caricatures, with their shameful innuendo, were ever seen by Mr Trollope; nor whether Anthony ever saw them or knew about them, then or afterwards.

Mr Trollope, with Tom, got back to Harrow Weald in spring 1829. It was a whole year later that Henry came home, on his own and exhausted. He turned up at the farmhouse one April night at half-past midnight. His ship had docked at Liverpool; he had taken the coach to London and walked home from there.

Everything had gone wrong in Cincinnati, and Henry had been gravely ill. As Mrs Trollope wrote in *Domestic Manners of the Americans*: 'a bilious complaint, attended by a frightful degree of fever, seized him, and for some days we feared for his life. The treatment he received was, I have no doubt, judicious, but the quantity of calomel prescribed was enormous.' Henry (now nineteen) was also subjected to 'repeated and violent bleeding'.

Mr Trollope wrote in exasperation asking why Henry had come home; America had been intended to furnish him with a career. Mrs Trollope replied not to her husband but to Tom, spelling it out. The bazaar had failed utterly. The enterprise was far too ambitious, comprising not only a shop but a picture gallery, refreshment room, ballroom and concert hall, in a tall building designed in vaguely Moorish style based on the Alhambra,* topped by a dome. The profit from the little they had sold – Mr Trollope had sent out £2,000 worth of goods, but nothing that the American West seemed to want – went towards paying their debts. Even their beds had been taken by creditors, and they had to board with a neighbour – Mrs Trollope and the girls in the one bed, Henry and Hervieu on the floor – in exchange for their parlour carpet. Cecilia, aged fourteen, had no shoes, or so her mother said. One might suppose that she was exaggerating their plight were it not for the many spiteful squibs that followed the publication of her book about America. *The Trollopiad*, for

---

* In this, she was in tune with contemporary taste. Washington Irving's hugely popular *Tales of the Alhambra* came out the same year as her book about America.

example, a verse satire that appeared in New York in 1837, contained the lines:

> She in the garments of a slattern dress'd,
> A TROLLOPE is, a trollop stands confest.

Mrs Trollope was pinning her hopes on her 'beloved son' Tom – 'Let me *hear* of you! I am sure you have to have the stuff in you to become something' – on her book, and on Hervieu. 'He seems only to live in the hope of helping us. He has set his heart on getting us home without drawing on your father's diminished purse.' She was writing to Tom from Washington, from the home of one of the Garnett girls (now Mrs Stone), collecting material for her book, which 'will have great advantages from Hervieu's drawings'.

It does not sound as if she wrote to her youngest son at all. 'My poor dear Anthony will have outgrown our recollection! Tell him not to outgrow his affection for us. No day passes, – hardly an hour – without our talking of you all. . . . God bless you, my dearest Tom.'

Anthony loathed the Harrow Weald farmhouse. He described it in his autobiography as 'one of those farmhouses which seem always to be in danger of falling into the neighbouring horse-pond. As it crept downwards from house to stables, from stables to barns, from barns to cowsheds, and from cowsheds to dung-heaps, one could hardly tell where one began and the other ended.'

Just fifteen, he was taken away from Winchester, for financial reasons, shortly after Henry returned from America in 1830. He was sent back to Harrow again as a charity boy. There was a new headmaster, Dr Longley, who unlike Dr Butler 'never said an ill-natured word'; he later became Archbishop of Canterbury. When Anthony was planning out his novel *The Way We Live Now* and listing the characters, he scrawled the words 'old Longley' against the name of his fictional Bishop of Elmham – a model bishop, as the narrator says in the novel. 'But I doubt whether he was competent to teach a creed, – or even to hold one, if it be necessary that a man should understand and define his creed before he can hold it.'

Since day boys were sent home for lunch and Harrow Weald

was three miles out, Anthony had twelve miles' walking each day, on top of the horror of school. 'Perhaps the eighteen months which I passed in this condition, walking to and fro on those miserably dirty lanes, was the worst period of my life,' he wrote in his autobiography. 'I had not only no friends, but was despised by all my companions. . . . What right had a wretched farmer's boy, reeking from a dunghill, to sit next to the sons of peers, – or, much worse still, next to the sons of big tradesmen who had made their ten thousand a-year? The indignities I endured are not to be described.' The other boys would not let him join in any games. 'Nor did I learn anything, – for I was taught nothing.' Old Harry must have given up on him.

One person to whom he did turn, or perhaps who sought him out, was Mr Cunningham, the much-mocked evangelical vicar, who had a very sympathetic manner. (His memorial in Harrow church praises his wise counsel, his kindness, his 'unfeigned love'.) Frederick Faber,* who was at Harrow with Anthony, told Mrs Trollope when he met her in Florence in 1846 that Cunningham 'gave him his first religious thoughts – but that he always had a sort of misgiving that he occasionally talked nonsense'.

To judge from what Anthony wrote alongside his mother's poem about the Allegra Byron episode, Cunningham betrayed him in some way: 'I used to talk to Cunningham a good deal at one time, and recall he always used to be very civil to me, but he is a most cringing hypocrite and a most confounded liar. . . .' He added the trenchant note that Cunningham's refusal to have a memorial tablet put up in memory of Allegra was 'for fear it should teach the boys to get bastards'.

Tom, already twenty years old, was hanging about for a place at New College which never materialised. He was frequently quarrelling with his father, who insisted on arguing even when people agreed with him, 'a very difficult man to live with'. Henry's relations with his father were even worse. He got a place at Caius College, Cambridge, but stayed up only a short time. Then he started half-heartedly to read for the Bar. Any enterprise involved

---

* Frederick William Faber, 1814–63. A friend of Newman at Oxford, he became a Roman Catholic in 1845. In 1849 he was appointed head of the London Oratory (called the Brompton Oratory from 1854).

rows with Mr Trollope who, while painfully ambitious for his boys, expected them to get educated on no money at all, since he had none to give them.

Tom finally gained a place at Oxford. His father chose Alban Hall, where the principal was Richard Whately, a liberal intellectual theologian (and Archbishop of Dublin from 1831) who transformed what had been known as 'the Botany Bay of the university' into a lively community. But to be in a hall as opposed to a college was, it seemed to Tom, social suicide as well as academically third-rate. Tom blamed his father for everything – for picking Alban Hall, and then for getting him sent down by keeping him back at the beginning of a new term for some reason of his own and refusing to pay the ensuing fine. Tom got taken in by Magdalen Hall* – another refuge, as he saw it, for waifs and strays.

'I have, as it were, been educated to dirt, and taken out my degree in outward abominations,' Anthony wrote in *North America*, thirty years later, when faced with the same primitive conditions in the American West that his mother had endured in his boyhood. He was referring to those months in the barely furnished, dirty and ill-lit farmhouse with his melancholy father, when Tom was at Oxford and he himself passed his 'most jocund hours in the kitchen, making innocent love to the bailiff's daughter'.

He and his father, he observed in his autobiography, ate less well than the bailiff's family. His father was half the time in bed, suffering from bilious headaches, and any hours that he could spare from the farm he shut himself up in the parlour with his work. He, like Mrs Trollope, was writing a book. He had madly embarked on an *Encyclopaedia Ecclesiastica*, a Church history that would explain all ecclesiastical terms, rites and ceremonies, and all the orders and subdivisions of monks and nuns. 'Under crushing difficulties, with few or no books of reference, with immediate access to no library, he worked at his most ungrateful task with unflagging industry.'

Sometimes he made time to coach an uncooperative Anthony in his Greek and Latin. 'As I look back on my resolute idleness and fixed determination to make no use whatever of the books

* Later Hertford College.

thus thrust upon me . . . and as I bear in mind the consciousness of great energy in after-life, I am in doubt whether my nature is wholly altered, or whether his plan were wholly bad.'

Anthony's nature did not wholly alter. At Harrow Weald his 'great energy' was blocked by unhappiness, loneliness and a sense of failure. But there was always mercy in his heart for his father, 'that suffering man', as there was not in Tom's. A bad childhood tends to flatten the emotions, and that is the classic response that the unresponsive, sullen, under-achieving Anthony apparently displayed. An unhappy and abused child can also develop an unusual sensitivity to the needs and moods of adults, if only because he has to be watchful for his own protection. This too was true of Anthony.

He often in his books described a sense of duality, something he called in *Ralph the Heir* 'a double memory, and a second identity'. It was what the heroine of *Ayala's Angel* experienced: 'She was unhappy because she knew that she could not rule herself to her own unhappiness; because, even at this moment, she knew that she was wrong. If she could only release part of herself from the other, then she could fly into his arms. . . .'

This feeling of alienation from one's better, happier self, and of the watcher and the watched within oneself, was expressed again through George Hotspur in *Sir Harry Hotspur of Humblethwaite*: 'He was able, though steeped in worthlessness, so to make for himself a double identity as to imagine and to personify a being who should really possess fine and manly aspirations with regard to a woman, and to look upon himself, – as that being; and to perceive with how withering a contempt such a being would contemplate . . . the real George Hotspur, whose actual sorrows and troubles had now become so unendurable.'

Anthony analysed such feelings frequently in his fiction – these are not the only examples – because he knew them so well. As a boy and as a young man he could only 'release part of himself from the other' in private, and his father could no longer do so at all. Yet with part of himself Anthony understood his father and suffered with him. 'In those days he never punished me, though I think I grieved him much by my idleness; but in passion he knew not what he did, and he has knocked me down with the great folio Bible which he always read' (*Autobiography*).

Mr Trollope had brought very few books from Julian Hill.

Anthony had only his schoolbooks. When Mrs Trollope was ill, during her second summer in Cincinnati, she read her way through all the novels of Fenimore Cooper, which in her feverish state gave her nightmares: 'An additional ounce of calomel hardly sufficed to neutralize the effect of these raw-head and bloody bones adventures.' Anthony too was reading Fenimore Cooper, but less comprehensively. Someone had left in the farmhouse the first two volumes of his novel *The Prairie*, which Anthony read in its incompleteness over and over again. In middle age, on one of his trips to America, he bought thirty-two illustrated volumes of the novels of Fenimore Cooper and shipped them home.

People who have endured a difficult childhood sometimes feel lucky, provided they are not broken by the experience, in that life afterwards can only get better. That is how it was for Anthony Trollope, and that is the theme of the autobiography he wrote when he was sixty. In structuring it he deeply cross-hatched the early shadows – not in self-pity, but with some anger, and a retrospective astonishment – in order to highlight what came after. He listed in his autobiography the precise sums of money he had made out of his books to date. This was partly the diffidence of one hesitating to claim the status of an artist, and partly because all his early miseries, he felt, arose from a lack of the stuff. From his late twenties on he was a fanatical keeper of accounts. Money and the efficient management of money were to be central to his feelings of security, along with the regular appearance of a sufficient dinner, and the reliable presence at home of a woman wholly devoted to him – though from the home, and the woman, he constantly absented himself, re-enacting the separation patterns of his youth.

Tom's memoirs were written after Anthony's death, and include a corrective, as Tom saw it, to Anthony's version of their early days. Tom wrote that the Harrow Weald farmhouse was not as dreadful as his brother suggested. Anthony had described it 'too much *en noir*. It had once been a very good house', and though shabby was not tumbledown, though 'forlorn enough' when only himself, Anthony and their father were in residence.

But how much more forlorn was it for Anthony when no one else was there? Tom was in America or in Oxford or on walking tours with college friends. All the Trollope boys were marathon walkers. Tom used to walk the forty-seven miles home to Harrow Weald from Oxford, a knapsack on his back. Once, around this time, Tom and Anthony walked all the way to a firework display at Vauxhall Gardens in south London, where 'Anthony danced all night' – Tom never danced – after which they walked home in the small hours, a round trip of about forty miles. Anthony's uninhibited dancing – and his evident ability to pick up partners – at a time when he was in the grip of adolescent depression reflects a disjunction between the inner and outer man that was to puzzle contemporaries in later life.

During much of the purgatory at Harrow Weald, Henry, as for a shorter time Tom, was with their mother in America. She was, wrote Tom, 'one of those people who carry sunshine with them'. It continued to be Tom to whom she wrote about her adventures, her hopes and her fears. He never had to doubt his central place in her life. That was the essential 'sunshine' that Anthony missed.

In the black scenario that he presented of school life, Anthony was forgetful of its positive legacies. Tom, who was proud of being a Wykehamist, described in detail in his rambling memoirs the daily routine at Winchester. It is from him that we know that the boys went regularly, for play and exercise, up St Catherine's Hill, site of an Iron Age fort and home for Chalk Hill Blue butterflies and badgers, which men and boys routed out of their setts with dogs. This noisy, brutal sport was recalled by Anthony in *The Three Clerks* as a metaphor for the way politicians behave in the House of Commons, each party taking it in turn to be dog or badger. The dogs up on the Hampshire downs, he wrote, could be horribly mauled by a badger, 'who rolls himself up with affected ease, hiding his bloody wounds from the public eye'. (Tom's Winchester nickname was Badger. He, like Anthony, had his wounds; but he also had his mother.)

At the foot of St Catherine's Hill runs the river Itchen, where the boys swam in summer. In the water meadows beside the Itchen is the Hospital of St Cross, an almshouse for thirteen poor men, the memory of which gave Anthony a model for Hiram's Hospital in *The Warden* (transposed to the West Country). He already knew the cathedral close at Exeter. The close at Winchester, to which the college almost seemed to belong, became familiar to him too; a family friend, Dr George Nott, a prebendary of the cathedral, kept in touch with the boys while they were there. Anthony said the memory of Dr Nott, an Italian scholar, dapper in white neckcloth and black gaiters, was the starting-point for idle, worldly Dr Stanhope in *Barchester Towers*.

In his autobiography, Anthony gave Winchester and its environs no more credit for its imaginative legacy than he gave Lincoln's Inn – because, at the time, there was no reason in either case to believe that there could be one. Lincoln's Inn meant desolation, and Winchester was an unpleasant interlude in the longer horror of Harrow.

At Harrow, Anthony wrote, he won no prizes. In fact, he won an English essay prize. This must have surprised everyone, since he was treated as a dunce. As when he danced all night at Vauxhall, Anthony for once 'released part of himself from the other'. But William Gregory,* two years younger, who 'became intimate' with him during the second spell at Harrow because they sat next to each other in class, confirmed Anthony's dismal view of himself: 'He was a big boy, older than the rest of the form, and without exception the most slovenly and dirty boy I ever met.' His work was 'a mass of blots and smudges'.

Mr Trollope's difficulties were well known, and a story went round the school, said Gregory, that Anthony's father 'had been outlawed, and every boy believed it was the duty of a loyal subject of the crown to shoot or otherwise destroy "old Trollope" if possible. Fortunately, he never appeared among us.' The public nature of the Trollopes' poverty was one of its most distressing features. As Anthony wrote in *Ralph the Heir*: 'In the midst of calamities caused by the loss of fortune, it is the knowledge of what the world will say that breaks us down; – not regret for those enjoyments which wealth can give, and which had long been anticipated.'

William Gregory did not dislike Anthony. 'I avoided him, for he was rude and uncouth, but I thought him an honest, brave fellow.' As Gregory – and Anthony – said, boys do not make allowances, 'and so poor Trollope was tabooed, and had not, so far as I am aware, a single friend'.

But what about John Merivale, whom Anthony had known

* Sir William Gregory, 1817–92, of Coole Park, Co. Galway: MP for Galway for many years, Governor of Ceylon 1871–77. His much younger second wife, Augusta, was the collaborator of W. B. Yeats and a leading figure in the Irish Revival. Quotations from his *Autobiography*, ed. Lady Gregory (1894).

since he was ten, who was at both Sunbury and Harrow with him, and who remained a close friend all his adult life? At Winchester, what about Walter Awdry, always in trouble, 'whom I dearly loved', wrote Anthony in his autobiography, when writing about their rackety life together in London? Maybe at school Merivale and Awdry had problems enough of their own and, like William Gregory, avoided Anthony and the contagion of his unpopularity. Merivale's father, Mr Trollope's legal friend, was a Commissioner in Bankruptcy which, under the circumstances, might have been an embarrassment.

Anthony's subfusc all-male world may also have been an indistinct one. As an adult he was extremely short-sighted, and wholly dependent on his spectacles. Myopia generally develops in adolescence. Yet with all his disadvantages Anthony was not a coward. He recalled in his autobiography a moment of rebellion at Harrow, 'a great fight – at the end of which my opponent had to be taken home for a while'. He hoped that some school contemporary might still be living 'who will be able to say that, in claiming this solitary glory of my schooldays, I am not making a false boast'.

It was not a false boast, and it was remembered. There was a day boy called Thomas Baylis who sometimes walked to school with Anthony, and he told Anthony's first biographer T. H. S. Escott all about the famous fight, which had lasted a whole hour. And in Australia in 1881 Anthony's younger son Fred met a government official 'who says he was your fag at Harrow. I had a long yarn with him and he said that you once had a great fight and at last beat your man.'

Such anecdotes lighten the dark picture of Anthony's schooldays, as does his throwaway mention of flirting with the bailiff's daughter at home. Anthony appreciated pretty girls. When an old Harrovian of the next generation asked an education specialist what, in his experience, was the distinctive characteristic of Harrovians, the expert said, 'a certain shy bumptiousness'.* Maybe Anthony had a certain shy bumptiousness.

He also had hidden resources. From the age of fifteen he had the 'dangerous habit' of keeping a journal, and kept it up for ten years. (Tom discovered and read it once at Winchester, and made it the occasion for a special beating, with a cricket stump.) He preserved

* *Collections and Recollections* by One Who Has Kept a Diary, Smith, Elder (1898).

these journals until 1870, and then destroyed them. 'They convicted me of folly, ignorance, indiscretion, idleness, extravagance, and conceit.' In a less formal context he conceded they were 'a heartsick, friendless little chap's exaggeration of his woes'. The journals were an emotional outlet and part of his apprenticeship; they 'habituated me to the rapid use of pen and ink, and taught me how to express myself with facility'. His handwriting, from earliest young manhood, was flowing and graceful. Blots, smudges and slovenliness were for school-work.

Another kind of secret life began even earlier. 'Play of some kind was necessary to me then, as it has always been.' So he played alone, in his mind. In *Barchester Towers* the authorial voice breaks into a description of the high, elaborately carved bishop's throne in the cathedral: 'Ah! how often sitting there, in happy early days, on those lowly benches in front of the altar, have I whiled away the tedium of a sermon in considering how best I might thread my way up amidst those wooden towers, and climb safely to the topmost pinnacle!' And in *Is He Popenjoy?* Jack de Baron, mooning over an unattainable married woman, wandered into Barchester cathedral and recalled how as a child he had got through a long sermon there by planning how he could 'climb to the pinnacle which culminated over the bishop's seat, and thence make his way along the capitals and vantages of stonework, till he would ascend into the triforium and thus become lord and master of the building'. But this was only the beginning of Anthony's imaginings.

He had a habit, he wrote, 'that I often regarded with dismay when I thought of the hours devoted to it, but which, I suppose, must have tended to make me what I have been.' The habit was daydreaming. He called it 'building castles in the air'. He daydreamed on the interminable long walks to and from school, in class, and through the tedious evenings at Harrow Weald.

For weeks, even months, 'I would carry on the same tale, binding myself down to certain laws, to certain proportions, and proprieties, and unities.' Nothing impossible, nor even violently improbable, was allowed. 'I was of course my own hero', but he never made himself a king or a duke. 'But I was a very clever person, and beautiful young women used to be very fond of me. And I strove to be kind of heart, and open of hand, and noble of thought, despising mean things; and altogether I was a very much better fellow than I have ever succeeded in being since.'

It was, he thought in retrospect, a most 'dangerous mental practice'. All the terms he chose, in his autobiography, to describe both this solitary play and the anxiety he felt about it, have sexual overtones. The daydreaming evidently involved sexual release as well as the emotional release 'of part of himself from the other'. The excitement of release through daydreaming was linked – by him – with the addictive excitement of writing novels, for 'I have often doubted whether, had it not been my practice, I should ever have written a novel.' Unlike the journal-writing, the daydreaming was never abandoned, though its nature changed.

The daydreaming habit was 'the occupation of my life', he wrote, for six or seven years before he joined the Post Office – which means that it became his refuge and comfort around the time his mother went away.*

Every now and then in his novels something happens which is so like a boy's daydream that it must have its source in early castles in the air, unforgotten. Obscure young Johnny Eames (a daydreamer himself) in *The Small House at Allington* gallantly rescued the Earl de Guest from an attack by a dangerous bull, after which the grateful earl took him up and became his patron; in *Marion Fay*, George Roden the despised young Post Office clerk discovered he was really the Duca di Crinola. Though Anthony said he never made himself a duke, an Italian title, being a lesser thing, was maybe allowed. He had cheated a little anyway by giving his humble clerk a name with noble connotations. There was a real-life Earl of Roden, with estates in the north of Ireland.

Mrs Trollope, with Hervieu and the girls, docked at Woolwich, home at last, in August 1831. Mr Trollope had driven the gig to London to enquire after their ship. As he would, he missed them, and they were at Harrow Weald when he got back. It was more than three and a half years since Anthony had seen his mother and sisters. He was a child when they left, a hulking youth when they returned.

Mrs Trollope, like her daughters, arrived home in tatters, and was appalled by the conditions at Harrow Weald. Tom, she told her friend Julia Garnett,† was sleeping in a garret with no pillow

* For a sensitive analysis of the masturbatory element in both the daydreaming and the novel-writing of Anthony Trollope, see J. Hillis Miller, *The Ethics of Reading*, Columbia University Press, 1987.

† The second of the Garnett girls from Bristol who had lived in Paris. Julia was by this time married to Dr Pertz, royal librarian and archivist in Hanover.

to his head. Henry, who had abandoned his law studies, and Anthony, who would have left Harrow had there been anything else for him to do, were both 'without destination'.

Mrs Trollope prepared for her next leap in the dark. From the day of her return she embarked on a non-stop literary career that lasted for twenty-five years. She wrote over forty books; Hervieu illustrated six of them. (His illustrations were adequate but unremarkable.) Her change of life was a change for the better; her entry into authorship, at the age of fifty-one, released unused mental capacities. She wrote with feeling in *Paris and the Parisians* about how, for English girls, 'the terror of being called learned is in general much more powerful than that of being classed as ignorant.' There was no stigma of that kind in France, 'whereas for us, the dread of imputed bluism weighs down many a bright spirit, and sallies of wit and fancy are withheld from the fear of betraying either the reading or the genius with which many a fair girl is endued who would rather be thought an idiot than a BLUE.' The bright spirit of Mrs Trollope, as Miss Milton, must have been weighed down in this way. Now she would put it to profitable use. Writing was one of the few money-making options open to women, or rather to ladies. As Anthony – never an advocate of careers for women – put it in his story 'Mrs Brumby', authorship 'seems to be the only desirable harbour to which a female captain can steer her vessel with much hope of success'.

The room where Mrs Trollope worked was labelled 'the sacred den', for which she paid for her own coal and candles as she laboured to finish her book about America. Outside the den there was little tranquillity. Anthony had another satisfactory fight, this time with Tom, who had brought home two singlesticks with basket handles. They tried them out, each trying to hit the other while defending himself. One singlestick broke at once, so they substituted 'a tremendous blackthorn'. Anthony was no longer the passive pupil in relation to Tom, who acknowledged in his diary that 'Anthony is far my superior in quickness and adroitness, and perhaps in bearing pain too.' Anthony had had a lot of practice in bearing pain.

The failure of Mr Trollope's farming enterprises cannot be ascribed wholly to his own mismanagement. The agricultural south of England was much harder hit by the post-war recession than the north, where the new factories and mills absorbed surplus labour. Farm labourers were pauperised by low wages, which were supplemented by a dole paid out of parish rates. This enraged everyone except the landowners – the labourers because they wanted a living wage, and the independent parishioners because they had to subsidise them. Although death penalties for minor offences were repealed during the 1820s, after the end of the war fierce game-laws had been introduced, which meant that poor country people risked deportation even for poaching rabbits.

The ruling, landed class – with the terrifying example of the French Revolution still in living memory – saw any combination of workers as potentially seditious and revolutionary. A few months before the introduction of the electoral Reform Bill, in the winter of 1830 when Mrs Trollope was still in America, farm labourers south of the Thames smashed up thrashing machines and marched aggressively for improved wages. Three were hanged, and thousands deported to Australia. The Reform Bill, finally passed in 1832, was not a democratic measure so much as an appeasement of 'the mob' and a measure to give the growing middle classes some stake in government, as well as an effort to stabilise the essentially landed base of the British political establishment. It left labourers, artisans and most of the lower middle class still without a vote. The franchise was considered a privilege, and a reward for material success. The uneducated and ignorant were 'unfit' to take part in government, and the idea of a secret ballot was thought to be sneaky and un-English.

In the run-up to the passing of the Bill, there was widespread unrest and, in London, an epidemic of cholera which killed over 5,000. It was not just the unlettered rural poor who were up in arms, but the growing class of aspiring urban working-class Radicals who took advantage of the new Mechanics Institutes, where the evangelical seriousness and the syllabus of science and modern subjects was in marked contrast to the classical studies of the public schools. There were Radical riots in Bristol, where Mrs Trollope had friends and relations, and the bishop's palace and the prison there were set on fire.

Hervieu wrote to Tom at Oxford: 'I have been for nearly three weeks now vexed beyond the power of my mild temper. First this cursed Reforms Bill' – and then, the difficulty of getting lithographic stone from Paris for his illustrations. 'Your poor Mamma has been floating about from incertitude to incertitude, cholera morbus and revolution spread their wings over everything we meet.' He fell ill, and Mrs Trollope nursed him. Mr Trollope rescued an old friend from a madhouse in Salisbury and installed him temporarily in the farmhouse.

Mrs Trollope had the energy to cope with all this. It was the lack of money that worried her sick, and the noisy scenes between Mr Trollope and the unemployed Henry. She took laudanum and green tea to keep herself awake to write. Hervieu 'insisted on my having his room to write in at night' – taking a smaller one for himself, she hastened to add, to Julia Pertz.*

Reunion with her husband did not mean reconciliation. He declined to show tenderness, on principle, and was too far gone in depression. Some relief came when he immersed himself anew in his *Encyclopaedia Ecclesiastica*. 'He really seems quite another being; – and so I, in consequence,' Mrs Trollope wrote to Tom. Hervieu was undertaking the illustrations for Mr Trollope's book as well as hers – pictures of monks and nuns in the habits of their orders. Thinking about Mr Trollope, it is impossible for readers of Anthony's novels not to remember tragic Mr Crawley in *The Last Chronicle of Barset*, 'mulling over his costly upbringing, his scholarship and learning, his vocation, his devotion – and his poverty'.

There was the possibility that Anthony's father might get a paid job, a police magistracy. Uncle Adolphus Meetkerke called on Lord Melbourne, the Home Secretary, and Lord Melbourne wrote a note to Mr Trollope which convinced him that the post was as good as his. Mrs Trollope felt the note implied no such thing, and she was right. Mr Trollope did not get the magistracy; but he managed to interest the publisher John Murray in the first volume of his *Encyclopaedia*, covering the letters A (for Abaddon) to F (for Funeral Rites). It was the only volume he ever completed,† and was probably accepted for his wife's sake; at the

* It seems unlikely that Mrs Trollope and Hervieu were ever lovers. She was infatuated by him, and co-opted him as a confidant and a male arm to lean on. He, having thrown in his lot with the family, and pinned his career hopes on them, was perhaps a bit in love with them all.

† Both Tom and Anthony, as middle-aged men, were friends with George Eliot and spent much time in her company. It is possible that their stories about their father's ambitious and doomed opus contributed to her creation of Mr Casaubon and his equally ambitious and doomed 'Universal Mythology' in *Middlemarch*. The dates of the Trollopes' friendship with her and of her creation of Casaubon support this supposition. There was however a real-life Casaubon, a seventeenth-century mediaevalist who collected manuscripts and records from monasteries destroyed by Henry VIII – see Alice Chandler, *A Dream of Order* (1969).

interview with Murray, to which Mrs Trollope accompanied him, the publisher showed much more interest in her future as an author than in his.

When *Domestic Manners of the Americans* came out from the publishers Whittaker, Treacher in March 1832 Mrs Trollope found herself, like Byron after the publication of *The Corsair*, famous overnight.

Travellers' tales about North America were already an established genre, but it is impossible to overestimate the furore that her book caused. Impression after impression was sold. 'I suspect that what I have written will make it evident that I do not like America,' she wrote in her conclusion. What she did not like was 'the total and universal want of manners' and the 'coarse familiarity, untempered by any show of respect'. She could not see why the girl she hired to help in the house in Cincinnati wept because she was expected to eat alone in the kitchen. Mrs Trollope had no money, and she sometimes looked like a tramp, yet expected to be instantly recognised as a 'lady', and treated accordingly, by the democratic citizens of the United States. She took offence, and she gave offence. If she did have any ill-formulated ideas about the romance of what she now called 'sedition', she was thoroughly cured.

She also, to her credit, berated the Americans for their treatment of slaves and Indians. Americans were 'most lamentably deficient in every feeling of honour and integrity. . . . You will see them with one hand hoisting the flag of liberty, and with the other flogging their slaves.'* But in the long backwash of the French Revolution and the American War of Independence, it was her anti-republicanism which polarised her readers. If Napoleon had been a name with which to frighten children, democracy was a word to frighten English Tories. Her book delighted them, and enraged pro-American Whigs and Radicals.

Her so-called coarseness added an extra frisson. She wrote about corsets, about women breast-feeding in public, and about the 'universal defect in the formation of the bust, which is rarely full, or gracefully formed'. She complained about the obscene graffiti on nude statues in the Pennsylvania Academy of Fine Arts,

* Slavery throughout the British Dominions had been abolished in 1825.

to which she was admitted on her own, the insulting implication being that she would like to 'steal a look at what was considered indecent'. She described the sexual frenzy which the hell-fire sermons of itinerant preachers aroused in young girls, and told how seven 'saved' girls were left pregnant after one lascivious evangelist left town. She did not use the words 'sexual' and 'pregnant', but her circumlocutions were neat, and sarcastic. It was this robust refusal to see any subject as taboo that made younger people call her 'vulgar'; she was a child of the eighteenth century.

After the first dinner party given for her by the publisher John Murray (she churned out no less than four books over the next two years – he finally secured the fourth), the invitations rolled in. Mrs Trollope was lionised and she loved it. In order to go to the parties she was asked to by lords, ladies and literati, she took lodgings for a while in London, in Thayer Street off Manchester Square, taking Cecilia with her. As the Reform Bill agitation raged, she moved among high Tories who, she told Tom, 'appear to me to do nothing but lie on their sophas [sic] and groan'. She assured him that the time she was giving to social life was 'not lost, professionally'. Cecilia was already making a fair copy of her second book, a novel.

Through his mother's new contacts Henry was made a Fellow of the Geological Society. Aged twenty, he spent the summer of his mother's triumph walking alone in the West Country. The letters which he wrote then to his mother are the closest we can get to this sad, dissatisfied elder brother of Anthony's. He wrote facetious, defensive letters – as if he suspected his parents were relieved he was out of the way, and might not much want to hear from him – laced with good French. His base was Cousin Fanny Bent's hospitable house in Exeter, which he reached one July night having walked the thirty-four miles from Taunton. 'What a beautiful road it is, I am almost ashamed to write the word beautiful yet I must repeat it till you are heartily sick of the repetition.' Thirty miles was his daily average. Fanny Bent gave a party and the pretty girls of the neighbourhood came. A Mrs Cross brought 'a most *beautiful* niece, but married, so don't be afraid, ma!'

Fanny Bent, no longer young, climbed to the top of the

cathedral tower with him, and walked with him on Dartmoor and up High Torr. Henry loaded his knapsack with stones and specimens, and with black oxide from the manganese mines at Upton Pyne. 'I am in good health – and very happy – oh yes I am very ha-a-py, when first I set out I little thought ever to be so ha-a-py.' (Mrs Trollope, in the face of the worst misfortunes, frenetically commanded her children to 'be happy'.) He visited his Aunt Mary Clyde at Ottery St Mary, and walked on towards Cornwall.

Visiting the caves at Buckfastleigh, Henry was invited to dinner by a stranger, Captain White of Buckfast Abbey, who lent him a coat and waistcoat for the occasion. The name Trollope, because of the notorious book, was an Open Sesame. 'To your fame oh illustrious mother do I owe this honour and this dinner.' He visited a copper mine, and walked on to Plymouth; but the weather had broken, and he had a pain that he called rheumatism in his right shoulder. His shoulder hurt, his feet hurt. The letters became plaintive, perhaps in response to plaintive ones from home. 'I am expensive mother because I cannot enjoy myself without it a little.'

The following spring there was a great flu epidemic and everyone in the family caught it. Hervieu was delirious, and the doctor bled Anthony with leeches until he fainted. But it was Henry who failed to recover properly. He got a temporary job as a tutor, in Fulham on the south-west outskirts of London, where Mrs Trollope's brother, also a Henry, and his family lived; it was probably this uncle who found him the job, and Henry stayed in his house. What kind of a tutor can Henry have been? He had left Winchester at fifteen as a failure, but as with Anthony, his school performance bore no relation to his accomplishments or capacities.

Mrs Trollope made £1,000 in the first year from *Domestic Manners of the Americans*. (She gave Hervieu half the proceeds of the second impression.) Six months after it came out she moved the family back to Julian Hill – 'one long turmoil', as she wrote to her friend Mrs Bartley, the pretty actress wife of George Bartley, manager of Covent Garden Theatre; 'but *it is done* and here we are once more enjoying our beautiful view from Harrow Hill.' The children were put to work. 'When we were young,' wrote Anthony in *Thackeray*, 'we used to be told, in our house at home, that "elbow-grease" was the one essential necessary to getting a tough piece of work well done. If a mahogany table was to be made to shine, it was elbow-grease that the operation needed.' Julian Hill was 'an Eden' to Anthony, 'as compared to our abode at Harrow Weald'; and he had only half a mile to walk to and from school instead of twelve miles a day. Mrs Trollope could afford to buy food and household essentials. It was like the transformation scene in a pantomime. The daily intimacy with the Grants next door was re-established, and friends poured through the house again. They started a family magazine called *The Magpie*, edited by Henry.

Remembering his mother at this time, Anthony wrote: 'Of the mixture of joviality and industry which formed her character, it is almost impossible to speak with exaggeration. The industry was a thing apart, kept to herself.' She got up to write at four in the morning and her stint was done before the family woke up. 'Work sometimes came hard to her, so much being required; – for she was extravagant, and liked to have money to spend' (maybe she was as much to blame as Mr Trollope for the extravagant house-building of their early Harrow years, as for the exotic multi-tiered bazaar in Cincinnati); 'but of all people I have known she was the most joyous, or, at any rate, the most capable of joy.'

He wrote those words in his autobiography, but even as a boy he knew that the capacity for joy – which his mother had, and his father had not – was good, and important. In September 1833, when he was eighteen, he annotated a copy of Burke's *Philosophical Enquiry into the Origins of Our Ideas of the Good and the Beautiful*, which he was reading for his own pleasure. A man might be fond of the romance of grief, he noted, but if so it is only the romance he enjoys. 'NO ONE CAN LIKE GRIEF.'

CHAPTER THREE

I N the summer of 1833 Mrs Trollope went on a trip to
Belgium and West Germany for another travel book, taking
Hervieu (with his sketchbook*) and Henry (with his geological hammer). Hervieu got on particularly well with Henry; they
had been through a great deal together during the American
adventure. Henry wrote in one of his letters from the West
Country that he wished Hervieu could be with him, to sketch the
scenery. Neither Tom nor Anthony left any record of their feelings
about their mother's friend. They sometimes referred to him in
letters as 'Heirview', but this may have been a joke about the
English pronunciation of his name rather than about his possible
expectations of benefits to come.

The three stayed in Ostend with the Fauches. Mr Fauche was
the British consul, and his wife Mary, née Tomkisson and the
daughter of a piano manufacturer, was one of Mrs Trollope's
younger friends and supporters. Mrs Trollope had other friends in
Brussels, 'long valued and long lost', as she wrote in her book.
These were the Rev. William Drury and his wife. Both William
Drury and his father Mark got into serious financial trouble in the
late 1820s and had to leave Harrow; William Drury became
clergyman to the large British community in Brussels and ran a
school there for boys.

'Old Harry' Drury went bankrupt as well. The number of
'smashes' among the Trollopes' acquaintances alone shows
the toughness of the times and the vulnerability of people in
the professions. There was absolutely no safety net for the
unlanded, other than the charity of friends and relations.
The Trollopes accepted handouts when they had to. Anthony was

---

* Mrs Trollope appended a regretful note to her *Belgium and Western Germany in 1833*: 'The
sketches by Mr *Hervieu*, so frequently alluded to in the following pages, were intended to
accompany this publication; but the expense of engraving them in the style they deserved
was found so great, that the idea was abandoned.'

writing from family experience, in *The Last Chronicle of Barset*: 'None but they who have themselves been poor gentry, – gentry so poor as not to know how to raise a shilling, – can understand the peculiar bitterness of the trials which such poverty produces.' Their sufferings were different from those of what he called the 'normal' poor. Poor gentry rarely had to face the workhouse, but 'The angry eyes of unpaid tradesmen, savage with an anger which one knows to be justifiable; the taunt of the poor servant who wants her wages . . . the neglected children, who are learning not to be the children of gentlefolk; and, worse than all, the alms and doles of half-generous friends, the waning pride, the pride that will not wane. . . .'

What struck Mrs Trollope about Belgium was its cheapness, for English people. It was half the price of Paris – a city that, as she wrote in *Paris and the Parisians*, was considered 'so favourable an expedient in cases of diminished or insufficient fortune'. The point about Paris was that 'It is not the necessaries of life, but the luxuries of life that are cheaper here' – wine, wages, wax candles, fruit, books, 'handsome apartments'. Whereas in Belgium, the necessaries were cheaper too. It was at this point that she began making contingency plans for yet another leap in the dark.

She could pay for the necessaries of life at Julian Hill out of her earnings, but she could not save her husband from personal financial ruin. Lord Northwick, Mr Trollope's landlord, had run out of patience. Northwick complained to Quilton, his bailiff, that he was not doing enough to collect overdue rents, and threatened to dock his salary. Quilton tried to persuade his employer to reduce the rents, since none of the tenant farmers on the estate could possibly pay them, in spite of better harvests for the past couple of years.

Mr Trollope wrote to Lord Northwick personally, saying that in the seventeen years he had held his lease, the produce of the land had never sufficed to cover the rent. Northwick sent him a dusty answer, suspecting him of combining seditiously with the other tenants, and put a distraint on his crops. In late 1833 another Northwick tenant farmer was caught trying to do a moonlight flit, and had the law brought down on him. If the Trollopes wanted to do the same thing, they would have to have a plan.

—— * ——

Anthony, already eighteen, was only vaguely aware that discussions were going on about a flitting. He was still unsuccessful at Harrow, still daydreaming, still cut off from his parents emotionally. 'My mother was much from home or too busy to be bothered. My father was not exactly the man to exact confidences' (*Autobiography*).

He tried for scholarships and exhibitions to both Oxford and Cambridge, and failed. He kept his griefs to himself, like poor Arthur Wilkinson in his novel *The Bertrams*, who also was a school failure:

> Boys on such subjects are very reticent; they hardly understand their own feelings enough to speak of them, and are too much accustomed both to ridicule and censure to look anywhere for sympathy. A favourite sister may perhaps be told of the hard struggle and the bitter failure, but not a word is said to anyone else. His father, so thinks the boy, is angry at his failure; and even his mother's kisses will hardly be warmed by such a subject. We are too apt to think that if our children eat pudding and make a noise they require no sympathy. . . .

In Arthur Wilkinson's case too, in *The Bertrams*, 'It was a great object with his father that he should get a scholarship at New College. . . . When his time came, he was all but successful – but he was not successful.' The fictional Wilkinson was reprieved – his father paid for him to go to Balliol – but there was no possibility of Mr Trollope paying for Anthony.

By virtue of his age Anthony was near the top of the school, but he was still an outsider.

> I coveted popularity with a covetousness that was almost mean. It seemed to me that there would be an Elysium in the intimacy of those very boys whom I was bound to hate because they hated me. Something of the disgrace of my schooldays has clung to me through life. Not that I have ever shunned to speak openly of them as openly as I am writing now [in his autobiography], but that when I have been claimed as schoolfellow by some of the many hundreds who were with me either at Harrow or Winchester, I have felt that I had no right to talk of things from most of which I was kept in estrangement.

51

Yet he was grateful and even proud, afterwards, to have been educated at two great public schools. He left his mark at Harrow, scratching his signature on a cupboard door of the headmaster's desk in the Fourth Form Room, as Byron had done before him. Years later, he gave the manuscript of *Framley Parsonage* to the library at Harrow, in his capacity as a distinguished Old Harrovian. When in the early 1860s the Clarendon Commission investigated the public schools, in consequence of a debate in the periodicals about the quality of the education they provided, Anthony Trollope came to the schools' defence in the *Fortnightly*. Their great merit, he wrote, was that rich boys and less rich boys (such as those educated, like himself, 'on the foundation') met in later life as friends and 'on an absolute equality as gentlemen'.

This point about meeting on an equal footing as gentlemen is the key. The only topics that exercised the nineteenth-century English mind so much as the class system were religion and the politics of religion, and for the same reason. Both were under stress from new and destabilising ideas.

It was not so much a question of class as of tribe. Servants and the lower classes, Anthony always said, were good judges of who was and was not a gentleman; deference was accorded to a gentleman, whatever one's private opinion of him. It was extremely difficult to challenge a gentleman's authority, in the deference society.

Gentlemen recognised one another by complex codes of dress, gesture, taste, use of language and shared references. Gentlemen not only acknowledged and accepted one another, they selected one another – as friends, as suitable husbands for their sisters and daughters, as the holders of commissions, posts, church livings, official positions, parliamentary seats, high office.

To be a gentleman was to have access to power, influence and 'society'. It was not a trivial matter because no one perceived it as a trivial matter. For a man to lose caste, and not to be a gentleman if his father had been a gentleman, seemed an exile of an almost metaphysical order, like losing his faith – only reversed: it was the world that lost its faith in him. Radicals, artists and mavericks who contested or wholeheartedly rejected class demarcations were true rebels. Anthony did not conform at Harrow because he could not. He was a rebel only by default. But he was an outsider within the system, and that gave him his cutting edge.

Gentlemen secure in their status and identity knew each other, or each other's friends, from childhood, and important friendships were made not only at Oxford and Cambridge but at Eton, Winchester, Harrow or one of the lesser public schools. To have been at a public school was a passport, doubly important to Anthony since he did not go to a university. Mr Elias Gotobed, the eponymous non-hero of *The American Senator*, speaking of the difference between the English and the Americans, remarked that 'They meet as might a lad from Harrow and another from Mr Brumby's successful mechanical cramming establishment. The Harrow boy cannot answer a question, but he is sure that he is the proper thing, and is ready to face the world on that assurance.'

For Anthony, the mere fact that he went to Harrow was an assurance to himself and to others that he was 'the proper thing'. He needed that assurance badly. In the frequent allusions, in his fiction, to whether one could make a silk purse out of a sow's ear, the reverse proposition hovered fearfully between the lines: adverse circumstances could make a sow's ear out of a silk purse.

There runs throughout Anthony's novels an ongoing debate about what constituted a gentleman, or a lady. Mary in *Doctor Thorne*, the illegitimate daughter of a gentleman, asks herself: 'What makes a gentleman? What makes a gentlewoman? What is the inner reality, the spiritualized quintessence of that privilege in the world which men call rank, which forces the thousands and hundreds of thousands to bow down before the few elect? What gives, or can give it, or should give it?'

Mary Thorne is a high-minded girl, and her answer is, 'Absolute, intrinsic, acknowledged, individual merit must give it to its possessor, let him be whom, and what, and whence he might. Beyond this it could be had but by inheritance, received as it were secondhand, or twenty-second hand.' That was the ideal view, the moral high ground.

It wasn't so simple, in practice, as glimpses into Anthony's novels at once prove. The Rev. Samuel Prong, the evangelical clergyman in *Rachel Ray*, who had been educated 'at Islington', was 'a devout, good man', wrote Anthony editorially, 'but deficient in one vital qualification for a clergyman of the Church of England; he was not a gentleman. May I not call it a necessary qualification for a clergyman of any church? He was not a gentleman. I do not mean to say that he was a thief or a liar; nor do

I mean hereby to complain that he picked his teeth with his fork and misplaced his "h"s. I am by no means prepared to define what I do mean, – thinking, however, that most men and most women will understand me.'

This uncertainty about who was and who was not a gentleman or a lady preoccupied Anthony's fictional characters, sometimes facetiously, sometimes farcically, sometimes painfully, sometimes quasi-theologically, like a point in scholarship. His English women were every bit as aware of the demarcations as the men. It was an American girl, Caroline Spalding in *He Knew He Was Right*, who, thinking of her English suitor, 'had probably never questioned the fact, whether Mr Glascock was a gentleman or not, and now she did not analyse it. It probably never occurred to her, even at the present time, to say to herself that he was certainly that thing, so impossible of definition, and so capable of recognition. . . .'

The impossibility of definition made for infinite complexity, spitefulness and anxiety. In the last short story Anthony ever wrote, 'The Two Heroines of Plumplington', the provincial bank manager Mr Greenmantle knew that 'the one great line of demarcation in the world was that which separated gentlemen from non-gentlemen.' As for himself, 'there could be no doubt that he was on the right side of the demarcation', and he raised a storm when his daughter wanted to marry the son of a brewer. However, the great man of the town, Dr Freeborn, who traced his lineage back to the days of Charles I, 'did not see the difference between the banker and the brewer nearly so clearly as did Mr Greenmantle. He would probably have said that the line of demarcation came just below himself.' So would many people.

It was not a question of wealth. Gentlemen were acknowledged as gentlemen even in degraded circumstances. Pauperised, disgraced, half-mad Mr Crawley in *The Last Chronicle of Barset* is moved and comforted beyond measure when sleek Archdeacon Grantly pays him the supreme compliment of saying, 'We are both gentlemen.' This is an embarrassing scene for us; the intensity of the manner seems too heavy for the matter. The intensity was Anthony's own, but it would not have struck a false note with his contemporary readership.

The drama of the hierarchical English class system was in its porosity. Families or individuals could rise into the gentleman category, and fall from it into obscurity. Blood and breeding were acquired characteristics, over time: 'I have heard that it takes three generations to make a gentleman,' wrote Mrs Trollope, grand-daughter of a saddler and daughter of a clergyman. Anthony, echoing what must have been the accepted wisdom, put the same words into the mouth of Mrs Freeborn, the doctor's wife, in 'The Two Heroines of Plumplington': 'It always does take three generations to make a gentleman.'

Whether a gentleman let himself and his family down by marrying a woman who was not a lady, or not quite a lady, was central to many of Anthony's novels. He was not a slave to the class system, as his own choice of a wife would demonstrate. But then, like his fictional Reginald Morton in *The American Senator*, he believed in the doctrine that a man 'could raise a woman to his own rank, whereas a woman must accept the rank of her husband'.

In *Lady Anna* Anthony gave his eponymous heroine the choice between marrying an attractive earl and marrying the young tailor to whom, in a time of trouble, she had pledged her troth. While the novel was being serialised in the *Fortnightly* and before Lady Anna's final decision had been divulged Anthony's friend Lady Wood wrote to say she hoped Lady Anna was going to do the right and sensible thing – dump the tailor and marry the earl.

Anthony explained to her that the story of Lady Anna 'was originated in my mind by an idea I had as to the doubt which would, (or might) exist in a girl's mind as to whether she should be true to her troth, or true to her leneage' [sic, for lineage: Harrow did not teach Anthony to be a reliable speller]. 'Of course,' he wrote, 'the girl has to marry the tailor.' He had decided that 'in such a case she ought to be true all through'.

That is the pure Trollopian dogma. Lady Anna might betray her class and drive her mother literally insane by her choice, but she was honest and true and therefore more of a 'lady' than if she had become the wife of an earl. (It must be admitted that, in the frequently recurring dilemma of cross-class attraction, Anthony sometimes let everyone off the hook by revealing in his final chapters that the humbler lover had unexpectedly inherited a fortune, or a noble heritage, to ensure a comfortably happy ending for all.) 'The horror which was expressed to me at the evil thing I had done,' he wrote in his autobiography, 'in giving the girl to the tailor, was the strongest testimony I could receive of the merits of the story.'

Honesty was part of being a gentleman, or a lady. Self-discipline, fortitude, good manners, fastidiousness, a degree of reserve, a sense of duty and the habit of command were the gentlemanly virtues; though very young gentlemen must be allowed to sow their wild oats. There was hypocrisy in this double standard. Sensitive youths valued 'purity' as highly as young girls were taught to do, and suffered agonies of guilt when they fell from grace.

The fact remained that gentlemen often lied, gambled, brawled, fornicated or cheated at cards, and high-born ladies were sometimes grossly unladylike. The unscrupulous Arabella Trefoil in *The American Senator* was the niece of the Duke of Mayfair, but Lord Rufford should not have imagined he loved her, said the horribly ladylike Miss Penge: 'Because you are a gentleman, and because she – is not a lady.' Anthony Trollope's novels are full of voices, sometimes his own, defining, refining, defending and attacking England's class structure, a source of both comedy and tragedy.

The creation of Barchester was inspired, because it united in a microcosm and in a common discourse the two great preoccupations, class and the politics of religion, which Anthony shared with his contemporaries. It was only in England, Anthony wrote in *Australia and New Zealand*, that the clergy constituted 'a distinctive social class'. In this, whether he realised it or not, he was, as so often, echoing his mother, who wrote in *Paris and the Parisians*: 'The clergy of England, their matronly wives and highly educated daughters, form a distinct caste.'

Mrs Trollope developed this idea. Within this distinct caste, she wrote, 'are mingled a portion of every other; yet it has a dignity and aristocracy of its own', within which were blended 'the high blood of the noble' and 'the learning which has in many instances sufficed to raise to a level with it the poor and needy'. This was a wordy way of saying that while many men of gentle birth became clergymen, a clever non-gentleman could advance himself in society by becoming a clergyman; and that the Church, as an institution, provided a gilded ladder with clearly marked rungs.

She capped this perfectly rational analysis by adding that

wherever clergymen and their families are, 'the canker of known and tolerated vice is not'. She cannot have known much about what went on at Harrow.

When Anthony was writing his later books, the wider, looser fabric of society, the spread of education and the rise of immigrants and self-made men had introduced new variables into the already clotted argument about ladies and gentlemen, involving a closing of the ranks on the part of some, and radical thinking about social levelling from others.

Those who could least face wholesale social levelling were not necessarily aristocrats, but middling people who knew their middling niche and found comfort in the status quo – like muddle-headed Mrs Bluestone of Bedford Square in *Lady Anna*: 'I think that a girl who is a lady, should never marry a man who is not a gentleman. . . . Otherwise everything would get mingled, and there would be no differences. That is the meaning of being a gentleman, – or a lady.' On the other hand Mrs Masters, the provincial attorney's wife in *The American Senator*, deploring the emotional turbulence among the young people, ascribed it irritably to 'all that question of gentlemen and ladies, and of non-gentlemen and non-ladies!'

That question of gentlemen and ladies, and non-gentlemen and non-ladies, amused and exercised Anthony Trollope to the end of his days. He continued to believe, as he said in his autobiography, that there were 'places in life which can hardly be well filled except by "Gentlemen" ', even though he knew that this opinion 'almost subjects one to ignominy'. For throughout Anthony's life the divine rights of the old upper class, a tiny minority, were being questioned and eroded by shifts in the base of economic power and by an increasingly educated, articulate majority. (Nevertheless, the class system was to prove uncannily durable and adaptable.)

Anthony approved heartily of self-improvement, of bettering oneself, and of the increasing fluidity of the class system. 'The gates of the one class should be open to the other; but neither to the one class nor to the other can good be done by declaring that there are no gates, no barrier, no difference.' He had direct experience of the gates and barriers, in his impoverished, unhappy boyhood.

Whatever the ambiguities, a gentleman could always be

recognised by his familiarity with the classics. It was a sign that he had been educated in the old-fashioned way, probably at a public school. A casual quotation from Juvenal, Ovid, Virgil, Horace, in print or in speech, was a word to the wise. Though even this could be faked: 'The getter-up of quotations from books which he has never read, – how vile he is to all of us!' (*Travelling Sketches*). Anthony was lavish with Latin quotations, but not from books he had never read. Sometimes he overdid it, especially when in elevated company and anxious to belong. This anxiety, which he recognised as craven, was bred into him at school.

Anthony's parents had left him marking time at Harrow for too long. He could hardly be left there for ever. It was decided he must leave in summer 1834, by which time he would be well into his twentieth year. But the crisis came sooner than that.

Mrs Trollope, assuming perforce the position of authority in the family, had to determine, with the help of her brother Henry Milton, what income could be salvaged. The family affairs were in chaos. Mr Trollope had done unbelievably stupid things, such as lodging the lease of his house in Keppel Street as security against a loan without obtaining a receipt. One did not borrow money from banks, but from friends or professional money-lenders. Mr Trollope was caught in a web of IOUs and 'bills' which he had signed against loans – bills which could be sold on from hand to hand, the interest rising exponentially until the last in the chain attempted to collect some impossible total from the initial borrower.

Mrs Trollope had brought to the marriage £900 a year of her own, but her husband's muddles had swallowed it up. She had a small additional private income, from rents in Somerset held in common with her sister Mary Clyde. There had been a marriage settlement drawn up before her wedding to Mr Trollope; a settlement was the only legal way that a woman's personal money could be protected from an improvident husband. All a wife's money not tied up by a settlement belonged to her husband, by law. Even with a settlement, the wife had use only of the income (which she might choose, or be prevailed upon, to give to her husband). The capital – £1,300 in her case – should have remained intact, but something untoward had happened to it. Marriage settlements were administered by the Court of Chancery, which was Mr Trollope's own branch of the law.

When what remained was salvaged there was enough for Mrs Trollope to buy an annuity of £250 a year, for herself and her daughters. If she failed to keep up her writing they would be in trouble. The crucial matter was to separate her own affairs from those of her husband before his landlord Lord Northwick and other creditors called in the law.

Mrs Fauche was deputed to find a house in Belgium for them. It was arranged that Mr Trollope should be got safely out of the country first, in April (1834), and that Mrs Trollope, Henry and the girls would follow. Tom was in his last year at Oxford and Anthony was meant to see out the school year at Harrow. In the event, one March morning Anthony was hauled out of bed early and told to drive his father to London. Only when they were on their way did he learn that he was to take his father to the boat for Ostend. 'It was not in his nature to be communicative and to the last he never told me why he was going to Ostend' (*Autobiography*).

Mr Trollope got away only just in time. If he had stayed he would have been arrested and imprisoned for debt. As Anthony was nearing home on the way back he was intercepted by their former gardener and warned that the sheriff's men were already at Julian Hill on Lord Northwick's orders, removing all their possessions. If he turned up with the horse and gig they too would be taken. Anthony drove on up the hill into the village and sold horse and gig to the ironmonger, for £17 – which was the sum the ironmonger said the family owed him, so Anthony walked home with nothing.

'When I got back to the house a scene of devastation was in progress, which was not without its amusement.' While the bailiff's men carried furniture out at the front Cecilia, Emily and the three Grant girls were surreptitiously collecting up anything they could carry – china, glass, books, silver – and running with them through the gap between the two gardens into the Grants' house. Anthony joined in. 'I still own a few books that were thus purloined.' So not everything was lost; and Mrs Trollope was able to buy back, with her own money and at the official valuation, some of the furniture that was carted away.

She called on Lord Northwick, though it is hard to imagine what she could have said to him. She wrote to Tom at Oxford: 'Nothing, surely, of equal importance was ever left in such a manner (unless it were the bazaar at Cincinnati).' Colonel and

Mrs Grant, 'that dearest of all women', as Anthony called her, took them in. The Rev. Mr Cunningham – who had twelve children, and had moved into Julians, the Trollopes' original white elephant of a house – offered to give Cecilia and Emily a home. The Rev. Henry Trollope, a Lincolnshire cousin who was also a brother-in-law (he was married to Mr Trollope's sister Diana), lent £100. Uncle Henry Milton helpfully corrected the proofs of *Belgium and Western Germany in 1833*.

They were all packed and ready to leave the country when Henry's state of health worsened. He had TB. The doctor said the damp Belgian coast in winter might be fatal for him. So Mrs Trollope, in great distress, took him down to Devonshire and left him by the sea in Dawlish in the care of Fanny Bent. The other children sailed alone, and their mother joined them later. Auguste Hervieu stayed behind.

The Trollopes and their luggage travelled from Ostend to Bruges by barge. The house Mrs Fauche had found for them was large and square and modern, just outside the Smeeden Port, one of the old stone gates of Bruges, in the hamlet of St Baess. Called the Château d'Hondt, it was not a château but a large suburban villa. Tom, when he went back to take a look at it more than thirty years later, found it 'as uncompromisingly ugly, as solidly compact, as comfortable and as defiant of the pretty or the picturesque as ever.' At the beginning of June Mrs Trollope wrote a long letter about their new life to Colonel Grant in Harrow:

> As the days and weeks roll over us, my beloved friend, we begin to get fitted into the places that fate and fortune have been pleased to chuse [sic] for us, and so blessedly flexible is the – fancy, spirit, imagination, or whatever I should call that part of us which best endures change, that we have each of us learned to fix ourselves in some selected corner of our different rooms, and believe ourselves at home. The old desks have found new tables to rest upon, and the few favourite volumes that could not leave us are made to fill their narrow limits in orderly rows that seem to say – 'here we are to dwell together'. All this is very well – I am quite satisfied with our house and have almost learnt to think the square garden, with its labyrinth walks through overgrown shrubs, a very pretty bocage.'

What she most missed was 'the cheering sound of some of your dear voices on the lawn'; not seeing the Grants every day cost her more than 'the loss of my whole visiting list from A to Z'. The house was too large, and to make believe it was furnished she was 'plotting and planning from morning to night how to make one table and two chairs do the work of a dozen'. She was worrying about Henry, not having heard from Dawlish by the last mail. She was worrying about Tom, who was leaving Oxford with a third-class degree, and needed paid employment. She did not mention Anthony – nor Emily, who was showing signs of the same disease that had attacked Henry.*

The resilient Mrs Trollope drew what was pleasant around her like a magnet, as Tom put it, and she soon had a busy social life among the many English people living in Bruges, Brussels and Ostend mostly for the same reason as the Trollopes and the William Drurys – because they could not afford to live in their own country, or were evading their creditors, or in some cases because their private lives were unorthodox. Divorce was so complicated and expensive, requiring an act of Parliament, and caused such scandal, that some incompatible couples separated unofficially, and one of them would repair to the Continent (giving delicate health as a reason) where he or she maintained a second relationship.

Tom remarked that these expatriates constituted 'a queer and not very edifying society', and that even the married couples 'seemed to be continually dancing the figure of *chassée croisée*' (i.e., changing partners). Mrs Trollope had a strong sense of the proprieties in some areas – she did not think young girls should be allowed to read the novels of Richardson or Fielding – but she had a gossip's appetite for sexual irregularity. In her *Belgium and Western Germany* she described watching on a Rhine steamer 'a handsome woman, but not quite young, and a magnificent *militaire*, not quite old. They were certainly not married.' And of a pretty woman dining alone in a hotel in Baden: 'No gentleman ever attended her into the room, but when she left it, she was generally accompanied by two or three.' Mrs Trollope could weave whole novels out of vignettes such as these – a skill inherited, or picked up, by Anthony.

* Tuberculosis was the scourge of the nineteenth century, affecting all classes. Between 1838 and 1842 the annual mortality per million of population from pulmonary tuberculosis was 3,782. The mortality rate fell gradually as the century progressed.

He too exploited, long afterwards, his knowledge of the English in Belgium. In *Mr Scarborough's Family* the snooty wife of the British Minister in Brussels complained about English people 'who had come to live there as a place at which education for their children would be cheaper than at home', and she did not see why she, as the Minister's wife, 'should be expected to entertain all the second-class world of London'. But there were plenty of Belgians who found the society of the expatriates amusing, like M. Grascour, 'thoroughly a gentleman', in the same novel: 'As is the case with many Belgians, he would have been taken to be an Englishman were his country not known. He had dressed himself in English mirrors, living mostly with the English. He spoke English so well that he would only be known as a foreigner by the correctness of his language.'

There were two English churches in ·Brussels, and two English-language newspapers. Charles Lever, a young Irish doctor and aspiring author whom Anthony was to meet a decade later, arrived in Belgium in 1836, attracted like everyone else by its cheapness. He set up in practice as physician to the English community and, cutting through the English class system as only an Irishman could, rose rapidly both socially and professionally, boasting that he had lords and ladies as patients; he was one who did pass muster with the British Minister of the time,* becoming his medical attendant and a pet of his wife and family, 'really at the top of the ladder', as he put it.

Lever said that before he arrived in Belgium – which was the year after the Trollopes left – there was only one English doctor in Brussels, a man who was frequently in gaol for debt. Of Bruges, Lever noted that it was one of the cheapest places not only in Belgium but on the whole Continent – 'and no English doctor, though a qualified man could make £400 to £500 a year'.†

The Trollopes could have done with a friendly English doctor. The Château d'Hondt was a house of sickness. Henry joined the family in July, having been instructed by his mother to bring out soap and '6 lb of wax ends' – the stubs of wax candles from hotels and big houses, sold off cheap. Tom saw Henry off at the docks, and thought he looked desperately ill.

---

* Sir Hamilton Seymour.
† Edmund Downey, *Charles Lever: His Life in His Letters*, Blackwood, 1906.

At fifty-five, Mrs Trollope re-established her routine of writing her books by night, helped by laudanum and green tea. The famously drug-addicted writers of the period such as de Quincey and Coleridge were not exceptional except in degree. Harriet Martineau,* writing in her autobiography about the 1830s and 40s, claimed that 'a clergyman who knew the literary world well' told her that 'there was no author or authoress who was free from the habit of taking some pernicious stimulant; either strong green tea, or strong coffee at night, or wine or spirits or laudanum. The amount of opium† taken, to relieve the wear and tear of authorship, was, he said, greater than most people had any conception of; and all literary workers took something.' (Except of course the high-principled Miss Martineau.)

What is important, for understanding Mrs Trollope's habit, is the parity of perniciousness accorded at the time to tea and coffee, and to opium. Cohabitation was a far worse crime, in the public estimation, than drug abuse.

Anthony was only in Bruges for about six months. He felt there that he was 'an idle, desolate hanger-on, that most hopeless of human beings, a hobbledehoy of nineteen, without any idea of a career, or a profession, or a trade. As well as I can remember I was fairly happy, for there were pretty girls at Bruges with whom I could fancy I was in love. . . .' (*Autobiography*).

Bruges was not a bad place for a nineteen-year-old to fancy that he was in love and to build castles in the air. A short walk from the house brought Anthony through the city gate, over the encircling canal and up a street of narrow, steep-gabled houses to the heart of the little Flemish city. The quietness was broken quarter-hourly by the clangour of the carillon in the tower on the market square – with its waterways, barges and breweries, humped stone bridges, convent closes, cobbled courts and squares, decaying mediaeval palaces and brand-new neo-classical fishmarket. Bruges is a Catholic town; in the basilica in the Burg Square, a reliquary holds drops of the Holy Blood. Nuns treated patients in a hospital hung with paintings by Memling and Van Eyck. Milk

* Harriet Martineau, 1802–76. Journalist, novelist and pamphleteer, political economist and indefatigable social reformer.
† Laudanum is a tincture of opium.

was sold in the streets from carts pulled by dogs; animated flea-markets lined the banks of the canals. Anthony was free of 'the real misery of school', but he was aimless: 'as to my future life I had not even an aspiration.'

In this situation almost anything would do. There came 'from some quarter' – no doubt from one of Mrs Trollope's new acquaintances – the offer of a commission in an Austrian cavalry regiment. The only qualification necessary was fluency in French and German. (In neither language was Anthony ever proficient. In French, 'I have been able to order my dinner and take a railway ticket, but never got much beyond that.')

Anthony was not averse to the idea. He was aware that he was doing nothing at home to help his mother. He and Cecilia were in good health, but there were three invalids in that house – Henry, Emily and Mr Trollope, who had suffered two mild apoplectic seizures, or strokes, before he left England, and who was broken not only in body but in mind. Henry's condition was the most agonising for Mrs Trollope. 'I have written many novels in many circumstances,' wrote Anthony in his autobiography, 'but I doubt much whether I could write one when my whole heart was by the bedside of my dying son.'

Mrs Trollope had to try to keep Emily away from Henry, who was unaware of his true condition. The burdens she had to bear were expressed in severe pains in her shoulders, made worse by long cramped hours at her writing-table. Anthony marvelled in retrospect at 'her power of dividing herself into two parts, and keeping her intellect by itself clear from the troubles of the world'. Henry was an irritable and exigent invalid. He had taken up carpentry, and hammered away frantically in his room. He also had a set idea that he would get better if he were sent to a tropical climate, but there was no money for that, and anyway it was too late.

In September 1834 Mrs Trollope took Henry and Emily briefly to London, on borrowed money, for a consultation with their own Dr Harrison, in Lisson Grove. He told her that Henry was mortally ill and Emily 'precarious', and he took no fee. Mrs Trollope went for a long walk in Regent's Park with Tom and told him the situation. (Anthony was never told anything.) Back in Bruges, in desperation, she wrote to Dr Harrison: 'For the last few days [Henry] has expectorated much less than usual, and complained of great oppression and pain on his chest. . . . He also wishes me to mention that every thing he eats causes him great pain as soon as it reaches the stomach, so as almost to make him dread taking any nourishment.'

By that time Anthony was no longer in Bruges. In order that he might learn the required languages, he was taken on by the Rev. William Drury as a classical usher – a junior master – in his school. 'To Brussels I went, and my heart still sinks within me as I reflect that anyone could have entrusted to me the tuition of thirty boys.' The idea was that he should be paid not in money but in French and German lessons, though he did not remember ever being given any.

Meanwhile his mother had other strings to her bow. She was an uninhibited string-puller, like all dutiful parents of her class. Careers and professions were entered through family influence, or purchase, or patronage. There were no competitive examinations outside the universities, and so no other way in. There was no embarrassment at all in pulling strings, only in having no strings to pull.

Mrs Trollope had a connection with the Freeling family dating back to Bristol days. The old man, Sir Francis Freeling, ruled the Post Office as Secretary, and had done so since before the mail coaches were first sent clattering down the newly macadamised roads of England in the 1780s. Sir Francis had secured places for both his own sons. The elder, George Henry Freeling, was also in the Post Office, as Assistant Secretary. The younger, Clayton Freeling, was Secretary at the Stamp Office. Mrs Trollope's personal contact was with Clayton Freeling's wife; and that lady successfully petitioned her father-in-law for a place in the Post Office for Anthony. Mrs Trollope left no stone unturned. The publisher John Murray also put in a word for Anthony with the Freelings.

Mrs Clayton Freeling communicated the good news to Tom, who was in lodgings in London, getting some work as a private tutor. Tom passed it on. His mother replied, 'I am happier receiving this news than I thought anything just now could make me.' Anthony had only been at the school in Brussels six weeks when he heard about the offer. 'I accepted it' (*Autobiography*).

Mrs Trollope wrote apologetically to William Drury to thank

him for 'your kindness to dear Anthony who I assure you feels very sensibly the friendly manner in which you have permitted him so hastily to leave you – nothing would have induced him to do so, but the absolute necessity of immediately presenting himself to Sir Francis Freeling, who was himself doubtful if he could keep the situation he had offered open for him till next week – the interest making for it, being very great.'

Anthony went home to Bruges first, where Emily, aged sixteen, was now unmistakably ill. 'Of course she was doomed,' like Henry, wrote Anthony in his autobiography. 'I knew it of both of them, though I had never heard the word spoken, or had spoken it to anyone. And my father was very ill, – ill to dying, though I did not know it.' Mrs Trollope had already sent eighteen-year-old Cecilia home to England, to Uncle Henry Milton in Fulham, to keep her away from infection. The mother was left to nurse three terminally ill people and to support the family by non-stop writing. Anthony got away, to start his life in London. He never saw Henry or his father again.

CHAPTER FOUR

THE Houses of Parliament burned down in October 1834, three weeks before Anthony came to London. Watching the blaze was Tom Trollope, perched dangerously on the balustrade of Westminster Bridge, crushed by a disrespectful crowd that cheered and jeered to see the headquarters of their legislators burn. Tom lived in a narrow alley between Regent Street and Soho called Little Marlborough Street, in the house of a tailor and his mother – a queer old house disconnected from the row and standing in its own court. He was the only lodger, and Anthony joined him there.

Fifteen years before Anthony was born the population of Greater London was just over a million; by the time he was twenty-five it had all but doubled. Even so, in the 1830s the country still began north of Bloomsbury. There was hunting in Regent's Park, and a few years earlier hounds had chased a stag up the front steps of a house in Montague Street. Hyde Park was like a common, where sheep grazed, and most of the houses on Park Lane, which was not particularly fashionable, turned their backs to it and their fronts to the Mayfair streets.

Smart young bachelors, the 'curled darlings', lived in chambers in Albany off Piccadilly, or in St James's – the streets between Piccadilly and Pall Mall – in rooming-houses often run by retired butlers who had married housekeepers. Upper-class families lived in the country and came up to their town houses in Mayfair (or rented someone else's) for the season, which coincided with the sitting of Parliament. They could shop at Fortnum's, the Piccadilly grocers, and buy books at Hatchard's close by. The drapers Dickins and Jones, like Swan and Edgar, had been established before Anthony was born. The impecunious heroine of *Lady Anna*, which is set in the early 1830s, bought clothes for a country visit at Swan and Edgar's: 'Marshall and Snellgrove [sic] were not then, or at least had not loomed to the grandeur of an entire block of houses.'* The plane trees in Berkeley Square were already thirty-five years old, and Anthony, on his evening wanderings, could have heard nightingales singing.†

The Haymarket was a haymarket (and a haunt of whores). Cows and sheep were driven through the streets to Smithfield Market, where they were slaughtered, causing bloody mess and foul smells. Old Brompton, where the streets and squares of South Kensington were not yet a gleam in a developer's eye, was an area of market gardens, and down the Bayswater Road there was a racecourse where the terraces of the Ladbroke estate would soon rise. Only nine years before Anthony joined the Post Office the gallows had been removed from Tyburn, near the junction of the Oxford Road (later Oxford Street) and the road to Edgware.

St Paul's Cathedral, a stone's throw from the General Post Office where Anthony worked, was London's highest building.‡ Nash's stucco terraces around Regent's Park, and Regent Street itself, had recently been completed. The classical grandeur of Regent Street failed in its purpose in one respect; the curved colonnades called the Quadrant at the Piccadilly end rapidly became shelters for loiterers, and the little shops became gambling dens.§ The United Service Club and the Athenaeum, brand new, outfaced one another across Waterloo Place. Two more new gentlemen's clubs, the Travellers and the Reform, spread their frontages along Pall Mall. The British Museum, which had been under construction since 1823, was finished three years after Anthony came to London.

Leicester Square, or Leicester Fields, was a wilderness of weeds, desolation, starving cats and human filth (there were no public privies and, in poor quarters, no private ones either), surrounded by broken railings, with a headless statue of George I in the centre. From time to time exhibitions, dioramas, panoramas, panopticons and other entertainments were mounted there. Around Leicester Fields, and in the villainous streets running back to Seven Dials and Soho, lived impecunious

---

* Marshall and Snelgrove opened in 1837.
† The last report of nightingales singing in Berkeley Square was in 1850.
‡ St Paul's remained London's highest building until the 1960s.
§ The Quadrant was demolished in 1848. Nash's Regent Street was redeveloped entirely in the twentieth century, following the original street-line.

foreigners, mostly French. The prostitutes around Leicester Fields were much 'lower' than those in the Haymarket.

Trafalgar Square was a building site. Five years back, this uneven, irregular, sloping tract of ground had supported a shanty-town slum. Now the National Gallery was being built where royal stables and the St Martin's graveyard had been, on the northern edge. Nelson's Column did not go up until 1843, and by then Anthony was no longer in London.

From this new square the old thoroughfare of the Strand ran into Fleet Street under Temple Bar, in a congestion of carts, hansoms and coaches up to Ludgate Hill and the City. The Strand, gas-lit by night, was brilliant and rowdy with shops and taverns. The streets off the Strand to the north led to the greater rowdiness of Covent Garden, but those to the south, at the City end, were dim cul-de-sacs ending in the sewage-tainted mud of the river, inhabited by minor lawyers and lodging-house keepers. Anthony's Miss Mackenzie, in his novel of that name, lived in Arundel Street, 'one of the quiet streets leading down from the Strand to the river', with her brother, who was a clerk at nearby Somerset House – a majestic warren of government departments, where Anthony's Uncle Henry Milton worked in the War Office and where Anthony sited his imaginary Department of Internal Navigation in *The Three Clerks*. The overcrowded but still used graveyard of St-Mary's-le-Strand was a scandal, with rotting coffins and the bodies inside them rearing into view.

Most tradesmen and professional men lived where they worked. Over 100,000 people had their homes in the courts and narrow lanes of the City itself. Though it was a hive of commercial and financial dealings there were no purpose-built office buildings apart from banks. The commercial streets were loud with horse traffic and the shouts of street-sellers. 'Jew boys' sold oranges and lemons; Jews and Quakers were recognisable by their distinctive dress.

Beyond the City were the spreading mean streets of the East End, already beginning to swallow up villages with endless terraces of small houses, 'creating wonder in all thoughtful minds', as Anthony wrote in *Castle Richmond*, 'as to whom can be their tens of thousands of occupants'. The Rotherhithe Tunnel under the Thames was still under construction – a barrel-vaulted, gas-fumy, dripping-wet pedestrian passage lined by booths where in the mid-century unhealthy girls sold trinkets, and sometimes themselves.

Bloomsbury, where the Trollopes had begun their lives, clung to its gentility with gates at the entrances to its squares and streets, manned by liveried porters who only admitted residents and superior tradesmen. What the respectables were afraid of were the rookeries of St Giles to the south-west, between Holborn and Covent Garden, swollen in population since the Trollopes lived there – tottering, vermin-ridden tenements in a network of courts off stinking alleys, inhabited by the diseased, violent and predatory poor. They seemed only half-human to clean and well-fed people, who made long detours rather than walk through St Giles, a no-go area even to the new police, in their blue swallow-tail coats and high chimney-pot hats with waterproof tops. People feared that St Giles would erupt in revolution. The Duke of Wellington had the windows of Apsley House covered with iron shutters against attacks by hostile crowds during the pre-Reform Bill unrest, and he did not have them taken down afterwards.

Gentlemen's houses could be barricaded against an angry mob, but nothing would keep out the 'blacks' – smuts which came in through every nook and cranny, covering antimacassars, toilet-covers, collars and cuffs, towels, beds. The 'blacks' were particles of soot from hundreds of thousands of coal fires and the growing number of manufactories. The rain was filthy, and the winter streets squelched with detritus and horse-droppings. In summer, the air you breathed choked you with dust and specks of dried dung and straw. Ladies and gentlemen changed their clothes several times a day not only for ceremonial reasons. To wear white muslin dresses in London, as young ladies liked to, was a luxury made possible only by armies of laundresses. What all Trollopian young men dreading marital poverty feared most was not being able to afford outside laundering. There was nowhere and no way, in the poky rooms of lodging houses, to wash and iron sheets, intimate linen, and white shirts and dresses.

The first railways were being built when Anthony came to London, necessitating the demolition of whole areas, adding to the noise and dust and to the number of homeless. Euston Station and its great neo-classical arch were under construction. Even the General Post Office was only five years old – a huge building in St

Martin's-le-Grand, housing over a thousand employees, close to
St Paul's Cathedral.

Clayton Freeling, whom Anthony already knew and liked, took
him along to the General Post Office and introduced him to his
brother Henry Freeling, the Assistant Secretary. The job was not
his yet; he had to be examined and approved. 'I was asked to copy
some lines from the *Times* newspaper with an old quill pen,* and at
once made a series of blots and false spellings. "That won't do,
you know," said Henry Freeling to his brother Clayton.' Next, he
was asked if he could do arithmetic. He had never even learned
the multiplication tables, but mumbled that he knew a little. 'The
story of that examination is given accurately in one of the opening
chapters of a novel written by me, called *The Three Clerks*,' wrote
Anthony in his autobiography, and the humiliations of Charley
Tudor in that novel are Anthony's own.

He was told to come back next day and bring in a better sample
of his handwriting, and be tested in arithmetic. Back with Tom in
their lodgings, he made under Tom's supervision a careful copy of
some pages out of Gibbon, and took them to the office next day
'with a faltering heart'. But all idea of examining him was
forgotten. No one even looked at what he had brought, and he was
shown his desk and put to work. There still exists† the document
dated 4 November 1834 appointing Mr Anthony Trollope as
'Junior Clerk in the Secretary's Office in the room of Mr Diggle'
(the word 'dismissed' is scribbled in pencil beside the name of Mr
Diggle) on the recommendation of the Secretary himself, Sir
Francis Freeling.

Patronage, not discernible merit, got him his job. Anthony was
always violently and vocally opposed to competitive examinations for entry into the Civil Service, which were introduced in
1855 after years of heated debate. His main reason was that
examinations can be passed by cramming but cannot test the
qualities of a good and responsible civil servant (or of a
gentleman), such as honesty. Anthony believed that promotion

---

* The unfairness was not that he was given a quill pen but that he was given an old
one. Quills – goose-feathers – were bought in large bundles, and sharpened and slit in
the office. They lasted no time at all, and were more expendable than the cheapest
ball-point today.
† In private hands.

To *Mr Anthony Trollope*

HIS MAJESTY's POSTMASTER GENERAL has been pleased to appoint you *Junior Clerk in the Secretary's Office* —————

in the room of *Mr Diggle* *dismissed*

on the recommendation of *myself* —————

and you are, without loss of time, to furnish the Solicitor of this Office with the Names of two responsible Persons to become bound with you in the Sum of *Two hundred* Pounds, for the due and faithful discharge of your Duty.

GENERAL POST OFFICE,
4 Nov. 18*34*

Entered,

Secretary.

The enclosed is the form of the Oath which you are to take to qualify you for your employment.

Anthony's official letter of appointment as a junior clerk in the Secretary's Office in the Post Office, at the age of nineteen. The signature is that of Sir Francis Freeling.

should go by seniority in the service, provided the man in question was capable. He knew that he would certainly not have got in if competitive examinations had been the method of entry in 1834. He became, in time, a good and efficient civil servant; but he was a late developer. In retrospect this seemed to him to be no bad thing. Englishmen of the 'gentleman' class, he wrote in middle age, 'are boys for a more protracted period of their life, and remain longer in a state of hobbledehoyhood, than the youths probably of any other nation. They are nurtured on the cold side of the wall, and come slowly to maturity; but the fruit, which is only half ripe at the end of summer, is the fruit that we keep for our winter use. I do not know that much has been lost in life by him who, having been a boy at twenty, is still a young man at forty' (*Travelling Sketches*). When he wrote that he was thinking about his own immature elder son, and hoping for the best. When he himself was a hobbledehoy he had no such perspective.

Henry died on 23 December 1834, when Anthony had been in London about seven weeks. Mrs Trollope wrote to Tom begging him to come to Bruges at once, and to bring Cecilia, for Emily's sake. 'Give our most affectionate love to dear, dear Anthony. Tell him I will write to him in a day or two, but *cannot* do it now.' Cecilia was staying with the Milmans* at Pinner, near Harrow; she and Tom left at once but arrived too late for Henry's funeral. Mrs Trollope came back to London alone a few weeks later to make arrangements with a publisher for a book about Paris, and Anthony, who must have had a wretched Christmas, however hospitable his Milton aunt and uncle may have been, saw her then.

He moved into 22 Northumberland Street (now Luxborough Street), off the Marylebone Road. His small room there faced the windowless back of a workhouse. His mother had lodged in the same house when she brought Henry and Emily from Bruges to consult the doctor in nearby Lisson Grove. This was the part of London to which the Trollopes gravitated when looking for

* The Milmans were good friends to the Trollopes. Lady Milman was the widow of a royal physician. Her son Henry – poet, dramatist, and later Dean of St Paul's – was a particular friend of Mrs Trollope and spoke up in her defence at a dinner party where Harriet Martineau, who had herself just returned from the United States, was running down Mrs Trollope and her America book.

somewhere cheap to live. It was familiar to them as the first built-up area coming in from the Harrow Road. 'Lodgings in London are always gloomy. Gloomy colours wear better than bright ones for curtains and carpets, and the keepers of lodgings in London seem to think that a certain dinginess of appearance is respectable. I never saw a London lodging in which an attempt at cheerfulness had been made, and I do not think that any such attempt, if made, would pay' – because the lodging-seeker would suspect that 'something was wrong'. When Anthony wrote that, he was referring to the rooms taken by Squire Dale for himself and Lily in Sackville Street, in Mayfair (*The Last Chronicle of Barset*). Anthony's lodgings were meaner and gloomier still. He later had the Rev. Joseph Emilius, bigamist and unconvicted murderer in *Phineas Redux*, going to ground as a 'valued lodger' in this seedy Northumberland Street house 'opposite to the deadest part of the dead wall of the Marylebone Workhouse'.

Anthony's starting salary was £90 a year, rising to £110 after three years. He worked for seven years in a room with the other junior clerks, supervised by an older man. The clerks, as a group, were chiefly interested in smoking, drinking and playing cards. There was an upstairs room where they played *écarté* after lunch (which was sent in from a pot-house) for an hour or two, and adjourned again in the evenings to play again and smoke; some clerks actually lived in the building. The work was simply copying. They copied letters into the letter books and minutes into the minutes books. Those who got promoted dealt with the official correspondence, writing letters at their superiors' instruction. The office day began at ten and Anthony was always late – not because he had a three-mile walk from his lodgings, but because he simply could not be punctual and was, he said, 'in possession of a watch which was always ten minutes late'.

Instructions from Sir Francis Freeling, the Secretary, were issued in the form of memos, to be circulated and signed by each clerk to show that he had understood. Anthony's signature heads the list of names on a memo reminding the clerks that the first hour of the office day was for work, not for eating breakfast. His lateness nearly brought about his dismissal very early on; Mrs Clayton Freeling, 'with tears in her eyes, besought me to think of my mother'. Anthony was not a success as a junior clerk. Tom, in the spring of 1835, had through an old schoolfriend the chance of a teaching job at King Edward's School, a grammar school in Birmingham, and hung around in London while the decision about his appointment was endlessly deferred. He spent part of his time with the Grants and part with Anthony, 'who was doing – or rather getting into hot water for not doing – his work at the Post Office. He was, I take it, a very bad Post Office clerk.'

Thomas Anthony Trollope, their father, died in Bruges at half-past three in the afternoon of 23 October 1835. The death was registered by the clerk of the Protestant Chapel and the local policeman. He had been bedridden for several months, attended by Dr Herbout, an old army doctor who had served under Napoleon. Tom and Cecilia were with their mother. No one pretended to excessive grief. As Tom said, his father would have liked to have been loved, and knew he was not.

Mrs Trollope, after burying her husband in the Protestant section of the cemetery at Bruges near Henry,* went straight to London to consult Dr Harrison about her younger daughter Emily. They joined Anthony at 22 Northumberland Street, from where she wrote to her publisher Richard Bentley in Great Marlborough Street explaining how Mr Trollope had died the day after she sent him her manuscript of *Paris and the Parisians*. 'This melancholy and unexpected event – for I believed all danger over – has rendered me very incapable of working.' If Mr Bentley would call, she would arrange for him to meet Mr Hervieu, 'as he is desirous of being introduced to you'. Hervieu's lodgings were close by at 15 Nottingham Street, which runs into Northumberland Street.

Tom and Cecilia stayed on in Bruges to close up the house. Mr Trollope had died intestate. When the Trollope goods and chattels were shipped home they were immediately seized and granted by the Prerogative Court of Canterbury to George Barnes, 'a Creditor'. In the margin of the court order is a note, 'Sworn under £50', which presumably means that there was nothing there for Mr Barnes to take, and that Mrs Trollope and

---

* When Tom returned to Bruges in 1867 he visited the cemetery and found the two graves in good repair. I went there in 1989. The Protestant section had been reorganised, there was no attendant to ask, and after long searching I failed to find the graves.

Tom got out everything that was worth having by some other means.

Over Christmas 1835, which was spent in Northumberland Street, Mrs Trollope had a new idea in keeping with her increasingly Tory views. She tried to interest Bentley in launching a periodical, to be edited by her, but chiefly it seems for Hervieu's sake, 'as a means of bringing his pencil into notice'. Bentley was famous for the care he took over illustrations. Stressing Hervieu's talent as an artist and etcher, she proposed a monthly magazine containing in each issue 'a travestie in verse' of radical speeches in the House of Commons, to be written by herself, and political anecdotes, 'embellished with a Hogarth style of caricature (all on the right side remember)'. She had discussed it, she said, with no one but Hervieu and her two sons. It sounds as if she were planning a family venture along the lines of *The Magpie* of Julian Hill days, but on commercial lines.

It was not wholly unrealistic since her popularity as a writer was high and still rising, but her uninhibited pushing of Hervieu, and her whimsical tone, did not inspire confidence. It was always her way, when racked by anxieties, to throw herself into some ambitious enterprise. She did not easily abandon this one. More than two years later she was still urging on Bentley the possibility of her editing a new '*decidedly strong saucy* conservative publication', an 'anti-radical, anti-jacobin' monthly magazine.

By that time Richard Bentley, in his early forties and born and bred to the printing and publishing trades, had his money on another horse so far as a periodical was concerned. He had met Charles Dickens, and had become one of his publishers. He also got Dickens to agree to edit a monthly magazine, Bentley's *Miscellany*, which first appeared in 1837. Dickens left the editorship after a couple of years, but the *Miscellany* survived.

The Trollopes' dreams of a periodical seem naïve in comparison. Mrs Trollope's plans for it sound like those for 'The Panjandrum', a non-starter of a magazine in a short story of that name which Anthony published in 1870. In the story, a little group of young men, headed by the dominating Mrs St Quinten, each agreed to bring manuscript articles of twenty-one pages to the next meeting. Our hero could not come up with an article, but walking round Regent's Park in despair and the pouring rain he followed a woman with a little girl, overheard a tantalising scrap of their conversation, and was inspired by it to write – a story.

Mrs Trollope found a house in Hadley, a village on the borders of Hertfordshire and Middlesex just beyond Barnet on the Great North Road. It was a good house, with drawing-room, dining-room, library and, as she said when attempting to let it for an exorbitant 180 guineas for four months, 'ten beds, garden kept up, and cows'. Here she wrote one of her most successful novels, *The Vicar of Wrexhill*.* Anthony kept on the lodgings in Northumberland Street but spent some free time at Hadley. 'The amusements there were not of a very exciting nature; but London was close, and even at Hadley there were pretty girls with whom he could flirt,' wrote Anthony of George Bertram in *The Bertrams*.

In that novel, the future suicide Sir Henry Harcourt wooed calculating Caroline Waddington at Hadley. Describing their walk together, Anthony reminisced: 'There is – or perhaps we should say was; for time and railways, and straggling new suburban villas, may now have destroyed it all; but there is, or was,† a pretty woodland lane, running from the back of Hadley church, through the last remnants of what was once Enfield Chase. How many lovers' feet have crushed the leaves that used to lie in autumn along that pretty lane!'

Anxiety about Emily overshadowed flirtations. Emily was fair-haired, blue-eyed, and had been high-spirited. In *The Three Clerks* Charley loved lively Katie Woodward, sixteen years old, and watched her sicken, leaning against her mother on the sofa, bravely pretending to read, insisting she was 'only tired'. The months passed and Katie 'lived beneath a stethoscope, and bore all their pokings and tappings with exquisite patience. She herself believed she was dying. . . .'

Anthony, in *The Three Clerks*, did not let sweet Katie Woodward die. But Emily Trollope died, on 12 February 1836. She was not quite eighteen.

Tom was away, and it was Anthony who wrote, the same day,

---

* It is generally assumed that the character of her Vicar was a skit on Mr Cunningham of Harrow, but she hotly denied this in a letter to Tom – 'and as for the very unjust assertion that I have quarrelled with him, I will only say that if I *had* I would never have written the book at all, for fear this very thing should be said of me.'

† The pretty path through the back of the churchyard is still there, leading on to Hadley Common.

to tell him: 'She died without any pain, and without a struggle. Her little strength had been gradually declining, and her breath left her without the slightest convulsion, or making any change in her features or face. Were it not for the ashy colour, I should think she was sleeping. I never saw anything more beautifully placid and composed.'

It was better, Anthony felt, that Emily should die this way than that she should live longer only to 'undergo the agonies which Henry suffered'. Cecilia was with the Milmans at Pinner and had not yet heard. 'I shall go for her tomorrow. You went to the same house to fetch her when Henry died.'

They buried Emily in Hadley churchyard, against the back of the flint-built church.* In *The Bertrams*, Caroline and Harcourt married in Hadley church, and the wedding bells rang out – at which point their creator made another personal interpolation: 'I know full well the tone with which they toll when the soul is ushered to its last long rest. I have stood in that green churchyard when earth has been laid to earth, ashes to ashes, dust to dust – the ashes and the dust that were loved so well.'

'God is good to us, and heals those wounds with a rapidity which seems to us impossible when we look forward, but which is regarded with insufficient wonder when we look backward' (*The Bertrams*). Mrs Trollope picked up her life and spirits yet again. Five months later, in the summer of 1836, she took off for Vienna to research her next travel book. She took Tom with her, and a college friend of Tom's, and Hervieu, and her faithful maid Mrs Cox. Anthony saw them all off. In Paris they picked up Cecilia, who was with the Garnetts. After six months, Tom had to return home to take up his teaching job at Birmingham, but the rest of the party were away for almost a year.

Mrs Trollope professed to hate cant, and indeed she always

* Emily's grave is untended but the headstone is in good condition. Hadley churchyard is full of Trollopian echoes, which during the Trollopes' brief residence were unrecognisable signposts towards the future. Buried at Hadley was William Makepeace Thackeray, died 1815, a forebear of the author, the friend of Anthony's middle age. The Bertrams were buried there; Anthony was to use the name as the title of one of his novels, partly set in Hadley. The little son of a John Tilley, who died in 1809 aged four, lay there; Cecilia Trollope's future husband was another John Tilley. There was near where Emily was buried the grand tomb of the Rev. David Garrow, a former rector of Hadley, who died in 1827; he was a cousin of Joseph Garrow, whose daughter Theodosia was Tom's first wife.

spoke her mind, but her mind at this time inclined strongly towards great personages towards whom her attitude might, were she a less able woman, be called sycophantic. In Europe, as a travelling literary celebrity, she had access to the grandest dinner tables. Because she was not rich, nor beautiful, nor well- born, this was not the case in London, once the first flurry of her notoriety had subsided. In England, the story of Mr Trollope's misfortunes was against her.

In Vienna, at the house of the British Ambassador, Sir Frederic Lamb, she was taken in to dinner by Prince Metternich, Foreign Minister and Chancellor of Austria, the big man of Europe – and before the end of the evening she had been invited, with Tom, to dinner with the Prince and Princess the following Monday, an invitation that was subsequently repeated. (Metternich did not eat the dinners; he nibbled thin slices of brown bread and butter, and told stories about Napoleon.) Mrs Trollope saw more of the Princess than of the great man himself, and after Hervieu had finished his 'very clever engravings' for her book, she obtained for him permission to paint a portrait of Princess Metternich, 'and I sit with her generally through all her sittings. She is a lovely woman, and a very charming person in all ways,' she told Julia Pertz.

The problem for Anthony in London was how to live on his inadequate salary, and how to occupy his free time without getting into trouble. He knew very few people, and Uncle Henry Milton's house down the Fulham Road was a four-mile walk away. 'I had no friends on whom I could sponge regularly.' He was always in debt. When his mother was at home, 'She paid much for me, – paid all that I asked her to pay, and all that she could find out that I owed. But who in such a condition ever tells all and makes a clean breast of it?'

He should, he said in his autobiography, have stayed in his lodgings in the evenings, drinking tea and reading good books. While Charles Dickens, only three years older than Anthony Trollope, was getting £750 from Richard Bentley for the serialisation of *Oliver Twist*, with illustrations by Cruikshank, Anthony Trollope was hanging about the late-night oyster houses, taverns and seedy 'free-and-easies' of Haymarket and the Strand. (So was young Thackeray, a Bar student, who was addicted to gambling and frequented the same night-hour dives as Anthony, but the two did not know one another.) The lads in *The Three Clerks* have no money but are 'one and all addicted to Coal Holes and Cider Cellars; they dive at midnight hours into Shades, and know all the back parlours of all the public houses in the neighbourhood of the Strand.'

'Can it be', Anthony wrote in *The Small House at Allington*, 'that any mother really expects her son to sit alone evening after evening in a dingy room drinking bad tea, and reading good books? And yet it seems that mothers do so expect, – the very mothers who talk about the thoughtlessness of youth!' Did it never occur to these mothers, who were so concerned with 'under flannel shirting, with books of devotion and toothpowder', that provision should be made 'for amusements, for dancing, for parties, for the excitement and comfort of women's society? That excitement your sons will have, and if it be not provided by you of one kind, will certainly be provided by themselves of another kind.'

Anthony had to find his dinner every night, and restaurants as such were non-existent. When his mother, in Paris, saw well-behaved family parties in inexpensive restaurants, she was amazed. It could never catch on in London, she was sure; it was impossible that 'such places, open to the public, should continue a reputable resort for ladies for a week after its doors were open.' Any woman out on the London streets at night, let alone in the Blue Posts, the Coal Hole or the Cider Cellars, was definitely not a lady. As Anthony wrote, 'There was no house in which I could habitually see a lady's face and hear a lady's voice. No allurement to decent respectability came my way. It seems to me that in such circumstances the temptations of loose life will almost certainly prevail with a young man' (*Autobiography*).

Decent society, he said in his own authorial voice in *The Three Clerks*, 'is the first requisite which a mother should seek in sending her son to live alone in London; balls, routs, picnics, parties women, pretty, well-dressed, witty, easy mannered, good pictures, elegant drawing-rooms, well got-up books. Majolica and Dresden china – these are the truest guards to protect a youth from dissipation and immorality.' Repeatedly, in different novels, he implied that it was a mother's duty to set up a social life for her young adult son. This was unreasonable. He was expressing a displaced, generalised resentment. Hobbledehoys 'never get petted, though they may not be the less esteemed, or perhaps loved' (*The Small House at Allington*).

Anthony's dissipations were no worse than any other young man's and far less so than some. It was a matter of late nights, rough company, cheap drink, girls, and normal time-wasting. Many young men in his position would have enjoyed the freedom, but Anthony, because he was unhappy in himself, did not. He longed for the world from which he was excluded. In *Lady Anna*, the well-bred girl promised to the tailor was half-seduced not only by the young earl's desire for her but by his cleanness and grace. When he kissed her,

> It was to her, as that sunny moment passed across her, as to some hard-toiling youth who, while roaming listlessly among the houses of the wealthy, hears, as he lingers on the pavement of a summer night, the melodies which float upon the air from the open balconies above him. A vague sense of unknown sweetness comes upon him, mingled with an irritating feeling of envy that some favoured son of Fortune should be able to stand over the shoulders of that singing syren, while he can only listen with intrusive ears from the street below. And so he lingers and is envious, and for a moment curses his fate. . . .

From Anthony's envious lingerings under the open drawing-room windows of Mayfair grew castles in the air that led, in time, to ice-blonde Lady Dumbello and her cold flirtation with Mr Palliser, to Lady Laura Kennedy and her doomed love for Phineas Finn, and to Lady Glencora's mad waltz with the dangerous Burgo Fitzgerald.

In actuality, Anthony's mother did what she could for him. Perversely (since he complained about not having any) he avoided 'suitable' social contacts. He was asked out – by Mrs Clayton Freeling, by the Casewick Trollopes when they came to London, by Henry Taylor* and John Forster,† who had both

---

* Later Sir Henry Taylor (1800–95): an official in the Colonial Office, who in the year that Anthony started in the Post Office published a verse drama, *Philip Van Artevelde*, which Anthony admired extravagantly. He came to know Taylor well in the 1860s.

† John Forster (1812–76): author and editor, only three years older than Anthony. From 1837 to 1860 he was literary adviser to Chapman & Hall, who were to be Anthony's major publishers. Close friend of Charles Dickens.

known his father – but he would not go, and when he was not racketing around with his fellow clerks he was much alone.

In *The Small House at Allington*, he relived those lonely times in the person of Johnny Eames, a hobbledehoy like himself. There is a class of young men, he wrote, 'who do not come forth in the world as Apollos, nor shine at all, keeping what light they have for inward purpose. Such young men are often awkward, ungainly, and not yet formed in their gait; they straggle with their limbs, and are shy; words do not come to them with ease, when words are required, among any but their accustomed associates.' The hobbledehoy wanders about alone, 'taking long walks in which he dreams of those successes which are so far removed from his powers of achievement', feeding an imagination 'for which those who know him give him but scanty credit, and unconsciously prepares himself for that later ripening, if only the ungenial shade will some day cease to interpose itself'. He feared snubs and condescension.

A junior clerkship in the Post Office did nothing for Anthony's self-esteem. It was all very well to be a civil servant, but in the hierarchy of the Civil Service the Post Office was at the very bottom. The imaginary Internal Navigation Office in *The Three Clerks* was less smart than some, but 'not so decidedly plebeian' as the Post Office. George Roden, the Post Office clerk in *Marion Fay*, one of Anthony's last novels, was loved by the daughter of the Marquess of Kingsbury. The girl explained to her angry father that Mr Roden had first been invited to the house by her brother, Lord Hampstead:

> 'It was very foolish of Hampstead to bring him, – very foolish, – a Post Office clerk.'
> 'Mr Vivian is a clerk in the Foreign Office. Why shouldn't one office be the same as another?'
> 'They are very different . . .'

A snooping clergyman reported to the Marquess that George Roden was 'vulgar, flippant, ignorant, impudent, exactly what a clerk in the Post Office might be expected to be', and he presumed that Roden 'was sent about with the Post Office bags', delivering letters.

When Mrs Trollope and Cecilia returned to Hadley from Vienna, life picked up again. The only real friends they made in the village were the doctor, Mr Hammond (and, through him, J. H. Green, who had been Coleridge's surgeon and literary executor), and the Thackeray family – Mr Thackeray, a connection of the future author, was the rector at Hadley. But Mrs Trollope asked her own and her sons' friends out from London, and her hospitable routine of parties and picnics – combined with her daily pre-breakfast four hours of writing – was re-established.

Anthony was not expected at Hadley every weekend, as of right. His mother wrote to Tom, apropos one August weekend, 'Please to tell Anthony *not* to come down on Saturday, because all the Thackeray family will be from home.' She was writing from the rectory; this was the time she was trying to let her own house. Mrs Trollope, in her expansive phases, spent a lot of money. She tested the patience of wine-merchants, to whom she wrote polite but defensive letters when they sent in their bills. If Anthony was always in debt, that was nothing unusual in his family.

Anthony had more fun than he let himself believe. One house where he, like Tom, was always welcome, was the Grants'. They had moved to Hayes – no further than Harrow from London, but still a long way for a poor Post Office clerk. Those happy families in Anthony's early novels consisting of a devoted, attractive mother always at home, and two or three adorable girls – the Woodwards in *The Three Clerks*, Mrs Dale and her daughters in *The Small House at Allington* – are Anthony's romantic tribute to the Grants.

The boating accident on the Thames in *The Three Clerks*, when Charley Tudor rescued Katie Woodward from drowning, reflected Anthony's own weekend adventures. His mother reported to Tom that 'Anthony went on the river with Mr Bond, and fell into the water as he got out of the boat on the return, which was in the middle of the night, after which he had to walk dripping wet from Westminster bridge to Hervieu's lodgings in Nottingham Street. . . . I think by his description of the adventure it would have killed most people.' Her sons had had a bad meal together somewhere, and Mrs Trollope commiserated: '. . . I pretty well know how it would make you feel. Poor Tony is marvellously unlucky in his feeds.'

There is evidence that Anthony went to the races once, in a boisterous mixed party; a letter has survived from him to 'My dear Miss Dancers': 'Like a man of honour I send you what I owe – that horrid white and pink which ought never to have won the race!! If the gloves do not fit pray let me know – & I will procure another pair.' He asked her to thank 'Ellen' for all her kindness; he had 'her flowers blooming on my desk the envy of all the Clerks in the Office – tell her also that I have still the pin which she wanted, but was not able to purloin.' Yet another young lady, Emma, was, he hoped, 'consoled for the loss of the gingerbread man – tell her that she should never allow grief for anyone to prey upon her spirits for long. It is very bad for the complexion.' And finally, 'I think Mr G.T. must have been hid in that cupboard yesterday evening – else Emma would not have been so *very* angry with me. . . .'

There was also the Tramp Society, which consisted of Anthony, his friend John Merivale (now a law student*) and Walter Awdry, who was a Winchester friend of both Anthony's and Tom's. Awdry had been in trouble both at school and at Oxford;† Anthony, who loved him, described him as perverse, 'bashful to very fear of a lady's dress' (not like Anthony), 'unable to restrain himself in anything, but with a conscience that was always stinging him' (like Anthony); 'a loving friend, though very quarrelsome; and, perhaps, of all men I have known, the most humorous.'

The three friends went wandering on foot in the country around London. 'Southampton was the furthest point we ever reached; but Buckinghamshire and Hertfordshire were more dear to us.' These were his happiest times, he said. They slept rough, and terrorised villages by the 'loudness of our mirth'; they got into scrapes, played practical jokes on farmers, and pretended to be escaped lunatics. But the fun, wrote Anthony, was the fun of Awdry, 'and would cease to be fun as told by me'.

Tom, meanwhile, was bored stiff at the grammar school in Birmingham, teaching Latin and Greek to the sons of tradesmen. It was not so much fun as swanning round the courts of Europe with his enterprising mother. He found it hard to keep order, and there was nothing to do in the evenings except sit in his lodgings

---

* John Merivale ended up as Registrar in the Court of Chancery.
† Awdry became a school usher, then a clergyman, and died young and in poverty.

with 'my book, my teapot, and my pipe'. When he voiced his discontent to his mother, she panicked. She had a dread of her sons being unemployed and unleashed a spate of letters, begging him to find the 'strength of mind and resolution' to stick it out at least for a while.

'If I live a few years longer with the power of making money I will risk something rather than let you remain in a situation that is so distasteful to you – and distasteful, *certainly*, with good reason.' But he must be patient. 'You know what very heavy up-hill work I have hitherto had.' She dreaded him giving up 'a certain maintenance' – Tom was earning £200 a year, more than twice Anthony's salary – 'before I have cleared myself of the claims that are still upon me'. She did not dismiss the unspoken suggestion that she ought to rescue her able twenty-seven-year-old son from a situation that he found tedious. She was used to fixing things for everyone, and found it specially hard to refuse Tom anything. She depended on his companionship, looking forward to his return home for the holidays. 'I shall want you to *trot me out* sometimes, as in days of yore.' Meanwhile, 'Take regular exercise dearest and above all things use cold water *abundantly* every morning.' Tom had a new idea – he might become a clergyman. Mrs Trollope was consulting the Drurys, who had the ear of the Bishop of Lichfield.

Tom was also thinking of writing as a career. All the Trollopes did, seeing the success their mother had made. Their involvement in her idea for a monthly magazine was only part of it. Tom had made a beginning when still a schoolboy, with an article about Winchester for a Hampshire magazine. In the summer holidays of 1837 he went on a tour of Normandy and Brittany and wrote up his impressions. His mother wrote to her own publisher Richard Bentley saying that she had read the first three chapters, which were written in 'a popular, and to my judgement in a very pleasing style', and asking whether Tom might come to see him. Bentley resisted. A year later, Tom himself wrote to Bentley with the abysmal suggestion that he should write a book about his own impressions of the United States (impressions already ten years old), to be illustrated by Hervieu and written with Mrs Trollope's assistance, using her old notebooks, and with the benefit of her 'perusal and corrections'. Bentley resisted this too.

Mrs Trollope involved her sons in the practical details of her

career, using them as her agents and messenger boys when she
was abroad and even when she was at Hadley. Most of this fell on
Anthony, since Tom was out of London, and most of Anthony's
surviving early correspondence is with her publishers – business
letters about the delivery of her manuscripts, proof-reading,
arrangements for translations and, above all, about the urgency of
paying money due to her on her novels and of adequate advances
for her travel books. For a shy and inexperienced young man,
writing such letters and calling on publishers was testing. He did
it well, and it meant that he learned much about the business side
of authorship long before he himself became an author.

Not that literary work was ever far from his mind, or from his
mother's, as a way of supplementing his tiny income. As soon as
he joined the Post Office she wrote to John Murray asking
whether her son Anthony could be useful in any capacity, such as
proof-reading. Nothing came of this, but as Anthony wrote in his
Thackeray, writing 'requires no capital, no special education, no
training, and may be taken up at any time without a moment's
delay'. The idea comes to a man that 'as he has the pen and ink,
and time on hand, why should he not write and make money?'

When he had been in the Post Office only six months, Anthony
called on Richard Bentley to report that the printers were failing
to send the proof sheets of his mother's new novel, and a few days
later wrote to reiterate the complaint, adding on his own account:
'Is it in your power to lend me any assistance in procuring the
insertion of lucubrations of my own in any of the numerous
periodical magazines &c which come out in such monthly swarms
– I am not aware whether you are yourself the Proprietor of any
such – My object of course is that of turning my time to any
account that I am able, and if you would put me into the way of
doing so, & excuse the liberty I am taking you would much oblige,
My dear Sir, Yours truly, Anthony Trollope.'

His pomposity betrays his embarrassment and inexperience.
Bentley, besieged by Trollopes, did nothing.*

Mrs Trollope's advice to her sons was to read and read before
ever they considered setting pen to paper themselves. Anthony
had been brought up in a family where everyone read and talked
about what they read. Anthony's general knowledge was impres-

---

* But he published Anthony's sixth novel, *The Three Clerks*, in 1858.

sive, even though at school he had learned only Latin and Greek and not much of either. Uncle Henry Milton was a connoisseur of painting and had published an account of the contents of the Louvre – Napoleon's collected loot – in 1815. The Trollope children had been acquainted since childhood with the major paintings in the Louvre, through engravings. Anthony, who in London spent time in the old National Gallery in Pall Mall, was no ordinary hobbledehoy. (His knowledge of a better kind of life only made him more depressed, feeling condemned by circumstances and his own failures to choose the worse.)

At nineteen, Anthony said in his autobiography, 'I could have given a fuller list of the names of the poets of all countries, with their subjects and periods, – and probably of historians, – than many others; and had, perhaps, a more accurate idea of the manner in which my own country was governed. I knew the names of all the Bishops, all the Judges, all the Heads of Colleges, and all the Cabinet Ministers, – not very useful knowledge indeed, but one that had not been acquired without other matter that was more useful.'

He had read Milton, Shakespeare, Scott and Byron, and thought *Pride and Prejudice* the best novel in the English language, with *Ivanhoe* a close second. When, depressed in London, he thought about his own future, he did not see himself remaining in the Post Office. He saw himself as a novelist – by default. His fictional George Bertram thought there were only two worthwhile occupations. 'A man should be known either as a politician or an author. It behoved a man to speak out what was in him with some audible voice, so that the world might hear.' Of himself, Anthony wrote that 'Parliament was out of the question. I had not means to go to the Bar. In official life, such as that to which I had been introduced, there did not seem to be any opening for real success. Pens and paper I could command.' Success with poetry, drama, history or biography seemed beyond him. 'But I thought it possible that I might write a novel' (*Autobiography*). What tortured him was his failure even to make the attempt.

He did read and read. He did spend evenings in his dingy lodgings with the bad tea and the good books. He had with him in Northumberland Street his old Harrow texts, and worked on them to such good effect that he realised one day, with a burst of triumph, that he was reading Horace for pleasure. Soon after he started at the Post Office he began a 'commonplace book', which went into two volumes, in which he made notes about authors and their books, arranged alphabetically. Like his father, he had a penchant for lists and systems.

Since he also wrote down what he felt when reading the books, there was a 'journal' element to the enterprise, of a self-flagellating nature. He began a long critique of Pope's *Essay on Man* with the comment: 'I read this some three years ago and fancied I understood it – perhaps I did but I can hardly do so now – Since that time by idleness – dissipation – & riot of my mind I have lost in a measure the power of thinking and reflecting. . . .' Under 'O' he wrote 'Order – Method – ' and then: 'I am myself in all the pursuits (God help them) & practices of my life most disorderly and unmethodical.' And under 'B', about the novels of Sir Edward Bulwer, he described the nature of his conflict:

> I feel a want when reading novels of something which will more occupy my heart or mind. When I read anything more abstruse or which takes any labour or thought, I get fatigued & leave it, but yet I am still more ennuyé by the continued idleness in which my mind is left while I am reading novels – In the same way, when reading, I long to be writing – & attempting to write, I become weary of the labour, & do nothing; I am not contented with mediocrity – want the perseverance to accomplish superiority, & therefore fall into utter inferiority.

His performance in the office was getting worse. Sir Francis Freeling, who had always been friendly to Anthony, died in 1836. He was replaced as Secretary by Colonel William Leader Maberly, 'who was certainly not my friend'. Writing his memoirs at sixty, Anthony still remembered 'the keenness of my anguish when I was treated as if I were unfit for any useful work'. He caricatured Maberly as the windbag Sir Boreas Bodkin in *Marion Fay*. Anthony did try – not with the work, which, he said in his autobiography, was so simple as to be done without trying – 'but to show that I was willing to do it. I do admit that I was irregular.'

Maberly, then in his forties, an absentee Irish landlord with a smart Anglo-Irish wife who wrote novels, was on half-pay from the army all the time he held office, and received a salary, in the

Post Office. His handwriting was illegible, and he was a martinet who resisted all change. Edmund Yates, who joined the Post Office a decade later, blamed Anthony for his failure to get on with Maberly; Anthony's manner 'was not conciliating'. Yates described the heavily built Colonel Maberly sitting in a big chair with his handkerchief over his knees, reading his private letters while the clerk tried to read him the official ones. The clerk was expected to answer these with no more guidance than 'Tell him to go and be damned, my good fellow!'*

Anthony was continually on the mat – for unpunctuality, for failing to copy and send off letters, for chronic carelessness, for overstaying a weekend leave, for failing to log office expenditures, for mislaying bank-notes. He was punished by threats to dock his pay, by being kept in to work overtime, by losing the points of seniority which led to promotion. 'How well I can remember the terror created within me by the air of outraged dignity with which a certain fine old gentleman, now long since gone,† could rub his hands slowly, one on another, and look up to the ceiling, slightly shaking his head, as though lost in the contemplation of my iniquities! I would become sick in my stomach, and feel as though my ankles had been broken' (*The Small House at Allington*).

Anthony was not only unpunctual in the office, he was unpunctual in paying his bills, because he had no money. When he signed a tailor's bill for £12, the bill found its way to the hand of a professional money-lender, and Anthony got deeper into trouble as he borrowed £4 more, and then more, and by the end paid back over £200, because of the astronomical interest exacted by the money-lender. 'With that man, who lived in a little street near Mecklenburgh Square, I formed a most heart-rending but a most intimate acquaintance.' This 'little, clean old man' even turned up at the office looking for the money due to him, and stood behind Anthony's chair whispering, 'Now I wish you would be punctual. If you only would be punctual, I should like you to have anything you want.'

---

* *Edmund Yates: His Recollections and Experiences*, Richard Bentley, 1884.
† Anthony's wording was intentionally ambiguous. Maberly was long gone from the Post Office when Anthony wrote that, but he was still alive. He outlived Anthony, dying aged eighty-seven in 1885.

That is in his autobiography, but it all went into *The Three Clerks* as well – the money-lender's intrusion into the office, and the 'weary, useless, aimless walks' to the horrible room in the house near Mecklenburgh Square, where Mr Jabez M'Ruen always kept Charley Tudor waiting, staring at 'the rickety pembroke table, covered with dirty papers', the horsehair-bottomed chairs, the 'broken bits of filthy crockery, full of whisps of paper' on the chimney piece, the pictures on the wall representing three of the four seasons, behind cracked glass. Charley Tudor kept no records of the 'double-fanged little documents' he signed for Mr M'Ruen. He had 'even been so preposterously foolish as to sign them in blank'.

Anthony described in the same meticulous detail the dark public house in the City, in an alley behind the Exchange, where Charley Tudor had further assignations with the revolting M'Ruen. He knew such places only too well. He described in *The Last Chronicle of Barset* the 'killing sense of shame' of these appointments, and the necessity 'to be civil, almost suppliant, to a cunning knave whom the borrower loathes; to be refused thrice, and then cheated with his eyes open on the fourth attempt . . .' He described the money-lender's tactics: the 'piteous manner', the 'assured demand', the 'sudden attack'. Anthony, student of the brutal politics of personal relations, added to this passage the startling judgement that 'A man who desires to soften another man's heart, should always abuse himself. In softening a woman's heart, he should abuse her.'

His experience with money-lenders made good copy, but at the time it was a nightmare. There was another nightmare, and another unwelcome visitor stumping up the stone stairs of the GPO. 'A young woman down in the country', he wrote in his autobiography, 'had taken it into her head that she would like to marry me. . . .' He was not, he said, to blame. 'The invitation had come from her, and I had lacked the pluck to give it a decided negative; but I had left the house within half an hour, going away without my dinner' – a genuine sacrifice, that – 'and had never returned to it.'

In *Ralph the Heir*, Mr Neefit the breeches-maker was owed money by young Ralph, and it was Mr Neefit's daughter Polly with whom Ralph became entangled. Mr Neefit was prepared to forget the debt if Ralph would make a lady out of his daughter by marrying her. Invited to the Neefits' 'villa residence' at Hendon, Ralph unlike his creator ate his way through the whole dinner (boiled salmon and lamb), thus raising parental expectations even higher. Fortunately Polly Neefit did not share her father's aspiration: 'I'm not going to be given away, you know, like a birthday present, out of a shop.'

In real life, according to Anthony's autobiography, the dinner from which he fled was followed by a stream of letters from the girl – and then her mother turned up at the Post Office. 'My hair almost stands on my head now as I remember the figure of the woman walking into the big room in which I sat with six or seven other clerks, having a large basket on her arm and an immense bonnet on her head.' The office messenger had tried to make her wait outside, but she followed him into the room and said in a loud voice: 'Anthony Trollope, when are you going to marry my daughter?'

In *The Three Clerks* the bonneted woman who sought Charley out in his office was the landlady of the Cat & Whistle in Norfolk Street off the Strand. The 'wronged' girl was the landlady's young cousin, with whom Charley had become too intimate during evenings spent drinking gin and water in the back parlour. But Anthony's fiction is riddled with young men, attracted and aroused, but desperate to avoid matrimony. Johnny Eames in *The Last Chronicle of Barset*, no longer a hobbledehoy but private secretary to the Chief Commissioner of the Income Tax Board, flirted dangerously with Miss Madalina Demolines, 'a bird of prey, and altogether an unclean bird', as his artist friend warned him. Caught by Madalina's mamma (in her dressing-gown) in an embrace with the young lady on the sofa, Johnny only escaped promising marriage by throwing open the window and calling out to a passing policeman.

One of the friends whom Anthony brought to Hadley to meet his family was John Tilley, a fellow clerk in the Post Office, and two years older. Tilley had entered the service at the age of seventeen; he was born in Camberwell, on the southern edge of London, the son of a merchant and his Scottish wife. There were seven children of the marriage, of whom only John and his elder sister Susanna, known as Susan, survived. Cecilia, in Vienna, had formed an attachment to a Baron Charles Hügel; but at Hadley in 1838 she and John Tilley fell in love.

The shape of the family was changing. Hervieu was no longer always at Mrs Trollope's side. It is impossible to know whether he had been distancing himself, and Mrs Trollope's involvement of him in her projects was an effort to keep him; or whether he expected and demanded her support and devotion, and it was she who began to disengage. The tone in which Tom's wife wrote about Hervieu, in her memoir of Mrs Trollope, suggests that the family, in the end, had had enough of him.

But Mrs Trollope needed someone, a man, to 'trot her out', travel with her, and be her confidential friend. The lot fell, of course, on twenty-eight-year-old Tom. With Emily gone and Cecilia soon to be off her hands, Mrs Trollope's financial commitments were much diminished. After long discussion, they – or rather she – decided Tom should leave Birmingham, abandon for the present all idea of an outside career, and devote himself to becoming 'her companion and squire', as he put it. He also became her agent and business manager. 'The decision was a momentous one,' wrote Tom in his memoirs, but he never regretted it.

'My brother Anthony,' wrote Tom complacently, 'used to say of me that I should never have earned my salt in the routine work of a profession, or any employment under the authoritative supervision of a superior.' They had in common, however, the habit of private industry. Tom, in his long life, wrote sixty books, and he could when necessary write even faster than Anthony. But he enjoyed idleness too. Anthony, in his maturity, found idleness painful. 'Work to him,' wrote Tom in his memoirs, correctly, 'was a necessity and a satisfaction. He used often to say that he envied me my capacity for being idle. Had he possessed it, poor fellow, I might not now be speaking of him in the past tense.'

Back in 1838, Anthony had no work that felt right to him. Tom was released from teaching, Cecilia was getting married, he was stuck in his junior clerkship and in a squalid, unworthy off-duty life. 'Could there be any escape from such dirt? I would ask myself; and I always answered that there was no escape. The mode of life was itself wretched. I hated the office. I hated my work. More than all I hated my idleness' (*Autobiography*).

CHAPTER FIVE

JOHN Tilley was promoted in 1838. He was appointed District Surveyor for the Northern District of England, responsible for deliveries, improvements, complaints and the efficiency of local postmasters and postmistresses. His starting salary was £300 a year, which made possible his marriage to Cecilia.

Mrs Trollope had only maintained the Hadley house, which she could ill afford, for the sake of her daughter. In late 1838, after perching for a while in Dover with one of her Bristol cousins who had married the rector, Mr Maule,* she moved with Tom, Cecilia and Anthony to rented quarters at 20 York Street, Marylebone, a few blocks west from Northumberland Street. (They wrote the address as 'York Street, Portman Square', which was pushing it a bit.)

A letter of invitation for Christmas 1838 survives from Mrs Trollope to an unknown friend – maybe John Tilley: 'Will you come and share our roast beef and plum pudding at *two* o'clock? In which case I shall rejoice for myself and my trio.' She gave her servants a holiday, she said, at Christmas, 'and we are literally to wait upon ourselves during the evening – but you shall have tea and coffee and cold chicken and punch at ten o'clock.'

Cecilia and John Tilley were married on 11 February 1839 at St Mary's, Bryanston Square, a modern church whose rector was an old acquaintance, that same Rev. Thomas Dibdin who had rhapsodised about Harrow's speech day. According to Tom, he preached 'trashy' sermons in a ludicrously theatrical manner. Mary and Kate Grant were bridesmaids.

Edmund Yates, who joined the Post Office in 1847, found John Tilley, whose life was now inextricably linked with the Trollopes, 'a shrewd, caustic, clever man . . . as unimpressionable as an

---

* Anthony was to borrow the surname Maule for a self-indulgent widower and his languid son (doggedly wooed and won by Adelaide Palliser) in *Phineas Redux*.

oyster',* cold and obstinate. But there was a generation gap between them; and by the time Yates knew him Tilley was scarred by sorrow. He and Anthony remained close until the end, surmounting periods of bitter professional disagreement.

Tilley was an austere person, and his friendship with Anthony was of that masculine kind astutely characterised in *The Vicar of Bullhampton*: 'that undemonstrative, unexpressed, almost unconscious affection which, with men, will often make the greatest charm of their lives, but which is held by women to be quite unsatisfactory and almost nugatory. It may be doubted whether either of them had ever told the other of his regard. "Yours always" in writing, was the warmest term that was ever used. Neither ever dreamed of suggesting that the absence of the other would be a cause of grief or even of discomfort.'

Close women friends, on the other hand, 'will always be expressing their love, always making plans to be together, always doing little things for the gratification of the other, constantly making presents backwards and forwards', and therefore wrongly assume that men, 'caustic, and almost ill-mannered' with one another, have no comparably strong feelings of friendship. In *The Last Chronicle of Barset* Johnny Eames was more openly sceptical about female demonstrativeness: 'When I see women kiss, I always think there is deep hatred at the bottom of it.' Like his father, Anthony distrusted effusiveness.

Anthony was close to his sister Cecilia as well as to John Tilley, before her marriage. She became very religious, attracted by the Oxford Movement within the Church of England, which arose in protest against theological liberalism; it counterpointed, from the opposite corner of the Anglican battlefield, the puritan austerity of the evangelical movement. The Oxford Movement sought to revive the doctrine of the apostolic succession and to draw the Anglican Church nearer to Rome, with the introduction into the liturgy of ritual, candles, incense, crucifixes and other practices, which became known as 'High Church', or Puseyism.†

---

* *Edmund Yates: His Recollections and Experiences*, Richard Bentley, 1884.

† The leaders of the Oxford Movement included the Revs. Edward Pusey, J. H. Newman, John Keble and Hurrell Froude. Their ideas were circulated in a series of 'Tracts for the Times', whence the word Tractarian for adherents of the movement. In 1845 Newman, after much soul-searching, left the Church of England to become a Roman Catholic, an event deeply shocking to the established church, and discussed in *Barchester Towers*. Newman was an enthusiastic admirer of the Barsetshire Chronicles.

Religion, and the practices and politics of the Church of England, were topics of intense interest and concern. Tom wrote to a lady friend in Paris in 1843 that 'Matters ecclesiastical always excite in England, as you must be aware, infinitely more attention in general society than they ever do in France. And all the world here are taking part on one side or the other in the great Puseyite controversy, – with the exception of a few lookers-on at the fight like myself.' When he added that Puseyism was 'filling every man's – (and woman's, worse luck) mind and mouth', it was his sister Cecilia that he was thinking about. Anthony, as his sympathetic treatment of the Rev. Francis Arabin in *Barchester Towers* suggests, fully understood the spiritual lure of the Oxford Movement.

Cecilia, and Anthony, read the Oxford Movement's literature. 'In those days the Tracts were new, and read by everybody, and what has since been called Puseyism was in its robust infancy,' he wrote in *The Bertrams*, set in the early 1840s. In *Doctor Thorne* he characterised, accurately if ironically, a High Church cleric in the person of the Rev. Caleb Oriel:* 'He delighted in lecterns and credence-tables, in services at dark hours of winter mornings when no one would attend, in high waistcoats and narrow white neckties, in chanted services and intoned prayers, and in all the paraphernalia of Anglican formalities which have given such offence to those of our brethren who live in daily fear of the scarlet lady.'

Anthony himself had been moved and impressed by hearing Newman preach at Oxford, presumably when he was attempting to win scholarships to the university or visiting Tom – Newman was a close friend of Whately, principal of Alban Hall – and had spoken with him. It was not the vestments and lace and incense, the superficial liturgical theatricality of 'the scarlet lady', that drew Newman himself towards Roman Catholicism, but a need for unequivocal doctrine and dogma, and a clear authority – all of which were deeply attractive to the unsettled, uncertain Anthony. In *The Bertrams* Anthony described with some passion a young man's overwhelming emotional desire to dedicate his whole life to

* Newman was a Fellow of Oriel College. Anthony's contemporary readers would have picked up the reference.

God – a desire that soon evaporated. Cecilia's piety was fundamental.

The young Tilleys moved north to a house called Fell Side, near Penrith, between the town and the beacon to the north. They were happy. A long incoherent letter survives* from Cecilia to Mrs Trollope announcing – or obliquely suggesting – her pregnancy; Cecilia was a modernly modest girl and did not share her mother's Georgian plain-spokenness.

> *Private.*
>
> I have made my husband promise dearest darling mother to frank this letter to you without reading it. That is a better plan than telling you anything by phrases preconcerted [?] – don't you think so, dearest. Now Mother you will know to what I allude without my telling you more explicitly what I want you to know for even though no one will read this but your own dear self I scarcely know how to put 'in black and white' as Hervieu calls it the communication I wish to make. Now I suppose mother dear you will be very glad and strange as it seems I am glad too. I really scarcely know why – I believe my husband too but I don't quite know for I was so frightened and cried so when I told him that I think he thought more of quieting me than anything else. . . . I am very well indeed, quite a different creature from what I was in town and when I have my husband with me it is impossible for anyone to be happier. I fear I am only too happy for it seems impossible that I should remain perfectly happy for a great while and now there is no single circumstance I could complain of if I sought for one. Much as I loved my own dear John before I was married and happy as I fancied I should be as his wife I had not conceived that I should be so completely happy for I did not know that I should love him infinitely more than ever.

The letter goes on, and on. Cecilia was a complicated young woman. When she too joined the family business and wrote a novel, *Chollerton*, five years or so after her marriage, she used it to demonstrate that love and domestic happiness were lesser things

* In private hands.

96

than chastity, good works and a life devoted to the Christian religion (as practised by High Church Anglicans). For her hero and heroine, marriage would have been a weakness, and virtue lay in suppressing desires.

Soon after Cecilia's wedding Tom and Mrs Trollope went – by train* – to Lancashire, where she did her research for *Michael Armstrong*, a novel about a factory worker (at the suggestion of Lord Ashley, later Shaftesbury), and on to the Lake District, where they visited Wordsworth – and came away unimpressed by his maunderings and his green eyeshade.

Then Tom, with Hervieu, went walking in France, to gather material for a book. Anthony sent £50 of their mother's money for Tom's travel expenses, adding: 'I have but little news of any kind. I do not think that Awdry will join you, as he says he shall have no money, but he is so uncertain and capricious that there is no guessing what he means to do. I trust you get on well in your tour, & your book. Give my love to Heirview.'

That's the very last we hear of the bewhiskered Frenchman. He drifted away.† Tom's first book, *A Summer in Brittany*, was published the following year, 1840, and received a favourable notice in *The Times*. In the same year, Uncle Henry Milton too published a book: a novel, called *Rivalry*.

While Tom was away Mrs Trollope and Anthony lived together in York Street. When Tom returned he went again with his mother up to Penrith to stay with the Tilleys; and in the autumn the two went to Paris, where they enjoyed the 'brilliant receptions' at the British and Austrian embassies and the parties given by Mary Clarke. 'I liked it better than teaching Latin to the youth of Birmingham,' wrote Tom.

Anthony, meanwhile, endured his daily drudgery at the Post Office. When in December Cecilia had her first baby, ten months and a day after her wedding, Anthony was one of the sponsors (i.e., a godfather) at the christening. The baby was named Frances, after her maternal grandmother.

* Mrs Trollope's first-ever train ride was when she went to the Grants' house at Hayes after Cecilia's wedding. It is not recorded whether Anthony went too.

† Hervieu continued to exhibit in London until the late 1850s. In 1866 Anthony told an unidentified correspondent that 'Hervieu still lives, & is I think in London. But I never see him.'

—— * ——

Back in spring 1835, when Mrs Trollope was researching her Paris book, she had taken apartments at 6 rue de Provence, near the Madeleine. The people she liked and cultivated in Paris were the ageing, fading figures of the *ancien régime* and their more 'rococo'* younger friends. Her most useful contact with them was Mary Clarke, already in her mid-forties but seeming girlish still, with her frizzed and tousled hair, 'saucy' ways, unconventional clothes and ideas.

Mary Clarke was a devotee of Madame Juliette Récamier, whose heyday as a young beauty was in the 1790s. After the restoration of Louis XVIII in 1815 her salon was one of the most distinguished in Paris. Napoleon's brother Lucien had been an admirer and Madame de Staël a friend. When the latter was exiled by Napoleon, so was Juliette Récamier. The Vicomte de Châteaubriand – author, Royalist, diplomat and melancholic – adored her. Her past was a scandalous extravaganza, though she was reputed to be a virgin; in the 1830s she was an exquisite icon, white-haired, dressed always in white, living up three ill-lit flights of stairs in a small apartment in a convent, the Abbaye-aux-Bois, on the rue de Sèvres on the Left Bank. Here she received the old guard of her admirers, in a darkened white and blue room crowded with her old Directoire furniture, a harp, and Gérard's painting of Mme de Staël as Corinne. The star guest was old Châteaubriand, bored, gloomy and ill; and the star turn was a reading from his unpublished autobiography, *Memoires d'Outretombe*.†

Mary Clarke went to the Abbaye-aux-Bois every day, and she obtained permission, after anxious consultations, to bring Mrs Trollope along for a special morning reading. No one was ever admitted but those who could be trusted to admire and applaud. There were about seventeen people in the room that day, including the Duchesse de La Rochefoucauld and the Duchesse de Noailles, and a grand-daughter of Lafayette, who sat on the sofa between her hostess and Mrs Trollope – who was asked again. She

---

* 'Rococo' in colloquial French means antiquated and old-fashioned. Mrs Trollope said she herself was 'profoundly rococo' and proud to be so.

† Châteaubriand did not read his work himself. The historian Jean Jacques Ampère read, while the author looked lugubriously on from his special armchair on the left of the fireplace, protected from draughts by a Louis XV screen.

took Cecilia and Emily with her, and presumably Hervieu, because he drew the scene for her book.

Mrs Trollope met the authors Benjamin Constant and George Sand, and heard Liszt playing the score of Mozart's *Don Giovanni* with Princess Belgiojoso, on two pianos. The Princess was a youngish woman devoted to the cause of Italian independence (from the Austrian Empire), and in exile in Paris. It was on that 1835 trip that Mrs Trollope organised a young people's picnic party to the woods of Montmorency. (She loved, as she wrote in her Paris book, 'that indescribable air of contented confusion and happy disorder which can only be found at a pic-nic'.) At the inn called the Cheval Blanc the party hired ponies and donkeys to ride into the forest. One of the young guests, an English student whose name Mrs Trollope never knew, fell from his mount on to a heap of stones and was feared dead. He was carried into the nearby château and made a total recovery, though he carried a scar on his face till his dying day. It was William Makepeace Thackeray.

In 1839, when Tom and Mrs Trollope returned to Paris, they had an even gayer time, 'overwhelmed with invitations and social attentions of all sorts'. Mrs Trollope was presented to King Louis Philippe, who had read her book about America. The salon and the readings at the Abbaye-aux-Bois were still going on. Mary Clarke was living with her old mother – and giving parties – on the upper floors of 120 rue du Bac, with Châteaubriand and his wife living on the lower floors. Mrs Trollope and Tom met Julius Mohl, the specialist in oriental languages, who was to marry Mary Clarke (ten years his senior) in 1847. Old General Pepe was in Paris, and they met Henry Bulwer, then first secretary at the British legation.

They also met Henry Bulwer's tempestuous sister-in-law, Rosina, estranged wife of Sir Edward Bulwer* (whose novels Anthony commented on in his commonplace book). Rosina was Anglo-Irish, from Limerick. Her mother was the daughter of an archdeacon, her father an alcoholic. The Bulwers' marriage was disastrous. Harriet Martineau (admittedly a hostile witness to all upper-class luxuriousness) described in her autobiography the

---

* When his mother died in 1844 and he inherited Knebworth in Hertfordshire, Edward Bulwer took his mother's maiden name and became Sir Edward Bulwer Lytton, the name by which he is known to posterity. He became Lord Lytton in 1866.

foppish Bulwer in the 1830s 'on a sofa, sparkling and languishing, among a set of female votaries'. He seemed to her 'a woman of genius enclosed by misadventure in a man's form'. His languor belied his infidelities, his vindictiveness and his wife-battering. He had removed the two children of the marriage from Rosina in 1838; in 1839 she established herself in Paris, at 30 rue de Rivoli, and like Mrs Trollope and Tom went to the parties given by the Granvilles at the British Embassy, causing a good deal of social unpleasantness, it was said, because of her brother-in-law's position there.

Rosina Bulwer had genuine and terrible grievances and was in anguish over the loss of her two children; but she was a hysterical, garrulous, melodramatic creature, and alienated sympathy. She was strikingly handsome, white-skinned, dark-haired, running to fat. She latched on to Mrs Trollope, who was fascinated by the domestic drama and became her ally and adviser – Lady Bulwer was twenty-two years younger. Mrs Trollope was sorry for Rosina, as she wrote to Cecilia, 'But she is not as quiet as I would wish her to be, in her grief – her lamentations compromise her dignity.'

This was the world into which Anthony, briefly, was plunged. In spring 1840 Tom was away from Paris in Anjou and Poitou – the area known since the Revolution as La Vendée – for another travel book, then in London sorting out the details with his publisher, Henry Colburn. Anthony took a break from the Post Office and went to Paris for a holiday, taking Tom's place as his mother's escort.

The contrast with his London life was so extreme as to be surreal. He went with his mother to Mary Clarke's salon in the rue du Bac, where she had one room for the adults and another with boisterous games for children. The adults were startling. Someone observed of Mrs Trollope's friend Princess Belgiojoso, glimpsed standing in a doorway during a party, that 'she must have been very beautiful when she was alive'. Anthony enjoyed going to 'so many good parties', Mrs Trollope told Cecilia, 'and to our incessant dissipation you must look as the cause of my long silence', adding that she was 'so perfectly tired' of long evenings, beginning with a dinner and ending with a ball; 'I go to bed almost when it is time to get up.' (She was sixty.) Anthony, she wrote, would be home by the time Cecilia (who was pregnant again) received this letter.

He left Paris at the point when Lady Bulwer's troubles, in which his mother was heavily involved, reached boiling point. Bulwer was collecting evidence against her character, and having her watched. Lady Bulwer went to court to prosecute her husband's attorney for attempting to steal her private papers, and the attorney's clerk (who happened to be a Mr Thackeray) for defamation.

The case came up in Paris the week after Anthony left, at the end of March; he could read all about it in London in the *Morning Post*. 'Mrs Trollope,' the paper reported, 'was present, and appeared to watch the proceedings with great anxiety.' Lady Bulwer, whose appearance 'created some sensation', entered with Mrs Trollope, who remained seated at her side throughout. Lady Bulwer succeeded in getting her husband's representatives banned from her house, but Sir Edward retaliated by putting a stop to her correspondence with her children.

As the law stood, children were as much a husband's property as was his wife's money. After the passing of the Infant Custody Act of 1839 the children under seven of a broken marriage could spend time with their mother – but only if the Lord Chancellor judged that the mother was 'of good character', whence Bulwer's efforts to prove that Lady Bulwer was not.

This very moderate concession was entirely due to the campaigning of another woman much in the public eye. Caroline Norton, Lady Bulwer's exact contemporary and grand-daughter of the playwright Sheridan, left her husband, another aristocratic wife-batterer, in the mid-1830s. (Her husband was heir to Lord Grantley. Anthony borrowed the name Grantley – minus the 'e', except when he forgot – for the worldly archdeacon in the Barchester Chronicles.) Caroline Norton was anything but friendless, and held court; Lord Melbourne was one of the admirers who visited her regularly; so, ironically, was Sir Edward Bulwer. Mrs Norton too had her children taken away from her when the marriage fell apart. Her husband, seeking to divorce her, named Melbourne (then Prime Minister) as co-respondent.

There was no evidence of adultery (and no adultery), and the jury threw the case out; but the scandal was enormous, and damaging to Mrs Norton. Her 'gentlemen callers' were held against her. Her life became one long struggle to change the law on child custody, and on married women's property, and to be allowed access to her three children. Mrs Norton earned money by writing. (As the law stood, her earnings could technically be claimed for his own use by the husband who repudiated her.) Lady Bulwer wrote too, using her marital troubles and her husband as raw copy for novels.

Anthony, like the great British public, followed the vicissitudes of these sensational, angry and unhappy women in the newspapers, but he also knew, in Paris, Lady Bulwer in the opulent and expressive flesh. When in 1867 he began writing *He Knew He Was Right* the scenes with which he had been regaled and the feelings they evoked in him as a young man of twenty-four were waiting to be exploited.

There is an added anguish in *He Knew He Was Right* in that Louis Trevelyan and his wife Emily were still in love with one another. They separated because of his obstinate insistence that she must not receive a certain gentleman, and her obstinate insistence that, since the relationship was innocent, she would give no such promise. Emily Trevelyan in the novel knew that her child could be taken from her. Both the law and public opinion would say he should go to his father.

'It is a very poor thing to be a woman,' she said to her sister Nora.

'It is perhaps better than being a dog,' said Nora; 'but, of course, we can't compare ourselves to men.'

'It would be better to be a dog. One wouldn't be made to suffer so much. When a puppy is taken away from its mother, she is bad enough for a few days, but she gets over it in a week.'

Mr Trevelyan set a private detective on Emily, as Sir Edward Bulwer did on his wife. In the novel, the baby was snatched from his mother after a nightmare drive through London in a cab which was really a kidnap vehicle. All the terror and despair of a mother went into Anthony's writing, and all the chill of the unjust law. 'If you care to obtain legal advice,' Emily's husband wrote to her, about the child, 'you will find that I as his father have a right to keep him under my protection.'

——— * ———

Mrs Trollope's life in Paris was lived at a different level – socially, economically, emotionally – than Anthony's in London. The contrast was hard to take; it was Tom, habitually and as if by right, who shared his mother's world. Anthony may not have enjoyed his visit all that much. As his mother wrote, Parisians would not speak English. Anyone who shrank from speaking French, she said, 'can have no hope of either speaking or being spoken to'. Anthony's French was execrable.

Anthony was never a francophile. In *The Three Clerks* he described Frenchmen escorting English girls at the Chiswick Flower Show, all modelled on their emperor Napoleon III, each with a 'long prickly-ended, clotted moustache which looks as though it were being continually rolled up in saliva'. In middle life he wrote disparagingly of French furniture, French clocks and French hotels. 'The dearest hotels I know are the French; – and certainly not the best. . . . In Paris grand dinners may no doubt be had, and luxuries of every description, – except the luxury of comfort' (*North America*).

His visit to Paris in 1840 was not the only one he made while his mother was there, but it was the most disturbing. The return to London – to dull work, poverty and seedy surroundings – may have reinforced his feelings of inadequacy and lowered his resistance. In April he passed his twenty-fifth birthday. In May and June he was dangerously ill.

Because he was so ill Mrs Trollope, with Tom, returned to England in June and took yet another temporary set of rooms in their usual area, at 3 Wyndham Street, which is where in Anthony's *Lady Anna* the heroine and her impoverished mother found rooms – 'in small close lodgings in Wyndham Street, New Road'. Mrs Trollope, as in York Street, improved on the address, heading her letters '3 Wyndham Street, Bryanston Square', whence she wrote to Lady Bulwer in Paris:

> My poor darling [Anthony] lies in a state that defies the views of his physicians as effectually as it puzzles my ignorance. It is asthma from which he chiefly suffers now; but they say this can only be a symptom, and not the disease. He is frightfully reduced in size and strength; sure I am that could you see him, you would not find even a distant resemblance to the being who, exactly three months ago, left

us in all the pride of youth, health and strength. Day by day I lose hope, and so, I am quite sure, do his physicians; we have had three consultations, but nothing prescribed relieves him, nor has any light been thrown on the nature of his complaint.

His loss of weight took place before she came back; wherever he was cared for, before her return, it was neither clean nor pleasant. Twenty years later, the 'dirt and abominations' of a public washhouse in Cairo, Illinois, where he was regarded with suspicion because he used his own comb instead of the public one, brought back memories of the squalid house where he had lain ill: 'I remember how an old woman once stood over me in my youth, forcing me to swallow the gritty dregs of her terrible medicine-cup' (*North America*).

He had a fever, and problems with breathing, but his illness did not seem to be tuberculosis. Mrs Trollope had lost three of her children. She prepared herself for the loss of a fourth.

Healthy young people fall gravely ill in Anthony's fiction when they are faced with a conflict they cannot resolve. In *The Claverings*, for example, Harry loved and proposed marriage to small, plain, 'meagre' Florence Burton in a provincial town, then became passionately involved with luscious Lady Ongar in London. Racked by guilt and indecision, he went home to his parents, told them nothing, and became ill 'with a low fever'. It is as if illness were a way of temporarily abandoning the problems and responsibilities of manhood, for women took over at such times: 'There are women who seem to have an absolute pleasure in fixing themselves for business by the bed-side of a sick man,' wrote Anthony in *Miss Mackenzie*. The sick man is like a baby and, 'in his prostrate condition, debarred by all the features of his condition from spontaneous exertion, feels himself to be more a woman than the woman herself.'

His parents had changed gender-roles in this way. It was a topic Anthony was to return to again and again. In *The Vicar of Bullhampton*, for example: 'When there is illness in a house, the feminine genius and spirit predominates the male. If the illness be so severe as to cause a sense of danger, this is so strongly the case that the natural position of the two is changed.' Anthony's illness forced his mother to take responsibility for his life, or death.

Anna in *Lady Anna* was committed by her sense of honour to marrying a tailor. Her devoted mother, desperate to regain for herself and her daughter their rightful social position, commanded her to break the engagement. Anna responded to the crisis by becoming very ill. So single-minded was the mother that she would rather see her daughter dead than married to the tailor. ' "Would it not be better that she should die?" said her mother to herself, standing over her and looking at her.'

Sick people, Anthony noted later, have preternaturally sensitive hearing. If he overheard his mother saying that she did not expect him to live, or realised that she was longing to get away back to her own life, it was a small step to imagining that he would be better dead. Not all his fantasies, his castles in the air, were triumphant ones. Like Johnny Eames in *The Small House at Allington*, he sometimes built 'pernicious castles in the air . . . black castles, with cruel dungeons, into which hardly a ray of light would find its way'.

When Mrs Trollope fell ill in the York Street house the previous year she had consulted Dr John Elliotson, a short, dark, dynamic man in his late thirties who was Professor of Medicine at the University of London, the founder of the Phrenological Society and the first doctor in Britain to use a stethoscope. He was a good clinical teacher and a popular lecturer, with a special interest in the nervous system – and in the occult and the paranormal. He was an ardent student of Mesmer. While not actually suggesting to his fashionable patients that he should mesmerise them, he employed the technique readily if they expressed any interest, and held sessions and 'exhibitions' at his house, which attracted a great deal of publicity.

He was practising what came, by the mid-1840s, to be called hypnotism. Mesmerists believed that there was an invisible fluid suffusing the universe, rather like electricity – it was sometimes called magnetism – and that it could be harnessed with therapeutic effect for both physical and psychological ills. There was a vogue for it; Harriet Martineau, who practised mesmerism in collaboration with her maid, believed that it had cured her of cancer.

Elliotson was a great friend of Charles Dickens, and physician to his family. It was when Dickens attended one of Elliotson's 'exhibitions' at University College, London, in early 1838 that he discovered that he too could mesmerise people, especially women. (Mrs Trollope met Dickens in the same year, at a party given by her actress friend Mrs Bartley.) Thackeray admired Elliotson, who successfully treated him (not by mesmerism) in 1849, and dedicated *Pendennis* to him.

Most of the patients who participated in Elliotson's experiments were adolescents and epileptics. Mrs Trollope was very interested. She had gone with Tom by invitation to see Dr Elliotson mesmerise two young patients, and was impressed by the total control he had over them when they were in trance.

Elliotson had two specially susceptible subjects, the Okey sisters, who were epileptics in their early teens. They were from a poor family, and Elliotson took them into his own house. His special rapport with adolescent girls raised a few eyebrows in the academic community, and shortly before Anthony fell ill Elliotson had been forced to resign his university chair. Nor, it appears, was Dr Elliotson called in to mesmerise Anthony even though, as Tom said in his memoirs, 'we were intimate with him at the time'. But the Okey girls, Tom remembered, were constantly in and out of 'Anthony's lodgings' (which suggests that he was not in the same house as his mother, but round the corner in York Street) during his illness. Mrs Trollope took a keen and watchful interest in them – recalling no doubt the way young girls had reacted to the evangelical preachers in America.

Before their 'fits' came upon them, she told her old friend Mrs Grant, they were decent working girls. Now 'they not only have lost all consciousness of their parentage, but have all their faculties developed under circumstances altogether unfitting them for the life to which they were born.' Elliotson, she believed, had an obligation to provide for them. 'They have all the innocence of children of three years old, joined to the natural intelligence of their real age.' Woe to anyone, she wrote, 'barbarous enough to use them ill!'

She became increasingly worried about 'those dear victimized girls' who, when Dr Elliotson tried to wean them from their dependence, were desolated, having become addicted to the 'exquisitely exciteable [sic] state' into which they were brought by

Julian Hill outside Harrow, the farmhouse improved and modernised by Anthony's parents in the 1820s. It was 'an Eden' to Anthony, but his father's rent-arrears resulted in a visit from the bailiffs and a final family 'flitting' in spring 1834.

Casewick Hall at Uffington near Stamford in Lincolnshire, the ancestral home of the senior branch of the Trollope family since the sixteenth century. Anthony's father was first cousin to Sir John Trollope, the sixth baronet.

Frances Trollope, Anthony's mother: a portrait by Auguste Hervieu, the young French artist who was for a decade her protégé and companion.

Cecilia Trollope, Anthony's sister, sketched by Hervieu. She married Anthony's Post Office colleague John Tilley, had five children, and died aged thirty-two.

Broad Street in 1829, and the spire of St Giles-in-the-Fields. This street (destroyed by the development of Shaftesbury Avenue in the late 1870s) marked the boundary between respectable Bloomsbury, where Anthony was born, and the overcrowded slums of St Giles.

'A Harrow School Boy (1805)', by Auguste Hervieu. The reference is to Lord
Byron, Harrow's most notorious former pupil; the lithograph was done in 1833
when the artist was living with the Trollopes and Anthony himself was a wretchedly
unhappy Harrow schoolboy.

General Post Office, St Martin's-Le-Grand: this impressive building within sight of
St Paul's Cathedral was completed only five years before Anthony started there as a
junior clerk in 1834. He worked in an upstairs office overlooking Goldsmith's Hall in
Foster Lane.

A recent photograph (1989) of the house near Drumsna, Co. Leitrim, which inspired Anthony's first novel, *The Macdermots of Ballycloran*. Already a desolate ruin in 1843, it fired his imagination with 'thoughts of the wrong, oppression, misery, and despair, to which someone had been subjected'.

The hotel by the river Shannon in Banagher, Co. Offaly, where Anthony lived and kept his horse when he took up his post as a Surveyor's Clerk in 1841. He brought his English bride, Rose Heseltine, back to this hotel after their marriage in 1844.

The house on the High Street in Mallow, Co. Cork, said to be the one leased 1848–51 by Anthony and Rose with their two small boys. Mrs Trollope senior visited them in Mallow, and they took in Anthony's little niece Edith here when her mother died.

Charles Bianconi, the Italian entrepreneur who achieved a virtual monopoly of road transport in southern Ireland, and was Anthony's introduction to the 'Melmotte' mentality.

An Irish 'outside car', on which the passengers perched facing outwards, with no protection from the weather. Bianconi's 'long cars' were extended outside cars. Anthony suffered equally in the 'altogether abominable affairs called inside cars', in which one faced inwards, but still had no cover from the rain.

The only known photograph of Anthony's wife Rose in her prime. She was from
Yorkshire, the daughter of a bank manager. There is no contemporary account of her,
only sparse references – to her prematurely white hair, to her liking for fashionable
dresses, to her pretty feet, to her devotion to her husband. In company, Anthony
held the floor. Privately, she had her say.

The Famine: the sick and starving clamouring for admittance to the workhouse at Clonmel, where Anthony and Rose were living during the worst of the famine period, and when painful scenes such as this, and worse, were being reported to the authorities in London.

The Famine: contemporary drawing of a gentleman sitting with dying peasants in their cabin, children begging at the door. Anthony later described a strikingly similar scene in *Castle Richmond*.

5 Seaview Terrace, Donnybrook, near Dublin: Anthony, Rose and their two sons
lived from 1855 to 1859 in this large, comfortable semi-detached house on what was still
a country lane. He travelled for the PO a great deal in these years, and referred to
Seaview Terrace as 'Home' in his travel diaries, as he had not with any of their
previous houses.

mesmerism. 'They are *all* nerves, poor dears.' Kind Mrs Grant was induced to part with money for the Okeys, and Anthony had had to cope with them while his mother was in Paris. 'I have letters from them both by Anthony,' wrote his mother, 'in which they speak with most grateful affection of all you have done.'

The Okey girls would remain under the influence of Elliotson's mesmerism for days at a time, and their paranormal faculties included what they called 'seeing Jack' at a sickbed, which apparently meant that the patient was going to die. They saw Jack beside Anthony as he lay ill in the lodging house, 'but only up to the knee', which was interpreted as meaning he would live.

'We are all of us fond of the marvellous,' Anthony wrote fifteen years later, commenting on mesmerism. 'It is the frailty of human nature.' For 'when we saw all the senses of a human creature brought as it were into a state of collapse, by the mere touchings or manipulations of another human creature; when we saw the movements and almost the instincts of one person placed under the control of another, at first we wondered, and disbelieved; and then we wondered and believed. The evidence adduced was too strong for disbelief. . . .' Mesmerism 'and its train of absurdities' was, he thought, a 'medical' phenomenon, imperfectly under-stood and exploited by men with 'more science than soundness' (*The New Zealander*). Medical science did not know how to use mesmerism, but 'medical charlatans' did.

At the time Elliotson's disturbed teenagers, '*all* nerves', as Mrs Trollope said, can hardly have been therapeutic company for a sick and depressed young man.

Besides watching over Anthony, Mrs Trollope and Tom were in constant communication with Lady Bulwer about her tangled affairs. Tom was acting on her behalf with Henry Colburn, who was to publish her next novel, *The Budget of the Bubble Family*, which she was dedicating to Mrs Trollope. She was difficult; Tom had to reproach her, with his customary elaborate courtesy, for her 'unreasonableness' in thinking that the £400 Colburn offered was a paltry price for her novel, and for nagging his mother over the matter. It was in fact a very good price, and reflected the author's notoriety rather than her literary gifts. Colburn was a cold little man who did no one favours, 'an embodied shiver' as Lady Bulwer called him.

Mrs Trollope wrote to Lady Bulwer on 3 July 1840: 'My poor Anthony is so very nearly in the same state as when I last wrote that I have not a word to say that can help to give you information of our future movements. Had I the power to move, my will is as fixed as ever on Italy.' She and Tom were longing to be abroad again, having arranged to meet Châteaubriand and Madame Récamier in Venice in the autumn. Tom wrote to Lady Bulwer on the same day, more optimistically: 'My brother is unquestionably *much* better. We must not, as his sententious Esculapius [i.e., his doctor] says, cry "Whoop" before we are out of the wood, but I am in great hope that he will now rapidly gain ground, and that our plans will resume their course.'

Writing to Lady Bulwer less than a week later, Mrs Trollope too was more hopeful. 'Anthony goes on decidedly improving, but so slowly as to make every morning's enquiry one of fear and trembling. Still I DO hope and believe that we shall be able to leave England early in September. . . . Could we not meet at *Venice?* Madame Récamier would not have *seemed* to like you had she not done so.'*

No mention at all was made of Anthony's frightening illness in the memoir of Mrs Trollope by Tom's second wife. She simply stated that in July 1840 Mrs Trollope went up for a long stay with the Tilleys in Penrith: 'She had the pleasure of seeing her son Anthony this autumn. He paid a flying visit to Cumberland.' In *Can You Forgive Her?* Anthony captured the quality of the late autumn light in Cumbria: 'It tells of the shortness of the day, and contains even in its clearness a promise of the gloom of night. It is absolute light, but it seems to contain the darkness which is to follow it. I do not know that it is ever to be seen so plainly as on the wide moorland. . . .' He set one of the most violent scenes between man and woman that he ever wrote – again in *Can You Forgive Her?*, where the 'wild beast' George Vavasor broke Alice's arm – on lonely Shap Fell, south of Penrith. Afterwards Vavasor had a terrible, stumbling walk, lost and alone, across the moor in the rain to Shap.

* The subsequent history of Lady Bulwer, who called herself Lytton from the time her estranged husband adopted the name, is too packed with sensational incident, drama and heartbreak to be summarised here. She was a deeply wronged woman. She was also unstable, garrulous, and difficult to help. Her story is told in *Life of Rosina, Lady Lytton* by Louisa Devey (1887).

'A man may be very weary in such a walk as that,' interposed the author's voice, 'and yet be by no means wretched. Tired, hungry, cold, wet, and nearly penniless, I have sat me down and slept among those mountain tracks, – have slept because nature refused to allow longer wakefulness. But my heart has been as light as my purse, and there has been something in the air of the hills that made me buoyant and happy in the midst of my weariness.' Cumberland was a good, tough, elemental place in which to convalesce.

Anthony was an uncle twice over now. Cecilia's second daughter, Cecilia Isabel, was born on 16 November. Mrs Trollope never did get to Italy that year. From Penrith she continued to agitate about the Okey girls, having decided that they should be rescued from the clutches of Dr Elliotson. She supported the girls' parents who were looking for a legally assured annuity for them, since they had been rendered unfit to earn their livings.*

Mrs Trollope was involved in a new and ambitious plan for her own life. She was going to build a house for her old age in Cumberland, near her daughter and grandchildren. It was, she conceded, 'very much on the windy side of reason' to start house-building again, 'but nothing in the shape of a comfortable residence was to be found within reach of Cecilia'.

She bought a field on high ground overlooking the ruins of Brougham Castle and the confluence of the rivers Eden and Lowther; the house, which she called Carlton Hill, took eighteen months to get built. The local landlord, Sir George Musgrave of Edenhall, was dismayed because in order to gain access to the road a water-course was diverted; he said it was bad luck. He was right. (Mrs Trollope was only to live at Carlton Hill for one winter and half a summer.) The Musgraves were superstitious. Longfellow wrote a poem about the 'Luck of Edenhall' – which would be broken were an ancient glass goblet in the house ever to be broken. 'I remember', wrote Anthony in *The Small House at Allington*, 'to have dined at a house, the whole glory and fortune of which depended on the safety of a glass goblet.' Sir George

---

* According to Tom, a daughter of one of the Okeys was employed as a maid by Anthony and his wife Rose years later when they were living in Waltham Cross.

Musgrave let visitors handle it, according to Tom, because otherwise the luck was not properly tested.

When Mrs Trollope abandoned Carlton Hill – ostensibly because her health would not stand the hard winters; actually, because 'she found the life dull' – she sold it to her son-in-law John Tilley. The area, over the years, became familiar to Anthony and dear to him. 'All the world knows', he lovingly wrote in 'The Mistletoe Bough', a story written in the early 1860s, 'that the Eamont runs out of Ulleswater, passing under Penrith Bridge and by the old ruins of Brougham Castle, below which it joins the Eden.' When he used Cumberland or Westmorland as a setting, he was extremely precise. Humblethwaite, for example, in *Sir Harry Hotspur of Humblethwaite*, is ten miles north of Keswick, with the river Caldbeck flowing through the grounds. To the south is Skiddaw and Saddleback, to the west Brocklebank Fell. He used the names of villages near Penrith (Sowerby, Greystoke) as names for fictional characters.

Anthony's illness was a turning-point. After it was over he was his own man. What remained of his family seemed to be regrouping up north; in fact, Mrs Trollope went on her first visit to Italy in April 1841, picking up Tom en route at the château of the Baroness de Zandt* in Bavaria, and it was in Italy that the two were to find their permanent home. On this initial trip, which resulted in Mrs Trollope's *A Visit to Italy* (her nineteenth book – she published one a year, and sometimes two), they were out of England for ten months.

Anthony was now earning £140 per annum, by reason of length of service, but there was no promotion in sight. With growing desperation came more marked insubordination. His name appeared even more frequently on the censorious memos from the Secretary. His lack of servility, all his professional life, looked like truculence.

In a lecture he later gave on 'The Civil Service as a Profession', he said that a craven attitude towards superiors used to be 'the disgrace of our calling'. He deprecated the obligation to be always 'agreeable'. 'He who at five-and-twenty can feel within his bosom

* Formerly Lady Dyer, a faithful friend from Harrow days who had lent Mrs Trollope the money to travel from Bruges with Henry to consult the London doctor.

that sort of dread for another man which a schoolboy has for his master, will probably feel it also at five-and-forty.' The way not to be craven, he said, was to give more than full value for money: 'For every half-crown that you receive be careful to give work to the value of three shillings and sixpence, and then do not care a straw for any man.'

When Anthony himself was twenty-five, he was unwilling to be craven *and* unwilling to work wholeheartedly, and therefore got into trouble. His father, as muddle and failure took over his 'outside' life, had embarked on an attempt at order and control in another sphere with his *Encyclopaedia Ecclesiastica*. Anthony, depressed and confused, now decided to compile a history of the literature of the western world from the Greeks onwards, in many volumes. It was a desperate undertaking. He made out reading lists and wrote a detailed outline. The work was to include fiction, poetry, science, mathematics, astronomy, history, philosophy, political economy, criticism, biography, the fine arts, periodical literature and 'miscellaneous'. His notes on his reading, from his journals, were to be incorporated. The outline was written some time in 1840 – we cannot know whether it was before his illness, and symptomatic of the stress that triggered it, or afterwards, in an effort to find *something* to which he could dedicate himself and of which he might be proud.

Luckily for him, he never had to write it. Providence, as he would say, intervened. The Post Office instituted a new grade of officer, called Surveyor's Clerks. (There were seven Surveyors in England – of which his brother-in-law John Tilley was one – and three in Ireland.) Anthony did not think of applying, knowing that he would never be successful. All the Surveyor's Clerks were duly appointed.

Then in August 1841 there came a report that the clerk who had been sent to assist the Surveyor in the west of Ireland was 'absurdly incapable'. By chance, Anthony was the first person to read the report when it reached the Secretary's office.

'I was at that time in dire trouble, having debts on my head and quarrels with our Secretary-Colonel [Maberly], and a full conviction that my life was taking me downward to the lowest pits. So I went to the Colonel boldly, and volunteered for Ireland if he would send me. He was glad to be so rid of me, and I went' (*Autobiography*).

When he told people that he was going to Ireland they were unenthusiastic, but did not try to stop him. 'I think it must have been evident to all who were my friends that my life in London was not a success.' He took the decision to go entirely on his own. His mother and Tom were abroad, and were not consulted. The only relative that he talked to was John Young, an elderly family lawyer, a first cousin of his father's on the Meetkerke side. From him Anthony borrowed £200 'to get me out of England'.

'But nobody then thought I was right to go.' He was twenty-six, and the salary was only £100 per annum – less than he was getting now in London. On the other hand, the job would involve a great deal of travelling, and he would have an allowance of 15 shillings a day for every day he was away from home, plus sixpence for every mile – and the cost of living was said to be 50 per cent lower. 'My income in Ireland, after paying my expenses, became at once £400. This was the first good fortune of my life.'

The move had other, immaterial benefits. It was a new start. He was escaping from his family even more definitively than they had seemed to be escaping from him; he was escaping from the office, and from his seedy London life; he was escaping from old failures and all the unhappy associations of his prolonged boyhood. Up to now he had been a high achiever who was achieving nothing. He was a man ready for great and sustained industry who was doing as little work as possible, a man with the capacity for happiness who rarely enjoyed himself.

> There had clung to me a feeling that I had been looked upon always as an evil, an encumbrance, a useless thing, – as a creature of whom those connected with him had to be ashamed. . . . Even my few friends who had found with me a certain capacity for enjoyment were half afraid of me. I acknowledge the weakness of a strong desire to be loved, – of a strong wish to be popular with my associates. No child, no boy, no lad, no young man, had ever been less so. And I had been so poor; and so little able to bear poverty.

When he wrote those sad words in his autobiography he was an ageing man, fearing he was past his peak and that the good times were about to slip away from him again, knowing too well 'how great is the agony of adversity, how crushing the despondency of degradation, how susceptible I am myself to the misery coming from contempt. . . .'

Not even that familiar dread could blur the memory of what his leap in the dark had done for him. From the time he set foot in Ireland, he wrote, 'all these evils went away from me. Since that time who has had a happier life than mine?'

CHAPTER SIX

ANTHONY arrived in Dublin on 15 September 1841. 'I went to a hotel which was very dirty, and after dinner I ordered some whiskey punch. There was an excitement in this, but when the punch was gone I was very dull. It seemed so strange to be in a country in which there was not a single individual whom I had ever spoken to or ever seen.' There he was, on his own, not for a holiday but for the foreseeable future. No one who has not had a similar experience can know quite how strange it feels. He was to be in Ireland, on and off, for the next seventeen years.

In the morning he went to see Augustus Godby, the Secretary of the Irish Post Office, and learned that Colonel Maberly had sent a reference damning him as worthless and unlikely to hold down the job. This was the last adhering scab of Anthony's London failure and it was quickly shed. Mr Godby assured Anthony that he would be judged on his own merits. Within months, Anthony knew that his services were valued, and within a year, as he wrote in his autobiography, 'I had acquired the character of a thoroughly good public servant.'

He was to be based at Banagher in King's County, now Co. Offaly, in the green Irish midlands. The only railway line in Ireland yet was the short one between Dublin and Kingstown. The waterways were Ireland's trunk roads, and the standard way to get to Banagher was by canal boat.

Anthony became used to taking the boat west on the Grand Canal from Portobello in Dublin. Towed by horses, covering only twenty miles a day, the boat worked its way eighty miles inland to Shannon Harbour, a few miles from Banagher, where Anthony disembarked. In the mainly poverty-stricken towns and villages along the way,* through which the canal passed, were un-

---

* We are used to thinking of the island of Ireland as agreeably uncrowded. But in 1841 the population of the island was more than double that of today – over 8 million, and rising.

expectedly large hotels; these would be put out of business when the railways came.

The canal boat was always overcrowded, and in *The Kellys and the O'Kellys* Anthony called it a 'floating prison'. It was impossible to read because of the noise, smells, rows, quarrels and general discomfort. Martin Kelly in the novel 'made great play at the eternal half-boiled leg of mutton, floating in a bloody sea of grease and gravy, which always comes on the table three hours after the departure from Porto Bello . . . huge collops of the raw animal, and vast heaps of yellow turnips', at two shillings a head.

Irish cooking continued to astound him. He described in detail, and doubtless at first hand, the repast after a wedding in his first novel, *The Macdermots of Ballycloran*. It consisted of two legs of mutton and a ham, each 'reclining on a vast bed of cabbage', and many dishes of potatoes. The mutton, again, was only half-cooked, and as plates were scarce the guests 'took the huge lumps of blood-red mutton in their fists'.

Half-cooked mutton was not the style at home. Tom in his memoirs described the mutton of Cumberland at this time as rich four-year-old meat, producing 'chocolate-coloured gravy' to which was added at table, after carving, some port, currant jelly and cayenne, the whole being reheated in a silver saucepan. In Ireland, celebrations apart, only the well-off could afford meat at all.

The conditions of the Irish poor shocked all newcomers from mainland Britain.* Only the exceptional traveller, such as the evangelical missionary Mrs Asenath Nicholson, saw enough to know that some cabins were models of 'perfect neatness'. She wrote that 'if few are scrupulously tidy, few are disgustingly filthy'.† Mrs Nicholson was a doughty fifty-year-old New Yorker who travelled through Ireland with almost no money in 1844 and 1845, investigating the conditions of the poor. She gratefully accepted hospitality in the poorest cabins, sharing space with pigs and fowl, picking her way to her sleeping-place between piles of turf, muddy potatoes, manure or 'noisome etceteras', dining on a

---

* This was partly because they came from the comfortable classes of society and did not know the wretchedness of their own country. Thackeray, for example, complained of the stinking dungheaps piled against Irish cottages, directly under the windows. He would have seen exactly the same thing in Haworth, where the Brontës were living, and in many other English villages too.

† A. Nicholson, *Ireland's Welcome to the Stranger* (1847).

potato held in the hand and a sup of milk if she was lucky. Though Anthony, like her, remarked on the wit and intelligence of the ragged children who grew up in these conditions, he was not motivated to experience the 'disgustingly filthy' at first hand, except as an observer.

In a typical village there would be a handful of solid slate-roofed houses and then, as Anthony described in *The Macdermots*, just 'hovels without chimneys, windows, door, or signs of humanity, except the children playing on the collected filth in front of them. The very scraughs of which the roofs are composed are germinating afresh, and, sickly green with a new growth, look more like the tops of long-neglected dungheaps.' He described what he saw inside one such hovel, once his eyes had got used to the smoke and darkness:

> A sickly woman, the tangled nature of whose insufficient garments would defy description, is sitting on a low stool before the fire, suckling a miserably dirty infant; a boy, whose only covering is a tattered shirt, is putting fresh, but, alas, damp turf beneath the pot in which are put to boil the potatoes – their only food. Two or three dim children – their number is lost in the obscurity – are cowering round the dull, dark fire, atop of one another; and on a miserable pallet beyond – a few rotten boards, propped upon equally infirm supports, and covered over with only one thin black quilt – is sitting the master of the mansion. . . . Squatting on the ground – from off the ground, like pigs, only much more poorly fed – his children eat the scanty earnings of his continual labour.
>
> And yet for this abode the man pays rent.

In England Banagher would be called a big village, in Ireland it is a town. At the top of the sloping street is the Protestant church of St Paul with its tall spire; a story has survived that Anthony Trollope, as a young Surveyor's Clerk, sometimes read the lesson there at morning service. It was in Banagher that Charlotte Brontë's widower, the Rev. Arthur Nicholls, later lived out his widowhood.*

* Mr Nicholls's family home was Hill House, Banagher, and he and Charlotte visited Banagher after their wedding in 1854. Mr Nicholls's brother was the manager of the Dublin to Banagher stretch of the Grand Canal, along which Anthony travelled.

The steep main street, over a mile long, runs down to the Shannon, which is the boundary with Co. Galway – and, in provincial terms, the boundary between Leinster and Connaught. Anthony lived in the hotel with a bulging front, like a half-barrel, at the Shannon end of the street. Within a week of his arrival he woke up to the noise and confusion of Banagher Great Fair, which lasted four days (and nights), filling the main street with horses for sale, carts, livestock, stalls and booths. A new bridge over the Shannon was being constructed during the time he was in Banagher; the foundation stone was laid by Lord de Grey, the new Viceroy appointed by the new Conservative government in England, the month before Anthony arrived.

The Post Office was up the street from his hotel on the left; it consisted of a two-storey double-fronted house with a fanlight over the door and a diminutive two-roomed cottage attached to it, where Anthony and his boss, George Drought,* had their private office. It was all as different from St Martin's-le-Grand and from sooty Marylebone lodging houses as could be imagined.

Anthony made himself valuable to Mr Drought, who was an idle and testy man, by doing most of the work. He shed his inertia along with his depression, which became occasional rather than chronic. He was subordinate to Mr Drought, but to no one else in the immediate vicinity. His job now was to inspect, not be inspected. He was part of that army of British administrators, officials and military – there was a garrison of redcoats in Banagher, down by the Shannon – who, with the landed Anglo-Irish, stood over the local population. He took to his new role with gusto.

His official manner was severe, gruff, barking. The native Irish officials too barked at underdogs – and at Mrs Asenath Nicholson, who remarked: 'I have observed throughout Ireland two classes of men with a superabundant capital of insolence – post-masters, and the agents of coaches and canal-boats.' She ascribed it to 'the hurry and perplexity of their business, and the pride of being so exalted above the spade'. That was the petty officialdom at which Anthony was now in a position to bark. He barked at those above

* Anthony used his name in the parliamentary novels: Sir Orlando Drought was a Conservative MP who resigned in opposition to the leadership of the Duke of Omnium.

him in the Post Office hierarchy as well, which was to cause him, and them, some problems.

Thackeray, three years older, was in Ireland writing a travel book the year before Anthony first arrived.* He noticed how English voices 'amidst the rich humming brogue round about, sounded quite affected (not that they were so, but there seems a sort of impertinence in the shrill high-pitched tone of the English voice here).' Anthony's voice was not high-pitched – it was beginning to boom – but was none the less unequivocally English.

His new manner was in part defensive. He was only twenty-six. Much of his work concerned postmasters' dodgy accounting, and Anthony knew nothing of book-keeping and had never been taught to manipulate figures. Before he had been in Ireland six weeks he was sent to Oranmore in Co. Galway to see a postmaster who was suspected of being unreliable over his accounts. The sums involved were small but the dealings were intricate. Anthony made the man explain to him exactly how the accounting should be done, and how the different forms were filled out. He got, in short, a series of free tutorials, in the course of which he saw exactly how the man had defaulted. 'Of course he was dismissed; – but he had been a very useful man to me. I never had any further difficulty in the matter' (*Autobiography*).

His skill in keeping accounts was sharpened by having to keep his own, in order to claim his all-important travel allowance. (He sent in a claim to London for his travel from London to Dublin, but it was disallowed.) Irish roads were appalling, Irish conveyances idiosyncratic, Irish weather wet. As Thackeray put it in his *Irish Sketch Book*, 'English waterproofs are not waterproof in *Ireland*.' Irish rain, wrote Anthony in *Castle Richmond*, was 'cold, light, drizzling rain, such a rain as gradually but surely makes its way into the innermost rag of a man's clothing, running up the inside of his waterproof coat, and penetrating by its perseverance the very folds of his necktie.' But he rarely caught a cold, he said, because there was no east wind.

In the standard Irish conveyance, a jaunting-car or 'outside car', where the passengers sat back-to-back facing outwards, at right angles to the horse, there was no way of avoiding the rain.

* Thackeray was based in Cork where his mother-in-law lived. He had his young wife and two small daughters with him. He was hoping, in vain, that the trip would cure his wife, who had become psychotic after the birth of her last child.

Then there were 'those altogether abominable affairs called inside cars, not because you had any of the comforts of an inside place in case of rain, for they have no covering, but because the inmates, sitting on each side, have full power to kick each other's shins, and no liberty to stretch their legs.' A covered 'inside car' was not much better: 'It is entered from behind, and slopes backwards. The sitter sits sideways, between a cracked window on one side and a cracked doorway on the other; and as a draught is always going in at the ear next the window, and out at the ear next the door, it is about as cold and comfortless a vehicle as may well be imagined' (*Castle Richmond*). There were also Bianconis, known as Bians (pronounced Bye-anns) and named after their Italian-born owner. As in the smaller outside cars, the passengers in Bianconi's 'long cars' travelled facing out, looking sideways on the world, and were provided with oil-cloth aprons to protect them from knee to chest. But the oil-cloth was often torn; and in wet weather one sat, on a leather cushion, in a puddle. Bianconi's fleet of cars also carried the mails.

The Irish postal services were, by English standards, casual, even though the Irish PO had been united with the PO of Great Britain in 1831 in an attempt to improve efficiency. Mail coaches were often robbed on unfrequented country roads; the guards on the mail cars carried bell-mouthed blunderbusses, and Godby in Dublin offered rewards for information leading to arrests. It was common in the 1840s, when sending bills (the equivalent of cheques) by mail, to cut them in half and send the two halves by separate posts, as a precaution. Bags of mail sometimes toppled off the mail cars, or were jettisoned.

In Cork, Thackeray tried to cash six five-shilling postal orders at the Post Office; it took four visits on four different days before they could collect up all the money for him. Meanwhile, he overheard a man who had no change to pay for his letter being told to leave the letter and pay another day. This sort of laxness shocked Thackeray, and it was part of Anthony's job to put a stop to it in his district, as well as to improve the inadequate delivery services to remote areas.

The friendliness and the disregard for forms and norms which underlay the Irish laxness were the most healing aspects of Ireland, for Anthony Trollope. National stereotypes are offensive and silly. In the nineteenth century the Irish stereotype of the ragged, ape-faced, idle, treacherous 'Paddy', so dear to the *Punch* cartoonists, was especially so. Yet stereotypes cannot exist if they do not capture some lowest common denominator of perceived truth.

There was a positive stereotype too in the chaste, brave and goddess-like figure of Hibernia, and in the English idea of the Irish as warm, witty and verbally agile. The Irish welcome and Irish hospitality and the convivial Irish 'crack' are conventions, and may conceal as much anxiety and resentment as the coldest, dimmest British gathering, or as much malice as English society gush. But they are beneficent conventions, the outward and visible signs of an ideal of cherishing acceptance – an ideal often realised.

It was just what Anthony needed to bring him out of his shell. In his later life, in England and America, many people commented on his noisy, boisterous social manner, which could be like that of Tony McKeon in *The Macdermots of Ballycloran*: 'Whenever six or eight were talking loud together, his voice might always be heard the loudest. Whenever a shout of laughter arose – and that was incessantly – his shout was always the longest.'

Some loved Anthony for this manner and some didn't. It was taken to be a particularly bluff, roast-beef kind of Englishness, and that is in the end what it became. But it was a mode he learned in Ireland where, as Thackeray found, 'the stranger is at once made happy and at home, or at ease rather'. For the first time in his life Anthony felt at ease. 'It was altogether a very jolly life that I led in Ireland' (*Autobiography*).

The greater part of his work was travelling around investigating complaints about the service made by members of the public. The complainers received a personal visit from the Surveyor's Clerk. This took Anthony into all kinds of houses, at all levels of society. He told in his autobiography about a large country house he had to visit in Cavan – outside his district, 'but I was young and strong' and the householder had written many times and in the strongest language. But when Anthony arrived, in a snowstorm, on an open jaunting-car, he was given brandy and water, and dinner, and a pleasant evening listening to the daughter of the house singing, and a bed for the night. Only after breakfast the next day could he broach the question of the postal service. His host had nothing to say, no complaint to make; 'Here I sit all the day, – with nothing to do; and I like writing letters.'

Mr Drought kept a pack of hounds at Banagher, though he did not hunt himself. Anthony knew how to ride. He had learned the hard way. 'It's dogged as does it,' the old countryman said, trying to instil courage into the despairing Mr Crawley in *The Last Chronicle of Barset*, and 'It's dogged as does it' could stand for Anthony's motto. He had learned to stay on a horse after much falling off; Tom put him up on a wretched pony, bareback, as a boy at Harrow Weald, and forced him to jump hedges and ditches. More recently he had ridden in Cumberland, when staying with Cecilia and John Tilley.

His Harrow Weald approach to riding lasted all his life. He called hunting 'the easiest of all sports', declaring that 'it is only necessary that a man should stick on the back of a horse, – or, failing that, that he should fall off' (*South Africa*). He was not long in Banagher before he bought a horse. He stabled it at the back of the hotel where he lived and hired a local man called Barney to be his groom.

Anthony was an upright, supple young man, good in the saddle. It is sad that there is no known photograph of him before he was middle-aged, bearded and balding. The perpetual spectacles veil his eyes, which were blue or blue-grey. Tom described himself in his memoirs as having no pretensions to good looks, 'thick and sturdy, ungainly', with good skin and 'pale-coloured lanky hair'. Anthony was two inches taller than Tom's five foot eight but shared his build. His face was broader-featured* and less aquiline than Tom's. When he was in the West Indies, Anthony's hair was described as *castaño*, which he rightly presumed meant 'chestnut', though *castaño* is also the Spanish word for any shade of brown. His hair too was probably lightish in colour and texture, English 'mousy' hair like Tom's.

Anthony always loathed having his photograph taken, as he loathed the later fashion for extracting photographs from celebrities and for exchanging photographs not only with friends, but with mere acquaintances. 'That bringing out and giving of

---

* 'No man with thin lips ever seems to me to be genially human at all points,' remarks his authorial voice in *Castle Richmond*.

photographs, with the demand for counter photographs, is the most absurd practice of the day,' he wrote in *Phineas Finn*. He was not enamoured of his own appearance. He spoke not only as an artist frustrated by his medium, but as an un-handsome man when he wrote in *Barchester Towers* that 'It is to be regretted that no mental method of daguerreotype or photography has yet been discovered by which the characters of men can be reduced to writing and put into grammatical language with an unerring precision of truthful description.'

The maddening irony, from posterity's point of view, is that living where he did in Banagher, at the back of beyond, he was within ten miles of a gifted pioneer photographer. At Birr, through which he passed constantly on his visits of inspection, was the newly remodelled Gothic castle of the earls of Rosse. The young third earl, whose father died the year Anthony came to Ireland, was during the 1840s constructing to his own design his 'Great Telescope', with which he discovered the spiral nature of the nebulae. It attracted astronomers from all over the world. In 1842 he sent off to London for equipment and materials for the newly discovered daguerreotype process, with the aim of photographing the moon as seen through his telescope.

But it was Lord Rosse's wife Mary, who came from Yorkshire and whose money paid for the telescope, who found the time (in spite of giving birth to eleven children) to teach herself the new art of photography. The Countess directed her lens at what was around her – the demesne, the town, her husband's telescope and the distinguished astronomers who made the pilgrimage to look through it, her family, her servants, her guests. Her most active years as a photographer were after 1845, the year the telescope was completed. By that time Anthony was no longer living so near.

The Rosses had special reason to be concerned with the functions of the local Post Office, since Lord Rosse's father, the second earl, had been joint Postmaster General for Ireland (with Earl O'Neill) for more than twenty years. The letters delivered to Birr Castle in Anthony's time were of great significance – from Sir Robert Peel and Lords Palmerston, Derby and Aberdeen and the Duke of Wellington, as well as from astronomers and scientists.

But even if, in her early photographic experiments, Lady Rosse happened to capture in one of her Birr street-scenes the blurred and distant image of the young Surveyor's Clerk going about his business, we would not recognise him.

At Birr were kennelled the hounds of the Galway Hunt, known as the 'Galway Blazers' since an over-exuberant celebration in Dooley's Hotel on the square at Birr ended with the hotel being set on fire. Now hunting became 'one of the great joys of my life'. He came to love it 'with an affection which I cannot myself fathom or understand'. The attraction was partly what he called its easiness, and also the fact that hunting was the one activity among those to which he gave himself unreservedly in which there were no winners or losers, no scoring or reckoning-up. He divided hunting men into those who rode to hunt and those who hunted to ride, and counted himself among the latter. It was not the kill that excited such a man, but the rare perfect run, 'a joy that he will remember through all his days' (*Autobiography*).

He had to squeeze his hunting in among his official duties, which only added to its charm. In later prosperous days he sometimes had six horses of his own at his disposal, and did not always enjoy himself. The 'moments of ecstatic delight' were few and far between. There are 'ordinary days', he wrote, 'on which those creamy moments of ecstasies are only hoped for . . . and do not come'.* It was in those first years, when he had only one horse and not much free time, that he felt he 'saw what hunting was' (*British Sports and Pastimes*). He enjoyed it then, he wrote, as he never did again to the same degree. When, later, he saw a young man out who had only one horse and only one day a week free, he envied him.

He learned to conduct himself well in the field by watching the experts and, on account of his short sight, by listening: 'Move as they move, and learn to hunt with your ears' (*British Sports and Pastimes*). The Galway still had the reputation of being a fierce hunt, with a field ready to risk their necks over six-foot walls. Anthony discovered this to be not so, 'and I found the six-foot walls all shorn of their glory, and that men whose necks were of any value were very anxious to have some preliminary knowledge

---

* The imagery of sexual release is not fortuitous or unconscious. In these matters, Anthony always knew what he was doing. And hunting was a mercifully permitted indulgence, not in the same category as 'drinking, swearing, gambling, bad society, naughty women, and roaring lions' (*British Sports and Pastimes*).

of the nature of the fabric, – whether for instance it might be solid or built of loose stones, – before they trusted themselves to an encounter with a wall of four feet and a half ' (*Hunting Sketches*).

Hunting was also, in a place where he had no contacts, a great way of making friends. The whole point of hunting, in Anthony's opinion, was that anyone could join in who had the use of a horse. It made all kinds and classes of people equal 'for a time' – butchers, bakers, apothecaries, auctioneers, barristers, landlords and their tenants. This social intercourse, he wrote, was 'the best half of hunting' (*British Sports and Pastimes*). As a young English gentleman, humbly employed, who knew almost no one in Ireland, Anthony gained from this social promiscuity.

The meets of the Galway and East Galway hunts were often held at the great houses of the district. In early 1844 the name 'Frenchpark' – a Palladian mansion in Co. Roscommon, the home of Lord de Freyne – begins to occur regularly in his diary, with an elaborately decorated capital letter H (for Hunting) beside it. There was a pleasant tradition, as men* hacked home along the roads at the end of the day, of asking one another in to their houses along the way.

This sociable dimension was not open to him straightaway. 'No one but an erratic fox-hunter such as I am,' he wrote in his Irish short story 'The Conors of Castle Conor', 'a fox-hunter, I mean, whose lot it has been to wander about from one pack of hounds to another – can understand the melancholy feeling which a man has when he first intrudes himself, unknown by anyone, among an entirely new set of sportsmen.' In this story, the young narrator Archibald Green† was welcomed by Mr Conor at the end of the day with open arms once he mentioned the name of a mutual friend in Dublin, and carried off to Castle Conor for a dinner and dance.‡

Unattached young men, especially if they would dance, were

---

* Women did not generally hunt in the early 1840s.

† 'Mr Green' was one of his favourite fictional disguises. When, in Anthony's short stories, Mr Green is the narrator, you may be sure it is Anthony himself. Maybe, like Mr Jingle in *Pickwick Papers*, he had a green coat.

‡ Mr Green in the story had no dancing shoes with him and when he sent to his hotel for them his servant gave the messenger heavy walking boots instead. How Mr Green got out of this embarrassment is the point and joke of the story and, Anthony said, something that actually happened to him.

gold dust in the country-house world of rural Ireland. When in *The Kellys and the O'Kellys* Lady Cashel of Grey Abbey in Co. Kildare was planning a ball she despaired of finding enough men. A surplus young lady in the house-party bewailed the uselessness of army officers, 'they are always going away; you no sooner get to know one or two of a set, and to feel that one of them is really a darling fellow, but there, they are off – to Jamaica, China, Hounslow Barracks' – and then, as she said, 'It's all to do over again' (*The Kellys*). A young English bachelor, once he became known, never lacked invitations to dances in big houses, or to hunt-balls, or to less exclusive balls after race-meetings like the one in *The Macdermots*, where there was 'little brilliancy, but a great deal of good humour'.

Anthony was a keen and vigorous dancer. Dancing was exciting, in that it involved physical contact. 'There is an intoxication quite distinct from that which comes from strong drink,' Anthony wrote in 'Miss Sarah Jack of Spanish Town', '. . . and in this way Miss Leslie was drunk that night. For two hours she danced with Captain Ewing' – and then, overwrought, undressing in her room at four in the morning, 'burst into violent tears'.

Dances changed with the fashion. Before Mrs Val Scott's ball in *The Three Clerks* her daughter Clementina declared that 'We only mean to dance one kind of dance – that new thing they have just brought over from Spain – the Contrabandista'; it was 'all the rage'. In *Is He Popenjoy?* 'a new Moldavian dance', the Kappa-Kappa, was to be demonstrated at Mrs Montacute Jones's ball. Lord George Germain did not want his wife to take part, but she did. The Kappa-Kappa involved some waltzing. Lord George felt she had disgraced him.

For the waltz, unlike the familiar formation dances such as the quadrille, was sexually arousing, potentially indiscreet, even indecent. In the waltz, couples swooped around rhythmically to the point of exhaustion, the man's arm clamping the woman's body to his own. In *Can You Forgive Her?* Burgo Fitzgerald and Lady Glencora Palliser – a married woman – recklessly infatuated, waltzed at Lady Monk's party under the baleful gaze of the disapprovers. George Hotspur, the fortune-hunting rake in *Sir Harry Hotspur of Humblethwaite*, waltzed with his heiress cousin, Emily: 'Cousin George waltzed well. All such men do. It is part of their stock-in-trade.' Emily was in bliss. One may imagine Anthony in Ireland as an enthusiastic if not a graceful waltzer.

He danced and he hunted. He wrote his first 'hunting chapter' in his second novel *The Kellys and the O'Kellys*, and thereafter contrived to bring his story around to a hunt in more than twenty more. As he wrote in his autobiography, 'I have dragged it into many novels, – into too many no doubt, – but I have always felt myself deprived of a legitimate joy when the nature of the tale has not allowed me a hunting chapter.' He allowed himself racing chapters as well; this was another and more risky pleasure he enjoyed in Ireland, followed by much deleterious drinking of whiskey punch – whiskey, sugar and boiling water. Nearly every Irish town got up horse-races. There were regular race-meetings, for example, at both Clonmel and Mallow, where Anthony lived after he married. Then as now, the Curragh in Co. Kildare was the prestigious centre of Irish racing. Frank O'Kelly in *The Kellys* was one of the Curragh stewards, and had a horse called Brian Boru which won the English Derby at Epsom.

But Anthony was not, in later life, attracted by the racecourse atmosphere, feeling maybe with disillusioned Captain Boodle in *The Claverings* that 'to be always spying into stables and rubbing against grooms, to put up with the narrow lodgings which needy men encounter at race-meetings, to be day after day on the rails after platers and steeplechasers' was no life at all. In the Trollope canon racing spells bad debts, incurred by foolish sons and paid off by heavy-hearted fathers. Racing was the downfall of the Duke of Omnium's sons in *The Duke's Children*; the younger was sent down from Cambridge for scooting off to the Derby, and the elder was persuaded to place a private bet of £70,000 with unscrupulous friends on a horse in the St Leger at Doncaster. The horse was nobbled and did not even run. This is a memorable and authentic-seeming episode, but Anthony asserted that he knew and cared little about racing. 'As the horses run, I never can distinguish the colours; I generally lose sundry small bets; and I don't like champagne' (*Australia and New Zealand*).

He never cared either for the other gentlemanly sports, shooting and fishing. As with hunting, he used fishing as a metaphor for the marriage game; Lady Milborough, pontificating in *He Knew He Was Right* about what a man expected of a girl, spoke as if the girl should be 'half-angler and half-bait'. Not that

Anthony knew anything about angling. 'I am not capable of fishing,' he wrote, baldly, in *North America*; and he described, in that book, declining an invitation to go duck-shooting in Chesapeake Bay: 'The fact of my never having as yet been successful in shooting a bird of any kind conduced somewhat to my decision.' As he got older, he liked less and less the people who did shoot. He was in sympathy with his young Lord Hampstead in *Marion Fay* in his revulsion against four or five men who 'in a couple of days would offer up hecatombs of slaughtered animals'; there was no excitement in it, 'simply the firing off of many guns'. Lord Hampstead also thought that 'the salmon with the hook in its throat was in a position certainly not intended by Nature. The fox, using all its gifts to avoid an enemy, was employed exactly as Nature had intended.' That was Anthony Trollope's position precisely.

In July 1842 Anthony was sent for two weeks to Kingstown (now Dun Laoghaire), a seaside place not far from Dublin to the south, on Post Office business. Kingstown was where the mail boats came in (at 5 a.m.). Thackeray in his *Irish Sketch Book* described it as 'a town irregularly built, with many handsome terraces, some churches, and showy-looking hotels; a few people straggling on the beach, two or three cars at the railway station, which runs along the shore as far as Dublin.' Kingstown was a favourite summer resort of Dubliners of a 'certain class', i.e. not the richest or smartest. 'The houses have a battered rakish look,' wrote Thackeray, 'and seem to be going to ruin before their time.'

Perhaps in his hotel, or perhaps 'straggling on the beach' in his time off from the Post Office, Anthony met Edward Heseltine, an English bank manager from Rotherham, a small town near Sheffield in south Yorkshire, on holiday with his daughters. It is possible that he had an introduction.*

Edward Heseltine was sixty years old, and a widower; the girls' mother had died the previous year from injuries sustained in a railway accident. There were four Heseltine girls. Eliza Ann and Mary Jane were already married, Eliza to an Irishman called

---

* The introduction could have come through the Bland family. Thomas Bland was a clerk at the Post Office in London, and was later posted to Ireland. Joseph Bland, Thomas's brother or cousin, was a clerk in Mr Heseltine's Rotherham bank and later married Isabella, the youngest Heseltine girl.

Samuel Anderton. Still on Mr Heseltine's hands, and with him in Ireland, were twenty-year-old Rose and eighteen-year-old Isabella.

Anthony fell in love with Rose.

The Heseltines stayed over a month in Kingstown. When the time allotted to Anthony's Post Office work there was over he had to go back to Banagher; but his annual leave was coming up. In the middle of August he returned to Kingstown for a fortnight. He was due to spend his holiday in Cumberland with the Tilleys, his mother and Tom. He applied for two weeks' extension of leave and went to Cumberland after his second fortnight in Kingstown – before the end of which he and Rose were engaged to be married.

One of the most frequently recurring authorial generalisations in Anthony's fiction is that while girls were, consciously or not, considering every man they met as a potential husband (because they had to; marriage was their only career option), it was different for men. 'It is not often that a man looks for a wife because he has made up his mind that he wants the article. He roams about unshackled, till something, which at the time seems to be altogether desirable, presents itself' ('Alice Dugdale'). The passage in *Doctor Thorne* which describes 'the absolute words and acts of one such scene', the only proposal of which the author claimed personal knowledge, and which must therefore be his own, has been often quoted, but it cannot be passed over. It takes place on a beach:

> Gentleman: 'Well, Miss —, the long and the short of it is this: here I am; you can take me or leave me.'
>
> Lady – scratching a gutter on the sand with her parasol, so as to allow a little salt water to run out of one hole into another: 'Of course, I know that's all nonsense.'
>
> Gentleman: 'Nonsense! By Jove, it isn't nonsense at all; come, Jane; here I am: come, at any rate you can say something.'
>
> Lady: 'Yes, I suppose I can say something.'
>
> Gentleman: 'Well, which is to be; take me or leave me?'
>
> Lady – very slowly . . . 'Well, I don't exactly want to leave you.'

—— * ——

Anthony's mother and Tom had been in Italy till that spring, when they went up to Penrith and stayed with the Tilleys at Fell Side while Carlton Hill was completed and Tom supervised the planting of hundreds of trees and shrubs. In July, while Anthony was at Kingstown, they moved into the new house, and it was to Carlton Hill that Anthony went at the end of August.

It is impossible to know whether Anthony told his mother about Rose. Given his character, it seems unlikely that he did. There was a great round of expeditions and drives and dinners between the households at Carlton Hill and Fell Side; the family found Anthony much changed – 'a very different man', as Tom wrote. 'I believe there is no period of life so happy as that in which a thriving lover leaves his mistress after his first success,' Anthony wrote in *Castle Richmond*. 'His joy is more perfect then than at the absolute moment of his own eager vow, and her half-assenting blushes.'

Tom and Anthony went for strenuous Trollopian walks over the fells, and when Anthony had to go back to Ireland, Tom went with him, for a holiday. Mrs Trollope 'missed Tom sadly' while he was away.

It was an important holiday for the two brothers. For the first time they met as equal adults, and became good friends. Tom was clever, industrious, immensely sociable and a great talker. He had been so much with his mother and her friends that his manner became adjusted to their age-group. He was pedantic. Tom's close friends, in later days, compared him with Anthony to Anthony's disadvantage. Alfred Austin, for example, thought that they were both delightful as companions but that Anthony, 'though brimming over with active intelligence, was in no active sense of the word intellectual, and as unhelpful and impatient an arguer as I ever met'. Tom, on the other hand, 'rejoiced in threshing out afresh the old metaphysical and theological problems, handling them with a rare dialectical skill'; Anthony did not appear to enjoy these 'serious intellectual deliberations'.*

* *The Autobiography of Alfred Austin*, Macmillan, 1911. Alfred Austin (1835–1910) was a tiny, dapper, spiteful man, a barrister who became a journalist, war-correspondent, magazine editor, and a bad, prolific poet. Through Lord Salisbury's influence he became Poet Laureate in 1896. Austin would have been aware of the relative obscurity of Anthony's life in Ireland, since his wife's family, the Homan-Mulocks, lived in a fine house called Bellair at Ballycomber, some fifteen miles from Banagher.

Tom was surprised, when they knocked on Mr Drought's door in the main street of Banagher, to find it opened by 'an extremely dirty and slatternly bare-footed and bare-legged girl'. He had not quite appreciated the differentness of Anthony's world. He observed that Anthony was in his chief's good books – because he did all the work of the district. 'The rejected of St Martin's-le-Grand,' wrote Tom in his memoirs, 'was already a very valuable and capable officer.'

Tom and Anthony went on a 'grand walk' together in the wild mountains round Killary harbour in the far west. It was an expedition that both always remembered, dwelling on how they got wet to the skin and ended up in an inn with roast goose and whiskey punch. Anthony's mind was full of Rose, Tom had a fond attachment to a lady in Paris whose name is not known. If Anthony told Tom about Rose, it's highly probable that sooner or later Tom told their mother.

Anthony was left to work out the consequences of his next leap in the dark on his own. Tom, who never criticised his mother, acknowledged that the only difficulty about living with her was her sudden switches of mood and her precipitate decisions. Having decided that she and Tom were bored at Carlton Hill, she did not want to stay another minute. Tom, writing to Anthony's son Harry years later about the way Anthony had dealt with this sudden flitting from Carlton Hill in his autobiography, said: 'The truth is that we found our neighbours dull and stupid. You need not mention this to Tilley; – not that we found him or my dear sister or his house dull; – but the neighbours were all his friends.' Anthony's reason for their leaving – 'the climate' – was, Tom said, 'an amiable euphemism'.

The summer of 1843 was appallingly wet and cold in England, and Mrs Trollope and Tom decided to make their home in Florence. They left England on 1 September, and stayed with their troubled friend Lady Bulwer in the Palazzo Passerini until her tiresomeness got them down. Then they took apartments on the second floor of the Casa Berti, next to the church of Santa Croce.

Mrs Trollope started giving regular Friday receptions and by early 1844 they were well established – being presented to the Grand Duke and Duchess of Modena and Parma at one of the weekly balls at the Pitti Palace, dining with the British Minister in

Florence, Lord Holland.* This was their preferred milieu now, not the solid, unadventurous gentry of rural Cumberland.

It was a year and eight months after the little scene on the sands at Kingstown before Rose and Anthony got married. His salary may have had something to do with the delay; he was not earning straight away the £400 of which he boasted.

Anthony was a good match, in worldly terms, for Rose Heseltine, but there was nothing about the idea of Rose to bring pleasure or pride to Mrs Trollope. Mr Heseltine, Rose's father, was born in Hull, a small fishing and freight port on the Humber estuary in north-east Yorkshire. He was one of the eight children of a merchant clerk, and became in due course a bank clerk and married, in Hull, a girl with the same surname, presumably a cousin. Their two elder daughters were born in Hull, and were baptised into the Church of England; Rose and her younger sister, born in Rotherham, were baptised at the Hollis Chapel as Unitarians – which suggests a parental conversion, which in turn suggests a serious commitment.

Mr Heseltine did not have a public school education or any concomitant social advantages of a kind to recommend his family to Mrs Trollope. The ironic comedy in Anthony's 'The Two Heroines of Plumplington' about the gentlemanliness, or not, of the bank manager, had its source in the ambiguity of Rose's father. A bank manager did not have the status or the salary of a bank director – he probably earned £300 a year, plus free living quarters – and Rose had no 'fortune', however modest, to bring to the marriage. She spoke, naturally enough, with a local accent; Anthony wrote that he had learned to love not only an Irish lilt but a 'northern burr'.

One of the employees in the Rotherham bank remembered Mr Heseltine as 'a chevalier of the old school', sunning himself in the doorway of the bank house in his blue coat with gilt buttons. The bank was the Sheffield and Rotherham Joint Stock Bank, on the High Street, and the manager and his family – which included

---

* This social success, wherever Mrs Trollope went abroad, was a tribute to her charm and to her determination. S. Baring-Gould, who was living on the Continent with his well-born parents at this period, remarked bitterly in his *Reminiscences* how hard it was to be received in good society abroad if one had not been presented at Court in England. Mrs Trollope had never been presented at Court.

Mary, one of the elder daughters, with her husband and baby girl – lived above the office, as was the custom. They had two female servants living in.

Mr Heseltine was a figure of note in his small town. His hobby was collecting armour, and he was a director of the Sheffield and Rotherham Railway, which opened in 1838. There was another fact about Mr Heseltine which, if Mrs Trollope had known it, would have made her blood run cold. What Rose and Anthony could not know, what nobody knew until 1853, was that ever since he became manager of the bank in 1836 he had been fiddling the books. Rose's father, like Anthony's, would end his life in despair and foreign exile.

The only memory of Rose as a child to have come down the years is a story that she and her sisters once stitched lace round the bottoms of their father's trousers as he slept in a chair. It sounds as if they were lively girls; but the bank on the High Street, between an apothecary's shop and a tailor's establishment, was not an idyllic place for Rose and the others to grow up in. The houses were old, the drains catastrophic. In 1851 Mr Heseltine gave evidence to a Board of Health enquiry into the sanitary conditions of the town, and said that he had lived in the house twenty years and had to have his cellar pumped out six or seven times a day. The effluvia gave the family fevers and caused servants to leave. The contents of half the water-closets in the High Street, he said, lay under the houses, unable to run away. 'I have been obliged during the last two years to raise the cellar floor, to prevent the foul water coming in. . . . If I were not obliged I would not live in the house.'

Anthony had become fastidious, perhaps as a result of the mud and filth of rural Ireland, perhaps because of his undiagnosed illness in London. 'There comes upon us some strange disease, and we bid Him stay his hand. But the disease, when it has passed by, has taught us lessons of cleanliness, which no master less stern would have made acceptable' (*Castle Richmond*). Mrs Trollope was an advocate of copious cold water for the curing of most ills, and Anthony, from the time he escaped from London lodgings, longed for houses, and personal linen, and people, to be clean. (Yet he was never smart in appearance, owing to his natural awkwardness and tendency to rush.)

Rose too must have longed to distance herself from the noisome atmosphere of her home. She was a North of England girl, and northern women are traditionally houseproud and what Anthony would call 'nice' in all their personal arrangements. He documented, with fascinated distaste, girls and women who were not in this sense 'nice'. Feemy in *The Macdermots*, who had 'that bold, upright, well-poised figure, which is so particularly Irish', was slatternly at home, reading novels all day with her hair in papers. 'Her back hair had been hastily fastened up with a bit of old black ribbon and a comb boasting only two teeth', her dress looked 'as if it had never seen a mangle';* the hem was torn as if she or someone else had trodden on it, some time ago; and 'it was too tight, or else Feemy had not fastened it properly, for a dreadful gap appeared in the back, showing some article beneath which was by no means as white as it should be. . . .' If only such girls would remember, wrote Anthony, 'that the change in a man's opinion and mind respecting a girl will often take place as quick as the change in her appearance' they would be more particular. 'Lovers will drop in at most unseasonable hours.'

In Anthony's fiction, a poor girl, in a simple brown dress and darned gloves, can be an object of adoration. But in novel after novel, sluttishness and grubbiness are deplored. Charley in *The Three Clerks* noticed with disgust that Norah's nails were dirty and that her hair smelt nasty even as he was drawing her to him to kiss her. In *Rachel Ray*, grim Dorothea Prime's black dress was 'disagreeable to the eye in its shape, as will always be the dress of any woman which is worn day after day through all hours'. Madame Gordeloup, up to no good in *The Claverings*, received gentlemen callers in 'a tumbled nightcap, and a dirty white wrapper, old cloth slippers, and objectionable stockings'; and when in *Miss Mackenzie* the girls' white muslin dresses went limp and their ribbons lost their freshness in the London heat and crush at the Negro Soldiers' Bazaar, the gentlemen lost interest. 'Men won't flirt with draggled girls. . . .'

Anthony hated messy women, and repeatedly in his novels the

---

* Younger readers may never have seen a mangle either – a contraption for wringing the water out of washed sheets and clothes by means of sliding them between two heavy rollers, turned by a handle. No one would expect lazy Feemy to iron clothes, but a dress could, with care, emerge from the mangle looking almost as if it had been ironed.

disarray to which women were reduced by train journeys seemed to distress him particularly. We know that Frank Greystock, infatuated to madness by Lizzie Eustace, will return to the faithful arms of Lucy Morris when we read – of Lizzie, sitting opposite him in the train to Scotland: 'She had been travelling all day, and perhaps the scrutiny was not fair. But he thought that even after the longest day's journey Lucy would not have been soiled, haggard, dishevelled, and unclean, as was this woman.'

He was asking a lot. The smoke and smuts of the railways made it impossible for women to remain spotless, as did the smoke and smuts of industrial towns such as Tankerville in *Phineas Redux* where, as Anthony wrote with a darting intimacy, 'even ladies who sat in drawing-rooms were accustomed to the feel and taste and appearance of soot in all their daintiest recesses.'

There are no photographs of Rose as a girl, and the one that survives from later years does not suggest that she was beautiful. Sexual attraction – which is what it was, plus some instinct for the right person – does not depend on beauty. Since Anthony loved Rose, we may be sure that she was 'nice' and neat, and proud of it, and that her whites were whiter than white, and that she scorned anybody's that were not.

She, who was to read everything that Anthony wrote before anyone else saw it, surely contributed to the technical details of what women wore. It was Rose's habitual, expert gesture that Anthony saw in his mind's eye when he wrote in *Sir Harry Hotspur of Humblethwaite*: 'Poor Emily Hotspur had not yet learnt the housewife's trick of passing the web through her fingers, and of finding by the touch whether the fabric were of fine wool, or of shoddy made up with craft to look like wool of the finest.' In his own way Anthony mirrored Rose's skills precisely. 'A clever Dublin lady,' wrote his first biographer, 'under whose eye Trollope made his earliest Irish observations, told me his close looking into the commonest objects of daily life always reminded her of a woman in a shop examining the materials of a new dress.'

Who was the clever Dublin lady 'under whose eye' Anthony passed so much of his time? The need for a loved woman to provide the ordered sweetness that he had hitherto lacked was strong in him. But he had always liked women, and Ireland was full of attractive girls. He had committed himself so soon and suddenly that it was likely that he would go on falling in and out of love, in her absence, in spite of himself.

Perhaps Rose had accepted him too quickly. 'What is there that any man desires, – any man or woman, – that does not lose half its value when it is found to be easy of access and easy of possession?' (*The Belton Estate*). As he wrote in *Framley Parsonage*, 'It is my belief that few young men settle themselves down to the work of the world, to the begetting of children, and carving and paying and struggling and fretting for the same, without first having been in love with four or five possible mothers for them, and probably with two or three at the same time.'

Because the majority of Irish girls were virtuous they allowed themselves a long rope in their relations with men. Anthony expressed this very well: 'Where does one find girls so pretty, so easy, so sweet, so talkative as the Irish girls? And then with all their talking and all their ease, who ever hears of their misbehaving?' ('The Conors of Castle Conor'). Like Fred Neville, the young lieutenant in *An Eye for an Eye*, Anthony had 'the spirit of adventure strong within him': 'When young men are anxious to indulge the spirit of adventure, they generally do so by falling in love with young women of whom their fathers and mothers would not approve.' Fred Neville seduced, impregnated and betrayed a poor, respectable Irish Catholic girl.

In at least a dozen of his novels, Anthony made authorial statements about the complications of committing oneself to another person, and to the pain of loving two people at once. The Ur-story of his romantic plots – sometimes the main plot, sometimes a subplot – involves an innocent, young, poor, respectable girl, usually in the country, who attracts a young man from elsewhere. In the heat of proximity and desire he spontaneously proposes to her, or half-proposes. Sometimes the girl demurs on account of her humbler status, but ultimately responds with an unconditional and passionate commitment. The young man returns whence he came – usually London – and has second thoughts. He becomes involved with another and more sexually sophisticated woman, who generally has money as well. He says nothing of his engagement.

From this point on the Ur-story takes various forms. The author enters with equal intensity into the feelings of both parties. The trusting girl in the country suffers hells of anxiety. The young man suffers hells of indecision and self-hatred. He does not always decide, in the end, for his first love. There are many variations on the theme.

The Small House at Allington can stand for all. Lily Dale at the small house loved a young Apollo, Adolphus Crosbie, who was visiting at the big house next door. He found her irresistible and, in the summer-holiday atmosphere, they became engaged. Then Crosbie got cold feet as he thought of penurious domesticity and babies, and of how he would no longer be able to move among countesses and their daughters, 'because it would be out of the question' to take Lily to their houses. Back in his own fallen and less simple world, he proposed to Lady Alexandrina de Courcy, who did not love him but who wanted to be married. The outcome is a tragedy for both Lily and Crosbie. This novel is typically Trollopian in that it runs along like a romantic comedy, but is, when you strip it down, shot through with desolation.

Equally Trollopian is its even-handedness. The author stresses that Crosbie was worldly and inconstant but 'not altogether a villain'; and that Lily, though she was her creator's darling, was naïve and inflexible in her assumption that love was for ever. The Ur-story is never a matter of awarding rewards and punishments, it is an exploration of a dilemma.

There is no question of treating this recurring scenario as a key for what happened between Anthony and Rose, or between Anthony and anyone else. If there was a girl in Ireland, we don't know who she was. The girls to whom Trollopian young men are betrothed, and from whom they stray, are always humbler in status and less sexually exciting than those with whom they become entangled. Rose Heseltine, by virtue of being English, would have seemed 'superior' to an Irish Catholic country girl, though not to the daughter of an Anglo-Irish family in a big house. The Ur-story remained alive in Anthony's imagination after they moved to England when, as a well-known author, he had access to influential and aristocratic drawing-rooms. In this later context, Rose was sometimes in the country cousin position.

We are grappling here with the fantasies and what-ifs of a susceptible man; but given that he and Rose were separated for months at a time, given Anthony's avowal, in *The Life of Cicero*, that a writer writes about 'what there is in his mind', and given the conspicuous non-preservation of any early correspondence with his 'Dearest Love' (which was how all his life he began his letters to Rose), it seems reasonable to believe that the time between the engagement and the marriage was not untroubled.

He said so little about his marriage in his autobiography that what he did choose to say is all the more telling. He wrote that 'as a bachelor in Ireland I had been received most kindly, but when I brought my English wife I fancied that there was a feeling that I had behaved badly to Ireland generally. When a young man has been received hospitably in an Irish circle, I will not say that it is expected of him that he should marry some young lady in that society; – but it certainly is expected of him that he shall not marry any young lady out of it. I had given offence, and I was made to feel it.'

Anthony's bachelor life in Ireland was not wholly fulfilled by Post Office work, hunting, racing and girls. 'For though during these three years I had been jolly enough, I had not been altogether happy. The hunting, the whiskey punch, the rattling Irish life . . . were continually driving from my mind the still cherished determination to become a writer of novels.' In London he had aspired to write, and failed. It was after he became engaged to Rose, spurred by the desire to prove himself and to make more money, that he began writing his first novel, *The Macdermots of Ballycloran.*

He spent some weeks in the late summer and autumn of 1843 at Drumsna, north of Banagher in the boggy lake country where the Shannon divides Co. Leitrim from Co. Roscommon, on Post Office business. He later exploited the events of his first night there (transposed to Co. Galway) in a short story, 'Father Giles of Ballymoy', in which the narrator (Archibald Green, again) arrived wet and tired. Still new to 'this savage land', he went to the hotel and was shown up steep narrow stairs, and into a bedroom. He awoke in the night to find another man moving about in the room. Green went for him, struggled with him, and threw him down the steep stairs – only to discover that the intruder was the local priest, whose rightful bedroom it was. (Bedrooms were regularly shared with strangers in Irish small-town hotels.)

During Anthony's weeks in Drumsna, John Merivale came to visit him for a couple of days. They went for a walk, away from the Shannon, 'along as dusty, ugly, and disagreeable a road as is to be found in any county in Ireland', as he wrote on the first page of *The Macdermots of Ballycloran*. After about a mile they came to a ruined bridge over a bog-stream and, on the right, a broken-down entrance, two brick pillars with no gates. A tall fir lay fallen across the avenue, which led to a ruinous house.

'Oh, what a picture of misery, of useless expenditure, and premature decay.' The roof was off, there were docks and sorrel all over what had been the garden, and local people were using the outbuildings to keep their animals and timber in. 'We wandered about the place,' Anthony wrote in his autobiography, 'suggesting to each other causes for the misery we saw there, and while I was still among the ruined walls and decayed beams I fabricated the plot of *The Macdermots of Ballycloran*.'* Soon after, a guard called McCluskie on the Bianconi coach that plied between Longford and Boyle told him the true story of the family that had lived in the ruined house. Between imagination and local lore, his own tale took shape. On 13 September, still in Drumsna, Anthony wrote in his travel diary: 'Began my first novel.'

It is not known if or when Anthony slipped across to Rotherham to see Rose and her family. He did not chart his private journeys in his travel diary. The first time Frank O'Kelly visited Fanny Wyndham as her accepted lover in her guardian's house, 'he was not comfortable, he did not amalgamate well with the family'. It is, complains the authorial voice-over, 'impossible to talk to one's mistress, in an ordinary voice, on ordinary subjects, when one has not seen her for some months. A lover is never so badly off as in a family party' (*The Kellys and the O'Kellys*). There was an added complication in that Mr Heseltine, during the engagement period, got married himself; his second bride, Charlotte Platts, the daughter of a Unitarian minister, was thirty years younger than himself and the same age as his own eldest daughter.

Rose perhaps was happy. Florence Burton, the engineer's

---

* Following the instructions Anthony gives at the beginning of the novel, you can still cross the bridge over the bog-stream and find the ruined house which inspired *The Macdermots*. Docks and sorrel still grow all around it. It is still used by local farmers for storage. The walls are more fallen, the ivy has a stronger grip. There is a treble suggestiveness about the place for today's visitor: is it the ghosts of the original owners you expect to meet in the avenue, or Feemy Macdermot waiting for her seducer Myles Ussher? Or Anthony Trollope and John Merivale, wandering around with their hands in their pockets?

daughter, showing off her gentlemanly fiancé in her father's small back parlour in an industrial town (in *The Claverings*), 'could perceive, though she never allowed her mind to dwell on the fact, that her lover was superior in many respects to the men whom her sisters had married'. To judge from his novels, the candid sexual triumphalism of girls secure in their love impressed Anthony and scared him too. 'Girls do triumph in their lovers,' he wrote in *Rachel Ray*, 'in their acknowledged and permitted lovers, as young men triumph in their loves which are not acknowledged or perhaps permitted. A man's triumph is for the most part over when he is once allowed to take his place at the family table, as a right, next to his betrothed. He begins to feel himself to be a sacrificial victim, – done up very prettily with blue and white ribbons round his horns, but still an ox prepared for sacrifice.'

This feeling of being trapped occurs again and again. Colonel Stubbs worshipped Ayala in *Ayala's Angel*, but did not enjoy the few days before his wedding. 'There is always, on these occasions, a feeling of weakness, as though the man had been subdued, brought at length into a cage and tamed, so as to be made fit for domestic purposes, and deprived of his ancient freedom among the woods; whereas the girl feels herself to be the triumphant conqueror, who has successfully performed this great act of taming.'

A further example, from many: Frank Greystock in *The Eustace Diamonds*, who was seeing more than he should of the seductive Lizzie, felt 'that he had crippled himself, – impeded himself in running the race, as it were with a log round his leg', by his engagement to sweet, adoring Lucy Morris. The author breaks into one of his generalisations: 'To be alone with the girl to whom he is not engaged is the man's delight; – to be alone with the man to whom she is engaged is the woman's. When the thing is settled there is always present to the man something of a feeling of clipped wings; whereas the woman is conscious of a new power of expanding her pinions. The certainty of the thing is to him repressive. He has done his work, and gained his victory, – and by conquering has become a slave. To her the certainty of the thing is the removal of a restraint which has hitherto always been on her.' But Frank found out what was good for him. By the last chapter he had seized Lucy in his arms, 'and was showering kisses upon her forehead, and eyes, and her lips'.

Anthony knew what was good for him too, and discovered, like Frank Greystock, a talent for life *à deux*. 'Perhaps there is no period so pleasant among all the pleasant periods of love-making as that in which the intimacy is so assured, and the coming event so near, as to produce and to endure conversation about the ordinary little matters of life.'

The fact that they hardly knew one another mattered to him, in retrospect, not at all. 'Dance with a girl three times,' he wrote in *Orley Farm*, 'and if you like the light of her eye and the tone of voice with which she, breathless, answers your little questions about horseflesh and music . . . then take the leap in the dark.' It takes years to make a friendship, he wrote, but a marriage can be made in a week, or a day. 'The young people meet each other in their holiday dresses, on holiday occasions, amidst holiday pleasures, – and the thing is arranged' (*Ralph the Heir*). Maybe that was better, and more exciting, he thought, than taking five years to discover whether they were suited.

A young man seeks a young woman's hand in marriage, as he wrote in *Phineas Redux*, 'because she has waltzed stoutly with him, and talked pleasantly between the dances; – and the young woman gives it, almost in gratitude'. The risk was far greater for her than for him, because his way of life, and his work, will go on much as before; he will 'take her to his sphere of life, not bind himself to hers'. But she, 'knowing nothing, takes a monstrous leap in the dark, in which everything is to be changed. . . .'

'There are some leaps which you must take in the dark, if you mean to jump at all' (*Ralph the Heir*). When it came to mating he put a high value on instinct. There might be no more vocal expression of feeling between a man and a woman than there was between two thrushes: 'They whistle and call to each other, guided by instinct rather than reason' ('Miss Sarah Jack of Spanish Town'). So Anthony and Rose, after some whistling and calling and circling, came home at last.

PART TWO

INTO
THE LIGHT

CHAPTER SEVEN

I T was in the spring of 1844, wrote Tom's second wife in her memoir of Mrs Trollope, that 'first tidings reached the Casa Berti' of Anthony's engagement to Miss Rose Heseltine. The tidings that actually reached the Casa Berti were that Anthony and Rose were going to get married in Rotherham, on 11 June. 'In May,' continued the memoir, 'Mrs Trollope and her son [Tom] went to England, in order to pay a visit to the Tilleys in Cumberland, and also, doubtless, for the purpose of seeing her new daughter-in-law at Carlton Hill in the course of the summer.' Thus Anthony's marriage was placed second to seeing the Tilleys, now settled at Carlton Hill.

All this flannel was just a late nineteenth-century way of gliding over the fact that in 1844 the Trollopes were not quite happy about what Anthony was doing. They could easily have gone to the wedding; Rotherham is only about a hundred miles from Penrith, and Tom and his mother were indefatigable travellers. Cecilia had a real excuse. She had three small children, and was pregnant again.*

'Married 11th June. (hurrah)' was how Rose began the chronology of their peripatetic life, which she compiled to help Anthony in 1875 when he was beginning his autobiography. He himself scrawled 'married' in pencil in his travel diary for 1844, which records that he was in Dublin from 15 May until 9 June, only two days before the wedding. They were married at All Saint's church; in the notice in the *Sheffield and Rotherham Independent* the bridegroom was described as 'son of the celebrated authoress, Mrs Trollope'.† He had a month's leave; they went off together to the Lake District, and on to Penrith – 'first met your

---

* Her third daughter, Anna Jane, was born in February 1842; Arthur William arrived at the end of December 1844.

† Rose was described in the paper as the fourth daughter of Mr Heseltine. According to the available records, she was his third daughter.

First page of Rose Trollope's chronology, starting with their wedding day. She wrote it to help Anthony when he was embarking on his autobiography in late 1875.

mother, Cecilia, Tom & John Tilley', as Rose noted in her chronology.

In most marriages the family of one of the spouses 'wins'. With Anthony and Rose it was the Trollopes, not unnaturally, who won. In her summary of their married life up to 1875 Rose never noted a single visit to or from her family, nor is there any reference to any of them apart from her sister Isabella and Florence, Isabella's daughter. This does not mean that she cast them off, but they did not become part of her husband's life. His people became her people.

When in *The Claverings* Harry took his prospective bride Florence to meet the grander members of his family in their country house, the author intervened to say that if any of his young lady readers had entered a house under such circumstances, 'she will understand how anxious must have been that young lady when she encountered the whole Clavering family in the hall. She had been blown about by the wind, and her cloaks and shawls were heavy on her . . . and she felt herself to be a dowdy as she appeared among them. What would they think of her, and what would they think of Harry in that he had chosen such a one to be his wife?'

If meeting her famous mother-in-law and the others for the first time was an ordeal for Rose, she never acknowledged it. When, in the 1890s, Tom's second wife was compiling her memoir of Mrs Trollope, Rose (by then long widowed) contributed her earliest recollections. 'Nothing could have been kinder or more affectionate than the way she received me – kind, good, and loving, then and ever afterwards.' She recalled how upright and full of energy Mrs Trollope was, and how firm her step; she was the chief mover in planning excursions and picnics, 'the life and soul of the party' after rising early, making herself tea, and writing her allotted number of pages. Once she brought up a cup of tea to Rose, in her bedroom, 'because she thought I had caught cold during a wet walk in the mountains'. By the time the breakfast-bell rang she was usually out in the garden, 'having filled her basket with cuttings from the rose-bushes for the table and drawing-room decorations'. Rose was justifiably impressed.

According to Tom's wife, Mrs Trollope 'was not long in recognizing the excellent influence of the young wife on her son's [Anthony's] life in every way'. This sounds like guarded enthusiasm, but it was good enough. The marriage was a *fait accompli*; and Mrs Trollope was, as Rose said, kind, good and loving. She was fond of Anthony and wanted him to be happy, she always got on well with younger women, especially those who presented her with no challenge, and she was not one to spoil anyone's fun, or her own. The most anyone could accuse Mrs Trollope of was a touch of condescension in her attitude to 'Anthony's excellent little wife'. Tom, in his own memoirs, said nothing about Anthony's marriage at all.

Anthony did not say much about it either, in his autobiography. 'My marriage was like the marriage of other people, and of no special interest to any one except my wife and me.' That is all. The statement begs the question: what is marriage like? No reader of his novels can ever again imagine there is only one way of seeing what we are and what happens to us, or that contented and satisfied husbands (or wives) may not at some level be discontented and dissatisfied. Marriages, like books, are open to multiple readings.

In his novels Anthony explored all such possibilities. He was not afraid of generalising about marriage, and some of his generalisations were bleak. When at the end of *Framley Parsonage* Lord Lufton wedded his modest Lucy after long opposition from his mother, the authorial voice breaks in with the following:

> I will not say that the happiness of marriage is like Dead Sea fruit, – an apple, which, when eaten, turns to bitter ashes in the mouth. Such pretended sarcasm would be very false. Nevertheless, is it not the fact that the sweetest morsel of love's feast has been eaten, that the freshest, fairest blush of the flower has been snatched and has passed away, when the ceremony at the altar has been performed, and legal possession has been given? There is an aroma of love, an indefinable delicacy of flavour, which escapes and is gone before the church portal is left, vanishing with the maiden name, and incompatible with the solid comfort appertaining to the rank of wife.

Once the wedding is over, he added, a man 'has already swallowed the choicest dainties of his banquet. The beef and pudding of married life are then in store for him, – or perhaps only the bread and cheese. Let him take care lest hardly a crust remain, – or perhaps not a crust.'

The part of the bride, Anthony wrote in *Lady Anna*, was easily played: 'It is her duty to look pretty if she can, and should she fail in that, – as brides usually do, – her failure is attributed to the natural emotions of the occasion.' The bridegroom's part was more difficult. 'He should be manly, pleasant, composed, never flippant, able to say a few words when called upon, and quietly triumphant. This is almost more than mortal can achieve, and bridegrooms generally manifest some shortcomings at the awful moment.'

In *The Bertrams*, written when he and Rose had been married nearly fifteen years, Anthony gave Arthur Wilkinson and Adela Gauntlet the same wedding day as their own, 11 June: 'Let us trust that the day may always be regarded as propitious.' Wilkinson was happy: 'He had so often wailed over his own lot, droning out a dirge, a melancholy *vae victis* ["Woe to the vanquished"] for himself!' Now for the first time he felt triumphant.

Anthony wrote this book during a long absence from Rose, and possibly the reference to their wedding day was intended to amuse and reassure her. But there is something withheld. Anthony presented his heroines' appearance in pleasurable detail, but not Adela's. 'Adela Gauntlet was – No; for once I will venture to have a heroine without describing her.'

There is too a passage in the authorial voice which it must have been painful for Rose to read – and to copy out for him, as she always did: 'We can still walk with our wives; – and that is pleasant too, very – of course. But there was more animation in it when we walked with the same ladies under other names.' For 'the full cup of joy, for the brimming spring-tide of human bliss, oh, give me back, give me back. . . !'

If even the love scenes between Wilkinson and Adela seem muted, it was partly because of the 'vagrant circumstances' under which Anthony wrote the book. No sooner was he back from his voyage than he was sent to Glasgow: 'I almost forget now what it was that I had to do there, but I know that I walked all over the city with the letter-carriers, going up to the top flats of the houses. . . . The men would grumble, and then I would think how it would be with them if they had to go home and write a love-scene. But the love scenes written in Glasgow, all belonging to *The Bertrams*, are not good' (*Autobiography*).

So far as Wilkinson and his Adela were concerned, 'He was not a bad man, as men go; but she was – . I must not trust myself to praise her, or I shall be told, not altogether truly, that she was of my own creating.' Adela, in the story, is tactful, loyal, discreet, long-suffering, candid and truthful. She waited a very long time for her lover to marry her, in the face of his mother's opposition. In the end she got what she wanted. 'Worthy or unworthy, he was all that she expected, all that she desired, bone of her bone, flesh of her flesh, the father of her bairns, the lord of her bosom, the staff of her maintenance, the prop of her house.'

Anthony and Rose were thoroughly married, for better for worse; and in marriage something other than love was at issue, at least for the man: 'not from love only, but from chivalry, from manhood, and from duty, he will be prepared always, and at all hazards, to struggle ever that she may be happy, to see that no wind blows upon her with needless severity . . . and that her roof-tree be made firm as a rock. There is much of this which is quite independent of love, – much of it that is done without love. This is devotion, and it is this which a man owes to the woman who has once promised to be his wife and has not forfeited her right' (*The Claverings*).

There is a mild threat, and many masculine assumptions in that formulation. Anthony's father had not given his mother the devotion and security which Anthony posited as due from a husband to a wife. Her roof-tree had never been firm as a rock. Anthony's marriage was not going to be like his parents'. He would be master in his own house. Sweetness and dependence in women attracted him and reinforced his own feelings of manliness. Dutiful, adoring wifeliness was what Anthony wanted from Rose.

The primary woman in his life, his mother, was a strong-minded and resourceful woman, and in another part of his mind Anthony despised female submissiveness. 'The obedience of women to men – to those men to whom they are legally bound – is, I think, the most remarkable trait in human nature. Nothing equals it but the instinctive loyalty of a dog' (*Castle Richmond*). That is by no means the only occasion in his fiction when the brutal authorial voice likens women's love to that of a dog. His other favourite image for women was of ivy needing a strong male support in order to thrive and grow.

In later life he met intelligent, exciting young women whose ideas of themselves did not include clinging or doglike wifeliness, and with fascination he began to write them into his novels. At the time he married Rose he could not have entered with such acuity and sympathy into the hearts of such women. In reality, at the beginning, it was he who needed emotional support.

Rose was bone of his bone, flesh of his flesh, a phrase he used repeatedly when describing strong marriages. He wandered off – geographically, in his endless journeys, and in fantasy, in his fiction, and he often wrote about marriage as slavery both for men and for women. He loved the company of women. 'There are men who, of their natures, do not like women, even though they may have wives and legions of daughters. . . . Others again have their strongest affinities and sympathies with women, and are rarely altogether happy when removed from their influence. Paul Montague was one of the latter sort' (*The Way We Live Now*). So was Anthony Trollope. He remained susceptible, and Rose knew it, like Mrs Grantly in *The Last Chronicle of Barset*; and whenever Mrs Grantly was made aware of 'the influences of feminine charms' she loyally blamed not her husband but the other woman.

Anthony could not have survived without the marriage, any more than Rose could. Rose gave Anthony the authentication and support he needed for the building of his self-esteem. 'What is it that we all live upon but self-esteem?' asked Emily Trevelyan in *He Knew He Was Right*. 'When we want praise it is only because praise enables us to think well of himself. Everyone to himself is the centre and pivot of his little world.' Rose made that little world a comfortable one for Anthony.

Anthony took Rose home to Ireland in July, but it was some time before he could provide for her a roof-tree as firm as a rock. He had work in Kingstown for a couple of weeks, and then Rose's introduction to Banagher was to be accidentally driven into the canal in the coach; nor was living in a rough sort of hotel the ideal way to start married life. It was a relief when, after one unsuccessful application for a transfer – Anthony longed to be based in Dublin – he got the job of Assistant Surveyor in the Southern District. 'I had not felt myself to be comfortable in my old residence as a married man,' he wrote. He was referring to the local resentment – particular or general, we do not know – occasioned by his bringing back an English wife. If he felt uncomfortable, it must have been even worse for Rose.

Anthony had completed the first of the three volumes of the novel he was writing before the wedding; in the upheaval he mislaid the manuscript. Mrs Trollope's first letter to her new daughter-in-law was written on 7 August: 'I cannot say in the usual phrase my dear Rose that "I hasten to answer your letter" for truly I have been a very long time about it. . . . I am very glad, dear Rose, that the library subscription is paid, and I hope you carry with you to Banagher a good package to comfort you in your retreat. I do not yet give up hopes of Dublin for you, but as yet we have nothing in the way of information on the subject.'

It sounds as if Mrs Trollope still pulled strings when she could. 'This delay is very vexatious and must be *very* vexatious for you – for suspense is always more tormenting than any certainty. I rejoice to hear that Anthony's MS is found and I trust he will lose no *idle* time, but give all he can, without breaking in upon his professional labours, to finish it. I enclose you a pocket handkerchief which our miserable coal-stained water has washed into a most lamentable colour – It was brought to me among a parcel of my own, and spying out your *ci-devant pretty* name, I set it aside for you.'

The Tilley children, Mrs Trollope went on, had not forgotten their Aunt Rose. 'Cecilia is but so-so, she cannot walk without suffering so much from fatigue that I content myself with taking her to a beach' (to inhale the iodine). She signed herself 'Your affectionate friend and mother Frances Trollope'. Nothing could be warmer or more accepting, and she wrote to her 'dear daughter' Rose yet again, in answer to another letter, the evening before she and Tom returned to Italy.

For the autumn of 1844 Rose and Anthony, on account of his new posting, moved to lodgings in Cork, then to Clonmel, a pretty and prosperous town with the remains of its Norman fortified walls and a population of around 13,000. Here they took first-floor rooms in what had been a good house, by then dilapidated, on the corner of the High Street (now O'Connell Street) and one of the narrow lanes which ran off it. The house was said to be the one occupied by Cromwell after he besieged the town in 1650.

There was a club in Clonmel for the 'Gentlemen of the County', and English soldiers garrisoned in the handsome seventeenth-century building known as Main Guard. The Post Office, Anthony's headquarters, was in Mary Street. The Protestant church was furnished with the tombs of the land-owning magnates who were the area's aristocracy;* a neo-classical Roman Catholic church was under construction in Irishtown, outside the old walls. There was a strong Quaker community and even a Unitarian chapel, built seven years before, though it is unlikely that Rose kept up the Unitarianism in which she was reared after her marriage. The wedding, after all, had been in church. It is hard to imagine Anthony tolerating anything else.

Clonmel is in Co. Tipperary, on the border with Co. Limerick. Sea-going vessels of up to 200 tons came up the Suir through Clonmel, and the quays were lined with mills and warehouses. Situated in the eastern part of the beautiful 'Golden Vale', Clonmel was altogether an improvement on Banagher. It was good for Anthony's hunting as well; the Tipperary foxhounds were based at Clonmel, and Barney, his servant and groom, had come with them from Banagher.

'All the world feels that a man when married acquires some of the attributes of an old woman – he becomes, to a certain extent, a motherly sort of being; he acquires a conversance with women's ways and women's wants, and loses the wilder and offensive sparks of his virility' (*Doctor Thorne*). The young Trollopes lived quietly. Thinking back to those days, he wrote in his auto-biography that in Ireland, once married, he 'lived but little in society. Our means had been sufficient for our wants, but insufficient for entertaining others.'

He had had more social life as an unattached bachelor camping in a hotel. One of his best contacts in his first posting had been Sir William Gregory (who had avoided him at Harrow). Gregory's

* The first Norman lords of the manor of Clonmel were the de Burgo family; later the lordship passed to the Fitzgeralds (the earls of Desmond) – whence, surely, the naming of Burgo Fitzgerald, the handsome, aristocratic rake introduced by Anthony Trollope on the hunting field in *The Small House at Allington*, and whom Lady Glencora found almost fatally irresistible in *Can You Forgive Her?*

151

house, Coole Park in Co. Galway, was forty miles or so west of
Banagher. Their situations were grossly unequal; Gregory, two
years younger, in 1842 became Member of Parliament for Dublin.
Peel, the Prime Minister, took the twenty-five-year-old up,
introduced him to the Speaker of the House of Commons, gave
him an open invitation to his own house, treated him like a
favourite nephew and generally groomed him for political
stardom.*

As Gregory's guest at Coole, the Assistant Surveyor listened to
the social and political gossip and did not forget it. He heard stories
about the doings and the personalities of famous men and of people
in public life long before he ever met such people himself. It was the
best possible fodder for a novelist. It is the scrap of a story, the half-
understood scandal, the suggestive reference from someone in the
know, that fuels the imagination. What he heard could be filled in by
reading the newspapers. He was also buying and keeping political
pamphlets of all kinds. It was the politics and the sexual scandals of
the 1840s, when he knew almost no one, which were to be the
starting-points for his fiction long after he left Ireland.

Through Gregory, Anthony met Lord Clanricarde, a powerful
and mostly absentee landlord in Co. Galway, who was later
Postmaster General. At Coole too he met Charles Lever, the Irish
doctor who had made such a success in Belgium; he was back in
Ireland with his wife and four children, and editing the *Dublin
University Magazine*. Lever abandoned medicine for writing popular novels with an Irish flavour, and already had two published by
the time Anthony met him.

In his autobiography Anthony referred to Lever as 'my dear old
friend', unaware that Lever had written to their mutual friend
John Blackwood, the publisher: 'I don't think Trollope pleasant,
though he has a certain hard common-sense about him and coarse
shrewdness that prevents him being dull or tiresome. His books
are not of a high order, but still I am always surprised that he
could write them. He is a good fellow, I believe, au fond, and has
few jealousies and no rancours; and for a writer, is not that saying
much?' It is indeed. Lever, for one, was not without jealousies
where Anthony was concerned, though in a subsequent letter he

---

* The meteoric rise in English political life of Trollope's eponymous hero Phineas
Finn is matched by Gregory's experience.

apologised to Blackwood for his remarks: 'I never had the slightest idea of attacking a friend, and a good fellow to boot.'

Apart from Lever there were other writers of novels with Irish themes and Irish settings to read,* and for Anthony to use as models, warnings, and points of reference for his own work in progress, and other writers near him whom he did not meet. Maria Edgeworth, nearing the end of her life, lived at Edgeworthstown, through which the coach from Boyle to Dublin passed and where, in *The Macdermots*, 'the guard pointed out to the Englishman the residence of the authoress of whom Ireland may well be so proud.'

No longer in demand socially, Anthony got on with his own 'Irish' novel – before his day's work, and maybe by candlelight after it as well – or rather, after his dinner. 'That, I believe, is always the first thought in the mind of a good wife when her husband returns home. Has he had his dinner? What can I give him for dinner? Will he like his dinner?' (*Framley Parsonage*). The Clonmel rooms were their first approximation to a home of their own. 'To neither man nor woman does the world fairly begin till seated together in their first mutual home they bethink themselves that the excitement of their honeymoon is over. . . . It would seem that the full meaning of the word marriage can never be known by those who, at their first outspring into life, are surrounded by all that money can give. It requires the single sitting-room, the single fire, the necessary little efforts of self-devotion, the inward declaration that some struggle should be made for that other one. . . .' (*The Bertrams*).

One significant new friend Anthony made in Clonmel was the burly, curly-haired mayor of the town, Charles Bianconi, then in his late fifties. He was the able man who ran the fleets of open 'long cars' which had been carrying the mails from 1815, when he bought up army horses cheap after the Battle of Waterloo. He was still expanding his mail, freight and passenger services when the Trollopes met him, with over a hundred horses – all known by name – covering most of southern Ireland daily pulling crimson and yellow cars, built in his own manufactories.

---

* Such as William Carleton, Samuel Lover, Gerald Griffin, John and Michael Banim.

The railways were to erode his near-monopoly of southern Irish transport; the Waterford-to-Limerick railway, passing through Clonmel, was opened in 1844. Bianconi duly bought shares in the Irish railways, and his cars later became a taxi-service, meeting the trains. He was a rich man; in 1846 he bought the estate called Longfield, at Goold's Cross on the Suir, and became a major local landowner.

Bianconi wanted the political influence that money bought. 'An Irishman in thought and feeling' who never lost his Italian accent, he was Anthony's first commercial magnate, even though a provincial one; the incongruous friendship contributed indirectly to the creation of Melmotte, the foreign tycoon in *The Way We Live Now*, written over thirty years later.

Bianconi was in the 1840s and 50s a key contact in Anthony's PO work. 'If he liked and trusted the post-office surveyor he would help him to get the public well served,' as Bianconi's daughter put it.* Anthony, in turn, paid tribute to the old entrepreneur in his account of the Irish Post Office published in the Postmaster General's Report for 1857: 'The old system of getting the cross mails carried by any animal that the conscience of the local postmaster thought good enough for such a service does not ... appear to have been interfered with by the authorities, but to have been gradually amended by the commercial enterprise of a foreigner.'

Bianconi had come to Ireland as a boy in the charge of a compatriot, a peddler of cheap holy pictures and frames. Soon he was dealing on his own account, with carving and gilding shops in Carrick-on-Suir and Waterford before settling in Clonmel. His picture frames and mirrors were still adorning local hotels at the end of the nineteenth century – it would not be impossible to come across a crumbling specimen today. His cars worked out of Hearn's Hotel in Clonmel, and Cummins's in Waterford; in *Castle Richmond* Anthony described a similar hotel in Cork, 'a small, dingy house of three storeys, the front door of which was always open, and the passage strewed with damp, dirty straw'. In the room where travellers ate and drank the single window was 'clouded by a dingy-red curtain', and in the sideboard Tom the

---

* Or, more likely, as Anthony's son put it; for Henry Trollope was the ghost-writer for the biography of Charles Bianconi by his daughter (Mrs Morgan John O'Connell) published in 1878.

one-eyed waiter kept 'knives and forks, and candle-ends, and bits of bread, and dusters'. When Anthony added that over the chimney there was a round, dust-encrusted mirror, 'the framework of which was bedizened with all manner of gilt would-be ornaments, which had been cracked, and twisted, and mended till it was impossible to know what they had been intended to represent', he was knowingly describing an example of Bianconi's original craft.

Though Anthony's first novel *The Macdermots of Ballycloran* centred on one family's dissolution and a young woman's fatal love affair, public affairs surround and infiltrate the private ones, as they did in his second novel *The Kellys and the O'Kellys* and in all his later greater books. In the year he was engaged and separated from Rose the great Daniel O'Connell, the Liberator,* had been holding his 'monster meetings' in Ireland calling for the repeal of the Union with Britain.

If he listened to his mother, Anthony did not come to Ireland with any positive feelings about O'Connell; she was maddened, on the Continent, by hearing him talked about with reverence, not only as if he were about to take over Ireland, but England as well. Bianconi enlarged Anthony's political education. Bianconi was loud for Catholic rights, and pestered successive Viceroys about jobs for Catholics. He adored O'Connell, who stayed with him in Clonmel; his daughter was to marry a nephew, and his son a grand-daughter, of the great man.

Bianconi was a director of the Clonmel branch of the National Bank established as the 'poor man's bank' by O'Connell. A hard man when it came to money – he noticed an error of eight pence in his accounts when on his deathbed – Bianconi tried to help O'Connell untangle his confused private finances. He was also on intimate terms with William Smith O'Brien,† who joined O'Connell's Repeal Association in 1844.

* Daniel O'Connell (1775–1847): protested against the Union of Ireland with Great Britain from 1800, the year of its establishment. Founder of the Catholic Association 1823, elected MP for Co. Clare 1828, causing the crisis which culminated in Catholic Emancipation, 1829; agitated for reform throughout the 1830s and founded the Repeal Association 1840.

† William Smith O'Brien (1803–64): MP for Co. Limerick 1835–48. A Protestant country gentleman from Co. Clare, educated at Harrow, who strongly opposed the Union but also opposed some of O'Connell's political strategies.

In October 1843 the climactic mass demonstration against the Union, called by O'Connell at Clontarf on the north side of Dublin, was banned. O'Connell cancelled the event but was nevertheless arrested on a conspiracy charge two weeks later. Freed on bail, he was tried at the Four Courts in Dublin in January/February 1844 and found guilty, but sentence was postponed and he returned to the House of Commons. Anthony began *The Kellys and the O'Kellys* with O'Connell's trial, and a vivid tableau of his fictional Kelly brothers talking outside the Four Courts as the excited crowds buzzed around them.

On 30 May 1844, when Anthony was in the Dublin area for the month before his marriage, O'Connell was sentenced to a £2,000 fine and a year's imprisonment, but the sentence was quashed in September on appeal to the House of Lords. Bianconi was heavily involved with the question of O'Connell's imprisonment and appeal, and was prominent at the great celebrations on his release at the Liberator's house in Merrion Square and at the Rotunda, in Dublin.

Although Anthony may not always have been quite in the right place to witness these historic events at first hand they were central to anyone in Ireland, as indeed in Europe; and Bianconi, as their friendship developed the following year in Clonmel, was one of Anthony's chief sources of Irish nationalist argument and anecdote. Bianconi was the horse's mouth for one view of affairs, as William Gregory and Anthony's other ascendancy acquaintances were for the other. It was the personal cult inspired by O'Connell that made Anthony believe that political agitation in Ireland began and ended with him: 'O'Connell and Irish agitation were co-existent, coeval, and inseparable.'* The Irish, Anthony felt, were not a political people, and were naturally submissive to authority. He was misled, like many outsiders, by the natural (and sometimes ironic) courtesy of the Irish, which he also remarked, but failed to interpret correctly.

Anthony liked Ireland and was all his life prejudiced in favour of its people, but he was not sentimental about any section of Irish society. His first two novels were pre-Famine stories, which dramatised the conditions and the social structure which made the disaster uncontainable. Absentee landlords were represented

* Letter to the *Examiner*, 15 June 1850.

in *The Macdermots* by the fictional Lord Birmingham, who owned Mohill,* an impoverished town of primitive cabins 'without business, without trade, without society', unvisited by the good lord, well known in England for his charities. Mohill rents and the produce of Mohill's lands were the source of much of his wealth. 'Is he not responsible for these people?'

Resident landlords were not necessarily any better. Lord Cashel in *The Kellys* sat all day in his book-room in Grey Abbey 'throned amid clouds of awful dullness, ruling the world of nothingness around by the silent solemnity of his inertia' while his indulged elder son Adolphus squandered £80,000 on the turf and at cards.

The dispossessed Catholic Irish aristocracy had nothing to squander. The Macdermots lived in squalor, degraded and de-classed, all refinement and all hope lost. Anthony said that when he described how they lived he thought of Harrow Weald; and the father of the Macdermot family, apathetic and senile at fifty, is the first of many despairing, suffering older men, ghosts of the ghost of Anthony's own father, whose sadness darkens the pages of his fiction.

Other lasting Trollopian preoccupations took shape in his first two novels: the ambiguous relations between a brother and sister, with sadistic overtones; sexual betrayal and cross-class marriage; and the formidable woman who is more of a man than any man. She is there in the widow Mulready presiding over the shebeen in the candle-lit, earth-floored, two-room cottage in Mohill where the rebel conspirators met in *The Macdermots*; she is there in Mrs Kelly, who kept the grocery-cum-pub in Dunmore. Anthony described the shebeen in documentary detail, as he did Mrs Kelly's kitchen, making the latter the occasion for a disquisition on Irish filth. In an English house, he wrote, the kitchen was likely to be the cleanest room in the house. The Irish kitchen was a temple to the 'deity of dirt':

> It is not that things are out of their place, for they have no place. It isn't that the floor is not scoured, for you cannot scour dry mud into anything but wet mud. It isn't that the chairs and tables look filthy, for there are none. It isn't that

* A real place, not far from Drumsna, and almost entirely owned by the Earl of Leitrim.

the pots, and plates, and pans don't shine, for you see none to shine. All you see is a grimy, black ceiling, an uneven clay floor, a small darkened window, one or two unearthly-looking recesses, a heap of potatoes in the corner, a pile of turf against the wall, two pigs and a dog under the single dresser, three or four chickens on the window-sill . . . and a crowd of ragged garments, squatting, standing, kneeling, and crouching, round the fire, from which issues a babel of strange tongues.

And yet the kitchen was 'a place of hospitality', and out of its unfathomable depths 'proceed in due course dinners'. It was not the primitive and the poor whom Anthony blamed for the state of the country, but their upstart exploiters – 'superior' Irish tenants who thought work degrading, and sublet their land at high rents in small subsistence plots; or men like the agent Simeon Lynch in *The Kellys* who grew rich enough to send his son to Eton by robbing his employer's estate. Such men, as he wrote in another context, 'dubbed themselves estated gentlemen, and betook themselves to the race-course and the fox-covert', their social pretensions 'aided by the cheapness with which gentility is maintained in Ireland'.*

He disliked too the civil servants who ruled through informers, an infamous system which led to revenge killings. He knew these people, as he knew Mrs Kelly's kitchen and the dark shebeen and the wild mountains above Lough Allen where Thady Macdermot fled from arrest for murder.

In most places, Irish was spoken by the poorer people; all the Irish, when speaking English, brought to it the intonation, syntax, idioms and imagery of their native tongue. Anthony transcribed this Irish-English in his dialogue, and though dialect in novels is generally tiresome, the confidence he brought to the attempt carries the day. In retrospect he was sure he had it right, as he was sure that Thackeray in *Pendennis* did not. Thackeray, said Trollope in his book about his fellow author, mistook pseudo-English genteelisms for the real Irish speech and 'established a new language which may not improperly be called Hybernico-Thackerayan'.

—— * ——

* Letter to the *Examiner*, 30 March 1850.

In the early months of 1845 Anthony and Rose were transplanted once again, to Milltown Malbay in Co. Clare. 'Cliffs of Moher and Kilkee,' noted Rose in her chronological summary. (She always noted dramatic scenery, and was a good walker, if not quite in the Trollope league. Anthony used the cliffs of Moher as a setting in his short novel of passion and betrayal, *An Eye for an Eye*, written twenty-five years later.) In the hot summer of that year they went again to Penrith to join Mrs Trollope with the Tilleys at Carlton Hill. He took with him his completed first novel, which no one had read except Rose ('She, I think, has so read almost everything, to my very great advantage in matters of taste' – *Autobiography*), and entrusted it to his mother, who would try to place it with a publisher.

It was around now that Rose became pregnant. Maybe, with the novel finished, it seemed a propitious moment.

Anthony and his mother agreed 'that it would be as well that she should not look at it [the novel] before she gave it to a publisher'. In his autobiography he was defensive to the point of bitterness about his family's attitude to his writing. Given the encouragement his mother gave him, as we know from her letter to Rose, and given that she was prepared to put herself out yet again on his behalf, this seems unfair; but he never grew out of the feeling that he was excluded, and insufficiently valued. That is why Rose's unconditional loyalty and support were crucial.

He 'knew', he wrote in his autobiography, that his mother 'did not give me credit for the sort of cleverness necessary for such work. I could see in the faces and hear in the voices of those of my friends who were around me at the house in Cumberland – my mother, my sister, my brother-in-law, and I think, my brother – that they had not expected me to come out as one of the family authors. There were three or four in the field before me, and it seemed to be almost absurd that another should wish to add himself to the number.'

There were no doubt a few family jokes, which Anthony would not find funny. 'My mother had become one of the popular authors of the day. My brother had commenced, and had been fairly well paid for his work.' Cecilia's 'High Church' novel was already in manuscript. 'I could perceive that this attempt of mine was felt to be an unfortunate aggravation of the disease.'

Mrs Trollope took *The Macdermots of Ballycloran* to Thomas

Newby, a publisher in a small way with an office at 72 Mortimer Street, near Regent's Park. He had never published any of Mrs Trollope's own books, and was not a good choice. He was an untrustworthy, unpopular man. The only justification for her choice was that Newby had already published novels with Irish settings, notably by William Carleton and Gerald Griffin, and so might be expected to look favourably on Anthony's.

Newby wrote to Anthony in Ireland in September (1845) proposing to publish 400 copies of the book; Anthony would receive half the profits after expenses were covered, which would require a sale of 190 copies. At the same period Newby was negotiating with Emily and Anne Brontë (under their aliases Ellis and Acton Bell) for their respective novels *Wuthering Heights* and *Agnes Grey*. He required each of them to put up £50 towards the cost of production – which suggests that even though his arrangement with Anthony was less than generous, he had higher hopes of *The Macdermots* than he did of *Wuthering Heights*. Another interpretation is that he dreamed of a *quid pro quo* in the form of a manuscript from Anthony's successful mother, which he did not get. He managed, however, in his promotion of *The Macdermots*, to suggest (by omitting the author's first name) that it was by Mrs Trollope and not by her unknown son.

In the same month it was observed that the potato blight reported in August in the Isle of Wight had appeared in the Dublin area. The potato crop had failed before. There was no reason to panic. In October the blight spread south-west, to Cork and Kerry.

Newby said he would publish Anthony's novel the following February, 1846, but failed to do so. He was not only mean but dilatory and inefficient. Mrs Trollope was also trying to get Cecilia's *Chollerton* into print,* and wrote to her in August 1846, while the negotiations were in progress: 'I have seen Newby about Anthony's book. He, like *every*body else gives a most wretched account of the novel market. It is, I fear, but too true. He has offered to print Anthony's book at half profits – but declared that he had *no* hope that there would be anything above the expenses.

* *Chollerton, A Tale of Our Own Times*, by 'A Lady', was turned down by John Murray and published in 1846 by John Ollivier of Pall Mall. Ollivier had been the publisher of Henry Milton's novel *Rivalry* in 1840.

He says that he thinks it is very cleverly written – but that *Irish* stories are *very* unpopular.'

The word 'Ireland', to the average English reader, spelled religious and political problems, violence and, in literature, an unfamiliar and barbaric brand of regionalism. Meanwhile Anthony and the pregnant Rose moved about for weeks at a time at the Post Office's behest between Kilkee, Kilkenny and Fermoy. Anthony started his second novel, *The Kellys and the O'Kellys.*

It was not only in Ireland that crops were failing in the 'hungry 40s', and Irish landowners still refused to admit there was a crisis. At Banagher the Commissariat officer was told that there was always shortage at that time of year. Agrarian unrest, arms caches, illicit stills, secret societies of subversives (like the group with which Thady Macdermot became involved in Anthony's novel) and the assassination of landlords were nothing new either; the previous owner of Bianconi's country estate had been murdered.

It was true that emigration was at a high level even before the Famine, and even in a 'good' year, two and a half million people in Ireland were half-starved. But by February 1846 more serious distress and unrest were reported, due to the failure of the potato crop. Lord Clanricarde introduced in the House of Lords a Coercion Bill enabling the imposition of martial law in any area of Ireland. William Smith O'Brien, MP for Limerick, attacked the Tory government in the Commons for sending soldiers to Ireland, not food.

The Trollopes only settled back into their rooms in Clonmel, after a spell in Fermoy, a fortnight before the baby was born on 13 March 1846 – a boy, Henry Merivale Trollope. The baby was called Harry, in the family. It is to be hoped that Rose was not in the hands of such a doctor as Dr Colligan in *The Kellys*, who was 'excessively dirty in his person and practice; he carried a considerable territory beneath his nails; smelt equally strongly of the laboratory and the stable; would wipe his hands on the patient's sheets, and wherever he went left horrid marks of his whereabouts.'

Anthony was in Clonmel the day Harry was born, but three days later was away on business to Fethard until 8 May, and all through the baby's first year was away in different towns around his area for days and even weeks at a time. The distances were never vast; it paid him, however, to stay away sometimes rather than return overnight, from the point of view of travel expenses. Rose was much alone, with the baby and whatever well-meaning and red-petticoated, red-legged, barefooted (except on Sundays) servant-girl she had to help her and keep her company.

Anthony recorded the ecstatic indulgence in what he called 'baby worship' – 'Diddle, diddle, diddle, dum, dum, dum' – in *Barchester Towers*, and described Emily Trevelyan in *He Knew He Was Right* going through 'such a service in baby-worship as most mothers will understand' ('How is his mother's dearest, dearest, darling duck?') on the basis of Rose's response. For her, transplanted in a strange country with no permanent home and no relations or familiar friends, having the baby to love and look after must have made a huge difference. 'How precious are all the belongings of a first baby; how dear are the cradle, the lace-caps, the first coral, all the little duds which are made with such punctilious care and anxious efforts of nicest needlework to encircle that small lump of pink humanity!' (*The Three Clerks*).

Rose was a great novel-reader – she and Anthony were in agreement about the particular excellence of Thackeray's *Henry Esmond*; and the girl who once stitched lace round her father's trouser-bottoms was creative in a practical way, always having 'work' on hand – sewing for herself and her small family, embroidery, knitting, petit-point. Anthony brought these skills of hers into his novels with affectionate amusement. There is play made in *The Kellys and the O'Kellys* about Sophy and Guss O'Kelly's obsession with Berlin woolwork, and whether it would be better to decorate a sofa-cover with flowers, 'gorgeous macaws' or a cross- bar pattern. Lady Cashel in the same book had trouble tidying up 'the wool and the worsted, and the knitting-needles, the unfinished vallances [sic] and interminable yards of fringe', when visitors were expected. (To go on stitching when someone called, as did cold Lady Aylmer when her prospective daughter-in-law arrived in the house in *The Belton Estate*, was a calculated snub.) Harry in *The Claverings*, telling his troubles to his attractive future sister-in-law, was 'pulling her worsteds and threads about the while, sitting in idleness while she was working', and snipping and snipping at a scrap of worsted with her scissors as he talked.

—— * ——

In April 1846 starving people began collecting in crowds in the towns, and hijacking carts of meal. At Clonmel, food for export leaving by barge had to be guarded by fifty cavalrymen and eighty infantrymen on the canal bank. Lord de Freyne of Frenchpark, where Anthony had often been to meets of the hunt when he was living in Banagher, was hanged in effigy outside his own hall door. Parliament argued about relieving mass hunger by repealing the Corn Laws, which imposed tariffs on imported corn.

The Tory party was split over the matter; protection of British agriculture had virtually defined Tory policy, and there was a fear of admitting other radical measures along with repeal. The survival and unity of the Tory party was at least as burning an issue in the Houses of Parliament as was the fate of Ireland.

Sir Robert Peel the Prime Minister, tired and unwell, was in favour of repeal and found himself attacked in the House by the young MP for Shrewsbury, Benjamin Disraeli, who might have been expected to support his leader. Peel got the third reading of his Corn Bill through the House of Lords on 25 June; a few hours later his government was defeated in the Commons on the Irish Crimes Bill, and his Cabinet voted out of office. The conflict between 'men and measures', between political expediency and personal conviction, which was to be one of the central concerns in Anthony's parliamentary novels, was resolved by Peel in favour of measures, morality, and personal conviction, i.e. for the repeal of the Corn Laws, and he was punished by his party for it. Anthony's second cousin Sir John Trollope was one of the revengeful landowning Tory MPs who voted against his own party.

Meanwhile in Ireland it became apparent that the current year's potato crop could be as blighted as the last, and towards the end of that warm wet summer of 1846 it was clear that the whole of it was ruined and lost. As Anthony wrote, 'Early in the autumn of 1846, the disease fell upon the potato gardens like a dark mantle; before the end of September, entire fields were black, and the air was infected with the unwholesome odour of the blight; before the end of October it was known that the whole food of the country was gone.'*

In the summers of the Famine years, carrying on their lives almost

* Letter to the *Examiner*, 30 March 1850.

normally, Anthony and Rose took holidays with friends in the lakes of Killarney and on the wild coast at Glengarriff in west Cork – two of the worst-hit areas. Anthony liked to swim, from rocks not from a strand, and preferably not in mixed company: 'My idea of sea-bathing for my own gratification is not compatible with a full suit of clothing. I own that my tastes are vulgar and perhaps indecent; but I love to jump into the clear sea from off a rock, and I love to be hampered by no outward impediments as I do so' (*North America*). Nearly twenty years later he responded warmly to a letter from a painter friend who had been with him in the summer of 1845, saying that although 'I cannot run now as fast as we ran then over the bog', he remained 'just as fond of waterfalls, and of broken bridges by moonlight'.

Anthony, continuously on the road for his work between towns and villages, was in a better position than most to see what was going on during the Famine, but he was curiously anxious to play down the horror stories that appeared in the press. At home the Trollopes were half-insulated at first, like many middle-class urban people, from the disaster around them. Those higher in the social scale, the big landlords, could not ignore what was happening. Their tenants, too hungry and ill to tend their crops, or dead, could not grow the oats and wheat that paid their rents. Landlords had to bear the loss in income, or evict, which meant sending men to pull down the cabins and throw the inhabitants out on to the road.

In many places in the south-west, poor people rioted – while they had the strength – and looted. Outdoor relief had been disallowed, and men marched on the poorhouse demanding to be let in. Public works were initiated to provide paid employment, some of it useless – roads going nowhere, sections of canals which never carried water, attempts to level hills and humps in roads which left them in worse condition than before. Some of the public works were worthwhile, and the miles of stout stone walls enclosing demesnes still to be seen along Irish roads are often 'Famine walls'.

Still men marched on the poorhouses demanding to be admitted, and starving families roamed the countryside in ragged bands. In November, most unusually, it snowed; the winter of 1846–47 was the coldest anyone could remember. The Relief Inspector reporting on the Clonmel soup kitchen in January 1847

broke off in distress, saying simply '*I have witnessed such scenes.* . . .'
The nightmarish armies of diseased, homeless, desperate and
dehumanised people, and their dying children, could not all be
fed, nor accommodated in the overflowing poorhouses which had
to be opened to the destitute.

Anthony's friend William Gregory, MP for Dublin, was
responsible for the notorious 'Gregory Clause' in the Poor Law
Extension Act, which denied relief to anyone farming more than a
quarter of an acre, which meant that such people had to abandon
their homes if they accepted aid. There were horrible stories of
starving dogs and cats eating babies. The bad weather went on
until April. Anthony later wrote that 'those who were in the
country during the period will never forget the winter of 1846 and
the spring of 1847. The sufferings of the poor were awful. . . .' He
also remarked that while Irish landlords shrieked to the government for aid, they were at this stage unwilling to sacrifice their
own comforts: 'no carriages were abandoned, no hounds
destroyed, no retinues reduced.'*

Even in the worst of the Famine time there was food in the
markets for those who were linked into the money economy. The
Trollopes, again, were all right in this respect; but the poor lived
on the potatoes they grew themselves. An able-bodied labourer
might eat fourteen pounds of potatoes a day. Now there were
almost none. The government brought in yellow Indian meal,
which was hard to cook and which the people hated both for itself
and for its associations with previous periods of dearth.

After the public works were discontinued the government
authorised soup-kitchens – which in most cases did not dispense
soup but a porridge made from the Indian meal. In *Castle
Richmond* Anthony described the gently reared young people from
the big house working in such a soup-kitchen, learning 'exactly
how much turf it takes to boil fifteen stone of pudding'.

Whether Rose helped out in that dreadful, heartbreaking
soup-kitchen in Clonmel, it is impossible now to discover. During
that cruel weather of early 1847 she conceived her second child.

Anthony was then working mainly in Midleton in Co. Cork,
where since the previous November the second scourge, which

* Letter to the *Examiner*, 30 March 1850.

was to kill perhaps ten times more people than the hunger, was raging – 'famine fever', typhus and cholera. It reached the hitherto unscathed classes: in Waterford, the Sub-Inspector of Police, the bank manager, the wife of the Protestant clergyman and one of the doctors all died of it. The smaller Protestant gentry in Ireland had always shared, to a greater or lesser extent, in the hardships and improvisations of the majority. 'A well-nurtured lady,' Anthony wrote in *Castle Richmond*, 'the wife of a rector in the county Cork, showed me her larder one day about that time. It contained two large loaves of bread, and a pan full of stuff which I should have called paste, but which she called porridge. It was all that she had for herself, her husband, her children, and her charity. Her servants had left her before she came to that pass. . . . Poor lady! The struggle was too much for her, and she died under it.'

That was the spring when Harry, now a year old, was ill, and when *The Macdermots of Ballycloran* finally came out (three volumes, price £1.11.6). It is hardly surprising in the circumstances that after its publication, as Anthony acknowledged in his autobiography, 'I never said a word about the book, even to my wife.' He thought no one in Ireland was even aware it had appeared. He was sure it would fail, and it did. No one spoke or wrote to him about it, there was no further communication – and no money – from Mr Newby. What Anthony did not know was that Newby had not even distributed all the 400 copies he had printed; he kept half back, and reissued them the following year in the guise of a second edition.

Anthony claimed in his autobiography that there were no reviews. But there were – in the *Spectator*, *John Bull*, the *Athenaeum* and a few lesser journals, and all of them at least half-favourable. Both the *Spectator* and *Howitt's Journal* mentioned his relationship with the illustrious Mrs Trollope, which might have been annoying had not the *Spectator* praised the son at the mother's expense, saying his story had less 'forced contrivance' than she generally displayed. The *Athenaeum*, praising his humour, suggested he change his name to avoid the inevitable comparisons. *John Bull* praised the novel's realism; and *The Critic*, which was not an important paper, rudely wondered whether the novel's author was a boy or a man, and feared that 'if he have already reached maturity of years, his case is hopeless'.

Anthony was thirty-two. His second son, Frederic James Anthony, known as Fred, was born in Clonmel on 27 September 1847. Rose and Anthony had no more children after this. Anthony wrote so often and so vehemently in his novels about the domestic misery caused by having more children than one could support that it is possible that they limited their family by design.*

Three weeks after Fred's birth Anthony was writing to another publisher, one well known to his family, Richard Bentley, offering him his second novel, which was nearly finished. He wanted to be paid for it outright: no more 'half-profits'. Bentley looked at the incomplete manuscript and declined to take it on Anthony's terms. Anthony turned to Henry Colburn (Lady Bulwer's 'embodied shiver'), who agreed to take him on – but on the hated half-profits system again. Anthony gave in and accepted. Colburn was definitely an improvement on Newby.

Henry Colburn, who lived in a large house in Bryanston Square and worked from premises in Great Marlborough Street, was a shrewd businessman, no longer young, with a background in bookselling and speculative magazine publishing. In 1817 he had started the *Literary Gazette*, the first reputable English weekly dedicated solely to literature and the arts; he had been involved in the birth of the *Athenaeum* in the 1820s, and had an interest in the *Sunday Times*. His series 'Colburn's Modern Standard Novelists' – who included Bulwer Lytton, Captain Marryat, Lady Morgan, Theodore Hook – had contributed to his considerable fortune; and he had some interest in Irish novels, having published some of the works of John and Michael Banim. Colburn, famous for his uninhibited 'puffing' of his star authors, also published most of Disraeli's novels, including *Sybil, or The Two Nations* in 1845 and *Tancred* in 1847, the year he took Anthony on. Disraeli too was published on the half-profits system – with the difference that there were profits to be divided.†

---

* The barrier methods of contraception then in use were vaginal sponges and condoms made of sheep-gut; these last were expensive and not easy to get. Rubber condoms were introduced after the development of the vulcanisation process in the 1850s. The remaining options were withdrawal, or an understanding of the 'safe period' which, though not yet scientifically codified, could be arrived at by experience and common sense.

† *Sybil* sold 3,000 in the three-volume edition, and earned its author about £1,000. *Tancred* sold 2,250, netting him £750. See Robert Blake, *Disraeli*, Eyre & Spottiswoode, 1966.

Richard Bentley had started out as one of Colburn's printers, and had briefly been in partnership with him in the publishing business. The two parted as far back as 1832, and since then had been arch-rivals as publishers. Mrs Trollope, after publishing seven books in four years with Bentley, moved in 1840 to Colburn and had just made a new three-book agreement with him when Anthony made his approach. The maternal connection probably influenced Colburn in his favour, as it had Newby.

In the summer of 1847, on her regular visit to Penrith, Mrs Trollope found Cecilia seriously unwell. She had not after all escaped the tuberculosis that had killed Henry and Emily. Cecilia, aged thirty-one, had five children now: a fourth daughter, Edith, was born in November 1846. The week that Fred was born in Clonmel, Mrs Trollope and Tom took Cecilia back to Italy with them in the hope that the climate would halt the disease.

They also took back with them a young woman of twenty-two called Theodosia Garrow with whom Tom, her senior by fifteen years, was in love. In Rome, which was judged more salutary for Cecilia than Florence in winter, Tom and Theodosia became engaged. Tom had known her since 1844, when the Garrows came to the Casa Berti with an introduction. Her father Joseph Garrow was, said Tom, 'the son of an Indian officer [i.e., an English officer serving in India] by a high caste Brahmin woman, to whom he was married'. Mr Garrow was musical and artistic, and his uncle had been a famous judge.

Mr Garrow's rich wife had been one of three famous musical sisters, the Misses Abrams, of German Jewish origin. She was a widow, past fifty, when she married Mr Garrow; she had an elder daughter by her first marriage, Harriet Fisher, who was neither clever nor pretty but universally beloved, and devoted to her little half-sister Theodosia. Mr Garrow, like Harriet, doted on Theodosia; but 'I am afraid,' wrote Tom, 'that Mrs Garrow did not love her second daughter at all.'

If the records are correct, Mrs Garrow, 'a woman of coarse feeling and violent temper', was fifty-nine when she gave birth to Theodosia, the daughter she did not love. It was a miracle of human biology. There is another possible explanation. One must draw one's own conclusions as to who Theodosia's real mother might have been.

Theodosia (known as Theo), with her mixed Scottish, Jewish and Indian blood, was not, Tom said, beautiful as regards features and complexion; but she had huge grey eyes and wonderful long, rippling, copper-brown hair. They could not marry at once. Mr Garrow was violently against the match, not wanting to lose his treasure; Theo was his close and devoted companion, as Tom was Mrs Trollope's. Theo was delicate, self-distrustful and easily cast down. Her father was 'awfully savage', as Tom wrote in his diary, and made 'terrible scenes'.

Mrs Trollope, who wanted to keep Tom just as much as Mr Garrow wanted to keep Theo, was much, much cleverer. Left to themselves, the young couple had not a penny to their names. On the last day of 1847 Tom wrote in his diary that his mother had 'gladly promised to give my wife a home as long as she should live'. So the two became three, and Tom and Theo were married on 3 April 1848 in the British Minister's chapel in the Palazzo Ximenes in Florence.

CHAPTER EIGHT

I N March 1848, Mrs Trollope's reactionary old friend Prince Metternich was thrown out of Vienna. England, in this year of revolutions in Europe, seemed immune, though the Chartists kept up their agitation – for annual parliaments, universal male suffrage, the ballot, no property qualifications for MPs, salaries for MPs and equal electoral districts.

In Ireland the 'Young Ireland' movement, whose leaders included a few middle-class Protestants, Catholic intellectuals, and the country gentleman William Smith O'Brien, were pressing for repeal of the Union, with a faction advocating armed rebellion. In May, William Smith O'Brien was tried for sedition in Dublin but was cleared after a brilliant defence speech by Isaac Butt.* More and more British troops went into Ireland. A fleet stood off Cobh, and two warships off Kingstown. O'Brien returned to the fray, touring the country in an attempt to raise an armed force, and using Young Ireland's newspaper the *Nation* to get the message across.

Anthony was sceptical, even contemptuous. It was 'frequently only on receipt of that paper', he wrote, 'that ladies learnt that they had been moving about in the midst of an armed insurrection!'† From which we may deduce that Rose neither saw nor heard anything to disturb her.

Anthony's inclination was to play down the unrest both in Ireland and on the continent of Europe, as he played down the horrors of the Famine. 'Everyone now magnifies the rows at a distance from him,' he wrote to his mother in the spring of 1848. Letters from England asked him if he were not afraid for his wife

---

* Isaac Butt (1813–79): co-founded the conservative *Dublin University Magazine*, 1833. Professor of political economy, author, barrister, MP. He began as an opponent of O'Connell and repeal, but he had strong nationalist impulses and later led the Home Rule movement in the House of Commons.

† Letter to the *Examiner*, 15 June 1850.

and children in Ireland, 'whereas all I hear or see of Irish rows is in the columns of the *Times* newspaper'. The concept of social revolution, he assured her, was not understood in Ireland. There were just 'rows' between those who had nothing to lose and those who had something to lose. 'My own idea is that there is no ground to fear any general rising either in England or Ireland.' He thought there was 'too much intelligence in England for any large body of men to look for any sudden improvement; and not enough intelligence in Ireland for any body of men at all to conceive the possibility of social improvement.'

Anthony had a passion for politics but he had no political passion, which is something quite different, and he could never fully enter into the minds of those who had.

It is true that O'Brien's bid for revolution in Ireland in 1848 was a pitiful failure. The chivalrous, humourless, forty-five-year-old Old Harrovian had no resources and no organisation. Those that answered his call were mere boys, or came in the expectation of being fed. When in July 1848 he finally attempted an armed rebellion in the village of Ballingarry in Co. Tipperary, his band of 500 men, on being told to provision themselves with oatmeal, bread and hard-boiled eggs for a four-day stand, melted away. (Tipperary was subsisting on handouts of Indian meal.)

O'Brien, left with 38 followers, attacked a posse of 46 policemen staked out in a cottage outside the village; this abortive little encounter in Widow McCormack's cabbage garden became known as the 'Cabbage Patch Rebellion', and it seemed to prove Anthony right. Rose was sufficiently interested to note 'Smith O'Brien rows' in her chronology – the only reference she ever made to a political event in Ireland. But then O'Brien was a local hero. After his arrest by a railway guard at Thurles station he was tried at Clonmel in the autumn and sentenced to death for treason; the sentence was commuted to transportation.

According to Rose's chronology, she and Anthony and the children had left Clonmel in the spring for lodgings in Killarney, and spent some of the wet summer of 1848 in Dunmore. *The Kellys and the O'Kellys* came out in June. In September they moved to Mallow, a pretty, relatively prosperous town in Co. Cork, on the Blackwater river, where for the first time they rented a whole house – one of the tall Georgian houses on the High Street, near the Post Office which was Anthony's headquarters. From here Anthony hunted with the Duhallow; he could also go out with the Limerick to the north, the Muskerry to the south, and the United Hunt to the east.

The Duhallow was the oldest hunt in Ireland, reputedly the best, and Mallow was the best centre for it – in bank country, with pasture predominating and some gorse coverts.* Anthony was to describe a run with the Duhallow, and its fictional master Sam O'Grady,† in *Castle Richmond*; and as his young hero Owen Fitzgerald watched the kill, and the hounds (or dogs, as Anthony called them) growling over the 'bloody fragments', he thought all the time of the girl he loved – the first of many Trollopian equations between hunting a fox, which 'justifies almost anything that men can do', and a man's heated pursuit of a woman, or vice versa. The object of desire as 'prey' – whether the lure was money or sexual passion – is one of his recurring images.

Anthony's second novel *The Kellys and the O'Kellys* did no better than the first. His publisher Henry Colburn wrote in November to say that the sale had been so small 'that the loss upon the publication is very considerable'. The evidence suggested that 'readers do not like novels on Irish subjects so well as on others. Thus you will perceive, it is impossible for me to give any encouragement to you to proceed in novel writing.' (On the back of this letter, Anthony wrote 'Oh!!!') Only 140 copies of *The Kellys* were sold.

Frustration and disappointment are bad for the temper. To say that Anthony pursued his duties in the Post Office energetically is an understatement. In December 1848 he had a noisy row with a mail guard whom he was determined to keep out of the post office at Fermoy. Both parties complained in writing to the Postmaster General, Lord Clanricarde, in London; and the Secretary,

* The Duhallow met regularly at Bowens Court, the family home of the novelist Elizabeth Bowen. When the Trollopes moved to Mallow her grandfather Robert, not yet twenty, was living at Bowens Court with his mother and grandmother, and Anthony must have known them. There is no evidence that Elizabeth Bowen was aware of this connection, but a century later, in 1946, during World War II, she wrote a dialogue for radio, set in a railway-carriage, between the 'ghost' of Anthony Trollope and a young soldier.

† When Anthony moved to Mallow the Duhallow master was Robert Delacour of Bearforest, Mallow; in 1849 Mr Courtenay of Ballyedmond, Midleton, took over.

Anthony's old enemy Colonel Maberly, who like Clanricarde (the owner of large estates in the west of Ireland) was familiar with Ireland and the Irish,* advised the mail guard that superior officers should be treated with 'becoming deference and respect', while warning Anthony to be more careful, so as not to give rise to 'unpleasant charges' against him. Anthony, unable to leave well alone, wrote complaining about Maberly's tone, and was told for his pains that Maberly believed him to have been in the wrong all along.

Anthony was capable of violence. Tom told a story of his brother riding by night to visit a postmaster he suspected of stealing a valuable letter, rousing the man and, when told the keys of the desk were mislaid, *kicking* the desk in – and finding the missing letter. His violent streak is reflected in his fiction – in murders, muggings, garrottings, in quarrels where a man is left with his head broken against a fireplace or slumped against railings on a dark street, in shootings and attempted stabbings by both men and women; in suicides; in physical brutality of brother to sister; in frequent authorial regrets that the days of duelling are no more. The violence in his novels is not the compensating fantasy of a peaceable man; it comes from the imagination of a man who knows what it is to see red.

Anthony was already working on a third novel, to be called *La Vendée*. The publisher Colburn had ended his discouraging letter by saying that he hoped Anthony would 'favour me with a sight of it when convenient'. Anthony in his autobiography said that he 'took in good part Mr Colburn's assurance that he could not encourage me in the career I had commenced. I would have bet twenty to one against my own success. But by continuing I could lose only pen and paper; and if the one chance in twenty did turn up in my favour, then how much might I win!'

La Vendée, set in France in 1792, was not to be the lucky shot. It is the least readable of all his novels. 'La Vendée', the part of France where the Royalists held out after the French Revolution, was the post-Revolutionary name for Anjou and Poitou. Anthony

* In 1847 Mrs Maberly, the Secretary's Tipperary-born wife, published a thirty-page pamphlet entitled *The Present State of Ireland and its Remedy*. Her analysis centred on badly run agriculture and the shortcomings of the Irish character. She was in favour of mass emigration (to America, not England), and stringent law enforcement.

had never been there, and as he said in his autobiography he 'knew, in truth, nothing of life in the La Vendée country'; his local colour was borrowed from Tom's early French travel writing.

The book is notable not for its story but for its topic, defending as it does – in the context of events in Ireland, and in the wake of 1848 – the values of the *ancien régime*. Its thesis is that one doesn't need a bloody revolution to break down social barriers; common interest and shared loyalties will forge bonds of comradeship. Even so, class divisions remain, and in Anthony Trollope's view must remain.

He articulated in *La Vendée*, not for the last time, the theoretical and limited radicalism of the moderate man, in the person of De Lescure: 'Liberty and fraternity had been with him principles, to have realized which he would willingly have sacrificed his all; but at the commencement of the revolution he had seen with horror the successive encroachments of the lower classes, and from conscience had attached himself to the Crown.'*

It may be hard for the modern mind to accept that Anthony was not being ironic in his use of the word 'conscience' here.

Anthony sent the completed manuscript of *La Vendée* to Colburn in early 1850 and it was published that June. He received £20 down, with more to come if sales topped 350 copies. That £20 was all he got – 'And, indeed, I was well aware that I had not earned that; but that the money had been "talked out of" the worthy publisher by the earnestness of my brother, who made the bargain for me' (*Autobiography*).

His brother Tom was having better luck. In autumn 1848 his mother-in-law Mrs Garrow's daughter by her first marriage, Harriet Fisher, contracted smallpox and died. She had a lot of money to leave, under the terms of her mother's marriage settlement, and she left it all to Tom's wife Theodosia. 'As usual my cards turned up trumps!' was Tom's comment. Theo's money, combined with his literary earnings, enabled him to collect the books and Italian antiquities that became his passion.

It seemed that the Tilleys were in luck too. In September 1848 John Tilley was promoted again, and became Assistant Secretary

* In the 1874 reissue of *La Vendée* Trollope added a passage confidently looking forward to the re-establishment of the monarchy in France. He was never a good political prophet.

to the Postmaster General, Lord Clanricarde. The job had been half-promised by Clanricarde to Thackeray,* who had no Civil Service experience, and the proposition was vetoed by senior PO officials. Anthony, beavering away in Co. Cork, had still never met Thackeray, but when in 1879 he wrote the life of the fellow author he came to love, he was contemptuous of the idea of him as a senior civil servant.

If Thackeray had got the job, Anthony wrote, 'he would surely have ruined himself.' Thackeray would not have understood the work, nor had the application to learn it, and the appointment would have been unjust to men who had worked their way up in the service. Thackeray intended to go on writing novels, and 'an aptitude for continuous task work, a disposition to sit in one's chair as though fixed to it by cobbler's wax, will enable a man in the prime of life to go through the tedium of a second day's work every day; but of all men Thackeray was the last to bear the wearisome perseverance of such a life.' (He himself, as Anthony was saying without actually saying it, was among the few who had proved himself capable of this double work-load.)

Thackeray's loss was John Tilley's gain. He and Cecilia – still very ill – left Penrith and moved with their children to London, where they took a house at 6 Allen Place, Kensington.

Fanny Tilley, aged nine and the eldest of the five, was unwell and causing anxiety. Because Cecilia was so sick, John Tilley's unmarried sister Susan came to nurse Fanny. Mrs Trollope wrote on 5 January 1849 to thank Susan Tilley for sending her 'the first *intelligible* account that I have yet had of our darling Fanny. God grant that all your kindness and care may be rewarded by seeing her recover!'

In Italy there were violent uprisings against the forces of the Austrian Empire, who cracked down hard in retaliation, though in Florence a predominantly democratic provisional government was formed. In her letter to Susan Tilley Mrs Trollope referred to demonstrations and upheavals: the Grand Duke and Duchess had left Florence (so 'no balls, concerts, or receptions of any kind') and 'the dear good Pope too, who received us so kindly just one year ago in his splendid palace in the Quirinal is now a banished

---

* *Vanity Fair* had appeared in monthly numbers the previous year, but Thackeray still felt the need of a regular income.

man. . . .'* Only England seemed safe to Mrs Trollope, 'and there do I most heartily hope to be ere many months are past.'

She was in England sooner than she planned. Cecilia Tilley was dying, in a sickroom set up in the back drawing-room at Allen Place. When he learned how ill his sister was, Anthony made a flying visit from Ireland to see her in February 1849. To relieve the pressure in the Allen Place house he took the youngest Tilley child, Edith, back to Ireland with him. Edith was just over two, Harry Trollope was rising three and Fred was around eighteen months old. Rose had her hands full.

Mrs Trollope arrived at her daughter's bedside on 10 March. On 2 April John Tilley wrote to his sister Susan that Cecilia had taken a terrible turn for the worse. 'I cannot think that she will survive the next twenty four hours. Nor can I hope that she will do so as her death will be a happy release. Mrs Trollope is more calm *and* resigned than I expected.' On 4 April 1849 Cecilia died. She was thirty-two.

Anthony wrote to John Tilley that 'I cannot say that I have been sorry to get your last letter. I have felt so certain, since Cecilia's last relapse, that she could never recover, that I have almost wished that her sufferings should end. I know, that although you have expected her death, it will still come to you as a great blow, but you are not the man to give way to sorrow.' He urged Tilley to come over to Ireland with 'mama': 'it will be infinitely better for you – for you both – than remaining alone in the house which must for a time be so sad a place to you.' He was sorry not to come over for Cecilia's funeral, 'but I could not do so without crippling myself with regard to money, in [a] way which not even that object would justify, and I am sure you would think me wrong to do so. It is a great comfort to me to have seen her so shortly before her death.'

This may seem an unfeeling letter, particularly in the matter of citing expense as the reason for not attending his sister's funeral. It is all in keeping with Anthony's insistence on avoiding cant. There was no lack of feeling in the closing sentence of his letter to his brother-in-law: 'God bless you my dear John. I sometimes feel

---

* Pope Pius IX fled in disguise in November 1848, but the Republic declared in Rome in February 1849 only lasted until July. Correspondence in this section with and between the Tilleys is in private hands.

that I led you into more sorrow than happiness, in taking you down to Hadley.'*

His signature to this letter was out of control. He was moved and upset. But Anthony thought that social convention imposed prolonged demonstrations of grief which were often false, and forced the bereaved to act in bad faith. He wrote with irony in *Framley Parsonage* that 'If a man's wife be dead, he should go about lugubrious, with a long face, for at least two years, or perhaps with full length for eighteen months, decreasing gradually during the other six. If he be a man who can quench his sorrow, – put out the fire as it were, – in less time than that, let him at any rate not show his power!' Tilley was to 'show his power' in just this way.

Anthony hated too the ostentation of bereavement, particularly widows' weeds – enveloping black crêpe garments which went rusty brown as the dye faded, and made women ugly, like Lady Clavering in *The Claverings* who made herself 'a mass of ill-arranged widow's weeds' on behalf of a husband who had rejected her, or Laura Kennedy in *Phineas Redux* who 'clothed herself in the deepest of mourning, and made herself a thing of sorrow by the sacrificial uncouthness of her garments' for a husband she had never loved.

He liked women – and therefore Rose – to wear light fabrics and bright colours: 'What a blessed thing it is for women, – and for men too certainly, – that there should be a positive happiness to the female sex in the possession, and in exhibiting the possession, of bright clothing' (*The Vicar of Bullhampton*). He gave full marks in his novels to women who managed to look fresh and frisky even in mourning or half-mourning, as Rose must have done, the year after her mother's death, when he first met her in Kingstown. Rose's clothes-consciousness can be glimpsed in Anthony's description of Margaret Mackenzie, officially in mourning but transformed by a sophisticated kinswoman's gift of 'a muslin covered all over with the prettiest little frecks of black' and 'the gayest, lightest, jauntiest, falsest, most make-believe mourning bonnet that ever sprang from the art of a designer in bonnets' (*Miss Mackenzie*).

It was the falsity of make-believe grieving that really sickened

---

* There are some minor variations in this letter as quoted, from the version in the published *Letters*. The original is in private hands.

Anthony, believing as he did that 'sorrow should be allowed to bar out no joy that it does not bar out of absolute necessity, – by its own weight, without reference to conventional ideas; that sorrow should never, under any circumstances, be nursed into activity, as though it were a thing in itself divine or praiseworthy' (*The Belton Estate*).

These views reflect his mother's precepts and practice. In later life he came to see that formal exhibitions of grief did have a function. If the emotion were sometimes affected, 'even such affectation has its own rights and privileges' (*The Way We Live Now*). When he was young, taking the cue from his mother, he discounted not only the formal conventions of mourning but made it a virtue to throw off his own griefs by an act of will. This did him some harm. There had been so many heartbreaking deaths in his family, and the insistence on never giving way to sorrow meant that he never mourned the losses completely. His griefs lay buried, unexamined, and contributed their weight to the sudden angers and depressions that troubled him, off and on, all his life.

Cecilia was buried on 11 April 1849 at Fulham, 'in a grave close to the grave of Bishop Blomfield,* shown by a small plain cross bearing the initials of the name'. A letter Mrs Trollope wrote to Rose from 6 Allen Place on 20 April has survived: 'Your letter, my dearest Rose, gave me pleasure in every way, and thankful am I again to feel that I can take pleasure in anything! I have indeed suffered, more than I can express, more even than I expected.' She took comfort, she wrote, in knowing that Rose and Theodosia – 'the only daughters I have left' – had known Cecilia and loved her as a sister. 'I am very *very* glad that my darling Anthony saw her on her death bed. The impression left on his mind, however painful at the moment of receiving it, will remain with him for ever more as consolation, than sorrow. John Tilley is not a demonstrative man as Anthony knows – but his eyes filled with tears as he

---

* From a memo in private hands. Bishop Charles James Blomfield did not join Cecilia in the churchyard at Fulham until 1857. His significance for Cecilia was that he strove to hold the Church of England together while it was rent by controversy over the Tractarian movement to which she passionately adhered; he was therefore regarded by some as a trimmer. In *The Warden* the Grantlys' eldest son was called Charles James, an 'exact and careful boy' who 'never committed himself'. The other two Grantly boys were also named for contemporary bishops.

read your mention of his poor little Edith – God bless you for all your kindness to her, my dear daughter! We shall none of us ever forget it.'

Susan Tilley, wrote Mrs Trollope, was taking lodgings near Allen Place to help with the four children, 'and we mean to have a *day* governess. . . . This will leave our evenings free from the annoyance of a stranger, whom one would want to make comfortable, without exactly knowing how to set about it.' The suggestion that she and John Tilley should visit them in Ireland 'is rarely out of my head'.

Three months after Cecilia's death Anthony found himself in a court of law. In autumn 1848, shortly before his row with the mail guard which led to the trouble with Maberly, he had received complaints about letters and cash getting lost in the mails that went through Tralee, Co. Kerry. At home in his Killarney lodgings, Anthony composed a letter from a fictitious Mr Payton in Newcastle, Co. Limerick, to a fictitious Miss Jemima Cotton, enclosing a sovereign he had scored with his pen-knife, and posted it to Ardfert. (The Ardfert mail was sorted in Tralee.) Anthony then betook himself to Ardfert and waited for the letter – which did not arrive. He returned to Tralee with a policeman and a search warrant, and the marked sovereign was found in the purse of Mary O'Reilly, the postmaster's assistant.

O'Reilly's trial in the Tralee court house was on 26 July 1849. She was young and pretty, and her friends had arranged for her to be defended by Isaac Butt, the barrister and future Home Rule politician who had so successfully defended William Smith O'Brien on a graver charge. Anthony was the principal witness for the prosecution. The trial became an entertaining battle of skill, readiness, and temper between the clever counsel and the equally clever witness.

Butt was described by Thomas Carlyle as 'a terrible, burly son of earth' with a 'big bison-head, black, not *quite* unbrutal'; Carlyle was unmoved by Butt's charm. Butt's cross-examination of Anthony turned into an entertaining double-act. The two were much of an age, both were quick-witted, neither lost his temper, each capped the other's jokes. The transcript in the *Kerry Evening Post* showed the proceeding to be much interrupted by '(laughter)'. Flatteringly, Butt brought a copy of *The Macdermots of*

Ballycloran into court and read aloud passages from Thady Macdermot's trial.* 'I dreamed of you,' said Anthony to Isaac Butt, who asked whether he saw his fictional lawyer as 'the beau ideal of a good cross-examiner'. The exchange ended thus:

> *Mr Butt*: Fine imagination.
> *Mr Trollope*: Admirable cross-examiner.

The jury, after all this, were unable to reach a verdict, and pretty Miss O'Reilly got off. But she was dismissed from the Post Office.

Directly after the trial Mrs Trollope and the bereaved John Tilley came to stay in Mallow with Rose and Anthony for three weeks, while Tom and Theo went to the Garrows in Torquay, much to Mrs Trollope's displeasure. It was '*very* painful to me', she wrote to Tom from Mallow, not to have them with her. 'Anthony and his excellent little wife seem as happy as possible.'

Rose remembered, for the benefit of her mother-in-law's biographer, something of the visit. 'We took her to Killarney,† with which she was enchanted. She walked through the gap of Dunlo as easily as if she had been twenty-nine instead of sixty-nine.' They also got her on to one of Bianconi's cars to Glengarriff, 'after much protest on her part against the ramshackle looking machine'.

The excursion to Glengarriff, a renowned beauty spot of rocks, islands and cascades, where holiday-makers sailed boats and watched the seals in Bantry Bay, was not a success. Glengarriff, dear to Anthony and Rose, was not yet even a village; there was a house which served as the Post Office, a primitive hotel and 'people selling things'. For once Mrs Trollope was unable to enjoy herself. 'She was tired with her journey; the tea was rubbish; the food detestable; the bedrooms pokey; turf fires disagreeable, and so on.'

What with Irish food, Irish hotels and the devastated state of south-west Ireland it is easy to appreciate how unspeakable everything must have seemed to an elderly and celebrated woman whose idea of pleasant entertainment was a ball at the Pitti

---

* Isaac Butt wrote novels and stories too. He published a novel in 1848, called *The Gap of Barnesmore*. It did as badly as Trollope's first novels, selling only 171 copies.
† Mrs Trollope used Killarney as a setting in her 1851 novel *Second Love*.

Palace. 'And now looking back on it all,' wrote Rose, 'I feel that she had grounds for complaint; and I should vote it – nasty.' At the time, Rose and Anthony were mortified. 'However the next day was better. . . .'

Mrs Trollope brought glory on the family in Mallow by giving a silver sixpence to 'an astonished old pauper' breaking stones in the road outside the house – an act of generosity exaggerated in the stories of Barney, the Trollopes' groom and servant, to a largesse of half-a-crown a day. 'The mammy', as Barney called her (an Irishism adopted by her whole family), did not go to Ireland again, and Anthony was never able to persuade Tom and Theo to visit him there either, though he tried.

Mrs Trollope wrote nicely enough to Rose from her sister Mary Clyde's house in Charmouth in Dorset after 'a nasty, rolling passage' back by sea with John Tilley to Liverpool, and a smooth onward journey by train: 'Truly rail roads are a blessing. . . . I glided on by Birmingham, Gloucester, Bristol and Taunton positively without any fatigue at all, and only suffering a little from want of a due supply at fitting intervals of new-laid eggs, salmon curry, Irish potatoes (1849)* and bread and butter, together with a little honey and a little coffee and a little porter from the same green land – not to mention a few other trifles all singularly beneficial in the family complaint to which we have been so particularly subject of late. . . .'†

In early 1850 a young woman, Mary Anne Partington, came to run the sad little household in Allen Place for John Tilley, and little Edith went home. Rose and Anthony did not want to lose her. '*We are very sorry,*' Anthony wrote to his mother. 'But we have no right to complain. Indeed, the incurring the chance of losing her at any moment after we had become fond of her, was the only drawback to the pleasure of taking her.'

Mrs Garrow, Tom's unpleasant old mother-in-law, died in September 1849, and Mr Garrow was trying to persuade Tom and Theo to make their home permanently with him in Torquay.

* A reference to the first post-Famine crop. Not that the crisis was over; a cholera epidemic raged throughout the first half of 1849, emigration and evictions were continuing to rise and at the end of the year the philanthropist Sidney Godolphin Osborne 'frequently' saw dead bodies by the side of the road in the west of Ireland.
  † Asthma and bronchitis.

This was a horrifying prospect to Mrs Trollope. She felt 'my separation from you to be almost too painful under my present circumstances', as she wrote to Tom. 'For very nearly forty years, my dear son, you and I have lived together in more perfect harmony than is often found, I believe, in any connection in life.'

Now, when she most needed him, she was without him. Mrs Trollope felt abandoned and her bronchitis got worse. She went to Pau in the Pyrenees in early 1850 on her own, for her health's sake. She had spent time in Pau before, in the winter of 1847–48, when she had impressed a teenaged English boy, Sabine Baring-Gould, who was there with his family, as 'a good-humoured, clever, somewhat vulgar old lady. She took much notice of me.' The English residents of Pau were wary of her for fear she would put them in her next novel. When challenged on this, she replied: 'Of course I draw from life – but I always pulp my acquaintance before serving them up. You would never recognize a pig in a sausage.'

During the 1850 visit to Pau Sabine's mother invited Mrs Trollope to her house many times and admitted that 'I try to leave as pleasant an impression on her mind as possible on each repeated visit that she makes' – so that if Mrs Trollope were to put her in a novel 'she may give a pleasant portraiture of me to the world.'* Mrs Trollope may have been glad of this carefully calculated hospitality. Her brother Henry Milton died while she was in Pau, adding to her sense of loss. It was left to Anthony to sort out his uncle's affairs.

Anthony wrote to Tom on the death of his mother-in-law: 'I cannot pretend to condole with you on Mrs Garrow's death, for it is impossible that it should be a subject of sorrow to you. But of course Theodosia must feel it.' Theo was not strong, and her doctor advised living in the south of Europe. This was the best possible news for Mrs Trollope.

It was decided at Torquay that Mr Garrow should live with the young couple in Florence. Mrs Trollope could tolerate this – just so long as she too was part of the household. Mr Garrow needed some persuasion on this point, and she urged Tom to stress the contribution she could make – *'the entire household furniture'*.

So it was arranged. Tom and Theo returned on their own to

---

* S. Baring-Gould, *Early Reminiscences*, The Bodley Head, 1923.

Florence, where Austrian troops had restored order and the Grand Duke returned. By spring 1850 they had found what they wanted; and by autumn they had completed, with Theo's legacy, the arrangement of what had been a half-built house on the Piazza Maria Antonia (later the Piazza dell'Independenza) and the Villino Trollope was established.

Mr Garrow and Mrs Trollope learned to get on with one another. She felt safe, home at last and for ever. Anthony wrote to her: 'I am very glad you are suited with a house. I hope we may live to see it! At any rate I hope nothing will prevent our all meeting under the shadow of some huge, newly invented machine in the Exhibition of 1851. I mean to exhibit four 3 vol. novels – all failures!'

This was just before *La Vendée* came out, and he was edgy. He was making lists – an activity which, like his synopses of histories of world literature or of fiction, or his periodic catalogues of great writers, was a nervous reaction, an obsessive ordering, reflecting back to the hopeless encyclopaedic pedantry of his father; and with Anthony, it was always a bad sign. This time he asked his mother, Tom and Theo each to 'make out six lists each containing thirteen names', the categories being great men, great women, men of genius, great captains, great rebels and statesmen. They obliged, and in a subsequent letter he quarrelled with their choices. 'So much for the lists,' as he said.

With three unsuccessful novels to his credit, he searched around for other kinds of writing. He proposed to his mother's old admirer the publisher John Murray a handbook on Ireland, and spent half a year writing up Dublin, Killarney, and the route in between – about a quarter of the proposed book. 'The roll of MS. was sent to Albemarle Street, – but was never opened.' Nine months later it was returned without a word, 'in answer to a very angry letter from myself'. 'In all honesty,' added Anthony in his autobiography, 'I think that had he been less dilatory, John Murray would have got a very good Irish Guide at a cheap rate.'

He also plunged into polemical journalism, going public with his thoughts on the Famine. He had been infuriated by a series of letters about Ireland in *The Times* in June and July 1849 signed S.G.O. (for Sidney Godolphin Osborne) describing scenes of horror in poorhouses and unburied corpses on roadsides, and criticising the British government for its mismanagement of the disaster. When he went to London to see Cecilia for the last time he had called on John Forster in Lincoln's Inn Fields; Forster was the new editor of the *Examiner*, an old-established liberal weekly. Anthony did not aspire to have his letters taken by *The Times*: 'At this time I knew no literary men. A few I had met when living with my mother, but that had been now so long ago that all such acquaintances had died out.' So he said in his autobiography; but he was still using his mother's name to open doors when he had to. Anthony offered Forster a series of considered articles, in the form of letters to the editor, on the subject of Ireland.

Seven of his pieces, under the heading 'The Real State of Ireland', were published in the *Examiner* between the end of August 1849 and the end of May 1850. There is an indignant tone about them; the English, Anthony thought, understood nothing about Ireland. In his first letter he insisted that the worst was over, and that the public works, abortive though some of them may have been, were useful. 'Government has never yet got credit for the good their measures did.' He was violently against instilling what he saw as habits of idleness and fraudulence in the people, and against reinforcing the idea that if they did not work to feed themselves others would do it for them. For him, independence was the first virtue, and the aim, in 1850, should be to 'awake a manly feeling of inward confidence in the country'.

He explained the pernicious subdividing of land into too-small holdings, and the resulting profiteering. He condemned the poor-rates system, which caused farmers to evict their employees and beggared the already mortgaged landlord who 'can neither live himself, nor allow others who are dependent on him to live'. Landlords who lowered their rents got paid, but many a landlord could not live on the reduced income, and retreated into his 'dirty crumbling mansion' to starve with his family. Trollope was not however in favour of subsidising such gentlemen, but praised the Encumbered Estates Acts of 1848–49, which freed property from legal entails and allowed compulsory purchase by creditors, enabling 'a new landed proprietary' to replace the 'old disabled landlords'. (His friend Bianconi acquired many additional acres by this means.)

The chief characteristic of the letters is a defiant optimism. Political agitation, he insisted, died with O'Connell in 1847. Nothing was as bad as was claimed. Anthony Trollope had witnessed terrible things, but: 'During the whole period of the famine I never saw a dead body exposed in the open air either in a town or in the country. I never saw a dead body within a cabin which had not been laid out in some rough manner,' even though 'I visited at the worst period those places which were most afflicted.' (It is just possible that he did not. It does not disprove the evidence of the reports of others.) What is more, now the workhouses were opened to the destitute, 'ejectments have lost their horror, and the landlord, in endeavouring to obtain possession of his property, can do so without subjecting wretched paupers to starvation.' He was 'glad to say' that there was growing agreement that deaths from disease resulting from the Famine far outnumbered those which were attributable to starvation.

The pathological insensitivity of some of his perceptions and attitudes, among much that was sensible and accurate, needs some explanation. Anthony's core belief – often hard to sustain, but the one on which his sanity rested – was in a benign and purposeful Providence. A corollary belief – equally hard to sustain – was that no one was given more to bear than he was capable of bearing. 'God tempers the wind to the shorn lamb,' as he frequently and reassuringly quoted – from Sterne's *Sentimental Journey* – in his fiction.

It was 'the severity of the circumstances ordained by Providence' that caused the distress in Ireland, not the incompetence of government. His images are of purging and bleeding. Ireland would be the better for the Famine, in the long run. (This was and is a tenable point of view, but cold comfort in the short run.) The trust in the 'all-powerful and unerring hand of Providence' was a widely held contemporary philosophy, firmly upheld by his mother.* It was her, and his, personal strategy for remaining buoyant in the face of serial sorrows and troubles. To acknowledge the reality of hell on earth was to face despair and the void. Anthony, in his boyhood, had been near the edge. His instinct, once he began to be happy, was to steer clear of that edge.

Besides, on the pettier, personal level, where such feelings are

---

* Anthony Trollope was also fond of quoting 'Whatever is, is good', from Pope's *Essay on Man*. Tom Trollope took this aphorism, translated into Latin, as his personal motto to accompany the family crest, instead of the Trollope family motto 'Audio sed tacio' ('I hear but keep silent'), which was singularly inapposite for either brother.

185

accessible, his own family had faced eviction and poverty, and no welfare system had rescued them, and Providence – via his diligent mother – had provided. And he was an Englishman in Ireland, and beginning to turn his eyes longingly towards home. The *Examiner* letters betray his ambivalence about his situation. In April 1850 he turned thirty-five. Was he fated to pass his whole life as a Post Office employee in the stricken sister-island?

When a decade later Anthony returned to the subject of the Famine in his novel *Castle Richmond*, set in the Blackwater valley not far from Mallow, he still stressed the providential qualities of the disaster. Famine, pestilence and emigration were 'the blessings coming from Omniscience and Omnipotence by which the black clouds were driven from the Irish firmament'. His authorial voice opined that 'the measures of the government were prompt, wise, and beneficent'. He had a go at the government's critics – 'and then the business of the slashing, censorious philanthropist is so easy, so exciting, so pleasant!'

Yet he revealed too in *Castle Richmond* how impossible it was not to be touched by individual misery. He described a wild-eyed woman 'involved in a mass of rags' and her five emaciated children, their limbs like yellow sticks, begging outside Desmond Castle. It had been settled by the local Relief Committee that all money given should go to the general fund. 'But the system was impracticable, for it required frames of iron and hearts of adamant.' The young gentleman, Herbert Fitzgerald, gave the woman a shilling and two sixpences.

On another occasion Herbert Fitzgerald, caught in a squall, sheltered – plus his horse – in a one-roomed cabin ('people are more intimate with each other, and take greater liberties in Ireland') where in the dank darkness a half-naked woman with dirt-clotted hair squatted on the earth floor, 'and the head and face of the child which she held was covered in dirt and sores. . . . There was a naked child dead in the straw in a dark corner.' It was Herbert who closed the dead child's eyes, and put his handkerchief over the body (and gave the woman a silver coin).

Whether this grim scene was written from direct experience or not, it ran counter to Anthony's irritable assertion in the *Examiner* that nowhere had he seen 'a dead body that was not laid out in some rough manner'. He too would have given shillings and sixpences to the starving, against his own theoretical conviction that men must work for pay, and his knowledge that there were no potatoes for the poor to buy. 'It was impossible not to waste money in almsgiving.'

Anthony left one surreal and unforgettable image of the Famine landscape. He mentioned in his first *Examiner* letter the 'curious mountain of wheelbarrows' at Killaloe which 'S.G.O.', in a letter to *The Times*, had used to illustrate the pointlessness and waste of the public works. Anthony too had seen those abandoned wheelbarrows. By the time he wrote *Castle Richmond* the wheelbarrows had multiplied in his imagination, and 'legions of wheelbarrows were to be seen lying near every hill; wheelbarrows in hundreds and thousands. The fate of those myriads of wheelbarrows has always been a mystery to me.'

John Tilley, the undemonstrative man, had an appalling couple of years after his wife died. The Tilley children were infected with Cecilia's tuberculosis. A year after her death, on 13 April 1850, his second daughter Cecilia Isabel died, aged nine. A month later, on 18 May, he married Mary Anne Partington, who had come to look after the children.

Mary Anne wrote to her new sister-in-law Susan Tilley thanking her for the 'kind reception' of her into the family, 'and I hope I shall not disappoint the good opinion you have so kindly formed of me. I trust we may spend many sisterly days together and see our cherished little Fan grow up into a healthy little lassie.' She had so many letters to write that 'I am quite "worn out" as dear little Arthur would say.' Three days after the quiet wedding, on 21 May, that dear little Arthur, Tilley's fourth child, died. He was five. On 3 August, Tilley's daughter Anna Jane died. She was eight.

In December 1851 Mary Anne Tilley gave birth to a son, whom they named Arthur Augustus. Anthony, closer than ever to his brother-in-law, was godfather. This second Arthur lived. It was his mother Mary Anne who died, a week after his birth. In the same week John Tilley's own mother died. In June of the same year, 1851, his eldest child Fanny, the first of them all to have caused concern, died aged eleven.

In the space of two years John Tilley lost two wives and four children. It was maybe his family tragedies that confirmed Rose and Anthony in their decision, if decision there was, to limit their family to the healthy pair they already had and to avoid multiplying the risk of heartbreak, as well as the danger to Rose. It was to be another ten years before John Tilley, left with Cecilia's Edith and Mary Anne's Arthur, risked marrying for a third time.

Anthony and Rose spent the whole summer of 1850 at Queenstown (Cobh), which provided sea air for Rose and the boys, and from where Anthony continued to criss-cross the southern counties in the course of his duties – he covered around 700 miles a month at this time. Twelve years later, on the way back from the United States, Anthony's ship stopped in at Cobh on its way to Liverpool and he 'went ashore at the dear old place which I had known well in other days. . . . I spent a pleasant summer there once in those times; – God be with the good old days!'

Meanwhile, during the days which in retrospect would become the good old days, he continued to cast about desperately for alternatives to novel-writing. In 1851 a review article he wrote on the first two volumes of a history of the Roman Empire by Charles Merivale was published in the *Dublin University Magazine*; the Rev. Charles Merivale, the future Dean of Ely, was an elder brother of Anthony's close friend John. Anthony sent the review in unsolicited and got nothing for it, the proprietor of the *DUM* telling him that 'articles written to oblige friends were not usually paid for'.

Not that Anthony's review was particularly obliging. He did a lot of enthusiastic homework on the subject, particularly on Julius Caesar, studying the *Commentaries* and, as he said in his autobiography, doing 'a mass of other reading which the object of a magazine article hardly justified'. He found himself 'anxious about Caesar' and 'desirous of reaching the truth as to his character', a matter on which he disagreed with Charles Merivale.

He was proud of his review, and let Tom know when it came out in the *Dublin University Magazine* – 'a periodical which, I presume, has not a large sale in Florence!'* He told Tom that Charles

---

* The *Dublin University Magazine* had far higher standing and a wider circulation throughout the British Isles than its title would suggest. It was the research Trollope did for this review, and a second review of subsequent volumes of Charles Merivale's *History of the Romans Under the Empire*, which laid the foundation for his own paraphrase-translation, *The Commentaries of Caesar* (1870).

Merivale had sent word that it was 'the best review' he had had; 'Certainly it is by no means the most laudatory.' Anthony did not tell Tom about his other project, which was just as well. 'I wrote a comedy,' he confessed in his autobiography, 'partly in blank verse, and partly in prose, called *The Noble Jilt*',* and sent it to George Bartley, the Covent Garden theatre manager, now retired. Bartley and his wife had been good friends of Mrs Trollope's; Anthony thought that 'for my own sake and for my mother's' he could count on a serious professional judgement.

Anthony was in England for the Great Exhibition in June 1851, but Bartley avoided meeting him. 'I am sorry I did not see you on Monday but as I was obliged to remain in Town until this afternoon, I occupied myself in carefully perusing your M.S. and feel myself bound, as you ask for my opinion, to give it candidly.'

Letters that begin like that never contain what the recipient hopes to hear. Bartley's response was long, embarrassed and negative. He found 'the serious parts deficient in interest, and the comic ones overlaid with repetitions'. There was no wholly sympathetic character, no hero, an unattractive heroine, and no real villain. Anthony had asked for an honest opinion, 'and I have too much regard & respect for your excellent & highly gifted Mother, and all her family, not to give them candidly as they are – and am most truly sorry they are not more favourable.'

As Anthony wrote, this was 'a blow in the face'. Even though Bartley stressed that he might be quite wrong (as people in such difficult situations always must), Anthony accepted his judgement, 'and said not a word on the subject to anyone. I merely showed the letter to my wife, declaring my conviction, that it must be taken as gospel.' He shared his humiliations with Rose. That speaks well for Rose, and for the marriage.

Their excitements focused on trips out of Ireland. Both Anthony and Rose were keen to see the Great Exhibition which opened in Paxton's massive crystal palace in Hyde Park in May 1851. '*We* intend going to see the *furriners* in June. I think it will be great fun seeing such a crowd. As for the Exhibition itself, I would not give a straw for it, – except for the building itself, and my wife's piece of work which is in it.'

* He cannibalised the plot in 1863–64 for his novel *Can You Forgive Her?* The play remained unpublished until edited by Michael Sadleir (1923).

John Tilley was involved in the organisation and was infectiously enthusiastic; at this time his second wife Mary Anne was pregnant, and life for him was temporarily less bleak.* Anthony repeatedly tried to persuade Tom to come over and join the party: 'Will there be no such thing as a cheap trip from Florence by which a man could come to London and go back within a fortnight or so?'† He and Rose were 'all agog about going to London. Rose is looking up her silk dresses, and I am meditating a new hat!'

Any commercial firm or private individual could send in contributions of art, craft or manufacture to local committees to be considered for the Exhibition, and written descriptions of the accepted items were then forwarded to juries of experts in London. Most exhibitors were professional designers, manufacturers or inventors, and every class of artefact had its place, from industrial engines and machinery to the revolutionary new rubber corsets and the 'cuffs, hand-spun and knitted, from the wool of French poodle dogs' exhibited by a Deborah Dawson from Newtownbarry. Pioneering technology apart, the Great Exhibition, visited by over six million people from all over the world, was like a gigantic jumble sale. The catering in the refreshment area was by Messrs Schweppe.

Anthony could not have entered his unsuccessful novels even had he seriously wanted to do so; there was no literature section, only 'Paper, Printing and Bookbinding'. Rose's successful entry in Class 19, 'Tapestry, Carpets, Floor Cloths, Lace and Embroidery, etc',‡ displayed upstairs in the South Central Gallery, was a folding screen of tapestry work. She won a bronze

---

* But his daughter Fanny died on 17 June, during the time that Anthony and Rose were in London for the Exhibition. No letters from Anthony about the Exhibition have survived, perhaps because a trip which should have been all enjoyment was overshadowed by this sadness.

† Thomas Cook (1808–92), the pioneer of mass tourism, was already arranging trips and excursions by train and boat within the British Isles; he helped 165,000 visitors to attend the Great Exhibition. There was a Cook's excursion across the Channel for the Paris Exhibition of 1855, and the first Cook's tour of Europe in 1856. So Anthony, though he was joking, was only anticipating what was to come.

‡ The Deputy Special Commissioner in charge of the jury for Class 19 was, of all people, Sir Stafford Northcote, best known as joint author of a report on the reform of the Civil Service, leading to the recommendations of the Civil Service Commission (1853–54), with which Trollope was to disagree strongly. He introduced Stafford Northcote into *The Three Clerks* under, as he himself conceded, the 'feebly facetious name' of Sir Warwick Westend.

medal. In *The Three Clerks* the two ambitious young civil servants Alaric Tudor and Harry Norman spent an evening walking up and down between the works of statuary in the great central aisle of the Exhibition, talking 'with something like confidence of their future prospects'.

Maybe that is what Anthony and John Tilley did too. An opportunity was offered to Anthony which brought him back to England for a while, and which was to be so demanding that all thoughts of writing were temporarily abandoned. On the strength of the reputation for energy and effectiveness which he had won in Ireland, and at the request of Rowland Hill, Secretary to the Postmaster General and Tilley's immediate superior, Anthony was seconded to reorganise the rural posts in south-west England. He and Rose returned to Mallow after the Exhibition, but on 1 August they made the crossing to Bristol and found themselves in yet another temporary home, this time in Exeter.

CHAPTER NINE

FROM Exeter, Anthony wrote to Tom again urging him to come to England. He and Rose intended visiting Florence, 'but I should greatly prefer your coming here, as I have such very heavy work on hand. You would, moreover, see Rose and Harry, who are with me. I should so much like you to see little Harry.' Fred had been left behind in Ireland.

The Trollopes went home to Mallow for Christmas, believing that their English sojourn was over. Anthony worked in his old district for three months, and then Rowland Hill recalled him to extend his reorganisation of services in south-west England and South Wales. This time both the children returned to England with Rose and Anthony. Over the next two years they made temporary homes in Bristol, Carmarthen, Cheltenham and Worcester, with many short stays elsewhere.

Since Anthony joined the Post Office the service had been transformed by two innovations – the penny post, inaugurated in 1840, and the railways, which in England began carrying the mails from 1841. Before 1840, the price of sending a letter depended on the distance. Letters within London, for example, cost twopence, and those between London and Birmingham ninepence. The postman, or 'letter-carrier', was paid on delivery.*

The penny post was the brainchild of Rowland Hill, the son of a Birmingham schoolmaster. He wrote a pamphlet on Post Office Reform while Secretary to the South Australian Colonisation Office. He was then appointed temporary special adviser to the Treasury and worked on his scheme in cramped quarters and in the face of much scepticism from the Whig administration and senior PO personnel. Colonel Maberly, predictably, thought the

---

* Letter-boxes in front doors came in with the penny post, since letter-carriers no longer had to knock at the door to collect the money.

idea of a penny post preposterous and heartily disliked 'the man from Birmingham'; poor Hill had later to work alongside the old die-hard in an awkwardly contrived dual secretariat until 1854, when Maberly was shunted off to the Audit Office.

Hill's hesitant manner at the time he was canvassing support for the penny post did nothing to help him; but a Select Committee of the House of Commons supported his proposals. The gamble, which paid off, was that the ease and cheapness of the pre-paid penny post would vastly increase the bulk of mail, and therefore the PO's revenue. Radicals such as Richard Cobden supported the proposal, since one of Hill's arguments was that the existing system was so expensive that working-class people could not afford to receive letters from children and relatives working away from home.

In the event, it was commercial houses and the middle class who chiefly availed themselves of the new service.* The penny post speeded up business transactions, friendships and love affairs. It opened up new possibilities of intensity and a whole new field of anguish. When in *The Claverings* Florence Burton fretted because she had not heard from her lover, her brother Theodore said to his wife:

> 'I used to think myself the best lover in the world, if I wrote once a month.'
> 'There was no penny post then, Mr Burton.'
> 'And I often wish there was none now,' said Mr Burton.

Rowland Hill was a brilliant, difficult man, slight and bald, with deep-set eyes behind spectacles, and a grave expression; he was fifty-six when Anthony took up his temporary post. Anthony's brief was to create 'a postal network' in the rural south-west, reorganising the letter-carriers' 'walks' and ensuring that every letter was delivered direct to its recipient's home. (This was what he had already done in his Irish district.)

He was subordinate, as in Ireland, to the local Surveyor, but 'I spent two of the happiest years of my life at the task. I began in Devonshire; and visited, I think I may say, every nook in that

* Within two years, UK letters posted increased from 75 million p.a. to 196 million. By 1849 the figure was nearly 329 million. In Ireland, in the first year of the penny post, there was an increase of 119.2 per cent, which continued to rise.

county, in Cornwall, Somersetshire, the greater part of Dorsetshire, the Channel Islands, part of Oxfordshire, Wiltshire, Gloucestershire, Worcestershire, Herefordshire, Monmouthshire, and the six southern Welsh counties.'

No 'walk' might be established on which insufficient letters were delivered to justify the postman's wages, so some remote places still could not receive mail daily. No postman, it was decided, should walk more than sixteen miles a day, which would have been easy to calculate had they kept to the roads. 'But my letter-carriers were here and there across the fields. It was my special delight to take them by all short cuts' – which Anthony discovered for himself, on horseback, travelling up to forty miles a day. The task fascinated him. 'It is amusing to watch how a passion will grow upon a man. During those two years it was the ambition of my life to cover the country with rural letter-carriers' (*Autobiography*).

A letter, in Trollope's novels, is not just written and received. It has a trajectory, and a destiny as well as a destination. In *Framley Parsonage* the Rev. Mark Robarts, seduced by high society, wrote defensively to his wife from Chaldecotes, the country seat of Nathaniel Sowerby MP, to explain why he was going on to a house-party at Gatherum Castle instead of coming home; and his letter

> went into Barchester by the Courcy night mail-cart, which, on its road, passes through the villages of Uffley and Chaldecotes, reaching Barchester in time for the up mail-train to London. By that train, the letter was sent towards the metropolis as far as the junction of the Barset branch line, but there it was turned in its course, and came down again by the main line as far as Silverbridge; at which place, between six and seven in the morning, it was shouldered by the Framley footpost messenger, and in due course was delivered at the Framley Parsonage exactly as Mrs Robarts had finished reading prayers to the four servants. Or, I should say rather, that such would in its usual course have been that letter's destiny.

The delay in Fanny Robarts receiving the letter was not the postman's fault; and Mark Robarts duly got her reply at Gatherum Castle, enclosing the ten-pound note he had requested, 'whereby strong proof was given of the honesty of the post-office people in Barsetshire'.

Anthony became an expert on his region, and fond of it. The prettiest scenery in all England, he wrote, was in Devonshire, 'on the southern and south-eastern skirts of Dartmoor, where the rivers Dart, and Avon, and Teign form themselves, and where the broken moor is half-cultivated, and the wild-looking upland fields are half-moor'. Those who disagreed with him, he said, did not know the locality. 'Men and women talk to me on the matter, who have travelled down the line of railway from Exeter to Plymouth, who have spent a fortnight in Torquay, and perhaps made an excursion from Tavistock to the convict prison on Dartmoor. But who knows the glories of Chagford? Who has walked through the parish of Manaton? Who is conversant with Lustleigh Cleeves and Withycombe in the moor? Who has explored Holne Chase?' ('The Parson's Daughter of Oxney Colne'). He did, he had.

This enthusiastic covering of the ground had its customary secondary motive. 'I was paid sixpence a mile for the distance travelled, and it was necessary that I should at any rate travel enough to pay for my equipage. This I did, and got my hunting out of it also' (*Autobiography*). Barney the groom had come with them from Ireland; Anthony kept two hunters, and sometimes hired a third. Country postmasters, and families in rectories, farmhouses and cottages, were startled to find themselves roused in the morning by a big, loud-voiced man in a red coat and full hunting rig, who interrogated them about how and when they got their letters delivered. Whether it was a hunting morning or not, he was always in a hurry to move on, and spent no time explaining fully what he was about as he took notes in his little book. 'I became thoroughly used to it, and soon lost my native bashfulness; – but sometimes my visits astonished the retiring inhabitants of country houses.'

The country postmen's walks were meticulously timed, and not only in the first years of the service. In *An Old Man's Love*, written in the last year of Anthony Trollope's life, William Whittlestaff was irritated because although 'the postman was really due at his hall-door at a quarter before nine', he was always ten minutes late. There were unsatisfied customers like the Rev. Frank Fenwick in *The Vicar of Bullhampton*; his house was 'at the end of the postman's walk', so that the mail rarely arrived before 11 a.m., and Mr Fenwick carried on 'a perpetual feud with the Post-office authorities, having put forward a great postal doctrine that letters ought to be rained from heaven on to everybody's breakfast-table exactly as the hot water is brought in for tea. He, being an energetic man, carried on a long and angry correspondence with the authorities aforesaid' – 'the authorities' in real life being the Surveyors.

Anthony exploited his knowledge of Cornwall and its tin-mining in *The Three Clerks*, in which it is clear that he had himself been down a tin-mine, feeling perhaps like that 'absolute dragon of honesty' Mr Fidus Neverbend: 'His spectacles had gone from him, his cap covered his eyes, his lamp had reversed itself. . . .' He described too the kind of hotel breakfast he got in such places, 'tea made with lukewarm water, and eggs that were not half-boiled'. To revise the rural posts in Cornwall was, according to a contemporary PO employee there, 'about as easy for a stranger in those days as to lay out a post road on the Upper Congo'.

In one place Anthony, booted and spurred for hunting, terrified both the maiden lady in charge and the rustic messenger whose walk he proposed to test. But in Penzance he met his match in a postmistress who told him he was no gentleman and ordered him out of the house. In Mousehole, the sub-office was kept by a fearless Quaker lady, Elizabeth Trembath, whose spirited rustic utterance was reproduced by the postmistress Mrs Crump ten years later in *The Small House at Allington*: 'Oh, letters! Drat them for letters. I wish there weren't no sich things. There was a man here yesterday with his imperence. I don't know where he come from, – down from Lun'on, I b'leeve: and this was wrong, and that was wrong, and everything was wrong; and then he said he'd have me discharged the sarvice. . . . Discharged the sarvice! Tuppence farden a day. So I told'un to discharge hisself, and take all the old bundles and things away upon his shoulders.' Here the author butts in: 'I may here add, in order that Mrs Crump's history may be carried on to the farthest possible point, that she was not "discharged the sarvice," and that she still receives her twopence farthing a day from the Crown.'

Another PO employee in a small town in South Wales recalled Anthony striding in announcing that he had walked the twenty-four miles from Cardiff and enquiring for the best hotel. On being informed, he strode out again, saying 'Back soon, going to have a raw beef steak.' The giant, refreshed, returned to the office, declared his identity, and settled to business.

Anthony and Rose had to put off their proposed trip to Florence in 1852, though as he wrote to Tom, 'a twelvemonth does not seem so long to wait now as it did ten years ago. . . . But somehow, the months and years so jostle one another, that I seem to be living away at a perpetual gallop. I wish I could make the pace a little slower.'

Anthony Trollope is commonly credited with the introduction into Britain of pillar boxes for posting letters.* It would be more truthful to say that it was his persistence and enthusiasm that resulted in their adoption. Rowland Hill among others had considered the idea.

When he was reviewing postal services in the Channel Islands, three months into his new job, Anthony wrote a long official report to his immediate superior in the Western District which included a recommendation to try out in St Helier, Jersey, the French plan 'of fitting up letter boxes in posts fixed at the road side. . . . Iron posts suited for the purpose may be erected at the corners of streets . . . and I think that the public may safely be invited to use such boxes for depositing their letters.' He had already marked the likely sites in red ink on a plan of St Helier, 'should the Postmr Genl be willing to sanction this experiment'.

Within a month he had the authority to go ahead, and immediately pressed for pillar boxes in St Peter Port in Guernsey as well. The pillar boxes were established in the Channel Islands the next year, and the year after that (1853) they began to appear in mainland Britain. The very first was in Carlisle. London did not get them until 1855, and there were initially only five in the capital. Rectangular, sage-green,† with a large ball on top, they were placed in Fleet Street, the Strand, Pall Mall, Piccadilly and Rutland Gate (Kensington).

Pillar boxes gave freedom to over-protected girls to carry on private correspondences, like the heroine of *Marion Fay* who dropped her love-letter 'by her own hand into the pillar letter-box which stood at the corner opposite to the public house'. Old-

---

* Before the pillar box, letters had to be taken in to the nearest receiving office, which could be several miles away.

† They were not painted the familiar 'pillar-box red' until 1874.

fashioned people, such as Miss Jemima Stanbury of Exeter in *He Knew He Was Right*, did not trust the system. She carried her important letter to her sister all the way to the main post office. 'As for the iron pillar boxes which had been erected of late years for the receipt of letters, one of which, – a most hateful thing to her, – stood almost close to her own hall door, she had not the faintest belief that any letter put into one of them would ever reach its destination.'

In August 1852 Anthony sent Rose and the children (at a cost of £2.11s, as he noted) away on holiday, where he joined them later. From Haverfordwest he wrote to his mother: 'We are now living, or staying for a while rather, in South Wales. Rose and the bairns are at a place on the sea-side called Llanstephen [on the Carmarthenshire coast], where there is plenty of air and bathing. We shall stay in Carmarthen during November, and then go to Gloucester for the winter.* Harry and Freddy are quite well, and are very nice boys: – very different in disposition, but neither with anything that I could wish altered.'

Harry was six and a half, Fred was five that September. Their parents' theory of child-raising may be deduced from Anthony's later remarks about American children, who seemed to him 'an unhappy race'. 'They eat and drink just as they please; they are never punished; they are never banished, snubbed, and kept in the back ground as children are kept with us; and yet they are wretched and uncomfortable.' He wondered whether it were not true that children were happier 'when they are made to obey orders and are sent to bed at six o'clock, than when allowed to regulate their own conduct; that bread and milk is more favourable to laughter and soft childish ways than beef-steaks and pickles three times a day; that an occasional whipping, even, will conduce to rosy cheeks?' (*North America*.)

Anthony had not heard from either Tom or Mrs Trollope for two months when he wrote to his mother: 'We have heard a rumour (some one told John Tilley in Kensington Gardens) that Theodosia is about to make Tom a father. If so, why has not Tom told us what we should have been so glad to learn from him?' Tom

---

* He changed his mind. They went to Charmouth on the Dorset coast in November, and thence to Cheltenham by Christmas, where they stayed till April (1853).

and Theodosia had been married for over four years. This was
news indeed.

Florence was a sink of gossip, where 'scandal holds its festival' as
Charles Lever put it, and the rumour was that Tom was not the
father. But if Tilley's informant in Kensington Gardens had
passed this on, would Tilley have retailed it to Anthony? Possibly.
They were very old friends and neither of them had yet met
Theodosia. Fifteen years later, when Theodosia was dead and
Tom was married to his second wife and they were temporarily
apart, there was gossip in the London clubs that he and she were
estranged because of revelations about the child's paternity, and
someone told the poet Robert Browning that he had heard about
it from Anthony himself. 'I take it,' wrote Browning, an arch-
gossip, 'that people's tongues, never very tight, were absolutely
loosened by Theo's death.'*

His correspondent Isa Blagden, who had known Theo
intimately, told Browning the story was absolute nonsense. Its
interest, for us, is in the light it sheds on the circumscribed, over-
leisured and bitchy world of the cultivated English in Florence,
and in the surprise people evidently felt, for whatever reason, that
Tom and Theodosia were about to become parents.

Theodosia, always delicate, felt ill during her pregnancy, and
'was not consoled for her ill health by the prospect of maternity',
as Tom put it in his memoirs. Anthony heard from Tom about the
expected event within a week of writing to his mother – the letters
crossed – and sent his brother a most peculiar response:

> I am glad you are to have a child. One wants some one to
> exercise unlimited authority over, as one gets old and cross.
> If one blows up one's servants too much, they turn round,
> give warning, and repay with interest. One's wife may be too
> much for one, and is not always a safe recipient for one's
> wrath. But one's children can be blown up to any amount
> without damage, – at any rate, for a considerable number of
> years. The pleasures of paternity have been considerably
> abridged, since the good old Roman privilege of slaying their
> offspring at pleasure, has been taken from fathers. But the

* E. C. McAleer (ed.): *Dearest Isa: Robert Browning's Letters to Isabella Blagden*,
University of Texas Press/Nelson, 1951.

delights of flagellation, though less keen, are more enduring. One can kill but once; but one may flog daily, and always quote Scripture to prove that it is a duty.

This painful facetiousness perhaps stemmed from embarrassment; perhaps too the thought of Tom having charge of a child reminded Anthony, consciously or not, of Tom's proven capacity to 'flog daily'. He had flogged Anthony daily, at Winchester.

'A daughter, I fear, does not offer so much innocent enjoyment,' continued Anthony. 'But some fathers do manage to torment their daughters with a great degree of very evident and enviable satisfaction. I have none, and therefore have not turned my attention to that branch of the subject.'

Anthony did, however, in his later years have Rose's young niece Florence Bland as proxy daughter and amanuensis. She worked with him in the early mornings, and over late breakfast Florence was once asked if her uncle beat her during their sessions. Anthony laughed, banged the table, and roared that such a remedy was long overdue.

Anthony had a common-sense attitude to the routine corporal punishment that was part of nearly every nineteenth-century child's upbringing. Underneath, the memory of humiliation stirred, and a flicker of lickerish excitement. Lady Glencora Palliser, bored by her husband and aroused by Burgo Fitzgerald in *Can You Forgive Her?*, wondered whether it might not be preferable to be 'beaten by him [Burgo] than to have politics explained to her at one o'clock at night by such a husband as Plantagenet Palliser'. Lady Laura Kennedy, married to a 'cold tyrant' in *Phineas Finn*, said to her brother, about to be married: 'And remember this, there is no tyranny to a woman like telling her of her duty. Talk of beating a woman! beating might often be a mercy.' The duty she was talking about was connubial duty. These passionate women, it seems, would find being beaten more exciting than no sex, or dead sex. That was their creator's fantasy; in the real world, beating was an uneasy subject for his jokes.*

Theodosia gave birth to a daughter on 8 March 1853. She was christened Beatrice, and always called 'Bice' for short, pro

---

* One could make too much of this. I do not believe that Anthony ever struck Rose, or any woman.

nounced the Italian way, 'Beechay'. She was the apple of old Mrs Trollope's eye and adored by both her parents, though Tom had to adjust to a change. During the first five years of his marriage, he wrote, 'I think I may say that she [Theo] lived wholly and solely in, by, and for me.' Theo's 'intense worship' of Bice meant that he now 'came second in her heart. But I was not jealous of little Bice.'

Anthony's secondment in England was coming to an end. He did not really want to go back to Ireland, and in autumn 1852 he – or his mother – involved their kinsman Sir John Trollope MP in using his influence with the new Postmaster General, Lord Hardwicke. 'And I believe he [Sir John] has done what he could do,' Anthony reported to his mother. 'But I ought not to want any private interest. The more I see the way in which the post-office work is done, the more aggrieved I feel at not receiving the promotion I have a right to expect. However, this does not really annoy me. I can't fancy any one being much happier than I am, – or of having less in the world to complain of. It often strikes me how wonderfully well I have fallen on my feet.' He did not want to seem sorry for himself, nor to have his mother brooding over his marginalised career.

In November 1852 he formally applied to Hardwicke for the vacant post of Superintendent of Mail Coaches. 'I have been 18 years in the service, and I believe I may confidently refer your Lordship to any of the officers under whom I have served, and especially to Col Maberly, as to my fitness for the situation.' There is no record of Maberly's reference, though he had written most praisingly to Hardwicke earlier about Mr Trollope's effectiveness in revising the services of the south-west, and recommending that he be retained to complete the job in South Wales. Anthony did not get the Mail Coaches job. It went to a man who had already been twenty-six years in the Mail Coach department – which ought to have satisfied Anthony, who strongly believed that preferment should follow length of service, all other things being equal.

Meanwhile the Trollopes, or rather Rose and the boys, settled in Cheltenham for the winter. Anthony was all over the place – in the Cotswolds, the west Midlands, Wales. The difficulties of their vagabond existence, especially for Rose, can be glimpsed in the request Anthony sent from Llandilo to the postmaster at Bristol, about belongings that had been shipped from Ireland back in the spring: 'Mrs. Trollope wishes to have the lumber which at present burdens you at Bristol, sent by luggage train to her present address. No. 5 Paragon buildings Cheltenham – I dont know how many articles there are. . . . There are I believe some maps – a case of maps – That had better be sent by post, addressed to me – "to be kept at the post office till Mr. Trollope's arrival".'

If he were to wish the good Bristol postmaster 'all evil', added Anthony, 'I could wish you nothing worse than a residence in South Wales for the rest of your life.' The only novel he set in South Wales was *Cousin Henry*, written, or rather dictated to his niece Florence, in 1878; the story centres on a hidden will in a country house overlooking the sea on that same Carmarthenshire coast where he, Rose and the boys had spent the summer of 1852. In *Marion Fay* he punished Lady Amaldina Hauteville by giving her an unattractive husband with a joke-Welsh name – the Marquis of Llwddythlw, a less than ardent bridegroom who found his wedding a disagreeable operation: 'It might, perhaps, have saved pain [to Lord Llwddythlw] if, as Lady Amaldina had said, chloroform had been used.'

When considering the opposite end of the Welsh social scale, Anthony expressed his horror of the 'strange and monstrous villages which in late years have sprung up on the hill-sides of Glamorganshire' – the coal-mining villages whose 'dusky denizens' worked underground. Talking to the miners, no one could possibly think 'that British energy is well cared for, and well rewarded' (*The New Zealander*). But he expressed the same feelings, in the same passage, about the brutish existence of Wiltshire farm-workers. Anthony did not romanticise pre-industrial labour. He saw too much rural deprivation, too many rural slums.

If rural Barsetshire seems a lost paradise to modern readers, it was paradise by default. From the late 1840s on there was a stillness and silence in English country towns and villages that was to last until bicycles, then motor cars, began to venture out on to the neglected high roads and penetrate the lanes. Anthony did not live to hear the silence broken.

It was not only that the exodus to the industrial cities had begun. Country towns had lost their economic base with the coming of the railways. The coaching business was at its height when Anthony was a boy; stage coaches trundled, mail coaches (which also carried passengers) bowled, and young men in the latest kind of carriages raced, all over the country along the smooth, newly macadamised roads. There was *traffic*. The inns in the towns through which it passed enjoyed good and regular trade – feeding and stabling horses, providing meals and beds for an endless supply of travellers.

Then the trains came, slicing through the countryside and carrying off the mails, and the passengers, and the business. Anthony in the West Country witnessed and deplored, with many an 'Alas!', the resulting stagnation.

In *Doctor Thorne* he described the Red Lion in the centre of Courcy, 'and here, in the old days of coaching, some life had been wont to stir itself at those hours of the day and night when the Freetraders, Tallyhoes, and Royal Mails changed their horses. But now there was a railway station a mile and a half distant. . . . And how changed has been the bustle of that once noisy inn to the present death-like silence of its green court-yard! There, a lame ostler crawls about with his hands thrust into the capacious pockets of his jacket, feeding on memory. . . .'

The courtyard was green because grass now grew between its untrodden cobbles. In *The Belton Estate* Anthony wrote about the quiet main street of Perivale: 'To me, had I lived there,' he interpolated, 'the incipient growth of grass through some of the stones which formed the margin of the road would have been altogether unendurable. There is no sign of coming decay which is melancholy to the eye as any which tells of a decrease in the throng of men.' This street 'had formed part of the main line of road from Salisbury to Taunton, and coaches, wagons, and posting-carriages had been frequent on it; but now, alas! it was deserted.' The Rev. Frank Fenwick in *The Vicar of Bullhampton* enquired after the delinquent Carry Brattle in the Bald-Faced Stag off the Marlborough to Devizes road 'which, in the days of the glory of that branch of the Western Road, used to supply beer to at least a dozen coaches a day, but which now, alas! could slake no drowth but that of the rural aborigines.'

It is in the context of this torpid provincial uneventfulness that we must think of Barsetshire's politics, snobberies, rivalries and taboos, and of bright and well-brought-up Trollopian girls, Lucy or Mary or Fanny or Lily, trying to find meaning in life. For them, any diversion – a fête, a picnic, a scandal, a visit from relatives, a trip to London, above all the arrival of an agreeable unmarried young man in the neighbourhood – carried a disproportionate emotional charge.

'1853 At Cheltenham until we went abroad first time middle of April,' wrote Rose in her chronology. The Trollopes went at last to Florence, and John Tilley, widowed for the second time, went with them.

This first experience of 'abroad' awoke in Rose an enthusiasm for travel and for regular holidays which could sometimes be a trial to Anthony. He would scrawl 'Alas!' or 'Ah me!' on his work-sheets across periods when he had done no writing because of even a week or so away on holiday with Rose – although the beauty-spots they visited often came in useful as settings for short stories or for episodes in his fiction. Rose's chronology is a laconic document; only when it came to charting the longer journeys they made together was she lavish with detail. Her spelling, especially of foreign places, was unreliable:

> To London. Paris by night mail. Three custom house officers. Paris one night. To Lyons by rail as far as Chalons sur Saone – canal boat. Lyons John Tilley ill. Night diligence to Chambery over the Echelles. The Mt Cenis [pass over the Alps] to Turin – one night in Turin – rail part of way to Genoa omnibus. Tom meets us at Genoa – scolds us because 4 hours behind time. Two days in Genoa. We post to Pisa via Sestra [Sestri Levante] Spezza [Spezia] Petro Santo [Pietrasanta] – row with the driver when we start. Florence in May. Return via steamer Leghorn & Genoa – with the Langheims. One night at Allesandra [Alessandria]. The Novara. Arena [?Acana] and over the Lago Maggiore to Belenzena [Bellinzona]. Post to [?]Arosa. Diligence and sledges over the St Gothard [pass]. Places taken from us by two Germans. Down to Altoff [Altdorf]. To Lucerne. You [i.e. Anthony] John Tilley and Mr Langheim go up the Rigi. To Basle –Mannheim – down the Rhone to Cologne. Antwerp Ostend and home to London.

It all meant a lot to Rose. She provided the same kind of

scrambled itinerary, reconstructed from her own illegible record in her loose, cheerful handwriting, sometimes with a surreal detail that only she and Anthony could interpret – 'Cross to Boulogne – ("Why did the man in the White Hat go to Basle")' – for every foreign 'tour', as they called these arduous trips, which they took over the years.

In his *Travelling Sketches* Anthony described the English pater-familias, i.e. himself, battling with Continental travel, 'paying the bills, strapping up the cloaks, scolding the waiters, obeying, but not placidly obeying, the female behests to which he is subject, and too frequently fretting uncomfortably beneath the burden of the day, the heat and the dust, the absence of his slippers, and the gross weight of his too-matured proportions'. To have crossed the mountains and heard the whistle of a steamer on an Italian lake, 'to have done these things so that the past accomplishment of them may be garnered like a treasure, is very well; – but oh and alas, the doing of them – the troubles, the cares, the doubts, the fears. . . .' It was 'our wives', he wrote, who enforced the performance of this duty, 'even when from tenderness of heart they would fain spare us'.

But that was more than ten years later. In *He Knew He Was Right*, written after the railway had tunnelled under the Alps between France and Italy, Anthony reminisced nostalgically about the days when the cold night journey through the mountains was 'still made by diligences, – those dear old continental coaches which are now nearly as extinct as our own'. The only trouble was that more tickets used to be sold by the Paris agents than there were places in these diligences, and 'it would generally be the case that some middle-aged Englishman who could not speak French would go to the wall, together with his wife.'

On their first and longed-for tour in 1853 they stayed at the Villino Trollope in Florence, and met Theodosia and the two-month-old Bice for the first time. Tom, with Theodosia's inheritance, had bought more ground and made a garden and an orchard of orange and lemon trees. He did his literary work* standing up at a high desk, in a library looking on to the shady loggia which was the family meeting-place. The eldest of the three

---

* Tom was working at this time on *The Girlhood of Catherine de' Medici*, the first in a long series of books on Italian historical themes.

Mrs Trollopes, aged seventy-three, was very much the mistress of the house, and it was she who made Rose welcome.

'She took me about everywhere,' wrote Rose, 'and explained everything to me. And she made me happy by a present of an Italian silk dress. She also gave me a Roman mosaic brooch, which had been a present to her from Princess Metternich during her stay in Vienna. It is a perfect gem.'

In *Barchester Towers* Anthony lent this brooch to the Signora Vesey Neroni (born – or *nata* as she affectedly said – Madeline Stanhope, daughter of the dilettante vicar of Crabtree Canonicorum); the Signora wore it at Mrs Proudie's reception, on a red velvet band across her brow, 'a magnificent Cupid in mosaic, the tints of whose wings were of the most lovely azure, and the colour of his chubby cheeks the clearest pink'.

The Signora, back in Barchester with a flurry of pretensions and ambiguous marital status, is a measure of the amusement that Anthony derived from the Italianate expatriates. She aimed 'to create a sensation, to have parsons at her feet, seeing that the manhood of Barchester consisted mainly of parsons, and to send, if possible, every parson's wife home with a green fit of jealousy'. There was something wrong with her legs (a consquence, it is hinted, of marital violence), and she always lay upon a sofa. Anthony Trollope was free with the word 'legs' in a common-sense way which, nevertheless, left open the possibility of what his contemporaries called indelicacy – as in this exchange about the Signora between the bishop, his wife Mrs Proudie, and their daughters:

'She has got no legs, papa,' said the youngest daughter, tittering.

'No legs!' said the bishop, opening his eyes.

'Nonsense, Netta, what stuff you talk,' said Olivia. 'She has got legs, but she can't use them. She has always to be kept lying down, and three or four men carry her about everywhere.'

'Laws, how odd!' said Augusta. 'Always carried about by four men! I'm sure I shouldn't like it. Am I right behind, mamma? I feel as if I was open'; and she turned her back to her anxious parent.

'Open! to be sure you are,' said she, 'and a yard of petticoat strings hanging out.'

The bishop was left 'dying with curiosity about the mysterious lady and her legs. . . .'

Elizabeth Barrett Browning also held court from a sofa. She was, with her husband, a valued acquaintance of the family at the Villino Trollope in Florence. When the Brownings were planning to settle in Florence, Robert Browning had written to his wife about the perils of the 'large and vulgar' English colony there. 'There is that coarse, vulgar Mrs Trollope – I do hope, Ba, if you don't want to give me the greatest pain, that you won't receive that vulgar pushing woman who is not fit to speak to you.' But Mrs Browning did receive Mrs Trollope at her weekly receptions in the apartment on the *piano nobile* of the Casa Guidi, initially for her daughter-in-law's sake: Theodosia, in her poetical girlhood, had sat at Elizabeth Barrett's feet in Torquay.*

It was Mrs Trollope, rather than Theo, who was hostess at the weekly evening receptions at the Villino Trollope, at which she had her own special whist-table. 'I thought her the most charming old lady who ever existed,' wrote Rose to Tom's second wife, long after. 'I do not think she had a mean thought in her composition.' Nor had Rose – who found her mother-in-law generous, impulsive and, if sarcastic, not ill-natured.

Other members of the close Florence circle included Robert Lytton, attaché at the British Embassy and son of Mrs Trollope's old friend Rosina; and the high-spirited and sociable Irish writer Charles Lever.† Mrs Browning found Lever fascinating; Lever however was never at ease with clever women, and was particularly nervous of old Mrs Trollope. Their friends watched with amusement as he avoided her undisguised manoeuvrings to secure him as her whist partner.

Frederick Tennyson (brother of the more famous Alfred) also lived in Florence with his Italian wife at the Villa Torregiani. When Alfred and Emily Tennyson stayed there in 1851, old Mrs

---

* Theodosia had been encouraged not only by Elizabeth Barrett but by Walter Savage Landor. She worked as hard and seriously as any born Trollope; she continued to write poetry, contributed to Lady Blessington's annual *The Book of Beauty*, and her articles published in the *Athenaeum* were collected in 1861 under the title *Social Aspects of the Italian Revolution*.

† Lever said he had 'no word but ecstasy' to express his enjoyment of Florence society. In 1858 he obtained the sinecure of British Vice-consul at La Spezia, and continued to spend most of his time in Florence. He died in Trieste in 1872.

Trollope called on them – 'a kind motherly sort of body & not at all coarse as one would expect from her works', noted Emily Tennyson. Then there were the American sculptors – young Harriet Hosmer, whose work 'The Clasped Hands' was a model of the hands of Mr and Mrs Browning, and Hiram Powers, whose 'Greek Slave' had been prominent in the Great Exhibition (Mrs Browning had composed a sonnet about it); Mrs Trollope and Tom had known Powers as a young man in Cincinnati.* Anthony mentioned both Hosmer and Powers in *He Knew He Was Right.*

There was the old poet Walter Savage Landor, and small, dark Isa Blagden, nearing forty, who was, like Theodosia's father, the child of an Englishman and an Indian woman, but with no known family. Isa was an intimate of both the Brownings and the Tom Trollopes; she lived with her dogs and a series of women friends in a series of rented villas on the hill at Bellosguardo, wrote verse and romantic novels and loved, unrequitedly, the handsome, blue-eyed Robert Lytton. Both Anthony Trollope and Robert Browning (who went up to visit her in the evenings when his wife was settled in bed with a book) helped Isa Blagden to get her novels published. Rose's comment, when the second came out, was: 'I hope it will have more common sense than the former one – it can't well have less.'†

Rose and Anthony were to visit Florence many times, but it was in Venice that the family met up again two years later (May 1855); and though Mrs Trollope then still climbed stairs and walked everywhere she was growing nervy and found travelling tiring, and being in a gondola in a storm on the Lagoon frightening. Her great energies were, at last, beginning to flag. Her last and forty-first book, a novel called *Fashionable Life: or London and Paris*, into which she introduced her experience of séances, was published in 1856. Mrs Trollope laid down her pen with the same determination and stoicism with which she had taken it up.

---

* Hiram Powers (1805–73) collaborated with Mrs Trollope and Hervieu in Cincinnati on a commercial venture which, unlike her bazaar, made some money. It was a series of tableaux (with sound-effects) representing Dante's Infernal Regions, with sets painted by Hervieu and figures modelled by Powers. By the 1850s Powers was very respectable and famous. Browning was a great admirer.

† Rose Trollope to Kate Field, quoted in *Dearest Isa: Robert Browning's Letters to Isabella Blagden*, ed. E. C. McAleer.

——— * ———

'The Rev. Septimus Harding was, a few years since, a beneficed clergyman residing in the cathedral town of—; let us call it Barchester. Were we to name Wells or Salisbury, Exeter, Hereford or Gloucester, it might be presumed that something personal was intended. . . .' That is how *The Warden* begins, floating Barchester and its environs into existence in parallel to the West Country that Anthony Trollope now knew so intimately, and superimposing its alternative life, and its map, on the real map.

Anthony began writing his fourth novel on 29 July 1853, when they were back from Italy and he happened to be staying in Tenbury, a village north-west of Worcester. The story had been in his mind for over a year. He was working in Salisbury the previous May, and while wandering one warm evening 'round the purlieus of the cathedral' stood for an hour on the bridge and conceived the story of *The Warden* – 'from whence came that series of novels of which Barchester, with its bishops, deans, and archdeacon, was the central site' (*Autobiography*).

His West Country posting had given him Barsetshire. But he had to stop writing again almost immediately. His new appointment, not what he would have chosen, was as acting Surveyor in the Northern District of Ireland, based in Belfast, where the family was duly settled by early September, with Harry sent south to a boarding school in Cork. 'The work of taking up a new district, which requires not only that the man doing it should know the nature of the postal arrangements, but also the characters and the peculiarities of the postmasters and their clerks, was too heavy to allow of my going on with my book at once.' By the end of the year he was back into it – writing about Barchester from Belfast, whence rural England was dream and memory.

Before the Famine, Belfast had seemed to Thackeray, in his *Irish Sketch Book*, 'as neat, prosperous and handsome a city as might be seen'. Since then it had suffered with the rest of the country, but as Ireland's largest industrialised town, and a busy sea-port, it made a quicker recovery. It was a tough, fast-growing city of ship-building, rope-making, tobacco factories, brewing, linen-manufacture, and the iron-foundries that made the power-looms and other great engines of industry, enriching their Protestant masters: Houston & Hamilton, the MacAdam Brothers. The imagery of furnace and foundry that recurs in Anthony's *The New Zealander* is owed to Belfast. Huge linen-spinning mills, their thousands of windows lit up after dark, ringed the red-brick town in its saucer of land between high hills and Belfast Lough, leading to the sea. The neo-Tudor Queen's College* and the surrounding housing developments were new when the Trollopes moved there; the neo-classical Custom House was under construction; banks, warehouses and offices were springing up. Belfast was full of activity, but as a place to live, it was not greatly to the Trollopes' liking.

During Anthony's time in the Northern District the Belfast Post Office moved to a new building in Queen's Square. Anthony complained loudly about the inaccurate records kept of the times postmen returned from their rounds; the clerk concerned explained that he had no watch, and could not afford to buy one, and that there was no clock in the new building. Anthony growled, but put in a request for a clock of an ingenious design. It was placed in the window, and was double-faced – the larger face looking outwards, so that the mail coaches could check their timekeeping, and the smaller one facing into the office.†

Anthony's professional hopes were pinned on becoming a Surveyor. He was still, technically, only a Surveyor's Clerk. He got what he wanted in 1854, though not without much anxiety and delay, and was immensely relieved: 'I trust my state of vassalage is over,' he told Tom. It was not quite over; he was not given leave to take September off for another holiday in Italy, as he and Rose had planned.

His mother, from a distance, was intimately concerned in all his efforts to improve his position – and his income. (Shortly after his appointment in 1854, Surveyors' basic salaries went up from £650 to £700 a year.) Before the promotion was confirmed, Anthony wrote to her excitedly: 'Then comes the important question of residence – Where shall we live? We both dislike the north – & the districts may all be changed – but this also we must discuss on a gondola. We wont buy our furniture at any rate till we have

---

* Now the Queen's University. Queen Victoria had visited Belfast on her Irish excursion in 1849; nearly everything built in the following few years was named after her.

† This clock is now in the Ulster Museum in Belfast.

discussed with you the color of the drawing room curtains.' In this letter he told her about the children: 'Harry came home from Cork today – with such a Cork brogue – & such a pair of cheeks – & no shoes to his feet – They must both go to some school here in the North after midsummer – We are all now going to the sea side for a month. Fred is somewhat delicate – he is so miserably thin – he is like a skeleton – but full of life and spirits. . . .'

He signed the letter, 'ever your own little boy, A.T.' The big, balding, thirty-nine-year-old roaring martinet of provincial post offices wanted her love and approval as much as ever. In this he was no different from most mothers' sons, and with more reason than many.

Mrs Trollope wrote to Anthony from the Baths of Lucca a month later saying that a letter from him had been sent on from Florence, with a note from Tom – which she read first – expressing his indignation about the treatment Anthony was getting. 'Whereupon,' wrote their mother to Anthony, 'I immediately took it into my head that the hopes, *all* hopes, of the Surveyorship had been melted into air, and there I sat, resting my head upon my hands as if on purpose to prevent my reading any farther, as miserable a poor soul as you can paint to yourself, let your fancy be as dolorous as you will.'

In fact, the cause of Tom's indignation was merely the annoying postponement of the September reunion in Venice, now rescheduled for the following May (1855). Anthony's family in Italy were unflatteringly pessimistic about his career prospects. 'And I have no belief in your promotion, till you get it. Damn them all!' wrote Tom. His mother, just before Christmas 1854, told Anthony that 'I am looking forward to our Venetian trip as the great event of the coming year.'

It was after the Venice trip that Mrs Trollope and Tom returned with Rose and Anthony for a visit to London. The Florence circle of artistic British and American expatriates amused themselves with ambitious private theatricals, as well as whist; but spiritualism, in Florence as in England, was the latest craze. (Mrs Browning was piqued because Mrs Trollope obtained better results at table-turning than she did.)

Mrs Trollope and Tom spent much of their time in London attending the séances of the famous twenty-one-year-old medium

Daniel Home.* As Theodosia, from Florence, reported to a friend: 'They have made the acquaintance of Mr Hume [Home], who is staying with a Mr and Mrs Rymer at Ealing, to avoid being teased by enquiring visitors.' Home planned to visit Italy, so, continued Theo, 'we shall thus have the desired opportunity of seeing and hearing the wonders of the Spirit world with our own eyes and ears. His friends have with *real* kindness pressed the Mammy to go and stay with them for a few days to investigate the phenomena more closely.' Tom, she said, though not staying at the Rymers, was going to attend the séances.

Anthony went too, at least once; Rose considered it worth noting in her chronology that 'You [Anthony] go down to see Home at Ealing.'

'We all went to see these wonders,' he wrote in *The New Zealander* very soon afterwards, 'and messages were brought to us direct from the other world by the recalled spirits of our departed friends' – but only on condition that one sat obediently round a table and never looked beneath it. 'Men who cannot believe in the mystery of our Saviour's redemption can believe that spirits from the dead have visited them in a stranger's parlour, because they see a table shake and do not know how it is shaken; because they hear a rapping on a board, and cannot see the instrument that raps it; because they are touched in the dark, and do not know the hand that touches them. . . . Oh – to what has that soul come that can believe in such visitings as these; that can put credit in spirits crouching among visitors' legs, and rapping tables with due assistance from some kind American medium?'

He, or rather his inane Archie and Doodles (Bertie Wooster prototypes) returned to the subject in *The Claverings*, playing billiards in their club, idly wondering whether Madame Gordeloup might be 'one of those spirit-rapping people':

> 'There are people who think,' said Doodles, 'that the spirits don't come from anywhere, but are always floating about.'
>
> 'And then one person catches them, and another doesn't?' asked Archie.

* Daniel Dunglas Home (1833–86), born in Scotland. His father was said to be a natural son of the tenth Earl of Home. His mother emigrated with the boy to America, where he 'came out' as a spiritualist medium. Many well-known people attended his séances in Ealing in 1855, including Lord Brougham, Sir Edward Bulwer Lytton and Robert Browning, who made his adverse opinion of Home clear in his poem 'Mr Sludge the Medium'. In 1871 Home was taken up by the Czar, and he married, in succession, two aristocratic Russian women.

'They tell me that it depends upon what the mediums or medias eat and drink,' said Doodles, 'and upon what sort of minds they have. They must be cleverish people, I fancy, or the spirits wouldn't come to them.'

'But you never hear of any swell being a medium. Why don't the spirits go to a prime minister or some of those fellows? Only think what a help they'd be.'

They gravely agreed that Madame Gordeloup, like all mediums, was not quite respectable, and Archie concluded that 'If I were a spirit I wouldn't go to a woman who wore such dirty stockings as she had on.'

Rose did not approve of spiritualism at all. She could not understand how her clever mother-in-law could be so credulous: 'It appears very strange that a woman with so much strong common sense, should have placed faith in these absurdities. But her imagination and romance got the upper hand.' This was to be Mrs Trollope's last visit to England. Her health began to fail seriously that autumn. Rose thought her obsession with spiritualism had accelerated her mental and physical deterioration, but it was probably the other way around.

Theodosia's health also gave cause for anxiety, but 'as to Miss Beatrice', Mrs Trollope wrote to Anthony, 'she is (of course) a species of prodigy. All jesting apart, however, she is undeniably a *very* extraordinary little brat.' Before she was two, Bice talked fluently, hummed in tune, danced and loved pictures. '*De plus* she really is very pretty. . . . Give my affectionate love to dear Rose. I would that Henry and Fred could understand what it meant if I sent the same to them! God bless you my dear dear Son.'

Anthony's children could never have the same place in her heart as Tom's little daughter, whom she saw every day, though Harry, Anthony's eldest, was encouraged to write to his grand-mother. In July 1856 Mrs Trollope told the ten-year-old that his letter 'gave me much pleasure because it made me know that your dear Papa and Mama had talked to you about me. . . . Your Papa tells me, dear Henry, that you are going to a new school, and I have therefore sent you a *sovereign** to add to your stock of pocket

* She apologised to Anthony in a covering letter for not having repaid him yet for 'the fitting up of the Naples chess table', and '*Moreover* I must borrow of you in addition the sum of one golden sovereign which I have told dear Harry in the enclosed is to assist his reserve fund of pocket money when he goes to his foreign school.' (The school was in England, at Chester.)

money when you are further away from home.' His little cousin Beatrice 'would very much like to see you and Fred'.

Anthony finished *The Warden* – working title, 'The Precentor' – and on 8 October 1854 sent it to the publisher William Longman. Anthony had done no good for Colburn, his previous publisher, nor Colburn for him. He was striking out on his own for the first time, in that Longmans had no connection at all with Mrs Trollope; Anthony met William Longman, who had published Charles Merivale's *History of the Romans*, through John Merivale and his mother. Longmans was the oldest publishing house in London, established in its offices in Paternoster Row since 1724. They published the poems of Sir Walter Scott, Tom Moore, Wordsworth, Coleridge and Southey, and made a fortune out of Thomas Macaulay's multi-volume *History of England*. Fiction was definitely not their priority. The head of the family firm was Thomas Longman, who spent much time working on his own sumptuously illustrated edition of the New Testament.

William Longman, with whom Anthony dealt, was nine years younger than his brother Thomas and only a couple of years older than Anthony himself. William had worked in the family firm since he was sixteen and was not only a good publisher but an interesting and pleasant man – athletic and rugged, a keen mountaineer and one of the earliest members of the Alpine Club when it was founded in 1857. He was scholarly as well as sporty, with an informed interest in mediaeval history, languages and natural science, especially entomology. Altogether William Longman was a more worthwhile person with whom to be associated than was old Henry Colburn, who died the following year.

Within four days of receiving Anthony's manuscript, the Longmans reader Joseph Cauvin had sent in a very favourable report. The subject, Cauvin wrote, was not promising: 'But such is the skill of the author that he has contrived to weave out of his materials a very interesting and amusing tale. . . . The characters are well drawn and happily distinguished; and the whole story is pervaded by a vein of quiet humour and (good-natured) satire. . . .' *The Warden* was published in January 1855.

The Warden, a short novel, is like a musical theme played on a solo instrument – a violoncello* – at the beginning of a concerto. The simple arrangement of notes is the foundation of the whole. No one hearing the theme for the first time has any notion of the variations and developments, the changes in mood, pace and dynamics, or the complexity of texture that will come with the complete orchestral work. As Anthony Trollope himself later understood, '*Barchester Towers* would hardly be so well known as it is had there been no *Framley Parsonage* and no *Last Chronicle of Barset*.'

Each novel in the Barchester sequence, like each glimpse of a familiar Barsetshire personage in novels outside the sequence, adds to the meaning of what has gone before. In life outside books we know some friends, or enemies, intimately for a while, and then the ways part. We hear about them, with sudden intense curiosity, or see them unexpectedly – older, and changed – years later.

It is like that in the world of Trollope's fiction. People who will be central in the parliamentary sequence or in other later novels are first glimpsed, their significance unrecognised (even, sometimes, by their creator) in the Barchester novels. It is not the chronicles of Barset that make up a great concerto, it is his work as a monumental whole.

In 1855 no one knew that this was how it would be, and the optimism of William Longman's reader – 'In one word, the work ought to have a large sale' – was not justified. Longmans printed 1000 copies, of which fewer than 400 were sold in the first half-year. 'The novel-reading world did not go mad about *The Warden*,' as Anthony wrote in his autobiography, 'but I soon felt that it had not failed as the others had failed.' The review in the *Examiner*, probably by John Forster himself, was welcoming but condescending, with several references to 'bad taste': '*The Warden* is a clever novel, though we are not quite content with it.' The *Athenaeum* said that 'The whole story is well and smartly told, but with too much indifference to the rights of the case.'

But that was the whole point for its author, at the time of writing it. If, as has been suggested earlier, there is an Ur-story in

* Mr Harding in *The Warden* loved to play his violoncello, 'that saddest of instruments', to the assembled pensioners of Hiram's Hospital. Anthony wrote to Mary Holmes in 1873: 'I remember well, when I was quite a young man, being moved to weeping by hearing a solo on the violoncello by [Robert] Lindley.'

Trollope, there is also an Ur-notion; it is that 'in this world no good is unalloyed, and that there is but little evil that has not in it some seed of what is goodly', as he put it in *The Warden*. He wrote in *Barchester Towers*, having established the slimy careerism of hypocritical Mr Slope: 'And here the author must beg it to be remembered that Mr Slope was not in all things a bad man. His motives, like those of most men, were mixed. . . .' Even Mrs Proudie, the domineering, interfering virago, had 'a heart inside that stiff-ribbed bodice. . . .' As for Lady Carbury in *The Way We Live Now*, 'The woman was false from head to foot, but there was much of good in her, false though she was.'

It was a point he stressed about the people in his books over and over again, from the beginning of his oeuvre to its end. He continued to see not only the good in the bad, but the bad in the good. In *Mr Scarborough's Family*, completed two years before he died, he described how all virtues 'may be said to be tarnished by faults'. 'Unselfishness may become want of character; generosity essentially unjust; confidence [in the sense of trustingness] may be weak, and purity insipid.'

The idea for *The Warden*, and the Ur-notion, arose from hostile press reports about ancient endowments intended for charitable purposes which had become, over the years, subverted into providing incomes for idle clergymen. Anthony recognised this as an evil, but 'the second evil was its very opposite'; that was, the violence with which the press attacked the clergymen in question, because 'when a man is appointed to a place, it is natural that he should accept the income allotted to that place without much inquiry.' The newspaper attacks seemed to him simplistic and dishonest. 'Satire, though it may exaggerate the vice it lashes, is not justified in creating it in order that it may be lashed' (*Autobiography*).

However, as the doctor in Baslehurst in *Rachel Ray* said, 'If in this world we suspend our judgment till we've heard all that can be said on both sides of every question, we should never come to any judgment at all.' Anthony, counsel for both the defence and for the prosecution of the people in his books, and rarely their judge, was like his barrister Frank Greystock in *The Eustace Diamonds*: 'As a large-minded man of the world, peculiarly conversant with the fact that every question has two sides, and that as much may often be said on one side as on the other, he has probably not become violent in his feelings as a political partisan.'

This same Frank Greystock got into an appalling moral mess by being so uncommitted emotionally that he became heavily involved with two women at once – a recurring predicament in Trollope's fiction which combines the Ur-story with the Ur-notion of even-handedness, in a closed system of stresses and balances.

'Yes – I should prefer to be employed in England, but we can't get all we want – & failing that I should prefer the South to the North of Ireland, preferring on the whole papistical to presbyterian tendencies,' Anthony wrote to his old colleague the Bristol postmaster in November 1854. By the following spring he had obtained permission to run his Northern District from Dublin; and in June 1855 the family moved south.

They rented 5 Seaview Terrace, in the village of Donnybrook, on the outskirts of Dublin. Seaview Terrace, which ended then with No 6, next door, was a Georgian development of town houses along a country lane. The house had three storeys over a basement, with steps up to the front door, a stone-flagged hall, Venetian windows up the curling stair, heavy double doors and marble fireplaces in the L-shaped main rooms on the ground and first floors. There was a medium-sized square room on the half-landing for Anthony to have as a writing-room, with a closet off it. The semi-basement, housing scullery, pantry and kitchen looked out on to the yard, stables and coach-house, with a hayloft and a room for Barney above. Beyond was a narrow garden enclosed by stone walls. Mary and Ella, the maids, slept downstairs, off the kitchen. Only from the room at the top of the house – probably the boys' room – could they glimpse the bright strip of sea-view that gave the terrace its name.

Before Seaview Terrace, Anthony in his travel diary had written 'Clonmel' or 'Mallow' or wherever, when he returned to base. Now, for the first time, he always put 'Home'.

He could take the train to Belfast, with connections to other northern towns, from Amiens Street Station in Dublin. He had begun writing *Barchester Towers* in the month *The Warden* was published. He wrote to an unknown correspondent at this time: 'Pray know that when a man begins writing a book he never gives over. The evil with which he is beset is as inveterate as drinking – as exciting as gambling.' He was spending many hours in trains, travelling on Post Office business, and found a way of using the time for his own purposes. 'A man's seat in a railway carriage is now, or may be, his study,' as he wrote in *The New Zealander*. He explained in his autobiography how he made himself* 'a little tablet' or writing-slope, and found after a few days' practice 'that I could write as quickly in a railway-carriage as I could at my desk'. He worked in pencil, and Rose made a copy in ink afterwards. 'In this way was composed the greater part of *Barchester Towers*' (*Autobiography*).

At the same time he was writing a non-fiction work, called *The New Zealander*. William Longman turned it down.† And when he submitted *Barchester Towers* to Longman, he got another rebuff.

Longman's reader Joseph Cauvin did not think the new novel matched up to *The Warden*. He found it too long and uneven. It was, he said, so unequal in execution 'that while there are parts of it that I would be disposed to place on a level with the best morsels of contemporary novelists, there are others – and unfortunately these preponderate – the vulgarity and exaggeration of which, if they do not unfit them for publication, are at least likely to be repulsive to the reader.' Cauvin praised the easy, natural style – but not the spelling. (That was Rose's fault. She was a worse speller than Anthony.) The chief defect of the work was the 'vulgarity' of the chief characters. 'There is hardly a "lady" or "gentleman" among them.' As for the Signora Neroni, 'a most repulsive, exaggerated and unnatural character', she was 'a great blot on the work'.

These strictures belie any conventional supposition that Anthony Trollope was always in tune with his times, or that he deliberately tailored his work to the acceptable standard. His off-key, or off-colour, sense of humour reflects how little opportunity he had had to become conditioned by the assumptions of the 'polite' English world – which, in artistic terms, was to his advantage and ours.

He was hurt by the report, asking William Longman to believe 'that nothing would be more painful to me than to be considered an indecent writer.' He flatly refused to shorten the novel, as

---

* He wrote 'made myself' – but it is more likely that he had it made. This writing-slope is displayed in the Ulster Museum, Belfast.

† *The New Zealander* was not published until 1972, in an edition by N. John Hall for the Clarendon Press.

Longman requested, but agreed to some changes: 'At page 93 by all means put out "foul breathing" and page 97 alter "fat stomach" to "deep chest". . . . I write in a great hurry in boots and breeches, just as I am going to hunt. . . .'

CHAPTER TEN

'IT'S gude to be honest and true.'

That line from a Scottish ballad is quoted like the text of a sermon at the beginning and end of *The New Zealander*, the book that Anthony interrupted work on *Barchester Towers* to write, and which Longman declined to publish. This rejected work represented both his doubt about whether he could make a success with novels, and his desire as a marginalised Englishman to place himself at the centre of national debate. The title came from a famous article written twenty-five years back by Macaulay, in the *Edinburgh Review* of October 1840, about a sophisticated New Zealander in some future age standing on London Bridge and surveying the ruins of the once-great capital city and the collapse of its civilisation. What had gone wrong? Was England, even now, asked Anthony Trollope, 'in her decadence'?

In *The New Zealander* he examined British institutions – the political hierarchy, the press, law and medicine, the army and navy, the church, Parliament, the Crown, society, literature, art. Everywhere he found hypocrisy, greed and dishonesty. (His sense of probity was sharpened by his own disappointments: 'Success is necessary to excellence. Such is the motto of the present age; and in the very motto is proof of dishonesty.') The aristocracy, through idleness, was losing its justification: take any sporting marquis, wrote Anthony, 'who is that and *nothing else*, and any great working Railway Contractor, and it will be found that of the two, the Railway Contractor has the most to say towards the ruling of the country.' Just why Anthony was preoccupied with the influence of railway contractors will become clear.

So far as the press was concerned – and 'on speaking of the English Press, it is impossible to do other than speak of The

Times* alone' – it had too much power, and abused it. Newspaper writers, like clergymen, went in for 'mock indignation' and promulgated a false code of morals by preaching doctrines higher than those by which they themselves lived. 'It is, alas, so easy to fall into pretences; so vitally necessary to avoid doing so.' Church services were nothing but the pointless repetition of prayers: 'I will not calumniate a parrot by likening the religious observances of many Christians to its gabble.' The churches encouraged 'religious rancour, the depth of religious contempt, the fascinating warmth of religious hatred' towards those who worshipped in other ways. Parsons who liked good dinners and wished to see their daughters marry well preached the vanity of worldly things; they taught that the body was vile and worthless, 'and we sit tediously to hear the tidings, bedizened in our silks and satins'.

As for the law, a barrister 'can find it consistent with his dignity to turn wrong into right, and right into wrong, to abet a lie, nay, to create, disseminate, and, with all the play of his wit, give strength to the basest of lies, on behalf of the basest of scoundrels.' In the House of Commons, lying and intrigue 'are necessary and permitted'. As for the House of Lords with its hereditary peers: 'It is this worship of the dead, of things that are dead as well as men, that has so often been the ruin of nations.'

And so on. It is important to know the fierceness of his moral disgust, since churchmen, the aristocracy, lawyers and MPs are so central in his fiction. Dishonesty – in sexual as in commercial and public life – is the quintessential Trollopian sin. His outrage lies like a chained bull behind his comedy. But 'It is impossible not to be hopeful for one's country,' he wrote in *The New Zealander*. 'No latter-day pamphlets will drive him to despair.'

That was a dig at Thomas Carlyle's *Latter-Day Pamphlets*, which Anthony bought and read in 1851, telling his mother that he thought he had wasted his money. Carlyle, Anthony told her, 'has one idea, – a hatred of spoken and acted falsehood; and on that he harps throughout the whole eight pamphlets.' It was Carlyle's

* *The Times* and the *Athenaeum* were the only English papers that Anthony and Rose took in Ireland. He had parodied *The Times* as the 'Jupiter' in *The Warden*. It was widely believed that the 'Jupiter''s leading writer, Tom Towers, was a skit on *The Times*'s editor, J. T. Delane; but as Anthony wrote, 'at that time, living away in Ireland, I had not even heard the name of any gentleman connected with *The Times* newspaper, and could not have intended to represent any individual by Tom Towers.'

pessimism and hectoring censoriousness that antagonised Anthony, and it was for these qualities that he parodied Carlyle as Dr Pessimist Anticant in *The Warden*.* Dr Pessimist Anticant never recognised 'that in this world no good is unalloyed, and that there is but little evil that has not in it some seed of what is goodly.'

Nevertheless, *The New Zealander* was too like Carlyle's famous *Pamphlets* to be comfortable, which was why Longmans rejected it. As the publisher's reader reported, 'All the good points in the work have already been treated of by Mr Carlyle, of whose *Latter-Day Pamphlets* this work, both in style and matter, is a most feeble imitation.' *The New Zealander* was conceived by its author not as an imitation of Carlyle but as a robust corrective. It is of interest to posterity because it reveals Anthony's preoccupations; but it is perfectly understandable that at the time his book seemed just a pointless re-hash of a better-known writer's work.

Anthony Trollope believed passionately in the basic soundness of British institutions, and his novels are freighted with tenderness for their traditions and an understanding of the frailties of the men and women who abused them. No man was more 'honest and true' than he, but he did not disassociate himself superciliously from the evils he excoriated. It was not possible for him to do so. Dishonesty and moral chaos lay too close to home. In *The New Zealander* he was concentrating on public and social immorality; but the full stanza of the ballad from which he took his 'motto' was about the private immorality which lay behind the Ur-theme of his novels. The Signora Neroni sang it jeeringly to her slippery admirer in *Barchester Towers*:

> It's gude to be merry and wise, Mr Slope,
> It's gude to be honest and true;
> It's gude to be off with the old love – Mr Slope,
> Before you are on with the new.

In the public domain Anthony had direct experience of moral muddle – not only in the past, with his father's mismanagement of

---

* In *The Warden* Trollope also made fun of Charles Dickens as Mr Popular Sentiment, author of a novel called *The Almshouse*, which was *The Warden* as Dickens, with his simplistic attitudes to human character (the good people so very good, the bad people so very bad), would have written it. Trollope 'reviewed' the first instalment of *The Almshouse* but did not attempt to parody Dickens as he did Carlyle.

the family affairs, but recently, in the case of his unfortunate father-in-law.

Rose's father Edward Heseltine had retired from the Rotherham bank, aged seventy-two and in poor health, on 31 December 1852, and moved south to Torquay in Devon. There is no record of any family reunions, and Rose and the children were living in Cheltenham that winter; but it is most unlikely she did not see her father and stepmother, unless all communication had been broken off. Charlotte, Mr Heseltine's young second wife, had borne him two sons, Ned and Frank, who were much the same ages as Harry and Fred Trollope.

Mr Heseltine had always enjoyed considerable independence at his branch when it came to advancing money and authorising overdrafts, though towards the end of his career there were questions asked by the bank's directors about the wisdom of some of his decisions. But he had served the bank as manager for twenty-five years, and at the annual general meeting in February 1853 the directors agreed that he should receive a pension, or 'retiring allowance'. Then in late April 1853 – when Rose and Anthony had just left for their first trip to Italy – the new manager, Mr Dyson, reported to his directors 'large deficiencies' in the Rotherham branch's accounts.

Subsequent investigations revealed that the accounts began to go badly wrong from the time Rose's father took over the branch back in 1836; by June that year the deficit was already nearly £4,000. There was some puzzling evidence that not all the defalcations had been for Mr Heseltine's personal gain, but his whole career had been a combination of dishonesty and muddle.

The directors invited Mr Heseltine back to Rotherham at the bank's expense to assist the new manager in squaring up the books. Mr Heseltine declined to return, so bank officials visited him in Torquay, taking the bank's books with them, and pointed out the 'fictitious Items'. Mr Heseltine 'strongly averred that he never took a shilling of the money', but was unable, or unwilling, to account for its disappearance.

He decamped to Plymouth, but was traced; and Mrs Heseltine wrote to the bank to say that her husband was too unwell to travel north to face questioning. They flitted again, to Bristol; and again, a week later, to Gainsborough, only twenty-five miles from

Rotherham, where two of the directors finally caught up with him. They found him 'very ill and wholly unable to attend to business . . . the symptoms being great prostration physically, and such pressure on the brain as to impair his faculties so that attention to the Rotherham books at present was impossible'. His wife agreed to keep in touch and let the bank know if his health improved. 'It was also Resolved [by the directors] that the question of paying the 1st quarter's pension cannot be entertained.'

Charlotte Heseltine had a married sister in Manchester, and possibly the two little boys were left with her. Inconclusive negotiations between the bank and the now penniless Heseltines went on for another year. Finally, with the threat of criminal proceedings hanging over the demented man's head, the couple fled to Le Havre in northern France.

It is hard to see how Mr Heseltine kept what was going on from his clerks, or from Mr Dyson, who had been cashier before he took over as manager; or maybe cooking the books had come to seem normal in the Rotherham bank. No one has ever suggested what it was that Mr Heseltine had done with the missing thousands, though the answer seems obvious.

He was a director of the tiny Sheffield and Rotherham Railway – the journey between the two towns took just over a quarter of an hour – which was authorised by Act of Parliament in the year he took up his post at the bank, and opened in 1838. At Sheffield this little line fed into the more ambitious north-south North Midland Railway, which was always in trouble. George Hudson, the 'Railway King', declined to join its board of directors in 1841, and was a member of a committee of enquiry into its operations in 1842. After effecting stringent economies, Hudson added the North Midland to his empire, amalgamating it with other north-south lines as part of his plan to control the Edinburgh-to-London trunk route. By 1846, the little Sheffield and Rotherham branch line was also under Hudson's control.

Hudson ran his ever-expanding railway empire by means that would land him in gaol today, but in the 1840s company law was in its infancy. Accounts were carelessly kept and manipulated, falsely favourable balance sheets were presented, non-existent subscribers were listed, and investors were attracted by high dividends paid out of capital, not revenue. Votes, shares, contracts and transfers were rigged. Money was cheap, and there was an orgy of railway speculation in all ranks of society. Hudson, whose personality was as powerful as his ambition, was one of the most famous men in Britain and idolised as a public benefactor.

He was also chairman of the York Union Bank, which serviced his financial dealings. What happened to the manager there, Mr B. T. Wilkinson, is instructive. He was Hudson's *protégé*, or tool, and as a matter of course used the bank's money to speculate in railways on his own account. (He was discovered when Hudson's empire crashed in 1849, and resigned.) Mr Heseltine probably did exactly the same as Mr Wilkinson. Being a railway director as well as a bank manager, he had even greater opportunities for buying shares – and if he bought them in the local Midland line they were among the first to fall disastrously as the bubble burst. Mr Heseltine was one of the thousands who swindled in a small way in the shadow of George Hudson – millionaire, master-swindler and entrepreneur of genius.

This supposition is confirmed by the fact that the customer to whom Mr Heseltine had lent money without security, thus disturbing his superiors in the bank, was Thomas Badger, a Rotherham solicitor, and a respectable pew-owner in the church where Rose and Anthony were married. Badger was solicitor to the Sheffield and Rotherham Railway, and no doubt over-extended himself in his own speculations. Mr Heseltine, in the same racket, obliged a fellow gambler. The other transactions questioned by the bank's directors concerned repeated unsecured advances made to a local manufacturer of railway wagons.

All those directors of railways who were not Hudson's cronies were his puppets. In charity, it is possible to believe that Mr Heseltine was leaned on. No wonder his lips were sealed. He could not explain his activities without exposing other, more powerful people. Perhaps this was what Mrs Heseltine meant when she suggested to the bank that certain matters might be revealed 'when Mr H. was no more'. Mr H. died at Le Havre on 15 September 1855. Just a few weeks earlier, on August 12, another Mr H., George Hudson himself, his empire in ruins, had also fled to the Continent.

Though there is no evidence that Rose and Anthony knew about Rose's father's disgrace, it is inconceivable that they did not. Rose's younger sister Isabella was married to Joseph Bland, a senior clerk in the Rotherham bank, and it was the clerks who went back over the books documenting the irregularities of their former manager, Joseph's father-in-law and Anthony's. Rose was in contact with her sister Isabella, who came to stay with her in Seaview Terrace when Anthony was away.

Anthony wrote in *The New Zealander*: 'It is not of swindlers and liars that we need to live in fear, but of the fact that swindling and lying are gradually becoming not abhorrent to our minds. . . . Could the career of that wretched man who has lately perished have been possible, had falsehood, dishonesty, pretences, and subterfuges been odious in the eyes of those who came daily in contact with his doings?'

The 'wretched man' in question was one John Sadleir, banker, politician and crook, who committed suicide on Hampstead Heath in February 1856.* Anthony's interest in such people foreshadows his later creation of the adventurer Ferdinand Lopez in *The Prime Minister* and of the great swindler Melmotte in *The Way We Live Now*, both of them suicides.

Ferdinand Lopez's was a 'railway' suicide: Anthony wrote few more powerful scenes than that at dusky Tenway Junction, where the lines converged 'with sloping points, and cross passages, and mysterious meandering sidings' in a 'wilderness of wagons', amid smoke and sparks of fire and shrieking whistles. Then 'there came a shriek louder than all the other shrieks, and the morning express from Euston to Inverness was seen coming round the curve at a thousand miles an hour.' Unhurriedly, Lopez stepped down under the engine – 'and in a moment had been knocked into bloody atoms'.

The career of George Hudson was another crucial element in the creation of the great Melmotte, to whom Anthony Trollope was to award suicide by prussic acid.† But in the mid-1850s, only

---

* Although *The New Zealander* was turned down by Longmans in April 1855, Anthony continued to tinker with it for over a year, and his father-in-law's troubles may have strengthened his anger against institutionalised dishonesty in commercial, public and official life. It is worth noting too that the most popular of Carlyle's *Latter-Day Pamphlets*, 'Hudson's Statue', mocked the greedy sycophants who closed their eyes to Hudson's practices while the dividends poured in, and turned on him when his frauds were revealed.

† George Hudson did not commit suicide. He ended up back in England, living on an annuity subscribed by his old supporters and reminiscing about the good old days in the smoking-room of the Carlton Club.

his pathetic father-in-law was on his mind; and behind him, in the unforgotten past, his own father.

'I sometimes look back, meditating for hours together, on his adverse fate,' wrote Anthony of his father in his autobiography. He was not given to exaggeration. If he said he thought about his father 'for hours together' then it is true. 'The touch of his hand seemed to create failure. . . . His life as I knew it was one long tragedy.'

Anthony's broodings fed his fiction, bleeding into all those suffering, despairing, unhinged older men who recur throughout his work. One can only give a few examples here. John Vavasor, Alice's father in *Can You Forgive Her?*, was like Thomas Anthony Trollope a failed barrister, with a dingy office near Chancery Lane. In *The Belton Estate* Clara's father, Mr Amedroz, was wholly given over to maudlin self-pity. Of Nina's father in *Nina Balatka* Anthony wrote: 'His state was such that no one could say why he should not get up and dress himself, and he himself continued to speak of some future time when he would do so; but there he was, lying in his bed.' In *Ralph the Heir* Sir Thomas Underwood had two pretty daughters at home in his Fulham villa, but hid himself from the pleasure of their company in his Chancery Lane chambers; he had been working on a life of Francis Bacon since he was twenty-five, but as yet had never written a word: 'Those who know the agonies of an ambitious, indolent, doubting, self-accusing man, – and of a man who has a skeleton in his cupboard as to which he can ask for sympathy from no one, – will understand what feelings were at work within the bosom of Sir Thomas Underwood.'

In *Castle Richmond*, written before all these, Sir Thomas Fitzgerald had a guilty secret for which he was being blackmailed. He dosed himself with laudanum, and sat at his table all day with his head on his arms. His malaise was not physical. 'Depression is, I suppose, the name that the doctors would call it,' said Sir Thomas's son Herbert. The doctor was aware 'how impossible it is to administer to a mind diseased. The mind of that poor man was diseased past all curing in the world, and there was nothing left for him but to die.'

Was this not true of Thomas Anthony Trollope, and of Edward Heseltine? The most painful and perceptive study of the perhaps-mad is that of Mr Crawley in *The Last Chronicle of Barset*, first introduced to the reader in *Framley Parsonage* as 'a stern, unpleasant man', which was how Anthony Trollope's father also presented himself. In *He Knew He Was Right*, apropos of the pathologically jealous Louis Trevelyan, Anthony wrote: 'There is perhaps no greater social question so imperfectly understood among us at the present day as that which refers to the line which divides sanity from insanity. . . .' This is what he thought about, when he meditated on his father, and on Rose's.

Now that he was a Surveyor, Anthony made regular trips from Ireland to London on Post Office business. There were new reforms to assimilate. In 1855, after years of debate, the system of entry into all branches of the Civil Service was changed, following a report by Sir Charles Trevelyan and Sir Stafford Northcote.

As Sir Gregory Hardlines (Anthony's alias for Sir Charles Trevelyan) believed in *The Three Clerks*, 'It was too notorious that the Civil Service was filled by the family fools of the aristocracy and middle classes, and that any family who had no fool to send, sent in lieu thereof some invalid past hope. Thus the service had become a hospital for incurables and idiots.' Anthony agreed that not many boys actually chose to go into the Civil Service; they were pushed in by their relatives, but necessarily, since young gentlemen without private money had to have security and an income. Now, however, there were to be stringent and c-ompetitive qualifying examinations.

This was not the democratic measure it seems at first sight, since young men, to pass the examinations, required not only intelligence but a classical, i.e. public school, education. Anthony Trollope, who had benefited from the corrupt old system but knew he was an efficient civil servant, was also a generalist who mistrusted 'experts' and professional elites, and he opposed the new system vociferously in an article in the *Dublin University Magazine* in October 1855, for which he was paid seven guineas. In *The Three Clerks*, which drew on his own experience as a junior clerk in London, he took the opportunity to devote a whole chapter to criticising, in polemical pamphleteering style, the competitive examination system and its instigators. This caused, as he said, 'official offence'.

This was not the only way in which he made himself difficult.

One of his crusades was to improve the quality of official writing; he took 'infinite pains' with his own reports, although never writing a preliminary draft. He thought that a first version conveyed 'the exact feeling' of a situation, and that to recopy and 'improve' on a report made it stilted. His lively efforts were not always appreciated by his superiors. 'I have heard horror expressed because the old forms were disregarded and language used which had no savour of red-tape.'

He even dared to write a memo to Rowland Hill, in answer to one from Hill defining Surveyors' duties, questioning Hill's ambiguities of style. Hill replied: 'You must be aware, Mr Trollope, that a phrase is not always intended to bear a literal construction. For instance, when I write to one of you gentlemen, I end my letter with the words "I am, Sir, your obedient servant", whereas you know I am nothing of the sort.'

With Rowland Hill, Anthony said in his autobiography, 'I never had any sympathy, nor he with me. . . . I have no doubt that I often made myself very disagreeable. I know that I sometimes tried to do so.' This must sometimes have been awkward for John Tilley, who came next in the PO hierarchy after Rowland Hill. It is probable that Rose backed her husband up heartily in all his confrontations with authority: 'Women love a bold front, and a voice that will never own its master to have been beaten in the fight' (*Castle Richmond*). It is equally probable that though he might voice outrage on any matter, whenever he wanted to, he did not like it when she did likewise. 'As a general rule, it is highly desirable that ladies should keep their temper; a woman when she storms always makes herself ugly, and usually ridiculous also. There is nothing so odious to a man as a virago' (*Barchester Towers*). Out of his fear of female dominance, female anger and female contempt had grown the tragi-comic Mrs Proudie, the Bishop of Barchester's wife.

Off-duty in London, Anthony was often at a loose end. It was so long since he had lived there that he knew relatively few people, and had 'no opportunities of becoming acquainted with literary life in London'. There were publishers to see, and John Tilley's house was open to him, and Uncle Henry Milton's widow was still living in Fulham. He joined with his old friend John Merivale in a 'Goose and Glee Club', which gave rise to some schoolboyish letters from Anthony in Ireland packed with mock-Latin puns about the all-male dining-club's motto, rules and procedures, and the unstable lavatory at the proposed venue, which might collapse under his weight: 'I am fast becoming a 15 stone man.' Like Archdeacon Grantly in *Barchester Towers*, 'his frolic humours were of a cumbrous kind'.

Anthony was adamant that recitations should not be part of the club's entertainments: 'No – if once you admit recitations – farewell then to all quiet harmony – farewell the genial song, the easy pipe, the hot tumbler.' Men would not, he told Merivale, come from far and wide to hear 'long stories tamely drawn out'. He always hated to be held captive while someone else had licence to talk; he avoided sitting through speeches, lectures and sermons all his life. 'There is,' he wrote in *Barchester Towers*, 'perhaps, no greater hardship at present inflicted on mankind in civilised and free countries, than the necessity of listening to sermons'; a preacher was 'the bore of the age'. As for the speeches made at the Thornes' sports party in the same book, 'either let all speech-making on festive occasions be utterly tabooed and made as it were impossible; or else let those who are to exercise the privilege be first subjected to a competing examination before the civil service examining commissioners.' He found even a grace before dinner hard to stomach.

It is not known how often the Goose and Glee Club met, but in London in the 1850s Anthony was often alone, like unworldly Mr Harding in *The Warden* up from Barchester to see a grand lawyer. The chapter-heading 'A Long Day in London' says it all. As Mr Harding looked for somewhere to eat lunch Anthony provided a vivid run-down of the unsalubrious eating-houses of the Strand,* and of Mr Harding's awkwardness and embarrassing choices. Mr Harding stayed at the Chapter Hotel and Coffee House† near St Paul's, and dined there alone. Anthony described the experience as one who well knew hotels 'where one plate slowly goes and another slowly comes without a sound; where the two or three guests would as soon think of knocking each other down as of

---

* All of them easily identifiable from man-about-town memoirs of the period.

† An alias for the Pater Noster Coffee House near St Paul's, where Charlotte and Emily Brontë stayed on their first journey to Brussels in 1842; once a fashionable literary meeting-place, but in Victorian days a dim hotel chiefly used by dons and clergymen.

speaking . . . what can be more melancholy than a mutton chop and a pint of port in such a place?'

Anthony (though not his Mr Harding) spent time in the National Gallery, which he called in *The New Zealander* 'a poor erection', criticising the bad lighting and dirty floors in its 'five dark rooms'. It had become 'a place of assignation, a shelter from rain, a spot in which to lounge away an idle ten minutes, a nursery for mothers who are abroad with their infants, a retirement for urban picnics. The place cannot be said to be often crowded, but it is always clear that of those who are there four fifths care nothing for the pictures.'* He preferred the Dulwich gallery, which was virtually unvisited by the public. He admired the new Houses of Parliament, which were nearing completion, doubting whether 'many nobler piles have ever yet been built by the hands of man'. He liked the 'very beautiful' new Treasury building in Whitehall, and the new polychrome brick church by Butterfield in Margaret Street. A bulky fortyish man, he roamed the London streets alone as he had done at twenty.

The year 1856 was the first in which profits from writing appeared in Anthony's accounts. He disposed of his meagre earnings from his fiction with gallantry: 'From Longmans June 29 £9.1.2. To Rose £9.1.2.'

He began *The Three Clerks* in February 1857 and finished it in August the same year, three months after the publication of *Barchester Towers*, for which Longmans, after some personal interventions on Anthony's behalf by John Tilley, gave him an advance of £100 against half-profits.

Barchester Towers had been designed as a standard three-volume novel. Its author, who along with the Grantlys, the Proudies, the Stanhopes, the Bolds and Mr Slope, is present in its pages ('I never could endure to shake hands with Mr Slope. A cold, clammy perspiration always exudes from him. . . .') made it clear in the novel that he found the formula difficult: 'And who can

---

* In view of the controversy in Britain about charging for entry to galleries and museums it is worth noting that Trollope advocated charging entry to the National Gallery on certain days each week, for the benefit of those who wanted to look seriously at the pictures; his undemocratic assumption was that all such people would be able to afford it. It is also worth noting that Mr Harding in *The Warden* had to pay twopence to get into Westminster Abbey 'as a sightseer'.

apportion out and dovetail his incidents, dialogues, characters, and descriptive morsels, so as to fit them all exactly into 462 pages, without either compressing them unnaturally, or extending them artificially at the end of his labour? Do I not myself know that I am at this moment in want of a dozen pages, and that I am sick with cudgelling my brains to find them?'

This playful distancing, 'showing the workings', was not popular with his publisher, but it was a measure of his rejection of all falsehood that he would not pretend that art was not also artefact; and he had, at the same time, an instinctive inhibition against revealing just how intimately 'real' his fantasies were to him. As he finally acknowledged in *The Last Chronicle of Barset*, 'to me Barset has been a real county, and its city a real city, and the spires and towers have been before my eyes, and the voices of the people are known to my ears, and the pavement of the city ways are [sic] familiar to my footsteps.' If any modern readers should doubt this, let them turn back to the chapter entitled 'Barchester by Moonlight' in *Barchester Towers*, in which the geography of the place, like the emotional territory under dispute among the young people sauntering out from the cathedral close, is perfectly understood and completely conveyed.

'In the writing of *Barchester Towers* I took great delight. The bishop and Mrs Proudie were very real to me, as were also the troubles of the archdeacon and the loves of Mr Slope' (*Autobiography*). The critics, unlike the Longmans reader, liked it very much. 'The former tale [*The Warden*] was good, but this is better,' said the *Examiner*. '*The Warden* was a remarkable book; *Barchester Towers* is still more remarkable,' said the *Leader*. '*Barchester Towers* is a very clever book,' said the *Saturday Review* – adding, 'Indeed it is, if anything, too clever. . . .' *The Times* remarked on its unpromisingly ecclesiastical tinge, 'Yet the subject is so fresh and the representation so vivid, that the contracted limits of the story are forgotten, and we are left to wonder that more has not long ago been made of such promising materials.'

Anthony, encouraged, was bullish about *The Three Clerks*, writing to William Longman from Ireland that he expected £200 advance this time, and if his expectation could not be met 'I fear it will hardly be worth while for you to have the MS. read. . . . Of course an unsuccessful novel may be worth much less – worth indeed less than nothing. And it may very likely be that I cannot write a successful novel, but if I cannot obtain moderate success I will give over, and leave the business alone. I certainly will not willingly go on working at such a rate of pay.' As Archdeacon Grantly remarked to Mr Harding in *Barchester Towers*, 'If honest men did not squabble for money, in this wicked world of ours, the dishonest men would get it all; and I do not see that the cause of virtue would be much improved.'

Anthony badly wanted to secure an agreement for *The Three Clerks* before he went off to Italy again with Rose and John Tilley in the autumn of 1857. When in August William Longman made it clear that he would not pay more than £100, the standard sum at the time for unknown authors, Anthony did not even bother to send him the manuscript. William Longman, charming though he was, had not in the event become a personal friend; because Anthony lived in Ireland there was no opportunity for them to get to know one another, and in letters Anthony never got beyond 'My dear Sir' with him.

Anthony desperately wanted to make money out of his novels, and Longman's prestige in the publishing world did not make up for the lack of it. As he wrote in his autobiography, 'I did think much of Messrs Longman's name, but I liked it best at the bottom of a cheque.' Longmans clearly did not think Anthony's probable future sales justified financial risk-taking; they were prepared to write large cheques in certain cases – Macaulay, in the year *The Warden* came out, was handed one for £20,000 for just two volumes of his *History of England*. Anthony may not have known that, nor that Thackeray had received initial payments totalling £1,200 from Smith, Elder for *Henry Esmond* in 1852; but he knew that his mother had been receiving upwards of £500 for a novel, back in 1840.

Anthony, in London just before the departure for Italy, returned to the familiar offices of the late Henry Colburn in Great Marlborough Street, now occupied by Hurst & Blackett, who had taken over Colburn's business. He was kept waiting, and departed. He trudged on to see Richard Bentley in New Burlington Street, and left the manuscript of *The Three Clerks* there while he was away. He agreed to sell the book outright to Bentley for £250 immediately after his return from the third tour with Rose and John Tilley over the Alps – to Como, Milan ('Hotels all full' noted Rose), Verona, Bologna, and by diligence over the

Apennines to Pisa and Florence, where they stayed for three weeks at the Villino Trollope.

Previously his mother had praised him for his unremitting industry: 'Tom and I agree in thinking that you exceed in this respect any individual that we have ever known or heard of – and I am proud of being your mother – as well for this reason as for sundry others.' But now in Florence 'she expressed to me her delight that her labours should be at an end, and that mine should be beginning in the same field' (*Autobiography*). This was gratifying. But Anthony could not resist adding bitterly that his literary labours had been proceeding already for a dozen years – 'but a man's career will generally be held to date from the commencement of his success'.

His earnings in 1857 were £793 gross (i.e., including travel allowances and expenses) from the Post Office, and £359 from the novels. His solid, undisputed success was established with his next book, *Doctor Thorne*, the third in the Barsetshire saga.

In Florence he was, as he put it in his autobiography, 'cudgelling my brain for a new plot', and it was Tom who sketched out the idea of *Doctor Thorne*. 'I mention this particularly, because it was the only occasion in which I have had recourse to some other source than my own brains for the thread of a story.' As the *Athenaeum* said in its review of *Barchester Towers*, 'Mr Trollope has a happier art of drawing sketches from life, and striking off pungent sayings hot and vivid upon the page, than of elaborating the action of a novel.' Characters and conversations proliferated in Anthony's imagination much more readily than plots, but his understanding of the importance of structure may best be expressed by borrowing from *Barchester Towers* his description of Mrs Stanhope's dress-sense: 'She well knew the architectural secret of decorating her construction, and never descended to construct a decoration.'

He began writing *Doctor Thorne* in Ireland in October 1857. Tom's plot centred on the predicament of a proud and lovely girl born out of wedlock. Mary Thorne was the daughter of a gentleman – the doctor's brother – and of an apprentice bonnet-maker. Railway speculation was still on Anthony's mind. The bonnet-maker's alcoholic brother Roger Scatcherd, who played a central part, had made a vast fortune as a contractor, having 'latterly had in his hands whole lines of railway'. Doctor Thorne reared his niece Mary to young womanhood and loved her deeply, but 'what man would marry this bastard child, without a sixpence, and bring not only poverty, but ill blood also on his own children?'

Within the context of a quiet village fifteen miles from Barchester, murder, delirium tremens, the corruption of party politics, and the cynicism of well-born ladies and gentlemen hunting one another down for loveless lawful wedlock ('instead of heart beating to heart in sympathetic unison, purse chinks to purse') form the background to Mary Thorne's discovery not only of the true love of Frank Gresham, the son of the big house, but of a convenient personal fortune. Yet even at her humblest, when most conscious of her illegitimacy and poverty, Mary Thorne's attitude to the Gresham family was spiked with anger and irony: 'If I humble myself very low; if I kneel through the whole evening in a corner; if I put my neck down and let all your cousins trample on it, and then your aunt, would not that make atonement? I would not object to wearing sackcloth, either; and I'd eat a little ashes – or, at any rate, I'd try.'

Anthony had only written the first eleven chapters of his story about this spirited heroine and her uncle Doctor Thorne when he was picked to go on a Post Office mission to Egypt.

He was sent to find out whether bags or metal boxes were more suitable for sending mail across Egypt and, more importantly, to negotiate with Nubar Bey* the use of Egyptian railroads, instead of camels, for British mail bound for India and Australia. He left Dublin in January 1858 and while being briefed in London tried to fix publication terms for *Doctor Thorne* with Richard Bentley. He asked for £400 this time. Bentley agreed, and then retracted, on the grounds that sales of *The Three Clerks* did not justify paying more than £300.

'I was intent upon the larger sum; and in furious haste, – for I had but an hour at my disposal, – I rushed to Chapman & Hall in Piccadilly, and said what I had to say to Mr Edward Chapman in a quick torrent of words.' The astonished Chapman agreed to

* Nubar Bey (1825–99): diplomat and civil servant, ten years younger than Anthony, he was in charge of transport between Egypt and India. He was instrumental in completing the rail-link between Cairo and Suez and, later, the Suez Canal. As Nubar Pasha he was to be three times Premier of Egypt.

Anthony's terms. 'I remember that he held the poker in his hand all the time that I was with him; – but in truth, even though he had declined to buy the book, there would have been no danger' (*Autobiography*). Edward Chapman, in his mid-fifties, was co-founder of the firm that owed its prosperity to that of Charles Dickens; Chapman & Hall had been the first publishers of *Pickwick Papers*, and were still Dickens's main publishers. They looked after their star author well, subsidising his sabbaticals and at times paying him a weekly salary as well as four-figure advances on his novels.

By the time Anthony burst in upon him in the back office at 193 Piccadilly, Edward Chapman was growing tired. His original partner William Hall had died, and Edward was giving more responsibility to his cousin Frederic, twenty years younger. It seems clear that Anthony liked the Chapmans, but they remain dim as personalities; perhaps that is why he managed to remain on good terms with them. The association with Chapman & Hall begun so impetuously on a cold January day in 1858 was to last until Anthony's death.

Having signed the agreement for *Doctor Thorne* with Chapman & Hall, Anthony started on his journey, stopping off in Paris where he met Tom. Anthony might be counting his literary earnings now in hundreds, but Tom had a greater windfall without turning a hand. Theodosia's father had recently died. 'It seems that Tom will get nearly £3000 by Garrow's death,' Anthony wrote to Rose from Paris, 'and as this £3000 is all over & above what he expected, it ought to relieve him from all his embarrassments. . . .' Mrs Trollope was no longer contributing to the household by her writing; Tom had overspent on the Villino Trollope, and had been planning to sell it. He had some of its exotic contents – 'a great heap of their things', as Anthony put it – with him in Paris, to be put in a sale. (Tom was becoming something of a dealer.)

Rose, at home in Seaview Terrace, was copying out the beginning of *Doctor Thorne*. 'You must of course be careful about the reading,' he told her, 'and also alter any words which seem to be too often repeated.' 'Do not be dismal if you can help it – I feel a little that way inclined, but hard work will I know keep it off.' Anthony had to do five pages of the book every day or he would not keep his deadline. 'As I journeyed across France to Marseilles, and made thence a terribly rough voyage to Alexandria, I wrote my allotted number of pages every day.' More than once, he said, he hurriedly left his papers on a cabin table, 'rushing away to be sick in the privacy of my state room'.

He was abroad from the beginning of February 1858 until mid-May. He sent in full reports on the postal situation and his dealings with tricky, charming Nubar Bey to Rowland Hill and his younger brother Frederic Hill (who, in the old unreconstructed tradition of nepotism, was Assistant Secretary at the PO); he also heard howling dervishes, visited the Pyramids and spent ten days on holiday in the Holy Land before returning home via Malta, Gibraltar and Spain, where he spent a week. This trip gave him material for a spate of short stories. Meanwhile, he finished *Doctor Thorne* in Egypt on 31 March, and on 1 April began writing *The Bertrams*.

The man who travels alone 'is not, I think, to be envied'. It was only tolerable if one had a job to do, 'even a teapot to convey' (*Travelling Sketches*). Anthony had a job to do; but sightseeing and staying in foreign hotels alone, without Rose, was a new experience, and an important one. He had to overcome what he called, in his story 'George Walker at Suez', 'that terrible British exclusiveness, that *noli me tangere* with which an Englishman arms himself, and in which he thinks it necessary to envelop his wife'. At the *table d'hôte*, the large table where all sat who did not dine in their hotel rooms, he had to talk to whoever he sat next to. 'But it certainly does seem to be happily arranged by Providence that the musty fusty people, and the nicy spicy people, and the witty pretty people do severally assemble and get together as they ought to' (*The Bertrams*).

Being alone changed the angle of his relations with the women he met, and how he looked at them – especially women travelling without a husband or chaperone. 'When you have been up the Great Pyramid with a lady,' he wrote in *The Bertrams*, 'the chances are you know more about her than you would do from a year's acquaintance fostered by a dozen London parties.' He wrote a short story, 'An Unprotected Female at the Pyramids', about a Miss Dawkins, exemplar of a type 'setting itself up as it were in opposition to the old-world idea that women, like green peas, cannot come to perfection without supporting-sticks'. The authorial tone is wary, chiefly because in spite of her vaunted independence Miss Dawkins had 'a strong inclination to use the arms and legs of other people when she could make them serviceable'. She was, in short, a sponger and a bore.

This was the old, i.e., the young, Trollope speaking. Solitary travel was to change his ideas. A couple of years later he wrote another story, 'A Ride Across Palestine', in which the narrator Mr Jones made a long horseback excursion from Jerusalem to the Wilderness of the Gospels in company with Mr Smith, an attractive, shy young man. The two rode and ate and slept on the way in a companionable and pleasing intimacy. 'I thoroughly hate an effeminate man; but, in spite of a certain womanly softness about this fellow, I could not hate him,' mused Jones the narrator. Young Smith asked Jones if he was married. 'Now the fact is, that I am a married man with a family; but I am not much given to talk to strangers about my domestic concerns, and therefore, though I had no particular object in view, I denied my obligations in that respect.' (Did Anthony sometimes do that too? Probably.)

This story is loaded with sexual ambiguity. Jones was at pains to point out that he was a ladies' man – and that it was Smith's feminine helplessness that appealed to him. 'A man, as a rule, has an amount of energy within him which he cannot turn to profit on himself alone. It is good for him to have a woman by him that he may work for her, and thus have exercise for his limbs and faculties. I am very fond of women. But I always like best those who are most helpless.'

Anthony, unlike his Mr Jones, was just beginning to perceive the attraction of women who were not helpless. In *Travelling Sketches* which he published in book form in 1866 he included a piece about 'The Unprotected Female Tourist', and she clearly attracted him a great deal. 'You find yourself talking to her of your mother, your sister, or your friend, – but not of your wife or sweetheart. . . . You find her to be very clever, and then think her to be very pretty; and if, – which may probably be the case, – you are in such matters a fool, you may say a word or two more than you ought to do, and the unprotected female shows you that she can protect herself.'

At the end of 'A Ride Across Palestine' Smith was revealed as a pretty girl in disguise. 'I confess,' said Jones, 'that the mistress of my bosom, had she known my thoughts at that moment, might have had cause for anger.' The mistress of Anthony's bosom was

never more distanced from him, figuratively as well as geographically speaking, than in 1858 and 1859. There is more frank
sensual appraisal of female attractiveness in *The Bertrams* than in
any of his previous novels – a Jewish girl glimpsed washing
clothes, and Caroline Waddington with the 'daring eyes', whom
the hero met with her aunt in a Jerusalem hotel: her full bust had
'that ease and grace . . . of which tight-lace stays are so utterly
subversive', and her mouth was all 'enticing curves and ruby
colour'. It was Caroline's free and graceful walk that provoked the
wildest authorial outburst: 'Alas! how few women can walk! . . .
They scuffle, they trip, they trot, they amble, they waddle, they
crawl, they drag themselves on painfully, as though the flounces
and furbelows around them were a burden too heavy for easy,
graceful motion; but, except in Spain, they rarely walk.'

In his fiction he always contrived to make it known to the
reader whether a young woman's bust was full or flat, and he
made it equally clear that his preference was for the former. In the
matter of women's walk, he became a connoisseur. He admired a
free, athletic step. The eponymous heroine of *Rachel Ray*, for
example, tall and fair, walked 'as though the motion were
pleasant to her, and easy, – as though the very act of walking were
a pleasure'. He noticed with distaste little American girls who
affected what he called the 'dorsal wriggle'. The 'dorsal wriggle'
was also to be seen, he wrote, 'on the boulevards in Paris. It is to
be seen more often in second rate French towns, and among fourth
rate French women. Of all signs in women betokening vulgarity,
bad taste, and aptitude to bad morals, it is the surest' (*North
America*).

He was both repelled and attracted by such blatant sexual
invitation. Of Jewish Rebecca, in *Nina Balatka*, for example: 'You
would think that if you were permitted to embrace her, the
outlines of her body would form themselves to yours, as though
she would in all things fit herself to him who might be blessed with
her love.' But Rebecca was bold-eyed and flashily dressed; hers
was 'a repellent beauty that seemed to disdain while it courted
admiration, and utterly rejected the idea of that caressing
assistance which men always love to give, and which women often
love to receive.' Thus he continually fell back on an ideal of
feminine helplessness, which flattered his sense of manliness and
did not challenge what he understood to be man's chief claim to

attraction: 'After all, power and will are the gifts which a woman most loves in a man,' he wrote in *The Bertrams*.

Anthony, full of exotic new experiences and accustomed to write about what was in his mind, strove vainly to avoid travelogue: 'I will not take my readers up the Nile; nor will I even take them up a pyramid,' he promised in *The Bertrams*. 'For do not fitting books for such purposes abound at Mr Mudie's?' Nevertheless he included in *The Bertrams* pages of description better suited to a travel book than to a novel, in which the observer is patently none other than the author, and within which his characters exist in suspension, sustained by a seemingly self-generated fictional reality. Travelogue was inevitable. As he wrote on his work-sheet for *The Bertrams*, the book was 'Begun in Egypt, and written in the Mediterranean, in Malta, Gibraltar, England, Ireland, Scotland, and finished in the West Indies.'

It was from *Barchester Towers* onwards that he drew up on lined quarto paper his much-folded, grubby work-sheets – charts divided into weeks in which he entered, day by day, the number of completed pages. The number depended on the demands of his PO work, his family life and his health ('BAD FOOT' he wrote across a non-writing week during *The Three Clerks*), and varied between 20 and 112 a week. 'And as a page is an ambiguous term, my page has been made to contain 250 words; and as words, if not watched, have a tendency to straggle, I have had every word counted as I went.' This method allowed for no waiting on inspiration. 'To me it would not be more absurd if the shoemaker were to wait for inspiration, or the tallow-chandler for the divine moment of melting' (*Autobiography*).

Anthony Trollope's fluent, regular output, and all this page-counting and word-counting, may seem idiosyncratic, but he was merely behaving professionally; the standard three-volume post-octavo novel had so many words to a line and so many lines to a page. In publishers' agreements, the phrase 'the usual number of pages' was regularly used, as if a novel were a product quantitatively understood, like a pound of sugar.

He was sincere in his contempt for the notion of waiting for inspiration, and in his often repeated comparison of writing with the prosaic craft of shoemaking. He was not unique in this. Both Thackeray and Dickens described themselves as writers in 'tradesman' terms. But it was only half the story. Anthony Trollope needed to write as he needed to eat. Like the day-dreaming of his youth, writing was an addiction. He himself compared it to drinking and gambling. Unlike gambling, to which writing has certain affinities, it was beginning to pay regular dividends.

Just how much psychological solace the fantasy life of his novels afforded him cannot be calculated. In his life of Cicero he questioned Cicero's assertion that he found no cure for grief in writing. 'In that he was wrong. He could find no cure for his grief; but he did know that continued occupation would relieve him, and therefore he occupied himself continually. . . . By doing so he did contrive not to break his heart.'

Doctor Thorne sold 700 copies almost at once. This was respectable if not world-shattering; but this novel represented the break-through because, as the review in the *Leader* put it, Trollope was now 'among the extremely select few who shine out like a constellation among the unnumbered lesser luminaries of the "circulating" firmament'. He had become popular – though already the critics were raising their eyebrows at the rapidity of his output, and a certain resulting carelessness.

'The "circulating" firmament' was a reference to the circulat-ing libraries, and in particular to Mudie's Select Library, without whose support no novelist or publisher could hope to make a living. If a book were not taken by Mudie's it was as good as dead. A listing in Mudie's catalogue was the only publicity worth having. Mudie's ordered huge numbers of books judged to be popular, and publishers' print-runs were determined by Mudie's order. New three- or four-volume novels were not always announced as being for sale but as being available in the libraries. This was because their usual sale-price was £1.10.6, which was very expensive, so relatively few were sold.

Charles Edward Mudie, a Scot, was only three years older than Anthony. There were other lending libraries, but none so successful as Mudie's. He began lending books from his stationery shop in Bloomsbury in 1842, exploiting the growing rail network, which allowed him to send books – with their bright yellow labels and Pegasus symbol – into middle- and upper-class homes deep in the country. Provincial families depended entirely for reading-matter on the continuous exchange of brass-bound boxes of books from Mudie's, and when they visited one another, they recognised the familiar yellow-labelled books on their friends' tables, which gave a sense of a reading community.

This might not always, however, be quite convenient. Mr Abel Wharton QC, in *The Prime Minister*, secretly read poetry and novels 'and even fairy stories' in his chambers, and attempted to conceal 'Mr Mudie's suspicious ticket' when predatory Ferdinand Lopez called on him. 'Barristers certainly never get their law books from Mudie, and Lopez at once knew that his hoped-for father-in-law had been reading a novel.'

The subscription was a guinea a year for one volume at a time, two guineas a year for four at a time. Until the end of Anthony's life, not to subscribe, for a middle-class family, was to lack an essential amenity. When in *Ayala's Angel* (written 1878) the orphaned Lucy Dormer had to go and live in comparative poverty with her Aunt and Uncle Dossett in 'a genteel house in Notting Hill' she was dismayed to find that Aunt Dossett did not subscribe. 'That Mudie's unnumbered volumes should come into the house as they were wanted had been almost as much a provision of nature as water, gas, and hot rolls for breakfast.'

In London, you could go into his establishment and change your own books; collections and deliveries were also made by Mudie's carts. The emphasis was on new books, and the key-word was 'Select'. Mudie did not stock rubbish. He guaranteed a public to serious writers such as George Eliot, as well as meeting the demand for romance and 'sensation' fiction. ('I don't subscribe to Mudie's,' complained Lady Linlithgow in *The Eustace Diamonds*, 'because whenever I asked for "Adam Bede", they always sent me the "Bandit Chief".')

Mudie stocked not only novels but books in almost every genre (except law books, as Ferdinand Lopez knew) and even periodicals. He was a religious man; some books were excluded for moral reasons, since everything had to be suitable for family reading. This did not exactly force the more ambitious novelists, such as Anthony, to exercise self-censorship, but compelled them to convey matter unsuitable for a sixteen-year-old vicar's daughter in such a way that it passed not only over her head but over the head of an innocent or shockable reader of any age or sex.

This took considerable ingenuity, and Anthony became very skilled at it.

High, fixed book-prices were good for the lending libraries. But in 1852 the Net Book Agreement was overthrown, producing a 'free trade' situation and allowing retailers to undercut prices. Most leading authors, including Dickens and Carlyle, publicly supported the change. (In 1852 Anthony was still virtually unknown, and not consulted.) In the event, it made absolutely no difference to Mudie, who in the same year moved to new and larger premises on the corner of New Oxford Street and Museum Street; and by 1858, when *Doctor Thorne* came out, he had 100,000 volumes in stock.*

Anthony Trollope was now a star of Mudie's solar system.

---

* Since Mudie charged by volume, he discouraged single-volume novels, and was largely responsible for the continuation of the convention for multi-volume novels and histories. This was burdensome in more ways than one. The 2,500 copies each of volumes 4 and 5 of Macaulay's *History of England* which Mudie ordered in 1855 weighed eight tons.

CHAPTER ELEVEN

ROSE met Anthony in London when he returned from his trip abroad in May 1858. They went off together to Ollerton, a village in Sherwood Forest south-east of Rotherham – Rose's part of the country, and probably the holiday of her choice. They travelled on to Scotland. Anthony's leave ended on 10 June, the day before their fourteenth wedding anniversary; Rose left him to return to Ireland, and he embarked on Post Office duties in Glasgow.

Doctor Thorne was doing well, but now he had a disappointment. Edward Chapman turned down his short novel *The Struggles of Brown, Jones, and Robinson*, which had already been rejected by Longman before he joined Chapman & Hall. The book was intended as 'a hit at the present system of advertising', but apparently failed to reach its mark.* This dreary period in Glasgow was when he wrote those unsatisfactory love scenes in *The Bertrams*, including the well-meaning reference to his and Rose's wedding date.

He made a brief return to Ireland at the end of June, but the Trollopes continued to be separated for most of the time during what was a famously hot summer. The reorganisation of the Scottish postal deliveries was so arduous that Anthony was separated from his writing as well; he wrote 'Ah me!' forty-three times that summer in the blank spaces in his work-sheet where each day's page-count should have been entered. The only

---

* What was wrong with *The Struggles . . .* was that while the 'hit at the present system of advertising' was fine, the story in which it was embedded was feeble. But the book is worth reading – first, for Trollope's comic skill in parodying contemporary copy-writing and outrageous publicity campaigns, and second, for his knowing evocation of the hideously 'modern' haberdashery shop, all plate-glass, magenta paintwork, and arched wrought-iron supports (also magenta) with slogans painted on them. Rose's input is to be discerned in the details of items for sale and their prices. Bad fiction provides nuggets of social history unobtainable elsewhere.

literary chore he accomplished was to abridge *The Three Clerks* for
a cheap one-volume edition.

His 'bachelor' life was destined to continue. At home in Dublin at
last that autumn (1858), 'I was asked to go to the West Indies, and
cleanse the Augean stables of our Post Office system there.' He
was to go on to Cuba and thence to Panama, to negotiate postal
treaties with the authorities.*

He was in London being briefed for the first two weeks of
November and was present when John Tilley, in the chair,
launched 'at great length' the Post Office Library and Literary
Association at a big meeting in the Returned Letter Room at St
Martin's-le-Grand on 6 November.† Anthony seconded the
resolution by default. It should have been a Mr Potter, but he
wasn't there. Frederic Hill spoke, also at length, and prominent
were two younger officials whose careers and personalities were to
impinge on Anthony's: Frank Scudamore‡ and Edmund Yates,
both of whom had literary talents themselves.

The meeting started at two in the afternoon and went on till the
late evening. Apart from the speeches, a long list was read of books
donated or promised; as Anthony said ruefully in his speech, 'I
thought the titles of all the books printed and published within the
last three centuries were going to be read out.' Having had no time
to prepare his address he spoke briefly, which pleased his
audience, and what he said was informal and jolly. He stressed the
socially cohesive function of the library and not, as did Tilley and
Hill, the value to be derived from reading good books. The

---

* International mails were governed by individual treaties negotiated between
the postal authorities of each country. As the volume of mail and choice of transport
increased, this led to a hopelessly confused multiplication of arrangements.
Anthony's missions abroad took place at the peak of this proliferating complexity: in
May 1863 delegates of fifteen states met in Paris for the first of several international
Postal Conferences, culminating in the establishment of a General Postal Union in
1875.

† The library was opened on 3 January 1859, with more than 2,000 books.
Charles Dickens, solicited by his young friend Edmund Yates, sent seventeen
volumes of the magazine he edited, *Household Words*, W. H. Smith & Son donated 300
volumes. *The Times* sent each day's paper free, and other periodicals followed suit.
Prince Albert lent his support. The annual subscription for PO employees was 12
shillings p.a., which included the right to one volume at a time from Mudie's Library.

‡ Frank Scudamore (1832–84) was a small, eager man who had organised the PO
Savings Bank; he became Assistant Secretary to the PO in 1863.

Reading Room, he said, 'should partake of the nature of a club. . . . There should be a very strong *esprit de corps*. "Money Orders" should know "Circulations", and "Circulations" should know "Secretaries". We should all know each other. . . .' He expressed the hope that the 'club' would be comfortable: 'You have all been sitting long on deal benches. I hope we shall get by degrees something better than deal boards – chairs with comfortable arms – a well-furnished room. We deserve it.'

Edmund Yates then made some courteous remarks about Tilley being the ideal chairman, not only by reason of seniority and distinction 'but in consequence of his intimate connection with literature'. He was referring to Tilley's relationship by marriage to 'a lady whose name is known throughout the length and breadth of the kingdom, and whose son is as great an ornament to the literary profession as he is to the department to which we all belong'. This was rather a backhanded compliment to Anthony; and the official who reported the meeting for the house magazine referred, as to a well-known fact, to Tilley's 'aversion to officers of the Department engaging in literary pursuits' – an interesting sidelight on Tilley which may have some bearing on why Anthony's PO career had not moved along faster than it did.

Ten days later Anthony set sail from Southampton, reaching the island of St Thomas on 2 December. On landing, a lady in pink gloves gave him a rose: 'That's for love, dear.'

He finished *The Bertrams* at long last in the West Indies on 20 December. On 25 January he wrote the first sentences of the best and liveliest of his travel books, *The West Indies and the Spanish Main*: 'I am beginning to write this book on board the brig —, trading between Kingston, in Jamaica, and Cien Fuegos, on the southern coast of Cuba. At the present moment there is not a puff of wind. . . .'

The *Linwood*, under sail not steam ('Flap, flap, flap! roll, roll, roll!'), was carrying salt fish, and the stench pervaded his cabin: 'Ugh!' The calm kept the boat rolling around in a stationary position for days, and the exasperated Anthony wrote in his travel diary:

[Jan] 26: At Sea – in the Linwood.
      27: At Sea Ditto – alas!
      28 At Sea Ditto Alas Alas!!
      29 At Sea Ditto Alas Alas Alas!!!
      30 At Sea   Alas alas alas alas!!!!
      31 At Sea   Alas alas alas alas alas!!!!!
Feb 1 At Sea   (on the rocks, rather), alas

The next day they docked in Cien Fuegos. Anthony was not impressed by Cuba, 'a slave economy' and ripe, he felt, for annexation by the USA. What he did admire was the way the Cuban women walked – 'but for travelling en garçon,* I should probably prefer the south of Spain'.

In the West Indies† and throughout this trip Anthony conspicuously enjoyed 'travelling en garçon'. His artlessness on the subject, in his book, verged on the artful. 'There is a feminine accomplishment so much in vogue among the ladies of the West Indies, one practised there with a success so specially brilliant, as to make it deserving of special notice.' This was 'the science of flirting'; the girls there flirted 'not only with the utmost skill, but with the utmost innocence also'. His imagery is that of deep waters – he was 'sucked in as my steps unconsciously strayed near the dangerous margin. . . . I have found myself choking in those Charybdis waters, have glanced into the Circe cave. I have been seen in my insane struggles. But what shame of that?'

He described evenings on Jamaican verandahs, under the stars: 'How beautiful a woman looks by their light, how sweet the air smells. . . .' He became accustomed to 'quick dances and long drinks'. Later, climbing a mountain in Costa Rica, an English-woman in the party told him the story of her marriage 'with that sudden intimacy which springs up with more than tropical celerity in such places'. Apart from the intrinsic interest of these sudden intimacies, they enlarged his understanding of how

---

* *En garçon*: without a wife or a lady companion.

† His itinerary on this trip included St Thomas, Jamaica, Cuba, the Windward Islands, Barbados, Grenada, Trinidad, British Guiana, Santa Marta, Colon, Costa Rica, Greytown, Bermuda; and New York and Niagara Falls. He gives an account of all these places in *The West Indies*, complete with administrative and economic facts, plus statistics – even though, as he said in the book, 'I utterly disbelieve in statistics as a science. . . . Figures, when they go beyond six in number, represent to me not facts, but dreams, or sometimes worse than dreams.'

Page from Anthony's travel diary and account book, written in exasperation when becalmed on the *Linwood* between Jamaica and Cuba at the end of January 1859.

women thought, felt and talked, and excited his novelist's imagination.

Anthony was nearly forty-four. 'I am not a very young man; and my friends have told me that I show strongly that steady married appearance of a paterfamilias which is so apt to lend assurance to maiden timidity.' The maiden in question told him all her sorrows, and 'I took her hand in mine . . .' (*West Indies*). Anthony was discovering that women were more accessible than he had believed. Middle age brought ease, and a renewal of an adolescent kind of susceptibility.

'There are words which a man cannot resist from a woman, even though he knows them to be false' (*Is He Popenjoy?*). What he called in *The Last Chronicle of Barset* 'the amusement of pretending to be in love' never ceased to interest him, whether the participants were married (to other people) or single. Sometimes, in his novels, flirting was a game of skill, with acknowledged rules; sometimes it was playing with real fire; sometimes it was the shabby pastime of a bored or destructive person. Adelaide Palliser, in *Phineas Redux*, defined flirting as 'the excitement of love, without its reality, and without its ordinary result in marriage'. Herself longing to secure in marriage the passionless Gerard Maule, she shrewdly identified a subtler kind of emotional fraudulence – 'playing at caring for each other'. This, as she said, had none of the excitement of flirting, 'but it often leads to the result [marriage], and sometimes ends in downright affection.' The comment was Adelaide's; the perception, and the shrewdness of it, can only be her creator's.

The seductive women on the verandahs were the wives and daughters of Europeans. The point about the pink-gloved woman on the quay and the troubled girl whose hand he held was that they were black. Anthony had never been in contact with black people before, and much of his West Indies book was concerned with working out his attitudes. The slaves on the sugar plantations had been freed twenty-five years earlier, which, along with the ending of trade protection, put an end to the princely incomes of the British sugar planters. Jamaica was no longer prosperous; Kingston was 'like the city of the dead'. Half the estates had reverted to bush, and the planters who remained clung to a reduced version of their old way of life. Anthony complained that he was given bad English food, mostly out of tins, instead of fresh local produce.

The black population, once freed, worked for what they needed but not more. Anthony was amazed by their lack of financial greed. 'At home, in England, one is apt to think that an extra shilling will go a long way with boots and chambermaid, and produce hotter water, more copious towels, and quicker attendance than is necessary.' It did not follow, in the West Indies.* Nor did the black servants respond to his peremptory orders. They took offence. Only when Anthony spoke with what he intended as heavily ironic courtesy did he get his bath filled. He did not know what to make of this innate self-respect. He was impressed; but it threatened the hierarchical philosophy which was part of his being.

His reactions tell us, in fact, as much about British social structure in the mid-century as about Jamaicans. 'There will be those who will say that I had received a good lesson; and perhaps I had. But it would be rather cumbersome if we were forced to treat our juvenile servants at home in this manner – or even those who were not juvenile.' The carefully trivial phrase 'rather cumbersome' deflects the argument from its proper seriousness.

He was always against slavery, but he thought it would take a very long time before black people would be the equal of whites. (He was well aware that those he called 'philanthropists' in England would disagree with him, and would resent his remarks.) The black man was a man and a brother, 'but he is the very idlest brother with which a hardworking workman was ever cursed'. He thought even the Christianity of the blacks was dubious, since they did not seem to apply its doctrines to their lives.

What he really meant was, they did not value either work or the accumulation of money for its own sake. The concepts of Christianity and of civilisation, and the right to vote and to legislate for oneself and others, were inextricably bound up for Anthony Trollope with the work ethic. On this trip, his responses

* Anthony, who put a high emotional value on money, was capable of gross insensitivity, mistaking disinterested kindness for venal servility. Crossing the Isthmus of Panama by road ('Mud, mud; mud, mud!') his party was given a meal, and fruit to take on their way, by an obviously poor German; on leaving, Anthony proffered him a dollar. His host 'let the dollar fall to the ground, and that with some anger in his face. The sum was made up of the small silver change of the country, and I felt rather little as I stooped under the hot sun to pick it up from the mud of the garden. . . . It is often hard for a traveller to know when he is wished to pay, and when he is wished not to pay' (*West Indies*).

were raw and instinctive. A decade or so later, writing about the Maoris, he stated his view as dogma: 'The desire of accumulating property, combined with the industry necessary for doing so, is perhaps of all qualifications for civilization the most essential' (*Australia and New Zealand*).

Only it wasn't as simple as that, and he knew it. There were many aspects of the civilising process of 'accumulation' which disgusted him. *The Struggles of Brown, Jones, and Robinson*, for example, mocked the great god Commerce: 'Thou civilizest, hast civilized, and wilt civilize. Civilization is thy mission. . . .' And this god's one commandment was, 'Buy in the cheapest market and sell in the dearest.' Anthony's own relationship with money was profound and complicated, resulting in the heightened tension with which he dwelt upon the making, keeping, losing, and final disposal of the stuff.

The resolution of this tension, reached for again and again, concerns the redeeming quality of work – the authentic investment of the self. A man who makes and sells a new kind of shirt, he wrote in *The Struggles. . .* , adds to the world's riches as well as his own. But if he only claims it is a new kind of shirt, when it has just been bought from the wholesaler down the road and given a new label, he adds nothing. (It's good to be honest and true.)

Another characteristic quality that baffled him about the West Indians was their elegance. 'In England, among our housemaids and even haymakers, crinoline, false flowers, long waists, and flowing sleeves have become common; but they do not wear their finery as though they were at home in it. There is generally with them, when in their Sunday best, something of the hog in armour.' (Again, we learn more about England here than about the West Indies.) With the black women there was none of this. They walked proudly, they had good figures, they had a natural skill with colours and materials. Anthony was impressed, attracted, repelled; and as always when baffled, he pontificated.

He was not a visionary. He was unable, generally, to imagine what might lie beyond his own horizons.* Yet he can never be dismissed, or hailed, as a typical Victorian. In his unqualified

---

* In *The West Indies*, for example: 'All mankind has heard much of M. Lesseps and his Suez canal. . . . I have a very strong opinion that such canal [sic] will not and cannot be made.' He held the same very strong opinion about the unlikeliness of the projected Panama Canal.

distaste for the idea of Empire he is nearer to us than to the generation that came after him. Though he deplored Peel's betrayal of the sugar planters of the West Indies by removing trade protection, he saw no virtue in retaining British control of the region. Some people, he wrote, might find this view un- patriotic, and 'one would then be driven back to ask whether patriotism be a virtue'. He conceded that we might still be sending out colonial governors 'to support the dignity of the throne of Queen Victoria's great-grandchild's grandchild. . . . To my thinking, it would be more for our honour that it should not be so.'

There were, he wrote, men 'mad enough to regret [the independence of] the United States', and many men 'mad enough to look forward with anything but composure to the inevitable, happily inevitable day, when Australia shall follow in the same path.' Unlike many of his contemporaries, he never deviated from his anti-imperialism, which he frequently restated in print. His imagery was that of a parent allowing her adult children – the colonies – to lead their own lives. He wrote in *South Africa* of the 'unnatural extension of our colonization', and said that 'the important person in South Africa is the Kafir and the Zulu, the Bechuana and the Hottentot; not the Dutchman or the Englishman.'

He allowed that some strategic spots in the world might be retained for security reasons – Malta, Gibraltar – and he made one big exception to his general theory: Ireland. For him, it was an integral part of Great Britain. He rejected the idea of Home Rule. He found justifications for this, but at root the reason was sentimental. He had invested years of his life in Ireland. His children had been born there. He was British. Ireland was 'his'. So Ireland was British.

Anthony undertook travelling with the same ferocious energy that he undertook writing a book or negotiating a postal treaty. He was extremely conscientious – knowing, for example, in New Zealand in 1872, that because he had not had time to see the west coast of South Island 'to my dying day the conviction will haunt me that when in New Zealand I did not see the one thing best worth seeing in the colony'. He was an anxious traveller, writing in the West Indies that 'the things which really occupy the mind' were 'Where shall I sleep? Is there anything to eat? Can I have my clothes washed?'

Some of the excursions he made were purgatorial. In Jamaica he climbed Blue Mountain Peak with six companions and a lot of rum. The weather was wet. At the summit, in a hut, they ate 'one of those wretched repasts in which the collops of food slip down, and get sat upon; in which the salt is blown away and the bread saturated in beer. . . . I was bound to be jolly, as my companion* had come there merely for my sake.'

He was bothered by the heat and by the mosquitoes. The ordinary kit of the travelling Englishman, according to Anthony, was 'a portmanteau, bag, desk,† and hat-box'. He hated to go without his daily cold tub. In Georgetown, British Guiana, the black chambermaid would not put down his bath, which she carried on her head full of water, till she had curtseyed to him. To open his door for her he leaped out of bed 'in my deshabille' and with British modesty hid crouching behind the door; but she looked about for him till she spotted him and, unembarrassed, performed her curtsey.

His clothes posed the worst problem. 'Oh, those weary clothes! If a man could travel as a dog, how delightful it would be to keep moving from year's end to year's end.' In Panama he bought 'a light straw hat, with an amazing brim' and draped it in white calico against the mosquitoes; in Costa Rica, where he rode for five hours at a stretch on mule-back, he wore 'short canvas smock-frocks, which would not come below the saddle, and coarse holland trousers'.

From Bermuda he sailed to New York 'in company with a rather large assortment of potatoes and onions'. He went north in mid-June (1859) to Albany and the Niagara Falls, where he was persuaded to 'put myself into a filthy oil-skin dress, hat, coat and trousers, in order that I might be conducted under the Falls'.

Once behind the wall of water he was as overwhelmed as his mother had been nearly thirty years earlier, and wrote a passionate passage about his feelings. 'Oh, my friend, let there be no one there to speak to thee then; no, not even a heart's brother. As you stand there speak only to the waters.' It was an experience

---

* Companion in the singular – because the other five were black, carrying the equipment.

† Desk in the sense of a portable sloping board, like the one he used on trains at home; sometimes the board formed the lid of a shallow box for papers.

of religious intensity, and he was to use his account of it again. 'On the United States I should like to write a volume,' he wrote on this occasion. In the event, he was to write two.

He returned to New York via Montreal and Saratoga Springs. He had been away from home for six months, fulfilled his postal missions, gained exotic material for short stories and produced a travel book which earned him £250, writing it as he went along. The money was not great, but 'the view I took of the relative position in the West Indies of black men and white men was the view of *The Times* newspaper at that period; and there appeared three articles in that journal, one closely after the other, which made the fortune of the book. Had it been very bad, I suppose its fortune could not have been made for it even by *The Times* newspaper' (*Autobiography*).

Anthony sailed home to Liverpool on the Royal Mail steamship *Africa*: 'And on board this most comfortable of vessels I have now finished my book, as I began it on that one, of all the most uncomfortable, which carried me from Kingston in Jamaica to Cien Fuegos in the island of Cuba.'

He discovered another of the pleasures of travelling alone: the shipboard romance. 'If you cross the Atlantic with an American lady you invariably fall in love with her before the journey is over' (*North America*). On board ship, as he wrote in a late book, *John Caldigate*, 'all who are worth anything are more or less in love by the end of the first week.' His own romances were innocent enough, however pleasurable or self-indulgent; he imagined them blossoming into intense attachments, which perished as soon as the ship reached port – as in an episode in *The Bertrams* and in one of his best short stories, 'Journey to Panama'.

On the *Africa* he struck up a friendship with Mrs Harriet Knower, from New York, and her daughter Mary, aged twenty. Seventeen years later, when Mary had just become a widow,* he wrote to Mrs Knower that 'I can see her now, as she used to be then, just springing out of childhood – almost too young to be treated by one like myself otherwise than as a child. . . .'

He reached Liverpool on 3 July 1859. Rose, stuck in Dublin,

---

* In 1866 Mary Knower married Samuel Penniman – who had also been on board the *Africa* on that voyage, as a young widower in his late twenties with two small children. Maybe there were more emotional undercurrents than even Anthony knew.

had not led a recognisable married life, with a husband working from home, since before Anthony's journey to the Levant eighteen months earlier. It was not much better now. He was due to be in Scotland for the second half of July. In London, he arranged an outing to Richmond with Mary Knower and her mother, plus another American couple, the Pardees, also from the *Africa*. He wrote to Mrs Knower that he was glad the Pardees could come, 'but even had they not I think we could have had a very pleasant evening together. I don't know that we have ever found each other stupid yet, – & I flatter myself we should not have been more so at Richmond than on board the Africa.'

The old life was almost over. In London, after his PO debriefing, Anthony was rewarded at last for his long service and his foreign missions. He and Rose were to live in England again, permanently.

'I had often longed to return to England, – with a silly longing,' he wrote in his autobiography about this release from what had come to feel like banishment. Without this release his marriage to Rose would not have foundered, but their relationship could have become formal and meaningless. They needed a joint project, of equal importance to them both, and the move home to England was it.

Anthony had requested, and been granted, the post of Surveyor to the Eastern District of England – which comprised East Anglia and parts of Bedfordshire and Hertfordshire. Within days of securing the appointment, on 20 July 1859, he saw and liked a house at Waltham Cross, in south-east Hertfordshire, near the borders with Essex and Middlesex and about fourteen miles north-east of central London. On 2 August he composed the following happily facetious missive to Rose in Dublin:

To ye. ladie of Waltham House in ye. Countie of Herts.
These –
Deareste Madame
   Havinge with infinite trouble & pain inspected & surveyed and poked manie and diverse holes in ye aforesaid mansion, I have at ye laste hired and taken it for yr. moste excellente ladieship – to have and to hold from ye term of St Michaels mass next comynge. The whiche Waltham House

255

is now the property of one Mistress Wilkins, who has let it to your lovynge Lord & husband for 7 – 14 – or 21 yeares, with manie and diverse clauses which shall hereafter as time may serve be explained to your excellent ladieship –

In ye. mean time I am with all true love and affection your ladieships devoted servant and husband

Anthony Trollope.

Then he was off north again on PO business. But he took two months' leave in the autumn of 1859; he, Rose and John Tilley travelled slowly, with many stops, to the Pyrenees, and Tom came from Italy to meet them. They stayed for a time in the spa town of Vernet in the eastern Pyrenees, and Rose noted 'La Mère Bauche' in her chronology – the title of a short story Anthony subsequently wrote, set in the hotel there. Rose made more tantalising notes: 'John Tilley and Tom try and get beds at Puigcerda – dance in the kitchen.' On the way home, 'John Tilley ill.' This was par for the course.

Anthony and Rose had a great deal to think about. The day after they got back to Ireland and Seaview Terrace, which was still home for the moment, Anthony worked out the finances of their new life. First, projected expenditure for the year to come, and in the parallel column his probable income:

Rose [housekeeping]	£320	Salary	£700
Rent	£150	Rent [for use of home	
Boys [school fees]	£220	as office]	£30
Groom, gardener,		Profit [travel expenses]	£50
& labourer	£100	Books	£800
Horses	£90		£1580
Sundries	£100		
Tour [holiday]	£100		
Clothes	£45		
Doctor	£20		
Insurance on life	£60		
Ditto for Fire	£10		
Taxes rates etc.	£50		
	£1300		

'Excess £280' he wrote at the end of this calculation. His projection of his earnings was unduly cautious. His travel expense-account was less, once he lived at Waltham Cross, than in Ireland, but his literary earnings (listed as 'Books') were on the increase. At the end of 1859 he calculated that he had for the first time made more from his writing – £1,008 – than from his Post Office salary plus travel expenses (£909.12.1).

At the beginning of August 1859, only two days after he agreed to take the lease of Waltham House (with effect from November), he began writing *Castle Richmond*, conceived as his farewell to Ireland. As he wrote in his first chapter: 'I am now leaving the Green Isle and my old friends, and would fain say a word of them as I do so. If I do not say that word now it will never be said.'

He conceded that writing about Ireland again would do little to endear him to readers. 'That there is a strong feeling against things Irish it is impossible to deny. Irish servants need not apply; Irish acquaintances are treated with limited confidence; Irish cousins are regarded as being decidedly dangerous; and Irish stories are not popular with the booksellers.' For all that, young Frederic Chapman of Chapman & Hall, on the strength of Anthony's recent successes, agreed to pay £600 for this one. As for Irish servants, 'I have had some in my house for years, and never had one that was faithless, dishonest, or intemperate' (*Castle Richmond*). Barney, who had been with Anthony since before he was married, loyally agreed to accompany the family to England.

In October, from Seaview Terrace, Anthony wrote a fateful letter to W. M. Thackeray, whom he had never met: 'I do not know how far the staff of your new periodical may be complete. Perhaps you will excuse my taking the liberty of offering to make one of the number if it be not so.'

The new periodical was the *Cornhill*, a shilling monthly planned by the publisher George Smith, head of the firm Smith, Elder & Co. It was to carry serial fiction, stories, articles and poetry, and would be illustrated. Thackeray had been persuaded to edit the magazine. Anthony in his letter offered not a serial novel but a series of five short stories, each 'intended to be redolent of some different country'.

Three days later, on 26 October, George Smith replied to Anthony with a businesslike letter, discussing terms for stories (£2 a page), but stating a preference for 'a continuous story' as long as an ordinary three-volume novel, for which 'we should be happy to pay you One Thousand pounds.' Anthony, always seeking recognition and better terms, had been moving backwards and forwards between publishers in a way that seemed assertive enough – but until he went to Chapman & Hall only between publishers like Newby, Colburn and Bentley whom he knew through his famous mother or, in the case of Longman, through the Merivales. Unsure of himself and unfamiliar with the current London literary world, he had been relying on the limited 'networking' available to him. His approach to Thackeray was another of his leaps in the dark and it had paid off.

The sum offered by Smith was marvellous enough; but two days later came a letter from Thackeray, as informal as if they had been colleagues for years, suggesting that 'My dear Mr Trollope' might contribute articles as well as fiction:

> You must have tossed a deal about the world, and have countless sketches in your memory and your portfolio. Please to think if you can furbish up any of these besides the novel. When events occur on wh. you can have a good lively talk, bear us in mind. One of our chief objects in this magazine is the getting out of novel spinning, and back into the world. Don't understand me to disparage our craft, especially *your* wares. I often say I am like the pastry cook, and don't care for tarts, but prefer bread and cheese – but the public love the tarts (luckily for us), and we must bake & sell them.

Then came the best part: 'There was quite an excitement in my family one evening when Paterfamilias [i.e. Thackeray himself] (who goes to sleep over a novel almost always when he tries it after dinner) came up stairs to the Drawing Room wide awake and calling for the second volume of The Three Clerks. I hope the Cornhill Magazine will have as pleasant a story. . . .'

This response to his overture was, as Anthony acknowledged in his autobiography, very pleasant; but Thackeray and Smith needed the first part of the serial novel within six weeks. Anthony rushed over to London and saw Smith, who bore most of the editorial responsibility for his new magazine, and offered him the half-written *Castle Richmond*. But Smith did not want an Irish story. 'He wanted an English tale, on English life, with a clerical flavour.' On the journey back to Ireland, Anthony was already getting down on paper the beginnings of what was to be *Framley Parsonage*.

Under this pressure he cannot have been much help in the packing up of Seaview Terrace. 'Who does not know how terrible are those preparations for house-moving; – how infinite in number are the articles which must be packed, and how poor and tawdry is the aspect of one's belongings while they are thus in a state of dislocation?' (*The Small House at Allington*). Yet it was he who wrote, possibly at Rose's dictation, to the agent at Waltham asking him to order 'as much coal as will fill, or nearly fill, the larger coal hole' in the new house, 'so as to avoid having the dirt again sooner than can be helped'. And 'If they have cut the oil cloth for the hall, do not let them put it down permanently before the furniture is in.'

Rose, Anthony and the boys moved into their new house, and their new life, on 23 November 1859. Three days after Christmas the *Cornhill* appeared, with the first instalment of *Framley Parsonage* in the place of honour. The magazine was an immediate success, selling 120,000 copies of this first issue.*

In March 1858, when Anthony was in the Middle East, his elder son Harry, aged eleven, started as a boarder at St Columba's College at Rathfarnham, outside Dublin. St Columba's, founded in 1842, was intended to provide the equivalent of Eton for the gentry of Ireland. Six months later, in September 1858, while Anthony was going backwards and forwards from Glasgow, Harry's younger brother Fred also started at St Columba's.

New plans had now to be made for the boys' education. Anthony did not inflict Winchester or Harrow on his sons. The latter school had gone from bad to worse. When in 1844 Dr Charles Vaughan took over as headmaster, the vicar of Harrow – that same evangelical Mr Cunningham who had taken over the house built by Anthony's father – advised him to sack the remaining sixty-nine boys and start from scratch. By the late 1850s Dr Vaughan had raised pupil numbers to over 500, and the

---

* This was a huge circulation for the time, and it settled down to 80–85,000. *The Times*, which was enormously influential, maintained its influence with a circulation of 60,000, though challenged by the *Daily Telegraph*, founded 1855, which was cheaper and sold more copies.

school's reputation was transformed. However, the constant and unconcealed sexual activity among the boys in the studies and dormitories was startling even by the standards of the day.

Better concealed was the crisis that took place around the time that Anthony was looking for a school in England for his boys. In 1858 one of the older Harrow pupils, the future author John Addington Symonds, discovered that the headmaster himself was sexually involved with one of the boys. In a ferment of jealousy and spite Symonds told his father, who wrote a threatening letter to Dr Vaughan. The two men met, and long, painful negotiations followed. The outside world was astonished when this respected and successful headmaster resigned at the end of 1859.

It is unlikely that Anthony knew the reason for Vaughan's departure;* but enquiries to parents may have elicited some unease, quite apart from Anthony's own unhappy memories of the place.

The sister school of St Columba's, in England, was St Peter's College, Radley; but Anthony chose Radley's rival and near neighbour, Bradfield College, in the wooded valley of the river Pang in Berkshire. Both were new schools, part of the mid-nineteenth-century expansion and reform of the public school system. Bradfield was the cheaper. It was founded in 1850 on the model of Winchester by the Rev. Thomas Stevens (who was both vicar and squire of Bradfield village, and a high-churchman), 'for the careful education of boys as loving children of the Church of England'. He was the Warden and benevolent despot of the school, with a headmaster under him.

The year 1859 was when Bradfield, ceasing to be a private institution, was reconstituted under a board of trustees; Gladstone was a member of its Council, though he never attended a single meeting. It was still a small school of about 120 boys. The celebrations in the summer of 1859 which the change in constitution occasioned, and the improvements that were taking place – a cricket professional from Eton had been engaged, and new buildings were planned – no doubt influenced Anthony's choice.

---

* Hardly anyone did, though both Vaughan and Symonds confided in one or two eminent advisers. Dr Vaughan was subsequently offered bishoprics, which he prudently declined in accordance with his bargain with Dr Symonds. The Vaughan Library at Harrow was built in his memory. He was by all accounts an admirable headmaster in most ways.

There was an awkwardness. Harry and Fred had left St Columba's under a cloud. Anthony and Rose visited Bradfield soon after they moved to Waltham, on 10 December 1859, and that same evening the Warden, Mr Stevens, wrote to the Warden of St Columba's, the Rev. John Gwynn: 'Mr Trollope has informed me that his son has been in disgrace with you and has been sent away for a breach of discipline and for lying to conceal his fault. If the occasion of these doings was a single instance of his want of good bearing with you and if you do not believe him to have habits of low tone or to be generally unprincipled it would seem to be unkind to shut him out from the chance of making good.'

He did not say which of the boys had been in trouble. Two boys a little older than Harry – Cornelius O'Callaghan and Frank Dunne – were expelled from St Columba's at the end of November. Neither Harry nor Fred had 'expelled' written against his name in the records as these others did, but then they were leaving anyway. Whatever trouble led to the expulsions must also have involved one of the young Trollopes.

The sons of Anthony Trollope, the popular author, would be valuable acquisitions to Bradfield. Dr Stevens wrote to a cousin on 15 December: 'The two Trollope boys are to come after Christmas – that Irish Warden is only fit to be employed in Ireland – an awful muff! A sort of donkey that would be likely to make hypocrites of honest boys. . . . I hope the boys will do well here. I have no fears for them.'

Anthony was evidently upset about whatever it was that had or had not taken place at St Columba's. (It may have reminded him of his unhappy experience at the Sunbury school, long before.) Mr Stevens wrote to him: 'I did sympathise very keenly with you in your distress about your boy.' He added that he thought Dr Gwynn's views of how to get the best out of boys was '*very foggy*'.

So Harry and Fred, with their Irish accents, started at Bradfield in an atmosphere of goodwill. There was a new headmaster, the Rev. Stephen Poyntz Denning, a portly, genial man of liberal views who widened the essentially classical syllabus to include maths, history, geography and French, and who encouraged (among pupils who were mainly clergymen's sons) the discussion of controversial topics such as evolution: Darwin's *Origin of Species* was published in 1859.

—— * ——

When Anthony in his novels discussed women's ways and domestic management his primary reference point was, necessarily, Rose. Her cavalier attitude to officialdom and her shrewdness seemed to him shameless. 'Why is it that commercial honesty has so seldom charms for women? A woman who would give away the last shawl from her back will insist on smuggling her gloves through the Custom-house. . . . Is not the passion for cheap purchases altogether a female mania?' To deny the shopkeeper his fair profit almost verged on dishonesty for Anthony: 'Would that women could be taught to hate bargains! How much less useless trash would there be in our houses, and how much fewer tremendous sacrifices in our shops!'

He was, when he wrote those words, seeing the world of shopping from the inside of the haberdashers' plate-glass windows, alongside his fictional Messrs Brown, Jones and Robinson; but clearly Rose had an eye for a bargain. The unorthodox nature of women's morality always surprised Anthony. Going through Customs with Rose must have been, repeatedly, an ordeal for him. 'It is, I think, certainly the fact that women are less pervious to ideas of honesty than men are. They are less shocked by dishonesty when they find it, and are less clear in their intellect as to that which constitutes honesty. Where is the woman who thinks it wrong to smuggle?' (*Miss Mackenzie*).

And what woman, he wrote in the second chapter of *Framley Parsonage*, 'ever understood the necessity or recognized the advantage of political honesty?' Lady Ushant in *The American Senator*, planning her will, planned too how to avoid death duties; she was a religious woman, 'but it never crossed her conscience that it would be wrong to cheat the revenue. It may be doubted whether any woman has ever been brought to such honesty as that.'

It was his amused, fearful observation of the divergent morality of women, starting with Rose, that empowered him in his creation of irresistible law-benders: Lady Mason in *Orley Farm*, and Lizzie Eustace, and Lady Glencora. What hope had the grand male simplicity of 'honest and true' in such company?

Rose had to put her shrewdness to use in furnishing Waltham House. It was a tall, plain, early eighteenth-century house built of red brick, with steps up to the porch of the front door and a lower wing each side – one was the stables, where Anthony kept his hunters. He had thought there would be no more hunting after he left Ireland, but the kennels of the Essex Hunt were at Harlow, ten miles from Waltham, and Anthony was soon hunting over the country known as the Roothings, famous for high fences and deep ditches. The other wing of Waltham House became an office for the Post Office clerks who worked under him organising the mails of the Eastern District.

The house had fine entrance gates and a gravel sweep, and enough land for them to keep livestock. There was a walled garden with a sundial and a square pond; and a wide lawn with cedars, and a summerhouse; and an orchard, and a good vegetable garden. 'We grew our cabbages and strawberries, made our own butter, and killed our own pigs' (*Autobiography*).

Anthony was particularly proud of their strawberries. Mention of strawberries and cream is frequent in his letters of invitation in the summers of their twelve years at Waltham. The strawberries grew all among the roses, in the flower garden. One of their first guests was young Mary Knower, who came to stay on her way back from France to take the boat home. 'I will be your humble slave, & come & fetch you at any time or point. I suppose you will not return by Paris or I might pick you up there,' wrote Anthony. By incorporating his female friends into his home life ('I and Mrs Trollope will be so delighted to have you'), Anthony saved himself from danger and secured friendships that could last.

He knew nothing about plants, and grew bored when being conducted round botanical gardens, 'because I am called on to listen to the names of shrubs conveyed in three Latin words, and I am supposed to interest myself in the locality from which they have been brought' (*Australia and New Zealand*). Yet he appreciated a well-designed, well-kept, useful garden.

He wrote in *Castle Richmond*, 'Let all those who have houses and the adjuncts of houses think how considerable a part of their life's pleasures consists in their interest in the things around them. When will the sea-kale be fit to cut, and when will the crocuses come up? will the violets be sweeter than ever? and the geranium cuttings, are they thriving? we have dug and manured, and sown, and we look forward to the reaping.' (Anthony had not personally dug and manured; though he was seen charging around the lawn with a heavy roller.) 'The very furniture which ministers to our daily uses is loved and petted; and in decorating our rooms we educate ourselves in design. . . . All men love these things, more or less, even though they know it not. And women love them even more than men.'

Inside Waltham House, the staircase was impressive and the main rooms large. Anthony's taste in cigars had become educated during his visit to Cuba, and now he imported them directly from Havana, over a thousand at a time. He had one wall of his library at Waltham fitted with small glass-doored cupboards, or bins, in which the cigars were stored. On wet days the glass doors were closed, and on dry days they were opened, so as to allow the air to circulate. A peg was stuck in a hole in the woodwork above the bin in use, and when it was empty the peg was moved along to the next, and the empty bin refilled from his reserve chest. He smoked a great deal, and his beard was a repository for fragments of cigar ash.

In Anthony's young manhood English gentlemen were clean-shaven. Beards were for eccentrics, bohemians and foreigners. Anthony's contemporary Albert Smith – author, traveller, lecturer and Alpinist, most certainly an eccentric, and a distin-guished one – was blackballed from the Garrick Club in 1855 because he had a beard. It was only after the Crimean War (1854–56) that both beards and smoking became fashionable, when our brave boys came back from besieging Sebastopol addicted to Turkish tobacco and with their lower faces smothered in hair. There was, at first, considerable variation; a fashion of the early 1860s was to have long side-whiskers dangling down each side of the face like displaced spaniels' ears, with a shaven chin in between.

Anthony wore a full beard. He probably grew it in 1857; Frank Gresham in *Doctor Thorne* had a new beard, and found it necessary to explain to his family at dinner, over the soup, that 'All I require is a relay of napkins for every course'; and then went to work, 'covering it with every spoonful, as men with beards always do'. Anthony's beard was well established – but still new enough to be worth mentioning – when he was in the West Indies. He told how on his Spanish passport it was described as *poblada*. Not having a Spanish dictionary, he had no idea what this meant. It means bushy.

So there he is at Waltham House, with his bushy beard, and his bulky body, and his balding head, straddling the hearthrug as he said all men do when they first come into a room (which means that he did), with his thumbs tucked into the armholes of his waistcoat, talking loudly in his deep voice, laughing his big laugh at his own joke, shouting cheerfully for some hot tea. He is wearing spectacles; he always does. 'There are spectacles which are so much more spectacles than other spectacles that they make the beholder feel that there is before him a pair of spectacles carrying a face, rather than a face carrying a pair of spectacles' (*Is He Popenjoy?*). Anthony's are not like that. His eyes are large, luminous and light-coloured, the spectacles are small and fragile on his healthy-coloured face. He has been up since half-past five or so; one of old Barney's jobs is to creep upstairs and wake him. Barney is paid an extra £5 a year for this service and Anthony wrote in his autobiography, 'during all those years at Waltham Cross he was never once late with the coffee which it was his duty to bring me.' Anthony gets his writing stint done before the official work-day begins.

And Rose, at Waltham House? 'All nice women are proud of their drawing-rooms, and she was proud of hers,' wrote Anthony of Fanny Robarts in *Framley Parsonage*. We glimpse Rose here; and again in the same book, in a description of Fanny Gresham doing the drawing-room flowers: 'And when she had grouped her bunches properly she carried the jar from one part of the room to another, backwards and forwards, trying the effect of the colours, as though her mind were quite intent upon her flowers . . . still giving a twist here and a set there to some of the small sprigs which constituted the background of her bouquet.'

Rose was nearly forty when they moved back to England. Anthony was emphatically not one to consign older women – and forty, then, was 'older' than forty is now – to sexual oblivion. He was tender and perceptive about older women in his novels, granting them not only desires but, sometimes, lovers. He was as fond of the mothers as of the daughters in the sentimental friendships he struck up on his travels. His authorial voice scolded Mrs Dale in *The Small House at Allington* for being more 'old' than she need. 'Let her who is forty call herself forty; but if she can be young in spirit at forty, let her show that she is.'

No one should underestimate Rose, or her importance for Anthony; but maybe in her forties she found it hard to know what note to strike. Her taste in clothes and decor, now that they had more money and moved 'in society', had to be discovered; there may be a painful subtext to Anthony's comment that 'in decorating our rooms, we educate ourselves in design.'

Maybe she was not proud of her drawing-room straight away. Perhaps mistakes were made. Anthony described a failed drawing-room in *Can You Forgive Her?*, where the professional decorator 'had chosen green paper, a green carpet, green curtains, and green damask chairs. There was a green damask sofa, and two green arm-chairs opposite to each other at the two sides of the fireplace. The room was altogether green, and was not enticing. . . .' Most of us, added the author, 'know when we enter a drawing-room whether it is a pretty room or no; and how few of us know how to make a drawing-room pretty!'

Anthony, for all his bulk and baldness, seemed young until he was about fifty. Rose's hair went white early. In January 1866, when they were staying for four days with Lord Houghton at Fryston, his country house in Yorkshire, a fellow guest was Lady Rose Fane, daughter of the Earl of Westmoreland, a clever woman in her early thirties. She described Rose Trollope, in a letter to her mother, as 'a quiet sort of woman and wd. be well enough only she has perfectly white hair which is coiffé en cheveux – in the most fashionable way with (last night) a little rose stuck in it wh: looks most absurd.'*

'*Coiffé en cheveux*' means that Rose didn't wear a piece of lace on her head, or a little cap – which would have been the convention for a woman of her age, especially one whose hair had turned white. A decade later the artistic Augustus Hare praised Rose in his journal as 'a beautiful old lady [then in her mid-fifties] with snow-white hair turned back.'† She would have arranged her hair simply, which in itself made her conspicuous in the 1860s and 70s.

Anthony's observation of the colour, smell, texture and arrangement of women's hair was so obsessional as to require a brief digression.

What he loathed, in women as in everything, was falseness and

---

* Lady Rose Fane was even more supercilious about Anthony, whom she found 'detestable – vulgar, noisy & domineering'. She wished she had never seen him, he was 'as unlike his books as possible' (Weigell MSS, Kent County Archives). The social manner that he had learned in Ireland, and which served him well there, did not always go down well in the chillier reaches of the English upper class.

† Augustus Hare, *In My Solitary Life* (1953).

William Makepeace Thackeray: novelist, humorist and first editor of the *Cornhill* magazine. Anthony's letter to him from Ireland in 1859, seeking to place his stories in the new magazine, was the first step towards a brief but important friendship which bloomed when Anthony moved to London and ended with Thackeray's death on Christmas Eve 1863. 'I regard him as one of the most tender-hearted human beings I ever knew' (*Autobiography*). Anthony and Rose considered Thackeray's *Henry Esmond* as the finest novel in the English language, and Anthony published a short biography of him in 1879.

Pillar boxes were introduced into
Britain at Anthony's instigation in the early
1850s. At first they were not red, but
sage-green.

Sir Rowland Hill: Inventor of the penny
post, and Secretary to the Postmaster
General from 1847 to 1864. He was a difficult
man, with whom Anthony got on
conspicuously badly.

Kate Field, the American whom Anthony first met in Florence in autumn 1860, when
she was twenty-two and he forty-five. She is the only woman known to have shaken his
emotional equilibrium seriously after he married. He wrote about her in his
autobiography, without giving her name.

Anthony aged just over forty, when he had only recently begun to wear a beard. The sprightly checkered trousers reflect his dislike of the dull dinginess of modern men's clothing: 'It is not permitted to the ordinary English gentleman to be anything but ugly' (*Castle Richmond*).

One of Millais's drawings for *Framley Parsonage*, depicting Lucy Robarts in emotional agony on her bed. Anthony protested that the illustration was 'simply ludicrous'. Lucy seemed not in despair but asleep, and the true subject of the picture was her exaggerated crinoline skirt. Anthony hated crinolines.

NEW OMNIBUS REGULATION.

'*Werry sorry 'm, but yer' l 'av to leave yer Krinerline outside.*"

Anthony complained about women heaving their 'misshapen, dirty mass of battered wirework' across men's knees in New York street-cars. *Punch* shows how crinolines caused trouble on London omnibuses too.

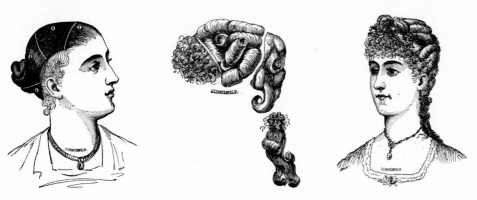

Anthony was disgusted by the female fashion of the 1860s and '70s for wearing quantities of artificial hair. Mr Gibson in *He Knew He Was Right* saw Arabella's false chignon as 'an abortion': 'It grew bigger and bigger, more shapeless, monstrous, absurd, and abominable, as he looked at it.'

The loggia of the Villino Trollope, the house of Anthony's brother Tom in Florence, about 1862: Tom standing protectively over his old mother on the left, his first wife Theodosia looking out into the garden on the right, and their daughter Bice sitting on the floor. Kate Field, a frequent visitor, described this terrace as where the 'real life' of the house took place, 'opening upon a garden, with its lofty pillars, its tesselated marble floor, its walls inlaid with terra-cotta, bas-reliefs, inscriptions, and coats of arms, and here and there a niche devoted to some antique Madonna.' Anthony and Rose stayed at the Villino Trollope on many of their holiday tours.

Frances Trollope, mother of Tom and
Anthony, near the end of her life.

Theodosia Garrow, Tom's first wife. She had
grey eyes and copper-brown hair.

Anthony's niece Bice, aged fourteen, when
she was at boarding school in Brighton.

Bice around the time of her marriage to
Charles Stuart-Wortley in 1880.

The Trollope brothers in the early 1860s: Tom (glaring, in profile) and Anthony, who sent this photograph to a female relative with the facetious but not untruthful comment, 'Here you have my brother and self. You will perceive that my brother is pitching into me. He always did.'

Tom (glaring again) and his much younger second wife Fanny Ternan. She was an elder sister of Ellen Ternan, the mistress of Charles Dickens, and became governess to Bice after Theodosia's death. Tom married her the following year. 'Yes, of course! I knew you would,' wrote Anthony.

pretence. 'With padding and false hair without limit a figure may be constructed of almost any dimensions. . . . The taste for flesh and blood has for the day given place to an appetite for horsehair and pearl powder' (*The Way We Live Now*). Like most older people at all periods, he felt that modern fashions represented a grotesque falling-away from the decent simplicities of his own young days. He retained a fondness for the hairstyles worn by women when he was young, though Jemima Blackburn, a near-contemporary of Rose's whom Anthony was to know later, thought that the way she and her friends did their hair in the 1840s was 'frightful': 'It was divided in the middle. Bunches of ringlets hanging down the cheeks was "front hair", and the "back hair" was drawn up tight . . . on the top of the head. Front and back hair were considered as separate parts of the body, as much as eyes and nose.'*

Jemima Blackburn also said that when she was young dark girls were much more admired than fair-haired girls.† When Anthony wanted to suggest sexual allure, he generally gave his heroines dark, glossy, unruly curls. Fair-haired Lily Dale in *The Small House at Allington*, rejected by Adolphus Crosbie, stood all unknowing at the point where gentlemen were beginning to prefer blondes. Dorothy Stanbury in *He Knew He Was Right* (1869) combined the best of the old ways and the new: she had flaxen ringlets, 'worn after the old-fashioned way which we used to think so pretty when we were young'. Aunt Jemima Stanbury was relieved to see her niece wore no chignon, and checked that she was not subject to headaches: 'How is a woman not to have a headache, when she carries a thing on the back of her poll as big as a gardener's wheelbarrow?'

Anthony was malicious in *The Three Clerks* – post-ringlets, pre-chignons – about Clementina Golightly, a large young heiress who danced with lumpish abandon. 'She had hair which was brownish and sufficiently silky – and which she wore, as all other such girls do, propped out on each side of her face by thick round

* Rob Fairley (ed.), *Jemima: The Paintings and Memoirs of a Victorian Lady*, Canongate, 1988.

† This is confirmed by Mrs Oliphant in *Phoebe Junior* (1876): 'How it comes about I cannot tell, but it is certain that there does exist at this present moment, a proportion of golden-haired girls which very much exceeds the number we used to see when golden hair had not become fashionable.'

velvet pads, which, when the waltzing pace became exhilarating, occasionally showed themselves, looking greasy. . . .' His real disgust, however, like Aunt Jemima Stanbury's, was to be elicited by chignons.

During the 1860s false chignons of larger and larger size, attached to the back of the head, became so fashionable as to be almost obligatory. The wearer's real hair was sleeked back, seldom washed, and made glossy with pomade. Anthony could not stand either the smell of pomade or the chignons. His heroines wore inconspicuous chignons – or no chignon at all, if he really approved of the girl. In *Mr Scarborough's Family*, written at the end of his life, Florence Mountjoy's hair was 'soft and smooth . . . and never redolent of peculiar odours. It was simply Florence Mountjoy's hair, and that made it perfect in the eyes of her male friends generally.'

Artificial chignons went with artificial colours as well as artificial smells. In *Is He Popenjoy?* the estranged wife of Lord George Germain brooded on the woman with whom he flirted, Mrs Houghton, whose back hair 'got bigger and bigger every month', and on her face, 'with the paint visible on it in the broad day, and her blackened eyebrows, and her great crested helmet of false hair nearly eighteen inches deep. . . .'

In *He Knew He Was Right* Anthony's obsession with chignons and pomades, transferred to Aunt Jemima and the Rev. Mr Gibson, reached its apogee. The culprits were two local belles desperate for husbands, Camilla and Arabella French, of whom Aunt Jemima said, 'You can see the grease on their foreheads when they try to make their hair go back in the dirty French fashion.'

Mr Gibson was almost ensnared by Arabella French when he became transfixed by the 'supplemental mass' of hair on the back of her head, the 'bale of goods' which she carried around. He was about to propose to her, but when he considered her chignon as 'a chignon that might possibly become his own, as a burden which in one sense he might himself be called upon to bear, as a domestic utensil of [sic] which he might himself be called upon to inspect, and, perhaps, to aid the shifting on and the shifting off', he panicked, thinking that 'never in his life had he seen anything so unshapely as that huge wen at the back of her head.'

Mr Gibson fled from the nightmare chignon. 'It grew bigger

and bigger, more shapeless, monstrous, absurd, and abominable, as he looked at it. Nothing should force upon him the necessity of assisting to carry such an abortion through the world.' This farcical, hallucinatory, phobic vision of the chignon as incubus gives the lie to any who still see Anthony Trollope as the chronicler of the prosaic.

Rose, who certainly wore no chignon, seems to have made little impact on visitors to Waltham House. Henry Brackenbury, a writer on military topics who was a good deal younger than she, mentioned her 'beautiful feet'.* Women who have beautiful feet generally have beautiful legs, but Mr Brackenbury had no way of knowing about that and neither do we. Mostly, Rose seems continually to be damned by faint praise. 'What I like best about Mrs T,' said the Rev. William Lucas Collins, a friend from the late 1860s, 'is her honest and hearty appreciation of her husband.'†
What were the unspoken things that he liked least about her?

She was a small woman but, in the only photograph of her in her prime that we have, her eyes are large, her features strong, her jawline a little heavy. In *The Belton Estate* much play is made of the pretty Alderney cow that Will Belton gave to Clara Amedroz, the girl he loved: 'and any man or woman at all understanding cows would at once have perceived that this cow was perfect in her kind. Her eyes were mild, and soft, and bright. Her legs were like the legs of a deer. . . .' In *The Last Chronicle of Barset* Lily Dale tried to persuade Grace Crawley to accept Major Grantly's love and support. He wanted to relieve Grace's troubles, said Lily, just as he would want to relieve his cow if she were sick. This was a contrived image, since Major Grantly was not noticeably bucolic, but it led into the following extraordinary exchange between the young women:

'I am not Major Grantly's cow.'
'Yes, you are.'

Looking at the photograph of Rose, if one had to pick an animal that she resembled, one might say – a nice heifer.

* Henry Brackenbury, *Some Memories of My Spare Time* (1909).
† Letter to John Blackwood, in *Letters of Anthony Trollope*, ed. N. John Hall, Stanford University Press, 1983.

—— * ——

The 1861 census reports the Trollope domestic staff as consisting of Bernard (Barney) Smith* the groom, aged 63; Anne Smith, aged 48, Irish, and maybe Barney's wife, described as the dairymaid; and Catherine Magnee, 32, also Irish, the housemaid. The cook was Rachel Robins, aged 43. There was also, in this middle-aged household, a twelve-year-old girl, Fanny Campbell, the 'under-cook'.† When inviting Bianconi's son-in-law M. J. O'Connell down to Waltham for a couple of days in May 1863, Anthony said the 'eating would be poor' because 'our cook has got drunk, – perpetually drunk. If there be nothing to eat we can do the same.' The cook was the only one of the servants – apart from the twelve-year-old – who wasn't Irish; she came from London. It may be presumed that she was soon sent packing. That weekend, which was to have been a house-party, was a frost anyway. The invited guests defaulted and went to the Derby. 'My wife was awfully disgusted as women always are when nobody comes to eat their pastries and sweetmeats.' The Trollopes had recurring cook-trouble. 'We have no cook, ours having gone blind, but it doesn't seem to make much difference,' wrote Anthony blithely, asking a friend down to Waltham in 1867.

For one of the Trollopes' pleasures, living at Waltham, was entertaining friends. It was easy for people to come out from London; as Anthony wrote to Kate Gould – who had been Kate Grant, Anthony's childhood friend from Harrow days – 'I am 14 miles out of town on the Norwich line of railway.' This was the Great Eastern line from Shoreditch (later called Liverpool Street) station. He asked people down to 'dine and sleep', advising them to take the 5.10 train. The journey took just over half an hour, and dinner at Waltham House was at 6.30, or at 6 in the summer, 'so as to get a cigar in the garden afterwards'. Fruit and wine would be laid out on a table under the cedar in the long twilight. Guests were encouraged to take the 10 o'clock train back to London the following morning. The house was half a mile from Waltham

* Doubt hangs over Barney's surname. It has been variously given as FitzPatrick and MacIntyre. Perhaps he wasn't sure himself, and 'Smith' was Anthony's jocular compromise.

† It was usual for working-class girls to go into service at this early age. With no secondary education available to them, such a position gave them a roof over their heads, regular meals, and a training. In country areas, it was the only prospect of earning an independent living.

station – Anthony called it 'five minutes' walk' or 'ten minutes' walk', rather vaguely; but a porter from the station would carry a visitor's bag all the way for him, or, as Anthony wrote to a Mr Gibbon, 'I shall have an old one-eyed Irishman [Barney] to meet you.'

They were not grand. Breakfast was late and ample, and lunch when there were no visitors was a brief matter of bread and cheese and cold meats; this was common enough, among people who dined in the evening. Anthony was amused and shocked, in the colonies, to find men doing no manual labour who were eating two heavy cooked meals a day.

If there was one thing Anthony loathed it was pretentious private dinner parties. They are described, and mocked, and excoriated, over and over again in his novels. You could fill an anthology with dreadful Trollopian dinner parties, with hostesses red-faced and hysterical because they did not know what was going on with the hired help in the kitchen, with overweening table-decorations and flower-arrangements, with disgusting, highly coloured desserts brought in from pastry-cooks at great expense, and everything else cold or burned.

Like his Doctor Thorne, Anthony consumed huge and numerous cups of tea, and hated the dainty cups he was passed at tea-parties, and then having to balance cup and sandwich-plate in his hand. Anthony also loathed the new system of dining 'à la Russe', which had become smart by the time he and Rose came back to England. It meant the dishes were offered or handed individually to each guest by servants, instead of each course of several dishes being placed on the table for everyone to help himself, the host carving the joints. He hated 'that handing round, unless it be of a subsidiary thimbleful of the best cognac when the business of the social intercourse has been dinner' (*Framley Parsonage*). 'Handing round' had become 'a vulgar and an intolerable nuisance' for people like himself, 'second-class gentry' who did not have a standing army of servants. It meant that he didn't get his potatoes until his mutton was eaten, or had gone cold, and that the wine did not come round often enough.

Anthony's objection rested on the pretence, discomfort and ostentation of it all. Not everyone agreed. Frederick Pollock, who was to be a friend of Anthony's in London, dined à la Russe for the first time in his own house in Montagu Square in 1858, 'and now I only wonder that we have not done so before. It is the greatest comfort to get rid of the carving on the table for a large party. I have always liked it at other people's houses, but there is still more reason for liking it at one's own.'* Waltham House was to be one place where Sir Frederick and his wife would have to be content with the old ways.

Dinner-party food, at the time when Rose and Anthony returned to England, was inclined to be heavy, with much emphasis on roast meat. Mutton was the staple, the more mature the better; a regular leg of mutton would weigh seven or eight pounds. Foreigners commented on the hot sauces and fiery condiments served in England. The British middle classes were timid about onions because of their smell, but used quantities of cayenne pepper, chilli vinegar and spicy commercial ketchups. The connection with India made curry very popular. Both curry powder and curry paste were available. Rose had given her mother-in-law curried salmon in Ireland; cookbooks of the time recommend curried oysters and curried macaroni. During the Irish Famine the Duke of Norfolk even suggested that in place of potatoes the poor should consume curry powder mixed with water, on which he appeared to believe the population of India was nourished.

The other sauce the average British household seemed to have taken to its heart was 'melted butter' sauce, which was melted butter mixed with flour and water to make a pale and pasty covering for fish and 'made dishes'. Salads were served undressed apart from a bowl of salt in which to dip the leaves, and vegetables were commonly overcooked; it was thought unhealthy to eat them crisp. Carrots, for example, were boiled for over an hour. Yet there were compensations. Vegetables were home grown except in the city centres, and therefore fresh and chemical-free. Bread from the baker was so bad that most middle-class households made their own, and the importance and function of bran and fibre were already understood; wholemeal flour was to be preferred for breadmaking on account of 'its slight medicinal effect which renders it valuable to many persons accustomed to have frequent recourse to drugs [i.e. laxatives]'.†

* Sir Frederick Pollock, *Personal Reminiscences*, Macmillan, 1887.
† Eliza Acton, *Modern Cookery for Private Families*, Longman, 1856.

Readers of Anthony's novels may easily infer what he liked to eat and how he liked it to be served. He did not like big dinner parties. 'A party of six is always a talking party. Men and women are not formed into pairs, and do not therefore become dumb. Each person's voice makes another person emulous, and the difficulty felt is not as to what one shall say, but how one shall get it in. Ten, and twelve, and fourteen are the silent numbers' (*The Bertrams*). He liked the table to be covered in a white cloth which was removed when the ladies left the gentlemen, who then settled down to their port over the mahogany.

When it came to the food, Anthony's priority was that there should be enough. 'Such a woman one can thoroughly despise, and even hate,' he wrote of wealthy, parsimonious Mrs Mason of Groby Park in *Orley Farm* – who served up for herself, her husband, their three daughters and the attorney Mr Dockwrath a lunch consisting of three 'scraps' of chicken and three 'morsels' of broiled ham, 'black-looking and very suspicious to the eye'. His approval of Johnny Eames's uncle Mr Toogood in *The Last Chronicle of Barset* is equally tangible: 'Mr Toogood did not give dinner-parties; always begging those whom he asked to enjoy his hospitality, to take pot luck, and telling young men whom he could treat with familiarity, – such as his nephew, – that if they wanted to be regaled à la Russe they must not come to number 75, Tavistock Square.' Mr Toogood's hospitality on this occasion consisted of soup, fish, roast beef, a couple of boiled fowls, 'and a glass of port such as you don't get every day of your life'. Anthony thought every dinner should begin with soup, ate mutton as readily as beef, and appreciated salads and vegetables too. For dessert, many a fruit tart is consumed in his fiction. But as a Frenchman visiting London in the 1850s observed, 'the funda-mental part of an English dinner is the fish and the roast, the rest is accessory.'*

Anthony, after a lifetime of disappointing dinners and lost homes and flittings and lodging houses and rented places, had come into his kingdom.† He was, in a modest way, a country gentleman, like

---

* *A Frenchman Sees the English in the Fifties*, adapted from the French of Francis Wey by Valerie Pirie, Sidgwick & Jackson, 1935.

† The kingdom has not survived. Waltham House was demolished in 1936.

his Trollope forebears. Rose, brought up in the sewer-scented rooms over the bank, had never lived in such style, not even in Seaview Terrace. They enjoyed domestic comfort and contentment on a scale which matched Anthony's limited pretensions and soothed his limitless insecurities.

His home life was rich in small pleasures. He wrote in *Framley Parsonage*: 'A man's own dinner is to himself so important that he cannot bring himself to believe that it is a matter absolutely indifferent to anyone else. A lady's collection of baby-clothes, in early years, or of house linen and curtain-fringes in later life, is so very interesting to her own eye, that she cannot believe but what other people will rejoice to behold it.' This domestic egotism – strong in Rose, who was at the 'house linen and curtain-fringes' stage of life – did not seem dull to him: 'For the most of us, if we do not talk of ourselves, or at any rate of the individual circles of which we are the centres, we can talk of nothing. I cannot hold with those who wish to put down the insignificant chatter of the world.'

If the insignificant chatter was feminine, so much the better. 'I protest that there is no place on the earth's surface so dear to me as my own drawing-room, or rather my wife's drawing-room at home; that I am not a man given hugely to clubs,* but one rather rejoicing in the rustle of petticoats. I like to have women in the same room with me' (*North America*).

And yet in *Framley Parsonage*, one of the most transparent of Anthony's books when it comes to discovering 'what there is in his mind', an anxiety about the 'tuft-hunting', or social climbing, of a devoted husband is at the root of the plot; as are his too-frequent absences from home. It was here that he wrote: 'It is no doubt very wrong to long after a naughty thing. Nevertheless we all do so.' It was here that Mrs Proudie made an appearance in her dressing-gown at breakfast, embarrassing her guests and lending a depressing and fearful gloss to the notion of informal domestic intimacy in her large, loose cap and large, loose wrapper.

In *Orley Farm* he wrote that 'for those who have managed that things shall run smoothly over the domestic rug' evenings at home were the happiest times in life; but Mr Furnival longed to be free to stay away if he pleased, even for a month at a time, without

---

* That was not to be true for very much longer.

'outward bickerings'. 'I have known other men who have dreamed of such a state of things,' mused the author, 'but at this moment I can remember none who have brought their dream to bear.'

When a dinner, or Post Office work, necessitated nights spent in London, Anthony stayed at Garlant's Hotel in Suffolk Street, off Pall Mall. At the GPO where he had started out so long ago, he had the use of an office. 'Make your man ring at the private door (?private!) – nearest to the gates at the South end, i.e. the end of Newgate Street. I hang out within that door,' he told *Cornhill*'s publisher George Smith, apropos the delivery of proofs. Anthony had a London life as well as a home life, a public life as well as a private life. His private life had a public aspect, and its guestly witnesses; and his public life in the great anonymous city had a private, or at any rate a '?private!' aspect.

PART THREE

MIDSTREAM

CHAPTER TWELVE

THE early and mid-1860s were good to Anthony Trollope. At the age of forty-five, he began to have the time of his life. It all happened very quickly, and through the *Cornhill*. In January 1860 the new magazine's publisher, George Smith, gave a great dinner for his contributors. 'It was a memorable banquet in many ways,' Anthony wrote in his autobiography, 'but chiefly so to me because on that occasion I first met many men who afterwards became my most intimate associates. It can rarely happen that one such occasion can be the starting-point of so many friendships.'

At that *Cornhill* dinner, the first of many, Anthony finally met Thackeray – not yet fifty but white-haired already, looking, with his tiny broken nose and considerable height, like a big baby. Their first meeting was not a success. Smith introduced the two with a proper sense of occasion, but Thackeray curtly muttered 'How do?' and turned on his heel – because, at that very moment, he was attacked by a spasm of acute pain in the gut. Anthony, not realising this, was mortified. 'He came to me the next morning,' remembered Smith, 'in a very wrathful mood, and said that had it not been that he was in my house for the first time, he would have walked out of it. He vowed he would never speak to Thackeray again, etc., etc.'* But soon the two men became good friends.

At that first dinner Anthony also met Thackeray's friend, the journalist and editor Robert Bell. He met G. H. Lewes (who wrote on scientific subjects for the *Cornhill*) and the artist John Everett Millais. He met the *Punch* artist John Leech, Millais's great friend, a grey-whiskered, melancholy Irishman, six foot eight inches tall and a great man on the hunting field. Leech hunted in Hertfordshire, and Anthony was soon to ride out with him. He met Sir

---

* Jennifer Glynn, *Prince of Publishers: A Biography of George Smith*, Allison & Busby, 1986.

Charles Taylor, sportsman and clubman, like Anthony a rough man rather than a smooth one who, after dinner, carried Anthony home with him for more talk.

Also at that first dinner was George Augustus Sala, a young journalist and the nominal editor of a rival magazine, *Temple Bar*. Sala left an alarming picture of an Anthony Trollope not quite in control, over-stimulated, 'very much to the fore, contradicting everybody; afterwards saying kind things to everybody, and occasionally going to sleep on sofas or chairs; or leaning against sideboards, and even somnolent while standing erect on the hearthrug. . . .'*

Sala had the perspicacity to realise that Trollope 'had nothing of the bear but his skin'. It was a thin skin. One of the paradoxes of this big, argumentative man was that he was still as thin-skinned as when he was a boy. He minded very much what people thought about him. When his son Harry read, in 1923, the draft of Michael Sadleir's *Trollope: A Commentary*, he wrote to Sadleir: 'I fancy you make too much of my father's aggressiveness. He was not aggressive. In general life few thought more of the opinions of others.'†

The old Whig statesman the Duke of St Bungay told the Duke of Omnium (the former Plantagenet Palliser) in *The Prime Minister*: 'A certain nervous sensitiveness, from which you should free yourself as from a disease, is your only source of weakness. Think about your business as a shoemaker thinks of his.' That was how Anthony insisted on thinking about the business of writing. The Duke of Omnium 'knew that he was too self-conscious, – that he was thinking too much about his own conduct and the conduct of others to him'. Both he and Phineas Finn are described as 'thin-skinned'. Anthony was sympathetically close to both these characters, though not uncritically so.

Anthony, out of his depth, made some mistakes when he first came to London. Boasting a little, maybe, of his new circle, he regaled Edmund Yates at the Post Office with a silly tale about

* George Augustus Sala, *Things I Have Seen and People I Have Known* (1894).
† Here is an extreme example from late in life. In 1880 he wrote to Gladstone, then Prime Minister: 'For some years I have thought that you had, not unnaturally, forgotten me. But latterly, – and again yesterday, – I have been made to suppose that you purposely shunned me.' Anthony's sensitivity was probably due to embarrassment about his disagreement with Gladstone's Irish policy.

something Smith had said at the *Cornhill* dinner, which seemed to betray an ignorance of literature. Yates repeated it in a gossipy article in a New York paper and the London *Saturday Review* took it up. This did Yates no good with Thackeray, who already had reason to dislike Yates, and had strong feelings about confidentiality; he wrote a riposte in the *Cornhill*. Anthony confessed his indiscretion to Smith, who was angry. For once, Anthony did not try to roar his way out of trouble. According to Smith, he said, 'I know I have done wrong, and you may say anything you like to me.' He was forgiven. 'Our friend won't sin again,' as Thackeray wrote to Smith.*

Of all these new friends Anthony loved and revered Thackeray most, 'one of the most tender-hearted human beings I ever knew'. He made joking reference to Thackeray, and to himself, in *Can You Forgive Her?*, making fun in his hunting chapter of a heavyweight 'sporting literary gentleman' who was himself:† a companion said, 'I'll bet half a crown that he's come down from London this morning, that he was up all night last night, and that he tells us so three times before the hounds are out of the paddock.' There was talk on the field of George Vavasor selling a horse to one 'Cinquebars' – who was, as Anthony admitted in a footnote, a character escaped out of Thackeray's novels. It pleased him to link his work with Thackeray's. In defining the false and unscrupulous Lizzie Eustace in *The Eustace Diamonds* as an 'opulent and aristocratic Becky Sharp' Anthony was forestalling critical accusations of 'copying', and paying tribute to his friend's creation.

George Smith, their host that first evening and the *Cornhill*'s publisher – tall and stout, with fine large eyes – was nine years younger than Anthony. He and his wife Elizabeth were living at 11 Gloucester Square when the first *Cornhill* dinner was held. In 1863 the Smiths moved to Oak Hill Lodge, Hampstead, where they were 'at home' on Friday evenings; their menu card was designed by George du Maurier, a regular guest. It was in the

---

* Jennifer Glynn, *Prince of Publishers: A Biography of George Smith*.

† He borrowed for the heavyweight sporting literary gentleman the name 'Pollock' from his friend Frederick (later Sir Frederick) Pollock. Every now and then we can pick up references and allusions such as this, once obvious to all in his circle; how many more must there be, that no one can now know?

Smiths' Hampstead garden, with its views across sloping lawns looking over towards Harrow, that Leslie Stephen courted Minny Thackeray, daughter of Anthony's new friend.*

At the Smiths' dinner table Anthony also met Albert Smith† (once, just before he died); Matthew Higgins, who wrote under the pseudonym Jacob Omnium, an old Etonian fiercely critical of Eton, and apparently six foot eight inches tall – like Leech. (It is odd that so many of this group were so tall. Thackeray was six foot three.) He met Wilkie Collins the 'sensational' novelist, then in his mid-thirties, whose most celebrated book *The Woman in White* came out that same year. Collins was not tall; he was short-legged, with a bulbous forehead, and as hopelessly short-sighted as Anthony himself. Collins's close friend was Charles Dickens, with whom he escaped on frequent jaunts – emphatically *en garçon* – to Paris. Because Collins was a close friend of Dickens, he was never a close friend of Thackeray. Anthony had to learn that it was hard to be the close friend of both.

George Smith had gone into the family firm of Smith, Elder & Co. at fourteen. The year after taking over, aged twenty-two, on the death of his father, he had published Charlotte Brontë's *Jane Eyre* (and later her subsequent books), and he looked after Charlotte when she visited London. He was Ruskin's publisher; he had known Thackeray since 1849 and was his original and main publisher. The first time Smith ever gave a four-figure sum for a novel was for Thackeray's *Henry Esmond*. He was able to pay his authors well because the publishing was subsidised by a second and quite different family business. Smith, Elder & Co. had banking and shipping interests, and also acted as agents, i.e. suppliers, to the British army, providing pistols, saddlery, provisions, books, and all kinds of essential equipment. Trade underpinned literature and both thrived.

Thackeray gave up as editor of the *Cornhill* after only two years, in May 1862, after which Smith ran it himself, with G. H. Lewes as consulting editor, until 1871 when Leslie Stephen took over. Thackeray's role had in any case been chiefly advisory, his main

---

* Leslie Stephen (1832–1904) married Minny Thackeray in 1867. She died in 1875. His daughters by his second marriage to Julia Duckworth were Virginia (Woolf) and Vanessa (Bell).
† The man who had been blackballed from the Garrick in 1855 for having a beard.

contribution being his own writing. Rumour said that the interference of Smith's wife Elizabeth had some bearing on his withdrawal from the office. She was a forthright and beautiful young woman, but more timorous than Anthony knew. George Smith said that when he and Elizabeth stayed at Waltham House, Anthony proposed, out of mere kindness of heart, that they should put a bar up and his wife might then relieve the dullness of her country visit by jumping over it on Anthony's favourite hunter for an hour or two each morning 'This was, for my wife, a very alarming proposition indeed.'*

Anthony, from the moment of the success of *Framley Parsonage*, was the star of the *Cornhill*, and nothing was too good for him. In September 1860, shortly before Anthony and Rose went on holiday to Italy, a large parcel arrived at Waltham House. Anthony in a letter to George Smith described how he opened it himself, working through layers of packing paper, till he reached a travelling-bag:

> 'I never ordered it,' said I angrily.
>
> 'It's a present,' said my wife.
>
> 'Gammon – It's a commission to take to Florence for some dandy and I'll be – '
>
> For a moment I fancy she imagined it was intended for her, but we came at once upon a brandy flask & a case of razors, and that illusion was dispelled.

This elaborately fitted bag was a gift from George Smith. Whether he would be able to use all those 'gold pins, silver soap-dishes, & cut glass', Anthony could not say. 'I feel a little like a hog in armour, but will do my best.' But he was touched, especially, as he told Smith, as he felt the debt was all the other way – 'seeing that you have brought me in contact with readers to [be] counted by hundreds of thousands, instead of by hundreds.'

Rose and Anthony duly went to Florence to stay with Tom and Theo, with the new travelling-bag. Anthony – without Rose? – called several times on the Brownings at the Casa Guidi. Both the Brownings thought Anthony 'first-rate' as a novelist (while deploring the sloppiness of his grammar), and liked both him and

* Jennifer Glynn, *Prince of Publishers: A Biography of George Smith.*

283

Tom. '*Framley Parsonage* is perfect it seems to me,' Mrs Browning wrote to her brother George Barrett, and added: 'Anthony has an extraordinary beard to be grown in England' – as if the beard were a horticultural specimen – 'but is very English in spite of it, simple, naif, direct, frank – everything one likes in a man – Anti-Napoleonist [Napoleon III] of course, and ignorant of political facts more than of course and not withstanding that, caring for *me*. . . .'*

Anthony met in Tom's house that autumn a young woman he was to care for in a much more intense and painful way. Kate Field was a twenty-two-year-old American, daughter of a Dublin-born actor and his actress wife. She was in Florence studying singing with Pietro Romani and writing articles for the Boston *Courier*, whose editor had given her introductions to the Brownings and the Tom Trollopes.

Kate Field left the best record we have of Tom's extravagant antiquarianism, in her description of the Villino Trollope with 'its marble pillars, its grim men in armour . . . its majolica, its old bridal chests and carved furniture, the beautiful terra-cotta of the Virgin and Child by Orgagna, its hundred *ogetti* of the Cinque Cento'. The real life of the house, the 'laughter and buzz of many tongues', took place out on the loggia – 'opening upon a garden, with its lofty pillars, its tesselated marbled floor, its walls inlaid with terra-cotta, bas-reliefs, inscriptions, and coats of arms, and here and there a niche devoted to some antique Madonna'. On this terrace, Kate witnessed the 'philosophic reasoning' of her host contrasting with the 'almost boyish enthusiasm and impulsive argumentation of Anthony Trollope, who is an admirable specimen of a frank and loyal Englishman'.†

There are three things to understand about Kate Field.

One, she was extremely attractive, slim and blue-eyed, with chestnut hair in loose curls, full of vitality, yet frequently in interestingly delicate health. She had a beautiful speaking voice, with a Boston accent. She moved and danced well, and she wore

---

* Paul Landis (ed.), *Letters of the Brownings to George Barrett*, University of Illinois Press, 1958.

† From her very fulsome recollections of George Eliot, published as a letter to the editor in the New York *Tribune*, 22 December 1880.

pretty clothes. There is reference to white tulle and blue ribbons, and to white tulle with silver lilies.

Two, she had strong feminist beliefs.* Browning, who liked her very much, told her that he read ambition in the glisten of her eyes. She was educated in art and science, and talented as a singer, a writer and an actress – but insufficiently talented to make an important name for herself in any of these arts, though she was to practise them all with some success.

Three, she collected the photographs of literary lions, and she collected the literary lions too, making herself irresistible to them – lionesses as well as lions. She loved Mrs Browning extravagantly, albeit on a short acquaintance. When Mrs Browning died, she left Kate a gold locket containing a lock of her hair twisted in the shape of two hearts.

In falling under Kate's spell Anthony was joining a cult. Robert Browning and Tom Trollope both wrote her long letters laced with sentiment and a mild, pseudo-fatherly suggestiveness. Another English literary expatriate, the poet Walter Savage Landor, became even more besotted. Landor was over eighty; the summer before (1859), Robert Browning had met him wandering aimlessly round Florence in the burning heat saying his wife had turned him out of their Fiesole villa. She had reason. He had absented himself from his family for thirty years, then suddenly taken it into his head to return. Browning felt responsible for Landor, who was an old friend and supporter of both his work and his wife's. So the intractable, noisy and irrational old man was installed on the first floor of the boarding-house kept by Mrs Browning's former maid Wilson. This was hard on Wilson. Landor was quite unmanageable.

The old poet undertook to teach Latin to Kate Field, 'and he feels', as Mrs Browning wrote to her, 'as we all do, that you are clever, dear, and good'. For Christmas 1860 Landor gave Kate his only copy of his two-volume *Collected Works* (1846), annotated with his corrections 'and doubly valuable on this account', as she

* Kate Field's journal, at seventeen: 'Oh, if I were a man. . . . There is not an ambition, a desire, a feeling, a thought, an impulse, an instinct that I am not obliged to crush. And why? because I am a woman, and a woman must content herself with indoor life, with sewing and babies. Well, they pretend to say that God invented women to be just what they are. I say that He did not, and men have made women what they are, and if they attribute their doings to the Almighty, they *lie*.' Lilian Whiting, *Kate Field: A Record* (1899).

wrote to her aunt in America. 'Was it not kind of the poor old man?' Landor's next gift to her was 'all the manuscript scraps in his possession, which I am to edit and publish after his death'.* This was rather more than Kate bargained for, as was his habit of visiting her every single morning. When she was leaving Florence, Landor came round with a vast album as a farewell present. It contained 140 engravings and drawings of great value – heads by Raphael, flowers by Leonardo, a Salvator Rosa landscape, sixteen sketches by Turner, some by Gainsborough, others by Claude Lorrain and Poussin. On Tom's advice Kate did not keep the album. Tom returned it to the offended old man, and as a compromise they agreed Kate should have it after Landor's death.

That autumn of 1860, when Kate was learning Latin with Landor, she wrote to her aunt in America: 'Anthony Trollope is a very delightful companion. I see a great deal of him.'

She did not mention Rose at all. Anthony, in a short story, 'Mrs General Talboys', written just after he returned from Florence (but set in Rome), described, under the playful guise of the fictional Mr and Mrs Mackinnon, more or less how he and Rose presented themselves in Italy. Mackinnon, who 'earned an ample living by his pen', was 'a big burly man, near to fifty as I suppose, somewhat awkward in his gait, and somewhat loud in his laugh. But though nigh to fifty, and thus ungainly, he liked to be smiled on by pretty women, and liked, as some said, to be flattered by them also.'

And his wife? 'Of Mrs Mackinnon no one did make much, and yet she was one of the sweetest, dearest, quietest little creatures that ever made glad a man's fireside. She was exquisitely pretty, always in good humour, never stupid, self-denying to a fault, and yet she was generally in the background. She would seldom come forward of her own free will, but was contented to sit behind her teapot and hear Mackinnon do his roaring.'

And she was never annoyed by his flirting. As often when Anthony in his fiction seemed obliquely to be praising Rose, his account sounds more prescriptive than descriptive. He said in *Orley Farm*, which he was writing at this time: 'The advantages of matrimony are many and great – so many and so great, that all

* Lilian Whiting, *Kate Field: A Record.*

men, doubtless, ought to marry. But even matrimony may have its drawbacks; among which unconcealed and undeserved jealousy on the part of the wife is perhaps as disagreeable as any.' In fairness to wives it should be remembered that this statement was made in the context of solicitor Mr Furnival's unusual interest in his client Lady Mason. Mrs Furnival's jealousy, though irritating, was not misplaced.

Kate wrote to her aunt that 'He has promised to send me a copy of the "Arabian Nights" (which I have never read) in which he intends to write "Kate Field, from the Author," and to write me a four-page letter on condition that I answer it.'

Anthony, back at Waltham House, was as good as his word, sending out through the good offices of George Smith a copy of the *Arabian Nights* to Kate in Florence along with an English saddle for Tom's daughter Bice, who went riding with the Brownings' son Pen. He wrote Kate a 'My dear Miss Field' letter: 'I am beginning to feel towards you & your whereabouts as did your high-flown American correspondent. Undying art, Italian skies, the warmth of southern, sunny love, the poetry of the Arno and the cloud clapt Apennines, are beginning to have all the charms which distance gives. I enjoy these delicacies in England – when I am in Italy in the flesh, my mind runs chiefly on grapes, roast chestnuts, cigars, and lemonade. Nevertheless let me council [sic] you in earnest not to throw away time that is precious.' She should, he said, see and study as much as she could while in Florence.

He also asked to be remembered to 'Cleopatra', a code-name for, possibly, the original of Mrs General Talboys in his short story. Mrs Talboys, who had 'soft peach-like cheeks' and 'a dimpled chin and a full bust' was outrageously provocative and free in her speech. She flirted with all the men and became intimate with a married Irish philanderer, urging him to be a free spirit and get a divorce. At a picnic on the Appian Way, after much wine had been drunk, Mrs Talboys and the Irishman disappeared together among the ruins. She emerged dishevelled and hysterical: O'Brien had taken her sexual invitation at face value. 'My wife,' Anthony wrote to George Smith, 'criticizing it [the story], says that it is ill-natured.'

Thackeray turned down 'Mrs General Talboys' for the *Cornhill* on moral grounds. It was just too explicit. Anthony accepted his decision. 'An impartial Editor must do his duty. Pure morals must be supplied.' He justified himself in a long letter, of which the burden was: 'I will not allow that I am indecent, and profess that squeamishness – in so far as it is squeamishness and not delicacy – should be disregarded by a writer.' Thackeray was having one of his attacks of gastric trouble when the letter came, and gave it to one of his daughters to read. Her verdict on Anthony was: 'He is an old dear and you should write him an affectionate letter.'

The friendship was unimpaired.* But in *Can You Forgive Her?*, written in 1863–4, Anthony allowed Kate Vavasor an outburst on the vexed question of delicacy: 'Oh, indelicate! How I do hate that word. If any word in the language reminds me of a whited sepulchre it is that: – all clean and polished outside with filth and rottenness within. Are your thoughts delicate? That's the thing.' Delicacy in sexual matters was maintained, ostensibly, so as not to offend feminine sensibilities; but Kate Vavasor, using a typically Trollopian image, made no exception for women: 'Delicacy with many women is like their cleanliness. Nothing can be nicer than the whole outside get-up, but you wouldn't wish to answer for anything beneath.'

George Smith paid £600 ('the hardest bargain I ever sold to a publisher,' said Anthony) to have the rejected *Struggles of Brown, Jones, and Robinson* slip serially through the *Cornhill*, sandwiched between articles on competitive examinations, the digestive organs, Liberalism, fish-farming, and poems, including one by Charlotte Brontë. (The *Cornhill* was nothing if not eclectic.) Thackeray's novel *Philip* had the place of honour in the front.

Anthony was a celebrity guest at what he called Mudie's 'great flare-up' – a reception in December 1860 to celebrate the opening of Mudie's new library, rebuilt on the old site on the corner of New Oxford Street and Museum Street. Mudie's new 'Great Ionic Hall' was a high, round neo-classical room under a dome, with

---

* 'Mrs General Talboys' was included in the second series of *Tales of All Countries* (1863) after publication in the *London Review* (2 February 1861). The *London Review* also published another story rejected by the *Cornhill*, 'A Ride Across Palestine', the one about the man who lived intimately with an attractive youth only to discover afterwards that the young man was a girl. These stories provoked violently disapproving letters from readers. Laurence Oliphant, one of the proprietors of the magazine, wrote a pompous letter to Anthony about the adverse response. Anthony wrote 'A wonderful letter' on Oliphant's missive. Perhaps he was being ironic; or perhaps he felt Oliphant had been generous, under the circumstances.

white columns and stucco decorations, the books ranged in tiers all round the galleried space, and semi-circular counters for customers. By now Mudie's library books, in tin-lined boxes, were being shipped to all corners of the colonies and the empire. This near-monopoly was not to last much longer. Authors were protesting against the tyranny of the multi-volume format, cheap reprints were making book-buying popular, and there was a growing number of public libraries.

Meanwhile Anthony was even more firmly established as one of Mudie's mainstays, each novel being rapidly published in book form after serialisation – apart from *The Struggles of Brown, Jones, and Robinson*, which first appeared as a book in a pirated version from Harper in New York; Smith, Elder did not bring out their edition until 1870. In May 1861, Thackeray was writing: 'I think Trollope is much more popular with the Cornhill Magazine readers than I am: and doubt whether I am not going down hill considerably in public favour.' The last years of Thackeray's life were made wretched by this conviction that he was out of date and that the public were tired of him. He grumbled sadly about it in his clubs, accepting no polite demurrals; but he showed no jealousy of Anthony, and praised him highly.*

Anthony was anxious to maintain the connection with Chapman & Hall as well as with George Smith. So it was Chapman & Hall, not George Smith, who published *Orley Farm* in 1862; and *Orley Farm* was serialised, between March 1861 and October 1862, not in a magazine but in twenty monthly numbers – paperbacked 'parts', costing one shilling, which could be collected and bound by the reader (once he had cut out the advertisements at front and back). Part-publication was an alternative method to magazine serialisation for publishers to profit twice from the same work, and was longer established: way back in 1836, Dickens's *The Pickwick Papers* had appeared in monthly parts and enjoyed a massive success. (Uncle Henry Milton used to bring the latest number up to Hadley in his pocket.)

Anthony was paid £2,500 for *Orley Farm*. The house and farm in the novel, which Lady Mason attempted to save for her son by

---

* John Vincent (ed.), *Disraeli, Derby and the Conservative Party: Journals and Memoirs of Edward Henry, Lord Stanley 1849–1869*, Harvester Press, 1978. Journal entry for 19 February 1863.

forging a will, were based on Julian Hill. 'I do not know that there is a dull page in the book,' wrote Anthony with justification in his autobiography. He was fond of this novel, in which he explored, indirectly, the shock of long-ago losses to his own family – the loss of the hoped-for Julians in Hertfordshire, and of their own Julians, and then Julian Hill, in Harrow. Lady Mason was a gallant, misguided woman whose personal morality was not the world's. She was also, at the age of forty-seven, fair and comely, capable of inspiring passion and with 'more of a woman's beauty' than when she was a bride.

Her neighbour Sir Peregrine Orme loved her deeply. There is in *Orley Farm* one of those sudden, shocking Trollopian scenes where emotion drives a properly decorous woman to abandon her decorum: Lady Mason confessing her guilt to her upright and elderly lover Sir Peregrine, falling on the floor and twining her arms round his knees. Another example of this sudden, shocking display of feeling occurs in *Phineas Redux*: Lady Laura Kennedy 'crouching prostrate on the floor' in her brother-in-law's drawing-room, when told that Phineas had been arrested for murder, having 'crouched down rather than fallen, as though it were vain to attempt to stand upright.' Such scenes were the normal stuff of contemporary melodrama, though in melodrama the stricken woman would have fainted. That agonised 'crouching' was inspired. In the doggedly unsensational Trollopian context, the effect on the reader is of witnessing something indecently private.

Mr Chaffanbrass, the Old Bailey barrister who made his first appearance in *The Three Clerks*, reappeared in *Orley Farm*, defending Lady Mason; he was later to defend Phineas Finn on the murder charge. A most unsavoury person – with his snuff-filled handkerchief, his habit of picking his teeth, his crooked wig, his grubby hands and linen and his sadistic cross-examinations – he was Anthony Trollope's most memorable fictional lawyer. Anthony made him MP for the Essex Marshes, the country across which he himself hunted.

On the Continent, families of substance lived in cities and retired to the country for the summer and in times of social or financial ill-fortune. In Britain, families of substance lived in their country houses and came up to London – where the seriously rich had their own houses, and the rest rented – during the Season. One of the results of the railway network was that gentlemen could travel up and down to London more quickly and easily, at any time. Gentlemen's clubs proliferated, in order to feed, water, contain and entertain them. This was greatly to the advantage of professional men who lived in or near London all the year round, and made great use of the clubs.

Then as (mostly) now, these clubs were all-male. One did not join at one's own whim. A man had to be proposed and seconded by existing members, and a card, or page in a book, was prepared for each candidate, which his friends in the club would sign in support. Even then, an aspirant could be blackballed at the decisive meeting.

Apart from the clubs, respectable hotels and dining places were at last beginning to open. At the London railway termini, ponderous station hotels were erected. Johnny Eames in *The Small House at Allington* had a grim dinner in the oversized and empty dining-room at the Great Western Hotel at Paddington, which was clearly all too familiar to Johnny's creator: 'What comfort are you to have, seated alone on that horsehair chair, staring into the room and watching the waiters as they whisk about their towels? No one but an Englishman has ever yet thought of subjecting himself to such a position as that.'

Cox's in Jermyn Street was cosier, a maze of small private dining-rooms, much used by people up from the country. This was where Lord de Guest entertained Johnny Eames in *The Small House at Allington*. Also in Jermyn Street was the Turkish Bath. Anthony used it in a short story, bequeathing to us a picture of himself as a purblind hippo; there was a necessity, when naked except for a couple of towels, of 'maintaining a certain dignity of deportment which has certainly grown upon you since you succeeded in freeing yourself from your socks and trousers. For ourselves, we have to admit that the difficulty is much increased by the fact that we are short sighted, and are obligated by the sudorific processes and by the shampooing and washing that are to come, to leave our spectacles behind us' ('The Turkish Bath').

The gentry still lived or lodged in Mayfair, though an alternative residential quarter was spreading west, down the Bayswater Road. Anthony disliked these new houses. They were all drawing-room, he thought, with nothing behind. In *The Last Chronicle of Barset* he put the nouveaux riches Dobbs Broughtons in a new, large Bayswater house, where Johnny Eames went to a pretentious dinner party, and where vulgar Mrs Van Siever (wearing false front hair and false curls, 'as to which it cannot be conceived that she would suppose that anyone would be ignorant as to their falseness') asked a fellow guest, Mr Musselboro, 'Why doesn't What's his name have real silver forks?' She was speaking of her host, within her hostess's hearing.

'What's the use?' said Mr Musselboro. 'Everybody has these plated things now. What's the use of a lot of capital lying dead?'

'Everybody doesn't. I don't. You know as well as I do, Musselboro, that the appearance of things goes for a good deal. Capital isn't lying dead as long as people know you've got it.'

So much for Bayswater. South Kensington too was being developed, and Adolphus Crosbie in *The Small House* thought of moving with his cold bride Lady Alexandrina to yet another recently developed area – the new squares fringing Belgravia and Westminster at Pimlico, near Vauxhall Bridge. But Pimlico too was socially dubious. 'For heaven's sake, my dear,' a friend said to Lady Alexandrina, 'don't let him take you anywhere beyond Eccleston Square!' Sir Frederick Pollock in his memoirs described seeing the Pimlico houses being built in 1856: 'In one place they were breaking up as old iron the columns designed by Nash for the Regent Street Quadrant – an instance of the mutability of things. A morticing machine, and one for executing mouldings in wood, were curious. All parts of a house are made on the premises – floors and doors, windows, grates, gas-fittings etc.' John Tilley and his children moved to one of these new houses – 73 St George's Square.

To see a bit of life, gentlemen (without their wives) still went east to the gas-flares and fish-smells and raucous, indecent street-life of Covent Garden and the Strand. But Simpson's in the Strand was setting a new tone for eating out. Like in a club, the table linen was clean, as were the waiters who pushed vast joints of meat around on trolleys. Simpson's was next to the old-established 'cigar divan', over a tobacconist's, where one paid a shilling for coffee, a cigar, a newspaper and the use of a chess or backgammon board.* The first tea-shop – the Aerated Bread Co. – opened in the

* Mr Harding in *The Warden* took refuge in the cigar divan during his long day in London.

Strand in 1861, as a temperance measure.

Late at night, for port and cigars, chaps went to the Blue Posts in Cork Street. Anthony enjoyed this place, and put it in *The Claverings*; the rascally Franco-Polish Count Pateroff took Harry Clavering to dine there, regaling him with a paean to good digestion which his creator's friend Thackeray would echo. To digest well, Pateroff said, was to be in Paradise: 'Adam and Eve were in paradise. Why? Their digestion was good. Ah! then they took liberties, ate bad fruit, – things they could not digest. They what we call ruined their constitutions, destroyed their gastric juices, and then they were expelled from paradise by an angel with a flaming sword. The angel with the flaming sword, which turned two ways, was indigestion.'

There was another Blue Posts in the Haymarket, which was more questionable; and next to the Haymarket Theatre, the Café de l'Europe, with a motley clientele; and next to the Café de l'Europe, the Raleigh Club, for billiards and broiled bones, and a private room upstairs for sex. (The police estimate of the number of prostitutes in London in 1860 was 6,940; this figure took account only of those circulating in the West End.) East of Temple Bar, in Fleet Street, were Dick's, Anderton's and the Cheshire Cheese, where customers superintended the cooking of their steak or chop. Further east still, in the City, down dirty alleys, were Reuben's and Joe's and Ned's, where one ate steak and a baked potato, squashed elbow to elbow with fellow diners. The place to go for breakfast, on the way home, was the White Horse Cellar in Piccadilly, where coaches from the west used to pull up before the railways came, and which still had cubicles like horseboxes and a sanded floor.

The clubs were the key to a pleasant and gentlemanly social life, and a wide circle of acquaintances. During his first summer back in England, Anthony asked Richard Monckton Milnes, an MP and a *Cornhill* contributor, to put his name up for the Cosmopolitan Club. He was not actually elected till the following April, 1861.

The Cosmopolitan met in two smoky rooms in Charles Street, off Berkeley Square, on Wednesday and Sunday nights, during the Season. On Wednesdays the House of Commons sat only from noon till six, so that was the night for society dinner parties – after which Cabinet ministers, editors, peers, journalists, artists might repair to the 'Cos' to smoke cigars and gossip. Members who had been asked to no dinner party at all dressed as if they had, and dropped in. Anthony put the Cosmopolitan into *Phineas Redux*, calling it the Universe: 'It was kept open only one hour before and one hour after midnight, and that only on two nights of the week, and that only when Parliament was sitting. Its attractions were not numerous, consisting chiefly of tobacco and tea. The conversation was generally listless and often desultory.' Even so, 'men liked to be members of the Universe'.

The Cosmopolitan was where public and private met. Thackeray was a member of the Cosmopolitan, though it was not really his sort of place, and Millais, and Browning. The young Prince of Wales enjoyed it. The Cosmopolitan was a fount of high gossip, and an ideal source of material for Anthony's parliamentary novels. Monckton-Milnes, Anthony's introduction to the 'Cos', who became Lord Houghton in 1864 (and in whose Yorkshire house the Trollopes were to be so uncharitably scrutinised by Lady Rose Fane), was described* as 'a politician who wrote poetry, a railway director who lived in literature, a *libre-penseur* who championed the Tractarians, a sentimentalist who talked like a cynic, and a philosopher who had elevated conviviality to the dignity of an exact science.' Because of his relaxed social manner, he was nicknamed 'The Cool of the Evening'. He had a notable collection of pornography.

The Cosmopolitan was sophisticated; but the Garrick was the favourite club of most of Anthony's friends, and their home from home. In *Phineas Finn*, the Hon. Laurence Fitzgibbon told Phineas that he should belong to Brooks's, 'and Phineas immediately began to feel that he would have done nothing until he could get into Brooks's.' For Phineas and Brooks's, we may read Anthony and the Garrick. He was elected to the club in 1862, proposed by Robert Bell and seconded by Thackeray, who belonged to lots of clubs, including the Athenaeum and the Reform; but he had belonged to the Garrick since 1833, when he was twenty-two. In a lonely, anxious life, the Garrick was Thackeray's chief refuge. He called it 'the little G'.

* In *Collections and Recollections* by One Who Has Kept A Diary, published by Smith, Elder in 1898.

The Garrick was founded in 1831 as a place where 'actors and men of education and refinement might meet on equal terms', and as a 'rendezvous for literary men'. When Anthony joined, it was still in its original premises at 35 King Street, Covent Garden. The congested alleys between King Street and St Martin's Lane were being cleared to form New King Street, on which a new and splendid Garrick Club was under construction; they moved in July 1864, and at the club's request New King Street was renamed Garrick Street.

The theatrical aspect of the Garrick appealed strongly to Anthony. His early attempt to write a play, *The Noble Jilt*, had been a failure. He recycled the plot for the novel *Can You Forgive Her?*, and in *The Eustace Diamonds* he sent Lizzie and her friend Mrs Carbuncle to the Haymarket Theatre to see – '*The Noble Jilt*, from the hand of a very eminent author.' 'The play, as a play, was a failure; at least so said Mrs Carbuncle.' But the women discussed the moral issues raised by the piece in the cab all the way home. This was all fun for Anthony; but maybe he really did have dreams of resuscitating his play. Was it the yellow manuscript of *The Noble Jilt*, or a later effort, his unperformed dramatisation of *The Last Chronicle of Barset* under the title 'Did He Steal It?', that he gave to the actor John Hare one day at the Garrick, asking for an opinion? The Garrick's historian* tells the story:

> A day or two later [Hare] encountered Trollope ascending to the cardroom. 'Well, young man – and what do you think of the play?' 'Oh, Mr Trollope,' stammered Hare, 'I'm afraid, I'm afraid – ' 'Don't like it, eh?' asked Trollope. 'Quite right young man,' patting Hare on the shoulder, 'I don't like it myself,' and he went up the stairs to his whist beaming through his glittering spectacles.

Anthony loved his whist in the smoking-room at the old Garrick in King Street, and afterwards in the new premises. Regular players included Thackeray, Dickens, the *Punch* contributors John Leech and Shirley Brooks, Millais, and Charles Reade. This last was an eccentric and cantankerous creature who filled large ledgers with historical information and anecdotes

* Guy Boas, *The Garrick Club* (privately published by the club, 1948).

which he copied into his novels; he collected violins, and other people's ideas. He was also an irritatingly slow card-player. Anthony, who greatly admired Reade's novel *The Cloister and the Hearth*, looked upon Reade as 'endowed almost with genius, but as one who has not been gifted by nature with ordinary powers of reasoning.' He meant, Reade could not tell right from wrong.

The Garrick and the Cosmopolitan were not Anthony's only clubs. He was a founder member of the Arts Club in Hanover Square, but resigned after a few years because he never went there; and he belonged, more from duty than from desire, to the Civil Service Club. In 1864 he was elected to the Athenaeum by special invitation, which was a great compliment. Later he joined the Turf Club, 'which I found to be serviceable – or the reverse – only for the playing of whist at high points' (*Autobiography*). But his heart was in the Garrick. In 1867 he paid £52.10.0 to become a life member; his certificate of life membership was signed by his convivial friend Sir Charles Taylor as chairman of the committee.

It was not just the theatre atmosphere, or the whist. It was, as he wrote in his autobiography, because he felt that he was popular at the Garrick. 'I have long been aware of a certain weakness in my own character, which I may call a craving for love. I have ever had a wish to be liked by those around me, – a wish that during the first half of my life was never gratified.' He recalled his 'pariah' status as a schoolboy and as a penniless young clerk in London. Ireland had been much better, but 'even in Ireland I had in truth lived but little in society'. Only after they were settled in Waltham had he 'begun to live much with others', and the Garrick Club 'was the first assemblage of men at which I felt myself to be popular'.

After knowing no one, but having heard of everyone, Anthony quickly got to know everyone, and everyone had heard of him. Any unpleasant comments about him may be ascribed to jealousy, and to the irritation of old-timers at having to adapt themselves to a new personality in their midst.

'Should I live to see my story [*Framley Parsonage*] illustrated by Millais no body would be able to hold me,' Anthony wrote to George Smith in February 1860. Millais, just over thirty, had recently abandoned the ideals and ideas of the Pre-Raphaelites. In the opinion of his critics, he had also abandoned his art, in favour of popular success and book-illustration. Anthony had been ambivalent about the Pre-Raphaelites, praising in *The Warden* their 'elaborate perseverance' and technique; but 'the lady with the stiff back and bent neck, who looks at her flower, and is still looking from hour to hour, gives us an idea of pain without grace, and abstraction without a cause.'

Millais had been a child prodigy, and was nicknamed 'the Child'. He had a mop of bushy bronze hair and was tall, thin and very handsome, even pretty. His friends continually used the word 'manly' in their descriptions of him, as if to stress that there was nothing effeminate about him. Not that there could be much doubt about his manliness. His wife Effie had been Mrs John Ruskin, before the marriage was annulled for non-consummation. As Mrs Millais, she produced eight children. Millais was boyish and charming, 'one of those good-natured individuals', his oldest friend the painter Holman Hunt told Edward Lear, 'who have a knack of always making other people carry their parcels'.*

Yet Millais was easily cast down, and suffered from depressions over his work, and over adverse criticism. This was another bond between them. Anthony rarely talked about his own depressions. It was to Millais that he wrote, 'It is, I suppose, some weakness of temperament that makes me, without intelligible cause, such a pessimist at heart.'†

Anthony liked his life and possibly did not understand why he was not 'happy' all the time, as Mrs Trollope had unrealistically exhorted her children to be. So he called his depressions and pessimism 'weakness of temperament' and his craving for love a 'weakness of character'. His self-knowledge was considerable but he does not seem to have made the connection between the depressions and the craving for love. His long-established insecurity was of the kind that cannot be assuaged. No amount or degree of reassurance could have satisfied him. A fat cheque from a publisher, a convivial evening at the Garrick, a gratifying chat with a pretty woman, Rose's reliable affection and support, were all balm to his soul – but not definitively. A lesser person, or someone without a fantasy life (which Anthony led in his fiction),

---

* Anne Clark Amor, *William Holman Hunt: The True Pre-Raphaelite*, Constable, 1989.
† Quoted in T. H. S. Escott, *Anthony Trollope: His Work, Associates and Originals*, John Lane The Bodley Head, 1913.

would have sought reassurance in trivial sexual conquests. This most worthwhile and lovable man needed to have his worth and his lovableness proved to himself and to the world over and over again.

Anthony was unlike Millais in that he learned not to be excessively upset by adverse criticism. He paid careful attention to reviews of his books, he wrote in his autobiography, and could recognise which ones were 'chaff', to be thrown to the winds whether they praised him or not, and which were 'corn' from which he could learn something useful. But his tendency to depression, and his recognition of the same tendency in Millais, was undoubtedly one of the bonds between them.

Millais illustrated *Framley Parsonage* and *Orley Farm*;* for the latter, he sketched, perhaps from a photograph, Julian Hill. In any case Anthony was anxious that no other house should represent Orley Farm. He gave the particulars to Chapman, the publisher: 'The house is at Sunbury† – on the London side of Harrow. There are two houses which did belong to my father, & were then called "Julians" – I doubt whether the name has been kept – In one, the larger, Mr Cunningham the rector of Harrow still I believe lives. The other which is a little lower down the hill, and a little further from the high road, is the house in question. I will however write to Harrow & learn the name of the occupier.' Anthony accepted Millais's depiction of his characters whole-heartedly. 'I have carried on some of those characters from book to book, and have had my own early ideas impressed indelibly on my memory by the excellence of his delineations' (*Autobiography*). In *Orley Farm* Anthony described Lady Mason as she sat alone in the house she risked losing, waiting for her trial, and referred, within the narrative, to the illustration: 'The idea, however, which the reader will have conceived of her as she sat there will have come to him from the skill of the artist, and not from the words of the writer.'

There was never a break in his affection for Millais. 'To see him

---

* Millais did more than eighty drawings in all for Trollope. Apart from the two novels mentioned, he illustrated *The Small House at Allington*, *Rachel Ray*, and *Phineas Finn*.

† Sunbury, which is where Anthony went to school, was a slip of the pen for Sudbury, the village at the foot of the hill up to Harrow. Julian Hill was, in fact, a school in 1860.

has always been a pleasure. His voice has been a sweet sound in my ears,' he wrote in his autobiography, which he did not intend to have published in his lifetime; thus his words would reach Millais from beyond the grave, 'and will tell him of my regard, – as one living man never tells another.'

G. H. Lewes became a familiar friend as quickly as did Millais. He was 'My dear Sir' to Anthony in July 1860, when Anthony obligingly asked the Postmaster General for a nomination as a PO clerk for Lewes's eighteen-year-old son Charles. He was 'My dear Mr Lewes' when Anthony wrote explaining that Charles, having been nominated, would have to take a test: 'For myself I should not dream of passing. I sd. break down in figures & spelling too, not to talk of handwriting.'

Young Charles Lewes was accepted by the PO as a 'supplementary clerk, second class' and, wrote Anthony to 'My dear Lewes', 'I hope I shall soon shake hands with him over his desk at the Post Office.' He told Lewes to remind his son that a government clerk 'may follow any pursuit without detriment to his public utility', citing various civil servants who were making their mark in literature, including one who plied 'a small literary trade as a poor novellist' – referring to himself, and demonstrating that his spelling was indeed shaky.*

Early in their friendship, Lewes questioned the opinion, vehemently expressed at the end of *Framley Parsonage*, that marriage was always a sad anticlimax and that 'the sweetest morsel of love's feast has been eaten . . . when the ceremony at the altar has been performed, and legal possession has been given.'†
Anthony said Lewes took him too literally. 'As to myself personally, I have daily to wonder at the continued run of domestic & worldly happiness which has been granted me; – to wonder at it as well as to be thankful for it.' His luck, he feared,

---

* Less than two years later he had a difficult letter to write to Lewes: 'I know my letter will grieve you, but I still think I had better write it. They tell me at the Post Office that your boy is not doing well.' Young Charles was careless, slow and lazy. 'I learn that his name has been taken off the list of candidates for the next step above him.' Charles sounds very much like Anthony Trollope at the same age, but he had no such glorious future; he stayed in the PO for the next twenty-five years, reaching the grade of Principal Clerk.

† Quoted fully above, page 146.

was almost too good to last. 'But no pain or misery has as yet come to me since the day I married; & if any man should speak well of the married state, I should do so.'

After this Lewes must have been eager to know Rose Trollope. He met her for the first time a week later, and wrote in his journal (15 April 1861): 'Went down to Waltham to dine and sleep at Trollope's. He has a charming house and grounds, and I like him very much, so wholesome and straightforward a man. Mrs Trollope did not make any decided impression on me, one way or the other.'*

But then, George Lewes lived with George Eliot – who was 'ardent, theoretic and intellectually consequent', as Eliot described Dorothea in *Middlemarch*. (They were, said Charles Dickens, the ugliest couple in London.) George Eliot's first novel, *Adam Bede*, had appeared to critical and popular acclaim in 1859.

In early July (1861) Anthony accepted an invitation to dine with Lewes '*and Mrs. Lewes*' at 16 Blandford Square – his underlining in his letter to Lewes stressed not only how much he wanted to meet George Eliot, but, with unsubtle wholeheartedness, his recognition of their unofficial marriage. He sent her a long, appreciative letter when *Romola* began to be serialised the following year in the *Cornhill*.† His admiration was genuine; so was his appalled astonishment at the amount of research she did, and his anxiety that her novels should not be so erudite as to be inaccessible. 'Do not fire too much over the heads of your readers.' But when *Romola* came out in book form he assured her that it would live on after her. 'The very gifts which are most sure to secure present success are for the most part antagonistic to permanent vitality.'

Because George Eliot and Lewes were not married they lived outside 'society'. They had their circle of friends and admirers, and George Eliot was idolised by ardent young women with progressive views. To Anthony the unorthodox nature of the union was, if anything, an additional attraction. 'Whenever I hear that there is a woman whom nobody visits, I always feel inclined

---

* G. S. Haight (ed.), *The George Eliot Letters*, Vol. III, Yale University Press, 1955.
† Smith offered George Eliot £10,000 for *Romola* – 'the most magnificent offer ever yet made for a novel', as Lewes crowed in his journal. Actually she got only £7,000, since she wrote the story in twelve instalments instead of the agreed sixteen.

to go and pay my respects to her,' as Theodore Burton said in *The Claverings*.

Lewes had a wife still living. Bigamy – as a dark secret, a blackmailer's opportunity, or a shocking discovery by a husband or wife – is a recurring theme in Anthony Trollope's novels, as it was (because of the virtual impossibility of divorce, and its social stigma) in contemporary life. Cohabitation was the alternative to divorce or bigamy. Women, above the lowest class, who cohabited without marriage faced ostracism, especially from other women. Men were free to take one another's sexual unorthodoxies on board, or politely to disregard them, as they chose.

Rose Trollope, one must deduce, was with the moral majority. There are numerous occasions in his novels where Anthony generalises with some heat about woman's inhumanity to woman on the subject of sexual irregularity. In *He Knew He Was Right*, 'a woman is always angry with the woman . . .' In *An Eye for an Eye*, 'Women in such matters are always hard against women . . .', and, in the same book, 'The hardness of heart of such women, – who in all other views of life are perhaps tender and soft-natured, – is one of the marvels of our social system. It is as though a certain line were drawn to include all women, – a line, but, alas, little more than a line, – by overstepping which, or rather by being known to have overstepped it, a woman ceases to be a woman in the estimation of her own sex.'

In a late novel, *Dr Wortle's School*, the new teacher Mr Peacock was constrained to confess to the headmaster, Dr Wortle, that he and his beautiful American wife were not actually married. Understanding the circumstances, Dr Wortle did not cast them out. Indeed, he was full of sympathy, and became dangerously fond of the *soi-disant* Mrs Peacock. Mrs Wortle, on the other hand, took the conventional position. She, 'who had no doubt as to the comfort, the beauty, the perfect security of her own position', was adamant: 'A woman should not live with a man unless she be his wife.'

Anthony's son Harry told Michael Sadleir in 1923 that 'I was struck in reading *Dr Wortle's School* with a likeness between the Doctor and my father. . . . The likeness was purely incidental, almost casual.' One suspects that there was a corresponding likeness between Mrs Wortle and Rose Trollope. Mrs Mackinnon, the fictional author's wife in 'Mrs General Talboys', when her husband worried that the attractive Mrs Talboys might get hurt by the Irish philanderer, announced that she would deserve anything she got. 'Why is it,' asked the authorial voice-over in this story, 'that women are so spiteful to each other?' Maybe this was what Rose had found 'ill-natured'.

Anthony saw George Lewes and George Eliot without Rose, and George Eliot did not come down to Waltham.

Anthony was particularly interested in *Romola* because of the involvement of his brother. For Tom Trollope knew Lewes and George Eliot, too. One of the benefits of living abroad was that 'interesting' English or American visitors arrived with a sheaf of letters of introduction, and once they met anyone in the expatriate community in Florence they met them all. Tom Trollope, convivial, hospitable and conspicuously well housed, made many friends in this way.

The Leweses became acquainted with Tom and Theo in Florence in spring 1860, soon after Lewes met Anthony at the *Cornhill* dinner. Lewes found Tom a 'frank, serious, interesting man'. The Leweses were again in Florence, for George Eliot to do more research for *Romola*, the following spring, 1861, and spent nearly every evening at the Villino Trollope, sitting out on the loggia and talking with other droppers-in (Lewes thought Isa Blagden was 'awful'). Tom, 'a most loveable creature', as Lewes now wrote in his journal, accompanied them on an arduous mountain expedition; and he was useful to George Eliot because of his knowledge of Florentine history. He read the proofs of the first part of *Romola* for her. On the Leweses' last night in Italy there were fond farewells; and little Bice, who had her mother's musical talent, sang for them. This friendship meant a lot to Tom, who dwelt upon it at length and lovingly in his memoirs.

On 5 July 1861 Lewes wrote to Tom: 'Yesterday Anthony dined with us, and as he had never seen Carlyle he was glad to go down with us to tea* at Chelsea. Carlyle had read and *agreed* with the West Indian book, and the two got on very well together; both

---

* The Leweses dined at 5 p.m., and tea was taken after dinner. Afternoon tea at 5 gradually became smart as dinner, among society people, was eaten later and later. A 5 o'clock meal was early even for the 1860s, and soon became known as 'tea'. The Underwood girls in *Ralph the Heir*, for example, 'habitually dined at two, calling the meal lunch, – then had a five or six o'clock tea, – and omitted altogether the ceremony of dinner.'

Carlyle and Mrs Carlyle liking Anthony, and I suppose it was reciprocal, though I did not see him afterwards to hear what he thought. He had to run away to catch his train.' (The last train to Waltham left London at 11.30 p.m.)

Anthony rushed home to his long-suffering Rose, and Carlyle no doubt had a grumble to his long-suffering Jane. He had been mocked by Anthony as Dr Pessimist Anticant in *The Warden* (and contested, though he didn't know it, in Anthony's unpublished *The New Zealander*). He had no reason to love 'Fat Trollope', as he called him. After Anthony wrote an unenthusiastic review of Ruskin's *Sesame and Lilies* in 1865, Carlyle wrote to his wife: 'A distylish little pug, that Trollope; irredeemably imbedded in commonplace, and grown fat upon it, and prosperous to an unwholesome degree.' There was more in the same vein; but then Carlyle was an irritable and discontented old curmudgeon.

The intricate network of literary and social friendships and enmities, into which Anthony erupted like a late-coming, middle-aged Phineas Finn, had all been formed in the 1850s or earlier. The central dramas of his new friends' lives were already over.

Wilkie Collins's liaison with Caroline Graves, the carpenter's daughter who some said was the original of the 'Woman in White', had been established in the mid-1850s. The crisis in the Ruskins' null marriage, and Effie Ruskin's remarriage to Millais, had been around the same time. And Anthony never knew either Dickens or Thackeray at his best.

Thackeray, by the time Anthony met him, was nearly finished both as a writer and as a physical specimen. His wife Isabella had been insane, and cared for away from home, since 1847. His passionate but unconsummated involvement with a married woman, Jane Brookfield, had been over for ten years. A sensual man, Thackeray had bought his sexual solace, hating the degradation of it. He was a compulsive gambler. He was constantly unwell, with digestive trouble (stomach spasms and sickness) and what he called 'hydraulics problems', the results of a venereal infection. He drank too much between these attacks, beginning his day with brandy and soda and ending it in the taverns of Covent Garden and the Strand. He was a genuine connoisseur of food, cigars and wine, in a way that Anthony Trollope – chiefly concerned with getting enough of these good things, at the hours and in the manner he wanted, and in amiable company – never was. Thackeray adored and cherished his clever daughters, and was presently involved in reconstructing an ambitious Queen Anne mansion at 2 Palace Green in Kensington; they moved there in March 1862. Minny and Anny Thackeray, when they were younger, used to go to the huge children's parties that the Dickenses gave at 1 Devonshire Terrace. Dickens and Thackeray had been friendly in the mid-50s, when Thackeray became godfather to one of the twin sons of Dickens's young admirer Edmund Yates.

The original quarrel between Yates and Thackeray was more than a year old by the time Anthony came to London, but it left a trail of antagonisms. In 1858 Yates had published in a gossip column a trivial profile of Thackeray asserting that his conversation was either 'openly cynical or affectedly good-natured and benevolent', and that his '*bonhomie* was forced'. Since Yates and Thackeray, according to Thackeray, had only ever spoken to one another at the Garrick, the older man saw the article as an ungentlemanly breach of club etiquette, and wrote a bitterly insulting letter to Yates – who wrote a reply reminding Thackeray of his own cruel remarks about real people in his novels and in the *Book of Snobs*. Dickens persuaded Yates not to post this letter.

Instead Yates wrote another, the insults continued ding-dong, Thackeray appealed to the committee of the Garrick, the committee came out on his side, Yates refused to apologise to Thackeray, Yates was expelled from the club, Dickens and Wilkie Collins stuck up for him, Dickens resigned from the club's committee,* Dickens and Thackeray no longer spoke to one another in the club, Yates published a self-justifying pamphlet. . . . Very tedious for everyone except the eminent members of the Garrick Club, all of them as temperamental as prima donnas.

Charles Dickens, like Thackeray, was going downhill fast by 1860. Only three years older than Anthony, he was tired, haggard and nervy. He had already embarked on the intoxicating routine of public readings that were to exhaust him fatally. It was in 1858, the same year as the Garrick row, that Thackeray had written to

---

* Dickens resigned from the Garrick finally in 1865 when his secretary, W. H. Wills, apparently 'lacking in social and literary distinction', was blackballed.

his mother: 'Here is sad news in the literary world – no less than a separation between Mr and Mrs Dickens – with all sorts of horrible stories buzzing about.' At the Garrick, some men said the cause was Dickens's intrigue with his sister-in-law. Thackeray put them right: 'No says I no such thing – it's with an actress.' Dickens heard about this and the relations between him and Thackeray worsened further. Dickens, a crazed man, placed a hysterical notice in *Household Words* and in *The Times* proclaiming the angelic innocence of an unspecified young woman and accusing his wife (whom he was abandoning) of being an unloving and unnatural mother. Thackeray made a point of befriending Mrs Dickens.

Anthony would have known about this particular half-veiled scandal, because of the newspaper publicity. He would also have heard that the young woman Dickens loved and saw constantly was an ex-actress called Ellen Ternan, even though Dickens kept his private life very private indeed, going to fantastic lengths to keep the object of his romantic passion out of the public gaze. (He was the very opposite of G. H. Lewes, who lived proudly and openly with his 'Polly', George Eliot.) But most things were known and said, or implied and inferred, within the walls of the Garrick.

Anthony had an actual link with Dickens's beloved, by way of Tom. The Ternans were theatre people through and through, clinging to the uneasy borders of respectability at a time when the words 'actress' and 'prostitute' were often used synonymously. Ellen Ternan's Irish father had been an actor, her widowed mother was an actress of repute, and her three daughters had all been child stars, singing, dancing, doing impressions. Ellen first appeared on the stage at the age of three. She had two elder sisters, Maria and Fanny, equally talented and versatile.

Fanny Ternan, the middle sister, was clever, a good linguist and a ready writer of poetry and prose. She lost her exquisite girlish good looks, took to wearing green spectacles, and aspired to be a serious professional singer. In September 1858 Charles Dickens paid for this ambitious sister of his beloved Ellen to go to Florence to study singing with Romani (exactly as Kate Field did; the similarity in their Irish theatrical backgrounds and professional aspirations must have occurred to Anthony), armed with letters of introduction, including one to old Mrs Trollope and Tom, whose meeting with Fanny Ternan was to have important consequences.

In March 1861 Anthony signed an agreement with Chapman & Hall for the travel book on America that he had been wanting to write since he returned from his first visit. The Civil War, or War of Secession as Anthony called it, had broken out, and 'from the first I interested myself very much in the question'.

Only after signing the agreement did he apply to the PO for leave of absence. He felt he deserved the nine months' sabbatical. 'During the period of my service in the Post Office', he wrote in his autobiography, 'I did very much special work for which I never asked any remuneration, – and never received any, though payments for special services were common in the department at that time.' But Sir Rowland Hill raised objections. Both Anthony and John Tilley had private words with the current Postmaster General, Lord Stanley of Alderley, and Stanley humiliated Hill by overruling his objections. Hill's private journals filled up with grumbling bitterness against Anthony. Hill felt that Anthony used the PO for his convenience, while speaking in public of earning his bread by his writing, as if that were his true profession. (In 1860 Anthony earned £751 from the PO and £2,228 from writing.)

On 25 August 1861 Anthony Trollope embarked for Boston. Rose went with him.

CHAPTER THIRTEEN

ON board ship they made another of Anthony's mother-and-daughter friendships, this time with a Mrs Cleveland and her Lily. The Clevelands kept up the connection; in December 1865, Anthony was writing to Lily: 'What am I to think of myself when on the above date I sit down in answer to your letter of 30 Sept.? And yet – I was so glad to get it, – as was my wife to have a note from your mother. We have by no means forgotten that passage in the Arabia when your party and ours were so pleasantly contiguous, – nor the times when we met again in Massachusetts.'

In Boston the Trollopes stayed at the Tremont House, on the advice of Kate Field. The first person to entertain them was Dr Samuel Lothrop, a Unitarian minister, with Charles Sumner, Senator for Massachusetts and a crusading reformer and abolitionist, as a fellow guest; and they were quickly in touch with James T. Fields, two years younger than Anthony, a partner in the Boston publishing house Ticknor & Fields and editor of the *Atlantic Monthly*. Anthony had met Fields at a *Cornhill* dinner the year before, and in Boston he and his much younger wife Annie Adams Fields became good friends of both Anthony and Rose. 'My kindest regards to your wife,' Anthony wrote to Fields from Cincinnati. 'I never saw a woman so ill used as she was that Sunday when you made her go down to dinner giving her only 30 seconds to brush her hair and do her fixings, – nor any woman who bore such ill usage so well.'

Annie Fields must at some point have pronounced Anthony to be a 'jolly fellow', for the day before he left America the following spring Anthony wrote to Fields: 'Goodbye, old fellow. Say ever so much to that dear wife of yours. I should call her a jolly fellow too, if I did not fear to shock the propriety of her Puritan citizenship. Nevertheless in good fellowship she is jolly; – and why not speak the truth openly?' In the same letter Anthony

307

reported to Fields that he had just seen J. B. Lippincott of the Philadelphia publishing firm and made an agreement with him for the book he was writing about America.

Lippincott was not offering generous terms – no advance, and royalties of 12½ per cent only after 2,000 copies were sold – but the alternative, for British writers in America, was likely to be nothing at all. Harper Bros, who had bought some of Anthony's short stories for *Harper's New Monthly Magazine* at £20 apiece, were in the habit of publishing his novels in America too, sometimes paying a derisory sum to his English publishers and sometimes not. Anthony had an unsatisfactory and acrimonious interview with Fletcher Harper, but in the absence of an international copyright law there seemed very little that could be done about this literary piracy.

Soon after Anthony first arrived in Boston, at dinner with the Fields at 148 Charles Street, he was introduced to the ageing heavyweights of the literary community – Dr Oliver Wendell Holmes (Harvard professor and author of *The Autocrat at the Breakfast Table*), James Russell Lowell (Harvard professor, diplomat, poet co-editor with Fields of the *Atlantic Monthly*), Nathaniel Hawthorne and Ralph Waldo Emerson. Holmes and Anthony got into a noisy argument. Literature was not the topic. Anthony pooh-poohed Holmes's pride in American connoisseurship of Madeira wine. Holmes pooh-poohed English peaches, and Anthony roared that England was the only country where such a thing as a peach or a grape was known. Hawthorne was appealed to, and ventured to remark: 'I asked an Englishman once who was praising their peaches to describe to me exactly what he meant by a peach, and he described something very like a cucumber.'*

Anthony, in *North America*, transposed the row about English peaches to Dubuque, Iowa. Or maybe he had the same argument wherever he went, sincerely believing 'that good peaches were to be got in England only' – unless, as he wrote, his insular ignorance prevented him from realising that 'a peach should be the combination of an apple and a turnip'. He was infuriated too by

---

* Hawthorne admired Anthony's novels; he had written to Fields the year before that they were 'solid and substantial, written on the strength of beef and through the inspiration of ale, and just as real as if some giant had hewn a great lump out of the earth and put it under a glass case, with all its inhabitants going about their daily business and not suspecting that they were made a show of.' Anthony copied this letter out in his own hand and reproduced it in his autobiography.

the American belief that there were no vegetables in England. All the glory of the garden at Waltham House was conjured up in his indignation: 'Do I dream, or is it true that out of my own little patches at home I have enough for all domestic purposes of peas, beans, brocoli [sic], cauliflower, celery, beetroot, onions, carrots, parsnips, turnips, seakale, asparagus, french beans, artichokes, vegetable marrow, cucumber, tomatoes, endive, lettuce, as well as herbs of many kinds, cabbages throughout the year, and potatoes? No vegetables!'

Lowell's impression of Anthony was of 'a big, red-faced, rather underbred Englishman of the bald with spectacles type. A good roaring positive fellow who deafened me (sitting on his right) till I thought of Dante's Cerberus. He says he goes to work on a novel "just like a shoemaker on a shoe, only taking care to make honest stitches". Gets up at 5 every day, does all his writing before breakfast, and always writes so many pages a day.' Anthony, in short, was doing his usual number. 'I rather liked Trollope,' added Lowell.* The opera singer Clara Louise Kellogg, who also met Anthony at the Fields', found him much too 'full of himself'.†

They went on to Newport, Rhode Island, a select seaside retreat, where they saw Anthony's young friend from a previous voyage, Mary Knower. (He also visited her mother in New York.) Anthony was astounded by the sheer size of the Ocean Hotel at Newport, which could accommodate 600 people. The public drawing-room, as he described it in *North America*, was a 'huge cavern', where no one spoke, and whence men escaped as soon as possible 'with a muttered excuse' to seek solace with a cigar. 'I confess that I could not stand the drawing-room . . . and that I basely deserted my wife.' They had been told in England that they would not need private sitting-rooms, but 'an Englishwoman cannot live in comfort for a week, or even, in comfort, for a day, at any of these houses, without a sitting-room for herself. The ladies' drawing-room is a desolate wilderness.' Anthony later found it 'disagreeable', in Western railway towns, to be asked by un-impressed hotel-clerks what he meant by a 'dressing room', and why he wanted one.

Rose and Anthony Trollope had put on weight in more senses

---

* H. S. Scudder, *James Russell Lowell* (1901).
† Clara Louise Kellogg, *Memoirs of an American Prima Donna* (1913).

than one since the days they were newly-weds in rented rooms in an Irish provincial town.

They retained some homely and economical habits. Laundry in the big American hotels cost 4d for every item, large or small. 'The craft of those who are cunning is shown I think, in little internal washings, by which the cambric handkerchiefs are kept out of the list, while the muslin dresses are placed on it.' There is a nicely conspiratorial marital intimacy in the reference to 'little internal washings', as there is in a letter Anthony wrote in 1864 to George Smith, just off to Paris with his wife: 'There is a shop in the Rue St. Honore devoted to Eau de Cologne, and in which as my wife thinks is the only true fountain. Will you bring her home the biggest bottle you can conveniently do. I think that they are about 12 francs. Tell your wife also that the Eau de Cologne if kept for a year or two, (as we always keep it,) is certainly the best I ever met.'

In Newport they hired horses, and from Magog took a steamer up the lake to the Mountain House, where they were told that 'young women' sometimes managed the two-mile climb from the hotel to the top of Owl's Head mountain. 'After that my wife resolved that she would see the top of the Owl's Head, or die in the attempt.' They set off at dusk in pouring rain, and on the way down again got hopelessly lost. 'I may confess now that I became much frightened. . . .' A search party from the hotel came out and guided them back.

They went on to Canada in October – Montreal, Ottawa and Toronto. The British should prepare, Anthony wrote, for the secession of Canada, and not suppose that her vast territories would be 'subject for ever to a veto from Downing Street'. He took Rose to Niagara Falls, and was overwhelmed all over again, and in his book repeated and elaborated upon the passionate passage he had written on Niagara in *The West Indies*, in images of sex, death and infinity.* Then on the train again, back over the border, to Buffalo, Detroit, Milwaukee, Chicago.

* 'You will hear nothing else, and think of nothing else. At length you will be at one with the tumbling river before you. You will find yourself among the waters as though you belonged to them. The cool green liquid will run through your veins, and the voice of the cataract will be the expression of your own heart. You will fall as the bright waters fall, rushing down into your new world with no hesitation and no dismay; and you will rise again as the spray rises, bright, beautiful and pure. Then you will flow away in your course to the uncompassed, distant, and eternal ocean.'

Anthony disliked there being only one class of carriage. 'If a first-class railway carriage be thought of as offensive, so should a first-class house, or a first-class horse, or a first-class dinner,' the pursuit of all of which was 'very rife' in America. But he was impressed by the folding beds in the sleeping cars, in which both he and Rose slept soundly. Rose was a doughty and enthusiastic companion but she did not travel light: on several occasions an overwrought baggage official suggested that their ten pieces of luggage were too many. When Anthony realised that every item had to be separately entered in a book, 'I did whisper to my wife that she ought to do without a bonnet-box. The ten, however, went on. . . .'

Anthony did not travel light either, even on his own. When that winter he visited a Federal army camp with an introduction to General Curtis, he had to carry his own bags: 'As I slipped about on the ice . . . burdened with a dozen shirts, and a suit of dress clothes, and three pairs of boots, and four or five thick volumes, and a set of maps, and a box of cigars, and a washing-tub, I confessed to myself that I was a fool.' He was a dogged but bad traveller, railing against discomfort and delay, unadaptable and wholly without fortitude. He missed his evening tea by the fire with a book, and preserves, and other light delicacies, 'the greatest luxury of an English inn'; he liked 'to have my tea-cup emptied and refilled with gradual pauses, so that time for oblivion may accrue, and no exact record be taken. No such meal is known at American hotels.'

At Chicago he was impressed by the Post Office which, like the hotel, was huge, 'though the postmaster confessed to me that the matter of the delivery of letters was one which could not be compassed'. In Cleveland he thought the red-brick houses good, but hated the colonial-style trim – 'vicious bits of white timber', tacked-on Greek porticos, with pediments and columns, 'an amount of bad taste that is almost incredible', 'the vilest of architectural pretences'.

Back on the train. 'If you cross the Atlantic with an American lady you invariably fall in love with her before the journey is over. Travel with the same woman in a railway car for twelve hours, and you will have written her down in your own mind in quite other language than that of love.' Did his English Rose wilt too on those long journeys, or did she remain good-humoured, spick and span? At Trenton Falls in New York State, men could walk along the channel of the river, but the descent was 'too slippery and difficult for bipeds laden with petticoats', i.e. for Rose. And so to New York, 'as grand as paint and glass can make it,' for ten days. On his visit to Harper's, where the printing, binding, publishing and selling of books took place under one roof, Anthony wondered whether the authors were not kept there too, up in the attics, scribbling.

'I have never walked down Fifth Avenue alone without thinking of money. I have never walked there with a companion without talking of it. I fancy that every man there, in order to maintain the spirit of the place, should bear on his forehead a label stating how many dollars he is worth, and that every label should be expected to assert a falsehood.'

The glory of New York, for him, was Central Park. On his map the streets went up to 154th Street, but there was not much built beyond 60th Street. 'I do not doubt that the present fashion of the Fifth Avenue about Twentieth Street will in course of time move itself up to Fifth Avenue as it looks, or will look, over the Park at Seventieth, Eightieth, and Ninetieth Streets.'

Anthony was worried that they were going to miss seeing Kate Field, who was only now returning from Florence. They finally arranged to meet in Boston soon before Rose was due to sail, alone, to England. 'You write about sending my wife home as tho' she were as free from impediments in the world as your happy self,' Anthony wrote to Kate. 'She has a house, and children & cows & horses & dogs & pigs – and all the stern necessities of an English home.' He was counting on Kate for their last fortnight in Boston, and wrote to her (with jocular use of American idiom): 'I have been real angry with you this week for not turning up.' In Boston, he heard Wendell Phillips lecture on abolition, and both Edward Everett (editor of the *North American Review*) and Emerson lecture on the Civil War, to enormous crowds. In the USA lectures, he perceived, were 'more popular than theatres or concerts'. There is no record of the first meeting between Rose and Kate. Rose sailed for England on 27 November.

Anthony called on Longfellow in Cambridge, and on 3 December 1861 left Boston, and Kate – '(oh that morning)' he wrote in his

312

journal – for Baltimore and Washington. He disliked Washington, the Federal capital, finding its newness ugly and pretentious, apart from a 'graceful' Post Office – the only one in the whole city, and no letter-boxes and no deliveries; people queued in the street to collect their mail.

Because of the war Washington was dominated by the army. 'I hate military belongings, and am disgusted at seeing the great affairs of a nation put out of their regular course.' His sourness in Washington was excusable. He had a boil on his forehead, and throbbed alone in his hotel. A doctor had 'chopped' his boil crosswise (he drew a picture of it for Kate), but 'the chops will keep healing and the thing which has collected itself inside will not come out. . . . I wish you were here to condole with me and get yourself scolded.'* He did his accounts for 1861: £734 from the PO, £3,038 from writing.

On 27 December he dined with William H. Seward, Secretary of State, and Seward's daughter put him down as 'a great homely, red, stupid faced Englishman, with a disgusting beard of iron grey'. It was an uncomfortable time for an Englishman, with or without a boil on his forehead, to be dining with Seward. A Northern vessel had intercepted a British steamship, the *Trent*, and arrested two Confederate envoys on their way to plead the Southern cause with the British government. This led to much anti-British feeling and increased fears that an outraged Britain might enter the war on the Southern side. Sumner was opposed to releasing the Confederate envoys; Seward was in favour. The envoys were released and British intervention averted. 'I dined with Mr Seward on the day of the decision, meeting Mr Sumner at his house, and was told as I left the dining-room what the decision had been. During the afternoon I and others had received intimation through the embassy that we might probably have to leave Washington at an hour's notice' (*Autobiography*).

Writing to Kate from Washington, Anthony scolded her for not having sent him a story she was writing, and for 'running after false gods' – political radicals and feminists. 'The blaze on my forehead has gone out, & I have been starring it about with all my

* Anthony's pleasurable intimacy with women often involved 'scolding', cf to Mrs Harriet Knower, 18 February 1866: 'I often think of the one evening when you sat on our lawn and complained that I scolded you.'

accustomed personal attractions.' He assumed Kate would have heard from Rose. 'She was very unhappy in her voyage, having resolved that she would be so – But now is at peace with her cows & pigs. Write to her.' That was 4 January 1862. Two days later, he wrote criticising some poetry of her own that Kate had sent. 'Poetry should be very slow work – slow, patient, and careless of quick result. That is not your character. Philanthropical ratiocination is your line, not philandering amatory poetising. . . . I am very fond of you, and it grieves me to pain you.' But he believed that she could write 'good nervous readable prose'.*

On to St Louis, where he met an acquaintance of Kate's, William G. Eliot, another Unitarian minister (and the grandfather of T. S. Eliot): 'I had some talk with Eliot about you. "Let her marry a husband," said he. "It is the best career for a woman." I agreed with him – and therefore bid you in his name as well as my own, to go & marry a husband.'

He had, he told her, 'another horrible carbuncle on the small of my back – (if my back has a small)', but went off to Pittsburgh, which was 'dirtier and blacker', he wrote in his book, than any Welsh mining-town. In the hotel, 'on coming out of a tub of water my foot took an impress from the carpet exactly as it would have done had I trod barefooted on a path laid with soot.' St Louis and Cairo, Illinois, were even dirtier.

He made for Cincinnati, where his mother, so long ago, had tried to restore the family fortunes with her bazaar, known as 'Trollope's Folly' – which, he was assured, was at the time of its erection considered 'the great building of the town'. He found it eclipsed now by 'great blocks'; it had become a Physico-Medico Institute, housing a quack doctor on one side, and a 'college of rights-of-women female medical professors' on the other. No one, he heard, had ever been able to make any money in that building.

He needed to get as near the war fronts as he could, for his book, but he longed to be back in Boston. He was there by 6 March. On 8 March he noted in his journal: 'Runaway sleigh.' On 9 March he left for New York – journal: '(Ah me, West St)' – and three days later sailed for home.

---

* He used a similar phrase in criticising the poems of Cecilia Meetkerke, wife of the Adolphus Meetkerke whose birth had deprived Anthony's father of Julians in Hertfordshire. 'Never use Italics,' he told her. 'They are the struggles of imbecility. Strong nervous language will always shew itself.'

Since he was writing his book as he went along, the passages about Boston are thick with emotion:

> I had promised myself, and had promised others, that I would spend in Boston the last week of my sojourn in the States. . . . The belief that men's arms and hearts are open to receive one, – and the arms and hearts of women too, as far as they allow themselves to open them, – is the salt of the earth, the sole remedy against sea-sickness, the only cure for the tedium of railways. . . . These matters are private, and should hardly be told of in a book; but . . . I should not do justice to my own conviction of the country if I did not say how pleasantly social intercourse there will ripen into friendship, and how full of love that friendship may become.

There was a great deal more of that. Too much. On a factual level, he explained in *North America* the 'runaway sleigh' diary-entry. All Boston was on sleighs, it was 'excellent fun', but the horses ran away with him, and he feared he was doomed to consign the lady with him (Kate) to 'a snowy grave'. He turned the adventure into a short story, 'Miss Ophelia Gledd', in which the English narrator Mr Green drove with the Boston belle in the sleigh at the end of the winter when the snow was slushy and 'the scene becomes one of peril and discomfort, though one also of excitement, and not infrequently of love.' As they started off, intimately close and enveloped in furs, Mr Green 'could not but think how nice it would be to drive on and on, so that nobody would ever catch us. There was a sense of companionship about her in which no woman that I have ever known excelled her. She had a way of adapting herself to the friend of the moment which was beyond anything winning. . . .'

Mr Green, in the story, swore that he was not himself in love with her. It was his English friend, 'a literary man of some mark, fifteen years her senior, very sedate in his habits, not much given to love-making', who had fallen for her charm, her sharpness, her easy American manners and her free speech. So the Boston belle and the English literary gentleman got married. 'Now comes the question; will she or will she not be received in London as a lady, as such a lady as my friend . . . might have been expected to take for his wife?' That was a displacement of the real question for Anthony Trollope. The question as posed had more immediate relevance to Rose than to Kate Field. The question about Kate, for Anthony, was: 'What would I have been, what would my life have been, if I had married someone like her?'

He wrote to 'My very dear Kate' after his return home: 'Tell me who you see, socially, & what you are doing socially and as regards work. I didn't at all understand how you are living, where – with whom – or on what terms. But I don't know that it matters. How little we often know in such respects of those we love dearest. Of what I am at home, you can have no idea: – not that I mean to imply that I am of those you love dearest. And yet I hope I am.'

His puzzlement over Kate's life was understandable. She did not belong to the interbred clan of high-minded, socially conscious Bostonians of the upper class. These women, many of them involved in work for abolition and for the education of women, shared her views. But unlike her they had 'old' family backgrounds, old money and distinguished names.*

Rose knew about her husband's infatuation, and was upset, then had her ample say about it in the privacy of the bedroom, in her deflationary north-country way.† In his novels Anthony repeatedly wrote that wives who had something to forgive felt, afterwards, more powerful and more loving. In *Is he Popenjoy?*, for example: 'I am sure that a wife's temper to him is sweetened by such evidence of human imperfection. A woman will often delight in being angry; will sometimes wrap herself in prolonged sullenness; will frequently revel in complaint; but she enjoys forgiving better than aught else. She never feels that all the due privileges of her life shall have been accorded to her, till her husband shall have laid himself open to the caresses of a pardon. But the man, till he be well used to it, does not like to be pardoned.' The feeling of being 'found out', he went on, was uncomfortable, 'but it is, I think, a step almost necessary in reaching true matrimonial comfort. Hunting men say that hard rain settles the ground.'

* Kate had been half-adopted and educated at a good school by a childless, rich uncle and aunt, Mr and Mrs Milton T. Sanford of Cordaville, Mass. Mrs Sanford was her actress mother's younger sister. Mrs Beal, another maternal aunt, lived on Beacon Street in Boston. Kate's financial support from her well-heeled connections was withdrawn because of their distaste for her feminist ideas and public appearances.

† I cannot prove that he told her, nor that she reacted as I say, but I am sure of it. The reader is free to disagree.

Harry Clavering, betrothed to Florence Burton in *The Claverings*, was in love with Julia Ongar. 'It was not that he had ceased to love Florence; but that the glare of the candle had been too bright for him, and he had scorched his wings.' Rose accepted Anthony's strategy of absorbing a dangerous friendship into the marriage. (It is harder for the 'wronged' spouse. The success of the strategy depends on the married couple liking, or trying to like, the third party with an equal intensity.) One letter from Rose to Kate has survived, written in December 1862. It suggests agitation and some sort of three-way crisis:

> Why don't you write to me? We are both really unhappy – I because I still think you are offended with me – My husband because he does not know why – I therefore will not wait for another week, and that will be certain to bring a letter – just as one takes out an umbrella & there will be no rain – but leave the thing at home & down it pours – He – my husband – not the rain nor the umbrella – has gone to hunt and on such days I always write heaps of letters because I dont like to be out of the way never knowing at what hour he may be in – Well at any rate if you are angry with me I am not going to care and shall torment you when the fit comes on. . . .

She signed off, 'Yours affly R.T.'

There is no reason to think that Kate felt as urgently and intensely about Anthony as he did about her. She was unhappily involved with an American she had met in Florence and remained so, off and on, for years. But it is possible that some Boston gossip about Anthony's liking for Kate had found its way back to Rose. Seven years on, Anthony wrote enigmatically to Kate: 'Touching the black phantom, I hope he has winged his way to distant worlds. He did not hurt me, – but a man is tough in these matters. It vexed you and teased my wife.'

The two volumes of *North America* make a big, baggy, undisciplined book. It was received more kindly in America than at home, but Anthony was not proud of it. Richard H. Dana, lawyer and author of *Two Years Before the Mast*, helped him with his chapters on the US Constitution and the judiciary but declined to have his contribution acknowledged in print, and was not impressed by Anthony as a person: 'says the most offensive things

– not a gentleman'.* Anthony's chief preoccupations in the book were American culture and technology, the Civil War, 'the tyranny of democracy' – and women.

He could not get over America's 'wondrous contrivances': 'In their huge hotels all the bell-ropes of each house ring on one bell only, but a patent indicator discloses a number, and the whereabouts of the ringer is shown. One fire heats every room, passage, hall, and cupboard, – and does it so effectually that the inhabitants are all but stifled. Soda-water bottles open themselves without any trouble of wire or strings. Men and women go up and down stairs without motive power of their own. Hot and cold water are laid on to all the chambers . . .' On the other hand he hated the 'damnable hot air pipes' which gave all rooms 'the atmosphere of a hot oven' and were responsible, he was sure, for the pale faces, lack of energy and early signs of ageing that he discerned in the American population.

So far as the war was concerned, he did not visit the seceding states, but in gross physical discomfort struggled out to look at Federal forts and gunboats and camps and barracks along the fighting fronts in Virginia, Kentucky and Missouri, hating every minute of it. He deplored the cost of the war and the ruin to agriculture and commerce at home and abroad. England had been dependent on supplies of cotton from the South for the Manchester textile trade. Besides this, there was romantic sympathy in England for Southern gallantry, and Anthony in the North met with some hostility.

He was sure the North would win, but thought that the South would secede all the same. In suggesting how painful this might be he used the parallel of divorce – not irrelevantly, given his emotional state: 'In common life it is not easy to arrange the circumstance of a divorce between man and wife, all whose belongings and associations have for many years been in common. Their children, their money, their house, their friends, their secrets, have been joint property and have formed bonds of union.'

He saw slavery as the 'real cause' of the war, and secession as

---

* It may be observed that a New England gentleman was and is more like the stereotype and ideal of an English gentleman than any English gentleman has ever been.

punishment for the 'curse' and 'blunder' of the institutionalisation of slavery; but he thought that to call for abolition during the war (as Kate and the Bostonian liberal intellectuals did) was either 'the deadliest of sins or the vainest of follies'. To free four million slaves, whom he believed to be as ignorant and helpless as children, would be to let loose 'such a hell on earth as has never yet come from the uncontrolled passions and unsatisfied wants of men'. A few months after Anthony's book was published, President Lincoln emancipated the slaves.

In *North America* Anthony described English society as a staircase, with most people congregated on the broad lower steps. He saw American society as a platform, higher than those lower steps but lower than the top ones. He himself enjoyed the benefits of hierarchy, but did not fool himself that it was good for those at the bottom of the staircase: 'We argue to ourselves that the dear, excellent lower classes receive an immense amount of consoling happiness from that ceremony of hat-touching.' He knew they did not, and that American artisans were better off. Nevertheless, he pined for 'the civility – for the servility, if my American friends choose to call it so, – of a well-ordered servant'.

As in the West Indies, he couldn't adjust to the fact that paying for a service entitled him to no deference. Democratic indifference seemed to him 'determined insolence'. 'I shall never forget my agony as I saw and heard my desk fall from a porter's hand on a railway station, as he tossed it from him seven yards off on to the hard pavement. I heard its poor weak intestines rattle in their death-struggle, and knowing it was smashed I forgot my position on American soil and remonstrated.' One can imagine the nature and volume of Anthony's remonstrance. 'The porter laughed, everyone laughed, someone said, "Guess you'd better get it glued". But those porters were better off than our porters' – not only materially, he conceded, but because they did not feel inferior to the man whose box they carried.

Also, they were literate. Everyone in America was reading newspapers, books and magazines. Anthony visited schools and saw sixteen-year-old girls – pretty ones – who knew all about the hypotenuse and could discuss Milton. He thought this admirable but a little absurd, and found it impossible not to make what he called 'a little innocent fun' of it.

American women threw him into disarray. They were good-looking, talkative, well-instructed – but unwomanly.* The women of New York in particular 'were, I must confess, too much for me'. They expected all a woman's privileges – such as taking a man's seat in a street-car – without fulfilling a woman's duty to be grateful, demure and attractive to the eye and nose. As the New York woman entered the street-car she 'drags after her a misshapen, dirty mass of battered wirework, which she calls her crinoline, and which adds as much to her grace and comfort as a log of wood does to a donkey when tied to the animal's leg in a paddock . . . striking it about against men's legs, and heaving it with violence over people's knees. The touch of a real woman's dress is in itself delicate; but these blows from a harpy's fins are loathesome [sic].'

But then, Anthony was vulnerable over crinolines. They were exciting because they made the 'lady' even more decorously ladylike, since any sudden movement could make the graduated hoops swing up fore or aft, and reveal legs. A lady had to sit down and get up slowly and smoothly. Walking, she had to glide. She needed space in which to turn, and a chair that would accommodate her, like lovely Lady Ongar's in *The Claverings*: 'It was a pretty chair, soft and easy, made with a back for lounging, but with no arms to impede the circles of a lady's hoops.' To embrace her closely was to displace the whole swinging bell.

In the same book, Madame Gordeloup in her dirty white wrapper said to her male visitor, 'You come early and I have not got my crinoline' – and smiled, 'and sat herself down suddenly, letting herself almost fall into her special corner of the sofa.' Anthony has said very little, but madame's graceless descent, the outline of her rear quarters, and the shape in the sofa made by previous graceless descents of her rear quarters, are to be inferred.

Though Anthony thought crinolines ridiculous in the late 1850s when they first came in, his eye like everyone's became adjusted to the expected, exaggerated silhouette. A woman who did not wear a crinoline was either a poor working woman or else eccentric. One was just not used to seeing the natural lines of the

---

* Men on both sides of the Atlantic chose to see the womanly ideal in their compatriots. Henry James's brother William to his sister Alice, in 1868: 'What pleases me most in the female of my dear country is her moral unstainedness – her proud, sensitive, & reserved nature – & a total absence of that worldly wisdom, or rather that muscular ability and joy to cope with all the commercial and material details of life which characterizes her european sister.' Jean Strouse, *Alice James*, Jonathan Cape, 1981.

lower body, which came to seem repellent in women who were not sexually desirable. Madame Max Goesler in *Phineas Finn*, foreign, dark and very thin, wore 'no vestige of crinoline'; this was intriguing, because she was attractive – and also in the bold vanguard of fashion, as crinolines were just beginning to go out by 1866–67.*

Anthony's early and only disagreement with Millais was about the drawing to illustrate Lucy Robarts throwing herself on her bed in despair (because she had, untruthfully, told Lord Lufton that she could not love him) in *Framley Parsonage*. 'The picture is simply ludicrous . . . a burlesque,' Anthony wrote to George Smith. What made Anthony angry was that the central and only subject of the drawing was Lucy's crinoline, a flamboyantly exaggerated mountain of flounces obscuring the bed and most of Lucy. A couple of months later, Anthony wrote to Smith that Millais's subsequent drawings were very good, and 'I will now consent to forget the flounced dress. I saw the *very pattern of that dress* some time after the picture came out.'

Anthony devoted a whole chapter of *North America* to 'The Rights of Women', quite apart from animadversions elsewhere in the book. Women's political rights, he conceded, were under discussion on both sides of the Atlantic; but only in America had he found their right of entry to the world of work being seriously claimed, or man's role as family breadwinner challenged.† He referred to the natural law and 'a higher power' in defence of the status quo. The best right of a woman, he wrote, echoing his advice to Kate Field, was 'the right to a husband'.

It did not occur to him, as it did not yet occur to many middle-class women, that male chivalry might be dispensed with, if the price to be paid for it were too high; nor that women might combine work with marriage. A woman with a profession did not expect to marry, or expected to abandon her profession if she did.

As a middle-class man, which he was by neither fault nor virtue of his own, Anthony stood only to lose by social change. 'When we express a dislike to the shoeboy reading his newspaper, I fear we

---

* Rose was still wearing a crinoline in 1872, in New Zealand. Walking down a hill in a snowstorm, 'her petticoats underneath became balled up with the soft snow. "She was an enormous size, and a wonderful sight to behold," ' said a witness. E. M. Lovell-Smith, *Old Coaching Days* (1931).

† He was referring to middle-class women. Poor women had to work.

do so because we fear that the shoeboy is coming near our own heels.' The woman question came even closer to home, eliciting a stark and primitive anxiety: 'If women can do without marriage can men do so? And if not, how are the men to get wives if the women elect to remain single?'

Not every woman could find a husband to support her, even if she wanted to. The numerical preponderance of women over men, both in parts of America and in Britain, was one of the social problems of the 1860s and succeeding decades.* Working-class women went into service or into factories. In England, they were not thought fit to be shop-assistants, largely because they had not been taught enough arithmetic to make up bills and give change. As late as 1880, Anthony wrote that women shoppers preferred male assistants because of the 'something of gallantry' that the sex difference brought to the transaction. He thought more women should be employed in shops, 'seeing that we are at our wits' end what to do with a certain number of thousands of women for whom the world finds it very difficult to afford employment', and that their working conditions should be improved. Nevertheless, 'We were assured by a man who had been long in the trade and had considered the subject thoroughly that even for the rolling of ribbon a man, though he cost much more, did the work at a cheaper rate per yard, and did it better' (*London Tradesmen*). The general belief, expressed by Anthony, was that although a woman might be equally intelligent a man had more patience and stamina, and was more manageable.†

Women above the servant class could not all be governesses, or work in the Post Office.‡ Anthony was respectful to spinsters in his

* In 1850 there were 20,000 more women than men in New England, where the Women's Movement took root, and the imbalance increased in the following decades. In 1851, there were 365,159 more women than men in England and Wales. The supply of marriageable men fell continuously as new colonies attracted settlers, civil servants and administrators. In 1862, when the question of redundant women was aired in the British press, the Female Emigration Society was established.

† It's an astonishing tribute to the power of irrational belief that men could reconcile this notion of woman's insufficient patience, perseverance and stamina with the crucifying physical labour and long hours put in by laundresses, seamstresses, servants, factory workers and the mothers of large families.

‡ The Post Office was the first Civil Service department to employ women on a large scale. In a late story, 'The Telegraph Girl', Anthony described his heroine working with 'eight hundred female companions, all congregated together in one vast room' in the Telegraph Office at the top of the GPO building in St Martin's-le-Grand.

novels, especially to those not in their first youth. The formidable Miss Dunstable in *Doctor Thorne* and *Framley Parsonage*, with her political influence, 'with her keen wit, her untold money, and loud laughing voice', was not to be pitied. The 'untold money' had a lot to do with the respect she commanded.

Anthony found a husband even for Miss Dunstable. He wanted women to be sexually happy. Embedded in the dense, intricate Trollopian narrative as a whole there are small, time-stopping tableaux – eternal moments. One such is in *The Small House at Allington* where Lily Dale, ecstatically secure in Crosbie's love (alas!), greeted him and her sister's suitor as they enter the house; she 'dropped a low curtsey before them, gently swelling down upon the ground with her light muslin dress, till she looked like some wondrous flower that had bloomed upon the carpet. . . . And then she gently rose up again, smiling, oh so sweetly, on the man she loved, and the puffings and swellings went out of her muslin.' After Crosbie abandoned her, Lily Dale insisted that, in her heart, she was married to him. 'When he kissed me I kissed him again, and I longed for his kisses. I seemed to live only that he might caress me.' Lily was too obdurate in her fidelity. But the point about the strength and fixity of women's sexual passion, once it was aroused, was made by Anthony again and again.

Another, subtler, eternal moment: the virginal, no-longer-young Miss Mackenzie looking in the mirror, alone in her bedroom, thinking she cannot accept decent John Ball ('The juices of life had been pressed out of him'): 'She pulled her scarf tighter across her bosom, feeling her own form, and then she leaned forward and kissed herself in the glass.' For a conventional woman, no marriage meant no sexual life. To the extent that Anthony felt, very strongly, that women could only truly fulfil themselves biologically his attitude was based on concern for their happiness. Miss Mackenzie did marry John Ball.

Those women who could not settle for a John Ball began to take matters into their own hands. Discussing working women in England in *North America*, Anthony cited someone he knew – Emily Faithfull, and her all-woman printing-press. Emily Faithfull, in her late twenties in 1862, had been referred to in a divorce case,* but she – 'that female Caxton of the age' as Anthony

---

* Gordon Haight in *George Eliot* referred to Emily Faithfull as 'a decidedly queer young woman', without explanation.

called her – was invited down to Waltham House along with his literary Garrick friends. Emily Faithfull and her companions enlarged for Anthony the new world of independent women to which George Eliot and Kate Field had introduced him.

Emily Faithfull had founded the Victoria Press at 9 Great Coram Street in 1860 to provide employment for women. She also published the feminist *Victoria* magazine and the *Englishwoman's Journal* from 19 Langham Place, which was the office for the Society of Promoting the Employment of Women and the social headquarters of a group of friends, mostly in their thirties, known as 'the ladies of Langham Place'. Not only Anthony Trollope but Tennyson, Thackeray and Matthew Arnold contributed to Emily Faithfull's high-quality Christmas annuals.

Barbara Bodichon, one of the ladies of Langham Place, born 1827, was the daughter of Benjamin Leigh-Smith, radical MP for Norwich; but he had never married Barbara's mother, and she was therefore excluded from smart society, like Emily Faithfull and George Eliot; and like George Eliot, she had in the 1850s been the mistress of the handsome, philandering editor of the *Westminster*, John Chapman. She was now married to a French surgeon working in Algeria. She and George Eliot were close friends. Barbara, a painter, was liberated and glamorous; she wore loose robes, no corsets, and had long Pre-Raphaelite hair. She had supported Caroline Norton's fight for a Married Woman's Property Act, which became law in 1857, and was co-founder of the Women's Suffrage Committee in 1866.

Barbara's family home was 5 Blandford Square, an undistinguished Marylebone square which by chance became a centre of radical action. The Leweses had lived in Blandford Square before the move to The Priory. Emily Davies, another of the ladies of Langham Place, had a brother, the Rev. Llewelyn Davies, whose rectory was in Blandford Square. He was a founder of the National Association for the Promotion of Social Science, which provided a platform for women, particularly on the subject of education for girls,* at a time when it was considered out of the question for 'ladies' to speak at public meetings. Both Emily Davies and Barbara Bodichon were supporters of Elizabeth

---

* Llewelyn Davies later became Principal of Queen's College, Harley Street, a girls' school with a properly demanding academic syllabus, and Emily Davies, with Barbara Bodichon's support, was the founder of Girton College, Cambridge.

Blackwell and Elizabeth Garrett, the first women in Britain to qualify, against violent opposition, as doctors. Anthony attended gatherings at the rectory in the early 1860s; his first contact with the group was through Emily Faithfull or Barbara Bodichon, whom he met at George Eliot's Sunday afternoon 'at homes'.

The elderly Madame Mohl, who had been Mary Clarke, the disciple of Madame Récamier, was a voice from Anthony's past which also made itself heard in this group. She paid annual visits to London, and held strong views about the disabilities of Englishwomen and the inadequacies of Englishmen. When in London, Madame Mohl stayed with Lord Stanley of Alderley, Anthony's acquaintance and the Whig Postmaster General. A younger and rather different kind of woman among the radical feminists in the 1860s was the Stanleys' fourth daughter, Kate. She married Lord Amberley, eldest son of Lord John Russell,* in 1864, when she was twenty-two and he was even younger.

Both the young Amberleys were humanists and deeply serious. Anthony met Amberley, who believed (as Anthony did not) in universal male suffrage and a secret ballot, at the Cosmopolitan Club. Amberley, horrified by the number of unwanted babies abandoned in London's parks, found himself in trouble in 1868 for publicly discussing birth control. Kate Amberley was a friend of Emily Davies and of Elizabeth Garrett, who delivered her second baby.† She appeared on public platforms, lecturing on 'The Claims of Women' and speaking at a great Women's Suffrage meeting at the Hanover Square Rooms in 1870.

Kate Amberley was also one of the rare wives in smart society who visited Lewes and George Eliot. She was appalled by them both at first: Lewes was, she wrote, 'desperately ugly, small, dirty looking', with long hair and a bad complexion. George Eliot was 'repulsively ugly', too large, with a long chin – 'but when she smiles it lights up amazingly and she looks both good and loving and gentle.'‡ Anthony dined several times with the young Amberleys and met most of the other women in the group at George Eliot's 'at homes' as well as in Blandford Square. (Men

* Lord John Russell, later Earl Russell, became Prime Minister for the second time on Palmerston's death in 1865.

† Her third baby, born May 1872, became the philosopher Bertrand Russell. He was brought up by his grandparents, as both Lady and Lord Amberley died young, she in 1874 and he in 1876.

‡ Bertrand and Patricia Russell (eds.), *The Amberley Papers*, Hogarth Press, 1937.

were not welcome at the Langham Place offices.) The younger women created a worshipful atmosphere round George Eliot. The prevailing attitude was reverential. Anthony's presence, sitting in his habitual chair opposite his hostess, one on each side of the fireplace, was incongruous, but seems to have been accepted by all.

It was from Kate Field in America and the ladies of Langham Place in England that Anthony began to learn about a different kind of woman – un-clinging, not looking to a man to justify her existence or to marriage as her religion, and ready to fight for her rights. They interested him but they did not convince him. They, or women like them, began to appear in his novels.

What continued to trouble him most was the feminists' resistance to marriage. He began to explore the female predicament through Alice Vavasor in *Can You Forgive Her?* (written in 1863–64), entering with a sceptical sympathy into her question 'What should a woman do with her life?'

Alice had 'a vague idea that there was a something to be done; a something over and beyond, or perhaps altogether beside that marrying and having two children – if only she knew what it was.' Alice was not very advanced. She did not want to be a lawyer or a doctor. 'She would have liked, I think,' wrote her creator, not even allowing her to speak for herself, 'to have been the wife of the leader of a Radical opposition, in the time when such men were put into prison, and to have kept up for him his seditious correspondence while he lay in the Tower. She would have carried the answers to him inside her stays. . . .'

He made fun of Alice Vavasor. He preached the same sermon that he had preached to Kate Field in *Miss Mackenzie*, which was begun within days of finishing *Can You Forgive Her?* He began *Miss Mackenzie*, he wrote in his autobiography, with the intention of *not* writing a love story, for once; but love, or at least marriage, crept in. The desire to get married was, he said in this novel, natural in women, and good for the world in general. 'There is, I know, a feeling abroad among women that this desire is one of which it is expedient that they should become ashamed. . . . Many of the most worthy women of the day are now teaching this doctrine, and are intent on showing by precept and practice that an unmarried woman may have as sure a hold on the world, and a position within it as ascertained, as may an unmarried man. But I confess to an opinion that human nature will be found to be too strong for them.' Which is why he made Miss Mackenzie marry John Ball.

Thus his first forays into the woman question, distorted by his anxiety that men might not be able to find wives to love and look after them, were modest. Clara Amedroz in *The Belton Estate* (written in 1865), complaining of her dependent status, said: 'I'm not prepared to alter the ways of the world, but I feel myself entitled to grumble at them sometimes.' This is the furthest any traditional Trollopian woman would go.

They, and their creator, grasped the nettle more boldly after 1866 and *Phineas Finn*, a book seething with the ambitions of both sexes. Lady Laura Standish, the tall red-haired daughter of a Whig peer, said to Phineas: 'You are going to the club, now, of course. I envy you men your clubs more than I do the House; – though I feel that a woman's life is only half a life, as she cannot have a seat in Parliament.' To get as near as she could to the sources of power, and to have the money that bought political influence, Lady Laura was prepared to marry a man she did not love – the greatest female sin in the Trollopian canon.

In the same novel the ambition of the exquisitely pretty Violet Effingham, too, was 'to be brought as near to political action as was possible for a woman without surrendering any of the privileges of feminine inaction. That women should even wish to have votes at parliamentary elections was to her abominable, and the cause of the Rights of Women generally was odious to her' – but she aimed to be 'politically powerful', and went so far as to say to Phineas, 'I wish I were in Parliament. I'd get up in the middle and make such a speech. You all seem to me to be so much afraid of one another that you don't quite dare to speak out.'

Such anarchic disregard for forms and norms was precisely what Anthony feared most in women. Lady Glencora Palliser, at a political country-house gathering in *Phineas Finn*, defiantly announced that she had been talking to the Radical MP Mr Joshua Monk before dinner about making men and women equal. Then, going into dinner, she whispered to her host that she did not think all people were equal, only that 'the tendency of all law-making and of all government should be to reduce the inequalities' – which was her creator's position exactly. He could without strain or very much irony share the unease behind Aunt Jemima Stanbury's outburst in his next major novel *He Knew He Was Right*: 'But now, what with divorce bills, and women's rights, and penny papers, and false hair, and married women being just like giggling girls, and giggling girls knowing as much as married women, when a woman has been married a year or two she begins to think whether she mayn't have more fun for her money by living apart from her husband.'

In all these novels of the 1860s a woman's discontents were tacitly presented as a problem of misapplied energy, to be solved by subordinating her life to a worthwhile man's and wielding power in private and behind the scenes. In *Ralph the Heir* the working-class Radical, Ontario Moggs, told his beloved Polly in a letter: 'I hope you think that women ought to have the franchise.' To which Polly wrote in reply: 'As for ladies voting, I don't think I should like that myself, though if I had twenty votes I would give them to you. . . .'

Anthony gave a lecture up and down the country in the late 1860s entitled 'The Higher Education of Women'. It was a riposte to a pioneering book of the same title published by Emily Davies in 1866. In it she scathingly cited Anthony Trollope as saying that 'we like our women to be timid'. Emily Davies must also have written a critique (untraced) of one of his novels, for an undated formal response to it from Anthony has survived in which his irritation was masked by facetiousness: 'Miss Davies no doubt knows a great deal more about love than Mr Trollope can pretend to do.'

Whatever Anthony's lecture was about, it was not about the higher education of women except in so far as he advised working at music or languages at home in the mornings rather than reading a novel from Mudie's. It is a painful document to read. He understood absolutely about the death-in-life of middle-class female idleness, yet his terror of women abandoning the domesticity which sustained men overruled his intelligent sympathy. Again, he appealed to the natural law, and to the idea that a woman could not acquire 'the gift of persistent energy' by which the world's work was done. Another argument was that if a woman were educated like a man there would be competition between the sexes: 'There are thousands of small household reasons which must crowd upon the minds of you all why that rivalry which is salutary between men, and between women also, should not be encouraged between men and women.' (Those 'small household reasons' are suggestive of clean shirts and dinner on time.)

His audience should 'divest their minds' of the idea of assimilating the sexes 'either as regards political privileges, social standing, or educational system. . . . As to women's rights, I have discarded them altogether.' A girl at home should contribute 'something to the comfort of her father; something to the ease of her mother'. He mentioned hemming handkerchiefs and darning stockings. He inscribed a printed copy of this lecture to the dearly loved niece who lived with them at Waltham, then in her early teens: 'Florence Bland: written for her special *edification*.'

In the 1860s Anthony Trollope was still overwhelmingly interested in love and passion, which did not sort well with the contemporary concept of the independence of women except in so far as a woman might desire some other man than her husband. The most heartstopping tableau in his novels of the 1860s came in *Can You Forgive Her?*, at a grand party. Lady Glencora Palliser, the beautiful, rebellious young married woman, and Burgo Fitzgerald were illicitly in love. Anthony as always set the scene precisely. There was a buffet downstairs; and upstairs, a gallery round the landing, and the reception rooms. Burgo was down in the supper room when Lady Glencora was announced. From the doorway he watched her go up the great staircase, and she turned to look back at him. 'How beautiful he was as he gazed up at her, leaning against the wall as she made her slow way up the stairs. . . . At this moment Burgo Fitzgerald looked as though it were possible that he might die of love.' He looks up at her, and she looks back at him, amid the crowd and noise of the party, for ever: another of Anthony Trollope's eternal moments.

CHAPTER FOURTEEN

ENERGY is a major component of genius. Anthony
Trollope had his Waltham House life and his London life,
his Post Office life, and the daily, early-morning writing,
which was both draining and sustaining. He did for himself
everything that an agent would do for an author today –
negotiating terms and agreements, rights, royalties, reissues,
translations, delivery dates, keeping records and accounts.

Between 1860 and 1871 he did a great deal of journalism and
editorial work, he wrote short stories, his book about America, a
version of Caesar's *Commentaries* (requiring a hefty programme of
study) and published no fewer than nineteen novels. These were
not all three-deckers. Those that were included some of the
greatest he ever wrote. The shorter ones were among his most
dramatic and unexpected. He embarked upon a history of English
prose fiction, with the aim of justifying and 'vindicating' both his
profession as a novelist and the public appetite for novels. He got
bogged down in this project and never finished it.

Something that became more of a duty than a pleasure was
turning out the 'Christmas stories' commissioned from all
popular authors for the Christmas issues of magazines and for the
illustrated annuals. 'I feel, with regard to literature, somewhat as
I suppose an upholsterer and undertaker feels when he is called to
supply a funeral. He has to supply it, however distasteful it may
be. . . . Nothing can be more distasteful to me than to have to give
a relish of Christmas to what I write' (*Autobiography*).

In spite of the Christmas jollities evoked in these stories, some
of them certainly based on festivities at Waltham, Anthony
disliked not only Christmas stories but the elaborate contemporary Christmas. He often was ill in bed over the festive
season, feeling perhaps like Felix Graham in *Orley Farm* that 'the
peculiar conviviality of the day is so ponderous. Its roast-beefiness
oppresses one so thoroughly from the first moment of one's

waking, to the last ineffectual effort at a bit of fried pudding for supper!' The funniest story he ever wrote was 'Christmas at Thompson Hall', for the *Graphic* in 1876; and the 'Christmas' element was minimal.*

'When I remember how many novels I have written, I have no right to expect that above a few of them shall endure even to the second year beyond publication' (*Autobiography*). Some reviewers muttered about 'overproduction', but Anthony believed that 'the work which has been done quickest has been done the best'.

He said he read all his work three times in manuscript and once, sometimes twice, in proof. 'In spite of this I know that inaccuracies have crept through, – not single spies, but in battalions.' Critics complained of carelessness and infelicities of style and grammar. He did write some dreadfully clumsy sentences and make careless slips,† but in an opus sufficiently vast they are sufficiently few to stand out. There were log-jams of Trollope novels from now on, with sometimes a long gap between completion and publication. 'As for *The Claverings*,' he wrote to the playwright Tom Taylor, 'it seems to be so long since I wrote it that I have forgotten all about it.' He finished that novel on the last day of 1864; it was being serialised in the *Cornhill* when he wrote to Taylor in February 1867, and had not yet appeared in volume form.

The 'overproduction' did not signify that he had to foist his work on the public. He was enormously in demand. He formed a Scottish connection; in 1862 he had a skittish letter from Dr Norman Macleod in Glasgow, asking him to write a serial novel for the monthly magazine he edited, *Good Words*. The magazine's publisher, Alexander Strahan, would be calling on him in London. 'You never perhaps heard of Good Words? . . . Enough, that our circulation is now 70,000 – & that *I* am Editor!'

---

* The story was about a dutiful wife who, confused by the room-numbers in a Paris hotel at night, returned to the wrong room and, in the dark, ministered to the wrong 'husband' in the bed. It was very much Rose's story – Anthony gave her the manuscript – and must reflect some near-adventure on one of their holidays.

† The carelessness is mostly a matter of bad editing. The church at Allington in *The Small House* has a tower in Chapter I and a steeple in Chapter II. In *The Eustace Diamonds* exactly the same sentence occurs twice at different points in Chapter X. In *The Way We Live Now* Daniel Ruggles starts out as Ruby's grandfather and ends up as her uncle. In Chapter XII of *The Prime Minister* both Phineas Finn and his creator forget that he is a Roman Catholic.

The Rev. Dr Norman Macleod, three years older than Anthony, was a chaplain to Queen Victoria and a popular preacher at the Barony Church in Glasgow. Anthony had met him in the context of the Gaiter Club, whose members (all men) went on walking tours in Scotland and met at an obstreperous annual dinner. The facetious Macleod was 'chaplain' to the Gaiter Club. *Good Words* was founded by its publisher Alexander Strahan, an ambitious Scots Highlander not yet thirty years old; Macleod, as well as editing it, had contributed in 1861 a serial novel of outstanding religious sentimentality, *Wee Davie*, a tear-jerker that had done wonders for the magazine's circulation. When Strahan came to see Anthony in London he was also arranging to move his publishing business south. *Good Words* was subsequently distributed from his Ludgate Hill premises, though its editor remained in his parish in Glasgow. Strahan borrowed heavily to effect the move, but it paid off. By the late 1860s *Good Words* (price sixpence) had outstripped the *Cornhill* and become the best-selling monthly in the English-speaking world.*

Anthony's first contribution to *Good Words* was a Christmas story, 'The Widow's Mite', which appeared in the issue of January 1863. He began the novel Macleod had asked for that March and finished it in three months flat. It was *Rachel Ray*, and it caused trouble. The Rays, in the book, were cottage-dwellers in a village outside Baslehurst, a small Devonshire town; and it was an 'Ur-story' novel, in that pretty Rachel Ray fell in love with Luke Rowan, a cut above the local lads, who came from London to work at the brewery in Baslehurst. Luke mixed with the local gentry. He was clever, susceptible and flirtatious. He returned to London. Would he be true to Rachel?

The novel pits Rachel's natural, overwhelming sexual awakening (Luke's words and touch were sweet 'with a sweetness which she had known in her dreams') against the punitive disapproval of her puritan elder sister. This sister, Dorothea Prime, made herself hideous with the rusty black of widowhood. 'Her caps were heavy, lumpy, full of woe, and clean only as decency might require, – not nicely clean with feminine care.' Mrs Prime was one of Anthony Trollope's grimmest, most frowsty and fanatical 'good women'.

* Patricia Thomas Srebrnik, *Alexander Strahan: Victorian Publisher*, University of Michigan Press, 1986.

'She liked the tea to be stringy and bitter, and she liked the bread to be stale. . . . She was approaching that stage of discipline at which ashes become pleasant eating, and sackcloth is grateful to the skin. The self-indulgences of the saints in this respect often exceed anything that is done by the sinners.' Mrs Prime was ecstatically religious in a low-church, killjoy way, and very close to the Rev. Samuel Prong, 'not a gentleman', whom she visited in his 'close little parlour in a back street' and even thought of marrying – only she feared he would get hold of her money.

The gentlemanly mainstream of the established church got less but no kinder attention in this story than did the bigoted evangelicals of the back streets. Rachel's simple-hearted mother sought advice from the rector, Mr Comfort, about whether Rachel should go to a dance where she would meet Luke, and where there would be waltzing. She had heard Mr Comfort preach, 'with all his pulpit unction', against the pleasures of the world and the flesh, which should be 'as nothing' to his flock. So she was bewildered by his realistic advice that Luke would be an excellent match for Rachel, and that she should certainly go to the dance.

It was no wonder that Macleod turned *Rachel Ray* down. To submit it to an avowedly Christian magazine, which *Good Words* was, amounted to provocation.

Macleod was reckoned a liberal (in Glasgow), and as editor tried to steer a course that could offend no particular religious clique or sect. In a long, pained letter, he complained that Anthony had shown only what was 'weak, false, disgusting' in the behaviour of Christians. 'You hit right & left – gave a wipe here, a sneer there, & thrust a nasty *prong* in another place . . . in short, it is the old story – the shadow over the Church is broad & deep, & over every other quarter sunshine reigns – that is the *general impression* which the story gives, so far as it goes. There is nothing of course bad or vicious in it – that *could* not be, from you. . . .' But there was enough, Macleod feared, 'to keep Good Words & its Editor in boiling water until either were boiled to death'.

The first instalment of *Rachel Ray* had been scheduled to appear in *Good Words* in July; Macleod filled the gaps that summer with his own *Reminiscences of a Highland Parish*, and *Rachel Ray* was never serialised. Strahan had promised Anthony £1,000 for it; he paid a kill-fee of £500, and Anthony got £1,000 from Chapman & Hall when they published it in two volumes in 1863. Anthony sent the book to George Eliot, with the comment: 'You know my novels are not sensational. In *Rachel Ray* I have attempted to confine myself absolutely to the commonest details of commonplace life among the most ordinary people, allowing myself no incident that would be even remarkable in ordinary life.'

None of the reviewers seemed offended by the book, and Anthony's depiction of commonplace life was, for some high-minded readers, just too commonplace. Young Kate Stanley, not yet married to Lord Amberley, was reading a book on Prussian education ('which excites and interests me so much') when her father persuaded her to break off and read *Rachel Ray* – 'which bored me to death'. It was, she said, 'a mere description of the feelings of a girl entering the world – I think one knows of them without reading of them'.

But George Eliot – no slouch on Prussian educational theory herself – wrote to Anthony that *Rachel Ray* was 'natty & complete as a nut on its stem' and, like all his books, 'filled with belief in goodness without the slightest tinge of maudlin'.* Anthony and Norman Macleod remained good friends, neither taking offence from the debacle over *Rachel Ray*. Anthony subsequently published more short stories in Macleod's *Good Words*, and the magazine provided in 1872 a much-needed home for his short novel *The Golden Lion of Granpere*, written in less than two months in autumn 1867.

It was not, he said, the fear of flooding the market but a desire to see whether he could establish a second literary identity that made him decide, again in the 1860s, to publish two short romantic novels anonymously. This is a ruse that rarely works. *Nina Balatka* was set in Prague and *Linda Tressel* in Nuremberg; he and Rose visited both these cities on their autumn holiday of 1865. George Smith turned down *Nina Balatka* for the *Cornhill*. 'All right about N.B.,' Anthony wrote to him, stoically. 'Would you kindly send her back – to Waltham? She won't mind travelling alone.'

---

* Readers who are also writers will know that friends' reactions to their books may be tokens of goodwill rather than considered criticism. But George Eliot consistently expressed enjoyment and approval of Anthony's work, and not only when writing to him – though she commented drily to a woman friend on the way his heroines devoted themselves to the men they loved: 'Men are very fond of glorying that sort of dog-like attachment.'

Through Joseph Langford, a member of the Garrick and the *Blackwood's* representative in London, John Blackwood of Edinburgh took *Nina Balatka* for serialisation in his Edinburgh-based magazine and subsequently published it, still anonymously, in book form.

Anthony had met John Blackwood in June of that year, 1865, at dinner with Samuel Warren 'at 7 pm *punctually*', as the host stipulated, at 16 Manchester Square. Warren was a barrister and former MP – a 'howling Tory' in the terminology of the time – as well as an author; his fame, of which he was very vain, rested on his novel *Ten Thousand a Year* which, published by Blackwood in 1841, had been a best-seller.

Nina Balatka was not so lucky. Blackwood sold fewer than 500 copies of it although, as Blackwood wrote to Langford, 'anxiety about the authorship shows that the book is telling although not selling.' Blackwood took *Linda Tressel*, too, which in spite of what Anthony called a 'frantic kissing scene', did not much better. When Anthony tried to persuade Blackwood to publish *The Golden Lion of Granpere* anonymously as well, the Scot declined: 'My wish naturally is to say yes and to give you as much as I can possibly afford, but on looking into the matter, I found as I feared that neither Nina nor Linda had on republication paid expenses as the enclosed memorandum shows.'

Another good Scottish friendship was established nevertheless, with John Blackwood and his wife. They visited Waltham to 'dine and sleep', and Rose and Anthony stayed at the Blackwoods' country house Strathtyrum, near St Andrews. Anthony's ebullience did not enchant a prim Presbyterian minister who was a fellow guest there in summer 1868. Trollope played golf for the first time. Affecting to faint with grief at a particularly bad shot, he crashed down on the green, forgetting he had a golf ball in his pocket, and 'started up again with a yell of agony, quite unfeigned'. Golf is a decorous game; his voice was heard all over the links. At dinner he appeared to the Presbyterian minister to be unkempt, 'and his clothes were wrinkled and ill-made'. He used bad language. He spoke ill of the novels of Sir Walter Scott, saying that if they were to be offered to any London publisher now they would be turned down because they were 'so dull'.* In short,

---

* A. H. K. Boyd, *Twenty-Five Years of St Andrews* (1892).

Anthony gave offence. He was talking for effect. It is clear from his autobiography that he considered Scott one of the great novelists of the generation before his own. As so often, strangers found it hard to reconcile this noisy, untidy, provocative man with the books he wrote. But his hosts were undisturbed. John Blackwood wrote that Anthony was 'great fun', and that after a farewell bathe in Loch Coruisk they parted 'almost with tears'.*

Anthony went again to America during this hyperactive decade, there were regular holidays with Rose at home and abroad, and in winter there was hunting. 'First one horse was bought, then another, then a third, till it became established as a fixed rule that I should not have less than four hunters in the stable. Sometimes when my boys have been at home I have had as many as six.' Few people, he said, 'have investigated more closely than I have done the depth, and breadth, and water-holding capacities of an Essex ditch' (*Autobiography*).

Women and girls now regularly went hunting too, adding greatly to the spice of the adventure. 'Hunting young ladies are very popular in the hunting-field,' he wrote in *Orley Farm*. 'I know of no place in which girls receive more worship and attention. . . .' Visitors to Waltham House in the hunting season were mounted and kitted out by their host. Anthony made himself, as he said, 'a slave to hunting,' even though he did not now always enjoy it.

Even he found the routine too much. In November 1862, apologising to George Smith for not sending back proofs on time, he explained that 'I have been very busy. I have been trying to hunt three days a week. I find it must be only two. Mortal man cannot write novels, do the Post Office and go out three days.' He was more often ill than in the past, ill enough to stay in bed. 'I wish you had my liver just for today,' he groaned to George Smith in February 1863.

He smoked, ate and drank too much in the clubs and at dinners. References to alcohol in his fiction are chiefly about the horror and degradation of over-indulgence. One of the sure signs of Louis Trevelyan's disintegration in *He Knew He Was Right* was his recourse to 'little drops of brandy in the mornings'. It had been the custom in Anthony's youth for gentlemen (such as

* Mrs Gerald Porter, *Annals of a Publishing House* (1898).

Archdeacon Grantly) to take port or claret when the tablecloth was removed after dinner, not to drink with the meal; but 'We take wine at dinner, sir', the Archdeacon's son informed him in *The Last Chronicle of Barset*, speaking for a more sophisticated generation.

Anthony began to develop a serious interest in wine, and in the 1870s some fine wine-snobbery crept into the novels. At the dinner party given by Mr Roby, the Admiralty Secretary in *The Prime Minister*, Lord Mongrober was given what his host claimed was a '57 Léoville claret. Mongrober grumbled that it might be good had it not been heated before the fire, or put in a hot decanter: 'Any man may get good wine, – that is if he can afford to pay the price, – but it isn't one out of ten who knows how to put it on the table.' In *The American Senator* it was a '57 Mouton that was abused – this time by ignorant guests who could not appreciate it. The authorial voice expressed sympathetic outrage: 'I, – who write this, – have myself seen an honoured guest deluge with the pump [i.e. add water to] my ah! so hardly earned, most scarce and peculiar vintage!' His taste was sufficiently assured by the end of the 1870s for him to name, in *Ayala's Angel*, his favourite: ' '64 Léoville, – which I regard as the most divine of nectars. . . .'

Since Anthony could not always drink tea it was hard not to take too much wine, especially in times of depression: 'There is an intoxication that makes merry in the midst of affliction; – and there is an intoxication that banishes affliction by producing oblivion. But again there is an intoxication which is conscious of itself though it makes the feet unsteady, and the voice thick, and the brain foolish; and which brings neither mirth nor oblivion' (*The Way We Live Now*). The problem was partially solved in 1872 by the ever-ingenious publisher George Smith, who in partnership with Ernest Hart* bought the British concession for the German mineral water Apollinaris. They marketed it as 'The Queen of Table Waters' with a label designed by George du Maurier, and within a decade were shifting 5–6,000,000 bottles a year, selling much of the 'British' consignment on abroad.† Anthony Trollope's Duke of Omnium (the former Plantagenet

---

* A Jewish doctor, journalist, sanitary reformer and collector of Japanese art.
† The profits from Apollinaris water funded George Smith's last and most monumental enterprise in the 1880s: *The Dictionary of National Biography*.

337

Palliser), as an unwilling Prime Minister in the novel of that name, drank Apollinaris as his wife's guests swilled and guzzled. The cold rascals who fleeced the no-good Mountjoy Scarborough at cards after dinner in *Mr Scarborough's Family* sipped Apollinaris while he grew fuddled on spirits. (Mountjoy was another lost soul who took brandy with his breakfast.)

Back in 1863, Anthony took himself in hand. He lost some weight by following William Banting's diet which, according to George Eliot, improved him both in body and soul. Banting was a grossly fat London undertaker who had worked out a diet that reduced his own bulk; he published a pamphlet on his method in 1863 which was so widely read and discussed that 'banting' passed into the language along with 'slimming', in response to the widespread corporeal evidence of mid-nineteenth-century prosperity and a growing awareness of the health risks. In Anthony's late novel *The Fixed Period* Mr Neverbend, listing the benefactors of humanity through the ages, included 'that great Banting who has preserved us all so completely from the horrors of obesity'. Anthony was joking. He did not maintain his weight loss.

As if he were not already doing enough, from 1860 on Anthony Trollope – the man who inveighed against sermons and speeches – himself spoke at dinners, gave lectures, and took on the time-consuming 'public service' aspect of the literary life which, for less committed writers, can become a full-time occupation in itself.

He had been maddened in the States to see how his books and those of other English writers were pirated, making money for opportunistic American publishers and nothing at all for their English publishers, nor for their authors, nor for honourable American publishers who bought the rights only to find themselves pipped at the post by pirated cheap editions. As it turned out, that was exactly what happened over his *North America*. When Anthony visited Harpers in New York he had exacted from Fletcher Harper an undertaking not to publish any book for which Anthony had secured a paying agreement; and Harper knew that Anthony had made such an agreement with Lippincott. Harper broke his word and rushed out a pirated 60-cent edition of *North America* before the appearance of Lippincott's more expensive edition, which left Lippincott and his colleagues '*positive losers* in the enterprise', as Lippincott wrote to Anthony.

So Anthony threw his weight into the campaign for an international copyright law, writing a long polemical letter to James Russell Lowell (citing his experience with *North America*) which was reprinted in England in the *Athenaeum*. He discussed the problem with Dickens, attended meetings on the subject in publisher John Murray's dining-room in Albemarle Street and, a decade later, sat on a Royal Commission on copyright law.

That was just one of Anthony's many activities. He gave lectures in London and the provinces, and organised a course of fortnightly fund-raising lectures for the Post Office Library and Literary Association, inviting all the speakers and giving the first address himself. He spoke at Royal Academy dinners, at Alpine Club dinners, at Royal Literary Fund dinners. The Royal Literary Fund is a charity started in the eighteenth century which helps indigent authors and their families. From 1864 Anthony (recruited by Robert Bell) was an active and conscientious member of the Fund's general committee, which met monthly at the offices in 4 Adelphi Terrace, the Strand, to deal with applications for grants.

He became one of the Fund's treasurers; a fellow treasurer was Frederick – later Sir Frederick – Pollock who, with his wife Juliet, became friends with both Anthony and Rose. The two men were exact contemporaries, and both of them Bloomsbury-born to barrister fathers. But Pollock's career had run smoothly – Trinity College, Cambridge, and the upper reaches of the law. The family were Conservative, and Frederick's father had been given a baronetcy. (Frederick's grandfather had been a saddler, like Dean Lovelace's father in *Is He Popenjoy?*, written in 1874–75.) Frederick Pollock had known for years all the sociable literary and artistic people – Lord Houghton, Thackeray and his daughters, Dickens, Millais, Forster, Browning. But he and Anthony had older ties in common – Mr Cunningham of Harrow, the mesmerist Dr Elliotson, and the Merivale family. Both Frederick Pollock and his wife wrote. In 1853 Chapman & Hall had published Frederick's translation of Dante's *Divine Comedy*; Juliet wrote children's stories and a book about the actor Charles Macready. Both Pollocks were keen on the theatre, and enthusiasts for amateur dramatics and playreadings.

They had other more unusual leanings. Juliet Pollock was a keen archer, and a member of the Toxophilite Society which held its tournaments in Regent's Park.* Frederick Pollock had an informed enthusiasm for physics, chemistry and technology, and was a friend of Charles Babbage, inventor of the calculating machine. Anthony was a scientific ignoramus; Frederick attended old Michael Faraday's lectures on electricity at the Royal Institution. The two friends were of one mind, however, about crinolines. Faraday's lectures were so popular and crowded that ladies who attended them were requested to leave off their hoops. 'Think of this,' Frederick Pollock wrote in his *Personal Reminiscences*, 'a piece of dress so monstrous that it cannot be worn with comfort in a place where fashionable and full audiences have assembled for the last fifty years. It is a frightful disfigurement.' One hears the tone of his voice, perhaps, in that. Henry James's sister Alice, living in London in 1885, recorded a Sunday evening 'made memorable by the advent of Mr [Sir Frederick] Pollock led in by his wife's rippling laughter'. (This was after Anthony's death, and Pollock himself was seventy.) 'He was quiet for the most part, but every now and then he suddenly jerked his profile round and shot forth a volley of deafening sound at the sideboard.'

Anthony was a very loud man; since Frederick Pollock was equally loud – 'deafening' – and Juliet Pollock talked and laughed a good deal, the two couples together must have constituted a noisy party. The Pollocks and the Trollopes met by design on holiday in the Isle of Wight in autumn 1864. Anthony and Rose crossed from Southampton on the same boat as Mrs Julia Margaret Cameron, the pioneer photographer, who lived on the island,† and William Allingham. On disembarking, as Allingham noted in his diary, 'I sat next Anthony outside the coach to Freshwater; he asked a great many practical questions about the houses and lands which we drove past – did not seem interested about Tennyson.' Allingham, the son of a merchant from Co. Donegal in Ireland, was a poet and a lover of poets, with a special devotion to Tennyson, who also lived on the Isle of Wight. Anthony was never part of that incense-laden cult.‡ Anthony and

---

* Anthony introduced an archery contest at a private garden party into his short story 'Alice Dugdale'.

† And who took a marvellous photograph of Anthony Trollope.

‡ The lack of interest was mutual. Tennyson said to Allingham in 1885 of Trollope's novels: 'But they're so dull – so prosaic: never a touch of poetry.' *William Allingham's Diary*, Centaur Press, 1967.

Rose stayed at Lambert's Hotel in Freshwater. During this holiday Frederick Pollock took Anthony for a walk to the Needles,* and the next evening Anthony (and presumably Rose – Frederick Pollock doesn't mention her in his diary-entry) went over to the Pollocks at Easton Farmhouse, where they regularly stayed.

Juliet Pollock informed Sir Henry Taylor (the retired civil servant whose early poetical work Anthony so much admired) that their first visit to Waltham Cross 'went off very satisfactorily'. She found her host a sympathetic and straightforward man but one 'to whom many devious, delicate turns and subtle ways of thought and feeling are not intelligible'. The weather was good, and they were much in the garden: 'a handsome stiff garden of the Queen Anne style, with a square pond at one end of it and a smooth grass lawn at the other. We walked round and round this garden many times, Anthony Trollope smoking and talking all the way.' The Trollopes went to dinner parties at the Pollocks' London house, 59 Montagu Square, in Marylebone. Fellow guests on different occasions included Mrs Cameron, Robert Browning, and the historians J. A. Froude and W. E. H. Lecky. Coming down to breakfast at Montagu Square after one of these parties, Anthony – who was then writing *Phineas Finn* and had risen early to work, as usual – surprised the company by announcing, 'I have just been making my twenty-seventh proposal of marriage.'

Anthony's work for the Royal Literary Fund involved yet more writing – letters setting out the needs and merits of applicants for fellow committee members and potential benefactors. As he wrote in his autobiography, the applications taught him all too much about the difficulties of his fellow writers, and stopped him from ever advising any young person to 'enter boldly on a literary career in search of bread'. He knew that he would have starved had his bread not been earned elsewhere when he first started.

But the Royal Literary Fund had social cachet as well as social purpose. Queen Victoria's son and heir the Prince of Wales, then

---

* The Needles are sharp upstanding rocks beyond the cliffs on the western point of the Isle of Wight. Anthony immediately put this dramatic and picturesque scene into the novel he was then writing, *The Claverings*: Count Pateroff pursued Lady Ongar on the cliff near the Needles ('Are you not rather near the edge?') and attempted to blackmail her into marrying him.

aged twenty-two, took the chair at its annual dinner in 1864. In 1868 Anthony was presented at Court, at one of the Prince of Wales's levees at St James's Palace, and thereafter maintained a friendly acquaintance with the Prince. In *Phineas Redux* Anthony had the Prince coming into the Universe Club on the night of Phineas's quarrel with Mr Bonteen. Everyone in the room rose from their seats momentarily in respect, but only those with 'peculiarly royal instincts', as Anthony ironically put it, edged closer and formed a little knot round the Prince, laughing loyally at the royal jokes. Anthony was not a republican,* but he did not have 'peculiarly royal instincts' either. He failed even to recognise the royal presence, or the royal voice saying 'Good evening, Trollope', when they passed on the stairs at the Turf Club one night. The Prince made a joke of it next time they met.

Anthony was generous privately, as well as through the Royal Literary Fund. In May 1862 Thackeray wrote to a hopelessly improvident younger friend of theirs, W. W. F. Synge: 'I have just met a Trojan of the name of Trollope in the street (your ingenious note of last night kept me awake all night, be hanged to you), and the upshot is that we will do what you want between us.' Thackeray and Trollope each lent him £900, and Synge's two young sons spent some time at Waltham.†

After Robert Bell's death in 1867 Anthony bought his books from the executors at a price fixed by himself, above the market value, in order to help the widow. 'I have bought the lot,' he told Chapman. 'I am told there are nearly 4,000.' That many extra books cannot be imported into an already book-filled house without trouble. Rose's comments are not recorded. But they had recently built a new large room on to Waltham House. Bell's library included rare collections of old English plays – Beaumont and Fletcher, Ford, Middleton, Marlowe, Otway, Congreve.

---

* The future of the monarchy was seriously questioned during Victoria's reign. The MP Charles Dilke, for example, called for a 'commonwealth', i.e. a republic, in a public speech in Newcastle in 1871. Kate Field wrote about the furore the speech caused, for the New York *Tribune*. Dilke was another of Kate's eminent admirers. He described her as 'a slightly outrageous person' and 'one of his closest friends'. Roy Jenkins, *Sir Charles Dilke: A Victorian Tragedy*, Collins, 1965.

† Synge was an unsuccessful author, employed in the diplomatic service. Anthony had met him in Costa Rica in 1859, and Synge had been a congenial companion on the arduous mule-back excursions from San José. Anthony remained very fond of him, sending him copies of his new books, and writing to him with special friendliness.

Over the following years Anthony read them all closely, annotating them with what amounted to mini-essays. His serious, continuous, eclectic reading has to be added to the long list of demanding activities that he fitted into his days. After finishing his work on Caesar's *Commentaries*, for example, he continued to read Latin for an hour each day so as not to lose his facility.

'Poor Bell worked hard at letters for over 50 years,' Anthony wrote to Wilkie Collins, asking him to sign a 'memorial', a petition for a pension for Bell's widow, to be presented to Lord Derby the Prime Minister. Charles Dickens signed as well, writing to Anthony: 'I had heard with much satisfaction that poor Mrs Bell had found a friend in you, for I knew she could have no stauncher or truer friend.'

What Anthony had no time at all for was inefficient private charity. He declined to contribute a story to a book to be sold to relieve poverty among the cotton-weavers in Lancashire on the grounds that the profit made by the volume would not represent the value of the work contributed: 'I should do better to sell my story, & give the money.' He loathed that most popular method of fund-raising, the charity bazaar. He disliked too the idea of lady 'inspectors' collecting the rents of the poor in order to instruct them on cleanliness and household management. As he wrote to George Lewes, 'You cannot inspect people into Godliness, cleanliness, and good grub. I do think you may educate them to it, and we are doing so, – only education won't go as quick as population. Then comes in Malthus & all the rest of it.'

The 1860s were a boom time for periodicals – and therefore for writers, illustrators and publishers. Between 1853 and 1861 the 'taxes on knowledge' – advertisement tax, newspaper duties, duty on paper itself – were abolished. Anthony was wooed unsuccessfully by the *St James's Magazine* and was offered the nominal editorship of *Temple Bar* for £1,000 a year. 'All the real work of editorship', he was assured, would be done by the sub-editor – Edmund Yates, Anthony's pushy young colleague in the Post Office. Anthony declined.

In 1863 George Smith, already owner of the *Cornhill*, started up another periodical, the *Pall Mall Gazette*,* in yet another set of

---

* The title was from Thackeray's *Pendennis*, in which the fictional *Pall Mall Gazette* was a journal 'written by gentlemen for gentlemen'.

premises* – in Salisbury Street off the Strand, sloping down to the muddy banks of the Thames, and liable to flooding. They had to have an arch cut into the ceiling over the staircase of that little house, so that tall Matthew Higgins could walk upstairs. The *Pall Mall Gazette* was a quality evening paper, a sort of evening *Times*. It never achieved a mass circulation, but it paid its way after the first three years and was politically influential. At *Pall Mall* dinners, Anthony said, he often met 'a crowd of guests who would have filled the House of Commons more respectably than I have seen it filled even on important occasions'. Anthony wrote articles for it – including, over the years, several light-hearted series, later published as *Hunting Sketches*, *Travelling Sketches*, *Clergymen of the Church of England*, *London Tradesmen* – and was almost as involved as if he were on the editorial staff.

His energies were still unsatisfied, and he was casting around for some further achievement: 'Excelsior!' as the ambitious young heroes of his novels frequently exhorted themselves. He was still reaching for 'the top brick of the chimney' in his own often-used phrase.

So in 1865 yet another periodical, the *Fortnightly Review*, was inaugurated by Anthony himself (as chairman, part-proprietor and regular contributor), Frederic Chapman and others, with capital of £8,000. George Lewes was persuaded, against his will, to be editor. The magazine was produced by Virtue & Co. in the City Road; Anthony made familiar reference to the firm in his story 'The Telegraph Girl', written for *Good Words* in the late 1870s, in which his heroine's fellow lodger in a Camberwell boarding-house had 'the care of a steam-engine in the City Road, – that great printing place'. The functions of printer and publisher were only gradually separated during the first half of the nineteenth century, and James Virtue was still both. He was yet another Scot, and a business associate of the entrepreneurial Alexander Strahan – who immediately countered the new *Fortnightly* by starting up another magazine of his own, the conservative *Contemporary Review*.

The first instalment of Anthony's novel *The Belton Estate* appeared in the first issue of the *Fortnightly*. The magazine, as

* He already had his original office in Cornhill in the City, and a West End office in Piccadilly.

Anthony told Herman Merivale, was to carry fiction, criticism, essays, politics 'and occasionally notices on art and science'. An essential accompaniment to all enterprises of this kind was a programme of jolly dinners for supporters and contributors: the *Fortnightly* dinners were held at the Star and Garter at Richmond.

The *Fortnightly* was too ambitious; it very soon became monthly, but retained its name. Lewes was not well, and after a year John Morley, aged twenty-eight, replaced him, and stayed fifteen years. When the money ran out at the end of 1866 Anthony and his colleagues sold the magazine to Chapman & Hall. Anthony's personal involvement evaporated after Lewes left. He wrote in May 1867, excusing himself from attending a meeting: 'I do not specially dislike Morley, but I do not care for his style of work, & cannot interest myself in the thing.'

Anthony broke with convention on the *Fortnightly* by including signed articles; anonymity had been the rule for serious journalism. What he had wanted to provide in the *Fortnightly* was a platform for ideas and opinions from all points of the political compass. This did not work out because, he discovered, conservatives would not consent to appear in the same paper with liberalism, free-thinking and open enquiry. 'As a natural consequence, our new publication became an organ of liberalism, free-thinking, and open enquiry.' Anthony in his autobiography implied that it went too far in that direction. John Morley was free-thinking and atheistic; a paper in the *Fortnightly* by Thomas Huxley, 'The Physical Basis of Life', caused a great stir in 1869. Under Morley's editorship the *Fortnightly* became a unique and influential forum for liberal debate.

Even this experiment was not enough for Anthony. In early 1867 he agreed with James Virtue to be the editor, for £1,000 a year, of yet another monthly magazine, to be called *Saint Pauls*. He needed a sub-editor to do the routine office work and invited Robert Bell to take the job. But this was just when poor Bell was dying; and the eventual sub-editor was a younger man, Edward Dicey,* who was paid £250 a year out of Anthony's £1,000. The mania for periodicals was already running into trouble. Alexander Strahan for one was over-reaching himself; in 1866 he had taken over the *Argosy* (to which Anthony contributed short

* Dicey afterwards became editor of the *Observer*.

stories) but could not make it pay, and sold it the next year to the popular novelist Mrs Henry Wood. Strahan, by now deeply in debt, wrote to Anthony in 1866 asking him to put his name up for membership of the Garrick: 'But if you don't think I would be a desirable member (as very likely I would not be) please let the matter drop and forgive me for suggesting it.' Strahan never became a member. But he had his ups as well as his downs; in 1869 he became exclusive publisher to the Poet Laureate Alfred Tennyson.

With magazine publishing now so competitive it was hardly surprising that under Anthony's editorship *Saint Pauls* did not become a commercial success. By 1869 James Virtue was trying to sell the magazine to Chapman & Hall. When that did not work out he transferred it to Alexander Strahan's company, of which he had partial control since he was Strahan's major creditor.* *Saint Pauls* struggled on until 1874, but Anthony was relieved of his office after three years. 'I was too anxious to be good, and did not enough think of what might be lucrative' (*Autobiography*). He was as vigorous in editorship as he was in everything else. He published the poems of the young Austin Dobson, thus giving a great boost to his literary career – but not before writing to Dobson pages of criticism, often suggesting alternative words and phrases. He felt paradoxically confident about criticising poetry. Writing with loving severity to Kate Field about hers, he said: 'I too have written verses, & have been told that they were nought.'†
He avoided publishing articles which he felt unqualified to assess, declining an article on ozone. As on the *Fortnightly*, he was unwilling to engage in controversy, other than political controversy. He wrote to one would-be contributor: 'I am afraid of the

---

* This meant that the copyright of *Phineas Finn*, serialised in *Saint Pauls*, ended up belonging to Strahan, who also owned the copyright of *He Knew He Was Right*. Copyrights were properties that could be passed or sold on from hand to hand. Since Anthony customarily sold his books outright, he had to write around to the various copyright-holders when his own books were being re-published, and accommodate them with a fee. Strahan's debts finally forced him out of his Ludgate Hill offices in 1872, and he found yet another business partner in Henry S. King, the brother-in-law of George Smith of Smith, Elder. The still evolving, constantly expanding, high-risk nineteenth-century publishing world operated in an intimate network of shifting alliances.

† Who told him so? Rose? Tom? Where are his verses now? The quatrains in his hand that remain among his papers, translations from Latin, are as graceful and easy as anyone could wish.

subject of Darwin. I am myself so ignorant on it, that I should fear to be in the position of editing a paper on the subject.'

What Anthony had wanted most of all in *Saint Pauls* was a strong political component. The world of parliamentary politics was interesting him, nagging at him, more and more. For him the House of Commons, which had always seemed out of his range, was the real 'top brick of the chimney'. By involving himself in these periodicals he was regrouping his energies for one last throw in that direction.

The 1860s saw regroupings within the extended Trollope family as well. In February 1861 John Tilley married again. His third wife was Susannah Montgomerie; within two years he was the father of two more children, a girl (called Cecilia) and a boy.

Rose's sister Isabella and Isabella's husband Joseph Bland both died. In March 1863 one of their daughters,* Florence Nightingale Bland, aged eight, came to live permanently at Waltham House. For Rose and Anthony she became the daughter they never had; and Florence, the northern bank clerk's daughter, became accustomed to a more ample and varied way of life, and celebrated visitors, and foreign holidays.

In 1863 Harry left Bradfield. The boys' academic careers there were not remarkable. A year before this, Anthony had been to see Lewes and George Eliot to discuss the possibility of sending his children to a German or Swiss school, like Lewes's sons. There seems to have been no talk of Harry going on to university. He wanted to travel, like his Uncle Tom before him. He was very like Tom, to whom he was always close; but unlike Tom he did not have a dominant mother in whose wake he could sail. In summer 1863 Rose, Anthony, Harry, Fred, and Anthony's niece Edith Tilley,† all went on holiday in the Bernese Oberland. Theo and her daughter Bice were with them: a big family party. Anthony and Harry accompanied Theo. and Bice back to Florence in September, and Harry stayed on in Italy, 'to begin life as a young man in Florence', as Anthony told Synge.

---

* Isabella and Joseph Bland had another daughter besides Florence, and two sons, the youngest of whom was three in 1863. Rose presumably felt she could take on only one extra child.

† Florence Bland, too young for such trips, must have been left at home with the servants to look after her.

Very soon after Anthony left, on 6 October (1863) old Mrs Trollope died at the Villino Trollope. She was eighty-three. The last letter from her to Anthony that has survived was written about five years before. It was very loving: 'My darling Anthony: You ask me to write – I and my pen have been so long divorced that I hardly know how to set about it – But you ask me to write and therefore I will – though I have no news to tell you other than that I love you dearly – I should like to see you again but can hardly hope it! God bless you my dear, dear Son! Your loving mother.'

Mrs Trollope had seen Anthony again, more than once, but she may not have taken it in. Her mind died before her body. She still doted on Tom, and depended on him: 'I want Tom to trot me out.' Her last words were, 'Poor Cecilia!'

Anthony requested an obituary article on her from the *Athenaeum*, and was pleased with the accuracy and the 'kindliness, heartiness, as well as excellent taste' of what they printed. He made no extravagant gestures or statements of grief, writing to Mary (Grant) Christie: 'My dear mother died full of years and without anything of the suffering of old age. For two years her memory had gone. But she ate & slept & drank, till the lamp went altogether out; but there was nothing of the usual struggle of death. I think that no one ever suffered less in dying.'

Mrs Trollope in her will, made in 1857, left to Tom and his heirs most of what she had: her interest in an estate at Bawd in Somersetshire, held in common with her sister Mary Clyde and the children of her late brother, Henry Milton (there would not have been much in that), and 'all such household furniture as may be left in his possession, and also the large china bowl now in the possession of my son-in-law John Tilley'. The bowl must have been left behind at Carlton Hill all those years ago – but not forgotten, perhaps, by Tom, who was her executor. Anthony and his heirs were left 'all shares in the Joint Stock London Bank* of which I may die possessed'. If she should leave any other money, her two sons were to divide it between them. But Mrs Trollope had not earned for eight years, and had never been able to save.

In his autobiography, Anthony summed up his mother's

---

* The bank shares were worth having. They brought in regular dividends (but not such high ones as Anthony's Garrick Club Debentures).

character and abilities with precision but little warmth: 'She was an unselfish, affectionate, and most industrious woman, with great capacity for enjoyment and high physical gifts. She was endowed, too, with much creative power, with considerable humour, and a genuine feeling for romance. But she was neither clear-sighted nor accurate; and in her attempts to describe morals, manners, and even facts, was unable to avoid the pitfalls of exaggeration.' His unresolved feelings about her made him uncharacteristically expressive in his grief for Thackeray, who died two and a half months after Mrs Trollope, on Christmas Eve 1863. Anthony had known this friend only a short time, but he felt his death, as he told Smith, as a very heavy blow. 'It has not been a merry Christmas with us,' he wrote to Chapman. 'I loved him dearly.' And to W. W. F. Synge: 'I saw him for the last time about ten days before his death. . . . How I seem to have loved that dear head of his now that he has gone.'

Anthony went to Thackeray's funeral at Kensal Green cemetery on 30 December, a sunny day. An astonishing number of people turned out – between 1,500 and 2,000. Millais wrote an account of it to his wife: 'It was a mournful scene, and badly managed. A crowd of women were there – from curiosity, I suppose – dressed all in colours; and round the grave scarlet and blue feathers shone out prominently! Indeed, the true mourners and friends could not get near. . . . There was a great lack of what is called "high society", which I was surprised at.'* Millais dined with artist friends that night. Anthony was not of the party. John Leech, who was, said he would never get over Thackeray's death, and nor did he; he died of heart disease the following year.

Anthony wrote at his own suggestion an appreciation of Thackeray for the *Cornhill*,† in which he said: 'One loved him

---

* Were the women in their scarlet and blue feathers the tribute of Babylon, a reflection of Thackeray's night-life? Not necessarily. Wilkie Collins's funeral at Kensal Green in 1889 was mobbed in the same way: 'There must have been at least a hundred of these unwholesome creatures, who call themselves women, who seem to live in graveyards. When the coffin had been lowered . . . there was a general rush of these people who . . . clawed the wreaths of flowers, and pulled about the cards which were attached to the wreaths, and laughed and cried and chattered until they were moved on by the graveyard police.' William M. Clarke, *The Secret Life of Wilkie Collins*, Allison & Busby, 1988.

† He took no money for this, only requesting a new copy of *Henry Esmond* for Rose ('my wife is mercenary, and requires payment') since their own copy was worn out.

almost as one loves a woman, tenderly and with thoughtfulness, – thinking of him when away from him as a source of joy which cannot be analysed, but is full of comfort.' Griefs and losses and longings merge, or become transposed. Around the time of his mother's death, Anthony had understood that Kate Field was married. Tom, knowing by then that she was not, wrote to Kate: 'My brother received cards in an envelope, – Mr and Mrs Carrol – née (as the damned idiots will write in french) Kate *P*. Field. He has no idea who could have sent them, and never knew any Kate Field than you, – As if there could be a second Kate Field!'

The tone of everything Anthony wrote about their mother in his autobiography grated on his brother. For Tom, she had been a source of joy and comfort always. It was common, he wrote in his memoirs, for a mother and daughter to live together for many years in so close a companionship, but 'it is not common for a son to do so'. For 'tête-à-tête walks, and yet more tête-à-tête home hours, we were inseparable companions and friends'. From the time he left the Birmingham schoolteaching job until his marriage, 'she was all in all to me!' The trouble with Anthony, he wrote, was that he did not really know her. From the time that he became a clerk in the Post Office until her death, 'he and my mother were never together but as visitors during the limited period of a visit.' As for Tom himself, 'I think I knew her, as few sons knew their mothers.'

Anthony always got Tom's work taken in the journals on which he had editorial influence; but Tom remained condescending. There had been some question of George Smith sending Anthony out to India to write a book in summer 1860, and Tom regretted that the idea was abandoned. 'I feel confident that the book would have improved your literary position, and given you a standing among government men, and such like, which the most successful novel-writing cannot do.' Sending to a relative in June 1864 a photograph of himself and Tom – the latter in profile, staring fiercely at Anthony, who looks straight at the camera – Anthony said: 'Here you have my brother and self. You will perceive that my brother is pitching into me. He always did.' Sibling rivalry did not die with their mother. Anthony could be condescending too. He told an author who sent him an abstruse work of fiction in 1869 that 'I often tell my brother, who knows more than any man I know and who is [a] man desiring to communicate his knowledge and convictions, that he is too didactic, too anxious to teach, to write a good novel.'*

Anthony was involved in petitioning for a memorial for Thackeray in Westminster Abbey,† and bought a 'dish', at a high price, as a memento of Thackeray when his great new house and its contents were sold up after his death. In summer 1864 George Smith gave Anthony one of the versions of Samuel Laurence's chalk portrait of Thackeray, which was hung in the library at Waltham House.

Smith commissioned Laurence to draw Anthony as well, that summer. 'Such a week I have had in sitting! Only that he is personally such a nice fellow, & has so much to say for himself, I should have been worn out,' Anthony told George Smith. 'I have been six times, or seven I think, & am to go again. He compliments me by telling me that I am a subject very difficult to draw.' He was delighted with the picture and, as he wrote to Smith, 'I did not tell you, I think, that my wife liked the portrait *very much indeed*. She seemed to have a fuller respect for me when she had seen it than ever before.' He returned to the pleasing topic in another letter to Smith: 'The picture is a very good picture & my wife declares it to be very like, – & not a bit more solid than the original. For your munificence we both thank you very heartily. . . .' The tribute came at a good moment; Anthony was going through a miserable passage in his Post Office career at that time, as we shall see in the next chapter.

Anthony and Rose remained on affectionate terms with Thackeray's daughters, particularly Anny. In the winter of 1865 Anny stayed at Waltham House, 'a sweet old prim chill house wrapped in snow', as she wrote in her journal. She heard Anthony being called by Barney at four o'clock 'in the bitter dark cold

* This was true. Tom was long-winded. His fiction is top-heavy with topography and architecture. But some of his novels did well. Many were historical, and set in Italy. *Lindisfarn Chase*, which Chapman & Hall published in 1866, was a proto-Anthony novel, complete with cathedral close, and went into at least four impressions. The heroine was called Kate and, Tom told Kate Field when he was writing it, she would be charming. 'You do not think that I could make a Kate, and make her anything but the dearest creature ever born!'

† A successful petition for a memorial to Anthony Trollope in Westminster Abbey was not made until 1991.

morning', to do his writing. This was an hour earlier than usual; but he was writing *The Belton Estate* for the *Fortnightly*, under pressure.

Anny Thackeray recorded the story of an excursion through the woods when she, and the Trollopes, were visiting John and Effie Millais at Sevenoaks, where they spent their summers. They came upon a painter at work under the trees. Millais looked at the painting, took the brush out of the artist's hand – 'Look, *this* is what you want' – and made one or two deft strokes. As they walked away, Anthony said the man should know it was Millais – and ran back and told him. Then someone else said that the man should know it was Trollope – and ran back and told him. Anny modestly did not say that it was she who was that 'someone else', nor that someone else again ran back to tell the unfortunate artist that it was Miss Thackeray. 'Greatly amused we all walked on through the woods to where the carriage was waiting.'*

Tom's wife Theo had been ailing, always, off and on. Robert Browning thought a great deal of Theo. When Elizabeth Barrett Browning died in 1861 it was Theo whom Browning first approached about seeking permission from the Florentine authorities for a tablet in her memory, which was placed on the wall of the Casa Guidi in 1863. Theo had 'true tact and taste, and feeling beside', Browning wrote to Isa Blagden, 'I am bound to her. She and her husband would smile if they knew the affection I have for them.'

Tom and Theo's great new friend in the spring of 1864 was the aspiring writer Alfred Austin, twenty-five years younger than Tom, who arrived in Florence with the usual introductions. In autumn 1864 Tom took Theo on the last of many health-seeking tours, to Lake Como. On 13 April 1865 she died, after weeks of pain, at the Villino Trollope in Florence. Walking away after the funeral in the English cemetery – where Mrs Trollope senior was also buried – Tom asked Alfred Austin to come and stay in the Villino Trollope, because he felt lonely. Austin moved in that afternoon for a protracted visit which was sustaining for them both.

Tom's daughter Bice was twelve when her mother died. She

---

* Hester Ritchie (ed.), *Letters of Anne Thackeray Ritchie*, John Murray, 1924.

was bright and precocious – Theo once referred to 'my *fast* daughter, who now rides daily and would smoke a cigarette if she could get it' – small for her age, pretty, with a sweet singing voice. 'But to ask Bice to study anything seriously was useless,' according to Alfred Austin. He remembered Anthony telling him that he promised a five-pound note to each of his nieces (Bice, Florence, and Edith Tilley) if they would learn Milton's 'Lycidas' by heart. Edith and Florence got their money. 'Bice never gave it another thought.'* She had been spoiled by her parents and their guests.

Anthony and Rose, as hospitable to the young as ever, did what they could. Anthony set off for Florence as soon as he heard of Theo's death and brought Bice home with him. 'The blow has been a *very* heavy one to me,' Tom wrote to Miss Dunlop, a friend of Theo's, in May 1865. Theo, he said, had not suffered at the end, 'but fell asleep as peacefully as a child in its mother's arms. . . . Bice is at Waltham Cross, near London with her uncle. He came to me immediately, and took her back with him. I would fain have gone too; but am detained here by business connected with the sale of this house. I *could* not live in it any longer. . . .'

Rose and Anthony now had two young nieces to look after. 'Drink all the cream you can,' Bice's father wrote to her, 'for you will get none when you come back to Italy, – or at all events none such.' Then began the first of countless little negotiations about money. Tom was endlessly correcting Bice, 'my own darling', for not paying postage, or for wasting her money. She was to tell her uncle that her father would pay half the hire of a piano for her, as Anthony had proposed.

As a music teacher for Bice, wrote Tom in his memoirs, he applied to 'a lady whom I might, at that time, consider an old friend', because of her sojourn in Florence three years before. This was the sister of Dickens's secret love: Fanny Ternan, now thirty years old. She had in the interim, according to Tom, 'through us made the acquaintance of my brother and his family, who all of them soon learned to value and esteem her as warmly as we did.' Fanny was to come to stay at Waltham every other weekend, and give Bice three singing lessons each time, for £2 a weekend.

When Anthony was away from Waltham on PO business he

---

* *The Autobiography of Alfred Austin*, Macmillan, 1911.

wrote Bice jolly avuncular notes: 'Your great-aunt Mrs Clyde, – my mother's sister, – who is a very old woman living in Exeter has sent you a present of ten guineas. We must have a great consultation between you, and aunt Rose, and papa, and Barney, and all the other wise people, as to what you had better buy. What do you say to a new cow? or perhaps ten guineas' worth of chocolate bonbons?' He signed himself 'Your own affectionate uncle T (for Toney [sic])'.

Anthony and Rose were worrying about their own children too. Their elder son Harry could not 'travel' indefinitely. His liking for foreign parts and aptitude for languages might however be put to use. In May 1864 Anthony wrote to Lord Houghton asking for help in getting a nomination for Harry to the Foreign Office. 'My son is now eighteen. He has been for the last eight months in Italy, with masters there. He will have a private tutor here for the next three months, and will spend the autumn & winter in Paris.' Nothing came of this. A year later, when George Smith asked Anthony to write an account of a May Meeting – an annual rally in support of charitable and religious causes – Anthony took Harry along, thinking to give him the chance to write it up; but the meeting bored Harry as much as it bored his father.

Fred, the younger son, left Bradfield in summer 1865. He was good at cricket and football, and had no academic ambitions. He was famous in the school for a long and bloody fight, like his father long ago at Harrow. In the summer term of 1862, when Fred was nearly fourteen, he attacked a boy called P. G. Ward, who was bullying a smaller boy, W. J. Richmond.* Ward was bigger, heavier and stronger than Fred, but Fred won – though he was so 'knocked about' that he was unable to go home for some days after term ended. Neither of the Trollope boys was tall, and both had been thin as children. Harry remained extremely thin, but the life that Fred chose broadened his back. Unlike Harry, he had a clear idea of what he wanted to do when he left school, and it was not what his parents would have chosen for him. Not yet eighteen, Fred was determined to emigrate to Australia and be a sheep-farmer.†

* W. J. Richmond became a clergyman and headmaster of Glenalmond.
† Of the first 1,000 boys at Bradfield (1850–88), 161 emigrated to the Empire. One in five left England permanently.

In the autumn of 1865 Rose and Fred went with Anthony on holiday to Germany and Austria, meeting Harry in Koblenz; then Fred left for Melbourne, and a sheep station at Barratta. 'This departure was a great pang to his mother and me,' Anthony wrote in his autobiography; 'but it was permitted on the understanding that he was to come back when he was twenty-one, and then decide whether he would remain in England or return to the colonies.'

Bice did not stay long with them at Waltham. Mourning her mother and missing her father, she longed to be back in Florence. Isa Blagden, the sociable mainstay of English families in Florence, wrote to her lovingly: 'My darling Beatrice you know I love you with all my heart, for your own sake and for my precious Theo's. She was my dearest friend, I may say in all these late years, almost my sister. . . .' With 'such a dear good Papa' and 'such an Uncle as loves you as your Uncle does' Bice would not want for affection; and she could always rely on Isa.

Once back in Florence, Bice grew even more depressed and lonely in the large house,* where her father stood at his tall desk writing all day.† So even though the Villino Trollope was not yet sold, the two moved to another house – a neglected, ancient, fifteen-room villa at Ricorboli, outside the Porta San Niccolo, south of the Arno. Since the Austrians were driven out in 1859 Italy had been in turmoil. The new kingdom of Italy was inaugurated in 1861, and in 1864 the provisional capital was established in Florence, which was good for Florentine society, Florentine business and Florentine property values. Tom began making ambitious improvements to the new villa. By means of the 'greasing of certain palms' he acquired ten purple marble columns on white marble bases that had been lying for centuries in the crypt of Florence cathedral, and built his grandiose new hall around them.‡ He was also building a library fifty feet long, to

---

* Tom had also bought the house next door, so that the Villino Trollope finally took up the whole of one side of the Via del Podere. The double garden extended all the way to the quiet road beneath the city walls.

† Tom's four-volume *History of the Commonwealth of Florence* came out in 1865 – perfectly timed, in view of Florence's new importance as the national capital.

‡ Tom's passion for dealing was growing on him. In 1866 he was still looking after the valuable album that Landor had given Kate Field. She was hard up, but he advised her it was a bad time to sell art. American Civil War memorabilia were a better bet. 'If you have any "war material" to dispose of, any belt leather, any ambulance carriages, any red cloth, I think I could find a market for you.'

house his 14,000 volumes. In his mid-fifties, 'in good health, young for my years, strong and vigorous in constitution', Tom realised that his life was not over.

Within five months of Theo's death rumours were running round Florence about a replacement. Browning, in London, wrote to Isa Blagden: 'You amuse me with the speculations about the new Mrs T: lord love us, how little flattering is women's love – that is, the collective woman's love – the *particular*, is another matter. It seems he may throw his handkerchief to anyone in Florence.'

Browning conceded that Tom took 'a real interest' in Bice, but the child needed a female companion. A French governess came, but stayed only until spring 1866. Bice took frequent refuge with Isa Blagden. Tom and Bice were still in touch with Fanny Ternan, who wrote to Bice, signing herself 'Fannina', about a ball she had gone to at Waltham House in February. 'Your aunt and uncle [Anthony and Rose] were kind enough to invite my sister Ellen and she accompanied me. Would you like to know our dresses? Well we were dressed quite alike in pale green silk with tarlatane of the same . . .' The dresses were trimmed with dewdrops, and both women wore scarlet geraniums – Charles Dickens's favourite flower – and white heather in their hair. It is impossible to know whether Rose Trollope was aware that Ellen, the sister of the music teacher, was Charles Dickens's beloved. The best guess is that Anthony, knowing her reaction to unorthodox arrangements, did not pass on all he knew.

That summer, while the villa at Ricorboli was being refurbished, Alfred Austin returned to Florence with his new young wife, and Fanny Ternan arrived too, as Bice's governess. The adults made a congenial foursome. Fanny Ternan, wrote Austin, 'though thoroughly feminine in every respect, had an almost masculine mind in the sphere of serious intellectual deliberations, in which, so different in that respect from his brother Anthony, Thomas Adolphus and I also greatly rejoiced.' Fanny's first novel was being serialised in Dickens's *All the Year Round*; but Tom Trollope and Fanny Ternan rejoiced in more than serious intellectual deliberations that summer.

Tom wrote in his memoirs: 'My brother, who had assisted in the negotiation which brought Miss Ternan to Florence, when I told him of my engagement, said, "Yes, of course! I knew you

would." ' Browning too gave the match his blessing, writing to Isa
Blagden: 'I am glad to hear that T. Trollope is about to marry
happily – quite right in him to try. I think him affectionate, good,
full of various talent, – all of which his wife will soon find out. Give
Bice my love, – I like the memory of her.' Browning loved a bit of
scandal. It was he who retailed to Isa the tattle in the London
clubs around this time about the doubts cast on Bice's paternity,
and maybe on Theo's.*

Anthony went out to Florence in the autumn of 1866 to
accompany Tom and Fanny to Paris, where the wedding was to take
place. A visit that Wilkie Collins had planned to make to Tom in
Florence had to be put off. 'I don't complain,' wrote Collins. 'I am all
for Love myself – and this sort of thing speaks volumes for women,
for surely a man of mature age, with a growing daughter, doesn't
marry again without knowing what he is about, and without
remembrances of Mrs Number One which surround as with a halo
Mrs Number Two.'†

Tom was fifty-six and Fanny, his Mrs Number Two, was
thirty-one. Fanny's elder sister Maria, now Mrs Rowland
Taylor,‡ travelled from Florence with the bridal party and
Anthony, and in Paris they were joined by Rose Trollope and
Harry, and by Ellen Ternan and Mrs Ternan. 'Bice might have
come with us also,' wrote Tom in his memoirs, 'but that she would
have been *de trop* after the marriage.'

Bice's trouble was that she was always *de trop* after the marriage.
During their long honeymoon tour, her new stepmother 'Fannina'
as well as her father wrote to her often, lovingly and bracingly. But
when all three were together again in Florence Bice made herself
difficult. She seemed happiest staying with Isa Blagden up at
Bellosguardo.

---

* See pages 168, 199.
† William M. Clarke, *The Secret Life of Wilkie Collins*. Collins's remark is interesting
in that he himself, two years before, had taken on a Mrs Number Two, or rather a
Mistress Number Two, without the intervention of a death. Caroline Graves and her
daughter (and his) were still solidly established in his life and remained so, bar a few
hiccups, when he took on Martha Rudd, a shepherd's daughter from Norfolk, by
whom he also had children.
‡ Maria Ternan too had put the stage behind her and made in 1865 a 'good' but
boring and unsuccessful marriage to Rowland Taylor, the son of an Oxford brewer.

The following summer, 1867, Tom and Fanny sent Bice to a boarding school in England, in Albany Villas at Brighton, kept by her former French governess Clara Collinet. 'Her terms are immensely high,' Tom told his daughter, 'including everything – £275 a year. But by leaving out several things it can be brought down to £146 – *which is quite as much as I can manage to pay.*'

Life was much easier for Fanny and Tom when Bice was away. They worked at their books and articles, entertained their friends and went on regular sightseeing tours. Bice did not like the Brighton school and let everyone know it. Anthony and Rose, necessarily, made themselves responsible to some extent for the unhappy girl.

Fortunately Harry seemed to be settled at last; by the autumn of 1867 he was, as Anthony announced with pride, 'a Cornet of mounted Yeomanry & is with his regiment. . . . I had to go up to London on Saturday to send him *dress spurs.*' Bice stayed with her aunt and uncle at Waltham that Christmas, to Tom and Fanny's relief. Fanny wrote that she had a letter from 'Uncle Tony' praising Bice's manners; she had been 'so nice and pleasant at Waltham' the last time that they said they had been sad to see her go.

Bice was at last made to feel wanted, with Rose and Anthony. Her father wrote about little else than the need for economy, and the cost of postage: 'You must not write to people abroad on such thick paper.' Tom, who was famously kind and jovial with his friends and who spent money lavishly on his houses and on summer 'tours', was completely neurotic about small sums. He was too mean to send on Bice's Christmas cards from Italy.

After Christmas Anthony wrote to Tom in some anxiety. 'He seemed to think,' Tom reported to his daughter, 'that you have hardly nourishment enough at Brighton. . . . Your uncle says he thinks it would be very good for you to have an egg every morning for breakfast, and a glass of sherry in the middle of the day.' He would consider authorising the egg, but not the sherry; she would need two glasses by the time she was eighteen, he said, and 'will not be able to get through the day without three before you are five-and-twenty.'* After a dance at the Tilleys, Bice got mumps. Rose looked after her.

* Tom was right in not encouraging a fourteen-year-old to become addicted to sherry. Tom was virtually teetotal. He drank milk, and guests drank home-made lemonade.

—— * ——

In 1865, a record year to date, Anthony made £6,945.7.0, of which
£5,866.15.10 was from his writing. He was able to buy the freehold
of Waltham House, for £3,500. In 1866 he made £7,446.14.10.
This was his all-time record; but then the Post Office accounted
for £700 of his annual income. In 1867, at long last and the age of
fifty-two, he gave up his Post Office work.

CHAPTER FIFTEEN

ANYONE who did not know the man might wonder why he stayed in the Post Office so long. His journeys around the Eastern District, charted in his diary, seem ever more irrelevant to his concerns and inclinations.

He was a lover of romantic mountain scenery and, in England, of the picturesque and varied West Country. The flat fens and fields and wide skies of East Anglia did not appeal to him, and the novels written during and after this posting reflect that antipathy. The most nightmarish household he ever described was that of Puritan Grange at Chesterton, outside Cambridge (in *John Caldigate*). 'Suffolk is not especially a picturesque country,' he opined in *The Way We Live Now*. Suffolk was 'very old-fashioned' and 'persistently and irrecoverably Conservative'. A picnic in East Anglia was his idea of torture. Unlike his mother, Anthony hated picnics, unless the situation was particularly idyllic and the company young and attractive. In *Can You Forgive Her?* Mr Cheesacre, a fat Norfolk farmer, was fond of picnics: 'The affair simply amounted to this, that they were to eat their dinner uncomfortably in the field instead of comfortably in the dining-room.' Describing Mr Cheesacre's windy picnic on the sands at Yarmouth in the same book, Anthony wrote scathingly of the dull flatness of the Norfolk seashore.

The endless train-travel involved in his work as a Surveyor had lost its charm for him too. He wrote in *The Belton Estate* that he personally knew 'no hours so terrible' as those passed waiting at stations. 'The mind altogether declines to be active, whereas the body is seized by a spirit of restlessness to which delay and tranquillity are loathesome.' In the waiting-room, everything 'is hideous, dirty, and disagreeable; and the mind wanders away, to wonder why station-masters do not more frequently commit suicide.'

But so far as the Post Office as an institution was concerned he was as committed as ever. During 1860 he sat on an internal committee of inquiry into PO inadequacies. There was a great row between Rowland (by then Sir Rowland) Hill, his brother Frederic Hill, John Tilley and the committee about exactly to whom and in what terms the committee should report. Anthony's manner on committee was never conciliatory. Edmund Yates remembered a Surveyors' meeting where he roared out: 'I differ from you entirely. What was it you said?'

Anthony's position with Hill was not improved by the lecture he gave to the Post Office Library and Literary Association on 'The Civil Service as a Profession' (afterwards published in the *Cornhill*) in which he challenged the reformed system of 'promotion by merit' instead of by seniority in the service. Anthony described 'promotion by merit' as a neat way of enabling those in authority to put forward their friends and special pets, and said that the staff should have been consulted beforehand anyway. This subversive stuff went down very well with his audience of PO employees.

Anthony was very far from being one of Hill's special pets. 'How I loved, when I was contradicted, – as I was very often and no doubt very properly, – to do instantly as I was bid, and then to prove that what I was doing was fatuous, dishonest, expensive, and impracticable. And then there were feuds, – such delicious feuds!' It was his pleasure, he wrote, to differ from Hill on all occasions, believing him to be 'unfit to manage men or to arrange labour' (*Autobiography*).

Anthony had agreed with Rose that he would leave the Post Office when he had saved enough to provide the same income as the PO pension to which he would be entitled at the age of sixty. This he had achieved by 1867. Now that he had undertaken the editorship of *Saint Pauls* he was patently doing too much, working on Sundays and at night on PO paperwork; but he would have stayed on with the Post Office, had he got the promotion he felt he deserved.

Sir Rowland Hill retired in March 1864. Anthony wrote him a courteous letter, praising him as one of the benefactors of the whole civilised world. (Hill was amazed. Anthony meant it; he was referring to the penny post.) John Tilley got Hill's plum job as Secretary to the Post Office. Anthony applied for his brother-in-law's former job as Assistant Secretary, but it went to Frank

Scudamore, eight years younger than Anthony and six years his junior in length of service. John Tilley, as the incoming chief executive, was instrumental in this decision.

It was a sensible appointment. Scudamore, besides his mild literary achievements, was a bright man and clever with money. The half-penny postcard had been his idea, and as Receiver and Accountant General to the PO he had set up the PO Savings Bank. As Assistant Secretary, he was to buy up the private telegraph companies, achieving a PO monopoly and expanding the service by the questionable means of diverting PO Savings Bank funds without authorisation.

In *The Way We Live Now*, poor little rich girl Marie Melmotte attempted to elope with Felix Carbury, who got drunk at the Beargarden Club and never even left London. Marie took the train, as arranged, and was humiliatingly intercepted at Liverpool station because of a telegram sent from London – which gave Anthony the opportunity to ask rhetorically whether the telegraph system had not added more to the annoyances than to the comforts of life, 'and whether the gentlemen who spent all the public money without authority ought not to have been punished with special severity in that they had injured humanity, rather than pardoned because of the good they had produced.' Who benefited, he asked, from telegrams? 'The newspapers are robbed of all their old interest, and the very soul of intrigue is destroyed.* Poor Marie, when she heard her fate, would certainly have gladly hanged Mr Scudamore.'

So would Anthony, in 1864. He had written with pre-vision in *Castle Richmond*: 'It is sad for a man to feel, when he is fast going down the hill of life, that the experience of old age is to be no longer valued nor its wisdom appreciated. When he was in his full physical vigour he was not old enough for mental success. He was still winning his spurs at forty. But at fifty – so does the world change – he learns that he is past his work. By some unconscious and unlucky leap he has passed from the unripeness of youth to the decay of age, without even knowing what it was to be in his prime.'

Anthony had come into his kingdom late; yet by the time he was

* He also blamed telegrams, as a future generation would blame the telephone, for the decline of the love-letter: 'the pith and strength of laconic diction has been taught to us by the self-sacrificing patriotism of the Post Office' (*Is He Popenjoy?*).

in his fifties he already wrote and spoke of himself as an old man, over-reacting to the inevitable diminution of the stamina on which he relied. His 'prime' seemed, to him, even shorter than most people's.

It was not the rise in salary he wanted – an extra £400 – but the status of a public man. He wanted a London office (no more trundling round a district) and official recognition of the quality of his thirty-three years' service.

Obviously, because of his writing he had not been single-minded in his devotion to the PO. But it was, he insisted, 'absolutely true that during all those years I had thought very much more about the Post Office than I had of my literary work'. Pathetically, he wrote in his autobiography that had he got the Assistant Secretaryship, 'I should have given up my hunting, have given up much of my literary work, – at any rate would have edited no magazine, – and would have returned to the habit of my youth in going daily to the General Post Office.'

A month after this disappointment the Surveyors, as a body, applied to the Postmaster General Lord Stanley of Alderley for a salary increase. It was refused via the new Secretary, John Tilley. The Surveyors had made the point that heads of department based in London, with responsibilities comparable to their own, had had a rise. Tilley's argument was that these increments had been for 'special services'. Anthony told a fellow Surveyor that Tilley's reply had been 'false as well as insolent', and he did not let the matter drop all through the spring and summer of 1864.

His personal resentments found expression in a long, angry memorandum he addressed formally to the Postmaster General Lord Stanley, but which was dealt with by John Tilley, as Anthony knew it would be. Anthony wrote that he had never seen a reply to any representation from civil servants so 'calculated to give offence' as Mr Tilley's. He was sceptical about the 'special services' which explained the London officials' pay increments. Mr Scudamore, he conceded, had performed special services* but 'with regard to the one of whose work I have known the most, – I mean Mr Tilley, I do not think that he will for a moment assert, – otherwise than with the general latitude of loose official

---

* This was a generous concession under the circumstances, but it was preferable to being accused of personal pique against Scudamore.

phraseology, that he, as assistant Secretary, performed any special services.' He kept harping on Tilley as an example of someone who had received preferential treatment, and he brought his own case into it: 'I believe no gentleman in the service, – always excepting Mr Scudamore, – has a better right to put forward a claim for special services than I have.'*

Tilley sent what he called 'this most intemperate letter' on to Lord Stanley, and replied to Anthony that his Lordship was 'at a loss' to know why only Mr Trollope had come forward with a complaint, in response to what had been a circular letter. 'He could only conclude that none of your colleagues felt aggrieved' or that none of them would put their names to such an improper letter.

Anthony, on holiday in Windermere – it must have been a grim holiday for Rose, with her husband seething and obsessed – then wrote, against all protocol, a personal letter to Lord Stanley, whom he knew in private life. He explained that he alone contested the circular letter because 'I chose to run a risk in which I could not ask them to join me.' He set out his grounds for complaint all over again. He said he had been treated like Oliver Twist when he asked for more – 'and I own that I thought Mr Tilley was very like Bumble in the style of the answer he gave us.' The Postmaster General behaved with official propriety. It was Tilley who answered Anthony's personal letter to Lord Stanley, informing him that his Lordship had nothing further to say.

The row fizzled out. John Tilley offered Anthony a mollifying nine months' trip on PO business to the Far East. Anthony turned it down, but he and Tilley were friends again: 'My dear Tony', 'My dear John'. In spring 1866 Tilley had a plan to reorganise the London postal districts, each under its own postmaster. Anthony was invited to make a feasibility study, working from the West London district office in Vere Street off Oxford Street.

He worked with his usual speed and commitment, exhausting his staff, barking at anyone who complained. One clerk assigned to Vere Street with Anthony described his 'method of attacking work': 'I have seen him slogging away at papers at a stand-up desk, with his handkerchief stuffed into his mouth, and his hair on

* Several of the other Surveyors, after Tilley's circular letter, put in applications for payments under the 'special services' rubric. Anthony never did.

end, as though he could barely contain himself.' During the same period he was writing *The Last Chronicle of Barset*.

The London assignment was completed in a matter of months and the new scheme put into operation. John Tilley offered Anthony the Surveyorship of the reconstituted Metropolitan district, but he declined it. The Post Office having let him down, he was ready to look beyond it. In early October 1867, already the editor of *Saint Pauls*, he sent in his resignation. John Tilley's official reply included the one assurance that, he knew, would mean most to Anthony. Tilley wrote that 'I have been especially glad to record that, notwithstanding the many calls upon your time, you have never permitted your other avocations to interfere with your Post Office work, which has been most faithfully and indeed energetically performed.' Anthony, copying this letter into his autobiography, noted with amusement the irony of that 'energetically'.

His resignation coincided with, and was perhaps precipitated by, a groundswell of unrest among PO employees. A weekly paper had just been founded called *The Postman*, devoted to 'the interests of Post Office Clerks, Sorters, Charge Takers, Messengers, Letter Carriers, Mail Guards, Auxiliaries, Supernumeraries, Mail Drivers, etc., etc.' Its function was to air grievances about pay and conditions, to unite the workforce nationwide against the 'tyranny and poverty connected with service under the Post Office authorities' and to publicise and solicit subscriptions for a public protest meeting of PO employees to be held at Exeter Hall in London in December. The paper questioned the government's monopoly of the mails; the reorganisation of London districts came in for particular criticism, as did the Surveyors as a group. Cost-cutting, which pleased their superiors and made the employees' tasks impossible was, according to *The Postman*, the chief priority of all Surveyors. John Tilley and his 'greedy, parsimonious, stupid officials' were not popular with *The Postman*; the days of Sir Rowland Hill were recalled with nostalgia.

So much can be gleaned from the issue of *The Postman* (16 November 1867) which reported Anthony Trollope's farewell banquet. He must have been pleased to be getting out for more reasons than one. 'The chaps in the GPO are going to give me a dinner on the 31st [October]. I suppose you couldn't come up – and take a part, & hear the speechifying, and help to make a row,' he wrote to 'My dear old fellow', some unnamed PO colleague from former days. The dinner, for nearly a hundred people, was held in the banqueting hall of the Albion Tavern, only a stone's throw from St Martin's-le-Grand. Frank Scudamore acted as host, with Anthony seated at his right hand and John Tilley at his left. There was musical entertainment from the Moray Minstrels.

Two unsigned accounts of the evening appeared in *The Postman*. The first was editorial, and politically flavoured, quoting Mr Scudamore's speech in which he praised Mr Trollope's 'strong rectitude of purpose, his manly confidence in himself, and the determination to do the very utmost what his post of duty required'. The writer of the article questioned whether those attributes were in themselves enough to gain advancement in the Post Office: 'That Mr TROLLOPE was a very praiseworthy, diligent, and dutiful servant we believe: but that he owes his present success entirely or mainly to the display of these qualities is much to be doubted. In the majority of instances Virtue in this world has to be its own reward, at all events in the Post Office: it is Talent, Genius, Influence, that are rewarded by others with worldly wealth and advancement.' The writer also implied that Anthony, in his reply to Scudamore, was a little incoherent, as may very understandably have been the case: 'Mr ANTHONY TROLLOPE . . . is a gentleman and a man of honour in every sense of the word, as well as a successful writer; and his reply-speech was most successful because of its effective word-painting; but even our friend got a little out of the ruck of strong sense. Perhaps it is the dinner; perhaps the wine; perhaps the excitement. Somehow, at least, post-prandial speeches spoil themselves by their excess of amiability and goodness.'

More about the evening can be learned from the second and less pompous account towards the back of the paper. There was 'immense cheering' when Mr Scudamore referred to Mr Trollope 'keeping half England breathlessly waiting to hear the Yes or No of Lily Dale' (a reference to the serialisation of *The Small House at Allington*), and 'Mr Trollope's speech . . . was excellent in every respect; characterized by his strong humour, but at the same time tinged with sadness.' He reminisced about his thirty-three years in the service and painted a picture of himself as a ' "junior assistant probationary temporary extra clerk" condemned to eleven years of preliminary service without any pay'. (If Anthony said that, he was indeed fuddled; he was poorly paid, but never unpaid.) Three of the five clerks who worked with him in the big square room at St Martin's-le-Grand in those days were, Anthony said, sitting near to him at the dinner table. Anthony's elder son Harry was also at the dinner; and Edmund Yates proposed the health of the visitors 'in a very neat and sprightly address'.

Anthony's farewell dinner after a third of a century's service was, however, a homely celebration compared with the grandiose farewell dinner given at the Freemasons' Hall two nights later for Charles Dickens, who was simply going on a reading tour of America. Anthony was asked to be one of the stewards at the dinner – 'I am not specially in that set, but having been asked I did not like to refuse.' He was required to respond to the toast to literature, which he did by defending the novel, as art form and moral influence.*

George Eliot, when she read in the papers that Anthony had resigned from the Post Office, wrote to John Blackwood that 'I cannot help being rather sorry, though one is in danger of being rash in such judgements. But it seems to me a thing greatly to be dreaded for a man that he should be in any way led to excessive writing.'

A huge chapter of Anthony Trollope's life had closed. He had, as he said in his autobiography, 'imbued myself with a thorough love of letters, – I mean the letters which are carried through the post, – and was anxious for their welfare as though they were all my own.'

He never wrote an epistolary novel, and disliked the classic example of that genre, Richardson's *Clarissa*. 'The fact that the writing of such letters is impossible wounds one at every turn.'† The language used by the letter-writers, he thought, was unnatural, and though their personalities were so different they expressed themselves in the same style.

The scores of letters that rustle through the pages of his own

---

* The possibly corrupting effects of novel-reading on young people were being discussed then as heatedly as were the effects of television a hundred years later. George Eliot fretted interminably about her 'influence', and so did Anthony.

† He wrote this in August 1868 to E. S. Dallas, who had just sent him his abridged version of *Clarissa*. Anthony wrote more in the same vein in an article on *Clarissa* in *Saint Pauls* (November 1868).

novels are deeds, events, things-in-the-world of which he was preternaturally conscious. They arrive, they don't arrive, they can be destroyed, or exploited, they are not always benign. 'Who does not know how odious a letter will become by being shoved on one side day after day?' he asked in *Marion Fay*. 'Answer it at the moment, and it will be nothing. Put it away unread, or at least undigested, for a day, and it at once begins to assume ugly proportions. When you have been weak enough to let it lie on your desk, or, worse again, hidden in your breast-pocket, for a week or ten days, it will have become an enemy so strong and so odious that you will not dare to attack it. . . . It makes you cross to your wife, severe to your cook, and critical to your own wine-cellar.'

With few exceptions, he kept the personal letters he received only until he had answered them. Then they were thrown out. He took trouble over his stationery; from the time of the move to Waltham House, he and Rose had headed letter-paper in a variety of sizes with the address engraved in red or black gothic lettering, and the family crest – a stag with an oak-leaf in its mouth – both on the paper and on the flap of the envelopes. His letters were written to inform rather than to charm. Hundreds and hundreds of them have survived and nearly all have been published. The majority of them are 'business' letters, even when the recipients were his friends.

Even if we had more of his personal letters it would not materially change the picture. Lord Hampstead in *Marion Fay*, finding it hard to compose a love-letter, thought that 'When a man is married, and can write about the children, or the leg of mutton, or what's to be done with his hunters, then I dare say it becomes easy.' Those were exactly the sort of letters that Anthony wrote to Rose. When Michael Sadleir was preparing his book on Anthony in the 1920s, Harry told him that both he and Fred thought that 'our father in his letters to us confined himself to the matter in hand and wrote shortly. He loved us both very dearly, but I think he had too much writing (PO works and books) to do to make him wish to dally pleasantly with his pen in writing to us. In talking he enjoyed heartily play of that kind, but writing savoured of business. . . .'

That makes sense so far as it goes. George Western in *Kept in the Dark* loved his estranged wife Cecilia, but wrote her an inexpressive letter: 'His dignity and his so-called manliness are always near to him, and are guarded, so that he should not melt into open truth.' There may have been something of this in Anthony, as there was in his father.

He had no time, in any sense, for the artificial bolstering of friendships by letter-writing. 'When there is something palpable to be said, what a blessing is the penny post!' he wrote in *Phineas Redux*. 'To one's wife, to one's child, one's mistress . . . one's publisher, if there be a volume ready or money needed. . . .' But for the maintenance of love and friendship, 'continued correspondence between distant friends is naught. Distance in time and place, but especially in time, will diminish friendship. It is a rule of nature that it should be so. . . .'

Angry letters, he said in *The Bertrams*, should be left unposted for twenty-four hours and then, preferably, burned. (Five years after this sage advice, he wrote – and posted – those angry letters to his superiors in the PO.) An angry letter was 'so much fiercer than any angry speech, so much more unendurable! There the words remain, scorching, not to be explained away. . . .'

'A pleasant letter I hold to be the pleasantest thing that this world has to give. It should be good-humoured; witty it may be, but with a gentle diluted wit. Concocted brilliancy will spoil it altogether. . . . It should be written specially for the reader, and should apply altogether to him, and not altogether to any other.' In *The Bertrams* he cited Walpole as an example not to be followed, and Byron as a model.

Here is Doctor Thorne gritting himself to propose by letter to Miss Dunstable, in *Framley Parsonage*: 'He would use the simplest, plainest language, he said to himself over and over again; but it is not always easy to use simple plain language, – by no means so easy as to mount on stilts, and to march along with sesquipedalian words, with pathos, spasms, and notes of interjection.' Nothing could be more simple, or more terrible, than Alice Vavasor's letter (in *Can You Forgive Her?*) to loyal, dull John Grey, who longed to marry her: 'What if I should wake some morning after six months living with you, and tell you that the quiet of your home was making me mad?'

The letters that Anthony wrote and posted were simple, even prosaic. Even to Kate Field he only touched the margins of his longing and did not 'melt into open truth'. Yet he was a very great letter-writer. His great letters are in his novels. He did not so much write his characters' letters for them as become his characters as they sat at their writing-tables. He wrote every kind of letter – passionate, treacherous, contrived, manipulative, poisonous, ingenuous, spontaneous, desperate, studied, cute, inhibited, blackmailing, artless, pompous, illiterate, confiding, titillating. Only the illiterate ones fail to convince; Anthony could not 'become' someone who had no command of language at all.

The written word was transparent, for Anthony. He admired Lord Palmerston but felt, with distaste, that his letters were written with a view to publication. 'They contain sententious morsels of didactic wisdom, which would not have been put there in the hurry of private correspondence unless they had been intended for other eyes' (*Lord Palmerston*). It is not easy to deceive, he said, in letters: 'A man or woman must have studied the matter very thoroughly, or be possessed of great natural advantage in that direction, who can so fill a letter with false expressions of affections, as to make any reader believe them to be true' (*Miss Mackenzie*). In *Mr Scarborough's Family* Peter Prosper had a hard time writing the letter extricating himself from his engagement to Matilda Thoroughbung: 'It had to be studied in every word, and rewritten again and again and again with the profoundest care. He was afraid that he might commit himself by an epithet. He dreaded even an adverb too much. He found that a full stop expressed his feelings too violently, and wrote the letter again, for the fifth time, because of the big initial that followed the full stop.' But she saw through it all. 'If you want to write naturally you should never copy a letter.'

Anthony demonstrated pseudo-spontaneity with a wicked knowingness. He was not mocking, exactly: he was saying, this is what people do. Francesca Altifiora in *Kept in the Dark*, working overtime to snare Sir Francis Geraldine, 'wrote him such letters, letters so full of mingled love and fun, that she was sure he must take delight in reading them.' She copied these out three times, the final version 'in such handwriting that it should have been the very work of negligence.'

Someone else who had 'studied the matter very thoroughly' was Winifred Hurtle, Paul Montague's American mistress, about to be cast aside in *The Way We Live Now*. In her dim Islington lodgings, she composed the letter that would bring him, temporarily, back to her arms. 'This letter took her much time to write, though she was very careful so to write as to make it seem that it had flown easily from her pen. She copied it from the first draught, but she copied it rapidly, with one or two premeditated erasures, so that it should look to have been done hurriedly. There had been much art in it.'

There was much art too (and, for the reader, high comedy) in the three different letters that the pot-boiling author Lady Carbury composed to three different literary editors, soliciting a kind review of her forthcoming book in the first chapter of *The Way We Live Now*. One of the editors had once kissed her; another was a dull family man who would be counting on her to review his own new book fulsomely; the third was a smart creature who hunted and dined. Each letter was tailored by Lady Carbury to its recipient.*

In his notes for *The Way We Live Now* Anthony wrote the name 'Shand' against the name of one of the fictional literary editors – the one who would expect Lady Carbury to give him a good review if he obliged her. Alexander Shand was a facile journalist and author, a friend of Laurence Oliphant and George Smith. One of Lady Carbury's many productions, in Anthony's novel, was called 'The Wheel of Fortune'; Shand, in 1886, published a novel called *Fortune's Wheel*. Perhaps he saw the joke.

Anthony always swore that he never drew characters from life, but like most novelists he used existing people, such as Shand, as a reference or jumping-off point, and like most novelists he was not always aware of the underground stream of memories and associations feeding his imagination. Harry Trollope told Michael Sadleir that when he said to his father that Lady Carbury reminded him of a Mrs E., 'He half jumped from his chair and said vigorously: "She is very like, but I was not thinking of Mrs E. when I wrote!" '

Mrs E. was probably Mrs O.† – Mrs Margaret Oliphant (a

---

* Lady Carbury's behaviour was part of 'the way we live now'. Harriet Martineau in her autobiography described how her publisher told her to 'write the notes' – explaining that all authors wrote notes to friends connected with periodicals 'to request favourable notices . . . all our authors do it'. Miss Martineau refused. Anthony in his autobiography was scathing of any author who 'goes to work among the editors, or the editors' wives, or perhaps, if he cannot reach their wives, with their wives' first or second cousins'.

† There's no point disguising a name by an initial if you give the right initial. Oliphant easily becomes Elephant, if one must seek a free association.

cousin of Laurence Oliphant), the author of over a hundred books* which she churned out in a desperate effort to support her family, as did the fictional Lady Carbury. Anthony serialised some of Mrs Oliphant's fiction in *Saint Pauls*. The Trollopes were on visiting terms with her, and she was friendly with Rose; Anny Thackeray in her diary for 1876, when she was living with her widowed brother-in-law Leslie Stephen in Hyde Park Gate, noted that 'Mrs Oliphant and Mrs Trollope walked in this afternoon most beautifully dressed.'

But whatever Mrs Oliphant's part in the creation of Lady Carbury may have been, no one can read about that driven, devoted, self-promoting literary work-horse without thinking of Anthony Trollope's mother.

The Way We Live Now is about the fakery and institutionalised deceptions of Anthony's modern world. Even young girls were infected, and letters played their part. When Anthony was young, and in his early novels, girls showed all letters they received to their mothers, as a matter of course. 'It is certainly a part of the new dispensation that young women shall send and receive letters without inspection.' He wrote many a paragraph in his novels of the 1870s describing, with fascination and some concern, the effects of this social change. The pillar box on the corner of the road, as he mentioned more than once, made private correspondences even easier for independent-minded wives and daughters.†

Gentlemen had no need of domestic subterfuge. Mrs Houghton in *Is He Popenjoy?* addressed her flirty notes (all but one) to Lord George Germain at his club: 'The secrecy which some correspondence requires certainly tends to make a club a convenient arrangement.' Lord George was too canny to send replies: 'The words that are written remain.' That could stand as Anthony Trollope's epitaph.

———— * ————

* Mrs Oliphant's novel-sequence of provincial life, 'Chronicles of Carlingford', mirrored Anthony's Barsetshire sequence. One of the Carlingford novels, *Phoebe Junior* (1876), expropriated much of the plot of *The Warden*. Yet Mrs O. had the nerve to have Phoebe say in that book that 'one reads Miss [Charlotte M.] Yonge for the Church. Mr Trollope is good for that too, but not so good.'

† Maybe Anthony felt a bit responsible. And certainly, in the story of the emancipation of women, the penny post and the pillar box have been paid insufficient attention.

1868 had begun with Bice getting mumps at Waltham House. It was Anthony who wrote to reassure Tom, Rose who stayed home to care for her. Anthony began his 1868 diary with the triumphant words, 'Free to Hunt!' On the sixth day of the year he took off to the Midlands for a week's sport, having sent his horses on ahead, and then went on for a few days to stay in Lincolnshire with the Trollopes of Casewick at the ancestral home. He had already started writing *He Knew He Was Right*.

He had still not quite finished with the Post Office. In April 1868 he left for more than three months in the United States, hired by the PO on a freelance basis (£5.5s. a day, plus expenses) to attempt an arrangement by which transatlantic mail should be carried exclusively by the Cunard Line.* John Tilley had recommended him strongly to the Postmaster General, the Duke of Montrose, as the man for the job.

Anthony did not make a great success of it. It is hard not to feel that he wanted to go chiefly in order to see Kate Field. (And for the money.) He also had a brief from the Foreign Office to negotiate an international copyright agreement, but nothing came of this either.

When his ship reached New York, Charles Dickens was in the harbour on board another one, about to sail home after his reading tour. Anthony got himself carried between the two ships on a mail tender just to say hello to Dickens: 'It was most heartily done,' wrote Dickens to Tom Trollope. 'He is a perfect cordial to me, whenever and wherever I see him, as the heartiest and best of fellows.' During his time in New York Anthony finished *He Knew He Was Right* and started, three days later, on *The Vicar of Bullhampton*.

His failure to resolve the postal problem was not his fault, since the US Postmaster General Alexander W. Randall was at first unwilling to engage on any serious discussions because of the impeachment of President Johnson,† intending to resign if

---

* Sir Samuel Cunard, the founder, had died in 1865. Anthony knew old John Burns, a partner in the Cunard Line, the original aim of which was to carry the mails, with passengers as an afterthought. John Burns's son George was a moving spirit in the Gaiter Club.

† Andrew Johnson was the only Southern senator to support the Union in the Civil War. Lincoln made him Vice-President in 1864 and he automatically became President after Lincoln's assassination in 1865. He lost control of the radical wing of the Republicans, who not only enfranchised blacks and disenfranchised Confederates against his veto, but passed a law prohibiting presidents from dismissing senior state officials without Senate approval. When, to test his authority, Johnson dismissed his Secretary of War, he was impeached before the Senate.

Johnson was convicted. Johnson was acquitted in mid-May, but when discussions began it became clear that the Americans would send their mail by whatever ships were cheapest, 'being less driven than we are in the matter of quickness and punctuality', as Anthony wrote to John Tilley. Anthony was disgusted with the impeachment and made his feelings clear to James and Annie Fields and to Kate, who was living with her mother on Joy Street in Boston.

Kate Field had been thrilled by Dickens's readings, and obtained an introduction to him. She wrote a short book, *Pen Photographs of Charles Dickens's Readings*, which Anthony tried to get published for her in England. Kate and Anthony were both in Washington during May, when Kate gave him her stories to criticise. Of one, he told her, 'It wants a plot, and is too egoistic.' He advised her not to use the pronoun 'I' in fiction. 'Your reader should not be made to think that *you* are trying to teach, or to preach, or to convince. Teach, and preach, and convince if you can; – but first learn the art of doing so without seeming to do it.'

Kate might well have countered that Anthony himself used 'I' in his fiction continually; but his authorial 'I' did not preach. 'I' aired likes and dislikes, and responses to everyday situations, building up a collusion with the reader which was reinforced by his trick of embarking on generalisations with the reader-embracing phrase 'Who does not know. . . ?'

Kate, nearing thirty, was going through a crisis when Anthony and she met in Washington and then New York. She abandoned hope of her long, unsatisfactory love affair at the end of May. She was aligning herself publicly with the more conservative wing of the feminists, under the aegis of Lucy Stone, a moving spirit in the American Woman's Suffrage Association. She had also become deeply interested in spiritualism. Anthony, who had been through all that with his own family, tried to dissuade her: 'I should like of all things to see a ghost, and if one would come and have it out with me on the square I think it would add vastly to my interest in life. . . . But when tables rap, and boards write, and dead young women come and tickle my knee under a big table, I find the manifestation to be unworthy of the previous grand ceremony of death.'

They went together to listen to the speeches in Congress, and he called on her in the evenings. Kate's diary-entries are laconic:

'Met Anthony Trollope. Same as ever.' And in New York: 'Mr Trollope came and remained an hour or two. Asked me to write a story for his St Paul [sic] magazine. If I can it will be a feather in my cap. If I can't – well, we shall see.' Her attitude to Anthony may be measured by the difference in her diary-entry about the middle-aged actor Charles Fechter, whom she met the following year: 'He is always sympathetic and *knows how to make love,** which is a luxury.'

Anthony called her Kate, she called him Mr Trollope. The protocol of names was heavy with significance. Gentlemen who were friends, but not related, called each other by their surnames: 'My dear Trollope', 'My dear Thackeray'. Ladies called one another by their first names, but for a man to use a woman's first name was a huge step. It carried a throb of intimacy which we can hardly imagine. It was quite intolerable to the woman if she did not like the man, and had the value of a caress if she did. It was a sexual advance – without making a move, without a touch. In *Ayala's Angel* it took time for Ayala Dormer to realise that Colonel Jonathan Stubbs was indeed her 'Angel of Light'. When finally they fell into one another's arms Ayala told him how terrible she had felt when, during an estrangement, he reverted to calling her Miss Dormer. 'I remember when you called me Ayala first. It went through and through me like an electric shock.'

On the question of novels and their 'influence' it is worth reflecting, in this context, on the peculiar and potent intimacy of novel-reading in Anthony Trollope's time. The hero and heroine were generally called by their first names in the narrative. The reader, if he or she were an isolated person, might have no one at all in his daily life whom he addressed other than as Miss Jones or Mr Brown. The Trollopian technique of carrying characters on from one novel to another over many years, making them grow older along with their readers, also contributed to the power that fiction such as his had in the inner lives of sheltered or impressionable readers.

To use someone's first name with social rather than sexual purpose was equally unacceptable. A case in point was Madame

* 'To make love' meant to flirt, to pay flattering attention and to make it clear that you found the other person attractive. Kate's diaries are quoted in *Kate Field: A Record* by Lilian Whiting, 1899.

Gordeloup in *The Claverings*. She latched on to rich Lady Ongar, whose name was Julia. Madame Gordeloup addressed her on all possible occasions not even as Julia (as her real women friends did), but as Julie, as in 'Julie and I are dear friends'. Her creator for once refrained from comment, but he may have cringed from those who sought to establish intimacy with him by calling him Tony, an abbreviation used by family and close friends, and not always even by them.

Cousins were family, and cousins of whatever sex could address one another by their first names. Yet attraction and marriage between cousins was not out of the question. 'A dear cousin, and safe against love-making!' thought Clara Amedroz comfortably of Will Belton in *The Belton Estate* – yet was wooed and won by him. Some of the most sexually charged relationships in Anthony Trollope's novels are between cousins: Alice and George Vavasor in *Can You Forgive Her?*, Anna and Frederick Lovel in *Lady Anna*, Mary Lowther and Walter Marrable in *The Vicar of Bullhampton*. 'The idea of cousinly intimacy to girls is undoubtedly very pleasant,' Anthony wrote in *The Vicar of Bullhampton*; and 'the better and the purer is the girl, the sweeter and the pleasanter is the idea.' Most Trollopian generalisations originate in the particular. Rose's niece Florence Bland, brought up with the Trollope boys, was growing up, and now there was Bice as well. Rose and Anthony watched the girls with their cousin Harry, wondering how it would all develop. 'Cousins are almost the same as brothers, and yet they may be lovers' (*The Vicar of Bullhampton*).

Not to use a first name when the occasion demanded it could be as significant as using it presumptuously. In *Castle Richmond* Lady Desmond, a mature woman, was in love with Owen Fitzgerald, the youth who loved her sixteen-year-old daughter. Lady Desmond declared her love, risking humiliation. Young Owen addressed her, throughout this agonising scene, as Lady Desmond. She begged him to call her by her real name. 'But so little familiar had he been with the name by which he had never heard her called, that in his confusion he could not remember it. And had he done so, he could not have brought himself to use it.' This was the subtlest and the most definitive form of sexual rejection, because unwilled.

A look at what Anthony wrote in *Castle Richmond* just before Lady Desmond's rash declaration of love illuminates both his method and his state of mind. He was meditating on the 'if only' of life, and on the regrets of 'most of us who have begun to turn the hill', using a game of rounders as an image. If he joined the young people in the game, he wrote, for a while they would be awestruck: 'and after that, when they grew to be familiar with me, they would laugh at me because I loomed large in my running, and returned to my ground scant of breath. Alas, alas! I know that it would not do. So I pass by, imperious in my heavy manhood, and one of the lads respectfully abstains from me though the ball is under my very feet. . . . Oh heavens! Is it not possible that one should have one more game of rounders? Quite impossible, my fat friend.'

This novel, completed just before he turned forty-five, and just before he met Kate for the first time, was riddled with the awareness of encroaching middle age: 'Young men are so apt to think that their seniors in age cannot understand romance, or acknowledge the force of a passion. But here they are wrong, for there would be as much romance after forty as before, I take it, were it not checked by the fear of ridicule.'

When Anthony did meet Kate, he was all too ready for romance one more time – and too self-aware to make a fool of himself. The close conjunction of the 'rounders' parable with Lady Desmond's avowal suggests an explanation for Anthony's unusually candid sympathy, demonstrated over and over again in his fiction, with the 'inappropriate' sexual longings of older women. It was not merely that he was in touch with the feminine principle within himself, though that made his strategy possible. He felt longings, as an older man, for young women – and transposed the genders.

So far as calling Kate by her first name was concerned, the age difference made it acceptable; Tom did it too, both of them 'imperious in their heavy manhood'. It was accepted quasi-paternal practice, which lent itself to the flirtatious kind of intimacy at which Anthony had become adept. In *He Knew He Was Right*, one of the factors that fed Louis Trevelyan's self-destructive jealousy was the way that the old family friend who wrote letters to his wife, and called on her rather too often, addressed her as 'Emily'. No one wrote or spoke even his own wife's first name, except to family and intimates. Rose, in Anthony's letters to most friends and all acquaintances, was 'my wife' or 'Mrs Trollope'. A compromise for the beginning of letters, between men and women who liked each other well, was 'My dear friend'.

—— * ——

377

Anthony Trollope and Kate Field had themselves photographed in New York (probably by Napoleon Sarony) and he ordered prints of himself to be sent to Kate, asking her in return: 'I should like one of you standing up, facing full front, with your hat. I think it would have your natural look. . . .' Maybe he and she were photographed together: 'I have got your section framed down to the mere hat and eyes and nose,' he told her. 'It is all I have of you except a smudged (but originally very pretty) portrait taken from a picture.'

Kate sent Anthony a cutting from the Boston *Daily Evening Transcript* which described him as a 'strange looking person' and his bald head as almost pointed – shaped like half a lemon, or a minnie ball.* 'His body is large and well preserved. He dresses like a gentleman and not like a fop, but he squeezes his small, well-shaped hands into a very small pair of coloured kids.' Since the writer of the piece also said that his 'general bearing' was like that of Dickens it seems that he may have got his notes on the two English authors mixed up. As Anthony wrote to Kate: 'If I saw the writer I should be apt to go off and let him know that I never wear gloves. What fools people are.'

He was writing in mid-July (1868) from Washington. The first time he was there it had been mid-winter. This time, hanging about to see the elusive US Postmaster General, he was crucified by the heat. 'Oh, Lord what a night I spent, – the last as ever was, – among the mosquitoes, trying to burn them with a candle inside the net!' he complained to Kate. 'I could not get at one, but was more successful with the netting. I didn't have a wink of sleep, and another such a night will put me into a fever hospital.'

He dropped hints that he would take off for Niagara or some cool seaside place if she would join him there, but nothing happened. The endings of his last two letters to her before he left are as expressive as he ever allowed himself to be. From Washington: 'Give my kindest love to your mother. The same to yourself dear Kate – if I do not see you again, – with a kiss that shall be semi-paternal – one-third brotherly, and as regards the small remainder, as loving as you please.' And from New York, two days before he sailed: 'God bless you dear, – I wish I thought I

* A minnie ball was a missile shot from guns in the American Civil War, shaped like a rugby ball.

might see your clever laughing eyes again before the days of the spectacles; – but I suppose not. My love to your mother.'

Home again, he wrote to Tom that the trip had been 'most disagreeable . . . so much so that I do not intend to go on any more ambassadorial business.' And to Kate, he said that his ever seeing her again depended on her coming to England. 'I am becoming an infirm old man, too fat to travel so far.'

A month later he was off to Beverley in Yorkshire, where he was standing as a parliamentary candidate. A seat in the House of Commons was his dream: 'the highest object of ambition to every educated Englishman', 'the top brick of the chimney'.

Charles Dickens wrote to Tom Trollope that Anthony's decision to stand for Parliament was to him 'inscrutable'. If Anthony had been a character in one of Dickens's own novels, Dickens would have understood. When Anthony was young, his Uncle Henry Milton had asked him what his hopes were for his future life. 'I replied that I should like to be a Member of Parliament.' Uncle Henry said in his dry sarcastic way that so far as he knew not very many Post Office clerks became Members of Parliament.

The memory of Uncle Henry's sarcasm still smarted when Anthony left the Post Office in 1867. He was well over fifty, he was not a particularly good public speaker, he lacked the patience for the slow small grind of practical politics. 'I was thus aware that I could do no good by going into Parliament, – that the time for it, if there could have been a time, had gone by. But still I had an almost insane desire to sit there, and be able to assure myself that my uncle's scorn had not been deserved' (*Autobiography*).

He was already in the House of Commons, in the parallel world of his novels. Anthony's fiction had always been about power politics, not only in regard to Parliament but in the sense that all institutions – from marriage and the family to the Church and the Civil Service – are political.

He said goodbye officially to the microcosm of Barchester cathedral close in *The Last Chronicle of Barset*.* 'Taking it as a

---

* Bishop Proudie and other Barsetshire figures were to be glimpsed, or spoken of, in later novels. Anthony continued to use the West Country (the landscape of Barsetshire) as a setting. In his last and very weak short story, 'The Two Heroines of Plumplington', he returned to Barsetshire, though it was based on Rose's girlhood in the Bank house in Rotherham. It was published posthumously in *Good Words*.

whole, I regard this as the best novel I have written' (*Auto-biography*).

The Last Chronicle gives the lie to any residual impression that the Barsetshire novels were reassuring reading-matter, tailored to reinforce a complacent, amused confidence in traditional English life and values. There is plenty of sardonic humour in it, and developments in the love-triangle of Lily Dale, Johnny Eames and Adolphus Crosbie. Above all there is the tragedy of the scholarly, gentlemanly, bone-poor curate of a rural parish, Mr Crawley, who was accused of stealing a cheque. So depressed and demoralised had he become that he could not be sure he was innocent. 'The truth is, that there are times when I am not – sane. I am not a thief, – not before God; but I am – mad at times.' Self-absorbed, self-pitying, arrogant, unhinged – but not guilty. Not innocent, either. 'There was something radically wrong with him, which had put him into antagonism with all the world, and which produced these never-dying grievances.' The ghost of Anthony's father, as of Rose's, was laid to rest by Anthony's unsentimental understanding of Mr Crawley.

Mr Harding, the former Warden of Hiram's Hospital, had grown old in *The Last Chronicle*, and his decline was slowly charted with the same ruthlessness and tenderness as was afforded to Mr Crawley: the shuffling and shambling about the room, sitting in one chair and then another, shrinking from the loud voice of his son-in-law the Archdeacon; opening his old cello case, passing his fingers across the strings; finally taking to his bed, and dying. But it is the death of Mrs Proudie that everyone remembers about *The Last Chronicle*.

She rampaged through the early part of the book, bullying her cowed husband, returning from evening service to terrorise lesser mortals 'in a brown silk dress of awful stiffness and terrible dimensions'. She is the ample forerunner of Wilde's Lady Bracknell, and of the terrifying aunts that P. G. Wodehouse inflicted on Bertie Wooster. Her husband the bishop trimmed and placated – until she went too far, and he withdrew into nervous breakdown and silence.

And then, although Mrs Proudie had not changed, she became pitiable, as she tried to win her husband back, going to him in his dressing-room at night and caressingly putting her hand on his shoulder – a tentative bed-time invitation which was both pathetic and horrible, and to which the bishop could not respond.* She was not without insight, she knew she had ruined his life and lost his affection. When she was found dead, 'the body was still resting on its legs, leaning against the end of the side of the bed, while one of the arms was close clasped around the bedpost.' She died with her eyes wide open.

Anthony said he only killed Mrs Proudie off because he was writing away at the book in the long drawing-room at the Athenaeum one morning and overheard two clergymen complaining about the way he reintroduced the same characters in his novels, with special reference to Mrs Proudie. 'I got up, and standing between them, I acknowledged myself to be the culprit. "As to Mrs Proudie," I said, "I will go home and kill her before the week is over." And so I did.' This story may well be apocryphal.

Sometimes, he said, he regretted having killed Mrs Proudie. He had come to know her so well. She was a tyrant and a vulgar bully, but, as he wrote in his autobiography, she knew it, and 'that bitterness killed her'. He never, he wrote, 'dissevered myself from Mrs Proudie, and still live much in company with her ghost'.

Within weeks of finishing *The Last Chronicle* he began *Phineas Finn*. He had introduced the characters who would be the major players (apart from Phineas himself) in *Can You Forgive Her?*, and prepared himself by listening to debates in the House of Commons from the gallery. The floor, lobby, corridors and committee rooms of the House were to provide the oxygen for new castles in the air, along with political dinner parties, and gatherings of Cabinet ministers, heiresses, and eager hopefuls at opulent country-house weekends.

Anthony called himself in his autobiography 'an advanced Conservative-Liberal', and said that he had been one ever since he had any political views at all. He was not a Conservative because, he said, the conscientious Conservative, believing the

---

* The spirit of Mrs Proudie lived on in Mrs Brumby, in Anthony's short story of that name, who, had she been a man, 'might have been a prime minister, or an archbishop, or a chief justice', and whose complexion, 'to a pondering, speculative man, produced unconsciously a consideration whether, in a matter of kissing, an ordinary mahogany table did not offer a preferable surface'.

inequalities of society to be of divine origin, saw it as his duty to preserve them. Anthony saw the Conservative's point of view: 'For the mind of the thinker and the student is driven to admit, though it be awestruck by apparent injustice, that this inequality is the work of God. Make all men equal today, and God has so created them that they shall all be unequal tomorrow.' Disraeli enunciated the aims and ideals of the Conservative party as 'the maintenance of our institutions, the protection of our Empire, and the improvement of the condition of the people'. Anthony disapproved of imperialism and disliked Disraeli. So he could not be a Conservative.

The conscientious Liberal, said Anthony in his autobiography, saw that inequalities could and should become less, 'and he regards this continual diminution as a series of steps towards that human millennium of which he dreams'. What the Liberal worked for was not equality – for the word suggested 'ideas of communism, of ruin, and insane democracy' – but 'a tendency towards equality'. The middle way, in fact, as was characteristic. All extremism or 'enthusiasm', from whatever quarter, smacked to Anthony of bullying and bigotry.

The Liberal party was the successor of the Whig party; the shift was not completed until Gladstone's Liberal administration, following the general election of 1868 in which Anthony stood for Beverley. The Radicals aligned themselves with the Whigs against the Tories in a partnership which brought a strong reforming and non-conformist element into the Liberal party. Anthony found non-conformism dreary; and, innocent of political passions himself, he tended to see Radicals as woolly idealists, trouble-makers, or motivated by a politics of envy.

Anthony in his fiction created an accurate conspectus of Radicals: opportunistic Quintus Slide, editor of the scandal sheet 'The People's Banner'; Ontario Moggs, the working-class hot-head with a chip on his shoulder; idealistic Joshua Monk, Phineas Finn's mentor and a man of honour and high principle; and Mr Turnbull,* who in *Phineas Finn* campaigned loud and long for

---

* The *Daily Telegraph* accused Anthony Trollope in a leading article of portraying the Radical leader John Bright as Mr Turnbull in *Phineas Finn*. Anthony denied it, naturally. Many other parallels have been drawn: Daubeny=Disraeli, Gresham=Gladstone, for example. The key word here is 'parallel'. Anthony depicted the real world of British politics. But to say Turnbull 'is' Bright is to misunderstand the high art of Trollope's castle-building fantasies, and the low cunning with which he judged how close to draw his parallels – which by definition can never meet.

manhood suffrage, the secret ballot, tenant rights, defence cuts, free trade and the disestablishment of the Church of England. 'It was his business to inveigh against existing evils, and perhaps there is no easier business.' Anthony himself was a Radical only in the sense that Luke Rowan in *Rachel Ray* was a 'radical at heart', not desiring 'the ruin of thrones, the degradation of nobles, the spoliation of the rich' but 'the gradual progress of the people': an advanced Conservative-Liberal, as he said.

This half-way position was not peculiar to himself. For most of his adult life the boundaries between the Whigs and Tories, or Liberals and Conservatives, had been blurred when it came to policies. Whiggery in his young days was not so much a political creed as a social caste – a Whig was born, not made. Lord Melbourne likened them to a special breed of spaniel; Disraeli, in *Coningsby*, called them a Venetian oligarchy. 'In former days, when there were Whigs instead of Liberals, it was almost a rule of political life that all leading Whigs should be uncles, brothers-in-law, or cousins to each other,' as Anthony wrote in *Phineas Redux*. Even when he was writing that book, in 1870, there was 'still a good deal of agreeable family connection'. The Whigs were grandees; some, like Lord de Courcy in *Doctor Thorne*, were what Anthony called 'court Whigs', the people who formed the Queen's circle at Windsor and Balmoral. Others, like the old bachelor Duke of Omnium in the same book, were far too superior to hang around the court. They sustained fiefdoms of their own in the tracts of country that they owned, especially when it came to elections; tenants voted for their landlord's chosen candidates, or else. The Whigs had carried the 1832 Reform Bill without, as Anthony slyly remarked in *Can You Forgive Her?*, losing their influence: 'The house of Omnium had been very great on that occasion. It had given up much, and had retained for family use simply the single seat at Silverbridge.'

The Whigs, true to the doctrine of *noblesse oblige*, had a developed sense of public accountability. The Tories were traditionally the smaller landed gentry, who feared all change and reform. The Greshams of Greshamsbury in *Doctor Thorne* were Conservatives. The Earl de Guest in *The Small House* was 'a thorough-going old Tory, whose proxy was always in the hand of the leader of his party; and who seldom himself went near the metropolis, unless called thither by some occasion of cattle-showing.' In *The Eustace Diamonds* Frank Greystock's father was an old-fashioned Tory, of the sort who 'enjoy the politics of the side to which they belong without any special belief in them. If pressed hard they will almost own that their so-called convictions are prejudices.' Anthony compared the Tory mentality to Buddhism; their belief was 'to have been always in the right and yet always on the losing side; always being ruined, always under persecution from a wild spirit of republican-demagogism, – and yet never to lose anything. . . .'

Party allegiance, in Anthony's vision, was a state of mind rather than a belief system, and the Tories trimmed in order to survive. Nothing, Anthony wrote in *The Bertrams*, 'stinks so foully in the nostrils of an English Tory politician as to be absolutely irreconcilable to him. When taken in the refreshing waters of office any such pill can be swallowed.' Survival accounted for the breaking-up of Whig solidarity too: it was a terrible shock to Plantagenet Palliser, as Duke of Omnium, when his son Lord Silverbridge announced he was a Conservative, in *The Duke's Children*. The father believed in the public interest, the son in self-interest: 'We've got to protect our position as well as we can against the Radicals and Communists.'

Elizabeth Barrett Browning thought Anthony was 'ignorant of political facts'. She, an ardent partisan for the unification of Italy, would have found his relativist approach incomprehensible. Though he intentionally made some parliamentary business seem trivial – Phineas Finn was put on a House committee which discussed legislation on potted peas – Anthony had a clear if idiosyncratic mental map of English politics. Phineas, in the Colonial Office at the apex of his five-year career curve, knew he was 'playing a great game', which he might lose – as he did. Politics was the game for men, just as sex and marriage was for women. (Lady Laura Kennedy, her marriage over and the man she loved – Phineas – unavailable to her, realised that 'A woman has a fine game to play; but then she is so easily bowled out, and the term allowed her is so short.')

The only valid reason to be in politics, Anthony wrote, was to improve the condition of one's fellow men. Anything else was intrigue, charlatanism, and self-promotion. 'If I go into Parliament,' announced Phineas Finn, 'I shall go there as a sound

Liberal, – not to support a party, but to do the best I can for the country.' But as clever Madame Max Goesler told him, when he met her for the first time at the Pallisers' dinner table, there is a great difference between theory and practice. What interested Anthony most intensely, in parliamentary politics as in sexual politics, was the inevitable conflict in the human heart between idealism and opportunism.

Phineas Finn was a young Irishman, the son of a doctor and a Roman Catholic, quick to learn and possessing immense personal charm and attraction. He made his way into English political life – greatly helped by the wives and daughters of statesmen, who fell in love with him and influenced decision-making behind the scenes – and climbed the greasy pole with astonishing speed. Anthony said it was pure chance that Phineas was Irish; he just happened to be on holiday in Ireland when he was thinking out the book. Nevertheless, Phineas's Irishness made sense of his meteoric rise. He was outside the English class system with its predetermining codes and signals, and so could not be summed up or boxed in. Scholars argue about Anthony's real-life model for Phineas Finn. The quest is irrelevant to understanding his creator. The adventurous career of Phineas Finn was Anthony's climactic, definitive castle in the air.

As far as honesty in politics was concerned, Phineas soon found that he had to support his party in the House even when he disagreed violently with its policies. He 'taught himself to understand that members of Parliament in the direct service of Government were absolved from the necessity of free-thinking'. The real questions were whether political honesty was not actually a disadvantage, and whether 'a candidate for office be more liable to rejection from a leader because he was known to be scrupulous, or because he was known to be the reverse'. Although Phineas longed most sincerely to 'exterminate' the last vestiges of parliamentary corruption, when it came to regaining a place in Parliament he took advantage of the safe seat procured for him by the besotted Lady Laura, through her father. His idealism was already buried deep beneath his ambition: 'He had taken up politics with the express desire of getting his foot upon a rung of the ladder of promotion. . . .'

As well as writing a political and sexual adventure story,

Anthony was conducting a funny, painful debate about honesty and intellectual independence, both for men and for women, in private as in public life. It is an Ur-story novel told from the man's point of view, with Phineas betraying the love of simple little Mary Flood Jones, back in Ireland, with rich, sophisticated, attractive young women from political families – not to mention the probably Jewish Madame Max Goesler, who in her pretty house on Park Lane offered herself and her money to him with a raw, brave frankness. In politics, compromise was the best solution: 'You must take the world as you find it, with a struggle to be something more honest than those around you.'

Phineas Finn was written between November 1866 and mid-May 1867, before Anthony left the Post Office. There was a time-lag between sending Phineas into Parliament and standing for Parliament himself (though the novel was still running in *Saint Pauls* as a serial during the Beverley election). In the interim Anthony wrote four novels of personal politics, concerned with freedoms and obligations as well as with honesty. Some readers and critics found the destruction of a marriage, anatomised in *He Knew He Was Right*, disagreeable. It was a more prolonged, but not a more merciless, investigation of possessive jealousy than that of the Kennedys' marriage in *Phineas Finn* – with the difference that the Kennedys' was a cold hell and the Trevelyans' a burning one.

He expected more trouble than he got from the critics for *The Vicar of Bullhampton*, in which the vicar befriended – and became sentimental about – a country girl, Carry Brattle. The vicar's wife warned him that there would be gossip if he saw Carry too often, and there was. Carry was a 'castaway': in modern parlance, she slept around, though not always for money.

Anthony made Carry blonde and pretty, 'such a morsel of fruit as men do choose, when allowed to range and pick through the whole length of the garden wall'. For the first time in his life he appended a preface, begging for understanding of Carry's predicament, especially from the 'pure' among her own sex: 'Cannot women, who are good, pity the sufferings of the vicious, and do something perhaps to mitigate and shorten them without contamination from the vice?'

Much more significant for the development of Anthony's understanding of women was the subtle depiction in the book of a 'suitable' marriage as no less degrading for a woman than Carry's prostitution of herself. The vicar and his virtuous wife could not see why their dear friend Mary Lowther should not accept the hand of their equally dear friend Harry Gilmore, even though she was not in the least attracted to him. Valuing herself little, Mary gave in to pressure, and to Gilmore's desire. Mary was described by her creator as a 'thing created for use', as a 'thing' that Harry Gilmore wanted. Ironically, it was when she extricated herself from the dishonourable engagement that she was punished by Harry Gilmore as if she were a 'castaway': 'If you were my sister, my ears would tingle with shame when your name was mentioned in my presence.'

The Vicar of Bullhampton was to have been serialised in Once a Week but was put off in favour of a novel by Victor Hugo, which infuriated Anthony, who found Hugo pretentious and 'untrue to nature'. The delay was a straw in the wind. The wheel of fortune was already beginning, imperceptibly, to turn, and Anthony's hypersensitivity to the shift reinforced his feeling that he was getting old. Publishers and editors were no longer falling over themselves in quite the same way to secure a new Trollope novel. There were so many of them. It made no difference that Anthony was at the height of his powers, working under the pressure of urgent creative energy. There is at all periods an irrational suspicion in the public mind that literary quality is in inverse proportion to quantity. Thus The Vicar became log-jammed; finished in November 1868, it did not appear in book form until 1870. The reviewers were unshocked by Carry Brattle.

Anthony however felt compelled, in his autobiography, to restate his sympathy for women like his Carry Brattle who became 'castaways'. His first point, give or take the use of the word 'sin', is still relevant: 'In regard to a sin common to the two sexes, almost all the punishment and all the disgrace is heaped upon the one who in nine cases out of ten has been the least sinful.' His other point was about the 'harshness' of virtuous women (Rose?) towards their fallen sisters. Virtuous women would be kinder, he said, if they had any inkling at all of the loneliness, contempt, disease, the 'slavery to some horrid tyrant', suffered by castaways. It was sufficient punishment. 'This is the life to which we doom our erring daughters, when because of their error we close our doors upon them. But for our erring sons we find pardon easily enough.'

—— * ——

A seat in Parliament for a division of Essex had been mooted for Anthony in 1867, through Charles Buxton, a great friend of Anthony's on the hunting field, whose family was deep in Liberal politics. Others in the county had other ideas, however, and finally Anthony was accepted for the borough of Beverley in East Yorkshire. The newly enfranchised working-class electors were mostly in the towns, and no one knew which way they would vote. Up till then Beverley, which returned two members, had been a safe Tory constituency, with the town's chief employer Sir Henry Edwards as one of the sitting members. Could Anthony Trollope, standing as a Liberal, overturn him? In his novels he had compared Members of Parliament in the House of Commons to the gods on Olympus, shaking the heavens and striking one another down with the wind and thunder of their oratory, objects of wonder to mere mortals. Now he aspired to join the Olympians.

CHAPTER SIXTEEN

FROM the very first moment, he hated it. There were two Liberal candidates and two Conservative candidates competing for the two seats. Disraeli's Reform Bill, passed the previous year, had introduced household suffrage, which meant that just under 4,000 men were eligible to vote in Beverley out of a total population of around 12,000. Both the sitting members were Conservatives. Sir Henry Edwards had held his seat for many years, establishing what Anthony euphemistically called 'a close intimacy' with the constituency; the Conservatives bribed the voters more heavily than the Liberals did and Beverley was a byword for corruption, 'one of the most degraded boroughs in England', as Anthony told Juliet Pollock. 'There was something grand in the scorn with which a leading Liberal there turned up his nose at me when I told him that there should be no bribery, no treating, not even a pot of beer on one side' (*Autobiography*). Under these circumstances there was no way that Anthony could win a seat, and his agent, a local solicitor, let him know it. Anthony's running-mate was a local gentleman, the Hon. Marmaduke Maxwell, son and heir of Lord Herries and a Roman Catholic.

Anthony went up to Beverley on 30 October 1868 to canvass, 'and spent, I think, the most wretched fortnight of my manhood'. His agent, to whom he paid £400 for expenses, and the other local activists seemed to him to be 'grinding vulgar tyrants'. He spoke at the Mechanics Hall, the Temperance Hall, and from a balcony above a tailor's in the market square. He had not prepared his speeches very thoroughly but spoke vigorously. He parried jokes about 'fiction', he abused the Tory leader Disraeli as a conjuror and a charlatan, and he told the townspeople it was 'unnatural' for them to vote Tory; it was a 'sin' that they must repent of and expiate. When he was not speaking he was being hauled round the town, 'exposed to the rain, up to my knees in slush, and utterly

389

unable to assume that air of triumphant joy with which a jolly, successful candidate should be invested'.

He unfortunately disagreed with some of his own party's policies, such as voting by secret ballot. 'I am too great a Radical to love the ballot.'* (He thought secrecy would make bribery or coercion even easier.) The chief national issue for the Liberals was Gladstone's policy of disestablishing the Anglican Church in Ireland. This Anthony did support, and had written an article to that effect in the *Fortnightly*; but that was no great matter in Beverley.

Anthony and his fellow Liberal longed to take a day off to go hunting. A Liberal publican told them it would lose them support, but Anthony went off nevertheless, conspicuous in his high boots and red coat, leaving his party workers slogging away. This was a mistake. Anthony longed to accept an invitation from Lord Houghton at nearby Fryston too, but was unable to take any more time off, as he wrote to Houghton, from 'that desperate work of canvassing, – than which no Life upon earth can be more absolute hell'.

The day before polling day all four candidates assembled on the hustings in the market square for the official nominations. The crowd threw lumps of wood and cobblestones at them. The ladies on the platform withdrew (Rose was not there), then Sir Henry and his running-mate Captain Edward Kennard withdrew, and Anthony Trollope and Marmaduke Maxwell stuck it out a little longer. It did not make any difference to the result. Next day, Sir Henry Edwards topped the poll with 1,132 votes. Captain Kennard came second with 986. Mr Maxwell was third with 895. Anthony Trollope was bottom of the poll with 740.

It was all over so quickly, 'water off a duck's back' as Anthony wrote bravely to a neighbour and writer-friend, Anna Steele,† when he had been home only three days. 'I shall have another fly

---

* The Ballot Act was passed in 1872.

† Anna Steele was the elder sister of Katharine O'Shea; Mrs O'Shea's liaison with Charles Stewart Parnell, who succeeded Isaac Butt in 1877 as leader of the Home Rule movement in Parliament, led to a divorce case that turned public opinion and his own Irish party against him. Anthony did not live to see Parnell's fall, nor his friend Anna Steele being named as co-respondent when Mrs O'Shea cited her husband's adultery with her sister, in a counter-case to Captain O'Shea's petition for divorce.

at it somewhere some day, unless I find myself to be growing too old.' He never did have another 'fly at it'.

There were some satisfactions. The Liberals in Beverley accused the Tories of corruption even before the poll had closed, and there were fist-fights. The election was declared void. Beverley was officially investigated for corrupt practices and the following autumn Anthony went back to the town and gave evidence before the commission. It was established that corrupt practices had prevailed at every election in Beverley since 1857, and the borough was disenfranchised.

The novel that Anthony wrote between April 4 and August 7 1869, *Ralph the Heir*, put his wretched experience to use. He had introduced elections into his stories before, with a lively and informed cynicism. But the election at Percycross in *Ralph the Heir*, in which gloomy Sir Thomas Underwood, a morose disappointed lawyer in middle age (more like Anthony's father than like himself) stood as a Conservative candidate, was drawn from life. 'Percycross and Beverley were, of course, one and the same place' (*Autobiography*).

Sir Thomas infuriated his fellow Conservatives at Percycross by protesting publicly against free beer and bribery: three half-crowns to each man was the going rate for a vote. 'The desire for the seat which had brought him to Percycross had almost died out amidst the misery of his position. Among all the men of his party with whom he was associating, there was not one whom he did not dislike, and by whom he was not snubbed and contradicted.'

The most popular candidate in Percycross appeared to be Ontario Moggs, the Radical working-class bootmaker from London, standing for the Liberals: 'He was great upon Strikes . . . held horrible ideas about co-operative associations, the rights of labour and the welfare of the masses.' However, on polling day Sir Thomas came second and won a seat, while Moggs was at the bottom of the poll: he had given out no beer or half-crowns.

Sir Thomas was not an MP for long. The Percycross election was investigated for corrupt practices. His own money had been misused without his knowledge, he had been 'a catspaw in the hands of other men'. Sir Thomas was horribly disillusioned, finding in political life 'convictions as to divisions, convictions as to patronage, convictions as to success, convictions as to

Parliamentary management; but not convictions as to the political needs of the people.'

Anthony was to return to the beastliness of electioneering in *The Duke's Children*: 'Perhaps nothing more disagreeable, more squalid, more revolting to the senses, more opposed to personal dignity, can be conceived.' Again he railed against the rain, the empty repetition of words and phrases, the quarrels and back-biting. 'To have to go through this is enough to take away all the pride which a man might otherwise take from becoming a member of Parliament. But to go through it and then not to become a member is base indeed!'

1868, the Beverley year, was not a good one. Poor Bice was still being parked with whoever could have her for the school holidays – her stepmother Fanny's sister Maria in Oxford, the Alfred Austins in Kent. Bice would feel 'fish-out-of-waterish' if she came home to Florence, Fanny assured her. 'If I continue to write as it appears in many ways desirable that I should, it would be impossible for me to devote my time to you.' There is a bleak shred of dialogue in *The Way We Live Now* between young Henrietta and her author-mother, Lady Carbury:

'Why do you speak of me always as though I were a burden?'

'Everybody is a burden to other people. It is the way of life.'

George Smith, having moved with his publishing business, his periodicals and his family to a fine big house on Waterloo Place, collapsed with a complete nervous breakdown and took two years to recover. It happened when he split his business and made over the non-literary, commercial side to his brother-in-law Henry S. King, in order to concentrate on publishing. It was not until he started up another side-interest – a ship-owning enterprise which caught his imagination and exploited his trading experience – that Smith was himself again. In his convalescence, he and his wife went to stay with the Tom Trollopes in Florence; but the breakdown coincided with a professional break between George Smith and Anthony. For whatever reason, Smith, Elder published no new novel of Anthony's after *The Last Chronicle of Barset* in 1867. In the following few years, when Anthony was involved in magazine-publishing with James Virtue and Alexander Strahan, he shifted for book-publication between a variety of firms: Strahan (for *He Knew He Was Right*), Blackwood (*Nina Balatka* and *Linda Tressel*), Virtue (*Phineas Finn*), Hurst & Blackett (*Sir Harry Hotspur* and *Ralph the Heir*), Bradbury & Evans (*The Vicar of Bullhampton*), Tinsley (*The Golden Lion of Granpere*) – before settling down once more in 1873 with Chapman & Hall for *The Eustace Diamonds* and many of his subsequent books.

In 1868 the Tilley family too were, once again, afflicted by illness. The elder of John Tilley's two children by his third wife Susannah, their daughter Cecilia, died in spring 1868, aged six, from 'water on the brain'.* Rose was her godmother. The Tilleys produced another baby in January 1869, John Anthony Cecil, to whom Anthony stood godfather. This child grew up to be an ambassador and lived until 1952.

Rose did not even mention the Beverley election in her chronology. She was more concerned with Fred's return from Australia, just after his twenty-first birthday, in time for Christmas 1868. Fred enjoyed a season's hunting with his father – who put an extra large helping into *Ralph the Heir*, set in his mother's home country around Heckfield, with much authorial animadversion about boots and saddles. The names of the horses in the novel were Brag, Banker, Buff and Brewer. Anthony had horses called Banker and Buff, and maybe Brag and Brewer were his as well.

Fred was determined to go back to Australia. Anthony did not countenance emotional farewells. 'When last days are coming, they should be allowed to come and to glide away without special notice or mention. And as for last moments, there should be none such. Let them ever be ended, even before their presence has been acknowledged' (*The Small House at Allington*). But he broke off work on *Ralph the Heir* for three days in April 1869 to go down to Plymouth and see Fred off, providing him with money to invest in a sheep station at Mortray, just north of Grenfell in New South Wales.

It was a turning-point of a year for all the family (11 June was

---

* Susannah and John Tilley's second child, William George, died in 1887 at the age of twenty-four.

the Trollopes' silver wedding. Rose's handwriting invaded Anthony's diary: 'Don't make an engagement on this day. R.T.'). Harry was changing direction yet again. He had not stayed long in the Yeomanry and afterwards opted to read law. He was called to the Bar in June but never practised. An opportunity came up elsewhere, created by Anthony. Frederic Chapman of Chapman & Hall was in need of a partner with capital. Anthony wrote to George Lewes in August 1869: 'My eldest boy Harry has gone into partnership with Chapman. I pay £10000 – (of course this is private) – and he has a third of the business. I have had an immense deal of trouble in arranging it, and will tell you details when we meet. It is a fine business which has been awfully ill used by want of sufficient work and sufficient capital.'

It was natural, Anthony wrote in *Phineas Finn*, 'that the father should yearn for the son, while the son's feeling for the father is of a very much weaker nature'. Fred's commitment to a life on the other side of the world, Harry's lack of commitment to anything at all, and the incapacity of either of them to finance themselves adequately, caused him grief.

What shines out of *Ralph the Heir* is the aching love of a father for his son, rewarded here by the idealised 'sweetness' of the young man's response: 'Ralph found it impossible to expostulate with his father. He could only take his father's arm, and whisper a soft feminine word or two.' When Ralph excelled himself on the hunting field the father's elation was excessive and embarrassing. 'He hardly carried himself with as perfect a moderation as his son would have wished. He was a little loud . . .', and the son stood aloof. The father's buoyancy, 'unless checked, might carry him too high among the clouds'.

Anthony observed, and inflated for fictional purposes, his own pleasure in Fred. The depiction of father-love in the novel is startling because over-compensatory. Ralph felt that 'No lover ever worshipped a mistress more thoroughly than his father had idolized him.' Anthony in retrospect thought that *Ralph the Heir* was 'one of the worst novels I have written', fearing that it justified the dictum that a novelist should not write love stories after the age of fifty. The lively romantic element in *Ralph the Heir* was based on his own errant young manhood in London, but the real love story in the book was between father and son. *Ralph the Heir* is revealing about the disappointments of middle age. It is hard to assess as a novel for those interested in Anthony Trollope. Second-rank works, in which personal experience and feeling are incompletely transformed, tell one much about an artist, if not much about his art.

With Fred away it was Harry who would be bearing the main weight of their father's concern. Anthony had been equally unmotivated as a young man, but Harry had loving parents with enough money to support him and could drift from one enterprise to another. Anthony, forking out, was like the Duke of Omnium in relation to his elder son Lord Silverbridge in *The Duke's Children*: 'It was for his son's character and standing in the world, for his future respectability and dignity, that his fear was so keen, and not for his own money.' Ironically, it was with *The Duke's Children* in the late 1870s that Anthony's own waning earning-power was brought home to him. It remained in the pipeline for three years before serialisation, and the ailing Chapman & Hall only paid him £1,400 for it – and still lost money on the deal. Anthony paid them back the loss.

Anthony did his best to establish Harry in the milieu he himself preferred: he got him elected to the Garrick. He hoped against hope that his elder son really was settled with Frederic Chapman, writing to John Blackwood that Harry was 'hard at work and comes home freighted with Mss. What he does with them I don't know; but . . . I fancy he goes to sleep over them with a pipe in his mouth.' To Mary Holmes,* who questioned what seemed to her the dangerous 'positivist and socialist' orientation of the *Fortnightly* and Chapman & Hall, he wrote that 'I should tell you that Chapman & Hall are in truth Chapman & Trollope, and that the Trollope is my son, – who, as it chances, is a very staunch Churchman.'

Throughout the 1870s a father's tender affection for his problem sons was to be a Trollopian topic, but especially in *The Duke's Children*. The Duke of Omnium discussed Silverbridge's future with him in the library of the Beargarden Club: 'Then the

---

* Mary Holmes was a clever, unmarried woman of his own age, a governess, a Roman Catholic and an unsuccessful writer who corresponded with authors. Thackeray had confided in her until she came to teach music to his daughters and he discovered she was plain. Anthony wrote to her seriously about her literary and musical aspirations and his own work. It was an exceptional friendship, given Anthony's attitude to letter-writing.

father looked round the room furtively, and seeing that the door was shut, and that they were assuredly alone, he put out his hand and gently stroked the young man's hair. It was almost a caress, – as though he would have said to himself, "Were he my daughter, I would kiss him." ' When Silverbridge reformed and became an MP, his father did put his arms round him and embrace him. This happy outcome fulfilled Anthony's dreams in fantasy but cannot have been comfortable reading for Harry.

The Beverley election marked a climacteric. It was an attempt on Anthony's part to marry his alternative world with the real one and to become a public man. A novelist is essentially a private person, however seriously he takes his influence on his readers.

Anthony Trollope was an outsider who became, almost, an insider. He achieved popularity and fame by exposing what had been, originally, his most secret life – his adolescent castles in the air about popularity and fame – to the public view; but he would never now achieve the synthesis. He lived, thought and wrote on the seductive frontier between private and public, inside and outside.

The divide existed in the real world, between the ordered sweetness of the middle-class domestic interior and the lust and risk of the night streets. Within those categories, there were further oppositional 'insides': marital misery and unhappy children in the smooth-running middle-class home, warmth and solace in the night-world outside.

Gentlemen watched their language in the presence of ladies (though Anthony, a boundary-crosser, would take the name of the Lord in vain in mixed company) and talked dirty among themselves. Thackeray, who piously turned down a story of Anthony's for the *Cornhill* on the grounds of its indelicacy, improvised rude limericks in private, rhyming 'her boobies' with 'her pubis'; and murmuring, as he contemplated the picture of a woman with large breasts: "'Tis true, 'tis titty, titty 'tis 'tis true.' Thackeray was not a hypocrite. He had a clear conception of the boundary between public and private.

This compartmentalisation was both reflected and defied in the serious newspapers. These carried morally sententious leading articles of the kind that Anthony Trollope liked to parody in his novels, and they also carried the police reports: explicit accounts of stabbings, poisonings, mutilations, rapes, adulteries, child prostitution, sadism, sexual slavery, domestic violence, homosexual violence, all the detritus of human passion and human misery gathered up from the overcrowded city. The police reports in the back pages of *The Times* or the *Daily Telegraph* were pornography, and used as such in the privacy of a respectable gentleman's study.

Louis Trevelyan in *He Knew He Was Right*, suspecting his wife of infidelity, pored obsessively over the police reports: could it be that she was 'so vile a thing, so abject, such dirt, pollution, filth? But there were such cases. . . .' In *The Vicar of Bullhampton* Mary Lowther turned down Harry Gilmore by letter. Frustrated in his longing to possess her, he put down her letter and picked up the newspaper, making a 'rush at the leading articles, and went through two of them. Then he turned over to the police reports' and read hard for a whole hour. Afterwards, 'he got up and shook himself, and knew that he was a crippled man, with every function out of order, disabled in every limb. . . .'

This last is an instance of Anthony Trollope tightrope-walking between the admissible and the inadmissible, writing in such a way that only those with ears to hear could understand what he was about. He was good at this. Syphilis killed or disabled more people in the nineteenth century than the equally terrible but socially acceptable scourge, tuberculosis.* Syphilis could not be named in public, and though men in private might make bleak reference to 'syph' many women would never have heard the word spoken. In *The Claverings* the knowing nineteenth-century reader might suspect that Lord Ongar, who was 'weak, thin, and physically poor' and of whom 'whispers were spread abroad darkly and doubtingly, as though great misfortunes were apprehended', was syphilitic. Or Sir Gregory Marrable in *The Vicar of Bullhampton*, who at forty was shambling and almost blind, described by his creator as 'unfit for use'; or twenty-eight-year-old Sir Florian Eustace, whom Lizzie in *The Eustace Diamonds* married for his money: 'He was vicious, and – he was dying.'

In these cases Anthony did the conventional thing, using no

---

* In 1860 one-quarter of the Foot Guards in London had syphilis and 46 per cent of surgical cases at the Royal Free Hospital were venereal, as were half of the outpatients seen at Bart's in 1868. In the late 1860s 20 per cent of patients at Moorfield Eye Hospital were suffering from advanced syphilis.

unacceptable words and leaving room for inference. In *The Last Chronicle of Barset* he sailed closer to the wind. He introduced a rakish Irishman called Onesiphorus Dunn, simply so that he could write that Mr Dunn was 'usually called Siph by his intimate friends'. He went on: 'A great many young ladies about London did call him Siph, and to him it was quite natural that they should do so.'* Anthony Trollope was banking on neither a fifteen-year-old rector's daughter, nor her mother, nor perhaps the rector himself understanding the allusion. Nor could any reviewer comment on it in a respectable journal. Thus a private joke was dropped with safety into a public text.

Another way of crossing the frontier was by omission. In a Trollope novel every move is charted. The reader knows which room the man and the woman are in, how she is sitting, what she is wearing, where he is standing and what he has done with his hat. When a married couple are talking in bed they are most thoroughly in bed; there is reference to pillows, bedclothes and bed-curtains. In *The Eustace Diamonds* Lord George de Bruce Carruthers and Mrs Carbuncle conducted a desultory, confidential conversation in an unspecified location. They were, obviously, in bed – which may cast light on the parentage of the 'niece' that Mrs Carbuncle had in tow – but Anthony could not put any of that into words.

'Words, my friend, are things, and often things of great moment' (*Nina Balatka*). Anthony went further, writing in *South Africa* that 'speech has been given to men to enable them to conceal their thoughts. In learning to talk most of us learn to lie before we learn to speak the truth.'

The divide between public and private was experienced in politics in the conflict between belief and expediency, and in another more paradoxical way. The House of Commons, in the old-fashioned view, was a private club for public men. The advanced Liberal Joshua Monk, Phineas's mentor, criticised the Radical Mr Turnbull (in *Phineas Finn*) for always seeking to address, in his speeches in the House, 'not the House only, but the country at large'. Mr Turnbull chose not to mark the difference

---

* Onesiphorus was not a made-up name. There was a Sir George Onesiphorus Paul (1746–1820), prison-reformer and friend of Sir Walter Scott. He had been named simply Onesiphorus, like his father before him, and added the George himself when he grew up, in self-defence.

between private and public discourse. Anthony, in his novels, sometimes chose likewise, as he did in his life – with John Tilley and his superiors in the PO, for instance.

In theory a man's private and public lives could be kept apart. Mr Masters in *The American Senator*, who did not have 'that great gift of being able to keep his office and his family distinct from each other', found as a result that his wife was 'very free with her advice'. The Duke of St Bungay told thin-skinned Plantagenet Palliser (the Duke of Omnium) that now he was Prime Minister he must go around and meet people and not bury himself with his family down at Matching. 'A man cannot be both private and public at the same time' – a key statement.

Sex, however, was the area where the fragile partition between public and private counted most. According to Anthony's first biographer T. H. S. Escott, who had several long conversations with him, one of his leading ideas was that 'the thinnest possible partition divides human contact in the most civilized society from primitive savagery', which was why constraints and conventions were so necessary. Society scandals which got into the newspapers were the tip of an iceberg of sexual irregularity which went unreported. If nothing was said, or read, nothing had happened. 'We often know, or fancy we know,' wrote Anthony in *Lady Anna*, 'who was in love with such a one's wife and how the matter was detected, then smothered up, and condoned; but there is no official knowledge. . . .'

Public silence was hard on un-public wives or lovers. Ellen Ternan, for example, lived in 'the gap between what could be said and what really happened'.* (Irregular private lives were led by Charles Dickens, Charles Reade, Wilkie Collins, to name but three in Anthony's immediate circle.)

A Frenchman in London in the mid-century observed that English correctness and reticence was entirely a matter of *words* – you could express any kind of indecency, so long as you did it elliptically or by a euphemism. ('Words, my friend, are things. . . .') The Frenchman also observed how fashionable ladies at Ascot races entered the lavatory-tent talking and laughing, and relieved themselves with the tent-flap wide open, so

* Claire Tomalin, *The Invisible Woman*, Viking, 1990.

that anyone could see in. (They did not name what they were doing: it was not happening.)

Men, as Anthony wrote in *Orley Farm*, might have a 'public and a private existence', and when it came to the pinch it was the private one, he said, that suffered. The woman's world was, in theory, interior and private, and her love a safe haven for her man when the world treated him badly. Adolphus Crosbie in *The Small House at Allington* abandoned Lily Dale 'because his outer world had seemed to him too bright to be deserted. He would endeavour to supply her place with Alexandrina, because his outer world had seemed to him to be too harsh to be supported.' An Englishman's home was his castle. Anthony, in his imagination, sought to see through the walls: 'How little do we know how other people live in the houses close to us! We see the houses looking like our own, and we see the people coming out of them looking like ourselves. But a Chinaman is not more different from the English John Bull than is No. 10 from No. 11' (*Ayala's Angel*).

There was part of a woman that the most uxorious husband could not touch, as Lady Laura Kennedy made clear to her husband in *Phineas Finn*: 'You cannot make a woman subject to you as a dog is. You may have all the outside and as much of the inside as you can master. With a dog, you may be sure of both.'

It was women, in Anthony's later books, who challenged the frontier, 'private and public at the same time', refusing to surrender their inner selves to men on the one hand, and on the other annexing and subverting the public arena.

The reader thinks of these women as real people; but it was their creator who empowered them to question the primal boundary: that between women and men. Trollopian women who are like men, and Trollopian men who are like women, do not embody any evolved Trollopian theory of androgyny. But in the sleep-walking 'inside' world of his novel-writing he explored ambivalence and ambiguity, his honesty pushing against the sexual stereotyping which society imposed and which he, in his 'outside' life, depended on for his comfort and self-esteem.

Mrs Proudie, more of a man than her husband the bishop, was unattractive, feared and unloved. Lady Glencora, who came into her own after Mrs Proudie was killed off, was deliciously pretty, and adored.

—— * ——

Anthony's outer and inner selves confused many who met him. How could this loud, obstreperous man be the Anthony Trollope who wrote with such extraordinary insight into the hearts of men and, even more extraordinary, of women? He was 'not at all like his books'. How was this possible?

It is a common problem. Proust wrote: 'We are dumbfounded when meeting socially with a great man whom we know only through his works', and have to superimpose what we know of those works on what we see before us, trying to reconcile them with 'the irreducible datum of a living body altogether different'. Books, he said, were 'the product of a self other than that which we display in our habits, in company, in our vices'. The self which produces the work is obscured 'by the other self, which may be very inferior to the outward self of many other men'.

Proust, out of his own self-knowledge, wrote of 'the gulf that separates the writer from the society man'. Books were written in solitude out of the 'deep self' (*le moi profond*). He also expressed the paradox that 'in actual fact what one gives to the public is what one has written when alone, for oneself', which gives Anthony's dictum that a writer is declaring to the world at large 'what there is in his mind' a deeper significance.

It is not in the events of a man's life, wrote Proust, but in his books that one finds the *moi profond*. If one accepts the Proustian model, biography is barking up the wrong tree altogether, and neither the writer nor the reader of biography can get anywhere near the writer's true self because 'the details of the outside life touch on precisely those very points where the writer's true self is not involved.'* This view of the artist was a romantic, aesthetic version of what was to become the critical orthodoxy of the mid-twentieth century with its exclusive focus on text.

Proust's idea was that writers were, as he put it, Dr Jekyll and Mr Hyde. The truth is, so are we all. To pursue Dr Jekyll and disregard Mr Hyde, or vice versa, is to settle for half the story. Anthony's private self was indeed different from his bluff, noisy public self, and as a novelist he inhabited a separate world when he sat alone at his writing-table. He had genius, which was released by another and related duality. The boy that he had been

* Marcel Proust, *Against Sainte-Beuve*, translation and introduction by John Sturrock, Penguin Classics, 1988.

lived on in the man: watchful, insecure, needy, addicted to fantasies about women and fame. But there seems no reason to insist that this was the 'real' Anthony, or any more 'real' than his everyday adult self. With all respect to Proust, a secret, less happy self has not, by virtue of being secret and less happy, some special and greater authenticity; but it is generally the one that powers great art.

After *Ralph the Heir*, which was full of hunting, Anthony conducted a public debate with the historian E. A. Freeman, whom he had never met, on the rights and wrongs of fox-hunting. Freeman sent in an article to the *Fortnightly* arguing aggressively that hunting was not a pastime for gentlemen and that it was wrong to take pleasure from the sufferings of animals. John Morley, the editor, published it in the issue of October 1869. In the light of his own connection with the magazine and his well-known passion for hunting, Anthony regarded Morley's action as 'almost the rising of a child against the father'. Morley's sympathies were with Freeman, and both knew that Anthony Trollope would reply.

Anthony's defence of hunting, in the December issue, was not brilliant. (A passion is not susceptible to justification.) Hunting was a fit pastime for gentlemen, he wrote, because it brought together all classes of society and because it encouraged the virtues of courage and persistence. Man killed animals for food 'in accordance with God's will'; and it was God's will that animals, and man, should hunt and kill each other. He went so far as to say that if there was an amusement which was in every way satisfactory, in which every person in the country could take part, but which resulted in the loss of one human life, that life would be well spent. Anthony put a very high value indeed on recreation.

The debate would have run and run had not Morley put an end to it. As it was, the issue was taken up by the *Saturday Review*, and Freeman carried it on in the *Daily Telegraph*. Those who joined in the debate in print mostly backed Freeman, but that was maybe because those who were on Anthony's side were all too busy hunting. Anthony returned to the fray six years later in *The American Senator*, where Reginald Morton of Hoppet Hall, invited to join an anti-blood sports association, let fly about 'a small knot of self-anxious people who think that they possess among them all the bowels [of compassion] of the world.' These 'philanimalists', raged Mr Morton, might include the lady 'whose tippet is made from the skins of twenty animals who have been wired in the snow and then left to die of starvation' and who justified 'the wires and the starvation because, as she will say, she used the fur. An honest blanket would keep her just as warm.'

Directly after the hunting debate in the *Fortnightly* Anthony plunged on to write one of his best novels, *The Eustace Diamonds*, and brought Phineas back from the obscurity to which he had sunk at the end of *Phineas Finn* in *Phineas Redux*. In between, he wrote the much shorter sexual drama *An Eye for an Eye*, set in Co. Clare, Ireland. These all had to be set aside for months, or more, waiting until the log-jam of his publications cleared. Unpredictably, he also produced a version of *The Commentaries of Caesar*.

John Blackwood was publishing a series of 'Ancient Classics for English Readers', edited by a clergyman, William Lucas Collins, and it was at Blackwood's suggestion that Anthony undertook the Caesar. He took only three months over it, time taken out from writing *The Eustace Diamonds*, but the project was painfully important to him. Scholarship, like politics, was a world in which he would like to have won honour. 'I do not know that I have ever worked harder. . . . I was most anxious, in this soaring out of my own peculiar line, not to disgrace myself. I do not think that I did disgrace myself' (*Autobiography*). He did not cover himself with glory either, even though he complied with all the tactful suggestions and corrections made by Blackwood and Collins.

'It is a dear little book to me,' he told Blackwood, to whom he made a present of the copyright. The best reward that Anthony got out of it was a good friendship with William Lucas Collins; he and Rose spent a weekend with Collins and his wife at their vicarage near Rugby after the *Commentaries* were finished, and afterwards Collins wrote to Blackwood: 'We like them very much, – him especially, he was so very pleasant to talk to, and at the same time so perfectly unassuming.' It was Collins who remarked to Blackwood that what he liked best about Rose was 'her honest and hearty appreciation of her husband'.

The worst result of the *Commentaries* venture was scholarly condescension. He sent an early copy of his book to Charles Merivale, Dean of Ely, the historian of Rome and elder brother of his great friend John. The learned Dean wrote back: 'Thank you for your comic History of Caesar.' The legend in the Merivale family was that Anthony wept, but how could they know? 'I do not suppose,' Anthony wrote in his autobiography, 'that he intended to run a dagger into me.'

A week after the *Commentaries* came out, in June 1870, Charles Dickens died. This was an occasion of national mourning; and it had implications for the Tom Trollopes. Fanny's sister Ellen was now free, but in a vacuum, having been 'invisible' for thirteen years.

Ellen went to stay with the eldest of her sisters, Maria, in Oxford, and Fanny came from Florence to be with them. Fanny wrote to her step-daughter Bice about the souvenirs of the great man that Dickens's family had given to her and Tom, and about going to see Dickens's grave in Westminster Abbey. She was careful not to suggest that there was any special link between Dickens and Bice's step-aunt Ellen, not even saying that Ellen's souvenir was the pen he had been writing with in his last days. Fanny Trollope had not been happy about her sister's liaison in recent years. Dickens said Fanny was 'sharper than the serpent's tooth'.

In September 1870 Rome finally fell to the Italian troops and Italian unification was complete. Rome would be the new capital. This was bad news for Tom. He had counted on Florence, the provisional capital, remaining the capital of all Italy. He had planned to sell the property at Ricorboli as building land and become, as he said, a millionaire. Fanny was anxious to live in England, where she was spending more and more time, and Anthony certainly assumed she would have her way and that Tom's Italian life was over. Tom put the villa on the market in 1871 and sold it the following year, losing £10,000 on the deal. He himself had no wish at all to return to England.

On 24 May 1871 Anthony and Rose sailed from Liverpool, known as the 'Port of Empire', to Australia.

This ambitious trip had been planned for over a year. It meant he missed seeing Kate Field in England; she reached Liverpool (with the corpse of her mother, who died *en voyage*) four days before he left and stayed six months, enjoying a considerable success lecturing, dining out, writing articles for the New York

Tribune and making further conquests: an unnamed literary man, not Anthony, began a letter to her, 'My dear Miss Field, Dear K.F., My dear Kate, My Lovely Passion Flower. . . .'

Anthony was in a renouncing mood. Waltham House had many attractions in the form of 'hunting, gardening, and suburban hospitalities'. It had been 'the scene of much happiness'. But it was no longer necessary for his work to live in that area, and his income was likely to decline rather than increase in the future. He was already being offered less for his novels than in the mid-1860s. 'Would not a house in London be cheaper?' (*Autobiography*).

Having made the decision, and knowing they would be away for eighteen months, Anthony and Rose prepared to 'flit', as he put it, with a promptness worthy of Mrs Trollope senior – though Anthony was characteristically ill in bed over Christmas and New Year of 1870–71. In January he fulfilled lecturing engagements in the Midlands, leaving behind at one place his knob-topped umbrella and his old brown purse (which would have been fatter by £10 or £15 for each lecture). In his lecture on 'English Prose Fiction as a Rational Amusement' he inserted an emotional reference to the loss of Charles Dickens; but what he thought privately about Dickens the man may better be judged from a letter he wrote to George Eliot and G. H. Lewes in 1872, apropos the first volume of John Forster's biography, which Anthony found 'distasteful': 'Dickens was no hero; he was a powerful, clever, humorous, and, in many respects, wise man; – very ignorant, and thick-skinned, who had taught himself to be his own God, and to believe himself to be a sufficient God for all who came near him; – not a hero at all.' But then, Anthony knew about Ellen.

At Waltham House there was 'a packing up, with many tears, and consultations as to what should be saved out of the things we loved'. All Anthony's books, and the best-loved pictures and bits of furniture, went into store. The rest was sold. George Smith and George Lewes probably got landed with a lot of cigars. Anthony was always pressing them to buy cigars off him. (To George Lewes, December 1869: 'I can send you a hundred of them, – strictly commercial – 4d a piece. I have a large parcel of unopened cigars, 12 hundred, – of which you shall have a box on trial instead if you prefer them.')

'I hope Mrs Trollope is well & likes the idea of the expedition as much as she did,' wrote John Blackwood in March 1871. 'Leaving old Waltham with its garden & all your comforts & pretty things there will be a wrench with which I have much sympathy.' The house itself was in need of repairs; no buyer was found for two years. The eventual sale was to William Paul, from a local family of nurserymen. The Trollopes' beloved garden was in good hands. William Paul was a famous rosarian and author of *The Rose Garden*, which remained the standard reference work for sixty years. Anthony's bookshelves were not wasted, either. Paul, who lived with his family at Waltham House until he died in 1905, had a large and distinguished collection of horticultural and general books.

The only pity was that Mr Paul did not buy the house sooner. No tenant was found to cover the two years it remained on the market, and Anthony lost £800 over the transaction. 'As I continually hear that other men make money by buying and selling houses, I presume I am not well adapted for transactions of that sort. I have never made money by selling anything but a manuscript. In matters of horseflesh I am so inefficient that I have generally given away horses that I have not wanted' (*Autobiography*). He sold one horse before he went to Australia, but his favourite hunters, Banker and Buff, were looked after by Anna Steele's brother. The one he called his 'little horse' was lent to Frederic Chapman. His much-loved niece Florence, who rode the little horse, was settled at a boarding school in France.

The date of their sailing was delayed, so he and Rose were 'homeless wanderers' for eighteen days, 'in all the misery of living about among friends and pot-houses', as Anthony told Alfred Austin, 'going through that very worst phase of life which consists in a continuous and ever failing attempt to be jolly, with nothing to do. . . .' On the final evening Anthony dined with his old Irish friend Charles Lever. It was the last time he would see him; Lever died suddenly during the Trollopes' time abroad.

'I went to Australia chiefly in order to see my son among his sheep.' He also had an agreement (for £1,250, with Chapman & Hall) to write a book about Australia and New Zealand. He offered *The Times* a series of articles as well, but they turned him down; he wrote them for the *Daily Telegraph* instead.

When he left, *Sir Harry Hotspur of Humblethwaite* had been out for a few months, *Ralph the Heir* was being serialised in *Saint Pauls*, *The Eustace Diamonds* was with John Morley awaiting serialisation in the *Fortnightly* and the finished manuscripts of *Phineas Redux* and *An Eye for an Eye* were stashed away in a strong-box for publication when the log-jam cleared. He regarded his unpublished books as assets, or insurance policies, ready to be cashed. He had a desk put up in his cabin and before they reached Melbourne on July 27 he had written the whole of *Lady Anna* 'at the rate of 66 pages of manuscript in each week, every page of manuscript containing 250 words' (*Autobiography*).

Yet another novel, a short one written back in 1867, *The Golden Lion of Granpere*, was to run in *Good Words* while he was away. Frederick Pollock undertook to correct the proofs of this for him but, as he wrote in his *Personal Reminiscences*, there was really nothing for him to do: 'Trollope's writing for the press was very distinct and regular, and entirely free from alterations or additions, etc. It seemed to have flowed from his pen like clean liquor from a tap.'

Young Fred Trollope was a squatter – an unpromising term for someone who had the opportunity to belong to Australia's most privileged group. 'The squatters here are what the lords and the country gentlemen are at home' (*Harry Heathcote of Gangoil*). Squatters were settlers who held massive tracts of virgin bush – unlawfully at first, subsequently on licence from the Crown, using it to graze sheep and later cattle. They were never landowners in the feudal British sense; this was a high-risk business, and they worked long hours alongside their men. But squatters who made money were able to build large and beautiful houses on their land or in the cities, and to establish dynasties. They became respectable and conservative, calling themselves graziers, pastoralists, or even squires: the colonial aristocracy.

In the 1860s, as a result of pressure to free for agriculture land held by the squatters, Selection Acts were passed. Up to 320 acres had to be released on demand to 'free-selectors', with no compensation paid, and the squatters had to buy the freehold of land they wanted to retain. The ensuing animosity and violence between squatters and free-selectors made the plot of the short novel of bush life that Anthony wrote for the Christmas 1873 issue of the *Graphic*, called *Harry Heathcote of Gangoil*. Fred, with Anthony's money, had bought his sheep run at Mortray outright to forestall further free-selection on it.

It was squatter gentlemen who gave Anthony hospitality in their homes, introduced him to their clubs in the cities, and supplied him with the introductions he needed to legislators, administrators, officials and experts. But he said, both in public in Australia and in his book, that the future lay with the free-selectors, the new waves of immigrants from Britain who would cultivate the land. When he first arrived in Australia he was fêted as a celebrity; but his outspoken judgements on Australian society, Australian boastfulness ('blowing'), Australian prospects and Australian womanhood, made in person and in the articles he was sending back to the *Daily Telegraph*, lost him some goodwill.

Rose spent several weeks with Fred at Mortray while Anthony toured Queensland. He saw the great sheep runs of the Darling Downs, and enjoyed the prosperous, friendly station life: 'I like having horses to ride and kangaroos to hunt, and sheep become quite a fascination to me as a subject of conversation. And I liked that roaming from one house to another, – with a perfect conviction that five minutes would make me intimate with the next batch of strangers.' He went to Gympie, a gold-rush town, developing a loathing of gold-diggings on account of the dreary, dirty work, the squalid surroundings, the risks, the unlikelihood of success and the meretricious nature of the enterprise.

Anthony was at Mortray with Rose and his son for a month in October and November 1871, during which time he worked on his book about Australia in the early mornings, sitting under a tree. Fred's sheep station was three days' drive from the nearest railway. He had a 250-acre horse paddock for his twenty horses, and 26,000 acres for his sheep. Riding for hours on end through the bush, Anthony hardly even saw any of Fred's 10,000 sheep, the acreage was so vast. His rides were taken alone; Fred was always busy.

Anthony described in *Australia and New Zealand* Fred's typical single-storey homestead by a creek, with its three rooms, and a verandah twelve feet wide all along the front and the two ends, where the life of the family took place. 'Here are congregated lounging chairs, generally very rough, but always comfortable, – with tables, sofas, and feminine nick-nacks, if there be ladies, till

the place has the appearance of a room open to the heavens.'
Fred's nearest neighbour was three miles away, 'which was a
great drawback to my friend's [i.e. Fred's] happiness, – for it was
inhabited by a free-selector and a publican. I rather liked the
publican, as he got up a kangaroo hunt for me', but Fred saw 'the
vicinity of grog' as a menace, as his men were apt to go on binges.

There was no social life. 'Squatters do not go out to dine, or ask
each other to dinner.' Fred had a Chinese cook for his shearers,
alongside whom he worked in the wooden wool-shed which was,
his father proudly wrote, 'the creation of his own ingenuity'.
Every meal, for everyone, was based on tea and mutton, though
efforts were made about soup and salad when Anthony was there.
Rose had gone to the extreme of bringing out from England a
young woman to cook for them, and she was, Anthony said,
invaluable, 'or would have been had she not found a husband for
herself when she had been about a month in the bush. But in spite
of her love, and her engagement to a man who was considerably
above her in position, she was true to us while she remained at
M[ortray], and did her best to make us all comfortable.'

Fred – aged twenty-four, lonely, isolated, overworked – needed
someone of his own to make him comfortable. He was already
engaged when his parents came out and, if they knew it already,
their journey would seem to have had an additional purpose. Fred
got married in Forbes, thirty miles from Mortray, on 14
December 1871. But Rose and Anthony were not at the wedding.

They were with Fred at Mortray until 9 November; they then
left for Sydney, where Anthony had engagements. He and Rose
were the guests of honour on a boat-trip and picnic down the
Hawkesbury River* on 9 December, and on 13 December – the
day before the wedding – they took ship from Sydney to
Melbourne, arriving on 16 December. Anthony's first important
engagement in Melbourne was to give his 'English Prose Fiction'
lecture, on 18 December. There seems absolutely no reason why
he could not have arranged, or rearranged, his schedule so that he
and Rose could attend their son's wedding. There was no question
of their being dissatisfied with Fred himself. From Mortray,
Anthony wrote to G. W. Rusden – a senior civil servant in

---

* In honour of that day, the stretch of the Hawkesbury River between Wiseman's
Ferry and Laughtondale is marked on the map as 'Trollope Reach'.

Melbourne, author, scholar and educationist, and the one close friend that Anthony made in Australia – that 'I find my son all I could wish, – steady, hardworking, skilful & determined.'

Fred's bride was Susannah Farrand, the nineteen-year-old daughter of the police magistrate* at Forbes. She visited Mortray while Anthony and Rose were there; Anthony had driven her the ten miles to Fred's place from Grenfell, and wrote in his diary-notes that Susie, as she was called, was much prettier than her photograph and 'a good humoured pleasant little girl who I think will make Fred a good wife'. Rose's comments are not recorded, though she must have been hoping that Fred would come home to England eventually and marry an English girl (a 'lady') – as John Caldigate did after repudiating the woman with whom he lived in the gold-fields, in Anthony's later novel of that name. Marriage to an Australian made Fred's return most unlikely.

Perhaps Rose did not take to Susie. Perhaps the prospect of the wedding at Forbes was too much for Anthony. Small towns in New South Wales, he wrote in his Australia book, exuded 'an apparent mixture of pretension and failure . . . which creates a feeling of melancholy sadness in the mind of a stranger.' Perhaps Fred took his marriage prosaically, and urged his parents not to upset their arrangements. Anthony in his Australia book set out the unromantically utilitarian reasons why a young squatter needed a wife. Without one, he had no female companionship. 'He will hardly get a woman who will cook for him decently, or who will sew a button on his shirt, when it is wanted. And he will soon care nothing how his dinner is cooked, and whether his shirt be with or without a button.' It cost nothing to marry: 'the thing is so easy that the young squatter simply goes out in his buggy and brings home the daughter of some other squatter, – after a little ceremony performed in the nearest church.'

Anthony and Rose did not get back to Mortray till June of the following year, and then only for a few days. They had a visit there from a neighbour of Fred's, Charles Dickens's fourth son Alfred,†

* Police magistracies were stipendiary magistracies, i.e. they carried a salary. A police magistrate generally had less social status than a magistrate who sat on the bench as an unpaid service to the community, and who was likely to be of the 'squatter' class.

† Later that year Alfred Dickens moved to Melbourne, and Fred missed him – 'one neighbour the less with whome [sic] you can exchange an idea', as he wrote to his brother Harry. Dickens's youngest son, Edward, also emigrated to Australia.

who had emigrated at the age of twenty in 1865. By this time Susie was pregnant, though pregnancy was not the reason for the marriage. (The baby, Frank Anthony, was born on Fred's birthday, 27 September. His Trollope grandparents did not see him; they were in New Zealand, en route for home.)

In the June evenings of 1872 Anthony and Rose, Fred and Susie, sat out on the verandah. 'I did endeavour to institute a whist table,' Anthony wrote in his Australia book, 'but I found that my friends, who were wonderfully good in regard to the age and points of a sheep, and who could tell to the fraction of a penny what the wool of each was worth by the pound, could never be got to remember the highest card of the suit. I should not have minded that had they not so manifestly despised me for regarding such knowledge as important.'

Anthony, sending Mary Holmes a copy of *Harry Heathcote of Gangoil* after it came out in book form, told her that 'the Harry Heathcote is my boy Frederic, – or very much the same'. He described in the story Fred's way of life, and his house, much as he had described it in *Australia and New Zealand*, with the added details of a striped awning over the verandah, and flowering creepers, and a picture of the young squatter himself, wearing, even for dinner in the evening, 'a flannel shirt, a pair of moleskin trousers, and an old straw hat . . . no coat, no waistcoat, and nothing round the neck'. He gave his young pioneer an adoring wife, for whom he was ready to work himself to the bone, even though 'the mental loneliness of his position almost broke his heart'. And this 'young patriarch in the wilderness' was only twenty-four, 'and had been educated at an English school!'

'He was not making money, nor has he made money since. I grieve to say that several thousands of pounds which I had squeezed out of the pockets of perhaps too liberal publishers have been lost on the venture' (*Autobiography*). Anthony did not think any of it was Fred's fault. He praised his son's 'persistent honesty' – persistence and honesty being prime Trollopian virtues – but mining (for gold, tin, copper) was the big new attraction in New South Wales, and it was difficult to get girls to help Susie in the house, difficult to get labour for the shearing. The labour Fred did get was rough. There was a murder in late 1872 on a nearby sheep station, in which two men who worked at Mortray were implicated.

411

Anthony did his best for Fred in the only ways he knew – subsidising him, and using his own famous name to pull strings. After the last visit to Mortray he wrote to Henry Parkes, the Premier of New South Wales, firming up an earlier request made through a mutual acquaintance to have Fred appointed a magistrate: 'He has become a zealous hard-working squatter, and I shall be much obliged to you if you assist him in this way to enter the position which I should be glad to see him occupy.' Parkes obliged. Fred was made a magistrate for the Forbes district a couple of months later, which enhanced his status in the community.

Anthony had not lost his stamina, but he was fat and ageing; he had his fifty-seventh birthday in Adelaide, where he admired the big Post Office. He was glad, he wrote, to see that the Australian colonies were more 'disposed to be splendid' in their Post Offices than in any other public buildings, 'for surely there is no other public building so useful'.

Nothing he had ever seen equalled Sydney harbour. 'Bantry Bay [in Ireland], with the nooks of the sea running up to Glengarriff, is very lovely', but not so lovely as Sydney. The Trollopes' base, however, was Melbourne, where Rose stayed with kind new friends or in a hotel when he went on his more arduous trips. In the cities and towns he assiduously visited schools, colleges, prisons, libraries and hospitals, and was uniformly impressed. 'Could a pauper be suddenly removed out of an English union workhouse into the Melbourne Benevolent Asylum, he might probably think that he had migrated to Buckingham Palace.'

He attended receptions, dinners and luncheons in his honour, although he was sometimes too tired to respond with the flattering graciousness required from visiting celebrities. At Gulgong where, in great trepidation, he allowed his bulk to be lowered 150 feet down the shaft of a gold-mine, he was given an official luncheon at which both he and the local police magistrate T. A. Browne spoke; Browne, under the pseudonym Rolf Boldrewood, was the future author of the classic Australian novel *Robbery Under Arms*.

Fred met Browne/Boldrewood at Dubbo a decade later, and reported to his father: 'He said that he met you at Gulgong. He scribbles a bit and has written several passable stories, if not especially clever at all events honest. . . .' Apropos of the honesty, Fred could by then have read Rolf Boldrewood's novel *The Miner's Right*, in which a luncheon was given for a visiting Briton called Anthony Towers: 'the old Turk gratefully acknowledged it in his book on Australia by a faint allusion and a statement that the cookery was better than the speeches.'* Rolf Boldrewood told Fred that he meant to plug away at his writing 'and quoted a saying of yours – "it's dogged as does it" [from *The Last Chronicle of Barset*] – and seemed to find some consolation in that.'

Anthony went from Gulgong to Ballarat, where he was joined by his new friend G. W. Rusden. Ballarat was one of the longest-established and roughest of the gold-towns. Anthony, accompanied by a policeman, saw the 'degraded life' in the Chinese quarter by night: 'They have no women of their own, and the lowest creatures of the streets congregate with them in their hovels. But this is far from being the worst of it. Boys and girls are enticed among them, and dwell with them, and become foul, abominable, and inhuman.' It was a relief to go on to the hospitality of Ercildoune, a large sheep station nearby owned by the Learmonth brothers, who entertained in simple, spacious comfort. Life in such houses, Anthony imagined, was 'very much as was that of an English country gentleman a century or a century and a half ago [i.e. in the first half of the eighteenth century].'

He visited the coastal regions of every colony† except the Northern Territory (in 1872 administered by South Australia, with a white population calculated at 600). He travelled around the coast by ship, he travelled by Cobb's coaches‡ and on horseback. There were only short lengths of railroad built, linking the coastal cities to nearby settlements. At Rosedale in Victoria he and Rusden hired horses to ride to the gold-mines at Walhalla,

---

* What Anthony wrote in *Australia and New Zealand* was: 'In the middle of the day there had been a public dinner or lunch, at which there was much speaking. I cannot say that the Gulgong oratory was as good as the Gulgong acting, or the Gulgong oysters.' (He had been to a lively theatrical performance, followed by an oyster supper, the night before.)

† Federation of the separate colonies was already being discussed when the Trollopes were there, but the Commonwealth of Australia did not come into existence until 1901.

‡ Cobb, an American, was the Bianconi of Australia.

and on to others at Jericho, Matlock and Woods Point. Anthony rode up to sixty miles a day through endless forests of gum-trees, with the necessities strapped to his saddle: 'Two changes of linen, a night-shirt, a pair of trousers, with hair-brushes, tooth-brush, and a pair of slippers.' He had learned, at last, to travel light, even though this meant that he appeared improperly dressed at dinners given in his honour.

By the end of February 1872, he was back in Melbourne from Tasmania, previously notorious as Van Diemen's Land. Anthony had interviewed, with shrewdness and sensitivity, one of the few remaining convicts* in the prison at Port Arthur. As he wrote in his book, for climate and scenery he preferred Tasmania to anywhere else: 'Were it my lot to take up my residence in Australia, and could I choose the colony in which I was to live, I would pitch my tent in Tasmania.'

'I am beginning to find myself too old to be 18 months away from home,' he told George Lewes and George Eliot. 'Not that I am fatigued bodily; – but mentally I cannot be at ease with all the new people and new things. . . . I am struggling to make a good book, but I feel that it will not be good. It will be desultory and inaccurate; – perhaps dull, & where shall I be then?'

He longed for good cigars, and good coffee, and to be writing 'with good ink at a comfortable table'. He was not impressed, he said in his book, by the Australian 'fine' wines. 'The best I drank were in South Australia but I did not much relish them. I thought them to be heady, having a taste of earth, and an after-flavour which was disagreeable.' The wine he liked best – 'both wholesome and nutritive' – was what he called the *vin ordinaire* of Melbourne, which came from Yering on the Upper Yarra. As for the brandy drunk by the working men in the public houses, it was 'a villainous, vitriolic, biting compound of deadly intoxicating qualities'.

Tired as he was, he still had the distant spaces of Western Australia to see. He travelled with a Scottish friend the 260 miles from Albany to Perth in a 'conveyance', sleeping in the bush at night, taking pride in proving that they could 'do without washing, and eat nastiness from a box [canned food]. . . . We lit

* Britain had stopped sending convicts to eastern Australia by the 1850s, when Van Diemen's Land became Tasmania. Western Australia was the last colony to accept convicts; the very last convict-ship reached Fremantle in January 1868.

fires for ourselves, and boiled our tea in billies; and then regaled ourselves with bad brandy and water out of pannikins, cooked bacon and potatoes in a frying-pan, and pretended to think it was very jolly. . . .'*

He missed his English hunting, though he got plenty of hunting in Australia, of an unfamiliar kind. On kangaroo hunts in the bush of Queensland and New South Wales, he was apt to crash into the gum-trees, not turning his horse quickly enough. He went out with the Melbourne Staghounds – a drag-hunt, over rough country and high fences, on a horse too small for his seventeen-stone weight. 'Blind as well as heavy,' as he said, Anthony did not notice a wire, and had another bad fall.

He was maddened to receive in Melbourne a letter from his whist-companion and fellow author Charles Reade in London saying that he had dramatised Anthony's novel *Ralph the Heir* under the title *Shilly-Shally*† and that since Anthony was not there to approve or otherwise, he was planning to stage it, putting both their names on the playbill as joint authors. Harry, in London, let his father down over this. He could, at least, have questioned Reade's right, when Reade got in touch with him, and later asked him to the first night.

The play had opened at the Gaiety Theatre before Anthony even got Reade's letter. Anthony shot off furious letters to Reade, to George Smith, to the *Pall Mall Gazette* and to the *Telegraph*. It was 'monstrous', he told Smith. Reade was 'by way of being an intimate friend of mine'. No longer: Anthony's anger, and Charles Reade's disgruntlement, lasted for five years. At the Garrick, that nursery-world of masculine squabbles, they glared at one another and never spoke, even managing to take part in the same four at whist without acknowledging one another's presence.

By the end of his antipodean tour, Anthony longed for home. 'I have interested myself very much with these colonial people . . .

* Anthony wrote so often in his later years about the necessity to *pretend* he was 'jolly' that one is inclined to believe his habitual manner was, increasingly, assumed, and masked a mild depression which was chronic rather than periodic.

† Reade in his adaptation focused on the romantic comedy, centring on Mr Neefit the breeches-maker and his efforts to make Ralph marry his daughter Polly. It ran for a month. A theatre critic attacked the play for indecency, upon which Reade sued him and was awarded £200 damages.

but in regard to social delights I cannot cotton to them thoroughly,' he confessed to Smith. In August he and Rose went on to New Zealand for a couple of months, covering the ground with now automatic assiduity. ('It's dogged as does it.') It was the depths of winter. The Trollopes travelled overland wherever possible, separated for long days from the bulk of their heavy luggage, which went by coastal steamer. Anthony, 'in a blue shirt and an old grey shooting jacket', felt at a disadvantage at dinner with the local aristocracy in the towns they passed through.

Rose's fortitude was tested. The journey from Queenstown to Dunedin, over the hills in thick snow, took six days instead of three. At one point, after leaving Tuapika, the coach and horses got stuck in a drift, everyone got out and the passengers helped to clear a way through the hip-high snow with shovels. Rose, her wide skirts encrusted and weighted down with balled-up snow, was in dire need of 'the kind hostess who took her to a fire and comforted her with dry stockings', while 'I got some dinner and brandy-and-water.'

One gets the impression that Rose put up cheerfully with the hard labour and gross discomforts of such journeys with Anthony because the alternative – being left behind in England – was even less appealing. Yet the drawback to New Zealand, Anthony wrote, was that after crossing oceans and travelling thousands of miles, the traveller felt that he 'had not at all succeeded in getting away from England'. This was to be a stock joke about New Zealand, along with the one about there being more sheep than people, which he also made.

He made one good prediction and one unfortunate one. He remarked on the lack of a harbour at New Plymouth, without which the settlement would not find prosperity. The sand of the coast here was 'composed chiefly of iron. . . . The sensation of weight when the soft stuff is gathered in the hand is very remarkable'. He felt that properly managed 'these sands would become the source of great wealth'. So it turned out, with steel mills on that very stretch of coast, south of Taranaki.

He was determined to see the lakes and hot springs south of the city of Auckland, to which there was no road. With an escort provided by the Governor, he and Rose took a fortnight over the trip, seven days of which were spent on horseback. On Lake Roto

Iti they stayed in a Maori house, ornamented with 'indecent carvings' – though, Anthony said, 'I doubt whether I should have discovered the indecency had it not been pointed out to me.' At Ohinemutu he bathed by night in a small hot pool, crouching among three 'Maori damsels' who jollied him along with little pats on his back.

He wrote ecstatically of the terraces of soft pink and white rock at Roto Mahana, and of wallowing in one warm, shell-shaped pool after another. 'It is a spot for intense sensual enjoyment. . . .' The time would come, he prophesied, when there would be 'a sprightly hotel at Roto Mahana, with a *table d'hôte*, and boats at so much an hour, and regular seasons for bathing. As I lay there, I framed the programme of such a hotel in my mind . . . fixing the appropriate spot as I squatted in the water, and calculating how much it would cost and what return it would give.'

This prophecy did not come true, or not for long. A tourist hotel was built at Te Waiora, the nearby Maori settlement. But in 1886 Mount Tarawera erupted. The village, the hotel and the lovely pink and white terraces were all obliterated under volcanic lava.

Travel did not broaden Anthony Trollope's mind. It is unnecessary to quote his opinions in *Australia and New Zealand* on black people, 'unfeminine' women, democratic manners, the undesirability of Empire and the inevitability of colonial independence. They had been expressed already in either *The West Indies* or in *North America* or both, in almost the same terms. He was fed in Australia with tales of the Aborigines' cannibalism and savagery, and so was reinforced in his belief that 'the negro cannot live on equal terms with the white man. . . .' He went further. 'Of the Australian black we may certainly say that he has to go. That he should perish without unnecessary suffering should be the aim of all who are concerned in the matter.'*

As for the Maori people, he had been enchanted by the 'damsels' who splashed with him so sweetly in the pool, but he saw no future for them. He saw the Maori as a 'gallant people'

* It was not so long since Aborigines had been shot like vermin by white settlers and the military. A policy of 'pacification by force' prevailed until the 1880s. The Aborigines were nomadic hunter-gatherers and did not practise cannibalism. Anthony's views are shocking to read, and it makes it no better to understand that they were widely shared by the British establishment.

who were gradually but inevitably melting away,* principally because their culture, like that of native Australians, was 'terribly subversive both of the desire and the power to collect wealth'. He restated his materialist religion: 'The desire of accumulating property, combined with the industry necessary for doing so, is perhaps of all qualifications for civilisation the most essential.'

Anthony gave offence in Australia and New Zealand, as he did in every non-European country, by treating as inferiors those who served or helped him. In European society, where social relationships were governed by status rather than by contract, they were inferiors by definition. Anthony, in New Zealand, accidentally knocked a young woman's washing off a line into the mud, and even though she was in tears she refused his money. 'Another girl told my wife, in perfectly friendly confidence, that she did not think she ought to take money.' He just could not come to grips with the fact that 'the offer of money is considered to be offensive', and found it noteworthy that when paying for a round of drinks he was expected to hand the money to the bar-tender and not to the men he was treating. He felt that the Australasian distaste for tips would 'doubtless be unlearned'. He was wrong.

Anthony knew the dangers of English ethnocentricity. 'As he would not buy gloves for his friend by the measure of his own hand, so he should not presume that an American will be well-fitted or ill-fitted in the details of his life according as he may or may not wear the customs and manners of his life cut after an English fashion' (*Australia and New Zealand*). In spite of himself, he did so presume. Nevertheless, his long, loose book constitutes the best and fullest account of travel in Australia and New Zealand at the period, and of homestead life, conditions in the gold-towns, and the atmosphere and appearance of the cities.

On 3 October 1872 he and Rose set sail for Honolulu; thence to San Francisco, arriving on 6 November. A stop-over in Salt Lake City for an abortive call on the polygamous Brigham Young, the Mormons' president, and then New York on 25 November. Home

---

* He was right in that the Maori population was falling rapidly, largely due to European diseases, throughout the nineteenth century. By 1896 there were only 42,113 left. Anthony could hardly foresee that by 1990 there would be 300,000 people registered as Maori.

by 17 December – only they had no home. Rose and Anthony
went into lodgings at 3 Holles Street, off Cavendish Square.

PART FOUR

TOWARDS
THE
FURTHER
SHORE

CHAPTER SEVENTEEN

NO sooner were Rose and Anthony home than Harry was packed off whence they came. Within a week of their return he was on a ship on his way to visit his brother in Australia. Such a visit had often been talked of, but this was very sudden.

Joe Langford, Blackwood's representative in London and a Garrick friend of Anthony's, reported on Christmas Eve 1872 to John Blackwood that Harry's departure 'will be attributed no doubt to a business quarrel [with Chapman & Hall] but the cause is one which has troubled our sex from the earliest periods and the young man has shown himself amenable to reason and obedient to parental authority. Trollope has behaved with his usual promptness.'

In *The Duke's Children* young Lord Silverbridge was reproached for loving the 'wrong' girl by his father the Duke of Omnium: 'Is there to be no duty in such matters, no restraint, no feeling of what is due to your own name, and to others who bear it? . . . Do you think that love is a passion that cannot be withstood?' And yet his children could stand up to him, if they really wanted to. 'They only had to be firm and he knew that he must be conquered.' Harry was not firm. He was, as Langford said, 'amenable'.

One would suspect from Langford's letter to Blackwood some homosexual involvement, were it not for what George Lewes wrote in his diary for 1 January 1873: 'Trollope came to lunch. Told me of his trouble with Harry wanting to marry a woman of the town.' A 'woman of the town' was the common euphemism for a prostitute. Other voices from the past mutter 'a French actress', which implied much the same thing. Anthony's fictional Vicar of Bullhampton may have 'built little castles in the air' on Carry Brattle's behalf, wishing for 'a loving husband' for the castaway, but Anthony was not prepared for his own son to be the loving husband of such a one.

Harry stayed less than five months in Australia. He returned in summer 1873 and withdrew his capital from Chapman & Hall. 'He remained there for three years and a half; but he did not like it, nor do I think he made a very good publisher,' wrote Anthony in his autobiography. Anthony remained heavily involved in the publishing policy of the firm, telling Mary Holmes that he was in their Piccadilly office 'almost daily'. Meanwhile Harry went off to the Continent for a year, with the idea of becoming – a writer.

Anthony celebrated his return home by a reunion with Banker (a dark chestnut), Buff (a blue roan) and the 'little horse', as well as buying a fourth. Starved, in Australia, of the release of fox-hunting and full of tension from the trouble with Harry, within a few days of his return he enjoyed in Essex 'the biggest bellyful of hunting I ever had in my life' – a run of nearly three hours ending in a kill. 'I never had such a day before. Buff carried me through it all as well as ever. But was *very tired.*'

For the next three seasons he kept up a gruelling routine of hunting from London three times a week, at first in Essex, where the daughter of a house in which he sometimes stayed recalled his wandering in and out of other men's bedrooms as they got ready, always talking; and talking, too, to bits of clothing he could not lay his hands on: 'Oh, Mrs Sock, where have you got to? Not under there? No. Perhaps in the chest of drawers. Why, I do declare, there you are hiding near the curtain. I've got you, ha! Now, Mr Top Boot, where is your twin? Can't go hunting alone, you know.' Plus snatches of song, out of tune.* He also hunted around Leighton Buzzard, where he followed Baron Meyer Amschel de Rothschild's deerhounds, and went fox-hunting with the Whaddon Chase.

Few landowners could now afford to subsidise the hunt as Master out of their own pockets; more and more hunts survived by combining, and charging subscriptions. Captain Glomax, the Master of the Ufford and Rufford United Hunt in *The American Senator*, received '£2000 a year from the gentlemen of the county' for the upkeep of the hounds. Farmers, who often loathed having to let up to a hundred and fifty horsemen rampage over their

* Mrs M. Evangeline Bradhurst, 'Anthony Trollope, the Hunting Man', *Essex Review*, 1928.

fields, smashing rails and fences, began in the 1870s to use wire –
even barbed-wire – as fencing. Wire was disastrous for short-
sighted Anthony.

He kept his horses in the country, having them transported to a
meet by a horse-box on a train. To get there himself from London
he had to get up in the dark, take a cab to the station, change
trains more than once – and then go through the reverse
performance after the hunt, in order to get home, exhausted and
often as not depressed, in time for dinner at eight. This costly and
arduous routine, as he said in his autobiography, was work for a
young, rich man, 'but I have done it as an old man and
comparatively a poor man.' Anthony was not a poor man, but he
was afraid of becoming one, if his writing failed.

By late January 1873 Anthony and Rose had found a house, 39
Montagu Square, north of Oxford Street and close to the dim
Marylebone streets where he had spent so many years of his
young manhood – 'not a gorgeous neighbourhood', as he told
Anna Steele, 'but one which will suit my declining years and
modest resources'. Their close friends Frederick and Juliet
Pollock had been living in the same square, at No. 59, for more
than twenty years. Frederick Pollock was at the peak of his legal
career, being in 1874 appointed Queen's Remembrancer* by
Disraeli. Anthony liked the bustle of London. 'I myself believe in
cities, – even though there should be dishonest ambition, short-
sighted policy, and rowdiness. The dishonesty, the folly, and the
rowdiness are but the overboiling of the pot without which cannot
be had the hot water which is so necessary to our well-being'
(*Australia and New Zealand*).

Tom was leading a hotel life in Florence while Anthony and Rose
were in the rented house in Holles Street. Christmas 1872 was an
anxious, lonely time for Tom, aged sixty-two, with his wife and
daughter in England and his house at Ricorboli and its opulent
contents being sold up. The sales cleared his debts with enough
over to assure him an income, but of only £300 a year. Tom had
nothing but an undesired return to England in prospect. Robert

---

* Queen's Remembrancer: not such a romantic post as it sounds. He was head of
the department in charge of Revenue suits – proceedings for the recovery of taxes,
rents, legacies etc due to the Crown. He also had charge of appointing the sheriffs of
counties.

Browning had written to Isa Blagden the previous year: 'As for [Tom] Trollope's cutting up his last thirty years of life by the roots, I feel no wonder at *that*: I always liked him – but money was worth all else in the world to him – and I never knew the chaffering* spirit so strong in a gentleman and person of culture.' (But against this, set the response of the wife of Lord Augustus Paget, British Ambassador in Rome: 'That year [?1878], Tom Trollope . . . brought his brother, Anthony, to see us. He was rough, heavy, persevering and rather vulgar, like his books, but interesting. My husband liked Tom, who was very cute and honest.'† People rarely appreciated both brothers equally.) Isa, so good a friend to both Robert Browning and Tom, died suddenly in Florence in January 1873, aged fifty-five.

Just when Rose and Anthony were buying 39 Montagu Square, Tom's life too took a new and welcome turn. His friend Alfred Austin had been since 1866 writing for the London *Standard*. Austin, by his own account, spoke to his editor, and Tom was offered the job of Rome correspondent of the *Standard*. He jumped at it, and was in Rome by mid-February 1873. Fanny joined him in March. After various temporary moves, Tom and Fanny established themselves in a spacious apartment at the top – up 141 stairs – of 367 Via Nazionale, a new building on a new street. Tom was soon amassing possessions again. 'They have just been selling off the property of Pius IX in the Vatican, everything from splendid jewelled crucifixes to empty bottles,' he wrote to Lady Westbury – widow of a former Lord Chancellor, who had a house in Italy – in early 1878. 'It was a very singular sight! I bought the embroidered cover of his habitual breakfast table, and Fanny bought a lot of lace.'

Bice, who was a young lady now – she turned twenty in spring 1873 – spent her time on an endless round of English and occasionally French visits, with nothing in view apart from a

---

* Chaffering: haggling, dealing. Browning had gone off Tom Trollope when he developed and decorated the villa at Ricorboli so extravagantly. Browning to Isa Blagden, 19 February 1868: 'I think T. Trollope, and always did, a goose despite his general good sense; he wastes his labour for that which is not bread: he works, when he might play, and for what or whom? So he always did, buying, selling, chaffering and wasting life.' E. C. McAleer (ed.), *Dearest Isa: Robert Browning's Letters to Isabella Blagden*.

† Walburga, Lady Paget, *Embassies of Other Days* (1923).

Waltham House at Waltham Cross in Essex, where Anthony and Rose lived from late 1859 until 1871. Standing by the gate is the servant Barney who had been with Anthony ever since his bachelor days in Banagher.

39 Montagu Square, south of the Marylebone Road, an area of London familiar to Anthony since his boyhood – 'not a gorgeous neighborhood, but one which will suit my declining years and modest resources'. Anthony and Rose lived here from 1873 until 1880.

Above: North End, South Harting, Sussex. Anthony and Rose moved yet again in 1880, when it seemed important to get out of London for his health's sake. North End was put together from several old cottages knocked into one at the very beginning of the nineteenth century. Additions included the tower which held the water-tank. Anthony did not admire the tower. There were seven bedrooms, and a good cellar for Anthony's store of wine. The Trollopes built on the long glass porch (visible behind the lady at the tea table), in order to provide a dry, covered way into the house from the gate. When Rose came to sell North End, the auctioneer's brochure made much of the modern technology involved in this porch – 'an Ornamental Conservatory, paved with Tiles, which is Heated by Hot Water Pipes communicating with a Hot Water Coil to give warmth to the Hall'. The house came with seventy acres, most of which they let out.

Facing page: Views of the double drawing-room and of the dining-room at North End. Since these pictures were reproduced in the auctioneer's brochure when Rose sold the property, it may be presumed that the furniture and paintings etc. as illustrated are the Trollopes', and that the rooms are arranged as they were when the family lived there.

From *How the 'Mastiffs' went to Iceland:* sketch by Jemima Blackburn of the 'Siege of the Deck Cabin', when the ladies attacked an unnamed gentleman (Anthony) for commandeering the cabin as a smoking-room.

Water-colour by Jemima Blackburn of some of the party in Iceland in early summer 1878, with Anthony in the middle of the group. The party comprised eleven gentlemen and five ladies, all of them Tories apart from Anthony, so he had some 'lively talks and arguments'.

Portrait photograph of Anthony in a stove-pipe hat by Herbert Watkins. There are pictures of him in a variety of headgear – conventional top-hats, bowler hats, and an informal, low-crowned, flat-topped hat with an upturned brim in which he looked decidedly raffish.

Caricature by 'Sem'. Versions of Anthony, a gift to caricaturists, appeared repeatedly in the public prints.

Portrait of Anthony by Samuel Laurence, commissioned by George Smith. Both Anthony and Rose were delighted with it.

John Tilley, Anthony's brother-in-law and his superior in the Post Office, who retired with a knighthood in 1880.

Tom Trollope in old age, inscribed by his widow Fanny to the sister of Charles Stuart-Wortley.

A characteristic study of Anthony from the late 1860s. He was deeply interested in and observant of the way women dressed, and regretted that a man who wore bright clothes was condemned as 'a popinjay', yet he never managed to wear his own clothes well or elegantly. Note the creases in the heavy material of the trousers, the rumpled waistcoat, and the straining button of the jacket. This was the angle from which he was most frequently photographed. Perhaps it was the one he preferred. Short sight rather than displeasure accounts for the deep frown-lines between his eyebrows, but he is not altogether at ease. Anthony disliked being photographed, and thought that the contemporary fashion for the 'bringing out and giving of photographs, with the demand for counter photographs, is the most absurd practice of the day' (*Phineas Finn*).

Rose in her widowhood in the late 1890s, posing on a sleigh against a studio backdrop in Kitzbühel, Austria.

Henry Merivale Trollope (Harry) the elder of Anthony and Rose's two sons. Neither of Harry's two children ever married.

Frederic James Anthony Trollope, their younger son, who emigrated to Australia. His descendants have inherited the family `baronetcy.

suitable offer of marriage. It sounds like a prolonged nightmare. Apart from a couple of months in Italy each winter she saw little of her father. Bice's contribution as a guest was her exotic charm and her singing voice; she was in demand to sing at evening parties. She had a disappointment that spring of 1873 in the defection of one Neptune Blood (who sounds like a character from one of her uncle's novels), the son of a house where she spent much time. 'The best would be not to forget him, but to remember him without any painful feeling,' her stepmother advised her from Rome.

The Montagu Square house became a safe haven for Bice, and a convenient base for London balls and parties. 'Your uncle seems to be a little afraid that, as you go out so much, you may over-do the singing, and tire yourself,' Fanny wrote in May 1874. Fanny tried to monitor, at long-distance, Bice's social circle: 'Where does Mrs Higford Burr live? Does your Aunt Rose visit her?' There was the eternal struggle over money. Bice did not know whether she should tip the servants at 39 Montagu Square when she left. Fanny wrote saying that 'Papa' advised giving something to 'your Aunt's maid (who I presume has attended on you) and the man servant if the latter has been sent out often on your business, or to take charge of you. He says you may give the man and maid fifteen shillings each', and if she did not have enough she was to ask her uncle to advance it.

Bice continually reproached Tom and Fanny for her poverty, saying she had nothing to wear. She had a good case: the money Tom was withholding was her own, left to her by her mother. A pompous, confused letter to her from Tom written in May 1876 sums up the situation:

> I pointed out to you when that arrangement [her allowance of £75 a year] was made, that in paying me £200 a year for your living *and journeys*, you would be paying much less than what they really cost, and less therefore than you ought to contribute to the joint family expenses, having the means of doing so. . . . You will reply that this money – £275 a year in gross – is yours. It is so. I might rejoin that I can not be expected to maintain by my labour, a daughter who has such an income of her own.

427

But since he was retaining £200 of Bice's money it was she who was subsidising *him*. She made the point, forcibly and in distress, feeling that she had simply made over her small fortune to him and Fanny, from which he doled out minuscule sums under protest.

The organising of her sterile round of English visits was another agony. 'Is anything settled about your visit to the Bagots; – or to Mrs Hay-Murray? – or to Madame Schmidt?' A new romance developed, with Madame Schmidt's son Herbert; but nothing came of it, and Tom reproached his daughter for talking 'incautiously and indiscreetly' about her abortive engagements.

Fanny's sister Ellen Ternan, having reinvented herself and shed fourteen years from her real age, married in 1876 a much younger man called George Wharton Robinson, who was told absolutely nothing about her years with Dickens. The couple took over a school in Margate, where Fanny and Tom Trollope often stayed with them. But there was rarely room there for Bice. 'I thought it likely,' Fanny wrote to her step-daughter, 'that some of the numerous friends who have often invited you, might receive you on a visit during our stay in Margate; for Nelly's house is not large enough to hold us all. If you get no invitation, I see nothing for it, but that you should go away with your Aunt [Rose] and Florence. . . .' When Harry and Florence were both at home, there was no room for Bice in Montagu Square either. Rose too had to hunt around among Bice's circle of acquaintances for somewhere she could go. How fortunate, wrote Tom on one such occasion, that Bice had found somewhere else. 'For you expected that you could remain at Montagu Square till your Aunt left London . . . you would have been simply on the pavé!'

Anthony was extremely fond of Bice. He was not a particularly musical man but his emotions were easily stirred. 'I wish you could hear our Bice play & sing,' he wrote to Mary Holmes. 'She affects me, as nothing else that I know in music.' Readers of his novels have to recognise Bice's pattern of life, though not her physical features, in that of Arabella Trefoil in *The American Senator*, written in 1875. Arabella, well-born but penniless, 'had long known that it was her duty to marry, and especially her duty to marry well'. She had been at the dreadful work for years, and was growing 'sick of the dust of the battle and conscious of fading strength', and sick of the effort to elicit invitations to the country houses where her current prey was to be staying. The authorial voice wondered 'which was the hardest part of the work, the hairdressing and the painting and companionship of the lady's maid, or the continual smiling upon unmarried men for whom she did not in the least care!'

Arabella Trefoil shamelessly placed herself in compromising situations with the sexually opportunistic Lord Rufford who, having kissed her in the heat of many moments (skilfully engineered by her), ought by convention to have married her. Skilled in the Trollopian letters-game, Arabella began a letter to him before they had even left Mistletoe, her ducal uncle's Lincolnshire seat, 'but the composition was one which required great care, and it was copied and re-copied till she had been two days in Hampshire'.

Humiliated by Lord Rufford's indifference, Arabella lost the remains of her beauty: 'She was haggard, almost old, with black lines round her eyes.' Arabella's mother very politely blackmailed Lord Rufford. He 'took a bit of paper and writing on it the figures "£6,000", pushed it across the table. She gazed at the scrap for a minute, and then, borrowing his pencil without a word, scratched out his lordship's figures, and wrote "£8,000" beneath them; and then added, "no one to know it." '

'I have been, and am still very unafraid of Arabella Trefoil,' Anthony wrote to Anna Steele before *The American Senator* came out in book form. 'The critics have to come, and they will tell me that she is unwomanly, unnatural, turgid, – the creation of a morbid imagination, striving after effect by laboured abominations.' Yet he swore to Mrs Steele that he had known Arabella Trefoil – 'not one special woman, not one Mary Jones or Sarah Smith, – but all the traits, all the cleverness, all the patience, all the courage, all the self-abnegation, – and all the failure.'

Whoever else contributed to the creation of Arabella, poor Bice had played her part. Anthony did not, he told Mrs Steele, see his Arabella as a damned soul. 'Think of her virtues; how she works, how true she is to her vocation [getting a husband], how little there is of self-indulgence, or of idleness. I think that she will go to a kind of third class heaven in which she will always be getting third class husbands.' (Bice was to be rewarded with a first-class husband, in this world, three years later.) The critics were not particularly upset by Arabella Trefoil. Only the New York *Nation* found her part in the story 'repulsive'.

When they first came home from Australia Anthony and Rose had been shocked by the rise in the cost of living. He could not get a good cigar for under eight pence,* and resolved to try pipe-smoking: 'Meat I have already given up, & clothes. I shall endeavour soon to live without coals. Tea and toast at the club for sixpence seems to be the only cheap thing left & I shall live upon that.' Agricultural workers, miners, tradesmen in the building industry, bakers and gas-workers had come out on strike during 1872: the 'deference society' was loosening up.

Anthony thought it was the mania for advertising that had sent up the price of coal. The coal merchants used once, he wrote, to push slips of paper through the letter-box; then the slips started to come in envelopes, marked 'Coal', and 'our wife, meaning to be economical, and thinking that something might be gained, would keep them, and they perplexed us by their reappearance.' As the 1870s progressed, coal merchants' advertisements were made to look 'like a private letter, and sent through the post'. Thus he identified and deplored, in *London Tradesmen*, the early manifestations of junk mail.

The new four-storey house had to be painted, papered and furnished. In Anthony's younger days, as he wrote to 'my dear Rusden',† his friend in Melbourne, a house could be modestly furnished for £200. 'Now I am told that £1500 for the rough big things is absolutely indispensable, and that prettinesses may be supplied afterwards for a further £500.'

Anthony's priority when they moved in to Montagu Square was to settle his 5,000‡ books on the new open shelves. (He and Florence evolved a ritual of dusting all the books twice a year.)

---

* By 1876 he was down from six cigars a day to a single one, which he said was like giving a horse a single straw a day.

† He put G. W. Rusden up for membership of the Garrick immediately on his return home, and wrote to him from the club in February 1873: 'You have been elected here without a single black ball. Perhaps that was because no one knew you. . . . God be with you, dear friend, and come over and teach the Garrickers billiards as soon as you can.'

‡ Tom had collected nearly three times as many, and sold 3,000 of them with his Florentine possessions.

The books overflowed into the double drawing-room on the first floor; in a recess at one end, where Anthony liked to sit for private talks, were shelved the old plays and theatre books he had bought from Robert Bell's estate. Some of these he gave away as a wedding-present to the Pollocks' son Walter in 1876.

While he was arranging his books he got Florence to compile a catalogue. It was not a very efficient catalogue, but then Florence, aged eighteen, had no experience. The books were listed alphabetically by title or author, indiscriminately. As well as English literary texts from the earliest times to his own contemporaries (both poetry and prose), the family's works, runs of periodicals, editions of the classics, topographical works, and masses of historical and political reference material, Anthony's library contained seventeenth-century cookery books, books on horse-doctoring and horse-management, on art, insects, witchcraft, Celtic languages; a Hebrew grammar; John Ball's *Peaks, Passes and Glaciers*, Townsend's *Facts in Mesmerism*, and a book (no author given) called *Diseases of Literary and Sedentary Persons*.

He had a few copies of the catalogue printed, to give to friends.* His library, or book-room, was in an extension at the back of the house between the ground floor, which housed the dining-room, and the drawing-room floor above. On the mantelpiece in his book-room lay a tangle of spectacles, amongst which he would rummage to find the pair he wanted. His daily routine was the same as ever, but pitched a good deal later. He still did his writing in the mornings before breakfast – but his breakfast was not until half-past eleven.

When the catalogue was done, 'and the new furniture had got into its place, and my little book-room was settled sufficiently for work, I began a novel, to the writing of which I was instigated by the commercial profligacy of the age.' This was to be the masterpiece *The Way We Live Now*. It is essence of Trollope. If he had written no other novel, *The Way We Live Now* would have ensured his immortality, though he could not have written it if he had written no other novel. It grew out of the compost of a lifetime's observation, anger, amusement and writing experience.

He embraced in his satire, with an understanding that

---

* A copy survives in the Forster Collection in the Victoria & Albert Museum, inscribed to 'John Forster – with kind regards from A.T. April 1874'.

bordered in some cases on affection, all his preoccupations – the corruption of the literary world, the Church of England and the flaccid beliefs of its adherents, the venal world of love and marriage, the financial world of insider dealings and City frauds, and the society world. Because he was Anthony Trollope, it is the people that we remember – the desperate authoress Lady Carbury, and the futile aristocrats, the Longestaffes, Grendalls and Nidderdales, and the betrayed heiress Marie Melmotte. Felix Carbury was after Marie's money, just as Lord Nidderdale was interested in a Miss Goldsheiner 'if the money's really there'. With a degree of realism, given the importance of a girl's 'fortune' in even the best of Trollopian marriages, Nidderdale remarked that 'It's a pity there shouldn't be a regular statement published with the amount of money, and what is expected in return. It'd save a deal of trouble.' The girls – though not Marie – were equally false in their own way, 'with padding and false hair without limit'.

Rich Jews were a feature of the new dispensation. Georgiana Longestaffe, on the marriage market for twelve weary years, accepted the proposal of a Jew, a decent person but 'absolutely a Jew; – not a Jew that had been . . . but a Jew that was', with dyed hair and beard. Her family were horrified; but daughters no longer deferred to their parents:

> 'It's worse than your wife's sister. I'm sure there's something in the Bible about it. . . . An accursed race; – think of that, Georgiana; – expelled from Paradise.'
> 'Mamma, that's nonsense.'

(Not that she married him.) And Melmotte, though he beat and abused her, could not in the end control his daughter Marie.

Jews were becoming part of the social fabric, as were Americans. The very English Henrietta Carbury, confronting her rival in love Winifred Hurtle, thought: 'How full of beauty was the face of that American female, – how rich and glorious her voice in spite of a slight taint of the well-known nasal twang; and above all how powerful and at the same time how easy and how gracious was her manner!'

Anthony's picture of the weakened, dishonoured English upper class was not misjudged. Moreton Frewen, a great-nephew of the Trollopes' old friend Madame Mohl, and a young man himself in the 1870s, recalled in his memoirs* how the landed gentry, their feudal functions eroded by two Reform Acts, degenerated into an army of 'rich, well-dressed, absolutely idle people' who lived only for sport and the social round, their ranks swollen by the equally idle sons of ironmasters and coal barons, who had become gentlemen, and did not work. The latter group were money-rich; the aristocrats were land-rich, and land was no longer the prime source of ready cash.

The 'new rich' were not a new phenomenon, but the 'new poor' – a phrase Anthony used in this novel, perhaps for the first time – were. The ball given by Madame Melmotte, the cowed Jewish wife of the foreign tycoon, in their house in Grosvenor Square, cost £60,000. All the aristocracy flocked to it. The Prince of Wales put in an appearance.

The lazy young scions of the landed gentry wasted their time in the clubs or became 'something in the City' – another Trollopian phrase much used in *The Way We Live Now*, and which like 'the new dispensation' has passed into the language. With their fathers they sat on Melmotte's board, lending respectability and what capital they had, understanding absolutely nothing and hoping for quick fortunes from foreign railways.

The shares were notional, the foreign railways very vague. 'Were I to buy a little property, some humble cottage with a garden, or you, O reader, unless you be magnificent, – the money to the last farthing would be wanted, or security for the money more than sufficient, before we should be able to enter in upon our new home. But money was the very breath of Melmotte's nostrils, and therefore his breath was taken for money.' Questions might be asked, but Melmotte had answers; the gentlemen did not understand the nature of credit. 'It was part of the charm of all dealings with this great man that no ready money seemed ever to be necessary for anything', whether shares, property or companies.

The Way We Live Now is a great shout in the long conversation that Anthony Trollope sustained, and sustains, with his readers about the betrayal of all that is 'honest and true'. Always, for him,

* Moreton Frewen, *Melton Mowbray and Other Memories*, Herbert Jenkins, 1924. Nicknamed Mortal Ruin, he was an example of the decadence he described, squandering the diminished fortunes of his aristocratic connections in disastrous investment schemes.

the worst aspect of individual dishonesty was that it corrupted the whole community by being perceived as success, and rewarded. 'If dishonesty can live in a gorgeous palace with pictures on all its walls, and gems in all its cupboards, with marble and ivory in all its corners, and can give Apician dinners, and get into Parliament, and deal in millions, then dishonesty is not disgraceful, and the man dishonest after such a fashion is not a low scoundrel. Instigated, I say, by some such reflections as these, I sat down in my new house to write *The Way We Live Now*' (*Autobiography*).

Kate Field was in London again in June 1873, and came to a dinner party at 39 Montagu Square on her second night in town. Robert Browning and Wilkie Collins were fellow guests, the latter writing to Anthony in answer to the invitation: 'Yes I have heard of the American lady – she is adored by everybody, and I am all ready to follow the general example.' Which he did, taking Kate subsequently to see his successful play *The New Magdalen* at the Olympic.

Browning called on her too, remembering old days in Florence, and read her a new poem, but Kate and Mr Browning no longer got on. (He had complained to Isa Blagden, during Kate's 1871 visit, that she was too tied up with sightseeing and 'Women's Rights, Anti-Contagious Disease agitation and so on' to see much of him.) Anthony called on Kate too, often, in the mornings, and she came again to Montagu Square: 'My wife has written to ask you to come and dine here. If you will come, (which pray do) we will discuss the album [Landor's] – But in truth I know nothing about it.'

Anthony added that two of Kate's 'wildest countrymen' were dining with him along with other friends at the Garrick the following week; they were Mark Twain and the poet Joaquin Miller, 'the Oregon Byron'. It seemed to Twain that both Anthony and another English guest Tom Hughes (author of *Tom Brown's Schooldays*) snobbishly paid more attention to The Hon. E. F. Leveson-Gower, a politician and the son of Earl Granville, than to himself or Miller. Not that Miller was silent: 'He and Trollope talked all the time and both at the same time, Trollope pouring forth a smooth and limpid and sparkling stream of faultless English, and Joaquin discharging into it his muddy and tumultuous mountain torrent.' It is unusual to see Anthony, for once, as the 'smooth' man.

So far as Kate was concerned the fire was not out, but the blaze had died down. Anthony felt old. When he and Rose were on holiday in Ireland for six weeks in autumn 1873, in the middle of the writing of *The Way We Live Now*, he became deaf. He wrote to Juliet Pollock, after seeing a doctor on his return: 'I fear I have lost the hearing of one ear for always.' He felt he was always about to be run over on the street, and people kept talking to him 'on the wrong side': 'I am told that a bone has grown up inside the orifice. Oh dear! One does not understand it at all. . . . Why should anything go wrong in our bodies? Why should we not be all beautiful? Why should there be decay? – why death? – and, oh, why, damnation? . . . When are you coming home? The square is desolate without you.'

In summer 1874 Rose and Anthony holidayed in Germany, Switzerland and Austria, taking Florence and Bice with them and meeting up with Harry in the Black Forest. Their favourite resort had become the pretty village of Höllenthal, near Freiburg. Höllenthal is maybe the 'Brunnenthal' of the story 'Why Frau Frohmann Raised Her Prices', written in the mid-1870s, which contains the most detailed and most dedicated description of a long, delicious dinner in all the food-filled Trollope oeuvre. As the author interpolated, 'And when a middle-aged man is taken away from the comforts of his home, how is he to console himself in the midst of his idleness unless he has a good dinner?' Not that Anthony was in idleness. Between April and mid-September he wrote *The Prime Minister*.

By the end of that September (1874) Anthony knew he would have to leave the comforts of home to make the long journey to Australia again. Fred was in financial trouble. As so often, Anthony was ill over Christmas and the New Year. 'A wretched attack of bile and deficient liver came to me in the middle of all that cold & very nearly upset me,' he told John Blackwood on 6 January 1875. 'At present I am so weak that I can only just crawl. But I am attaining to a slow but manly desire for mutton chops and sherry, and am just beginning to think once again of the glories of tobacco.' He explained that he was returning to Australia to give Fred 'a helping hand': 'I can see what money I can advance to him out of my small means, and settle certain things with him.' As for Harry (who came home for one week in September 1874 before taking himself off abroad again), he was 'coming out in the family line, having an article in February's Macmillan [*Macmillan's* magazine] on the French Stage, which of course I regard as the best thing ever written on that subject.'

But Harry quarrelled with *Macmillan's* about editorial changes, and withdrew his article. Anthony stepped in and sent Harry's article on to William Allingham, the editor of *Fraser's*, which ultimately published it. Anthony's feeling for his sons was not just a matter of family pride or paternal duty. It was unconditional, from the gut. A little more detachment on his part would have been better for both the boys.

He was hunting again within a week of his illness, and 'had an episode', as he put it to Alfred Austin: 'I got into a muddy ditch, & my horse had to blunder over me, through the mud. He trod three times on my head. When I saw the iron of his foot coming down on my head, I heard a man on the bank say – "He's dead." I am strapped up with plasters as to my forehead, but otherwise quite uninjured. You may imagine that in the scrimmage I had a queer moment.' His deafness, and the seriousness of his falls, brought on depression.

Then on 1 March, having corrected the proofs of *The Prime Minister*, he set off. He went via Italy, visiting Tom in Rome, and Tom accompanied him to his ship in Naples. 'Give my best love to Harry & Flo. God bless you. Keep up your heart & be as happy as you can,' Anthony wrote to Rose from Rome. And from Naples: 'God bless you dearest. . . . I have been troubled with sore throat, which has made me weak & I have been very glad of the quinine. I shall get rid of it when I get to sea.' Rose, accompanied by Florence, and with Harry as escort and guide, was to fill in the time by touring in Germany – 'We roam about', is how she unenthusiastically put it in her chronology.

As usual, Anthony had the ship's carpenter rig up a table in his cabin, 'and I have done my work very regularly.' He was writing *Is He Popenjoy?* (which he finished before reaching Melbourne). There was a mishap, which he reported to Rose as the ship approached Aden: 'You remember my big bottle of ink. When I unlocked the desk I found the bottle smashed to pieces inside the case. . . . There were three shirts on top to make things steady. I wish you could see those three shirts,' he wrote to his 'dearest, dearest love'. 'And there were 100 loose cigars. I have not yet tried how cigars, bathed in ink, smoke; but I shall try.' All his 'beautiful white paper' was now fringed with ink, 'black-edged'.

Not even Anthony could sell a second book about Australia; but he had arranged with Nicholas Trübner* to send back a series of twenty 'letters', i.e. articles, about 36,000 words in all, which Trübner sold on to the *Liverpool Mercury* and other provincial newspapers, paying Anthony £15 a letter, which was not generous.

These pieces are freer and funnier and more open to the democratic idea than his big Australia book, while covering much the same ground – some of it from memory, since he did not revisit all the colonies – and with the addition of an account of Ceylon. He enjoyed a two weeks' stop-over there, staying with his old friend Sir William Gregory, who was Governor. New surroundings still stimulated him; he made long uncomfortable excursions, excited by the beauty of the mountains, the flowers and the luscious vegetation. He understood the centrality of coffee in the country's economy – and also how it was threatening the ecology. 'The lovely sloping forests are going, the forests through which elephants have trampled for we do not know how many more than 2,000 years; and the very regular but ugly coffee plantations are taking their place.' He went on an elk-hunt, and conceived an uncharacteristic ambition to shoot a wild elephant. He never even saw an elephant, but came near to one, 'within thirty yards I would say, crushing his way through the jungle and flying from us down the steep mountainside. The growth was so thick that we could not catch a glimpse even of his tail.'

Once with Fred at Mortray (in Australia's winter), Anthony found a letter from Millais, full of gossip about Garrick feuds, and answered him on 30 June 1875: 'I wonder what you would think of the kind of life I am living here. . . . I write for four hours a day, then ride after sheep or chop wood or roam about in the endless forest up to my knees in mud. I eat a great deal of mutton, smoke a

---

* Nicholas Trübner (1817–84): literary agent, publisher, linguist, translator and distinguished orientalist, born in Heidelberg. Anthony's former publisher William Longman met him in Germany as a young man and started him off in London as 'foreign corresponding clerk' at Longmans. Trübner became a close friend of G. H. Lewes, through whom Anthony probably met him.

great deal of tobacco, and drink a moderate amount of brandy and water. At night I read, and before work in the morning I play with my grandchildren, – of whom I have two and a third coming.' He had begun writing *The American Senator* for serialisation in *Temple Bar*, which was owned by Bentley's. The Trollopes' old acquaintance Richard Bentley had died in 1871, and the publishing business was now run by his son George.

Susie and Fred's second baby was called Harry after his English uncle. Anthony's apparent integration in the family bears out what was passed down the generations; the youngest of Fred's eight children, Gordon Clavering Trollope, born after Anthony's death, wrote that Anthony showed Susie 'invariable respect and affection', liking to sit and hear her sing, 'and there are still in existence [1930] some of the lovely ballads of the day which he gave to her.' If there ever had been a coolness, it was forgotten. The coolness had probably been Rose's all along. Gordon Trollope, in the same family reminiscence,* referred to his grandmother as Anthony's 'little wife', who 'hated the country [Australia], and said many unkind things about it', for which Anthony got the blame.

Anthony's letter to Millais from Mortray continued sadly. Fred, he said, 'seems to me to have more troubles on his back than any human being I ever came across. I shall be miserable when I leave him because I do not know how I can look forward to seeing him without again making this long journey. I do not dislike the journey, or the sea, or the hardship. But I was 60 the other day, and at that age a man has no right to look forward to making many more voyages round the world.'

In one of his articles for Trübner, Anthony wrote that there was one class of person who should never emigrate to Australia. 'This is the young gentleman, who, finding that no one wants him at home, thinks that he may as well emigrate. Neither will anyone want him here. And here no [one] will pity him. At home he may get some compassion and some aid.' Anthony was bringing that compassion and aid out to Fred, whose problem was that his sheep run was too small and undercapitalised to survive drought and variable wool-prices.

After going through the accounts, he and his father decided

* Gordon Trollope, 'Trollope in Australia', *Sydney Bulletin*, April 1930.

Mortray would have to be sold. They went together to see the bank, and Anthony called his contacts into play – Sir James Martin, a former Premier of New South Wales, and Sir Patrick Jennings, both of whom had entertained Anthony on his previous visit. They and other bigwigs were kindly disposed towards Fred, but to little avail. Anthony gave a power of attorney to Sir Hercules Robinson, Governor of New South Wales, by which arrangement Fred, if he sold Mortray, would not embark on another speculation without informing his father, who would then tell Sir Hercules how much he could 'sign for' on Anthony's behalf. If Fred did sell Mortray, Sir Hercules was empowered to guarantee Fred's overdraft at the bank on Anthony's behalf to the tune of £7,000. This was generous to Fred, but also humiliating.

After Anthony was home again, he forwarded to Harry a long letter from Fred about his financial situation: 'The loss of money has been lamentable, – £4,600!! But it is a kind of misfortune which I can bear.' The son of a non-providing father, Anthony gloried, too much, in being able to provide. 'Poor dear Fred,' he added, to Harry. 'Do not suppose from what I have said on the other side that I blame him.'

Fred's intention was to become a 'managing partner' in some economically viable run; but the year after his father's visit, having sold Mortray, he part-paid for some 'back blocks' at Booroondara East, north-west of Mortray. He was discouraged and unwell, and could not complete the purchase. Susie produced their third child, another boy, called Freddy. Fred in desperation took a job as Inspector of Conditional Purchases – very apt – in the Lands Department. Susie and the children stayed in Sydney and he was posted miles away to Inverell, in the Grafton district.

Fred was twenty-nine, his pastoral dream had exploded, and in January 1878 he had to ask his father to give Sir Hercules Robinson renewed power of attorney to guarantee the money still owing on Booroondara, which he wanted to keep as an investment. Anthony agreed to back Fred's bill 'up to £700'.

As well as seeing Fred in 1875, Anthony fulfilled some public engagements in Sydney, speaking at a farewell lunch for the New Guinea Scientific Expedition, accompanying the Governor to a military parade on the Queen's birthday, appearing – ironically – on the platform at the O'Connell Centenary celebration, attending another river picnic in his honour, speaking everywhere with good humour and welcomed because, and sometimes in spite, of his Australia book.

He went home via San Francisco. 'I do not think that in all my travels I ever visited a city less interesting to the normal tourist.' Apart from 'the biggest hotel in the world' – not to his taste – he found nothing worth seeing. But he enjoyed the week-long train-ride to New York, with his priorities well catered for: 'an excellent bed and ample accommodation for washing the hands and face'.

Crossing the Atlantic on board the *Bothnia*, Anthony met another of the mother-and-daughter combinations he liked so well: wealthy Mrs Katherine Bronson, who lived partly in Venice, and her fourteen-year-old Edith. They became his boon companions on the voyage. In 1882, when he could no longer write easily, he dictated to Florence a letter to Mrs Bronson: 'I well remember our journey . . . and our innocent little card-playing, and more innocent little suppers.' When Anthony used the word 'innocent' in this gratuitous way it was a sign that his fantasy had been engaged.

Henry James, rising thirty and already a published author, was also on board the *Bothnia*, and reported on the English novelist to his family in Boston: 'We also had Anthony Trollope, who wrote novels in his state room all morning (he does it literally every morning of his life, no matter where he may be), and played cards with Mrs Bronson all the evening. He has a gross and repulsive face and manner, but appears *bon enfant* when you talk with him. But he is the dullest Briton of them all.'

Henry James often denigrated the British in his letters home, as a form of residual patriotism. He met Anthony again in London, at Edward Dicey's, and at a party at Lord Houghton's, and came to understand and appreciate him in spite of superficial in-compatibilities. Henry James was edgily astute about Anthony's writing because he was constructing in his own fictions, and in his own manner, a similarly broad sweep of social interaction as well as a similarly intimate sexual discourse. After Anthony died Henry James wrote for the New York *Century Magazine** a sustained and sensitive assessment of his genius – he used that word – which has never been bettered.

---

* Reprinted in *Partial Portraits* (1888). James's letter from the *Bothnia* is in Leon Edel (ed.), *Henry James: Selected Letters*, Belknap/Harvard University Press, 1987.

—— * ——

On board the *Bothnia* Anthony was writing not a novel but the first pages of his autobiography, the profit-and-loss account of his life and work. He continued it in the book-room at 39 Montagu Square. He was in a valedictory mood. 'I am hunting again with the fears as to frosts and trembles as to fast bursts; but I think this will be the last of it. I am over 60, and poor Fred will want some more money,' he told G. W. Rusden. 'Of whist and the clubs I am getting very sick. I generally play at the Athenaeum now; – but it is a dull set, and I am not happy there. After a man has done making love there is no other thing on earth to make him happy but hard work.'

This winter of 1875–76 was his last hunting season. Towards the end of his autobiography, he wrote: 'Now at last, in April 1876, I do think that my resolution has been taken. I am giving away my old horses, and any body is welcome to my saddles and horse-furniture.'

As for love. . . . It is hard not to assume that his sexual life with Rose had come to an end. He was to write in *Ayala's Angel*: 'Faith, honesty, steadfastness of purpose, joined to the warmest love and the truest heart, will not enable a husband to maintain the sweetness of that aroma which has filled with delight the senses of the girl who has leaned upon his arm as her permitted lover.' This awkward sentence suggests the woman's desire waning rather than the man's. Perhaps he reversed genders out of gallantry. He made a deliberate reversal of stereotypical wife-behaviour, to comic effect, in *The Last Chronicle of Barset*: 'A man must produce romance, or at least submit to it, when duly summoned, even though he should have a sore throat or a headache.' It is just possible that so much of his energy, including his sexual energy, was expended in writing fiction that there had never been enough left over for Rose. It is equally possible that his fantasies had hitherto found an outlet in his secret life with her and that he mourned the loss.

He inserted in the autobiography a paragraph which constituted, for a private man, a public declaration: 'There is an American* woman, of whom not to speak in a work purporting to be a memoir of my own life would be to omit all allusion to one of

* When Harry edited his father's autobiography for publication, after his death, he omitted the word 'American' in the interest of discretion, which only fuelled speculation.

the chief pleasures which has graced my later years. In the last fifteen years she has been, out of my family, my most chosen friend. She is a ray of light to me, from which I can always strike a spark by thinking of her. I do not know that I should please her or do any good by naming her. But not to allude to her in these pages would amount almost to a falsehood.'

Kate Field. Anthony did not intend that his autobiography should be published in his lifetime. Harry told William Blackwood, after Anthony's death, that his father had showed him the manuscript, and said, 'Now we'll lock it up and say no more about it,' and turned the key in a drawer of the writing-table in his book-room. He told Harry the main contents of a letter of instruction, dated 30 April 1876, which he locked up with the manuscript: Harry was to edit the autobiography after Anthony's death; he might omit any passage, but add nothing, except a preface. The book should be published, preferably by Frederic Chapman, as soon as possible after Anthony's death and 'ought to be worth some hundreds of pounds to you' – he mentioned £1,800 when locking the manuscript up – not as part of the general estate but as a personal gift to Harry made in Anthony's lifetime.

This was an emotional business, for Anthony. He ended the letter, knowing he would be dead when Harry read it, 'Now I say how dearly I have loved you.' He was dealing in realities – the manuscript, the money, his love for Harry. At the same time, his imagination was in play, just as if he were writing a novel. The autobiography was *An Autobiography*, and apparently and intentionally 'outer': 'It will not, I trust, be supposed by any reader that I have intended in this so-called autobiography to give a record of my inner life.' Towards the end of it, he listed his books to date and the money he made from each, adding up a grand total of £68,939.17.5. The autobiography was the romance of his life as he chose to tell it.

What Henry James was to call Anthony's 'gross fertility' was not yet exhausted. Eleven more novels, three biographical studies and a quantity of short stories and journalism lay ahead. But he would find them harder to place, and be paid rather less for them. As a notice of *The American Senator* in the *Spectator* put it in 1877, 'We take his more recent novels very much as we take English weather, – as something good in the main for health and amusement, though rarely offering special opportunities for either.' *The Way We Live Now*, first published in monthly numbers, did not come out in book form until July 1875, when he was with Fred in Australia, and few of the critics praised it, finding the characters vulgar and the tone cynical. Nevertheless Chapman & Hall had paid £3,000 for it. Anthony was never to get so much for a book again.

Only *The Times* reviewer did not take offence at the mirror held up to nature: 'As for Mr Melmotte, the vulgar millionaire, he is hero and heroine both in one. After all, love affairs are but child's play compared to the excitement and interest of floating a loan or forming a company, and men of the Melmotte type, who shoot every now and then with meteor-like suddenness across the London sky, are only too familiar to us all.' The reviewer was probably thinking of Baron Grant, born Gottheimer, a Jew from Dublin who was a pioneer of mass promotions and mail-shots, raising a million pounds in £20 shares (which never paid a dividend). Baron Grant built himself a huge house near Kensington Palace and, while Anthony was writing *The Way We Live Now*, he was developing the piece of waste ground that was Leicester Square, setting a statue of Shakespeare in the middle (which is still there). Grant, like Melmotte, dealt in dodgy foreign railways and mines. Like Melmotte, and like Hudson the Railway King, he crashed horribly – four years after *The Way We Live Now* was written.

Like an entrepreneur, every artist successful in his lifetime has a set span – whether twenty minutes or twenty years – during which his gift and the historical moment are in magic sympathy. This has no bearing on the quality of the work done before or after this set span, and the judgement of future generations is not affected. (We may, for example, rate *The Prime Minister* very highly, as contemporary critics mostly did not.) However, by the mid-1870s Anthony Trollope's significance for the mass of his contemporaries was waning. His historical moment was passing. He knew it.

Once he had written his autobiography he would have been content to die at any time. He was 'ready to go', and wanted no 'leisure evening of life', he told G. W. Rusden in 1876. He dreaded only 'physical inability and that mental lethargy which is apt to accompany it. No man enjoys life more than I do, but no man dreads more than I do the time when life may not be enjoyable.'

Two days after writing the valedictory letter to Harry and

locking the manuscript of the autobiography up in the drawer of his table (though he unlocked the drawer a few times over the next three years, and tinkered with the manuscript), he began writing *The Duke's Children*. The shock of this novel was, and still is, for his readers, that one learns in the first sentence that the Duchess of Omnium, the former Lady Glencora Palliser, has died. Her end counterpointed Anthony's anticipated end of his own story.

Lady Glencora was the love of his alternative life, and her marriage to Plantagenet Palliser, who became the Duke of Omnium, was his alternative marriage. 'By no amount of description or asseveration could I succeed in making any reader understand how much these characters with their belongings have been to me in my latter life,' he wrote in his autobiography – and, in one of his rare flashes of emotional flamboyance, 'they have served me as safety-valves by which to deliver my soul.'

'I think that Plantagenet Palliser, Duke of Omnium, is a perfect gentleman. If he be not, then am I unable to describe a gentleman. She is by no means a perfect lady; but if she be not all over a woman, then am I not able to describe a woman.' He developed their characters, growing older with them, like his readers, over thirteen years. 'To carry out my scheme I have had to spread my picture over so wide a canvas that I cannot expect that any lover of such art should trouble himself to look at it as a whole.' But *Can You Forgive Her?*, *Phineas Finn*, *The Eustace Diamonds*, *Phineas Redux*, *The Prime Minister* and *The Duke's Children* must be read in sequence, as he longed that they should be.

Lady Glencora and her husband move in and out of focus, sometimes in the foreground and sometimes in the background of the intricate tapestry of relationships between individuals and between 'sets' of people, sometimes central to the plot and sometimes peripheral. *The Small House at Allington* is really the story of Lily Dale and Johnny Eames, but here we met Plantagenet Palliser,* a grave twenty-five-year-old MP, heir to

* It's always interesting to speculate how Anthony Trollope found names for his characters. Thomas Palmer Eames, from a well-known family of West Country yeomen, was huntsman and Master of the Cotley Harriers, on the Somerset-Dorset borders, for thirty-one years from 1855. The family called Palliser owned Annestown, on the sea in Co. Waterford, Ireland, and hunted with the dashing Marquesses of Waterford. The artist Millais had a friend called William Pallisser (sic), who married one of his models.

the Duke of Omnium, engaging in a chilly flirtation with Lady Dumbello – who was Archdeacon Grantly's daughter Griselda, married and grown grand. (The Barchester novels cannot be separated from the Palliser novels; the Trollopian tapestry is indivisible.) We are told briefly that after this flirtation Mr Palliser married Lady Glencora MacCluskie, small and blue-eyed with 'short wavy flaxen hair, very soft to the eye', the daughter of the Lord of the Isles. And we learn that she is still in love with Burgo Fitzgerald, to whom she has given a lock of the flaxen hair.

Mr Palliser was an 'upright, thin, laborious man,' while Burgo was 'spendthrift, unprincipled and debauched' – and wildly handsome. The choice for Glencora was between the worthy man and the wild man, a choice echoed in the main plot of *Can You Forgive Her?*, which chiefly concerns not Lady Glencora but the proud and tiresome Alice Vavasor, torn between mild Mr Grey and her wicked scar-faced cousin George. Through Alice's eyes, we have a woman's-eye view of Lady Glencora: 'What a strange, weird creature she was, – with her round blue eyes and wavy hair, looking sometimes like a child and sometimes like an old woman! And how she talked! What things she said, and what terrible forebodings she uttered of stranger things that she meant to say.'

Glencora, in her early middle age, achieved her full efflorescence in *The Prime Minister*. Her husband, an unwilling Prime Minister, thin-skinned and consumed by self-doubt, shrank from fixing political appointments and dealing with applications for favour and office. Glencora gave dinner parties and house-parties and banquets, squandering her own fortune 'for his glory, – so that he might retain his position as a popular Prime Minister'.

Both husband and wife knew it was her spirit and cleverness that were keeping him in office. 'In such a state of things he of course, as her husband, must be the nominal Prime Minister.' He longed for a private life with her and their children, what she scathingly called 'a Darby and Joan life'. He told her he loved her for working to make him a great man. With candour, she replied: 'And myself a great man's wife.' He told her that he longed to share everything with her, but it was intolerable that she should interfere in public affairs, 'in all things there must at last be one voice that shall be the ruling voice'.

'And that is to be yours, – of course.'

'In such a matter as this it must be.'

'And, therefore, I like to do a little business of my own behind your back. It's human nature, and you've got to put up with it. I wish you had a better wife. I dare say there would be many who would be better. . . .'

'Oh, Glencora!'

Oh, Glencora. . . . Their relationship, like the Proudies', was the classic Trollopian conflict between public and private, and the male and female spheres. He: 'My enemies I can overcome, – but I cannot escape the pitfalls which are made for me by my own wife. I can only retire into private life and hope to console myself with my children and my books.' And she: 'I sometimes think, Plantagenet, that I should have been the man, my skin is so thick; and that you should have been the woman, yours is so tender.' To Mrs Phineas Finn she made the ultimate claim: 'They should have made me Prime Minister, and have let him be Chancellor of the Exchequer.'

In what way were the Pallisers 'safety-valves by which I have delivered my soul'? Anthony Trollope put into Plantagenet Palliser's mouth his own political philosophy of gradual social change, and created an honourable man unfitted to survive in public life by very reason of his high standards of honour. In a modest way, Anthony felt that about himself; but the weight of his grievance falls on the corrupting nature of public life. His politicians were no longer described as Olympians, as in his early novels. Lady Glencora expressed this disillusion in *The Prime Minister*: 'I remember when I used to think that members of the Cabinet were almost gods, and now they seem to be no bigger than the shoeblacks, – only less picturesque.' But their world still excited and attracted Anthony, as it did Lady Glencora.

He desired, admired, feared and pitied Lady Glencora. He felt she had taken a wrong turning. It was peculiarly perceptive of the anonymous *Times* reviewer to say that Melmotte, so bullyingly male in *The Way We Live Now*, was 'hero and heroine both in one'. He may have meant little by it. But the gender barriers which Anthony maintained so assiduously in his outside life melted in his fiction and, sometimes, in his private demeanour. The Rev. W. Lucas Collins wrote in his review of *An Autobiography** that

* W. L. Collins, 'The Autobiography of Anthony Trollope', *Blackwood's* magazine, November 1883.

Anthony's manner with friends who were ill or unhappy often 'had all the gentleness of a woman; and only those who knew him well were aware how much of this there was in his nature underlying a somewhat rough outside.'

Many of the women, however, whom Anthony created had very little gentleness about them; Collins's remark, perceptive though it is, accepts the conventional gender-stereotyping which Anthony, like a dog with a bone, worried over continually in his fiction. Often Anthony wrote from the viewpoint of a male supremacist under threat. Even in his later work, even after Lady Glencora, he could be merciless to card-carrying feminists. Yet he felt Lady Glencora's drive, her frustration and her sexuality as his own. Because he loved her he made her lovable.

CHAPTER EIGHTEEN

KATE Field spent much time in London in the late 1870s,
staying not far away from the Trollopes in New
Cavendish Street, off Portman Square. She ate her
Christmas dinner in 1876 at 39 Montagu Square. Inviting her,
Anthony said, 'I write because my wife is out of town – I add this
for the sake of propriety.' To Cecilia Meetkerke, wife of his
Hertfordshire cousin, he remarked ruefully on the way people
spoke about men of his age as if they were finished: 'In spirit I
could trundle a hoop about the streets, and could fall in love with a
young woman as readily as ever; as she doesn't want me, I don't –
but I could.'

Kate herself was not so young any more. In 1878 she turned
forty. In spring 1877 she appeared at the St James's Theatre in
London, under the stage-name Mary Keemle, in a comedy
translated from French by herself called *Extremes Meet*. She was
not a great actress; she was, they said, 'herself' on stage.
Spiritualism still absorbed her, and so for much the same reasons
('unknown forces' etc) did the telephone, about which she wrote a
score of articles after its first American demonstration in early
1877. She became a pioneer public relations officer, organising the
publicity and press releases for A. G. Bell when he brought the
telephone to London in 1878. At the press demonstration she was
in the forefront wearing a blue silk dress with rosebuds, and when
Queen Victoria commanded a private demonstration at Osborne
House on the Isle of Wight, it was Kate who sang 'Kathleen
Mavourneen' down the line to her from nearby Osborne Cottage.
(The Queen was not much impressed.)

Another of Kate's causes was the Shakespeare Memorial
Association, founded to raise money for a new theatre in
Stratford-on-Avon. The foundation stone was laid in spring 1877.
A year later Kate took part in the opening festival there, reciting
the inaugural poem in a Paris dress of silver-blue with water-lilies

dripping from her corsage, and later singing at a London benefit in creamy-white with pearls, and the locket given to her by Elizabeth Barrett Browning.

She was an effective fund-raiser, but failed with Anthony, who refused, with two exclamation marks, to send the requested five guineas. 'If there be any one who does not want more memorials than have already been given, it is Shakespeare. . . . Now don't you turn around and be cross with me. . . .' He had not many guineas to spare, he told her, and 'when I have I find so many mouths into which it can go; – mouths that want it, whereas neither Shakespeare nor Flower* want anything.'

In 1879 Kate went back to New York to found the Co-operative Dress Association on West 23rd Street, to provide employment for women making reasonably priced garments. It failed within two years. But the Bell Telephone Co. had paid her for her services in shares, which increased ten-fold in a very few years, so her money problems were over.

There was a lecture Kate gave, designed to combat the prejudice against women lecturing, which she sent to Anthony with a view to publication. He thought she protested too much. 'Who is the man of the world who exclaimed that "a lecturing woman is a disgrace to her sex"?' Perhaps he thought that she meant him. She had not, he said, addressed the real objections. These were (in his view) 'that oratory is connected chiefly with forensic, parliamentary and pulpit pursuits for which women are unfitted because they are wanted elsewhere; – because in such pursuits a man is taken from his home, and because she is wanted at home.'

One wishes that he had kept the letter from her which he answered, point by point, back in April 1870. 'You write as though I should find fault with your lecturing. I am not in the least disposed to do so. . . . I like your account of yourself, – with your handsome dress, looking as well as you can, and doing your work colloquially. I have no doubt you look very well. You could do that when you were not handsomely dressed, – and I should like to hear you lecture amazingly.'

Another point: 'I don't in the least understand why you should fly out against me as to matrimony. . . . I have said and say again

* C. E. Flower was the Stratford brewer behind the Memorial Theatre project, and himself contributed £30,000.

449

that I wish you would marry. But I have never advised you to marry a man for whom you did not care.' What he objected to, in principle, was her objection, in principle, to the idea of marriage. 'I do not like that tendency in you.' Married people, he said, had 'a better time' than bachelors and spinsters.

The next point: 'I never said you were like W. Petrie. I said that young woman did not entertain a single opinion on public matters which you could repudiate, – and that she was only absurd in her mode of expressing them – However we'll drop W.P. now.' Wallachia Petrie was the American poetess in Florence, 'the Republican Browning as she is called', in *He Knew He Was Right*: 'There were certain forms of the American female so dreadful that no wise man would wilfully come in contact with them. Miss Petrie's ferocity was distressing to [Mr Glascock], but her eloquence and enthusiasm were worse even than her ferocity.' Wallachia berated her friend Caroline Spalding for agreeing to marry Mr Glascock, which gave an opening for a weighty authorial sermon:

> We in England are not usually favourably disposed to women who take a pride in a certain antagonism to men in general, and who are anxious to show that they can get on very well without male assistance. . . . The hope in regard to all such women . . . is that they will be cured at last by a husband and half-a-dozen children. In regard to Wallachia Petrie there was not, perhaps much ground for hope. She was so positively wedded to women's rights, and to her own rights in particular.

There was no ambivalence about Anthony's opinion of the Wallachia Petries of this world, nor about his belief that masculine chivalry and babies were a fair exchange for women's subordinate role. Yet such were his empathy and intellectual honesty that he put into Wallachia's mouth words which expressed her viewpoint as trenchantly as anyone could: 'If you speak of a dog, you intend to do so with affection, but there is always contempt mixed with it. The so-called chivalry of man to woman is all begotten in the same spirit. I want no favour, and I claim to be your equal.'

As by now will be evident, his books are full of women who are equal, if not superior, to men. Sober-sided John Eustace in *The*

Eustace Diamonds conceded that Lizzie, because of her coolness and cleverness, was 'a very great woman; and, if the sex could have its rights, would make an excellent lawyer.' All the significant and intelligent women in the Palliser novels – Lady Laura Kennedy, Violet Effingham, Lady Glencora, Madame Max Goesler – expressed their frustration about the limitations placed on their activities by reason of their sex. Their creator did not mock them – because these women, like Lizzie Eustace, were attractive, and passionately involved with men. Contrary to what a modern reader might presume, Madame Max Goesler was not being wholly ironic in this exchange with Phineas Finn (she was referring to the ladies' gallery, screened with a grille, in the House of Commons):

> 'A poor woman, shut up in a cage, feels more acutely than anywhere else how insignificant a position she fills in the world.'
> 'You don't advocate the rights of women, Madame Goesler.'
> 'Oh, no. Knowing our inferiority I submit without a grumble; but I am not sure that I care to go and listen to the squabbles of my masters.'

To advocate the rights of women actively, and to appear on a public platform for that purpose, was a very different matter from Kate Field giving lectures to private gatherings in a pretty frock. Ladies who addressed public meetings were, to Anthony and all conventional people, vulgar and embarrassing. It was hardly respectable even to attend them. The first large public meeting on the subject of women's suffrage had been in 1868. There was a notable gathering of the Women's Suffrage Society in the Hanover Square Rooms in 1870, where Anthony's progressive young friend Lady Amberley was on the platform, supported by her husband.

Anthony had a field day with the feminist activists in *Is He Popenjoy?*, and with imaginary 'Rights of Women' meetings in Marylebone. The full title of his fictional organisation was the 'Rights of Women Institute for the Relief of the Disabilities of Females', commonly known simply as the Disabilities. Leading lights were Lady Selina Protest and Baroness Banmann from Bavaria, who had 'a considerable moustache', and a copious bust beneath her 'virile collar'. There was also Aunt Ju Mildmay, an aristocratic battleaxe in what was to be the Wodehouse mode, and the bespectacled Dr Olivia Q. Fleabody from New England, 'an enthusiastic hybrid'.

Lord George Germain said Lady Selina and Aunt Ju were 'two old maids who have gone crazy about Women's Rights because nobody has married them'. But Lord George's young wife Mary, unhappy and unsatisfied, went to the meetings (to her husband's horror – he was no Lord Amberley), sitting up on the platform before an audience of 'strongly-visaged spinsters and mutinous wives, who twice a week were worked up by Dr Fleabody to a full belief that a glorious era was at hand in which women would be chosen by constituencies, would wag their heads in courts of law, would buy and sell in Capel Court, and have balances at their bankers'. Dr Fleabody 'made proselytes by the hundred, and disturbed the happiness of many fathers of families'.

There are pages of facetiousness at the women's expense, particularly about their appearance and their petty rivalries. Mary stopped attending the meetings because she was disgusted by the malicious jealousy between Fleabody and Banmann, and because in the end she put her marriage first.

Anthony, like his unlikeable Lord George Germain, placed sexual frustration at the centre of the feminist question. The Germains' marriage had been sexually dead. Alone with her husband in a railway compartment, Mary leaned against Lord George, 'inviting him to caress her'. (Like most men of his period, Anthony found railway compartments sexually exciting.) Lord George responded in some inadequate and gentlemanly fashion. 'It might still be that she would be able to galvanise him into that lover's vitality, of which she had dreamed. He never rebuffed her; he did not scorn her kisses. . . . But through it all, she was quite aware that she had not galvanised him as yet.' He was in fact being galvanised by someone else, a flirtatious married woman who criticised Mary, saying: 'Nor is she – passionate. You know what I mean.'

The Germains separated – but she had become pregnant, which made all the difference, and they were reconciled. Public submission and obedience, private independence of mind – that was quite acceptable to Anthony. What was not acceptable, because it terrified him, was anything that disturbed the happiness of 'fathers of families'. In *The Bostonians* (1885) Henry James was to treat feminist activism, women's friendships, women in public life and the counter-pull of sexual passion and sexual submission with far greater subtlety. Henry James's feminist Dr Birdseye echoed Anthony Trollope's Dr Fleabody, both of them being loosely based on the real-life New England reformer Dr Elizabeth Peabody, Nathaniel Hawthorne's sister-in-law.

At the end of June 1877 Anthony went to South Africa to write another travel book for Chapman & Hall, who paid him £850. It was not a sensible thing to do, given his state of health and mind. He also negotiated another series of travel letters with Trübner, even less well-paid than before.

He primed himself before leaving by speaking with a recently retired Governor of Cape Colony, Sir Henry Barkly, and other old Africa hands, who provided him with the necessary letters of introduction. He read a lot of books, and 'were I to continue the list as to include all the works I have consulted I should have to name almanacks, pamphlets, lectures, letters and blue books to a very great number indeed.' The essence of these was regurgitated in the historical and economic sections of his *South Africa*.

On board the *Caldera* he wrote to Harry, who was briefly at home with Rose and Florence before going with them on a tour of the Tyrol. Anthony left his business affairs in Harry's seemingly casual hands, sending back insistent queries about the disposition of £500 due to him from Smyrna Railway shares (a rather Melmotte-style investment) and instructions about paying his horses' livery bills; Anthony may have sold his heavy hunters but he still needed horses for riding with Florence in Hyde Park and for drawing the family brougham. They were being brought up from the country to stables in Montagu Mews. The Trollopes now had a groom-cum-manservant called Ringwood, Barney having taken to drink in his old age and gone off home to Ireland – maybe without letting the Trollopes know. It was more than four years later that Anthony wrote to Harry: 'Barney has turned up again as fresh as paint. We wrote to the Protestant parson, and he says he saw him walking about Banagher every day, – only just a little the worse for wear.'

Anthony was losing his taste for ship-board life. From the *Caldera* he confessed to Harry that 'I don't like anyone on board, but I hate two persons. There is an old man who plays the flute all the afternoon and evening. I think he and I will have to fight. And there is a beastly impudent young man with a voice like a cracked horn, who will talk to me.' He wished Harry luck in his 'biographical labours' – Harry was embarking on the ghost-writing of the life of Charles Bianconi, ostensibly by Bianconi's daughter. 'I am sure your mother could help you a good deal if you would let her.' This was a measure of Anthony's respect for Rose's judgement, as was his advice to Harry about appending his name as 'editor' of the biography: 'If the book be good I should, and I should take mamma's advice as to the goodness for she is never mistaken about a book being good or bad,' he wrote from the Transvaal. Anthony could not bear to let Harry make his own mistakes or get the measure of his mediocre talent himself. He wrote from Pietermaritzburg (where he stayed with Sir Henry Bulwer, Governor of Natal): 'If you have not sent your Academy article to Bentley, keep it back till I am home. We will then touch it up and try the Fortnightly.' So far as is known Harry's Academy article, already turned down by *Blackwood's*, never got published.

On the ship, Anthony finished *John Caldigate* and posted it off to Frederic Chapman from Capetown, which he first saw in mist, with Table Mountain invisible. His first impressions, he told John Blackwood after only a day there, were of a 'poor, niggery, yellow-faced, half-bred sort of a place, with an ugly Dutch flavour about it.' He started on his investigations with his customary wholeheartedness, attending a debate in the Assembly, dining at the house of the Governor, Sir Bartle Frere, and starting the writing of his book straight away.

'The country is very large. We may say so large as to be at present limitless. We do not as yet at all know our own boundaries' (*South Africa*). Much of Africa was a mystery in the mid-1870s, and much of the interior unpenetrated by white men. Yet within a decade the whole continent was being carved up between Germany, Italy, Portugal, France and Britain. Anthony was there in the dawn of the scramble for Africa; he was actually in Grahamstown, in the Eastern Province of Cape Colony, when Sir Theophilus Shepstone high-handedly annexed the Transvaal. He stayed at Government House in Pretoria as a guest of Shepstone's, though his host was heavily engaged elsewhere and they never met; one of Shepstone's aides, who found Anthony 'obstinate as a pig', was the twenty-one-year-old future novelist Henry Rider Haggard.

Anthony's itinerary took him from Capetown through the Eastern Province of Cape Colony, thence to Natal, the Transvaal and the Diamond Fields in Griqualand West, the Orange Free State, and back through the Western Province of Cape Colony (where he was pleasantly surprised by the wine). He visited the Native Territories – parts of modern Namibia, Botswana and Mozambique. He was in southern Africa just under six months, travelling by train where possible, otherwise on horseback, and mostly in two-wheeled carts on bad roads, 'very rough indeed for old bones'.

There was the usual difficulty over laundry. In Pietermaritzburg 'It must be acknowledged that the washing is dear, – and bad, atrociously bad; – so bad that the coming home of one's linen is a season for tears and wailing.' There was, as in Australia, a dumping of his heavy luggage, with the result that, as in Australia, he attended formal dinners in his honour in the roughest of travelling clothes, which was interpreted as eccentric or lacking in respect. These dinners, and the whole trip, were too long and too tiring for him. In his private notebook he expressed real anxiety that he might not be able to stay the course. About to go sightseeing around Mossel Bay, between Port Elizabeth and Durban, he wrote to Harry: 'The grandest scenery in the world to me would be Montagu Square.'

The tone of his writing about black people had changed, because he was in a black man's country, by which he meant one where the blacks were so overwhelmingly in the majority. Extension of British colonisation had for him an 'unnatural' quality in South Africa. His animus here, as ever, was directed against philanthropists on the other side of the world who called for instant racial equality but who themselves 'never take the negro into partnership, or even make him a private secretary'. He said in *South Africa* that colour should be no bar to voting-rights: 'the privilege should be conferred on black and white alike, with such a qualification as will admit only those who are fit.' In Britain, fitness for the franchise was measured economically. That would not do in South Africa, where black men in the mines could already earn more than white men in white collars. Education, he thought, should be the test.

He had one piece of luck; he met in East London a young man whom he described in the book as 'a gentleman of about a third of my own age, who had been sent out by a great agricultural-implement-making firm' to sell to the farmers via promotional brochures. This was George Herbert Farrar, eighteen years old, who was later to become a director of the East Rand mines and a member of the Transvaal Legislative Council. He and Anthony bought their own cart and horses, hired a driver, and made the arduous journey to the Diamond Fields together. Anthony, always at his best with the attractive and resourceful young, enjoyed the adventure, even camping out with his young friend on the veld. (We may suspect that Farrar did most of the work.) They 'determined that the water [for tea] should boil, that the proper number of tea-spoon-fulls should be afforded, and that the tea should have every chance. We certainly succeeded. And surely never was there such bacon fried, or such cold tongues extracted from tin pots.'

The best writing in *South Africa* was his evocation of the great diamond-mine at Kimberley. 'I will not describe to you', he wrote to Harry, 'this most detestable place because I must write about it, and you must read what I write. I have been handling diamonds till I am sick of them. But the great hole out of which they come is certainly the most marvellous place I have ever seen.' Diamond-mining, like gold-mining, both of them 'picking through dirt', bored and disgusted him. He felt ill all the time in Kimberley: 'Much feared that I was going to be knocked up,' he wrote in his notebook. Yet he created a great set-piece in his description, in *South Africa*, of the oblong pit nine acres in extent and 230 feet deep, divided up into hundreds of tiny claims separated by dykes and low mud walls, the whole surrounded and overhung by engines and shafts, pulleys and buckets, for extracting the earth. He described it by moonlight, silent and empty; he described it by day, under the burning sun, the earth-removing contraptions all in action, and with 3–4,000 men working shoulder to shoulder all over the bottom of the great pit. He re-created a scene from Dante's *Inferno*.

It was 160°F in Kimberley – hotter than the infernal regions, he told Harry. The flies and the dirt were too much for him. Tuesday 11 December 1877: 'Started for home!!! Never so homesick in my life.'

J. A. Froude, the historian and biographer of Carlyle, was also working on a book about South Africa. He knew more about it, having undertaken at the request of Lord Carnarvon, then the Colonial Secretary, a feasibility study of confederating the three British and two Dutch states. Anthony got his book out first, and it was very well received, praised by the critics for its freshness and vigour and going into four editions in two years. His success turned his acquaintance with Lord Carnarvon* into a friendship, and he and Rose subsequently went to Highclere, the Carnarvons' country house in Berkshire, for weekends in distinguished company.

Back home in early 1878, he collapsed with flu. His next task was to negotiate with William Blackwood over the serial publication of *John Caldigate* in *Blackwood's*. The Blackwoods tended cannily to stress how poorly much of Anthony's work for them had sold, in order to pay him less and delay publication. John Blackwood was growing old and ill – from now on much of the firm's work was done by his nephew William – but the elder Blackwoods and the Trollopes remained good friends in private life. Anthony's framed photograph ornamented the Blackwoods' drawing-room at 45 George Street in Edinburgh, and the two couples enjoyed playing whist together. Mrs Blackwood was an erratic player. 'It's no good giving her a hint,' her husband wrote to Anthony, 'as she always does the very reverse', tossing down 'unsupported Kings with reckless daring'. Anthony replied that when Mrs Blackwood was next in town 'I will take her whist into my own keeping.'

In his extended critique of the manuscript of *John Caldigate*, Blackwood remarked that Caldigate himself was too cold and complacent to be a sympathetic hero, but 'the infernal narrow minded mother is a good picture'. Part of this novel was set amid the squalor and struggle of the Australian gold-fields. The eponymous Caldigate, a Harrovian, had gone out to try his fortune as an alternative to sitting alone in a desolate house with his unsympathetic widowed father – a late return to Anthony's unhappy adolescence. On the way out, Caldigate had a ship-board

---

* The Carnarvons' family name was Herbert; Anthony was at Harrow with Sidney Herbert, Florence Nightingale's great supporter. The first Lord Carnarvon in the seventeenth century had been called Dormer, a surname Anthony appropriated for the central family in *Ayala's Angel*.

romance with a woman of doubtful character, who accompanied him to the gold-fields. On his return to England, he married sweet Hester Bolton.

The plot turns on a blackmail attempt and a court case: was Caldigate's liaison in Australia in fact a marriage? Was he a bigamist? Was his and Hester's baby a 'bastard'? The 'infernal narrow minded mother' who impressed old John Blackwood was Hester's mother Mrs Bolton, who separated her daughter from Caldigate for moral reasons, thinking to save her soul. Mrs Bolton was the evangelical, self-punishing Mrs Prime from *Rachel Ray*, writ blacker. She was a woman who thought it wicked not to be uncomfortable.

Caldigate's marital status turned on a technical postal conundrum, concerned with the decoding of the minuscule markings on postage stamps which denoted the date of issue. (It appears however, when scrutinised by philatelists, to have been a fictional technicality.*) A keen clerk, Mr Bagwax, was despatched from St Martin's-le-Grand in London to Sydney, to inspect the evidence. The author added a footnote: 'I hope my friends in the Sydney post-office will take no offence should this story reach their ears. I know how well the duties are done in that office, and, between ourselves, I think that Mr Bagwax's journey was quite unnecessary.' Anthony never lost his proprietory interest in post-office matters. As he wrote in *South Africa*, wherever he went he dropped in and gave a little good advice. 'Having looked after post-offices for thirty years at home I fancy that I could do very good service among the Colonies if I could have arbitrary power given to me to make what changes I pleased. My advice is always received with attention and respect. . . . But I never knew any instance yet in which any improvement recommended by me was carried out.'

'I shall never dare to look you in the face again. I am going to Iceland!' Anthony wrote to Ellen Ternan, now Mrs Robinson, in June 1878, less than six months after his return from South Africa. (And to Mrs Knower, around the same time: 'I suppose I shall continue to go somewhere, till I take the Great Journey on some

---

* See article in *Mekeel's Weekly Stamp News* (Portland, Maine), 31 May 1926, by Frank E. Robbins, which points out that New South Wales stamps had no small letters printed in their corners in the 1870s, and that even on British stamps the small letters did not refer to year of manufacture.

nearly approaching day. I do not much care how soon I may start.') Because of his trip to Iceland, the Robinsons changed the date of the annual sports day at their school in Margate, so that Anthony could give away the prizes and make a speech, as arranged. Fanny and Tom were staying with the Robinsons; Fanny reported to Bice that the sports went off 'brilliantly' and that Anthony made 'an excellent speech'.

The two-and-a-half week expedition to Iceland was organised by his Scottish friend John Burns (later Lord Inverclyde), chairman of the Cunard Steamship Co. and a leading member of the exuberant and energetic Gaiter Club. The party (some of whom had never met before) of five ladies and eleven gentlemen, with a crew of thirty-four, sailed via St Kilda and the Faroes in Burns's Irish yacht, the *Mastiff*, from his home at Wemyss Bay on the Clyde. The voyaging took up most of the time; they were only in Iceland for four days. There, sixty-five ponies were hired to carry the party and all their food, crockery, pots and pans, tents, blankets, mattresses 'for the ladies' and all their luggage to their destination – the hot-water geysers, seven miles inland from Reykjavik. (Anthony had seen better ones in New Zealand.)

The best account of all this is in the memoirs of one of the ladies of the party, Mrs Jemima Blackburn.* She was a small, witty, indefatigable fifty-five-year-old; 'her deaf husband Hugh, a scientist, stayed behind at Roshven, their remote home on the Moidart peninsula in the West Highlands. She was a gifted artist, and in the fifteen days they were away produced fifty-six paintings and drawings, many of them humorous group-studies of her companions, including Anthony.

Mrs Blackburn was a clever and cultivated woman, the daughter of a former Solicitor General for Scotland. She had known Thackeray and Landseer, was a friend of Millais and Ruskin, and had illustrated Froude's fable *The Cat's Pilgrimage*. Her drawings frequently featured in Norman Macleod's *Good Words*. It is clear from her memoirs that her favourite male companions on the expedition were young Albert Grey (later the fourth Earl Grey) and a Captain Campbell Colquhoun, with Anthony, the oldest man there, running third. 'Anthony Trollope was one of the party, a rough spoken good sort of fellow; one

* *Jemima: The Paintings and Memoirs of a Victorian Lady*, edited and introduced by Rob Fairlie, Canongate, 1988.

wondered how he came to write such good novels.' But they had lively talks and arguments with him 'as he was a Liberal; all the rest of us were Tories'.

Jemima Blackburn and Anthony – she referred to him in her memoir as Tony – played chess together on the boat. They both published factual accounts of the expedition, she in *Good Words* and he in the *Fortnightly*.* Mrs Blackburn did not mention Anthony in her *Good Words* pieces, and all but one of the sketches of him in her original drawings were erased from the versions published with them. (Was that her idea, or his?) They collaborated on *How the 'Mastiffs' Went to Iceland* – written by him, illustrated by her, and privately printed in booklet form for the members of the party, paid for by John Burns. But it is only in Mrs Blackburn's private memoir that we glimpse Anthony's amused, intrigued liking for her: 'A.T. told me one day that I was not like anyone else he had known – I wish it had occurred to me to ask how so!'

Towards the end of his life Anthony wrote several compact single-issue novels, in which there was no plot worth the name, but a situation or a moral dilemma, which was revolved, restated, and acted upon, marginally, by one vacillating character after another, round and round, until resolution was achieved. One of these was *Cousin Henry*, written in two months in the autumn of 1878.†

Cousin Henry is about inheritance. Old Indefer Jones dearly loved his niece Isabel Brodrick, who lived with him, but felt after much soul-searching that he should leave his property to his nephew Henry Jones, the nearest male heir. The best of all worlds would be if Isabel would marry Henry Jones, but she could never love him. The old man died, and Cousin Henry came into his inheritance.

But Uncle Indefer had made another, more recent will, leaving the place to Isabel after all. Cousin Henry found it between the pages of Volume 4 of Jeremy Taylor's *Sermons* in the book-room of the house that was now his. Weak, selfish, indecisive, he tortured himself over a period of weeks but still did not declare his

---

* In June–September 1879 and August 1878 respectively.

† Others in the genre are *The Golden Lion of Granpere*, *Sir Harry Hotspur of Humblethwaite*, *Dr Wortle's School*, *Marion Fay*, *An Old Man's Love*.

discovery, until forced to do so in a strange scene of physical violence in the little book-room.

The point about Anthony Trollope and 'character' in fiction, highlighted in his single-issue novels, is that intense mental conflicts arise not through circumstances or situations, but because of the particular weakness or vulnerability of the person who finds himself or herself in these circumstances or situations. It is not what happens to you, in the Trollopian universe, that makes for drama; it is the person you are in relation to happenings which, to someone else, might be unproblematic and even unremarkable. *Cousin Henry* is almost dull, and yet disproportionately intense. It meant something to Anthony Trollope.

What it meant – apart from a lifelong preoccupation with the laws and customs of inheritance – was that Anthony was worrying about his own will. He began writing *Cousin Henry* on 16 October 1878 and signed his will on 29 October. It was witnessed by his solicitor Charles Richard Jones. The worry had been what he should do for Florence Bland, the beloved niece, now twenty-three, who had been part of his household since her childhood but who was not his own flesh and blood. He had given Sir Thomas Underwood the same anxiety back in 1869, when he was writing *Ralph the Heir*. Sir Thomas adopted his niece Mary and loved her as a daughter. But if he provided for her in his will, he must take something from his own children. 'That question of adopting is very difficult . . . a man feels that he owed his property to his children.'

If Florence Bland were to marry Harry, her cousin Henry, the problem would solve itself. Perhaps that was what Anthony wished might happen, but it did not seem to be on the cards. In his novel Uncle Indefer Jones, in the 'wrong' will by which Cousin Henry inherited the property, left his niece £4,000. That is exactly what Anthony willed to Florence.

It was a release to his own anxiety to write *Cousin Henry*, which was a coded message of apology and compensation to Florence. In part of his mind he would have liked Florence to have everything, after Rose. She was becoming, literally, his right hand. His own right hand, after the long years of daily writing, had seized up. From now on he dictated most of his work to her – *Cousin Henry* was the first novel she took down. Soon, as he wrote of Isabel in *Cousin Henry*, she would be writing 'all her uncle's letters . . .

unless there was, by chance, something very special to be communicated'. Anthony's life-in-his-books existed in its own universe. He surely made no reference, to Florence, to the parallels between the story he was dictating and her own situation.

We do not know what Florence was like. Anthony described her to Alfred Austin as 'clever but undemonstrative'. Her life was the very opposite of Bice's. Florence was the daughter-at-home (though she was only a niece). She was becoming not only her uncle's right hand but an indispensable companion and helper to both him and Rose, especially on journeys. No reader of Anthony's novels can doubt that he took an intense delight in the company, the looks and the conversation of girls. He was sensitive to their embarrassments and anxieties, and had a sense of their promise at all ages and stages, even in the awkwardness of adolescence: 'The plump, rosy girl of fourteen, though she also is very sweet, never rises to such celestial power of feminine grace as she who is angular and bony, whose limbs are long, and whose joints are sharp' (*Castle Richmond*).

There is in the public mind today an alertness to the possibility of the sexual abuse of young people which breeds a self-consciousness unknown to Anthony Trollope and his contemporaries. There are in his novels many instances of intense physical and emotional closeness between a girl and her father or uncle – Doctor Thorne and his niece Mary, or Michel Voss and his wife's niece Marie in *The Golden Lion of Granpere*: 'In all things she worshipped her uncle, observing his movements, caring for his wants, and carrying out his plans. She did not worship her aunt. . . .' When Uncle Michel put a stop to Marie's love affair with his own son, she was upset: 'When she crept so close to him and pressed his arm, he was almost overcome by the sweetness of her love and by the tenderness of his own heart.' The whole story is heavy with the caresses and endearments shared by niece and uncle. Whatever the ostensible course of Marie's love story, the real drama was between those two, as the aunt knew; she would much rather there 'might be no sentiment, no romance, no kissing of hands, no looking into each other's faces, – no half-murmured tones of love'. But it was a wife's tight-lipped disapproval, rather than an uncle's misjudgement, which seemed, almost with authorial defiance, to be pinpointed.

The physical contact was always oddly precise. Here, in *The American Senator*, is Mr Masters, in his study, trying to discover why his daughter Mary will not accept Lawrence Twentyman: 'Gradually he looked up into her face, still keeping her hand pressed on the desk under his. It was his left hand that so guarded her, while she stood by his right shoulder. Then he gently wound his right arm round her waist, and pressed her to him.' Here is Sir Thomas Tringle* in *Ayala's Angel*, trying to persuade his niece Ayala to marry his son Tom: ' "Why can't you be sensible, as other girls are?" said Sir Thomas, lifting her up, and putting her on his knee. . . .' If Ayala was old enough to marry, which she was, even Anthony's contemporaries might have felt she was too old to sit on her uncle's knee.

In *Mr Scarborough's Family*, which was being serialised in *All the Year Round* when Anthony died, Dolly Grey turned down a proposal of marriage, thinking that 'there was but one man with whom she could live, and that man was her father.' Her father said she should marry:

'If I could choose my husband.'
'Whom would you choose?'
'You.'
'That is nonsense. I am your father.'
'You know what I mean.'

She tells him it is her 'dear, dear, darling old father's fault' for being so perfect: 'You have made the bed and you must lie on it. It hasn't been a bad bed.' He had got into the way of discussing his business worries with his daughter. At an anxious time she went into his bedroom in her nightgown, and sat on the bed in which he lay, saying: 'I knew you would want me tonight.'

These are striking examples. Minor ones, throughout Anthony Trollope's fiction, are legion. Innocent sentimentality, erotic fantasy? However carefully we think about nineteenth-century literary conventions, about nineteenth-century modes of sexuality, and about the fantasy-life that fed Anthony's fiction, we can do no more than take note, and wonder. Florence had a friend

---

* Apropos of the ways Anthony Trollope found names for his characters: Tringle and Twentyman, from different novels but both mentioned by chance in this paragraph, were listed as householders on the page of the GPO *London Directory* on which his own name and address appeared.

from her schooldays called Ada Strickland, who stayed often in Montagu Square. Anthony rode with the two girls in Hyde Park, and took them with him to exhibitions. Ada wrote about Anthony to Michael Sadleir, in 1926: 'I knew him intimately as a young girl and was head over heels in love with him and used to have a furiously gay time at their house. . . .' Florence herself left no letters, no personal testament. We can only be glad for the 'furiously gay time'.

Sexuality between lovers or potential lovers in Anthony's fiction was signalled topographically, even though he is not generally thought of as a creator of symbolic landscapes. He and Rose, with or without Florence, continued to holiday in the mountain villages of Switzerland and Austria, but a favourite place in their own country was Bolton Bridge in Wharfedale, amid the North Yorkshire moors, a famous beauty-spot and 'the prettiest place in England' as Anthony wrote to Mrs Steele on their first visit in 1870. He used it as a setting in *Lady Anna*. 'There isn't a better inn in England than the Devonshire Arms,' said young Earl Lovel, planning a family party at Bolton Bridge to include his *déclassée* cousin Lady Anna. He desired her and would marry her, but she, though attracted, was engaged to marry Daniel Thwaite the tailor.

Close by Bolton Bridge is twelfth-century Bolton Abbey, beside the river Wharfe which, then as now, can be crossed by stepping stones. Anna stopped, scared, half-way across: 'The black water was flowing fast, fast beneath her feet . . .' but the earl told her she could not turn back. He led her up the steep path on the other side: 'It was very pleasant, very lovely, very joyous; but there was still present to her mind some great fear.' The climax came at the Stryd, which is, in Anthony's words, 'a narrow gully or passage, which the waters have cut for themselves in the rocks, perhaps five or six feet broad, but narrowed at the top by an overhanging mass . . . bridging over part of the chasm below.' The young earl leaped back and forth over the chasm, urging Anna to jump. She said she could not. He swore he would catch her. 'Then she stood and shuddered for a moment, looking with beseeching eyes up into his face. Of course she meant to jump. . . . Yes, she would jump into his arms.' Then she remembered Daniel Thwaite, stumbled and hurt her ankle, and the moment passed.

Chasms, rivers, torrents, waterfalls, high cliffs above the sea; falling, swimming, drowning; and bridges, stiles, passing-places. These were his metaphors for the ecstatic, engulfing, frightening surrender which was, it seems, his vision of sexual passion. Sometimes it was explicit as in *The Belton Estate* where Will Belton, who had already proposed to Clara Amedroz as they lingered on a bridge over 'slowly moving water', said to his sister that love was 'not like jumping into a river, which a person can do or not, just as he pleases': 'But I fancy it is something like jumping into a river, and that a person can help it. What the person can't help is being in when the plunge has once been made.'

More often the imagery was implicit. In *Can You Forgive Her?* the cousins Alice and George Vavasor, tense with mutual desire, were alone on the balcony overlooking the Rhine at Basle, watching swimmers 'glorying in the swiftness of the current'. That night, in the dark, leaning with the besotted pair on the parapet of the bridge over the Rhine, George's sister Kate (who loved both George and Alice) said she would like to go with the stream, and would not fear to drown. Alice only shivered. The heightened sexual atmosphere between the three climaxed in a hysterical scene in a hotel bedroom between Alice and Kate: 'Don't, Alice, don't; I don't want your caresses. Caress him, and I'll kneel at your feet, and cover them with caresses.'

Anthony was sexually sophisticated, on paper at any rate. He used the same spectrum of water-imagery to convey the black disgust of bad sex, as experienced by women. There are men, he wrote in *The Eustace Diamonds*, 'in whose love a good deal of hatred is mixed; – who love as the huntsman loves the fox. . . .' That was how coarse, brutal Sir Griffin Tewett loved Lucinda Roanoake. After avoiding his kisses, 'On a sudden she made up her mind, and absolutely did kiss him. She would sooner have leaped at the blackest, darkest, dirtiest river in the country. . . . Never before had she been thus polluted.'

It is no exaggeration to say that dozens of instances might be quoted where water, and bridges over water, are both the setting for and the substance of sexual crisis. Hoverings on the brink, leaps in the dark. The seasoned Trollope reader becomes conditioned to the strategy; the pulse quickens in anticipation. It is not useful to wonder whether the symbolism was deliberate. Symbolism is as old as language, and Anthony was skilled at transmitting subtextual messages. He was writing before Freud, a museum curator *manqué*, had prised apart the symbol and the symbolised and laid them out on display side by side, separately labelled. Freud did art no special service by putting artificial membranes between layers of the mind and weakening the diffuse potency of sexual imagery by insisting on the naming of parts. Words are things, as Anthony said.

If he is not commonly thought of as a creator of symbolic landscape, he is not thought of as a theorist of the novel either. Yet from his autobiography, and from the authorial asides in his fiction, a cluster of strong opinions about novel-writing and its techniques can be mined. He did not believe in violating 'all proper confidence between the author and his readers' by creating mysteries (*Barchester Towers*). 'I abhor a mystery. I would fain, were it possible, have my tale run through from its little prologue to the customary marriage in its last chapter, with all the smoothness incidental to ordinary life. I have no ambition to surprise my reader' (*The Bertrams*). Yet he did not go along with the categorisation that described him as a 'realist' and his friend Wilkie Collins as a 'sensationalist'. A good novelist 'should be both, and both in the highest degree' (*Autobiography*).

He knew that the construction of plots was his weak point, but questioned whether plot was central to the purpose. The novelist's aim should be to create a world: 'He desires to make his readers so intimately acquainted with his characters that the creatures of his brain should be to them speaking, moving, living creatures.' He disliked the terms 'hero' and 'heroine', since real heroes and heroines 'are not commonly met with in our daily walks of life' (*The Three Clerks*). 'Perhaps no terms have been so injurious to the profession of novelist as those two words, hero and heroine. In spite of the latitude which is allowed to the writer in putting his own interpretation upon these words, something heroic is still expected; whereas, if he attempt to paint from nature, how little that is heroic would he describe' (*The Claverings*).

'When I sit down to write a novel I do not at all know, and I do not very much care, how it is to end.' In this, he said in his autobiography, he was the opposite of his friend Wilkie Collins, who planned and plotted everything in minute detail before he began. Anthony was not quite telling the truth about himself; there are among his papers notes for some of his novels, with characters, situations and even the contents of chapters sketched out; but his 'day-dreaming' method imposed infinite flexibility, as in *The Eustace Diamonds*: 'I had no idea of setting thieves after the bauble till I had got my heroine to bed in the inn at Carlisle; nor of the disappointment of the thieves, till Lizzie had been wakened in the morning with the news that her door had been broken open' (*Autobiography*). He had not even decided whether Lady Mason in *Orley Farm* had forged her husband's will, until he wrote the chapter in which she confessed her guilt.

He did not sit down at his writing-table with no preparation at all. He needed to dream his scenes and conversations into existence, in solitude and silence. Noise, as he grew old, became an intolerable distraction. A barrel organ or a brass band* playing in Montagu Square 'altogether incapacitates me. No sooner does the first note of the opening burst reach my ear than I start up, fling down my pen, and cast my thoughts disregarded into the abyss of some chaos which is always there ready to receive them. Ah, how terrible, how often vain, is the work of fishing, to get them out again!'

He elaborated each new castle in the air on solitary walks, just as he had in his boyhood. Walking in woods was best for this purpose; but English woods were too small, too regimented, too fragmented, too full of tourists and gamekeepers. The limitless Australian bush had been ideal, and 'in Switzerland there are pure forests still'. Best of all were 'the dark shadows of the Black Forest' in Germany, where he could wander fancy-free – 'if that indeed can be freedom which demands a bondage of its own' ('A Walk in a Wood't).

Afterwards came the more laborious business of conveying his story to his readers, at the required length, without boring either them or himself. He often apologised in his novels for 'troubling' readers with the necessary details of his characters' family backgrounds. The old dramatists he loved were luckier, as he said in *The Eustace Diamonds*, for they could list the personages, and

---

* He was alluding to the German brass bands that were a feature of London street life. Anthony, trying to work, had violent altercations with them, and the police tried to keep the bands out of Montagu Square in order to keep the peace.

† Published in *Good Words*, September 1879.

even their blood relationships, and who was in love with whom; whereas in a novel 'the poor narrator has been driven to expend his first four chapters in the mere task of introducing his characters.' In *Is He Popenjoy?*, apologising again, he wrote: 'The plan of jumping at once into the middle has often been tried, and sometimes seductively enough for a chapter or two; but the writer still has to hark back, and to begin again from the beginning – not always very comfortably after the abnormal brightness of his few opening pages. . . .' He often called this technique of starting *in medias res* 'putting the cart before the horse', conceding in *The Duke's Children* that those 'bits of the horse' which could not be deduced by the reader would have to be shown sooner or later.

He admitted that he often groaned at the prospect of inventing the appearance of a young woman, yet again: 'And now looms before me the novelist's great difficulty. Miss Monsell, – or, rather, Mrs Mark Robarts, – must be described. . . . And now I must say a word about Lucy Robarts. If one might only go on without those descriptions how pleasant it would all be!' (*Framley Parsonage*). Another hazard was getting things wrong, from sheer ignorance. 'The poor fictionalist . . . catches salmon in October; or shoots his partridges in March. His dahlias bloom in June, and his birds sing in the autumn. He opens the opera-houses before Easter, and makes Parliament sit on a Wednesday evening. And then those terrible meshes of the Law. . . . But from who is any assistance to come in the august matter of a Cabinet assembly?' (*Phineas Finn*). He clearly found that assistance (at the club), for he proceeded to describe with confidence the dingy Cabinet room with its turkey carpet, its mahogany table on heavy carved legs, six heavy chairs, four armchairs, and four windows looking on to St James's Park. And after several mistakes about legal procedure, which he referred to ruefully in subsequent books, he took to checking out his law with friends such as Frederick Pollock. Publishers, in Anthony's day, simply published. They employed readers to report on manuscripts, but not line-by-line editors or fact-checkers. Some publishers, such as John Blackwood, took issue with Anthony over character and story-line, but he was exceptional. Mostly, an author was on his own.

Anthony's most perspicacious remarks about writing fiction, in the autobiography, concern dialogue. Ordinary conversation, he wrote, is carried on in 'sharp expressive sentences', which are frequently left unfinished. The novelist had to steer a course between 'absolute accuracy of language', which would sound pedantic and unreal, and 'the slovenly inaccuracy of ordinary talkers', which would be unacceptable in print. 'If he be quite real he will seem to attempt to be funny. If he be quite correct he will seem to be unreal. And above all, let the speeches be short.' He became so adroit at this that he ran ahead of his time. Many of his conversational exchanges between clever women (such as Lady Glencora and Madame Max), speaking candidly in private, have the startling, elliptical suggestiveness of Ivy Compton-Burnett or Henry Green.

He knew that readers picked up a novel to be entertained, and that 'instruction' must be concealed, as he said in *Ralph the Heir*: 'It is the test of a novel writer's art that he conceals his snake-in-the-grass; but the reader may be sure that it is always there. No man or woman with a conscience, – no man or woman with intellect sufficient to produce amusement, can go on from year to year without the desire of teaching' – and of influencing readers for their good.

Much of what he said in his lectures, his autobiography and his unfinished history of prose fiction was designed to 'vindicate' – a strong word – the writing and the reading of novels as a morally useful pursuit, over and over again. Novels were popular; they were devoured by anyone who could read. This was a modern phenomenon. He felt that the value of fiction, especially for young people, had to be defended and explained, in the face of a suspicion that anything so painlessly and universally accessible must be a waste of time. He saw too what we have seen in retrospect – the unprecedented intimacy generated between novelist and impressionable reader. The novelist, he wrote in *Thackeray*, 'creeps in closer than the schoolmaster, closer than the father, closer even than the mother. . . .'

Quite apart from the intrinsic validity of his arguments, Anthony needed to establish the worth of his life-work for his own self-esteem. It was to this end that he articulated so lucidly the processes and purposes that contributed to the making of his books.

Then, when a book finally came out, there were the reviews. He anatomised these in *The Way We Live Now*. There was the selling review, and the review which enhanced a reputation but did not sell the book; there was 'the review which snuffs a book out quietly; the review which is to raise or lower the author a single peg, or two pegs, as the case may be; the review which is suddenly to make an author, and the review which is to crush him. . . . Of all reviews, the crushing review is the most popular, as being the most readable.'

Literary criticism, he wrote in his autobiography, had become a profession and ceased to be an art. Yet however unfair or prejudiced a review might be, there was nothing to be gained for the author by making a fuss. 'To shriek, to scream, and sputter, to threaten actions, and to swear about the town that he has been belied and defamed . . . will leave on the minds of the public nothing but a sense of irritated impotence.' Writing about writing, and about the conditions and conduct of a writer's life, Anthony Trollope comes very close to us and to the way we live now.

CHAPTER NINETEEN

EAVING *Marion Fay* only just begun, Anthony sat down on 1 February 1879 to begin a short, popular book on Thackeray for the 'English Men of Letters' series, published by Macmillan and edited by John Morley. The fee was only £200, but it seemed a compliment to be asked. He was not an obvious choice, since he had not much track-record as a critic and none as a biographer.

Thackeray's family had no objections, principally because the book was to be brief; they did not want a full 'Life and Letters' done. 'I am delighted that it is to be,' Morley wrote to Anthony on 27 January, 'and particularly as we have such friendly assent from Stephen and his sister-in-law*. . . . I don't know how far you will feel free to tell his story, but I hope you will give us as much as you can in the personal vein, by way of background to the critical and descriptive.'

That was easier said than done. The help he got from Thackeray's daughter Anne – now Lady Ritchie – was limited; he submitted a list of factual questions to which she wrote minimal replies. He wrote around for memories and information to Thackeray's old friends, including Edward Fitzgerald,† who told Frederick Tennyson: 'I am glad Trollope has the job if to be done at all; he is a Gentleman as well as an Author – was a loyal friend of Thackeray's, and so, I hope, will take him out of any Cockney Worshipper's hands. . . .'

It took Anthony less than two months to write the book, but he

---

* Leslie Stephen had a say in the matter as the widower of Thackeray's elder daughter Minny. His sister-in-law Anne Thackeray had in 1877 married Sir Richmond Ritchie, many years her junior.

† Edward Fitzgerald, the translator, or adapter, of *The Rubáiyát of Omar Khayyám*, had been at Cambridge with Thackeray. He was a constant and enthusiastic reader of Anthony's novels. Quotation from A. M. and A. B. Terhune, *The Letters of Edward Fitzgerald*, Princeton University Press, 1980.

found it, as he told John Blackwood, 'a terrible job'. 'There is absolutely nothing to say, – except washed out criticism.' Anne Thackeray Ritchie did not put any family letters at his disposal; Fitzgerald, to whom Anthony appealed for information about the 1830s, said he had burned nearly all Thackeray's early letters and could not remember much anyway. 'But it has to be done, and no one would do it so lovingly,' Anthony wrote to Blackwood. It had to be done (as Thackeray's inner circle intended) with almost no material.

What he wrote was not so loving as to be hagiographical. He emphasised Thackeray's weaknesses at least as much as his strengths. Discussing the writing, he included generalisations that could apply equally to his own work. His own views, and anecdotes from his own experience, pad out the text.

Some of this material duplicated, and some of it amplified, what he wrote about narrative technique elsewhere. His remarks on what he understood by 'realism', for example, parallel what he wrote in his autobiography about dialogue. He wrote that both the sublime and the ludicrous were easier to achieve in fiction than the realistic, in that 'they are not required to be true'. And yet realism, in fiction, must be 'just so far removed from truth as to suit the erroneous idea of truth which the reader must be supposed to entertain'.

On Thackeray's literary mannerisms, he seemed to be writing about his own. Thackeray's besetting sin was 'a certain affected familiarity. He indulges too frequently in little confidences with individual readers, in which pretended allusions to himself are frequent'. In the course of this 'volubility' the narrator lays bare 'his own weaknesses, vanities, peculiarities' – and that, he wrote, robbed the narrative of its integrity.

The biographer shared, too, his subject's public joviality, and his private melancholy and self-doubt, his 'sense of imminent doom' and 'a certain feminine softness'. Where he differed from his subject, the divergence was expressed in a form that implicitly defined the biographer. Thackeray, he said, would have been incapable of sitting at an office desk day after day and doing a regular job at the Post Office; and Thackeray's grasp of Irish idiom, he said, was faulty.

Anthony had to be circumspect about his subject's private life. All he could say was that when Thackeray's wife's mind 'failed her' he became 'as it were a widower' till the end of his days. He could write about Thackeray's 'fits of painful spasms' but not about the night-roistering, the drinking or the long attachment to Mrs Brookfield which powered the love story in *Henry Esmond*. He sent the proofs of the biographical section to some of Thackeray's friends for comment. One of these was George Smith, who apparently asked to have something cut out, and another was Edward Fitzgerald, who also made some changes and corrections. Anthony had been working, Fitzgerald wrote to Frederick Pollock (another old friend of Thackeray's, as well as Anthony's neighbour), 'under Annie's eyes (who misinformed him in many ways)'. And to Lord Houghton, Fitzgerald wrote that 'Mr Trollope seems to me to have made but an insufficient Account of WMT, though all in gentlemanly good taste, which one must be thankful for.'

Thackeray got a bad review in George Smith's *Pall Mall Gazette*, which included a suggestion that Anthony had been guilty of bad taste in giving precise details of the 'comfortable income' (£750 p.a.) left by Thackeray to his family. Anthony, who saw a comfortable income as something to be celebrated as the reward of honest work, was upset not by the review but by the resulting chill between him and Anny, who appeared to agree with the reviewer even though she had supplied the figure. So he was pleased and relieved when, a couple of years later, they coincided one evening at George Smith's house in Waterloo Place. Anthony came over to Anny where she stood by the fireplace. She apologised, and so did he, and he called her 'my dear', and 'we smiled at each other, and we had a thorough good talk', as Anthony reported to Rose. 'I am very glad because my memory of her father was wounded by the feeling of a quarrel.'

Rose remained sensitive about the *Thackeray* episode on her husband's behalf. Harry's daughter Muriel (who never knew her grandfather) wrote to Michael Sadleir in 1926 that 'Grandma [Rose] never forgot that Anne Thackeray or rather Ritchie went to Grandpa at Waltham House and besought him herself to write it as she said no one would do it better than he. He did not want to write it. But to Anne's entreaties he finally yielded and then was cruelly abused by Richmond Ritchie in some article. Grandma told me, "Anne Thackeray nearly went down on her knees to your Grandfather in the Library at W. Cross." ' This is a very dubious

473

piece of family mythology. For one thing, the review was most unlikely to have been by Anny's husband; for another, the Trollopes were no longer at Waltham Cross when the Thackeray book was being discussed.

Anthony made two further brief biographical excursions. One was *The Life of Cicero*, which he told G. W. Rusden was to be 'the opus magnum of my old age'. He had been interested in Cicero ever since reviewing Charles Merivale's *History of the Romans* in 1851; he felt that Merivale had been unfair to Cicero and idealised Caesar at Cicero's expense. Anthony did all the research at home, having in his library 177 leather-bound volumes of the Bibliothèque Latine-Française, published in the 1820s and 30s. His annotations of the 36 volumes of the works of Cicero, and the detailed commentaries he pasted in at the end of each volume, formed the basis of his book. Anthony was already reading for this book in 1877 on his second visit to Australia,* and finished the writing after many interruptions in May 1880. It was Rose who took it down at his dictation, or at any rate made the fair copy, not Florence. Her involvement may be a measure of the long-standing significance this work had for Anthony; or Florence may simply have been away. Chapman & Hall published it in two volumes in September of that year. Frederic Chapman gave him no lump sum or advance for it, but made a modest royalty agreement.

For all his hard work and high aspiration, his *Cicero* is only worth reading for those who want to read everything ever written about Cicero. He wrote as Cicero's champion, refuting the critical analyses of previous writers (who included not only Charles Merivale but J. A. Froude and W. Lucas Collins, all known personally to Anthony). The only aspect of his hero's character he could not defend was his dishonesty – but then Cicero 'had not acquired that theoretic aversion to a lie that is the first feeling in the bosom of a modern gentleman.' In other respects, his Cicero was indeed a modern gentleman: 'What a man he would have been for London life! . . . How popular he would have been at the Carlton. . . . How crowded would have been his rack with invitations to dinner!' Enough said. But the book was received

* The seventh volume of his edition of Cicero's speeches contains this note in his own hand: 'this is the volume that was found out of doors at Forbes in N[ew].S[outh].W[ales].'

indulgently by some critics. Though no one praised Anthony's scholarship, most were warmed by his intimacy with his subject and felt, like the reviewer for *The World*, that 'there is little doubt that the *Life of Cicero* by the author of *Can You Forgive Her?* will be the most popular in the English language'.

His last biographical excursion was a short book about Lord Palmerston, Foreign Secretary, Home Secretary, and twice Prime Minister, who died in office in 1865. Anthony wrote it (for £200) during the winter of 1881–82 for the 'English Political Leaders' series published by William Isbister, a close colleague of Alexander Strahan and one of the proprietors of *Good Words*, for the same kind of non-specialist readership for whom *Thackeray* was intended. He had no access to original material; his chief sources were the existing biography by Evelyn Ashley, and the great Whig statesman's speeches.

Every gifted person longs to be admired for some expertise other than the one which is universally acknowledged. The areas in which Anthony would have loved recognition were classical scholarship and politics. He had always admired Palmerston and taken a special interest in his career, originally because of hearing him spoken of as a 'good' landlord in Co. Sligo in the 1840s. Palmerston and his active, attractive, Glencora-like wife had visited Ireland in 1841, the year Anthony himself arrived to take up his assistant surveyorship, and again in 1844, when they were conspicuously entertained by the Lord Lieutenant. Like his new biographer, Palmerston was a Harrovian, and had not begun to achieve his potential until he was forty-five.

Enacting in his own person, as always, the character about whom he was writing, Anthony stressed the vitality of the man: 'There is something almost ludicrous about the energy displayed by Lord Palmerston at the Home Office; and yet it was essentially useful. He visited prisons and wrote memoranda on the ventilation of cells. He arranged tickets of leave for convicts, and attempted to abate the nuisance of smoke in London. He built cemeteries, and fixed the winter assizes. Such matters are by no means ludicrous.'

Anthony admired Palmerston, who is best remembered as a great if eccentric Foreign Secretary, for putting the will of the people above party. In his fictional political world Anthony sustained his early badger-baiting image of politics by naming

475

successive Prime Ministers Lord Brock and Lord de Terrier. He characterised Palmerston, in the biography, in the same terms: 'His courage was coarse and strong and indomitable, like that of a dog.'

After he finished *Thackeray* he had taken Rose, in the particularly cold spring of 1879, for a holiday in William Lucas Collins's rectory at Lowick in Northamptonshire, the incumbent and his family being away. During the three snowed-in weeks they were there Anthony wrote the whole of *Dr Wortle's School*, using the house and its grounds as his setting and changing the name Lowick to Bowick.

In the mid-1870s Anthony had stayed at Lowick regularly, to hunt with the Pytchley and the Fitzwilliam. In those days Mr Collins had a young pupil living in the house, George Leveson Gower, whom he was preparing for Oxford. (Dr Wortle, in Anthony's novel, was similarly preparing young Lord Carstairs for Oxford; but if Harry is to be believed Dr Wortle was an unconscious portrait of the author, not of Mr Collins.) Leveson Gower recalled that he and Anthony 'always went out and often came home together. He brought down a string of seven hunters, which excited my envy. He was a big, bearded, red-faced jovial man with a loud voice and a hearty manner.'*

In the spring of 1879, from Lowick, Anthony wrote to his absent host: 'That I, who have belittled so many clergymen, should ever come to live in a parsonage. . . . You may be sure that I will endeavour to behave myself accordingly, so that no scandal shall fall upon the parish.' Would he be required to preach? he wondered. 'If they take to address me as "The Rural Anthony," will it be all right?'

He thought of himself as nearing the end of his life, preparing for the last 'Great Journey'. What did this man who had 'belittled so many clergymen' really believe? 'I may question the infalli- bility of the teachers, but I hope that I shall not therefore be accused of doubt as to the thing taught' (*Barchester Towers*). But it was not so simple as that. In the same novel, he defended

* Sir George Leveson Gower, *Years of Content*, John Murray, 1940. He was a nephew of Lord Granville; in his memoirs he claimed that the 'set of lawn tennis things' and the lawn tennis court that he laid out at Lowick Rectory in 1874 were the first ever seen in the neighbourhood, and 'made Lowick quite a fashionable centre'.

controversy. 'We are much too apt to look at schism in our church as an unmitigated evil. Moderate schism, if there may be such a thing . . . teaches men to think upon religion.' He thought upon it himself a great deal.

Our pastors, he wrote in *Phineas Redux*, are only human, 'and so they have oppressed us, and burned us, and tortured us, and hence come to love palaces, and fine linen, and purple, and, alas, sometimes, mere luxury and idleness. . . .' What, he asked, 'is a thinking man to do?'

The only one of his fictional 'heroes' to experience a religious epiphany was young George Bertram in *The Bertrams* who, on the Mount of Olives, determined to dedicate his life to God. Bertram, however, lost his faith: 'A man who has really believed does not lose by a sudden blow the firm convictions of his soul. But when the work has first commenced, when the first step has been taken, the pace becomes frightfully fast.' Bertram asked his ordained friend, 'How many of those who were sitting by silently while you preached really believed?' Bertram questioned the literal truth of the Bible, and the resurrection of the body.

The Bertrams, written in 1858, was set in the 1840s, when Anthony's devout sister Cecilia was still alive and an influence, and it was not so long since he had heard Newman preaching in Oxford. The novel reflected some loss of conviction on the author's part. Anthony did not believe in the literal resurrection of the body; he was, with Millais, one of the sixteen signatories of the founding document of the Cremation Society in 1874.*

He was not sure. . . . What he was sure about was that 'civilization, philanthropy, and brotherly love have come of the teaching of the Christian religion'; those who believed that, most firmly, were 'the very men who threw off from themselves, at first with dismay and then with disgust, unfathomable doctrinal points'. He could only say, like Lord Hampstead in *Marion Fay*, that 'No one, I think, has ever been put in [moral] danger by believing Christ to be a God.'

He was sceptical about faith in prayer; the clergyman in church might pray for a change in the weather, but 'Ask the clergyman on

---

* Cremation, which tacitly dispenses with the literal interpretation of 'the resurrection of the body', was made legal in 1884 in the interests of space and hygiene.

his way back from church what he is doing with his own haystack, and his answer will let you know whether he believes in his own prayers' (*The Life of Cicero*). He understood the uses of prayer only in a limited sense: 'We need not doubt this at least, – that to him who utters them prayers of intercession are of avail' (*Sir Harry Hotspur of Humblethwaite*). Religion, he thought, could not be taken up in an emergency, like a medicine: 'A religious man, should he become bankrupt through the misfortunes of the world, will find consolation in his religion even for that sorrow. But a bankrupt, who has not thought much of such things, will hardly find solace by taking up religion for that special occasion' ('The Courtship of Susan Bell').

He wished it were not so. As men grow older, he wrote in *Ralph the Heir*, in a passage that throws light on his own depressions, it becomes 'impossible to keep down the conviction that everything is vanity, that the life past has been vain from folly, and that the life to come must be vain from impotence. It is the presence of thoughts such as these that needs the assurance of a heaven to save the thinker from madness or from suicide. It is when the feeling of this prevailing vanity is strongest on him, that he who doubts of heaven most regrets his incapacity for belief.'

Rose had been brought up as a Unitarian, a denomination which, more than any other except the Quakers, dispenses with 'unfathomable doctrinal points'. Unitarians dispense, in the first place, with the doctrine of the Holy Trinity, and consider no doctrine, not even the divinity of Christ, to be above questioning. They adhere to no set creed and agree to differ even among themselves. The Unitarians of Anthony's day were prominent, socially responsible and intellectually respectable; many of the Boston intellectuals whom he had met were Unitarians. The strongly reformist ideals of even English Unitarianism would have been too advanced for Anthony; but if Rose retained the relaxed attitude to points of doctrine in which she had been raised, she may have both influenced him and solaced him in his difficulties. He was one of nature's Unitarians in his religious thinking, though not in his social and political orientation.

He had an inalienable affection for the faulty Church of England, but he was not anti-Catholic. He had seen the ugly face of Protestantism in Ireland, where it 'consists too much in a hatred of Papistry – in that rather than in a hatred of those errors against which we Protestants are supposed to protest' (*Castle Richmond*). The people he knew well in Ireland, and the priests who became his friends, had made bigotry impossible for him. In Ireland he had been happier with southern Catholics than with northern Presbyterians. Nevertheless there was in his last book *The Landleaguers* an explicit judgement that Catholicism was not a religion for 'gentlemen' – i.e., there was something vulgar and unsophisticated about it.

Yet he envied the simple certainty of Irish Catholicism, unequalled, he said, in Europe apart (remembering Bruges) from Flanders: 'I have met no Romanist Irishman who would express the remotest doubt as to any portion of the doctrines of the creed of his church – miraculous and difficult to believe as they are . . .' (*The Macdermots of Ballycloran*). Protestants would always have the edge on Catholics, he wrote in *North America*, in terms of wealth and progress. 'And yet I love their religion. There is something beautiful and almost divine in the faith and obedience of a true son of the Holy Mother. I sometimes fancy that I would fain be a Roman Catholic, – if I could; as also I would often wish to be still a child, if that were possible.'

He differentiated in his fiction between cultivated, sophisti-cated Irish Catholic priests, who had been trained in France or Italy, and their devout, less educated curates, often rough countrymen. In the last year of his life, in *The Landleaguers*, he identified a new kind of Irish priest, influenced by Irish-American political agitation and 'hot for Home Rule'. If he had chosen, and if there had been a market for it, he could have anatomised the Irish Catholic Church as intimately as he did the Church of England, which included not only the cathedral close at Barchester and the sunny lawns of country rectories, but a world that he hated – the prejudiced, priggish, anti-life (as he saw it) evangelicals.

No close reader of his work can doubt that his own beliefs were painfully vague, and that this troubled him. Equally, no one can doubt that he clung to a strong sense of God, something he also called Providence, or a 'superior power', which had to do with the natural law, and purpose and rightness, the grandeur of mountains and torrents and the immortality of the soul. His belief in this last is asserted in the course of a thumping male-supremacist remark he made in a letter to an unknown correspondent in

1879: 'The necessity of the supremacy of man [over woman] is as certain to me as the eternity of the soul. There are other matters on which one fights as on subjects which are in doubt, – universal suffrage, ballot, public education, and the like – but not, I think, on those two.' On both counts, he was maybe whistling in the dark.

His acceptance of the Established Church as an institution was comfortably irrational. 'I love the name of State and Church, and believe that much of our English well-being has depended on it. . . . Nevertheless I am not prepared to argue the matter. One does not always carry one's proofs at one's finger-ends' (*North America*).

Age was creeping up on all the old companions. John Tilley, who turned sixty-five in early 1878, touchingly wrote to Anthony to ask advice on whether he should retire from the Post Office. Anthony replied to 'My dear John' carefully and at length, stressing Tilley's health and strength, 'that of a man of forty'. Yet there might be some inner fatigue. 'You say of me: – that I would not choose to write novels unless I were paid. Most certainly I would; – much rather than not write them at all.' The two points Tilley should consider were his happiness and his duty. What did he propose to do in retirement? 'You cannot stand in a club window; you cannot play cards; you cannot farm. Books must be your resource' – but that only if the habit of reading had already been acquired. As to duty, John should only leave the PO if 'weariness tends to make your work unserviceable'. It was a good letter. This friendship had lasted more than forty years and survived many storms. Anthony ended: 'Your happiness is so much to me that I cannot but write about it much in earnest.' John Tilley stayed on at the PO for two more years, and left with a knighthood.

Tom, in England in 1878, was getting more and more difficult for Bice to get on with. She complained about his costiveness over her money to her Uncle Tony, who answered her diplomatically in October 1878: 'There are 4 ways in which you might proceed. I could write to your father. You could speak to him. You could get Fanny to speak to him. Or you could write to him.' If he were to write to Tom, 'it would make him *very* angry'. He was in favour of Bice herself writing to Tom very tactfully and, just as if she were a character in a novel, he drafted the letter for her. 'You had better see me again before you send it.'

In the late summer of 1879 Rose, Anthony and Florence met Tom and Fanny at Höllenthal, where they all stayed at the Hotel zum Stern. Tom, aged sixty-nine, was suffering agonies from sciatica. Morphine relieved the pain, but when the drug wore off he plunged into black depression. Anthony wrote a wonderful tribute to Fanny about the way she coped with Tom. He had expected as much – 'But your mental and physical capacity, your power of sustaining him by your own cheerfulness, and support-ing him by your own attention, are marvellous. When I consider all the circumstances, I hardly know how to reconcile so much love with so much self-control.'

Amid these signs of age and decay, he finished *Marion Fay* which, as if in defiance, was full of emblems of sexuality. There was great play with a poker, with which Marion absent-mindedly tended the fire when dining with Lord Hampstead at Hendon Hall. The young lord, in love with her, found great significance in the intimacy of this action; and after she died of consumption, he clasped his poker, as the only thing of his that she had touched. Rather less ludicrous, during the fire-poking evening, was Anthony's 'modern' image of 'electric sparks which, from Lord Hampstead's end of the wire, were being directed every moment against Marion Fay's heart.' Perhaps he was himself galvanised by seeing Bice in love. That autumn of 1879, aged twenty-six, she became engaged to be married.

'At all events the man you propose to entrust your happiness to is an English gentleman,' Tom wrote to her from Turin, on his way home to Rome. Bice's fiancé was the model of the ideal and well-connected lover that Anthony liked to award to patient heroines in his novels. He was Charles (Charlie) Stuart-Wortley, two years older than she, a barrister and budding politician, the grandson of Lord Wharncliffe and the son of a former Solicitor General in Lord Palmerston's first administration. Their worldly assets included a country place at Wortley in Yorkshire (no distance from Rotherham, where Rose's humbler home had been) and a London house, 6 Mandeville Place, off Wigmore Street. Anthony had met Charlie's mother and grandmother back in the 1860s; and in the absence of Tom it was Anthony who saw Charlie formally and welcomed him into the family.

There was a great fuss about whether Bice should take a maid with her on her first visit to Wortley, as her future mother-in-law expected her to, and whether she should also take a maid as a travelling companion when she went to her parents in Rome, to fill in the time until her marriage. Rose, as mother-substitute, became agitated. A letter survives from Bice to a girlfriend, written at 39 Montagu Square on 4 November 1879:

> ... there I have been interrupted in my letter by a long sermon from my Aunt *Rose*, the jist of it being that if I remain in England more than a week or two at most it will be a disgrace to me ever afterwards, that as it is, my engagement to Charlie has been talked of *much* too much, and that if after that I dangle on in England longer than a few days more it will be all rather shocking! Why that *absurd* tirade I can't tell! Probably the East Wind has got into her brain. Charlie dined here last night, thank God.

If, said Bice, 'my relations go on tormenting my life out with their most unnecessary advice, and compel me to engage a ruinous maid at a fabulous price to conduct me to the Paternal roof (where they are not a bit anxious to get me back) all the pleasant days wh: I might have in London before the terrible separation [from Charlie], must be put aside. . . .'

Back in Rome in the summer of 1880, Bice sent another letter to a friend which proves that the life she had been leading had not made her silly. She said she was bored, and did not go out. 'For, for the last three years, I have longed for an excuse to give up hateful balls and parties and to lead if not a useful life (that is impossible in this country of social slavery) an amusing one, according to my notions.' She was missing 'my boy' so terribly that 'the effort to keep down vain and useless wishes exhausts my body as well as my mind'.

Bice was safely married to her Charlie at the British Embassy in Paris (to save Tom and Fanny making the longer journey to London) on 16 August 1880. Rose and Anthony were there.

By that time Rose and Anthony were no longer living in London. The imminence of the move had been one reason why Rose had been so anxious to pack Bice off to Italy. As Anthony wrote in *The Landleaguers*, 'it may be observed that at any period of special toil in a family, when infinitely more has to be done than at any other time, then love-making will go on with more than ordinary energy.'

Anthony had thought to end his days in Montagu Square. The move to the country, effected in July 1880, was largely for his health's sake. The polluted air and filthy fogs of London exacerbated his breathing problems. He tired easily. His London life was as hectic as ever – Royal Academy dinners, Garrick dinners, Royal Literary Fund meetings and dinners, lecturing in the provinces. He was on the council of the Metropolitan Free Libraries Association, and chaired a couple of their meetings. In 1880 Chapman & Hall became a limited company; Anthony was one of the directors, which involved two long and anxious meetings every week. In early 1881 the firm moved from Piccadilly to new and cheaper premises at 11 Henrietta Street, Covent Garden.

The firm was in bad trouble. Frederic Chapman owed so much money that he was in danger of being declared bankrupt, and was forced to resign from the Garrick; Anthony tried, unsuccessfully, to get 'the poor fellow' reinstated. The change in constitution had been made as a means of raising capital. Both Anthony and Harry bought shares, which turned out to be a perpetual cause of anxiety. Anthony had deep feelings of loyalty and obligation to the man with whom he had been professionally associated for more than twenty years and who by 1880 had published twenty-nine of his books. Anthony was a very successful author; Chapman & Hall also owned Dickens's copyrights. Just what had happened to put Frederic Chapman, whose wife was said to have money, so deeply in the red is unclear.

Anthony loathed the board meetings and no doubt contributed to the painfulness of these sessions, which sometimes dragged on for five hours. He, who had made fun of people who made long speeches and had always been so succinct himself, was becoming long-winded and irritable on public platforms and committees. Lord Derby, son of the former Conservative Prime Minister, was president of the Royal Literary Fund from 1875; he was Foreign Secretary when he took on this duty. A decade younger than Anthony, Lord Derby was irritated at the meetings by Anthony's 'middle-class bumptiousness and lack of political acumen'.* This

---

* John Vincent, *Disraeli, Derby and the Conservative Party: Journals and Memoirs of Edward Henry, Lord Stanley, 1849–1869*, Harvester Press, 1978. Lord Stanley succeeded his more famous father to become the fifteenth Earl of Derby in 1869.

was particularly ironic since Lord Derby, a diffident and scrupulous man, shared many of the characteristics of Anthony's Plantagenet Palliser, even including an interest in decimal coinage.

During this difficult time Anthony also had to endure, in the pages of *Punch*, a reminder of his vulnerability as an ageing author and of the new and disrespectful generation snapping at his heels. Like all well-known people he had often been the subject of caricatures and parodies; he had even parodied himself, in a little book published for charity in New York in 1875 which he called *Never, Never – Never, Never* – a skit on Lily Dale's resistance to Johnny Eames (who appears as 'John Thomas') in *The Small House at Allington*. Earlier editors of *Punch* – Mark Lemon and Shirley Brooks – had been good friends of Anthony's, and the editor since Brooks's death in 1874 had been Tom Taylor, one of Anthony's first London friends and the one who had seconded Richard Monckton Milnes (who became Lord Houghton) when the latter put Anthony up for the Cosmopolitan Club back in 1861. Taylor was Anthony's contemporary, an ex-don and a lawyer who made a successful career as a popular playwright.

Taylor died in 1880, and the editorship of *Punch* passed to Francis Burnand, twenty years younger. Burnand, an old Etonian, was an irreverent humorist who had been contributing to *Punch* since 1863 as well as writing light burlesques and adaptations of French farces for the London stage. As an undergraduate at Cambridge he had founded the Amateur Dramatic Club, and converted to Catholicism. He toyed with the idea of the priesthood but the lure of the footlights, and of women, was too strong; he married twice and had thirteen children.

Burnand was confident and iconoclastic, with a gift for repartee. He said, in reply to the charge that *Punch* was not what it used to be, 'It never was.' He celebrated his accession to the editor's chair in 1880 by writing a parody of a Trollope novel – 'The Beadle – or, The Latest Chronicle of Small-Beerjester' by Anthony Dollop, celebrated author of 'Fishy Fin', 'The Prying Minister', 'Rub the Hair', 'The Way We Dye Now', 'Can't You Forget Her?' and 'He Knew He Could Write' among other works. Burnand ran this as a serial between May and October, beginning with a correspondence between Anthony Dollop and his publisher: 'DON'T call me "TONY." I don't like it. . . . You want a novel, on what you call an Ecclesiastical subject. That's the English of it, isn't it? Hey? You quote my titles incorrectly, and you omit *The Churchwarden*. Everyone liked *The Churchwarden*; and I think I've got just the thing for your readers, or rather for mine. How about *The Beadle*? Hey? Hasn't that the true smack about it? Hey? . . . You say terms are all right. That's business. Consider it settled. I'll do *The Beadle*, and throw in a couple of Bishops and a few new dignitaries for the money. Hey? Don't call me TONY again.'

The parody-novel itself was a conflation of *The Warden* and *Barchester Towers*, complete with Tooral-Looral-Rooral Deans, Vicars Chloral, an Archbeacon Overwayte, and a heroine called Morleena who was found by her lover in a tea-garden 'all among the Tea-roses and the buttercups and saucers, with her beautiful hair flowing in auburn masses down her back from under her bonnet, picking rosy-coloured shrimps'. The Signora Vesey Neroni appeared as the bedizened Columbina Crinolina, a member of a fairground troupe performing at the garden party of Mrs Dowdie, the bishop's wife. The fun with punning names was only part of it; like all good parodists Burnand knew his subject intimately and followed his model closely, packing 'The Beadle' with essential and not over-exaggerated Trollopian quirks and mannerisms. To be parodied in this way confirmed Anthony's status as a national institution, but it also turned him into an ancient monument. Would it have been any comfort to him to know that in 1881 Lord Acton was discussing with the Gladstone family the idea of giving him a peerage? Nothing would have pleased him more. But the idea was dropped on the grounds that he was 'noisy'.*

Getting out of town, under the circumstances, was a relief. The Trollopes moved to the Sussex-Hampshire border, to the small and unspoilt village of Harting, near Petersfield. The railway station at Rogate was only a mile away, so it was not hard to get up to London. The new house, North End, was described by the agents when Rose came to sell it as 'a Comfortable Cottage Residence', complete with stables, piggeries and cowsheds, a barn, wood-house, harness-room, coach-house, two enclosed

* Herbert Paul (ed.), *Letters of Lord Acton to Mary Gladstone* (1904).

yards – and 70 acres, which the Trollopes let out, keeping only one meadow.

They moved in, with Florence, in July 1880. Anthony told Cecilia Meetkerke that 'I hope to lay my bones here' – and that meanwhile 'I am as busy as would be one thirty years younger, in cutting out dead boughs, and putting up a paling here and a little gate there.'

The house had five family bedrooms and two servants' bed-rooms, one WC, a front staircase and a back staircase, a double drawing-room and a dining-room, and a smaller sitting-room. When they had been in a fortnight Anthony wrote to Harry, who was in Paris working on translations and compiling a guide-book: 'You may imagine what a trouble the library has been.' The bulk of his books were up on the shelves, and in their right order; but 'that which is not the bulk, but which forms a numerous portion, is all in confusion so that sometimes I am almost hopeless.' Who does not know – as Anthony so often prefaced his observations in his novels, drawing his reader ever closer – that hopelessness of accommodating books in a new house? There was a slight reproach in his complaints to Harry; in May, when they were plotting the move, he had told Harry he hoped he would come 'and put up the books for me. Oh the books – and oh the wine! I am beginning to tremble at the undertaking.'

Anthony's room at North End was larger than his book-room in London but 'two shelves lower', so took fewer books. 'If however I am in confusion with my books, I have got my wine into fine order, and have had iron bins put up in the cellar.' In January 1882 he told Harry that he was to consider 24 dozen bottles of Léoville claret and the same number of Beychevelle (both Médoc wines) as his own. 'It is 1874 wine and will not be fit for use until 1884 at the earliest.' He said John Merivale jokingly swore he would take an action against him over it, on the grounds that 'I held it in trust for my friends, and had no right to make it over secretly to a son.'

The Trollopes made North End comfortable. They built a long glass porch, heated by hot pipes, linking the entrance gate to the front door. A feature of North End is its tall Italianate tower. It is said that Anthony, on first viewing the house, announced 'I don't like that tower!' It housed at its summit a cistern, filled from a well by means of a hand-pump. The house had been remodelled in 1800 by one Joseph Postlethwaite, in whose family it had

SUSSEX,
ON THE BORDERS OF HAMPSHIRE.

PARTICULARS AND CONDITIONS OF SALE

OF

A CHARMING

Freehold Property,

KNOWN AS

"NORTH END,"

PLEASANTLY SITUATE

IN THE PARISH OF HARTING,

About one mile from Rogate Station on the London and South Western Railway, four miles from Petersfield, and 12 miles from the Cathedral City of Chichester,

COMPRISING

A COMFORTABLE RESIDENCE,

WITH

GARDENS, STABLING, FARM BUILDINGS,

AND NEARLY

70 ACRES

OF

PASTURE AND ARABLE LAND.

The House, although situate close to the junction of two roads, is, in consequence of being on a higher level and there being but a small amount of traffic, perfectly secluded, while having at the Front Gate ample room for carriage approach.

For Sale, by Private Treaty,

BY

Messrs. OSBORN & MERCER,

Estate Agents,

Of "Albemarle House," 28b, Albemarle Street, Piccadilly, London, W.,

OF WHOM PARTICULARS AND ORDERS TO VIEW MAY BE OBTAINED.

To view the Property, parties are advised to take conveyance from Petersfield Station to Harting.

Vacher & Sons, Printers, 29, Parliament Street, and 61, Millbank Street, Westminster

4 q

Page from the brochure for Anthony's last home, North End, Harting, produced by the estate agents when Rose put the house on the market in 1886. North End was sold to R.W. Oldham for £5,000.

remained. The pump wheezed and squeaked when operated: Rose declared that it was saying, 'I'm Postlethwaite's pump!'

There was a substantial greenhouse with a wrought-iron frame, a kitchen garden, an orchard and a 'Long Walk' up through the fields ending in a view over the downs. They made new friends in Harting, notably G. W. Frisby and his wife, who lived at the Manor House, and they were friendly with the vicar, who recorded that Anthony Trollope was 'the life of our school manager meetings, and a generous patron of the education of the poor'. 'We go to church and mean to be very good,' Anthony told Cecilia Meetkerke. According to the vicar, he attended church nearly every Sunday, 'an alert and reverent and audible worshipper'. He rode out daily on a big black horse, accompanied by Florence on a bay.

He was not content in this rustication. The first winter seemed very long. In the evenings he read aloud to Rose and Florence, as he had since the early 1870s. He pined for Harry, the one person for whose company he seemed to yearn. All his anxious hopes centred on Harry, who was, unfortunately for them both, an inadequate subject for vicarious ambition. 'I miss you most painfully,' he wrote to his son just before Christmas 1880. 'But I had expected that. . . . I finished on Thursday the novel I was writing [Kept in the Dark] and on Friday I began another [The Fixed Period]. Nothing really frightens me but the idea of forced idleness. As long as I can write books, even though they be not published, I think that I can be happy.'

Then, on Christmas Eve (1880), he heard from George Eliot's stepson Charles Lewes that she had died, and was shocked and grieved. 'I did love her very dearly,' he wrote to Charles Lewes. 'That I admired her was a matter of course.'

George Lewes had died on 30 November 1878, and Anthony went to his funeral at Highgate Cemetery, four days before finishing *Cousin Henry*. There had been a close, informal friendship between these two, and George Eliot was fond of Anthony partly because of his fondness for George Lewes. 'All goodness in the world bless you!' she had written to Anthony in 1866. 'First, for being what you are. Next, for that regard I think you bear towards that (to me) best of men, my husband. And after those two chief things, for the goodness both in word and act towards me in particular. . . .

The Little Man hopes to see you and speak to you on that tender subject, the Cigars, on Wednesday. . . .'

Another factor was that both Anthony and George Eliot craved affection and approval, and could rely on one another for ample supplies of both. Anthony wrote to her reverently about her books, but it was she, the person, whom he loved; his attitude to her work was ambivalent. Safe in the knowledge that she would not read it in his lifetime, he wrote in his autobiography: 'I doubt whether any young person can read with pleasure either *Felix Holt*, *Middlemarch*, or *Daniel Deronda*. I know that they are very difficult to many that are not young.'

'Daniel D. has been a trying book to me,' he confessed to Mary Holmes in 1876; 'You perhaps know how I love and admire her.' His complaint, in the autobiography, was that George Eliot was too cerebral and, sometimes, affected. 'She lacks ease.' Again he distinguished between the writer and the woman: 'Perhaps I may be permitted here to say, that this gifted woman was among my dearest and most intimate friends.'

It is not known what George Eliot made of Anthony's story 'Josephine de Montmorenci' which he published in *Saint Pauls* in summer 1870. In it, a susceptible magazine editor was beguiled by flirtatious letters from a female would-be contributor into walking across Regent's Park to Camden Town, to see where she lived. He spotted a pretty woman with a tiny blue parasol coming out of the house, seeming 'as some women do seem, to be an amalgam of softness, prettiness, archness, fun, and tenderness . . . fair, grey-eyed, dimpled, all alive'. If she hadn't been so pretty, he wouldn't have given the manuscript of her novel another glance.

But the pretty woman wasn't the letter-writing author. The pretty woman was a Mrs Puffle, married to Charles (the name of one of Lewes's sons) who worked in the Post Office (as Charles Lewes did) and was serious about cigars (as George Lewes was). The novelist was her sister, a plain, crippled little invalid, and Josephine de Montmorenci was just her pen-name. Her sister called her Polly (which was what George Lewes called George Eliot), and her real name was Maryanne (which was George Eliot's real name). Both sisters believed that the afflicted one was a genius. The editor became 'doubly interested' in the cripple: 'To teach her to be less metaphysical in her writings, and more straightforward in her practices, should be his care.'

What fascinated Anthony about George Eliot was that she was ugly and yet charming, intellectual (much too interested in German philosophy for his tastes), yet sexually alive. The story was partly about how a castle in the air can be built up from deceptive letters; it was also about the conflicting messages that he received from George Eliot. She did not fit into any of his ideas about women. She did more than Kate Field, or the ladies of Langham Place, to enable him to see women, or rather one woman (herself), as his equal, with whom he did not have to censor himself or behave stereotypically. There is a fragment of a letter he wrote to Cecilia Meetkerke in the 1870s: 'I own I like a good contradictory conversation in which for the moment the usual subserviency of coat and trousers to bodies,* skirts, and petticoats, may be – well – not forgotten – but for the moment put to one side.'

Anthony may have been as amazed as everyone else when in May 1880, as the Trollopes were organising their move to Harting, George Eliot, aged sixty, married John Cross, twenty years her junior and seemingly established in the role of an honorary 'dear nephew'.

Anthony knew Cross from before the marriage,† and seems to have accepted the changed situation. Not all the old friends did. But apart from visiting George Eliot and sitting with her for an hour in May 1879 – by which time her new intimacy with Cross was developing, though he could not have known that – Anthony had not seen her. She had been married only seven months when she died.

Kate Field, researching her tribute to George Eliot for the New York *Tribune*, wrote to Anthony for information about the circumstances of Eliot's liaison with Lewes. Anthony professed ignorance of the details, and reminded Kate sharply that George Eliot had clearly 'lived down evil tongues', since she had been invited to dine with Queen Victoria's eldest daughter the Princess Royal, the Crown Princess of Prussia‡ – and 'the English Royal

---

* A 'body' in this sense means bodice – a fitted blouse, or the top half of a dress.

† In the story discussed above, 'Josephine de Montmorenci', the editor's house was called Cross Bank. The Leweses had lived at North Bank. George Eliot first met Johnny Cross in Rome in 1860.

‡ This dinner was given on 31 May 1878 by George Goschen, the banker and Liberal politician. Twenty-two sat down to dinner, including J. A. Froude, John Morley and Anthony himself. More guests, who included peers and bishops, came in after dinner. The presence of Lewes *and* George Eliot in this company was, as Anthony suggested, a significant mark of social acceptance.

family are awfully particular as to whom they see and do not see'. Besides, George Eliot 'was one whose private life should be left in privacy, – as may be said of all who have achieved fame by literary merits'.

They were snowed in at Harting in early 1881, and Anthony could not go up and down to London. By the end of February he had finished *The Fixed Period*, a short, surprising novel set in an imaginary Australasian state in the future – 1980, to be exact. John Neverbend, the first-person narrator, the president of the Empire of the South Pacific, introduced a policy of compulsory euthanasia, to save society not only from the suffering but from the 'costliness' of old age. First, it was decided that sixty should be the end of the 'fixed period' of life; then sixty-five; and sixty-seven and a half was finally decided upon. (Anthony, when he wrote the book, was rising sixty-six.) The trouble was that the first man to reach the significant age after the law had been passed, a particularly hale and hearty fellow, did not in the least want to be 'deposited'.

Apart from the black humour involved, Anthony amused himself with inventing 1980s technology. He still thought in terms of coaches and horses, though Neverbend travelled around on a 'steam-tricycle'. In a cricket match with a visiting British side a 'mechanical steam-bowler' was wheeled into position, and the batsmen wore wicker helmets. The English ship communicated with the shore by means of a 'hair telephone', a thin metal wire linking the speakers. There was also a 'reporting telephone-apparatus' by means of which 'words as they fell from the mouths of the speakers were composed by machinery, and my speech appeared in the London morning papers within an hour of the time of its utterance.'

The Times, when *The Fixed Period* came out in book form (after its author's death, Blackwood having paid £450 for serial and book rights), called its main subject 'essentially ghastly'. Most critics took it as a cumbrous *jeu d'esprit*, but the reviewer for *Blackwood's* wrote: 'When an intimate friend ventured to refer to this Utopian euthanasia as a somewhat grim jest, he [A.T.] stopped suddenly in his walk, and grasping the speaker's arm in his energetic fashion, exclaimed: "It's all true – I *mean* every word of it." ' The reviewer was William Lucas Collins, and the 'intimate friend' was of course himself.

—— * ——

After this Anthony began *Mr Scarborough's Family*, another of his sagas of inheritance and illegitimacy, with a devious King Lear in the person of Mr Scarborough and an impeccable heroine called Florence – to whom he awarded a passionate husband, Harry Annesley, and a honeymoon in the Bernese Alps: 'He is to be my own, one absolute master, to whom I have given myself altogether. . . .' All her arrangements and belongings, declared Harry Annesley, equally ecstatic, must 'administer to my sense of love and beauty'. But she had to accept him as he was, all untidy. He did not snore, but even if he did she should put up with it, as her wifely duty: 'Those are the sort of things that must fall upon a woman so heavily. Suppose I were to beat you. . . .' This relationship was a late flowering of the essential erotic Trollopian daydream. In *Mr Scarborough's Family* he returned too to Hertfordshire, and to the circumstances of his father's lost inheritance, Julians.

With Rose and Florence, he went to Italy for two months, and visited Tom and Fanny. On their return in June 1881, Florence, in her mid-twenties, became seriously ill. Anthony wrote to Millais: 'There was one dreadful day during which I thought that the poor child would have died. They put her under chloroform and did dreadful things to her. But they saved her life. . . .' and she was now with him in his library, 'for a short time for a first short visit'.

He was not well himself. The diagnosis was angina pectoris. 'They tell me my heart is worn out,' he wrote to Tom, 'having been worked too hard. I cannot, among them, understand anything of it . . .' After the hard winter, the summer was unusually hot, and he found it difficult to work.

Then, in July, came news about Bice. At first the news was good. She was pregnant, and well cared for in the Wortleys' house in Mandeville Place. Her daughter was born during the heat-wave, in mid-July, with some trouble ('What an immense boon to humanity is that chloroform!' Tom Trollope wrote to Mrs Stuart-Wortley). Then Bice developed puerperal fever. Anthony went up to London to see her when he heard she was ill, but he was at Harting when she died, on 27 July 1881, aged twenty-eight. She was buried at Wortley.

Tom did not come from Rome for the funeral. Anthony attended, in a fatalistic, death-embracing frame of mind. Afterwards, he told Tom that even if Bice had lived, she would have been an invalid. This seems to have been his own pessimistic surmise. As for the baby, he wrote to Juliet Pollock, 'Is it to be wished that the poor motherless little baby should live?' His grief was dry. He was unsentimental in his assessment (to Lady Pollock, in answer to some query) of the pretty, clever, wilful niece to whom he had been such a loving support: 'I doubt whether you quite understand the antecedents of Bice's life. The fault was that she had been too much spoilt in every thing, – allowed to have her own way and to make a society for herself.' It was her own fault, he said, and not her father's or her stepmother's, if she was not happy with them. 'Everything was done for her that could be done; – but there were not carriages nor parties.* I say this in justice to my brothers [sic] wife, who has been very very good. The fault was my brothers in allowing her to have her own way, till her own way ceased to please her. Poor Bice! But her year of marriage was certainly a year of happiness.'

At North End, in the autumn of 1881, there was a bumper crop of apples. Harry was still in France, working on his translations and planning a book about Normandy. The slowness with which he operated, and the meagre results, worried his father: 'Your fault is in being somewhat too long a time, – not thinking quite enough of the days as they run by; and in being a little too timid as to the work as you do it.' Harry came to Harting for a short visit – to have a wart removed from his head by the local doctor.

Anthony longed for Fred's eldest son, Frank, to be educated at an English public school, and wrote offering to pay. Fred replied that Frank was not strong, and not as bright as his younger brother, and it might be a waste of time and money to send him over from Australia. Anthony itched to be fixing things for his descendants. He put Harry down for the Athenaeum Club, and when Harry's name was coming up for consideration in February 1882 he assiduously canvassed his friends for their support. He wrote to Rose, from the club: 'Dearest Love. They tell me Harry is safe. Though in truth a man is never safe; but in truth a great many more have written their names on his card.' Harry was

---

* Bice did have parties, perhaps too many. What Anthony meant was that Tom and Fanny could not provide a social life for her themselves.

elected a member on 13 February (1882). Anthony's letter to Harry, who was back in France, revealed just how agitated he had been: 'It was a jolly triumph. I was awfully nervous. But when the balloting began the Secretary came to me and told me that you would certainly get in. Knowing the club so well I suppose he understands all the whisperings. I remained there – as did Millais. And we did the best we could. Nevertheless up to the end I was in a funk.' The Secretary and a dozen other members came to him in the card room and told him the good news. 'Somebody said they had never remembered so large a majority.'

Unless there had been some serious objection to Harry as a person, the members could hardly have had the brutality to exclude him, knowing what it meant to his father.

Anthony had been following the activities of Charles Stewart Parnell, leader of the Home Rule party in the Commons and president of the Irish Land League, founded in 1879 – as famine threatened once again – to resist eviction and make landlordism unworkable, with the aim of bringing about a peasant pro-prietary. The Land League perfected a range of tactics – withholding rents, withholding labour, ostracism of land-grabbers by shopkeepers and tradesmen (called 'boycotting' after one of its first victims), death threats, murders and a variety of 'agrarian outrages' such as picketing the hunt and flooding fields, as in Anthony's *The Landleaguers*.

In October 1881 Parnell was jailed in Dublin and the Land League was outlawed. No resolution of the impasse seemed possible without Parnell; he was released, with a deal that exchanged his influence in quelling unrest for concessions to tenants. Within a few days of his release, in May 1882, the new Chief Secretary for Ireland, Lord Frederick Cavendish (who was the nephew of Gladstone's wife), and the Permanent Under-Secretary for Ireland, T. H. Burke, were murdered in Dublin outside the Viceregal Lodge in Phoenix Park. 'I do not know why the deaths of two such men as were then murdered should touch the heart with a deeper sorrow than is felt for the fate of others whose lot is lower in life. . . . But so it is with human nature' (*The Landleaguers*).

Anthony, unwell as he was, determined to write a novel about the crisis in the sister-island and, in June 1882, having completed

An Old Man's Love,* took off with Florence as companion and minder for over a month in Ireland. He travelled all round the country, talking to judges, officials, magistrates, landowners and, to judge from the novel, some of the nationalist clergy. He began writing *The Landleaguers* while he was still there. He missed one of Harry's visits to London: he 'evidently spends most of his time writing letters at the Athenaeum', Anthony complacently commented to Rose from Limerick. He and Florence stayed with the son of old friends, the de la Poers, near Clonmel, and he sent Rose news of the town that had once been their home. 'I am quite well as regards asthma, *except that I cannot stoop.* . . . When I get back I shall see whether the asthma returns at Harting.' From Recess in Co. Galway he asked for home news: 'How is the garden, and the cocks & hens, & especially the asparagus bed.'

He set his novel in Galway, which was a sound choice because, when the statistics emerged, the landowners in that county were shown to have suffered more murders and intimidations than in any other. Anthony was on the side of the responsible, 'improving' landlords, like his fictional Mr Jones of Castle Morony, and, as ever, against Home Rule.

He presented priests who stirred up the people as reprehensible, but scarcely less so than the 'thin, bigoted' Protestant clergyman or the Resident Magistrate who 'lived upon his hatred of a Landleaguer' and was as fixed in his 'devotion to an idea' as any nationalist. Prejudice, and its problematic relation to preference, devotion and loyalty, was Anthony's subject. The Irish-American Rachel O'Mahony said to Frank Jones, the son of Castle Morony: 'Papa says hating Jews is a prejudice. Loving you is a prejudice, I suppose.'

The love stories in the book are interesting only in that Anthony drew a tacit parallel between the proper relation between men and women, and the proper relation between Britain and Ireland. The Irish were by nature 'generous, kindly, impulsive, and docile, they have been willing to follow any recognized leader'. Anthony blamed American Fenianism for the troubles. The villain of his piece was Gerald O'Mahony, an Irish-American rabble-rouser. 'No educated man was ever born and bred in more utter

---

* He did not have the courage to write the book that was in him on this subject. His 'old man', who loved a young woman and renounced her, was only fifty.

ignorance of all political truths than this amiable and philanthropic gentleman.'

His other quarrel was with the policies of Gladstone. Here speaks Black Tom Daly, the Master of the Galway hounds: 'When they've passed this Coercion Bill they're going to have some sort of Land Bill, – just a law to give away the land to somebody. What's to come of the poor country with such men as Mr Gladstone and Mr Bright to govern it? They're the two worst men in the whole empire for governing a country.' Writing editorially (the novel, so far as it goes, becomes more political pamphlet than fiction), Anthony condemned the policy of alternating coercion and concession. With every government concession on land tenure and land purchase the 'mutineers' demanded yet more, and the government had recourse again to repression, and so on in a vicious circle. Anthony, characteristically, called for compromise.

He was back home writing *The Landleaguers* in July 1882 when Tom and Fanny came to stay for ten days. He went up to London with them, and the brothers parted at Garlant's Hotel in Suffolk Street. Tom and Fanny were returning to Rome, and Anthony, feeling that he needed more material, was going straight to Ireland yet again with Florence, for another exhausting month, ending with a quiet week at Kingstown.

Was he so very bored at Harting? Was he rehearsing or hastening his departure on the 'Great Journey' by these debilitating lesser journeys? Anthony wrote to Rose from Glendalough reporting 'a terrible attack of asthma'. Yet in the same letter he told her about enjoying 'the best dinner I ever ate' in the house of Sir Charles Booth, of Booth's Gin.

Even after this second trip *The Landleaguers* did not make progress. It was never to be finished. Harry was coming back to England for the winter, which meant more to Anthony than anything else. He determined to winter, with Harry, in London. 'I take quarts of medicine, and mountains of pills,' he told Tom from Harting after his first trip to Ireland. 'But I believe the fact to be that I am ill here and well in London – It is a bore.'

'For me I feel, – have felt for years, – tempted to rush on, and pass through the gates of death' (*The Fixed Period*). Some time in 1881 or 1882, he wrote to Tom that 'the time has come upon me of which I have often spoken to you, in which I should know that it were better that I were dead.'

In early October 1882 Anthony took the first and second floors of Garlant's Hotel as temporary quarters for himself and Harry. He spent his spare time and wrote his letters in the Athenaeum, only a stroll away. He went home to Harting at weekends ('I will bring 4lb of coffee, and some fish'), and there was talk of Rose coming up to attend the Lord Mayor's banquet at the Mansion House with him. He loved dining out, especially in company with Harry, but was at pains to make Rose feel that she would be welcome in London: she could use Harry's bedroom. 'He can go down to Harting, – or the Devil for that matter.' Rose would be able 'to see what sort of place I live in and would get your breakfast here with me. But we will talk about it.' She did not come – until 4 November.

On 8 October 1882 Anthony dined at the Garrick Club with Robert Browning, and planned a 'big dinner' with Browning, again at the Garrick, for 1 November. He went all the way down to Somerset to stay for a few days with Edward Freeman (with whom he had crossed swords over fox-hunting) near Wells – privately regretting bitterly that he had promised to go. Freeman introduced Anthony to two bishops, and took him for long muddy walks for which he was no longer fit, and argued with him about foreign politics and the geography of Barsetshire.

Anthony felt no better back in London. Some nights he could not sleep, and took chloral; as he wrote to Freeman, he could not write, 'as you see, because my hand is paralysed. I can't sit easily because of a huge truss I wear, and now has come this damnable asthma!* But I am still very good to look at; and as I am not afraid to die, I am as happy as most people.'

Cardinal Newman, an admirer of Anthony's novels, heard about the asthma and sent a message via Lord Emly† that a

---

* The truss was for a hernia. What Anthony called asthma was probably a symptom of his heart disease and high blood pressure.

† Baron Emly (1812–94), as William Monsell, had been at Winchester with Anthony and Tom. An Anglo-Irishman from Co. Limerick, he was MP for Limerick 1847–74 and Postmaster General 1871–78. A Catholic convert, he was a close friend of Newman. Anthony saw him in Ireland during his research for *The Landleaguers*.

treatment involving saltpetre and blotting-paper was particularly helpful. Anthony promised to try it, but 'I fear that it will not be efficacious, because no smoking, or nothing that touches my throat, is of any avail.' As he explained to Lord Emly, 'Great spasmodic want of breath is the evil which affects me, and which at night sometimes becomes very hard to bear.' He had given up wine, but still drank whiskey (which he spelled thus, the Irish way), and was smoking three small cigars a day. He saw his doctor William Murrell, a heart specialist, regularly; Sir William Jenner (one of the Queen's doctors), and the chest specialist Richard Quain,* who was also a friend, were called in as consultants.

The Garrick dinner on Wednesday 1 November went off well. 'We had a gay party,' Browning wrote to his dear friend Katherine Bronson – by whom Anthony too had been charmed, with her daughter Edith, on board the *Bothnia* in 1875 – 'and I thought him in his usual flood of health.' But Browning believed Anthony had been misapplying his 'wonderful capacities for work' of late, 'managing the disordered financial accounts of a bookseller's firm' – i.e., Chapman & Hall.

The next day, Thursday 2 November, Anthony met Freeman once more at dinner at the house of the publisher Alexander Macmillan, and 'talked as well and heartily as usual'. Macmillan lived out at Tooting – a long drive from central London and Suffolk Street.

There is a note in John Tilley's hand on the letter Anthony had sent him from Suffolk Street asking him to the Garrick on 1 November, for the Browning dinner: 'He dined with me on Friday 3rd Nov, & was taken ill at 10 o'clock that night just as he was leaving.'†

What happened after dinner at Tilley's house, 73 St George's Square, on the third consecutive night out, was this. Edith Tilley read aloud to her father and uncle from a new and funny novel which became a classic – *Vice Versa*, by F. Anstey. It is about

* Later Sir Richard Quain: Anthony's contemporary, born in Mallow, Co. Cork. He treated Carlyle, was painted by Millais, and belonged to the Garrick and the Cosmopolitan. He had a Co. Cork brogue. He was known for betraying his patients' confidences, and mentioned to Anthony's first biographer, T. H. S. Escott, Anthony's 'genial air of grievance against the world in general, and those who personally valued him in particular'.

† This letter is in private hands.

a father and son who swap identities, so that the authoritarian
father, trapped in a schoolboy's body, suffers the indignities and
miseries of school life. It is a farcical idea which appealed to
Anthony for obvious reasons. He roared with laughter. But as he
prepared to leave he was, as Tilley said, 'taken ill'. Though it was
not recognised at first, he had had a stroke. He seemed to recover,
and returned by carriage to Garlant's Hotel.

Paralysed on his right side, and unable to speak, he was taken
from the hotel to a nursing home at 34 Welbeck Street.

The Dean, in *Barchester Towers*, had suffered a stroke: 'The only
question was whether he must die at once speechless, unconscious, stricken to death by his first heavy fit; or whether by
due aid of medical skill he might not be so far brought back to this
world as to become conscious of his state, and enabled to address
one prayer to his maker before he was called to meet Him face to
face at the judgement seat.' Archdeacon Grantly 'looked on the
distorted face of his old friend with solemn but yet eager
scrutinising eye, as though he said in his heart, "and so some day
it will probably be with me". . . .'

Frederick Pollock enquired after Anthony every day, Millais
called at 34 Welbeck Street frequently, but did not see his 'dear
old Trollope'. The doctors issued bulletins to the newspapers
during the next weeks, but one must read Tom's letters to Harry
for the inside story of Anthony Trollope's decline. On 4 November
1882, after hearing by telegraph from Harry about the stroke,
Tom wrote from Rome: 'I agree with you that the varying
intonation of his voice must be taken to show that he is in
possession of his reason; the mischief is, I take it, physical in its
nature, and consists in inability to say the words he wants to
say. . . . Tell your mother how deeply we sympathize with her and
with you all in this terrible trouble.'

On 24 November, having heard from Rose and again from
Harry, Tom wrote that what struck him most painfully was
Harry's statement 'that your father wished and attempted to get
out of the carriage *while on his way* to your new house. This seems to
amount to mental alienation. . . .' Would it not be possible, he
asked, 'for Anthony to write with his left hand such few words as
would be invaluable as a means of communication with you?'

By 6 December Tom was expressing the hope that Anthony would not linger on with his mind impaired. He remembered their mother's last years. 'She frequently did things unreasonable in much the same degree as his wanting to undress in the dining-room. And her mind was in fact *gone*. But she certainly – I think I may say certainly – had no idea of this herself.' Anthony did not linger. He died at 34 Welbeck Street at about six o'clock that very evening, 6 December 1882. He was sixty-seven years old, plus nearly eight months – only just exceeding his Fixed Period of sixty-seven and a half years.

'But was there no transient return of mental lucidity quite at the last? That is very commonly the case.' The answer to Tom's question seems to have been in the negative. Rose was with him. Of course, wrote Tom to Harry, 'your mother feels all that I would fain to say to her if I knew how, and if the saying it could be of any comfort to her'. Tom had no ill will towards Rose, but there was no strong bond between those two.

Anthony was buried on Saturday 9 December at Kensal Green cemetery, 'in accordance with the deceased gentleman's strict instruction', as a newspaper said. Kensal Green cemetery is on the Harrow Road, along which Anthony travelled so often as a boy – along which, one distant dawn, he drove his silent father in the trap to the London docks and exile. Anthony knew the whole dreary area well. It was where, in *He Knew He Was Right*, the deranged Louis Trevelyan holed up in a squalid cottage with his kidnapped child: 'If you turn off the Harrow Road to the right, about a mile beyond the cemetery, you will find the cottage on the left hand side of the lane, about a quarter of a mile from the Harrow Road.' Anthony had attended Robert Bell's funeral at Kensal Green, and Thackeray's. As to Anthony's own funeral arrangements, Tom was right when he told Harry that Anthony would not have wanted a fuss. 'He was utterly above the sham and humbug of such things.'

It was just as well. Tom did not come to England for the funeral – 'that is – I *did think* of it, but decided against it. I would have given much to see him once again in his right mind, but I care little for funeral attendances, and would not wish any human being to cross the street to come to mine.' Not many crossed the street to come to Anthony's. The literary world did not turn out to bid him farewell. Perhaps his 'strict instructions' had enjoined that it should be a private occasion. Four mourning coaches and three private vehicles followed the hearse from Welbeck Street at noon. The service was conducted by the vicar of nearby St Peter's, with the Rev. William Lucas Collins in attendance and reading prayers. Tom was sent reports by his son-in-law Charles Stuart-Wortley and by Alfred Austin: 'Austin says there were but few people present.' It is not recorded whether or not the harpies in bright feathered hats who mobbed the graves of Thackeray and Wilkie Collins attended Anthony Trollope's funeral too.

Ladies did not normally attend funerals; Rose and Florence did not go, though Lady Trollope, Mrs Frederic Chapman and a Mrs Peto were present at the service in the cemetery chapel before the burial. Harry was at the graveside, with John Tilley, John Millais, Robert Browning, Frederic Chapman, Alfred Austin, Charles Stuart-Wortley, and a cluster of Trollope cousins. And a small somewhat arbitrary group of other friends, among them Edward Dicey, who had worked with Anthony on *Saint Pauls*, and Anthony's Australian friend G. W. Rusden, who had visited Harting earlier in the year.

As private and personal as the funeral were the words which Rose and Harry later had engraved on his tombstone, beneath his name and dates:

'He was a loving husband, a loving father and a true friend.'

CONCLUSION

ACCORDING to the will he made in 1878, Anthony appointed 'my eldest son Henry Merivale Trollope' to be his literary trustee and executor; and both Henry (Harry) and Rose as his general trustees and executors. He left Rose all his chattels – furniture, pictures, plate, linen, wine, etc – and £350 for her immediate needs. She gave Anthony's bust of Milton to the Athenaeum Club, Millais acting as the go- between. Harry got 'my library of books and pamphlets'. Profits from the sale of real and leasehold estate and all other monies were to be held in trust and invested.

His executors had discretion to keep or sell his stocks and shares as they saw fit, but new investments must not be in any companies outside the United Kingdom or its colonies and dependencies. (No more foreign railways.) Harry might make or vary no investment without Rose's consent in writing, and the income from the trust was hers for her lifetime.

Florence Bland, like Mr Indefer Jones's niece in *Cousin Henry*, was to get her £4,000, but not until after Rose's death; this may have been decided to ensure that Rose, bound to support Florence (unless Florence married, which she did not), would have a companion. Florence had made a will under her uncle's guidance the summer before he died, in which she made her cousins Harry and Fred her heirs. Perhaps he had settled a small annuity on her at that time.

The ultimate beneficiary of the trust was to be Harry, Florence's Cousin Henry, in equal shares with Fred, after taking into account Harry's legacy of the library (valued by Anthony at £1,000) and all the money that Anthony had advanced to Fred. He let Fred off all interest due on the loans.

Fred was always hard up; Rose packed up Anthony's coats, trousers, waistcoats and boots and shipped them out to Australia. Fred reported that the trousers needed taking in and the buttons on the coats needed moving back, but fitted him otherwise. The boots were a little big 'but not uncomfortable'; the only items he couldn't use were the black waistcoats. Rose also sent Fred a photograph of his father's gravestone: 'It seems to be handsome and massive,' commented Fred.

Anthony Trollope's estate was valued for probate at £25,892.19.3, with another £10,000 falling in later from copyrights. His custom of selling his books outright for lump sums meant that there was almost no long-term legacy of royalties.

Within months of his father's death, as if he had been waiting for the order of release, Harry, aged thirty-seven, became engaged to Florence's friend Ada Strickland. Ada's mother had a house in Jersey and a flat in Rome, where they spent the winter; Henry proposed to her in the Coliseum. 'I was kind to my husband,' wrote Ada to Michael Sadleir after Harry's death, 'and *liked* him because he was *Anthony's son* and only married him because he said if I refused him 50 times he would ask me as many times again!' They started their married life in spring 1884 at 121 Finborough Road, a street linking Fulham Road with the Old Brompton Road. The following year they had a daughter, Muriel Rose. She lived until 1953. A son, Thomas Anthony, was born nine years after Muriel. He died in 1931. Neither of Harry's children married.

Harry saw his father's autobiography through the press – not without difficulty. In the letter that Anthony locked up with the manuscript, he had written: 'I should wish the book to be published by Fred Chapman if he is in business at the time of my death; – but of course you will do the best you can as to terms, if not with him, then with some other publisher.' Chapman & Hall were still in business, but Frederic Chapman was controlled by his board; Tom advised Harry that Anthony would not offer them the book now 'had he to transact the affair himself'.

Harry recopied the manuscript and worked on a preface. He wrote to William Blackwood in Edinburgh in January 1883, telling him the story of the locking up of the manuscript and saying that his father had mentioned the sum of £1,800. Blackwood responded positively – but 'the sum you mention for the copyright appals me'. Harry came down to £1,500; they finally settled, in April, for £1,000 for an edition of 4,000 copies and a royalty of two-thirds of the profits of any further printing. In the event Blackwood only printed 3,000 copies, 'so as to get the éclat of a second edition early', as he told Harry.

An Autobiography was published in October 1883. Mudie's Library took 1,000 copies, but Blackwood was careful to stress to Harry that in spite of warm and gratifying reviews sales were 'sticky'. Harry wanted Blackwood to bring out a cheap edition – 5s or even 3s 6d. 'I fear,' wrote Blackwood, 'it will take a very large sale to make it remunerative at that price.'

Blackwood was equally costive about publishing *An Old Man's Love*. He said frankly that 'I would rather not have it. Your father's novels have somehow never taken a hold in the [*Blackwood's*] Magazine and without reading the MS I would be afraid to venture upon it.' He reminded Harry that *The Fixed Period*, which Blackwood's published in two volumes after serialisation in their magazine, had only sold 877 copies, leaving the firm out of pocket. In the end Blackwood bought *An Old Man's Love*, sight unseen, for £200.

Harry went to a new firm, Chatto & Windus, with *Mr Scarborough's Family* and sold the book rights to them for £600; Anthony had already made an agreement with Chatto for *The Landleaguers* shortly before his death, which suggests that he was indeed preparing to extricate himself from the doomed Chapman & Hall.

Harry wrote a novel himself, called *My Own Love Story*, which he got Chapman & Hall to publish in 1887, the year of the firm's definitive financial collapse. From Australia, Fred wrote to his brother: 'So you are going to publish a novel. I am sorry to hear Ada say that it is dull.' Ada was absolutely right.

Rose left North End House, Harting, soon after Harry married. She sold it in 1886 for £5,000; the auctioneer's brochure mentioned that 'the House will always possess a passing interest in having been the last residence of the popular author, the late Anthony Trollope. There are two Postal Deliveries daily and Telegraph Office at Rogate Station.' Rose had already moved with Florence, and her maid, 'the ancient Catherine', to London, to 6 Cheyne Gardens near the river in Chelsea. She spent frequent summers with Florence in Kitzbühl, 'an out of the world quaint old town in

Tirol [Austria] among the meadows and Pine woods', as she wrote to Anthony's old acquaintance the politician George Goschen, asking for an introduction for Fred to the Governor of New South Wales.

Rose let her London house profitably while she was away. Much of the material prosperity of which Anthony had been so proud, the fruits of his industry, died with him. 'Since the breakdown in the C & H company, I have to practice very close economy. . . .' All the Trollope family suffered through the failure of Chapman & Hall; Rose, Harry, Tom and Fanny (and her sister Ellen Wharton Robinson) had shares in the company, which ceased paying dividends in October 1887. The ordinary shares were then worth virtually nothing. In summer 1897, through Alfred Austin's intervention, Rose began drawing a Civil List pension of £100 a year. Like many old people she was sure she had no money; in fact, her investment income for 1896 was £538.

She was not indigent but she was not rich. She often sent small amounts of money to Fred. Perhaps she helped Harry and Ada as well; Harry never had a job, and his writing cannot have brought in much. Rose too in her widowhood made a stab at writing to increase her income. It was, after all, something that Trollopes, and those married to Trollopes, seemed to be able to do as a matter of course. In 1889, aged sixty-nine, she submitted to *Blackwood's* a story called 'The Legend of Holm Royde'. It was rejected.

Bice's widower Charles Stuart-Wortley, later Lord Stuart of Wortley, was Under-Secretary at the Home Office from 1885. He remarried in 1886. His second wife was Alice Millais, a daughter of Anthony's great friend. Bice's daughter, named Beatrice after her, married Arthur Cecil in 1906 and lived until 1973.

Kate Field never married. She remained a campaigner – for international copyright laws and temperance, and against Mormon polygamy and the US annexation of Hawaii. She died in 1896, aged fifty-eight.

Tom Trollope wrote his three volumes of reminiscences, having been 'first incited to attempt something of the sort by Geo. Eliot, who spoke to me about it on more than one occasion'. He and Fanny retired in 1885 to Budleigh Salterton in Devon. He had an income of £230 a year, and Charles Stuart-Wortley and Alfred Austin got him an additional £200 p.a. on the Civil List. Tom died on 11 November 1892 at 27 York Crescent, Bristol, where he and Fanny were stopping for a few days on their way to London. He was eighty-two. Fanny buried 'my own dearest, best, most loved and honoured darling' in Arno's Vale Cemetery in Bristol. A marble tablet to Tom was placed on their house, Cliff Corner, at Budleigh Salterton, with a Latin inscription: 'Scriptor copiosissimus, Amicus jucundissimus.'

Fanny Trollope busied herself in her widowhood by writing a memoir of the most famous Mrs Trollope, her mother-in-law, having inherited from Tom 'a great mass' of her letters and papers, going back seventy years. She told the publisher George Bentley that 'I cannot refrain from saying that, high as my respect for "the Mammy" (as we always spoke of her en famille) has been ever since I first heard or knew anything of her, it has been enormously increased by a perusal of these family papers.' Fanny, who died in 1913, spent her final years with her sisters Maria and Ellen in Southsea.*

Fred's eldest son Frank, aged ten, was sent to England the summer after Anthony died, as Anthony had wanted, but very much against his mother Susie's wishes. He went to the Wharton Robinsons' school at Margate, where he was not happy. As Fred had said, Frank was not strong, nor particularly clever; and he had, naturally enough, an Australian accent, which sounded common to his English relations. Tom commented to Harry that 'it is curious that a boy should come from Australia with a cockney accent! As for the hours in dressing and the maids [it is not known what young Frank did to the maids], I think I could cure that; – but it would be by processes altogether out of fashion in these days.' Tom had not changed.

Poor Fred wrote to his mother defensively. 'It troubles Susie that Frank speaks badly. He certainly was better than that when

* Bentley published *Frances Trollope: Her Life and Literary Work*, by Frances Eleanor Trollope, in 1895. The fact that Fanny moved in with her sisters accounts for the non-survival of so many Trollope family letters. After Ellen Wharton Robinson's death, the year after Fanny Trollope's, Ellen's son Geoffrey discovered evidence of his mother's true age, of her stage career and of her pre-marital association with Charles Dickens. He was so profoundly upset that he destroyed masses of letters and papers, which would have included some accumulated by Tom Trollope and Fanny. It is also likely that Fanny discreetly threw out some family letters after writing her memoir of her mother-in-law. See Claire Tomalin, *The Invisible Woman*.

he was at home.' Years later, Fred was still justifiably defensive. 'Your last letters or that part of them speaking of Frank made me unhappy and I may say angry especially when you blame Susie for what has taken place.' What had taken place was that Frank, when he was seventeen, joined the British Navy – which he simply used to secure a free passage home to Australia.

Later Frank went to South Africa, and fought in the Boer War; 'like most Australians', wrote his grandmother Rose to Charles Stuart-Wortley, asking for further favours for Frank, he '*can ride anything*'. Frank had led a rough life, but 'I must add that in spite of it having been a rough one he is a *gentleman*. . . . Have you any interest with Sir Evelyn Wood? My husband knew him in the old hunting days, but I seldom met him.' Rose was a tigress grandmother when it came to soliciting favours for Fred's children. Charles Stuart-Wortley was never allowed to forget his connection with the Trollope family. Fanny, Tom's widow, also sought his assistance. She wrote him charming, ladylike, begging letters.

Shortly after his father's death Fred Trollope accepted a clerkship in the Lands Department in Sydney, at a salary of £400 a year. This was only £50 more than he had earned before, but the work, since it did not involve inspecting a district, was less exhausting. Fred was respected and respectable, rising in his Department, but always socially isolated, apart from a period when he was chairman of the local Land Board in the small town of Hay. There, Fred was president of the Horticultural Society and vice-president of the Cricket Club.

Fred's career mirrored his father's – years travelling the roads, years as a reliable public official – but Fred lacked Anthony's buoyancy (and his genius). It appears that he was an irritable man, and a disappointed one. He abandoned England with a singular determination, but he was never fully at home in Australia either. He complained of the heat, he complained of the lack of service, and of his long run of bad luck.

Fred's flight from his father's world was ambivalent. When he first settled in Australia he sent home clippings of bad poems from local papers, in an attempt to show he was not without sensibility or culture. He read all his father's books and expressed opinions about them, and he named his Sydney house Clavering Cottage. The reference was not to the big house in *The Claverings*, Clavering Park, in which one of the coldest, bleakest marriages that

Anthony ever dreamed up slowly fell apart; but to the comfortable, well-ordered Clavering rectory, where lived a Clavering cleric-cousin and his wife: 'Her house was full of love.'

In 1903 Fred came back to England for the first time in over thirty years, to see his mother. He died before she did – in 1910, at the age of sixty-two. Since Harry had no grandchildren, Anthony's direct line died out in England. But Fred and Susie had eight children, the last two, Clive and Gordon, born after Anthony's death. Rose, in 1912, had a letter from her youngest grandson, twenty-six-year-old Gordon, telling her about his engagement to Mary Blacket,* 'the daughter of an engineer under whom I was once a pupil'.

Gordon Trollope's middle name was Clavering, and he wrote to his 'Dear Grandma' from his father's house, Clavering. A connection he may or may not have made was that in his grandfather's novel *The Claverings* young Harry Clavering, the son of the 'house of love', also married the daughter of an engineer whose pupil he had been. But Harry Clavering's father-in-law was a rougher diamond than Gordon Clavering Trollope's. Sir Edmund Blacket was an architect-engineer, responsible for some of Australia's most important nineteenth-century buildings.

Harry Trollope died at his house Greylands, at Minchinhampton in Gloucestershire, in 1926, aged eighty. In his last years he saw and corresponded with Michael Sadleir, who was writing his book *Trollope: A Commentary*. (This was published in 1927, and dedicated to Harry's memory.) Harry was not keen on the idea of the book at first; he felt Anthony and Rose would have been against it.†

---

* Of all Fred's children, Gordon was the only one that married. Owing to an accident of genealogy, the baronetcy of the Trollopes of Casewick in Lincolnshire passed sideways to Anthony's Australian grandson Frederick Farrand Trollope (who died unmarried in 1957) and thence to Sir Frederick's brother, this same Gordon (who married Mary in 1913); and thence to Sir Gordon's son and Anthony's great-grandson, Anthony Owen Clavering Trollope, whose house at Roseville, NSW, was also called Clavering. He died in 1987. The present baronet is his son and Anthony's great-great-grandson, Sir Anthony Trollope, born 1945, who breeds Rhodesian Ridgeback dogs and Anglo-Arab horses at Oakville, NSW. The house of Sir Anthony's younger brother Hugh, at Lindfield, NSW, is called Casewick Cottage. Since Sir Anthony only has daughters, the presumptive heir to the baronetcy is Hugh's son Andrew Ian Trollope, born 1978.

† Neither Rose nor Harry seems to have cooperated with T. H. S. Escott on *Anthony Trollope: His Work, Associates, and Originals* (1913) which was based on conversations with Anthony Trollope in his last years and on the reminiscences of friends and acquaintances.

Harry cautioned Sadleir against taking too seriously any of Ada's views about his father: 'My wife had a very great regard, even fondness for him; but apart from the enjoyment she does feel in reading a book her mind is not critical in a literary sense.' There does not seem to have been much mutual admiration in this marriage.

Harry remained a francophile and an occasional writer and translator, and published a life of Molière in 1905. The impression remains that, like Fred, he did not lead a wholly fulfilled life. But as the uncertain, uncommitted narrator of his dull novel said, 'It is not everyone who passes a life of thrilling adventure!'

Anthony had not found it easy or pleasant to be the son of Thomas Anthony Trollope. Harry and Fred, for different reasons, may not have found it easy to be the sons of Anthony Trollope. Harry, whom Anthony loved so much, remembered chiefly how irritable his father could be. Muriel told Michael Sadleir that 'Father [i.e. Harry] had inherited I think, a good deal of his Grandfather's [i.e. Thomas Anthony's] reticence and never really showed me what a lovable man, how good and generous yet impatient and brusque, how shy under the brusqueness and genuinely humble A[nthony] T[rollope] really was.'

Florence Bland died at Cheyne Gardens in 1908, aged fifty-three. Rose then moved in with Harry, Ada and Muriel at Minchinhampton. Rose saw things Anthony never dreamed of: motor cars, airplanes, short skirts, world war. She died on 25 May 1917. She was ninety-six. She never made a will. The gross value of her estate was £373.4.8.

Julian Hawthorne was right when he wrote of Anthony Trollope that 'his wife was his books', even though she was not 'literary' and even wished he were not a writer: ' "He never leaves off," she said complainingly, "and he always has two packages of manuscript in his desk, besides the one he's working on, and the one that's being published." But the good woman was always fashionably dressed, and money, unlike Dian's kiss, does not come unasked, unsought. But he and she were an affectionate couple; fox-hunting and matrimony cost him something, but he was faithful to both to the end.'* In point of fact Anthony did not sustain his fox-hunting to the end, as he had his marriage.

---

* *Shapes that Pass: Memories of the Past* (1928). Julian Hawthorne was the son of Nathaniel Hawthorne.

Rose had not been a doormat wife – in private. Anthony's novels are full of authorial generalisations about the gestures and silences that indicate wifely disapproval, and about the ways in which wives make dissent known. 'There be those who say that if a man be anything of a man, he can always insure obedience in his own household. He has the power of the purse and the power of the law; and if, having these, he goes to the wall, it must be because he is a poor creature. Those who so say have probably never tried the position' (*Orley Farm*).

Mrs Grantly deferred to Archdeacon Grantly at the dinner-table but spoke her mind beneath the bedclothes. The hold that Mrs Proudie had over her husband the bishop was at its most potent in the privacy of their bedroom, though we never learn exactly what she did to him there. If Rose lives on in the sweet, dependent, loyal Marys and Lucys and Fannys of Anthony's novels, she is there in Mrs Proudie as well. Mrs Proudie was 'not in the least a caricature', Anthony told T. H. S. Escott, 'but, stripped of her episcopal surroundings, the commonplace of most English households'.

There is an unguarded aside in *The Way We Live Now*: 'The man who succumbs to his wife . . . is as often brought to servility by a continual aversion to the giving of pain, by a softness which causes the fretfulness of others to be an agony to himself, – as by any actual fear which the firmness of the imperious one may have produced. There is an inner softness, a thinness of the mind's skin, an incapability of seeing or even thinking of the troubles of others with equanimity, which produces a feeling akin to fear. . . .'

In *The Fixed Period* the wife of Neverbend, the first-person narrator, lectured him as they lay in the marital bed. 'I hate these lectures. . . . I always find myself absolutely impotent during their progress. I am aware that it is quite useless to speak a word, and that I can only allow the clock to run itself down. . . . And I fear no evil results from her anger for the future, because her conduct to me will, I know by experience, be as careful and as kind as ever. Were another to use harsh language to me, she would rise in wrath to defend me.'

As would Rose, to defend Anthony. But their bedroom door is not open to us.

Dean Lovelace in *Is He Popenjoy?* gave his daughter this advice: 'A wife should provide that a man's dinner was such as he liked to eat, his bed such as he liked to lie on, his clothes arranged as he liked to wear them, and the household hours fixed to suit his convenience.' This will win from him 'a liking and a reverence which would wear better than the feeling generally called love, and would at last give the woman her proper influence.'

'A liking and a reverence', then? For thirty-eight years Rose was to Anthony everything traditionally associated with the word 'wife', with all its implications of comfort, trust, permanence, history, habit, irritation, boredom, limitation, affection, private references, family secrets – and the shared memory, like the foundations of a house, of passion. Bone of his bone, flesh of his flesh. He wrote in his autobiography, 'I have dishonoured no woman.' That must mean something. It must mean that he was never technically unfaithful to Rose.

He was honest and true. But in the virtual reality of his fiction he was a free man.

In real life too he absented himself constantly, in acts of abandon, and of abandonment. Of course she minded. When at the end of *The Fixed Period* Neverbend was leaving for the other side of the world, perhaps for ever, his wife, 'laughing gently under the bedclothes', did not seem to mind at all. She organised food for the journey and packed four pairs of flannel drawers for him. It was their son who said, 'Mother would like to have gone too.' Neverbend replied that there was too much for her to see to at home; but 'he knew that she would have liked to go with him. . . .'

What happens, in a long, stable marriage, to love? To the needy desire that Anthony Trollope felt for Rose Heseltine, the girl with the north-country voice whom he met on the beach at Kingstown in 1842? He asked and answered that question with definitive grace in *He Knew He Was Right*, through the young journalist Hugh Stanbury, sitting on a rock by the river Teign dreaming of his Nora. If love were attained, he wondered, what would be its pleasures?

> What is it all but to have reached the once mysterious valley of your far-off mountain, and to have found that it is as other valleys, – rocks and stones, with a little grass, and a thin stream of running water? But beyond that pressing of the hand, and that kissing of the lips, – beyond that short-lived

pressure of the plumage which is common to birds and men, – what could love do beyond that? There were children with dirty faces, and household bills, and a wife who must, perhaps, always darn the stockings, – and sometimes be cross. Was love to lead only to this, – a dull life, with a woman who had lost the beauty from her cheeks, and the gloss from her hair, and the fire from her eye, and the grace from her step, and whose waist an arm should no longer be able to span? Did the love of the poets lead to that, and that only?

Then he had an 'intimation' that the ultimate 'mysterious valley among the mountains' was not sex but the capacity to love. 'The beauty of it all was not so much in the thing loved, as in the loving.' Anthony Trollope was a loving man. That is not so common. Whatever the strains, Rose was lucky. So was he.

The last time Tom saw his brother was at Garlant's Hotel, on the August morning that he and Fanny left to return to Italy. But, as he wrote to Harry, 'what will most remain in mind will be the pleasant strolling up and down in the orchard at Harting, as we watched and laughed at his dog jumping for apples.' The eternal moment.

Those who read his books know him best. He ended his autobiography with them in mind: 'Now I stretch out my hand, and from the further shore I bid adieu to all who have cared to read any among the many words that I have written.'

NOTES AND SOURCES

I HAVE kept these notes to a minimum. Where possible I have given my sources in the narrative, either in the text or in footnotes. Other categories of material can be accounted for once and for all here and in the notes to Chapter One.

Letters written by Anthony Trollope and quoted in this book are taken from N. John Hall (ed.), *The Letters of Anthony Trollope* (two volumes, Stanford University Press, 1983) unless otherwise indicated. There are Trollope family papers in the Library of the University of Illinois at Urbana-Champaign and others elsewhere, as specified in the notes; but the richest repositories of Trollopiana are the Morris L. Parrish Collection and the Robert H. Taylor Collection in the University Library at Princeton University. Letters to or from members of the Trollope family and their correspondents are at Princeton unless otherwise indicated. Particularly important documents, letters or groups of letters are attributed specifically to the Parrish or the Taylor Collection in the notes. When not dated in the narrative, letters may be dated by month and year from the context. If a letter is quoted out of chronological context, this is made clear.

I include references only to those books and articles which I have found particularly useful or from which I have quoted, and which are not cited in footnotes. I have benefited in a variety of ways from the work of previous biographers of Trollope, to whom I would refer the interested reader: T. H. S. Escott (1913), Michael Sadleir (1927, revised edition 1945), Hugh Walpole (1928), James Pope Hennessy (1971), C. P. Snow (1975 – an illustrated essay rather than a full biography), R. H. Super (1988), Richard Mullen (1990), N. John Hall (1991).

I have had frequent recourse to Trollopian reference books: W. G. Gerould and J. T. Gerould, *A Guide to Trollope* (Princeton University Press, 1948); Donald Smalley (ed.), *Anthony Trollope: The Critical Heritage* (Routledge & Kegan Paul, 1969); R. C. Terry (ed.), *Trollope: Interviews and Recollections* (Macmillan London, 1987); R. C. Terry, *A Trollope Chronology* (Macmillan London, 1989). David Skilton, Claire Connolly and Christopher Edwards, *Anthony Trollope: A Collector's Catalogue* (The Trollope Society, 1992) provides an up-to-date conspectus of the considerable secondary and critical literature on Trollope as well as a complete Trollope bibliography.

The following notes are designed to be accessible and to suggest further reading as well as to identify my sources.

INTRODUCTION

For the intrigues of Lady Palmerston and Lady Jersey see F. E. Baily, *The Love Story of Lady Palmerston* (Hutchinson, 1938). For more about teeth see Michael Irwin, *Picturing: Description and Allusion in the Nineteenth-Century Novel* (Allen & Unwin, 1879).

CHAPTER ONE

Unless otherwise indicated, A.T.'s accounts of people and events throughout this book are from *An Autobiography* (Blackwood, 1883). His eldest brother Tom Trollope's versions are from his three-volume autobiography: Thomas Adolphus Trollope, *What I Remember* (Bentley, 1887), which includes excerpts from his diaries and from letters. The early letters between Thomas Anthony Trollope and Frances (Milton) Trollope are in the Taylor Collection. The memoir of her mother-in-law by Tom Trollope's second wife is *Frances Trollope: Her Life and Literary Work* by Frances Eleanor Trollope (Bentley, 1895). Some letters from Frances (Milton) Trollope which were later lost or destroyed are in this memoir.

The Trollope family history is traced by the Venerable Edward Trollope in *The Family of Trollope* (James Williamson, 1875). The Milton family background is described in Johanna Johnston, *The Life, Manners and Travels of Fanny Trollope* (Constable, 1979); Helen Heineman, *Mrs Trollope: The Triumphant Feminine in the Nineteenth Century* (Athens, Ohio, 1979); L. P. Stebbins & R. P. Stebbins, *The Trollopes: The Chronicle of a Writing Family* (Secker & Warburg, 1946).

See *The Victoria County History*, Vol. 4 (Middlesex), for details of T. A. Trollope's Harrow farm and his relations with Lord

Northwick. Sources for the Drury family and for Harrow School, here and in later chapters, include *The Dictionary of National Biography*; E. D. W. Chaplin, *The Book of Harrow* (Staples Press, 1948); Jonathan Gathorne-Hardy, *The Public School Phenomenon* (Hodder & Stoughton, 1977); John Chandos, *Boys Together: English Public Schools 1800–1864* (Hutchinson, 1984).

Tom Trollope's letter to Mary Grant Christie is in the Parrish Collection. Frances Trollope's 'Lines Written on the Burial of the Daughter of a Celebrated Author' with A.T.'s annotations are in the University of Illinois Library and have been published in N. John Hall, *Salmagundi: Byron, Allegra and the Trollope Family*, Beta Phi Mu Chapbook XI (Princeton University Press, 1975). The best brief account of the intellectual wing of the nineteenth-century evangelical movement in the Church of England is Chapter 5 ('Evangelicalism') of Noel Annan's *Leslie Stephen: the Godless Victorian* (Weidenfeld & Nicolson, 1984).

The anecdote about Robert Lowe beating the Trollope brothers is told without attribution in Asa Briggs, *Victorian People* (Odhams Press, 1954). For Fanny Wright and Nashoba see Margaret Lane, *Frances Wright and the 'Great Experiment'* (Manchester University Press/Rowman & Littlefield, 1972).

CHAPTER TWO

For Mrs Frances Trollope's experiences in the United States, and the reactions of Americans both to *Domestic Manners of the Americans* and to her as a person, see the biographies of her detailed under Chapter One; also Monique Parent Frazee's excellent *Mrs Trollope and America* (Université de Caen, 1969). The letters of A.T.'s brother Henry to their mother are in the Taylor Collection.

CHAPTER THREE

For a romantic account of the concept of the 'gentleman', see Shirley Robin Letwin, *The Gentleman in Trollope: Individuality and Moral Conduct* (Macmillan London, 1982). There were contrary views even in Trollope's time; Edmund Yates in his *Recollections and Experiences* (Bentley, 1884) quotes a subversive ballad of the 1850s:

There is a word in the English tongue
Where I'd rather it were not;
For shams and lies from it have sprung,
And heartburns fierce and hot.
'Tis a tawdry cloak for a dirty soul;
'Tis a sanctuary base,
Where the fool and the knave themselves may save
From justice and disgrace:
'Tis a curse to the land, deny it who can,
That self-same boast, 'I'm a gentleman!'

For careerism and patronage in the Church of England see Clive Dewey, *The Passing of Barchester* (Hambledon Press, 1991).

CHAPTER FOUR

The account of A.T.'s career in the Post Office, here and in later chapters, owes much to R. H. Super's monograph *Trollope in the Post Office* (University of Michigan Press, 1981). For nineteenth-century London's development and street-life, here and in later chapters, I have drawn chiefly on *Edmund Yates: His Recollections and Experiences* (Bentley, 1884); Alexander Shand, *Days of the Past: A Medley of Memories* (Constable, 1905); Robert Gray, *A History of London* (Hutchinson, 1987); N. T. P. Murphy, *One Man's London* (Hutchinson, 1989).

For A.T.'s grasp of the classics and how they were taught see Robert Tracy, 'Lana Medicata Fuco: Trollope's Classicism', in *Trollope: Centenary Essays*, ed. John Halperin (Macmillan London, 1982).

Thomas Anthony Trollope's death certificate is in the Taylor Collection. A.T.'s manuscript commonplace book is in the Beinecke Library at Yale and is included as Appendix A to A.T.'s *Letters*.

CHAPTER FIVE

For Mary Clarke (who became Mary Mohl), Madame Récamier and Mrs Trollope's Parisian circle, see *Madame Mohl, Her Salon and*

Her Friends (Bentley, 1885); M. C. M. Simpson (ed.), *Letters and Recollections of Julius and Mary Mohl* (Kegan Paul, 1887); and Mrs Trollope's *Paris and the Parisians in 1835* (Bentley, 1835). Madame Récamier's salon is described in an essay by Cynthia Gladwyn in *Genius in the Drawing-Room: The Literary Salon in the Nineteenth and Twentieth Centuries*, ed. Peter Quennell (Weidenfeld & Nicolson, 1980).

The career of Caroline Norton is well summarised in Margaret Forster's *Significant Sisters* (Secker & Warburg, 1984).

The letters from Mrs Trollope and Tom Trollope to Lady Bulwer, and Mrs Trollope's letters about Dr Elliotson and the Okey girls, are in the Parrish Collection.

A.T.'s proposal for a History of World Literature is in the University of Illinois Library and is published as Appendix B to A.T.'s *Letters*.

CHAPTER SIX

In researching Trollope and Ireland I have had frequent recourse to Mark Bence-Jones, *A Guide to Irish Country Houses* (revised edition Constable, 1988), which is a guide to Anglo-Ireland's genealogy and social history as well as to its architecture. James Pope Hennessy's *Anthony Trollope* is particularly informative about Banagher and its environs. W. M. Thackeray's impressions of Ireland are from *The Irish Sketch Book* (by 'Mr M. A. Titmarsh', 1843). For the pioneering photography of Mary Countess of Rosse see David H. Davidson, *Impressions of an Irish Countess* (Birr Scientific Heritage Foundation, 1989).

A.T.'s travel diaries, properly designated the Travelling Account Books, are in the Parrish Collection.

Contemporary accounts of Edward Heseltine are from *Reminiscences of Rotherham and District* by local contributors, reprinted from the *Rotherham Advertiser* (Henry Garnett, 1891). Heseltine's testimony about the drains is from William Lee's *Report to the General Board of Health . . . on the Sanitary Condition of the Inhabitants of the Townships of Rotherham and Kimberworth* (Her Majesty's Stationery Office, 1851). Documentation on the Heseltine family is from the Archives and Local Studies Section of the Brian O'Malley Central Library in Rotherham.

CHAPTER SEVEN

Rose Trollope's MS chronology is in the University of Illinois Library. Mrs Trollope's letters to Rose are in the Taylor Collection. Charles Lever's letter to John Blackwood is from Edmund Downey, *Charles Lever: His Life in His Letters* (Blackwood, 1906). Information about Bianconi from Mrs Morgan John O'Connell, *Charles Bianconi 1786–1875* (Chapman & Hall, 1878).

For the historical context of the Trollopes' life in Ireland and for political perspective on the Famine see R. K. Foster, *Modern Ireland 1600–1972* (Allen Lane The Penguin Press, 1988). The narrative details of the disaster, including eye-witness accounts of events in Clonmel, are from Cecil Woodham-Smith, *The Great Hunger* (Hamish Hamilton, 1962).

CHAPTER EIGHT

For hunts and hunting in Ireland and England see Raymond Carr, *The History of Foxhunting* (Weidenfeld & Nicolson, 1976) and J. N. P. Watson, *The Book of Foxhunting* (Batsford, 1977).

Henry Colburn's letters to A.T., like most of A.T.'s letters from publishers and editors, are in the Bodleian Library, Oxford. The Tilley family letters, and the Trollopes' letters to the Tilleys quoted in this chapter, are in private hands. A.T.'s Letters to the *Examiner*, edited by Helen Garlinghouse King, are reprinted in the *Princeton University Library Chronicle*, Vol. 26 (1964–65).

Material about the Great Exhibition of 1851 is chiefly from Asa Briggs, *Victorian Things* (Batsford, 1988) and from the *Official Catalogue of the Great Exhibition* (Spicer Bros, 1851).

CHAPTER NINE

Information about Rowland Hill and the penny post is from the *Dictionary of National Biography*, from R. H. Super, *Trollope in the Post Office*, and from Asa Briggs, *Victorian Things*. Memories of A.T. in Cornwall and South Wales by his PO contemporaries are collected in R. C. Terry (ed.), *Trollope: Interviews and Recollections*.

Rose's accounts of Mrs Trollope as an elderly woman are

quoted in her sister-in-law F. E. Trollope's *Frances Trollope: Her Life and Literary Work*. Robert Browning's letter to his wife about Mrs Trollope's vulgarity is quoted in virtually every book about either of the Brownings, including Betty Miller's excellent and neglected *Robert Browning: A Portrait* (John Murray, 1952). Emily Tennyson's contrary impression of Mrs Trollope is from Robert Bernard Martin's *Tennyson: The Unquiet Heart* (Oxford University Press/Faber, 1980).

CHAPTER TEN

A transcription of the report of Longman's reader Joseph Cauvin on *The New Zealander* is in the Bodleian Library, and is printed in A.T.'s *Letters*.

The details of Edward Heseltine's defalcation, his attempts to evade investigation and the letters from his wife, are taken from an unsigned article, 'Mr Trollope's Father-in-law', *Three Banks Review* (June 1865). Material on George Hudson is from Richard S. Lambert, *The Railway King* (Allen & Unwin, 1934).

A.T.'s work-sheets are in the Bodleian Library. For the mechanics of Victorian publishing and the lending-library system see Guinevere Griest, *Mudie's Circulating Library and the Victorian Novel* (David & Charles, 1971); N. N. Feltes, *Modes of Production of Victorian Novels* (University of Chicago Press, 1986); Peter Keating, *The Haunted Study: A Social History of the English Novel 1825–1914* (Secker & Warburg, 1989).

CHAPTER ELEVEN

The meeting to discuss the PO Library and Literary Association was written up forty years later in an article in the house magazine *St Martins Le Grand* (No. 12, 1902), reprinted as Appendix B in *A Trollope Chronology*. A.T.'s calculations of income and expenditure are in his travel diary for 1859 in the Taylor Collection. Thackeray's letter welcoming him to the *Cornhill* is in the Taylor Collection and reproduced in A.T.'s *Letters*.

The story of Dr Vaughan and Harrow is told in John Chandos, *Boys Together*. The expulsions from St Columba's and the dates of the Trollope boys' attendance there are from the school register. The Trollopes' connection with St Andrew's College, Bradfield, and the headmaster's letters, are from John Blackie, *Bradfield 1850–1975* (published privately by the Warden and Council, 1976).

Details of the garden at Waltham House are taken from James Pope Hennessy, *Anthony Trollope*, and the description of A.T.'s arrangements for storing cigars from Sir Frederick Pollock, *Personal Reminiscences* (Macmillan London, 1887).

CHAPTER TWELVE

Henry Merivale (Harry) Trollope's letters to Michael Sadleir, quoted here and in later chapters, are in Sadleir's papers in the Parrish Collection. Mrs Browning's letter to Kate is quoted in Lilian Whiting's *Kate Field: A Record* (Samson Low, 1899).

Letters from Thackeray quoted in this chapter are from Gordon N. Ray, *The Letters and Private Papers of W. M. Thackeray*, Vol. IV (Oxford University Press, 1946), and biographical material from Gordon N. Ray, *Thackeray*, Vol. II 'The Age of Wisdom' (Oxford University Press, 1958). See also John Carey, *Thackeray: Prodigal Genius* (Faber, 1977). Edmund Yates's own version of his rows with Thackeray is given in his *Recollections and Experiences*. The description of Lord Houghton is from *Collections and Recollections* by One who has Kept a Diary (Smith, Elder, 1898). A.T.'s certificate of life membership of the Garrick Club is in the Taylor Collection.

Dickens's comment on George Eliot and G. H. Lewes is quoted without source in Peter Ackroyd, *Dickens* (Sinclair-Stevenson, 1990). For Wilkie Collins, see William M. Clarke, *The Secret Life of Wilkie Collins* (Allison & Busby, 1988); Catherine Peters, *The King of Inventors: A Life of Wilkie Collins* (Secker & Warburg, 1991). For information about the Ternan family, here and in later chapters, I am deeply indebted to Claire Tomalin, *The Invisible Woman* (Viking, 1990). Sir Rowland Hill's journals are quoted in R. H. Super, *Trollope in the Post Office*.

CHAPTER THIRTEEN

The comment on A.T. by William H. Seward's daughter Fanny is quoted in *Trollope: Interviews and Recollections*. Rose's letter to Kate Field is in the Boston Public Library and is published in A.T.'s *Letters*.

For the ladies of Langham Place, see Sheila R. Herstein, *A Mid-Victorian Feminist: Barbara Leigh Smith Bodichon* (Yale University Press, 1985); W. P. Fredeman, 'Emily Faithfull and the Victoria Press', *The Library*, 1964; Daphne Bennett, *Emily Davies and the Liberation of Women* (Andre Deutsch, 1990); Gordon S. Haight, *George Eliot* (Oxford University Press, 1968). Material on the Amberleys and quotations from Lady Amberley's letters and journals are from Bertrand and Patricia Russell (eds.), *The Amberley Papers* (Hogarth Press, 1937).

CHAPTER FOURTEEN

Letters to A.T. from John Blackwood, the Rev. Norman Macleod, Alexander Strahan and James Virtue are in the Bodleian Library, Oxford. The complex business affairs of Macleod, Strahan and Virtue are ably disentangled by Patricia Thomas Srebrnik in *Alexander Strahan: Victorian Publisher* (University of Michigan Press, 1986).

George Eliot's letters to A.T. are in the Parrish Collection and are included in Gordon S. Haight (ed.), *The George Eliot Letters* (Yale University Press, 1955). The invitation from Samuel Warren is one of the specially treasured letters to her husband or herself that Rose Trollope kept after his death in a home-made red leather folder (Taylor Collection).

J. B. Lippincott's letter to A.T. is in the Bodleian Library and published in A.T.'s *Letters*. Alice James's description of the Pollocks is from Jean Strouse, *Alice James* (Cape, 1981). Thackeray's letter to W. W. F. Synge is from Gordon N. Ray (ed.), *The Letters and Private Papers of W. M. Thackeray*, Vol. IV (Oxford University Press, 1946). Dickens's about Robert Bell's widow, in the Taylor Collection, is printed in A.T.'s *Letters*.

Mrs Trollope's last known letter to A.T. is in the Taylor Collection, and her will in the University of Illinois Library.

Millais's description of Thackeray's funeral is from J. G. Millais, *The Life and Letters of Sir John Everett Millais* (Methuen, 1899).

Tom's condescending letter to A.T. about his 'literary position' (27 July 1860) is in the University of Illinois Library. The letters of Tom Trollope and A.T. to Kate Field are in the Boston Public Library and published in 'Kate Field and the Trollope Brothers', *More Books* (the BPL's monthly bulletin), July 1927. Browning's to Isa Blagden, here and in later chapters, are from E. C. McAleer (ed.), *Dearest Isa: Robert Browning's Letters to Isabella Blagden* (University of Texas Press/Nelson, 1951). Isa Blagden's letter to Bice Trollope is in the Parrish Collection, as is Fanny Ternan's to Bice about the ball at Waltham House.

Tom Trollope's letters to Bice Trollope, and Fanny Ternan's after her marriage to Tom, are here and in later chapters from the private collection of Bice's grandson Robert Cecil.

CHAPTER FIFTEEN

For the row over Surveyors' salaries and quotations from John Tilley's responses, see R. H. Super, *Trollope in the Post Office*. The memory of A.T. working with his handkerchief stuffed in his mouth appeared in an article in *St Martins Le Grand* (July 1896) and is reprinted in *Trollope: Interviews and Recollections*. Dickens's letters to Tom Trollope are from T. A. Trollope, *What I Remember*.

CHAPTER SIXTEEN

Details of the Beverley election are chiefly from Lance O. Tingay, *Anthony Trollope Politician: His Parliamentary Candidature at Beverley 1868* (Silverbridge Press, 1988). For a lurid account of nineteenth-century police reports and sensationalism in British newspapers see Thomas Boyle, *Black Swine in the Sewers of Hampstead* (Viking, 1989). For social attitudes to and incidence of syphilis see Richard Davenport-Hines, *Sex, Death and Punishment* (Collins, 1990).

The Rev. W. Lucas Collins's letter to John Blackwood about his visit to Waltham is in the National Library of Scotland and is included in A.T.'s *Letters*. Accounts of Kate Field's enterprises, here and in subsequent chapters, are chiefly from *Kate Field: A Record*. The relevance of Proust's *Against Sainte-Beuve* for understanding A. T.'s creative processes was brought home to me by a lecture given by Michael Wood at the 1991 Cheltenham Festival of Literature.

Australia: see Geoffrey Dutton, *The Squatters* (New South Wales, Currey O'Neill Ross, 1985). Accounts of Fred Trollope's career here and in later chapters owe much to P. D. Edwards, *Anthony Trollope's Son in Australia* (University of Queensland Press, 1982), in which are published the letters (from the University of Illinois Library) that he wrote home to his family. A.T.'s comment – first uncovered by N. John Hall – that Fred's fiancée was prettier than her photograph is from a diary fragment in the Houghton Library, Harvard University.

CHAPTER SEVENTEEN

J. M. Langford's letter to John Blackwood about Harry Trollope is in the National Library of Scotland and is included in A.T.'s *Letters*. G. H. Lewes's diary-entry on the same topic, also reproduced in *Letters*, is from *The George Eliot Letters*, Vol. V. Wilkie Collins's letter to A.T. about Kate Field is in the Taylor Collection and is included in A.T.'s *Letters*. For Mark Twain's account of the Garrick dinner with A.T. and Joaquin Miller see Bernard DeVoto (ed.), *Mark Twain in Eruption* (1940), reprinted in *Trollope: Interviews and Recollections*.

CHAPTER EIGHTEEN

For South Africa in the 1870s see Thomas Pakenham, *The Scramble for Africa* (Weidenfeld & Nicolson, 1991). A.T.'s South Africa notebook is in the Parrish Collection. His letters from John Blackwood are in the Bodleian Library.

CHAPTER NINETEEN

John Morley's letter to A.T. about the Thackeray biography is in the Bodleian Library, and is published in A.T.'s *Letters*. Muriel Trollope's letters are in the Parrish Collection, and Bice Trollope's in the private collection of Robert Cecil. The auctioneer's brochure (1886) for North End, Harting, is in the possession of the present (1992) occupants of the house. Robert Browning's letter to Katherine Bronson is published in Michael Meredith (ed.), *More Than Friend: The Letters of Robert Browning to Katherine de Kay Bronson* (Baylor University & Wedgeston Press, 1985). Tom Trollope's letters to Harry after A.T.'s stroke are in the University of Illinois Library and are published as Appendix D to A.T.'s *Letters*.

CONCLUSION

The letters from Fred Trollope to his mother are in the University of Illinois Library and published in P. D. Edwards, *Anthony Trollope's Son in Australia*. The letters from Harry and Ada (Strickland) Trollope to Michael Sadleir are in the Parrish Collection. The correspondence between Harry Trollope and William Blackwood about the publication of *An Autobiography* and A.T.'s last novels is in the Taylor Collection.

The letters written by Frances Eleanor Trollope and by Rose Trollope as widows are in the private collection of Robert Cecil. For the revelation of Rose's belated aspiration to write I am indebted to Richard Mullen's researches in the Blackwood papers in the Royal Library of Scotland.

ANTHONY TROLLOPE'S WORKS

* The Barsetshire novels
† The Parliamentary novels
(The place of publication is London unless otherwise stated.)

The Macdermots of Ballycloran, 3 vols., Newby, 1847
The Kellys and the O'Kellys, 3 vols., Colburn, 1848
La Vendée, 3 vols., Colburn, 1850
* *The Warden*, Longman, 1855
* *Barchester Towers*, 3 vols., Longman, 1857
The Three Clerks, 3 vols., Bentley, 1858
* *Doctor Thorne*, 3 vols., Chapman & Hall, 1858
The Bertrams, 3 vols., Chapman & Hall, 1859
The West Indies and the Spanish Main, Chapman & Hall, 1859
Castle Richmond, 3 vols., Chapman & Hall, 1860
* *Framley Parsonage*, 3 vols., Smith, Elder, 1861. Serialised in the
   Cornhill Magazine, January 1860–April 1861
Tales of All Countries, Chapman & Hall, 1861
Orley Farm, 2 vols., Chapman & Hall, 1862. Serialised in monthly
   parts, March 1861–October 1862
The Struggles of Brown, Jones, and Robinson By One of the Firm,
   Harper, New York, 1862 (pirated edition). Smith, Elder, 1870.
   Serialised in the *Cornhill Magazine*, August 1861–March 1862
North America, 2 vols., Chapman & Hall, 1862
Tales of All Countries, Second Series, Chapman & Hall, 1863
Rachel Ray, 2 vols., Chapman & Hall, 1863
* *The Small House at Allington*, 2 vols., Smith, Elder, 1864.
   Serialised in the *Cornhill Magazine*, September 1862–April 1864
† *Can You Forgive Her?*, 2 vols., Chapman & Hall, 1865. Serialised
   in monthly parts, January 1864–August 1865
Miss Mackenzie, 2 vols., Chapman & Hall, 1865

527

Hunting Sketches, Chapman & Hall, 1865. Reprinted from the *Pall Mall Gazette*, February–March 1865

The Belton Estate, 3 vols., Chapman & Hall, 1866. Serialised in the *Fortnightly Review*, 15 May 1865–1 January 1866

Travelling Sketches, Chapman & Hall, 1866. Reprinted from the *Pall Mall Gazette*, August–September 1865

Clergymen of the Church of England, Chapman & Hall, 1866. Reprinted from the *Pall Mall Gazette*, November 1865–January 1866

Nina Balatka, 2 vols., Blackwood, Edinburgh and London, 1867. Serialised in *Blackwood's*, July 1866–January 1867

The Claverings, 2 vols., Smith, Elder, 1867. Serialised in the *Cornhill Magazine*, February 1866–May 1867

* *The Last Chronicle of Barset*, 2 vols., Smith, Elder, 1867. Serialised in weekly parts, 1 December 1866–6 July 1867

Lotta Schmidt: And Other Stories, Strahan, 1867

Linda Tressel, 2 vols., Blackwood, Edinburgh and London, 1868. Serialised in *Blackwood's*, October 1867–May 1868

† *Phineas Finn: The Irish Member*, 2 vols., Virtue, 1869. Serialised in *Saint Pauls Magazine*, October 1867–May 1869

Did He Steal It? A Comedy in Three Acts, privately printed by Virtue, 1869.

He Knew He Was Right, 2 vols., Strahan, 1869. Serialised in weekly parts, 17 October 1868–22 May 1869

The Vicar of Bullhampton, Bradbury & Evans, 1870. Serialised in monthly parts, July 1869–May 1870

An Editor's Tales, Strahan, 1870

The Commentaries of Caesar, Blackwood, Edinburgh and London, 1870

Sir Harry Hotspur of Humblethwaite, Hurst & Blackett, 1871. Serialised in *Macmillan's Magazine*, May–December 1870

Ralph the Heir, 3 vols., Hurst & Blackett, 1871. Serialised in monthly parts and also as supplement to *Saint Pauls Magazine*, January 1870–July 1871

The Golden Lion of Granpere, Tinsley, 1872. Serialised in *Good Words*, January–August 1872

† *The Eustace Diamonds*, 3 vols., Chapman & Hall, 1873. Serialised in the *Fortnightly Review*, July 1871–February 1873

Australia and New Zealand, 2 vols., Chapman & Hall, 1873

† *Phineas Redux*, 2 vols., Chapman & Hall, 1874. Serialised in the *Graphic*, 19 July 1873–10 January 1874

Lady Anna, 2 vols., Chapman & Hall, 1874. Serialised in the
  Fortnightly Review, April 1873–April 1874

Harry Heathcote of Gangoil: A Tale of Australian Bush Life, Sampson
  Low, 1874. Published in the *Graphic*, 25 December 1873

The Way We Live Now, 2 vols., Chapman & Hall, 1875. Serialised in
  monthly parts, February 1874–September 1875

† *The Prime Minister*, 4 vols., Chapman & Hall, 1876. Serialised in
  monthly parts, November 1875–June 1876

The American Senator, 3 vols., Chapman & Hall, 1877. Serialised in
  Temple Bar, May 1876–July 1877

South Africa, 2 vols., Chapman & Hall, 1878

Is He Popenjoy?, 3 vols., Chapman & Hall, 1878. Serialised in *All the
  Year Round*, 13 October 1877–13 July 1878

How the 'Mastiffs' Went to Iceland, privately printed by Virtue,
  1878

An Eye for an Eye, 2 vols., Chapman & Hall, 1879. Serialised in the
  Whitehall Review, 24 August 1878–1 February 1879

Thackeray, Macmillan, 1879

John Caldigate, 3 vols., Chapman & Hall, 1879. Serialised in
  Blackwood's, April 1878–June 1879

Cousin Henry, 2 vols., Chapman & Hall, 1879. Serialised in the
  Manchester Weekly Times and the *North British Weekly Mail*, 8
  March–24 May 1879

† *The Duke's Children*, 3 vols., Chapman & Hall, 1880. Serialised in
  All the Year Round, 4 October 1879–14 July 1880

The Life of Cicero, 2 vols., Chapman & Hall, 1880

Dr Wortle's School, 2 vols., Chapman & Hall, 1881. Serialised in
  Blackwood's, May–December 1880

Ayala's Angel, 3 vols., Chapman & Hall, 1881

Why Frau Frohmann Raised Her Prices: And Other Stories, Isbister,
  1882

Lord Palmerston, Isbister, 1882

Kept in the Dark, 2 vols., Chatto & Windus, 1882. Serialised in *Good
  Words*, May–December 1882

Marion Fay, 3 vols., Chapman & Hall, 1882. Serialised in the
  Graphic, 3 December 1881–3 June 1882

The Fixed Period, 2 vols., Blackwood, Edinburgh and London,
  1882. Serialised in *Blackwood's*, October 1881–March 1882

Mr Scarborough's Family, 3 vols., Chatto & Windus, 1883.
  Serialised in *All the Year Round*, 27 May 1882–16 June 1883

The Landleaguers, 3 vols., Chatto & Windus, 1883. Serialised in
Life, 16 November 1882–4 October 1883

An Autobiography, 2 vols., Blackwood, Edinburgh and London,
1883

An Old Man's Love, 2 vols., Blackwood, Edinburgh and London,
1884

The Noble Jilt, Constable, 1923 (written 1850)

London Tradesmen, Mathews and Marrot, 1927. Reprinted from the
Pall Mall Gazette, 10 July 1880–7 September 1880

The New Zealander, The Clarendon Press, Oxford, 1972 (written
1855–56)

In 1987 the Trollope Society (9A North Street, London SW4) and
the Folio Society (202 Great Suffolk Street London SE1) in
association embarked on parallel programmes to republish
Trollope's forty-seven novels and five volumes of his short stories
by the end of the century, at the rate of four books a year. The
Trollope Society's uniform edition reproduces the original
illustrations, and the Folio Society has commissioned new
illustrations. Most of the novels are available in the Oxford
University Press 'World's Classics' series; all forty-seven will be
in print in 'World's Classics' by 1994. Penguin Classics are also
expanding their list of Trollope's works, and will have all the
fiction, the autobiography, and some of the travel books in print
by 1995. Never before, even in his lifetime, have Trollope's books
been so well published, so readily available, or so much in
demand.

INDEX

Canada 310
Carleton, William 153n, 160
Carlton Hill 109, 110, 129, 130, 159, 348
Carlyle, Jane Welsh 302
Carlyle, Thomas 179, 243, 302–3, 498;
 Latter-Day Pamphlets 221–2, 226n
Carnarvon, Lord 457
Casewick 6–7, 373
'castaways' 386–7
Catholic Association 155n
Catholic Emancipation 155n
Catholicism 478
Cauvin, Joseph 214, 215, 218
Cavendish, Lord Frederick 494
Cecil, Arthur 506
Cecil, Beatrice Susan (née Stuart-
 Wortley) 492–3, 506
Century Magazine 440
Ceylon xvii, 437
Chandler, Alice 44n
Chapman, Edward 235–6, 244
Chapman, Frederic 236, 257, 344, 394,
 395, 406, 442, 454, 474, 483, 501, 504
Chapman, Mrs Frederic 501
Chapman, John 324
Chapman & Hall 81, 235–6, 244, 257–8,
 333, 339, 345, 351n, 393, 395, 406, 423,
 443, 453, 474, 483, 498, 504, 505, 506
characters in AT's works: Adolphus,
 characters named 13, 157, *see also*
 Crosbie, Adolphus; Altifiora, Francesca
 370; Amedroz, Clara 269, 327, 376,
 464; Amedroz, Mr 227; Annesley,
 Florence 492; Annesley, Harry 492;
 Anticant, Dr Pessimist 222, 303;
 Arabin, Rev. Francis 95; Aylmer, Lady
 162; Bagwax, Mr 458; Ball, John 323,
 327; Banmann, Baroness 451; Belton,
 Will 269, 376, 465; Bertram, George
 77, 87, 477; Birmingham, Lord 157;
 Bluestone, Mrs 57; Bodkin, Sir Boreas
 88; Bolton, Hester 458; Bolton, Mrs
 458; Bonner, Mary 461; Bonteen, Mr
 342; Boodle, Captain ('Doodles') 126,
 212–13; Brattle, Carry 203, 386–7, 423;
 Brock, Lord 476; Brodrick, Isabel 460,
 461, 503; Bromar, Marie 462;
 Broughton, Dobbs 291; Brumby, Mrs
 381n; Burton, Florence 104, 138–9, 145,
 193, 317; Burton, Theodore 193, 301;
 Caldigate, John 410, 457–8; Carbuncle,
 Mrs 295, 398; Carbury, Felix 362, 432;
 Carbury, Henrietta 392, 432; Carbury,
 Lady 216, 371, 392, 432; Carruthers,
 Lord George de Bruce 398; Carstairs,
 Lord 476; Cashel, Lady 162; Cashel,
 Lord 157n; Chaffanbrass, Mr 290;
 Cheesacre, Mr 360; Cinquebars, Mr

281; Clavering, Archie 212–13;
Clavering, Harry 104, 162, 293, 317;
Clavering, Lady 177; Colligan, Dr 161;
Comfort, Rev. Charles 333; Conor, Mr
124; Crawley, Grace 269; Crawley,
Rev. Josiah 44, 54, 121, 228, 380;
Crosbie, Adolphus 136, 267, 292, 323,
380, 400; Crump, Mrs 196; Curlydown,
Mr 13; Dale, Lily 74, 136, 267, 269,
323, 366, 380, 400, 444, 484; Dale, Mrs
83, 265; Dale, Squire 74; Dale family
83; Daly, Black Tom 496; Daubeny,
Mr 382n; Dawkins, Miss 237–8; de
Baron, Jack 40; de Courcy, Lady
Alexandrina 136, 292, 400; de Courcy,
Lord 383; de Guest, Earl 41, 291, 383;
de Terrier, Lord 476; Demolines,
Madalina 91; Desmond, Lady 376–7;
Dockwrath, Mr 273; Dormer, Ayala
375463; Dormer, Lucy 242; Dormer
family 457n; Dossett, Aunt and Uncle
242; Drought, Sir Orlando 117n;
Dumbello, Lady (née Grantly) 81, 445;
Dunn, Onesiphorus 398; Dunstable,
Miss 323, 369; Eames, Johnny 41, 82,
91, 94, 105, 273, 291, 380, 444, 484;
Effingham, Violet 327, 451; Elmham,
Bishop of 32; Emilius, Rev. Joseph 74;
Eustace, Sir Florian 397; Eustace, John
450–1; Eustace, Lizzie 134, 139, 262,
281, 295, 397, 451, 467; Ewing,
Captain 125; Fay, Marion 481;
Fenwick, Rev. Frank 195–6, 203; Finn,
Phineas 81, 280, 290, 294, 303, 327,
331n, 342, 381, 382, 384–6, 403, 451;
Fitzgerald, Burgo 81, 125, 151n, 200,
329, 445; Fitzgerald, Herbert 186, 227;
Fitzgerald, Owen 172, 376; Fitzgerald,
Sir Thomas 227; Fitzgibbon, Hon.
Laurence 294; Fleabody, Dr Olivia Q.
452, 453; Flood Jones, Mary 386;
Freeborn, Dr 54; Freeborn, Mrs 55;
French, Arabella 268–9; French,
Camilla 268; Furnival, Mr 9, 274–5,
287; Furnival, Mrs 9; Gauntlet, Adela
147–8; Geraghty, Norah 133;
Geraldine, Sir Francis 370; Germain,
Lady George (Mary) 452; Germain,
Lord George 125, 268, 372, 452;
Germain family 8; Gibson, Rev. Mr
268–9; Gilmore, Harry 387, 397;
Glascock, Hon. Charles 54, 450;
Glomax, Captain 424; Goesler,
Madame Max (later Mrs Phineas
Finn) xx, 321, 385, 386, 446, 451, 469;
Goldsheiner, Miss 432; Golightly,
Clementina 267; Gordeloup, Madame
Sophie 133, 212–13, 320–1, 375–6;

of 287–8, 323, 377, 399, 429–30, 452;
teeth xxi-xxii; walking, manner of 239,
251; West Indian 247–9, 251; younger,
physical and emotional closeness in
novels 462–3; *see also* Trollope,
Anthony, Character, Interests and
Opinions: on marriage; sexuality
Women's Movement, in New England
322*n*
Women's Suffrage Committee 324
Women's Suffrage Society 451
Wood, Sir Evelyn 508
Wood, Mrs Henry 346
Wood, Lady 55
Woolf, Virginia 282*n*

Wordsworth, William 97
World, The 475
Wright, Camilla 25
Wright, Frances (Fanny) 22, 24, 25, 27

Yates, Edmund 89, 93–4, 245, 246, 280–1,
304, 343, 361, 367
Yeats, W. B. 38*n*
Yonge, Charlotte M. 372*n*
York Union Bank 225
Young, Brigham 418
Young, John 112

Zandt, Baroness de (formerly Lady Dyer)
110